This book is dedicated to Sian and Galen.
—Dan

This book is dedicated to Paul, Kristin, and Alison.
—Cal

Contents

About the Authors

Daniel Solis is a contract software engineer who has worked for a number of high-profile clients, including Microsoft Consulting Services, NASA, IBM, Lockheed Martin, and PeopleSoft. He has been programming and teaching object-oriented languages and development methods throughout the United States and Europe since the early days of C++. It was while teaching numerous seminars on various programming languages that he realized the immense power of diagrams in explaining programming language concepts.

Daniel has a bachelor of arts degree with majors in biology and English. He initially worked in a research lab studying the structure of bi- and tri-metal crystals, until he found that he enjoyed programming much more than working in a lab. He also has a master of science degree from the University of California at Santa Barbara, where he concentrated on programming languages and compiler design.

Cal Schrotenboer has been programming professionally for more than 20 years. Cal has worked as a contractor throughout this period, initially working on small, direct contracts and eventually graduating to enterprise-level contracts with Novartis, Instron, and 21st Century Fox.

For ten years Cal taught classes on the entire range of .NET subjects (WPF, WCF, Expression Blend, Silverlight, ADO) at Foothill Community College in Los Altos Hills, California. During this period, he also taught MCSE-type (Windows Server) classes at various California community colleges.

Cal's current position with the Fox Networks Group at 21st Century Fox involves all of the technologies that he taught for many years at Foothill Community College. Cal currently works remotely, giving him the opportunity to move to a new country every three to five months. He is more than 75 percent complete on his quest to visit every country in the world.

About the Technical Reviewers

Fabio Claudio Ferracchiati is a senior consultant and a senior analyst/developer using Microsoft technologies. He works at BluArancio S.p.A. (www.bluarancio.com) as a senior analyst/developer and Microsoft Dynamics CRM specialist. He is a Microsoft Certified Solution Developer for .NET, a Microsoft Certified Application Developer for .NET, a Microsoft Certified Professional, and a prolific author and technical reviewer. Over the past ten years, he's written articles for Italian and international magazines and co-authored more than ten books on a variety of computer topics.

Damien Foggon is a developer, writer, and technical reviewer in cutting-edge technologies and has contributed to more than 50 books on .NET, C#, Visual Basic, and ASP.NET. He is the co-founder of the Newcastle-based user group NEBytes (online at www.nebytes.net), is a multiple MCPD in .NET 2.0 onward, and can be found online at http://blog.fasm.co.uk.

Acknowledgments

I want to thank Sian for supporting and encouraging me on a daily basis, and I want to thank my parents and brothers and sisters for their continued love and support.

I also want to express my gratitude to the people at Apress who have worked with me to bring this book to fruition. I really appreciate that they understood and appreciated what I was trying to do and worked with me to achieve it. Thanks to all of you.

—Dan

Introduction

The purpose of this book is to teach you the syntax and semantics of the C# programming language in as clear a manner as possible. C# is a wonderful programming language! I love coding in it. I don't know how many programming languages I've learned over the years, but C# is by far my favorite. I hope that by using this book, you can gain an appreciation for C#'s beauty and elegance.

Most books teach programming primarily using text. That's great for novels, but many of the important concepts of programming languages can best be understood through a combination of words, figures, and tables.

Many of us think visually, and figures and tables can help crystallize our understanding of a concept. Over several years of teaching programming languages, I have found that the pictures I drew on the whiteboards were the things that most quickly helped students understand the concepts I was trying to convey. Illustrations alone, however, are not sufficient to explain a programming language and platform. The goal of this book is to find the best combination of words and illustrations to give you a thorough understanding of the language, and to allow the book to serve as a reference resource as well.

This book is written for anyone who wants an introduction to the C# programming language, from the novice to the seasoned programmer. For those just getting started in programming, I've included the basics. For seasoned programmers, the content is laid out succinctly and in a form that allows you to go directly to the information required without having to wade through oceans of words. For both sets of programmers, the content itself is presented graphically, in a form that should make the language easy to learn.

Enjoy!

Audience, Source Code, and Contact Information

This book was written for beginning and intermediate programmers, as well as for programmers coming from another language such as Visual Basic or Java. I have tried to remain focused on the C# language itself and give an in-depth description of the language and all its parts, rather than straying off into coverage of .NET or programming practices. I wanted to keep this book as succinct as I could while still covering the language thoroughly—and there are other good books covering those other topics.

You can download the source code for all the example programs from the Apress web site or from the web site for this book, which is www.illustratedcsharp.com. Although I can't answer specific questions about your code, you can contact me with suggestions and feedback about the book at dansolis@sbcglobal.net.

I hope this book helps make learning C# an enjoyable experience for you! Take care.

—Dan

CHAPTER 1

■ ■ ■

C# and the .NET Framework

Before .NET

The C# programming language was designed for developing programs for Microsoft's .NET Framework. This chapter gives a brief look at where .NET came from and its basic architecture. To start off, let's get the name right: C# is pronounced "see sharp."[1]

Windows Programming in the Late 1990s

In the late 1990s, Windows programming using the Microsoft platform had fractured into a number of branches. Most programmers were using Visual Basic, C, or C++. Some C and C++ programmers were using the raw Win32 API, but most were using Microsoft Foundation Classes (MFC). Others had moved to the Component Object Model (COM).

All these technologies had their own problems. The raw Win32 API was not object-oriented, and using it required a lot more work than MFC. MFC was object-oriented but was inconsistent and getting old. COM, although conceptually simple, was complex in its actual coding and required lots of ugly, inelegant plumbing.

Another shortcoming of all these programming technologies was that they were aimed primarily at developing code for the desktop rather than the Internet. At the time, programming for the Web was an afterthought and seemed very different from coding for the desktop.

Goals for the Next-Generation Platform Services

What we really needed was a new start—an integrated, object-oriented development framework that would bring consistency and elegance back to programming. To meet this need, Microsoft set out to develop a code execution environment and a code development environment that met these goals. Figure 1-1 lists these goals.

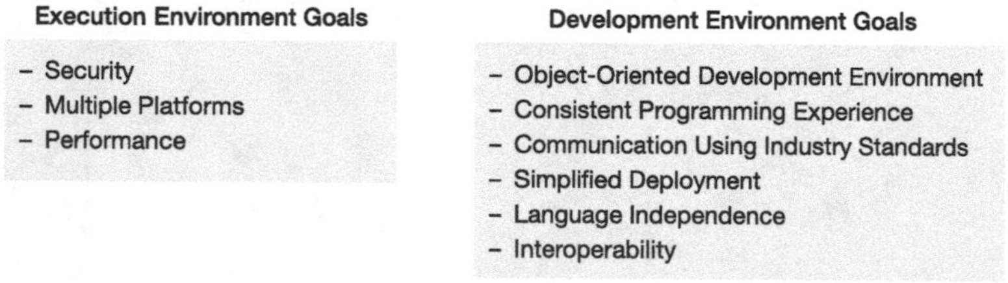

Execution Environment Goals	Development Environment Goals
– Security – Multiple Platforms – Performance	– Object-Oriented Development Environment – Consistent Programming Experience – Communication Using Industry Standards – Simplified Deployment – Language Independence – Interoperability

Figure 1-1. *Goals for the next-generation platform*

---

[1] I (Dan) was once interviewed for a contract C# position when the Human Resources interviewer asked me how much experience I'd had programming in "see pound" (instead of "see sharp")! It took me a moment to realize what he was talking about.

Enter Microsoft .NET

In 2002, Microsoft released the first version of the .NET Framework, which promised to address the old problems and meet the goals for the next-generation systems. The .NET Framework is a much more consistent and object-oriented environment than either the MFC or COM programming technologies. Some of its features include the following:

- *Multiple platforms*: The system runs on a broad range of computers, from servers and desktop machines to PDAs and cell phones.

- *Industry standards*: The system uses industry-standard communication protocols, such as XML, HTTP, SOAP, JSON, and WSDL.

- *Security*: The system can provide a much safer execution environment, even in the presence of code obtained from suspect sources.

Components of the .NET Framework

The .NET Framework consists of three components, as shown in Figure 1-2. The execution environment is called the Common Language Runtime (CLR). The CLR manages program execution at run time, including the following:

- Memory management and garbage collection

- Code safety verification

- Code execution, thread management, and exception handling

The programming tools include everything you need for coding and debugging, including the following:

- The Visual Studio integrated development environment (IDE)

- .NET-compliant compilers (e.g., C#, Visual Basic .NET, F#, IronRuby, and managed C++)

- Debuggers

- Web development server-side technologies, such as ASP.NET and WCF

The Base Class Library (BCL) is a large class library used by the .NET Framework and available for you to use in your programs as well.

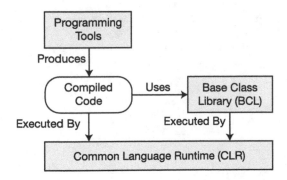

Figure 1-2. *Components of the .NET Framework*

3

An Improved Programming Environment

The .NET Framework offers programmers considerable improvements over previous Windows programming environments. The following sections give a brief overview of its features and their benefits.

Object-Oriented Development Environment

The CLR, the BCL, and C# are designed to be thoroughly object-oriented and act as a well-integrated environment.

The system provides a consistent, object-oriented model of programming for both local programs and distributed systems. It also provides a software development interface for desktop application programming, mobile application programming, and web development, consistent across a broad range of targets, from servers to cell phones.

Automatic Garbage Collection

The CLR has a service called the *garbage collector* (GC), which automatically manages memory for you. The GC automatically removes objects from memory that your program will no longer access.

With only a few exceptions, the GC relieves programmers of tasks they have traditionally had to perform, such as deallocating memory and hunting for memory leaks. This is a huge improvement since hunting for memory leaks can be difficult and time-consuming.

Interoperability

The .NET Framework was designed for interoperability between different .NET languages, the operating system or Win32 DLLs, and COM.

- The .NET language interoperability allows software modules written using different .NET languages to interact seamlessly.

  - A program written in one .NET language can use and even inherit from a class written in another .NET language, as long as certain rules are followed.

  - Because of its ability to easily integrate modules produced in different programming languages, the .NET Framework is sometimes described as language-agnostic.

4

- The .NET Framework provides a feature called *platform invoke (P/Invoke)*, which allows code written for .NET to call and use code not written for .NET. It can use raw C functions imported from standard Win32 DLLs, such as the Windows APIs.

- The .NET Framework also allows interoperability with COM. .NET Framework software components can call COM components, and COM components can call .NET components as if they were COM components themselves.

No COM Required

The .NET Framework frees the programmer from the COM legacy. If you're coming from a COM programming environment, you'll be happy to know that, as a C# programmer, you don't need to use any of the following:

- *The IUnknown interface*: In COM, all objects must implement interface IUnknown. In contrast, all .NET objects derive from a single class called object. Interface programming is still an important part of .NET, but it's no longer the central theme.

- *Type libraries*: In COM, type information is kept in type libraries as .tlb files, which are separate from the executable code. In .NET, a program's type information is kept bundled with the code in the program file.

- *Manual reference counting*: In COM, the programmer had to keep track of the number of references to an object to make sure it wasn't deleted at the wrong time. In .NET, the GC keeps track of references and removes objects only when appropriate.

- *HRESULT*: COM used the HRESULT data type to return runtime error codes. .NET doesn't use HRESULTs. Instead, all unexpected runtime errors produce exceptions.

- *The registry*: COM applications had to be registered in the system registry, which holds information about the configurations of the operating system and applications. .NET applications don't need to use the registry. This simplifies the installation and removal of programs. (However, there is something similar called the *global assembly cache*, which we'll cover in Chapter 22.)

Although the amount of COM code that's currently being written is fairly small, there's still quite a number of COM components in systems currently being used, and C# programmers sometimes need to write code that interfaces with those components. C# 4.0 introduced several new features that make that task easier. These features are covered in Chapter 27.

Simplified Deployment

Deploying programs written for the .NET Framework can be much easier than it was before, for the following reasons:

- The fact that .NET programs don't need to be registered with the registry means that in the simplest case, a program just needs to be copied to the target machine and it's ready to run.

- .NET offers a feature called *side-by-side execution*, which allows different versions of a DLL to exist on the same machine. This means that every executable can have access to the version of the DLL for which it was built.

Type Safety

The CLR checks and ensures the type safety of parameters and other data objects—even between components written in different programming languages.

The Base Class Library

The .NET Framework supplies an extensive base class library, called, not surprisingly, the *Base Class Library* (BCL). (It's also sometimes called the Framework Class Library [FCL]). You can use this extensive set of available code when writing your own programs. Some of the categories are the following:

- *General base classes*: Classes that provide you with an extremely powerful set of tools for a wide range of programming tasks, such as file manipulation, string manipulation, security, and encryption

- *Collection classes*: Classes that implement lists, dictionaries, hash tables, and bit arrays

- *Threading and synchronization classes*: Classes for building multithreaded programs

- *XML classes*: Classes for creating, reading, and manipulating XML documents

In programming, someone else has almost always needed to previously perform the same task that you are now faced with, particularly with respect to the most basic tasks. The idea of the BCL is to provide you with already built functionality for most generalized tasks so that your responsibility is limited to piecing together this functionality and writing whatever specialized code is required for your application. Don't worry—that remaining part still requires plenty of knowledge and skill.

Compiling to the Common Intermediate Language

The compiler for a .NET language takes a source code file and produces an output file called an *assembly*. Figure 1-3 illustrates the process.

- An assembly is either an executable or a DLL.

- The code in an assembly isn't native machine code but an intermediate language called the *Common Intermediate Language* (CIL).

- An assembly, among other things, contains the following items:

  - The program's CIL

  - Metadata about the types used in the program

  - Metadata about references to other assemblies

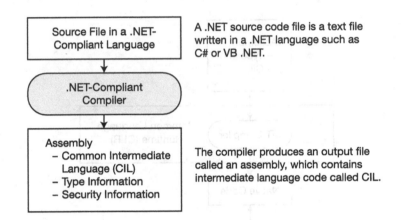

Figure 1-3. *The compilation process*

■ **Note**   The acronym for the intermediate language has changed over time, and different references use different terms. Two other terms for the CIL that you might encounter are Intermediate Language (IL) and Microsoft Intermediate Language (MSIL). These terms were frequently used during .NET's initial development and early documentation, although they're used much less frequently now.

Compiling to Native Code and Execution

The program's CIL isn't compiled to native machine code until it's called to run. At run time, the CLR performs the following steps, as shown in Figure 1-4:

1. It checks the assembly's security characteristics.

2. It allocates space in memory.

3. It sends the assembly's executable code to the just-in-time (JIT) compiler, which compiles portions of it to native code.

The executable code in the assembly is compiled by the JIT compiler only as it's needed. It's then cached in case it's needed for execution again later in the program. Using this process means that code that isn't called during execution isn't compiled to native code and that the code that *is* called needs to be compiled only once.

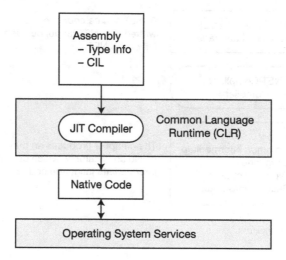

Figure 1-4. *Compilation to native code occurs at run time*

Once the CIL is compiled to native code, the CLR manages it as it runs, performing such tasks as releasing orphaned memory, checking array bounds, checking parameter types, and managing exceptions. This brings up two important terms.

- *Managed code*: Code written for the .NET Framework is called *managed code* and needs the CLR.

- *Unmanaged code*: Code that doesn't run under the control of the CLR, such as Win32 C and C++ DLLs, is called *unmanaged code*.

Microsoft also supplies a tool called the *Native Image Generator*, or *Ngen*, which takes an assembly and produces native code for the current processor. Code that's been run through Ngen avoids the JIT compilation process at run time.

Overview of Compilation and Execution

The same compilation and execution process is followed regardless of the language of the original source files. Figure 1-5 illustrates the entire compilation and runtime processes for three programs written in different languages.

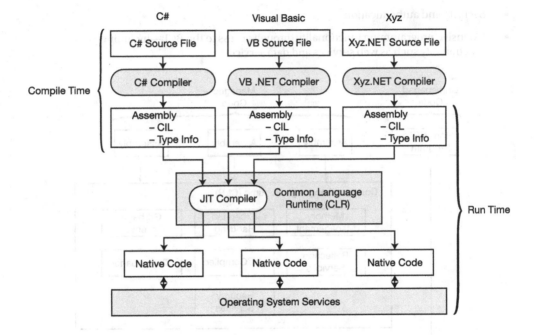

Figure 1-5. *Overview of the compile-time and runtime processes*

The Common Language Runtime

The core component of the .NET Framework is the CLR, which sits on top of the operating system and manages program execution, as shown in Figure 1-6. The CLR also provides the following services:

- Automatic garbage collection

- Security and authentication

- Extensive programming functionality through access to the BCL—including functionality such as web services and data services

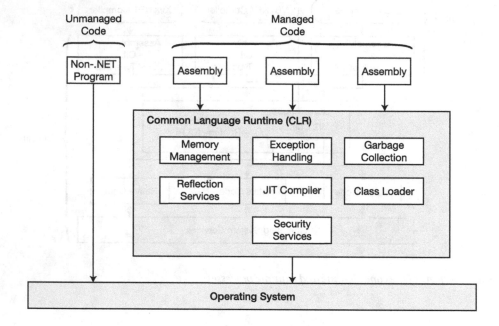

Figure 1-6. *Overview of the CLR*

The Common Language Infrastructure

Every programming language has a set of intrinsic types representing such objects as integers, floating-point numbers, characters, and so on. Historically, the characteristics of these types have varied from one programming language to another and from platform to platform. For example, the number of bits constituting an integer has varied widely depending on the language and platform.

This lack of uniformity, however, makes it difficult if we want programs to play well with other programs and libraries written in different languages. To have order and cooperation, there must be a set of standards.

The Common Language Infrastructure (CLI) is a set of standards that ties all the components of the .NET Framework into a cohesive, consistent system. It lays out the concepts and architecture of the system and specifies the rules and conventions to which all the software must adhere. Figure 1-7 shows the components of the CLI.

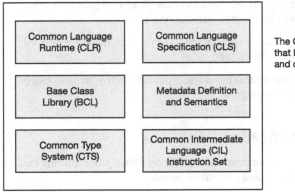

The CLI is a set of specifications that lays out the architecture, rules, and conventions of the system.

Figure 1-7. *Components of the CLI*

Both the CLI and C# have been approved as open international standard specifications by Ecma International. (The name "Ecma" used to be an acronym for the European Computer Manufacturers Association, but it's now just a word in itself.) Ecma members include Microsoft, IBM, Hewlett-Packard, Google, Yahoo, and many other corporations associated with computers and consumer electronics.

Important Parts of the CLI

Although most programmers don't need to know the details of the CLI specifications, you should at least be familiar with the meaning and purpose of the Common Type System (CTS) and the Common Language Specification (CLS).

The Common Type System

The CTS defines the characteristics of the types that must be used in managed code. Some important aspects of the CTS are the following:

- The CTS defines a rich set of intrinsic types, with fixed, specific characteristics for each type.

- The types provided by a .NET-compliant programming language generally map to some specific subset of this defined set of intrinsic types.

- One of the most important characteristics of the CTS is that *all* types are derived from a common base class—called object.

- Using the CTS ensures that the system types and types defined by the user can be used by any .NET-compliant language.

The Common Language Specification

The CLS specifies the rules, properties, and behaviors of a .NET-compliant programming language. The topics include data types, class construction, and parameter passing.

Review of the Acronyms

This chapter has covered a lot of .NET acronyms, so Figure 1-8 will help you keep them straight.

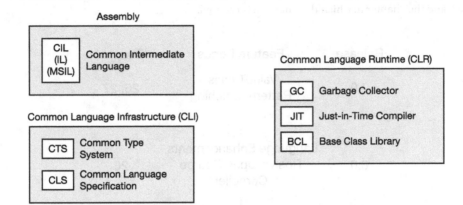

Figure 1-8. *The .NET acronyms*

The Evolution of C#

The current version of the language is version 7.0. Each new release of the language has generally had a specific focus for the new features added. Figure 1-9 shows the main feature focus for each of the releases of the language and the chapter in which that material is covered.

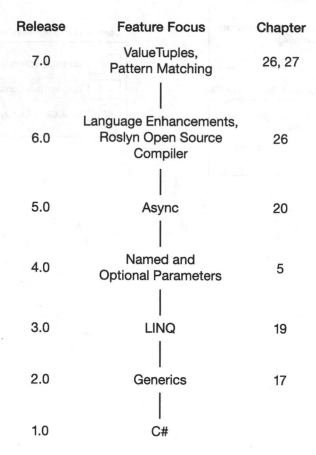

Release	Feature Focus	Chapter
7.0	ValueTuples, Pattern Matching	26, 27
6.0	Language Enhancements, Roslyn Open Source Compiler	26
5.0	Async	20
4.0	Named and Optional Parameters	5
3.0	LINQ	19
2.0	Generics	17
1.0	C#	

Figure 1-9. The primary focus of each feature set for the releases of C#

C# and the Evolution of Windows

The introduction of the iPhone in 2007 started a major trend in the industry toward portable devices. The iPhone was soon followed by the first Android device in 2008 and then by the iPad in 2010. Microsoft has also been involved in the portable device market, albeit less successfully, first with Windows Mobile (initially called the PocketPC), then with Windows Phone introduced in 2010, and currently with Windows 10 Mobile. As of this writing, the number of smartphones and tablets that have been sold is currently in the billions. Beginning in 2011, the quantity of portable devices sold annually exceeded the number of personal computers sold.

In response to these market shifts, Microsoft introduced Windows 8 in 2012. A major goal of this version of Windows was to introduce a user interface that was similar for both desktop computers and portable devices. Windows 8 was Microsoft's first operating system capable of working on both ARM-based tablets and traditional x86 PCs. It also gave a much greater emphasis to a touch-enabled user interface.

Developers for Windows 8 were encouraged by Microsoft to create "Metro apps," which could, with the appropriate customizations, be capable of running on both PCs and portable devices. Metro apps could be developed using any of the following:

- XAML and C# (or VB .NET or C++)

- HTML5, CSS3, and JavaScript

- DirectX and C++

Windows 10, which was introduced in 2015, included Universal Windows Platform apps as the next evolutionary step beyond Metro apps. The design goal of universal apps was to be capable of running on multiple Microsoft platforms with nearly identical code. These platforms include PCs, tablets, smartphones, Xbox One, and a number of more specialized devices. Universal apps do not, however, target either the Android or iOS platform.

Windows 10 Core (not to be confused with .NET Core) is a common platform present on every device running Windows 10. Universal apps are capable of calling not only the Windows 10 Core APIs that are common to all Windows 10 devices but also any APIs that are specific to individual device families, such as desktop, phone, and Xbox. This represents a significant integration over Windows 8, which required a considerably greater effort to create applications for different categories of devices.

Windows 10 has been generally well received and, as of this writing, has almost achieved the same level of penetration as Windows 7, the most successful of Microsoft's operating systems so far. Even though Microsoft's penetration in the smartphone and tablet market is considerably smaller than that of Android or Apple, universal apps nevertheless offer developers a nice extension on the marketplace for their applications.

The same programming languages listed earlier for developing Metro apps can also be used for developing Universal Apps. While there are also other options, C# is an excellent choice because of its integration with Visual Studio and support from Microsoft.

The 2017 Developer Survey on StackOverflow listed C# as the fourth most used programming language (after JavaScript, SQL, and Java) and the eighth most loved programming language (ahead of JavaScript, SQL, and Java). C# didn't even make the top 25 list of most "dreaded" programming languages (JavaScript, SQL, and Java, however, did make that list).

The conclusion is obvious. Tens of thousands of developers use C# on a regular basis, and a high percentage are very happy with it. It's an elegant language.

CHAPTER 2

■ ■ ■

C# and .NET Core

- ■ The .NET Framework Background
- ■ Why .NET Core (and Xamarin)?
- ■ Goals of .NET Core
- ■ Multiplatform Support
- ■ Rapid Development and Upgrades
- ■ Smaller Application Footprints, Simpler Deployment, and Reduced Versioning Problems
- ■ Open Source Community Support
- ■ Improved Application Performance
- ■ Fresh Start
- ■ The Development of .NET Core
- ■ Where Does This Leave the .NET Framework?
- ■ Where Does Xamarin Fit In?

© Daniel Solis and Cal Schrotenboer 2018
D. Solis and C. Schrotenboer, *Illustrated C# 7*, https://doi.org/10.1007/978-1-4842-3288-0_2

The .NET Framework Background

The .NET Framework was originally released in 2002. In terms of programming frameworks, that makes it "mature" in the sense that it contains virtually every significant, desirable feature currently available in major programming languages. Nevertheless, it would be a mistake to think that .NET has reached "old age"; "middle aged" would be a much closer description. After all, C and C++ have been around for far longer than C#.

While the .NET Framework is still an excellent choice for developing the type of applications that it was initially designed to create, the world of computing has changed a lot in the past 15 years, as will be described in the next section.

Why .NET Core (and Xamarin)?

The .NET Framework was created principally for developing applications to be used on computers (both server and client workstations) running the Windows operating system. At the time that .NET was introduced, Microsoft had a dominant position in operating systems for personal computers, and smartphones were still years away. Over time, however, both Unix and Apple managed to cut into Microsoft's market share in computers. Moreover, a much more significant development has been the massive shift toward mobile devices, an area where Microsoft's share (whether measured by hardware or software) has been negligible. A third major trend has been the increase in the share of web-based applications rather than desktop-based applications.

The effect of these three trends has been a reduction in the importance of Windows desktop applications in favor of web and mobile applications as well as desktop applications running on operating systems other than Windows. That, by no means, suggests that Windows desktop applications will be dying out any time soon; it's just that most people believe that the largest future growth will be in web and mobile applications.

With this in mind, Microsoft concluded that it could better address web development, as well as development for computers running Linux or macOS, with a cloud-enabled, cross-platform, open source derivative of the .NET Framework. It labeled that new framework .NET Core. At about the same time, Microsoft acquired Xamarin to address development on mobile platforms such as Android and iOS.

For the purposes of this book, the key thing to keep in mind is that whether you will be developing full .NET Framework applications, .NET Core applications, or Xamarin applications, in each case you can use the C# language.

Figure 2-1 shows the relationship between each of the frameworks in the .NET ecosystem.

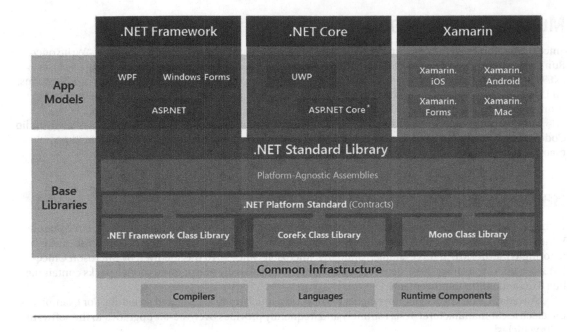

Figure 2-1. The .NET ecosystem

Goals of .NET Core

The following list summarizes the principal goals of .NET Core:

- Multiplatform support
- Rapid development and upgrades
- Smaller application footprints
- Simpler deployments
- Reduced versioning problems
- Open source community support
- Improved application performance
- Fresh start

19

Multiplatform Support

Since the beginning of the computer era, the holy grail of programming frameworks has been "Write once. Run everywhere." Even now that goal remains elusive, although most new efforts seem to bring us closer. .NET Core allows developers to create applications that will run on Windows and, with minor modifications, on Linux and macOS. At the time of this writing, there are beta versions of .NET Core that are capable of running on ARM processors (e.g., Raspberry Pi).

Multiplatform support also extends to developing on operating systems beyond Windows. Visual Studio Code is a new integrated development environment (IDE) created by Microsoft that can run on Linux, macOS, and Windows.

Rapid Development and Upgrades

In the past, it was common for software to experience major releases every two to three years. For example, Windows 95 was followed by Windows 98 and then Windows 2000. (Microsoft will probably thank us for ignoring Windows ME in this example.) Similarly, Microsoft Office 2010 was followed by Microsoft Office 2013 and Microsoft Office 2016. Between releases, there were usually one or more service packs containing bug fixes and minor improvements.

Nowadays, users expect improvements to come on a much more accelerated schedule. For example, the electric car manufacturer Tesla routinely and frequently provides over-the-air upgrades to the software in its vehicles.

The initial version of the .NET Framework was distributed in large measure via CD-ROM, and it was only a few years earlier that major software releases involved a large stack of floppy disks. When the Internet first reached public consciousness, dial-up speeds often were nominally 14.4 or 28.8 kilobits per second. Today, by contrast, most software is delivered over the Internet at speeds hundreds or even thousands of times faster than once was possible. Applications are programmed to check the server for available updates and, depending on user preference, either install those updates automatically or prompt the user for a decision as to timing.

Applications are typically designed in a modular fashion so that different components can be independently upgraded without requiring the entire application to be replaced. In this regard, .NET Core is highly modular, and upgrades can be performed automatically via NuGet packages, described in the next section.

Smaller Application Footprints, Simpler Deployment, and Reduced Versioning Problems

The distribution of .NET Core is based on NuGet packages. *Packages* are libraries of code that provide certain units of functionality. Packages are stored in the NuGet Gallery from which they are downloaded as needed. Developers can decide how modular the packages they create will be.

By contrast, the .NET Framework, which now contains more than 20,000 classes, must be installed in its entirety both on any development workstation and on each application user's computer. By specifying only relevant packages, the total footprint of a .NET Core application can be much smaller than the equivalent footprint of a full-fledged .NET Framework application. Admittedly, the .NET Framework itself only needs to be installed once per client workstation (per version), but that installation is, in contrast, quite lengthy.

Moreover, the requirement that all target computers for .NET Framework applications must have the identical version of .NET with which the application was developed may present problems if for any reason it's not possible to upgrade the .NET Framework on a target computer. This may be because of permissions, company policies, or other factors. This may require recompiling the application for that particular user or users with an earlier version of .NET.

By contrast, .NET Core applications do not suffer from this same constraint. The .NET Core framework can be distributed side by side with the application code, so there can never be a versioning conflict. In those cases where the .NET Core framework (in the appropriate version) already exists on a target computer, an application can optionally choose to use the existing code, thereby further reducing the application's installation footprint.

Moreover, since every application can have its own copy of the .NET Core libraries, it is possible to have multiple .NET Core applications running side by side on the same computer using different versions of .NET Core. This would allow different applications to be upgraded at different times rather than requiring all such applications to be upgraded simultaneously.

Open Source Community Support

It is generally perceived that the benefits of open source software are lower costs, greater flexibility (including customizability), greater freedom, higher security, and higher accountability.

The source code for proprietary software is generally a closely guarded secret. If that software contains a bug or an anomalous edge case behavior, users of that software have no way of knowing how the software works internally. By contrast, open source software can be seen by anyone with the appropriate tools in order to understand what might be causing the bug or anomalous behavior. With that knowledge in hand, developers can either fix the bug or modify their own code that interacts with that code to avoid undesirable results.

When hundreds or even potentially thousands of developers are available to fix bugs as soon as they are discovered, these fixes will likely occur much more rapidly than in the case of proprietary software. At least in theory, this can result in more secure and more stable code.

Developers are also free to modify or extend open source software. This gives users greater flexibility than in the case of proprietary software. Moreover, if these modifications or extensions are contributed back to the project, other users can benefit from these changes.

Improved Application Performance

In most cases, both .NET Framework applications and .NET Core applications use a just-in-time compiler to convert the IL code into machine-specific code on the fly when the application launches. While this provides a (generally) acceptable level of performance, .NET Core apps can be precompiled to native code on Windows, Linux, or macOS. While the results of this process will vary depending on a number of factors, in some cases this can result in significant improvements in application performance.

Fresh Start

By creating a new framework based on the existing .NET Framework but without abandoning the full .NET Framework, Microsoft is able to decouple obsolete and legacy elements while implementing a new framework design structure that is more suited to today's environment.

The Development of .NET Core

.NET Core 1.0 was released in June 2016 followed by version 1.1 in March 2017. Version 1.1 added support for several new OS distributions, a number of new APIs, and some bug fixes.

Version 2.0 was released in August 2017. This release included a substantial increase in the number of APIs as well as major performance improvements. This release also included support for Visual Basic .NET. As you can see, the pace of improvements in .NET Core is much more rapid than in the .NET Framework.

Where Does This Leave the .NET Framework?

Despite what you have just read, there's no need to worry about the fate of the .NET Framework. Microsoft has promised that the .NET Framework will continue to evolve and will continue to be supported in the current and future versions of the Windows operating system. As such, it will continue to play a critical role in the development of Windows desktop applications, particularly in the enterprise space (where, coincidentally, many of the highest-paying jobs reside). The advantages of .NET Core, described earlier, make it the platform of choice for web (ASP.NET Core) and Universal Windows Platform application development. At the same time, .NET Core is also generally the best option for developing applications designed to run on Linux or macOS.

Where Does Xamarin Fit In?

Xamarin is a platform that permits the development of native Android, iOS, and Windows applications using C# and the .NET libraries. On a PC, Xamarin development takes place within Visual Studio (after additional features have been enabled). On a Mac, development is done using Visual Studio for Mac, the successor to Xamarin Studio. Regardless of IDE and whether the targeted platform is Android, iOS, or Windows, the development language will be C#. Xamarin, therefore, provides another broadening of the locations where C# can be your development language of choice.

In 2016, Xamarin was acquired by Microsoft, and subsequently Xamarin has been bundled with Visual Studio. Even the Community (free) edition of Visual Studio includes Xamarin. The Xamarin SDK is now open source. Microsoft refers to Xamarin as ".NET cross-platform mobile." Technically, Xamarin's capabilities extend somewhat beyond that, but this is also beyond the scope of this book.

Figure 2-1, displayed earlier in this chapter, shows how Microsoft sees the relationship between the .NET Framework, .NET Core, and Xamarin.

CHAPTER 3

■ ■ ■

Overview of C# Programming

© Daniel Solis and Cal Schrotenboer 2018
D. Solis and C. Schrotenboer, *Illustrated C# 7*, https://doi.org/10.1007/978-1-4842-3288-0_3

A Simple C# Program

This chapter lays the groundwork for studying C#. Since we'll use code samples extensively throughout the text, we first need to show you what a C# program looks like and what its various parts mean.

We'll start by demonstrating a simple program and explaining its components one by one. This will introduce a range of topics, from the structure of a C# program to the method of producing program output to the screen.

With these source code preliminaries out of the way, we can then use code samples freely throughout the rest of the text. So, unlike the following chapters, where one or two topics are covered in detail, this chapter touches on many topics with only a minimum of explanation.

Let's start by looking at a simple C# program. The complete source code of the program is shown in the shaded area at the top left of Figure 3-1. As shown, the code is contained in a text file called SimpleProgram. cs. As you read through it, don't worry about understanding all the details. Table 3-1 gives a line-by-line description of the code. The shaded area at the bottom left of the figure shows the output of the program. The right side of the figure is a graphical depiction of the parts of the program.

- When the code is compiled and executed, it displays the string "Hi there!" in a window on the screen.

- Line 5 contains two contiguous slash characters. These characters—and everything following them on the line—are ignored by the compiler. This is called a *single-line comment.*

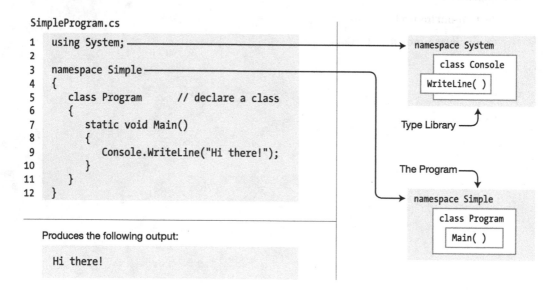

Figure 3-1. *The SimpleProgram program*

Table 3-1. *The SimpleProgram Program, Line by Line*

Line Number	Description
Line 1	Tells the compiler that this program uses types from the System namespace.
Line 3	Declares a new namespace, called Simple.
	• The new namespace starts at the open curly brace on line 4 and extends through the matching curly brace on line 12.
	• Any types declared within this section are members of the namespace.
Line 5	Declares a new class type, called Program.
	• Any members declared between the matching curly braces on lines 6 and 11 are members of this class.
Line 7	Declares a method called Main as a member of class Program.
	• In this program, Main is the only member of the Program class.
	• Main is a special function used by the compiler as the starting point of the program.
Line 9	Contains only a single, simple statement; this line constitutes the body of Main.
	• Simple statements are terminated by a semicolon.
	• This statement uses a class called Console, in namespace System, to print out the message to a window on the screen.
	• Without the using statement in line 1, the compiler wouldn't have known where to look for class Console.

More About SimpleProgram

A C# program consists of one or more type declarations. Much of this book is spent explaining the different types you can create and use in your programs. The types in a program can be declared in any order. In the SimpleProgram example, only a class type is declared.

A *namespace* is a set of type declarations associated with a name. SimpleProgram uses two namespaces. It creates a new namespace called Simple, in which it declares its type (class Program), and uses the Console class defined in a namespace called System.

To compile the program, you can use Visual Studio or the command-line compiler. To use the command-line compiler, in its simplest form, use the following command in a command window:

```
csc SimpleProgram.cs
```

In this command, csc is the name of the command-line compiler, and SimpleProgram.cs is the name of the source file. csc stands for "C-sharp compiler."

Identifiers

Identifiers are character strings used to name things such as variables, methods, parameters, and a host of other programming constructs that will be covered later.

You can create self-documenting identifiers by concatenating meaningful words into a single descriptive name, using uppercase and lowercase letters (e.g., `CardDeck`, `PlayersHand`, `FirstName`, `SocialSecurityNum`). Certain characters are allowed or disallowed at certain positions in an identifier. Figure 3-2 illustrates these rules.

- The alphabetic and underscore characters (a through z, A through Z, and _) are allowed at any position.

- Digits are not allowed in the first position but are allowed everywhere else.

- The @ character is allowed in the first position of an identifier but not at any other position. Although allowed, its use is generally discouraged.

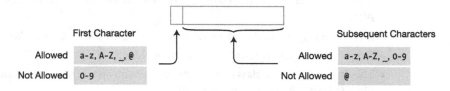

Figure 3-2. *Characters allowed in identifiers*

Identifiers are case-sensitive. For instance, the variable names `myVar` and `MyVar` are different identifiers.

As an example, in the following code snippet, the variable declarations are all valid and declare different integer variables. But using such similar names will make coding more error-prone and debugging more difficult. Those debugging your code at some later time will not be pleased.

```
// Valid syntactically, but very confusing!
int totalCycleCount;
int TotalCycleCount;
int TotalcycleCount;
```

We'll describe the recommended C# naming conventions in Chapter 8. The importance of using clear, consistent, and functionally descriptive terminology cannot be overemphasized.

Keywords

Keywords are the character string tokens used to define the C# language. Table 3-2 gives a complete list of the C# keywords.

Some important things to know about keywords are the following:

- Keywords cannot be used as variable names or any other form of identifier, unless prefaced with the @ character.

- All C# keywords consist entirely of lowercase letters. (.NET type names, however, use Pascal casing.)

Table 3-2. *The C# Keywords*

abstract	const	extern	int	out	short	typeof
as	continue	false	interface	override	sizeof	uint
base	decimal	finally	internal	params	stackalloc	ulong
bool	default	fixed	is	private	static	unchecked
break	delegate	float	lock	protected	string	unsafe
byte	do	for	long	public	struct	ushort
case	double	foreach	namespace	readonly	switch	using
catch	else	goto	new	ref	this	virtual
char	enum	if	null	return	throw	void
checked	event	implicit	object	sbyte	true	volatile
class	explicit	in	operator	sealed	try	when while

Contextual keywords are identifiers that act as keywords only in certain language constructs. In those positions, they have particular meanings; but unlike keywords, which cannot ever be used as identifiers, contextual keywords can be used as identifiers in other parts of the code. Table 3-3 lists the contextual keywords.

Table 3-3. *The C# Contextual Keywords*

add	ascending	async	await	by	descending	dynamic
equals	from	get	global	group	in	into
join	let	on	orderby	partial	remove	select
set	value	var	where	yield		

Main: The Starting Point of a Program

Every C# program must have one class with a method called Main. In the SimpleProgram program shown previously, it was declared in a class called Program.

- The starting point of execution of every C# program is at the first instruction in Main.

- The name Main must be capitalized.

The simplest form of Main is the following:

```
static void Main( )
{
    Statements
}
```

Whitespace

Whitespace in a program refers to characters that do not have a visible output character. Whitespace in source code is ignored by the compiler but is used by the programmer to make the code clearer and easier to read. Some of the whitespace characters include the following:

- Space

- Tab

- New line

- Carriage return

For example, the following code fragments are treated the same by the compiler despite their differences in appearance:

```
// Nicely formatted
Main()
{
    Console.WriteLine("Hi, there!");
}

// Just concatenated
Main(){Console.WriteLine("Hi, there!");}
```

Statements

The statements in C# are similar to those of C and C++. This section introduces the general form of statements; the specific statement forms are covered in Chapter 10.

A *statement* is a source code instruction describing a type or telling the program to perform an action.

A *simple statement* is terminated by a semicolon. For example, the following code is a sequence of two simple statements. The first statement defines an integer variable named var1 and initializes its value to 5. The second statement prints the value of variable var1 to a window on the screen.

```
int var1 = 5;
System.Console.WriteLine("The value of var1 is {0}", var1);
```

Blocks

A *block* is a sequence of zero or more statements enclosed by a matching set of curly braces; it acts as a single syntactic statement.

You can create a block from the set of two statements in the preceding example by enclosing the statements in matching curly braces, as shown in the following code:

```
{
   int var1 = 5;
   System.Console.WriteLine("The value of var1 is {0}", var1);
}
```

Some important things to know about blocks are the following:

- You can use a block whenever the syntax requires a statement but the action you need requires more than one simple statement.

- Certain program constructs *require* blocks. In these constructs, you cannot substitute a simple statement for the block.

- Although a simple statement is terminated by a semicolon, a block is not followed by a semicolon. (Actually, the compiler will *allow* it because it's parsed as an empty statement—but it's not good style.)

```
{              Terminating semicolon
                      ↓                                       Terminating semicolon
   int var2 = 5;                                                      ↓
   System.Console.WriteLine("The value of var1 is {0}", var1);
}
 ↑ No terminating semicolon
```

Text Output from a Program

A *console window* is a simple command prompt window that allows a program to display text and receive input from the keyboard. The BCL supplies a class called Console (in the System namespace), which contains methods for inputting and outputting data to a console window.

Write

Write is a member of the Console class. It sends a text string to the program's console window. In its simplest form, Write sends a literal string of text to the window. The string must be enclosed in quotation marks—double quotes, *not single quotes*.

The following line of code shows an example of using the Write member:

```
Console.Write("This is trivial text.");
                         ↑
                    Output string
```

This code produces the following output in the console window:

```
This is trivial text.
```

Another example is the following code, which sends three literal strings to the program's console window:

```
System.Console.Write ("This is text1. ");
System.Console.Write ("This is text2. ");
System.Console.Write ("This is text3. ");
```

This code produces the output that follows. Notice that Write does not append a newline character after a string, so the output of the three statements runs together on a single line.

```
This is text1.  This is text2.  This is text3.
     ↑                ↑                ↑
   First           Second            Third
 statement        statement        statement
```

WriteLine

WriteLine is another member of Console; it performs the same functions as Write but appends a newline character to the end of each output string.

For example, if you use the preceding code, substituting WriteLine for Write, the output is on separate lines.

```
System.Console.WriteLine("This is text1.");
System.Console.WriteLine("This is text2.");
System.Console.WriteLine("This is text3.");
```

This simple example illustrates the value of the Base Class Library, which contains a myriad of functionality that you can use throughout your program.

This code produces the following output in the console window:

```
This is text1.
This is text2.
This is text3.
```

The Format String

The general form of the Write and WriteLine statements can take more than a single parameter.

- If there is more than a single parameter, the parameters are separated by commas.

- The first parameter must always be a string and is called the *format string*. The format string can contain *substitution markers*.

  – A substitution marker marks the position in the format string where a value should be substituted in the output string.

  – A substitution marker consists of an integer enclosed in a set of matching curly braces. The integer is the numeric position of the substitution value to be used. The parameters following the format string are called *substitution values*. These substitution values are numbered, starting at 0.

The syntax is as follows:

```
Console.WriteLine( FormatString, SubVal0, SubVal1, SubVal2, ... );
```

For example, the following statement has two substitution markers, numbered 0 and 1, and two substitution values, whose values are 3 and 6, respectively.

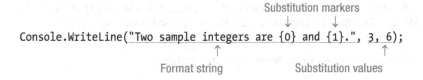

This code produces the following output on the screen:

```
Two sample integers are 3 and 6.
```

31

C# 6.0 introduced a simplified syntax to allow you to restate parameterized strings in an easier-to-understand manner. This syntax is referred to as *string interpolation* and consists of inserting the variable name directly into the substitution marker. In effect, the substitution marker tells the compiler that the variable name is to be treated as a variable and not as a string literal—provided that the string is preceded by the $ symbol.

```
int var1 = 3;
int var2 = 6;
Console.WriteLine($"Two sample integers are {var1} and {var2}.");
```

This code also produces the following output:

```
Two sample integers are 3 and 6.
```

The value of string interpolation becomes more evident when more complex examples are considered.

```
int latitude  = 43;
int longitude = 11;
string north  = "N";
string south  = "S";
string east   = "E";
Console.WriteLine($"The city of Florence, Italy is located at latitude {latitude}{north}
and longitude {longitude}{east}. By comparison, the city of Djibouti (in the country of
Djibouti) is located at latitude {longitude}{north} and longitude {latitude}{east}. The
city of Moroni in the Comoros Islands is located at latitude {longitude}{south} and
longitude {latitude}{east}.");
```

This code produces the following output:

```
The city of Florence, Italy is located at latitude 43N and longitude 11E. By comparison, the
city of Djibouti (in the country of Djibouti) is located at latitude 11N and longitude 43E. The
city of Moroni in the Comoros Islands is located at latitude 11S and longitude 43E.
```

As you can see, in complex cases it is easy to inadvertently switch variables.

■ **Note**   Throughout this text we will use examples of both the old and new string syntax. While the new syntax is easier to understand, the vast majority of the current C# code base uses the old syntax, so it's important that you be able to recognize and work with it.

Multiple Markers and Values

In C#, you can use any number of markers and any number of values.

- The values can be used in any order.
- The values can be substituted any number of times in the format string.

For example, the following statement uses three markers and only two values. Notice that value 1 is used before value 0 and that value 1 is used twice.

```
Console.WriteLine("Three integers are {1}, {0} and {1}.", 3, 6);
```

This code produces the following output:

```
Three integers are 6, 3 and 6.
```

A marker must not attempt to reference a value at a position beyond the length of the list of substitution values. If it does, it will *not produce a compile error but a runtime error* (called an *exception*).

For example, in the following statement there are two substitution values, with positions 0 and 1. The second marker, however, references position 2—which does not exist. This produces a runtime error.

Position 0   Position 1
          ↓   ↓
```
Console.WriteLine("Two integers are {0} and {2}.", 3, 6);        // Error!
```
                                   ↑
            There is no position 2 value.

Formatting Numeric Strings

Throughout this text, the sample code will use the WriteLine method to display values. Usually, it will use the simple substitution marker, consisting only of curly braces surrounding an integer.

Many times, however, in your own code, you'll want to present the output of a text string in a format more appropriate than just a plain number. You might, for instance, want to display a value as currency or as a fixed-point value with a certain number of decimal places. You can do these things by using format strings.

For example, the following code consists of two statements that print out the value 500. The first line prints out the number without any additional formatting. In the second line, the format string specifies that the number should be formatted as currency.

```
Console.WriteLine("The value: {0}."  , 500);     // Print as number
Console.WriteLine("The value: {0:C}.", 500);     // Format and print as currency
                                ↑
                         Format as currency
```

This code produces the following output:

```
The value: 500.
The value: $500.00.
```

Using string interpolation, the following code produces the identical result to that shown previously:

```
int myInt = 500;
Console.WriteLine($"The value: {myInt}.");
Console.WriteLine($"The value: {myInt:C}.");
```

The difference between the two statements is that the formatted item includes additional information in the format specifier. The syntax for a format specifier consists of three fields inside the set of curly braces: the index (or string interpolation variable), the alignment specifier, and the format field. Figure 3-3 shows the syntax.

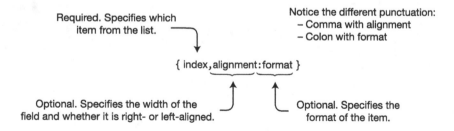

Figure 3-3. *Syntax for a format specifier*

The first thing in the format specifier is the index or a string interpolation variable. As you know, the index specifies which item from the list following the format string should be formatted. Unless a string interpolation variable is specified, the index is required, and the numbering of the list items starts at 0.

The Alignment Specifier

The alignment specifier represents the *minimum width* of the field in terms of characters. The alignment specifier has the following characteristics:

- The alignment specifier is optional and separated from the index with a comma.
- It consists of a positive or negative integer.
  - The integer represents the minimum number of characters to use for the field.
  - The sign represents either right or left alignment. A positive number specifies right alignment; a negative number specifies left alignment.

Index—use 0th item in the list
↓
```
Console.WriteLine("{0, 10}", 500);
```
↑
Alignment specifier—right-align in a field of ten characters

For example, the following code, which formats the value of int variable myInt, shows two format items. In the first case, the value of myInt is displayed as a right-aligned string of ten characters. In the second case, it's left-aligned. The format items are between two vertical bars, just so that in the output you can see the limits of the string on each side.

```
int myInt = 500;
Console.WriteLine("|{0, 10}|", myInt);      // Aligned right
Console.WriteLine("|{0,-10}|", myInt);      // Aligned left
```

This code produces the following output; there are ten characters between the vertical bars:

```
|       500|
|500       |
```

Using string interpolation, the following code produces the identical result to that shown earlier:

```
int myInt = 500;
Console.WriteLine($"|{myInt, 10}|");
Console.WriteLine($"|{myInt, -10}|");
```

The actual representation of the value might take more or fewer characters than specified in the alignment specifier.

- If the representation takes fewer characters than specified in the alignment specifier, the remaining characters are padded with spaces.
- If the representation takes more characters than specified, the alignment specifier is ignored, and the representation uses as many characters as are needed.

The Format Field

The format field specifies the form that the numeric representation should take. For example, should it be represented as currency, in decimal format, in hexadecimal format, or in fixed-point notation?

The format field has three parts, as shown in Figure 3-4.

- The colon character must be next to the format specifier, with no intervening spaces.

- The *format specifier* is a single alphabetic character, from a set of nine built-in character formats. The character can be uppercase or lowercase. The case is significant for some specifiers but not for others.

- The *precision specifier* is optional and consists of one or two digits. Its actual meaning depends on the format specifier.

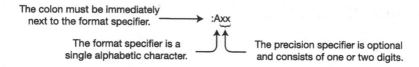

Figure 3-4. *Standard format field string*

The following code shows an example of the syntax of the format string component:

```
          Index—use 0th item in the list
                     ↓
Console.WriteLine("{0:F4}", 12.345678);
                     ↑
           Format component—fixed-point, four decimal places
```

The following code shows examples of different format strings:

```
double myDouble = 12.345678;
Console.WriteLine("{0,-10:G} -- General",                    myDouble);
Console.WriteLine("{0,-10} -- Default, same as General",     myDouble);
Console.WriteLine("{0,-10:F4} -- Fixed Point, 4 dec places", myDouble);
Console.WriteLine("{0,-10:C} -- Currency",                   myDouble);
Console.WriteLine("{0,-10:E3} -- Sci. Notation, 3 dec places", myDouble);
Console.WriteLine("{0,-10:x} -- Hexadecimal integer",        1194719 );
```

This code produces the following output:

```
12.345678  -- General
12.345678  -- Default, same as General
12.3457    -- Fixed Point, 4 dec places
$12.35     -- Currency
1.235E+001 -- Sci. Notation, 3 dec places
123adf     -- Hexadecimal integer
```

Using string interpolation, as shown in the following code, produces an identical result to that shown earlier:

```
double myDouble = 12.345678;
Console.WriteLine($"{myDouble,-10:G} -- General");
Console.WriteLine($"{myDouble,-10} -- Default, same as General");
Console.WriteLine($"{myDouble,-10:F4} -- Fixed Point, 4 dec places");
Console.WriteLine($"{myDouble,-10:C} -- Currency");
Console.WriteLine($"{myDouble,-10:E3} -- Sci. Notation, 3 dec places");
Console.WriteLine($"{1194719,-10:x} -- Hexadecimal integer");
```

Standard Numeric Format Specifiers

Table 3-4 summarizes the nine standard numeric format specifiers. The first column lists the name of the specifier followed by the specifier characters. If the specifier characters have different output depending on their case, they are marked *case-sensitive*.

Table 3-4. *Standard Numeric Format Specifiers*

Name and Characters	Meaning
Currency C, c	Formats the value as a currency, using a currency symbol. The currency symbol used will depend on the culture setting of the PC running the program. Precision specifier: The number of decimal places. Sample: `Console.WriteLine("{0 :C}", 12.5);` Output: `$12.50`
Decimal D, d	A string of decimal digits, with a negative sign, if appropriate. Can be used only with integer types. Precision specifier: The minimum number of digits to use in the output string. If the number has fewer digits, it will be padded with 0s on the left. Sample: `Console.WriteLine("{0 :D4}", 12);` Output: `0012`
Fixed-point F, f	A string of decimal digits with a decimal point. Can also include a negative sign, if appropriate. Precision specifier: The number of decimal places. Sample: `Console.WriteLine("{0 :F4}", 12.3456789);` Output: `12.3457`
General G, g	A compact fixed-point representation or a scientific notation representation, depending on the value. This is the default, if no specifier is listed. Precision specifier: Depends on the value. Sample: `Console.WriteLine("{0 :G4}", 12.3456789);` Output: `12.35`
Hexadecimal X, x Case sensitive	A string of hexadecimal digits. The hex digits A through F will match the case of the specifier. Precision specifier: The minimum number of digits to use in the output string. If the number has fewer digits, it will be padded with 0s on the left. Sample: `Console.WriteLine("{0 :x}", 180026);` Output: `2bf3a`

(continued)

Table 3-4. (*continued*)

Name and Characters	Meaning
Number N, n	Similar to fixed-point representation but includes comma or period separators between each group of three digits, starting at the decimal point and going left. Whether it uses a comma or a period depends on the culture setting of the PC running the program. Precision specifier: The number of decimal places.
	Sample: `Console.WriteLine("{0 :N2}", 12345678.54321);` Output: `12,345,678.54`
Percent P, p	A string that represents percent. The number is multiplied by 100. Precision specifier: The number of decimal places.
	Sample: `Console.WriteLine("{0 :P2}", 0.1221897);` Output: `12.22 %`
Round-trip R, r	The output string is chosen so that if the string is converted back to a numeric value using a `Parse` method, the result will be the original value. `Parse` methods are described in Chapter 27. Precision specifier: Ignored.
	Sample: `Console.WriteLine("{0 :R}", 1234.21897);` Output: `1234.21897`
Scientific E, e Case-sensitive	Scientific notation with a mantissa and an exponent. The exponent is preceded by the letter E. The E character will be the same case as the specifier. Precision specifier: The number of decimal places.
	Sample: `Console.WriteLine("{0 :e4}", 12.3456789);` Output: `1.2346e+001`

Both alignment specifiers and format specifiers continue to be available with string interpolation.

```
double var1 = 3.14159;
System.Console.WriteLine($"The value of var1 is {var1,10:f5}");
```

Comments: Annotating the Code

You've already seen single-line comments, so here I'll discuss the second type of inline comments—*delimited comments*—and mention a third type called *documentation comments*.

- Delimited comments have a two-character start marker (/*) and a two-character end marker (*/).

- Text between the matching markers is ignored by the compiler.

- Delimited comments can span any number of lines.

For example, the following code shows a delimited comment spanning multiple lines:

```
↓ Beginning of comment spanning multiple lines
/*
    This text is ignored by the compiler.
    Unlike single-line comments, delimited comments
    like this one can span multiple lines.
*/
↑ End of comment
```

A delimited comment can also span just part of a line. For example, the following statement shows text commented out of the middle of a line. The result is the declaration of a single variable, var2.

```
Beginning of comment
        ↓
int /*var 1,*/ var2;
            ↑
        End of comment
```

■ **Note**   Single-line and delimited comments behave in C# just as they do in C and C++.

40

More About Comments

There are a couple of other important things you need to know about comments.

- You cannot nest delimited comments. Only one comment can be in effect at a time. If you attempt to nest comments, the comment that starts first will remain in effect until the end of its scope.

- The scope for comment types is as follows:
  - For single-line comments, the comment will remain in effect until the end of the current line.
  - For delimited comments, the comment will remain in effect until the *first* end delimiter is encountered.

The following attempts at comments are incorrect:

```
↓ Opens the comment
/* This is an attempt at a nested comment.
    /*  ← Ignored because it's inside a comment
        Inner comment
    */ ← Closes the comment because it's the first end delimiter encountered
*/    ← Syntax error because it has no opening delimiter

↓ Opens the comment          ↓ Ignored because it's inside a comment
// Single-line comment    /* Nested comment?
                      */ ← Incorrect because it has no opening delimiter
```

Documentation Comments

C# also provides a third type of comment: the documentation comment. Documentation comments contain XML text that can be used to produce program documentation. Comments of this type look like single-line comments except that they have three contiguous slashes rather than two. I'll cover documentation comments in Chapter 27.

The following code shows the form of documentation comments:

```
/// <summary>
/// This class does...
/// </summary>
class Program
{
    ...
```

Summary of Comment Types

Inline comments are sections of text that are ignored by the compiler but are included in the code to document it. Programmers insert comments into their code to explain and document it. Table 3-5 summarizes the comment types.

Table 3-5. *Comment Types*

Type	Start	End	Description
Single-line	//		The text from the beginning marker to the end of the current line is ignored by the compiler.
Delimited	/*	*/	The text between the start and end markers is ignored by the compiler.
Documentation	///		Comments of this type contain XML text that is meant to be used by a tool to produce program documentation. This is described in more detail in Chapter 27.

While comments that do little more than repeat the name of a variable or method are generally of minimal value, comments that explain the purpose of a given block of code can be enormously useful during subsequent maintenance. Since all valuable code will eventually require maintenance, you can save a lot of effort by reading what the original developer had in mind with the block of code at issue.

CHAPTER 4

■ ■ ■

Types, Storage, and Variables

© Daniel Solis and Cal Schrotenboer 2018

D. Solis and C. Schrotenboer, *Illustrated C# 7*, https://doi.org/10.1007/978-1-4842-3288-0_4

A C# Program Is a Set of Type Declarations

If you were to broadly characterize the source code of C and C++ programs, you might say that a C program is a set of functions and data types and that a C++ program is a set of functions and classes. A C# program, however, is a set of type declarations.

- The source code of a C# program or DLL is a set of one or more type declarations.

- For an executable, one of the types declared must be a class that includes a method called Main.

- A *namespace* is a way of grouping a related set of type declarations and giving the group a name. Since your program is a related set of type declarations, you will generally declare your program type inside a namespace you create.

For example, the following code shows a program that consists of three type declarations. The three types are declared inside a namespace called MyProgram.

```
namespace MyProgram                    // Declare a namespace.
{
   DeclarationOfTypeA                  // Declare a type.

   DeclarationOfTypeB                  // Declare a type.

   class C                            // Declare a type.
   {
      static void Main()
      {
         ...
      }
   }
}
```

Namespaces are explained in detail in Chapter 22.

A Type Is a Template

Since a C# program is just a set of type declarations, learning C# consists of learning how to create and use types. So, the first thing you need to do is to look at what a type is.

You can start by thinking of a type as a *template* for creating data structures. It isn't the data structure itself, but it specifies the characteristics of objects constructed from the template.

A type is defined by the following elements:

- A name

- A data structure to contain its data members

- Behaviors and constraints

For example, Figure 4-1 illustrates the components of two types: short and int.

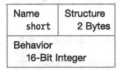

Figure 4-1. A type is a template

Instantiating a Type

Creating an actual object from the type's template is called *instantiating* the type.

- The object created by instantiating a type is called either an *object* of the type or an *instance* of the type. The terms are interchangeable.

- Every data item in a C# program is an instance of some type provided by the language, the BCL, or another library, or defined by the programmer.

Figure 4-2 illustrates the instantiation of objects of two predefined types.

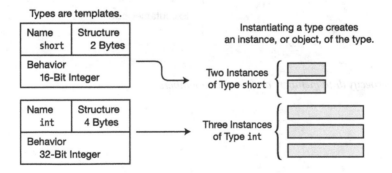

Figure 4-2. Instantiating a type creates an instance

45

Data Members and Function Members

Some types, such as short, int, and long, are called *simple types* and can store only a single data item.

Other types can store multiple data items. An *array*, for example, is a type that can store multiple items of the same type. The individual items are called *elements* and are referenced by a number, called an *index*. Chapter 13 describes arrays in detail.

Types of Members

There are other types, however, that can contain data items of many different types. The individual elements in these types are called *members*, and unlike arrays, in which each member is referred to by a number, these members have distinct names.

There are two kinds of members: data members and function members.

- *Data members* store data that is relevant to the object of the class or to the class as a whole.

- *Function members* execute code. Function members define how the type can act.

For example, Figure 4-3 shows some of the data members and function members of type XYZ. It contains two data members and two function members.

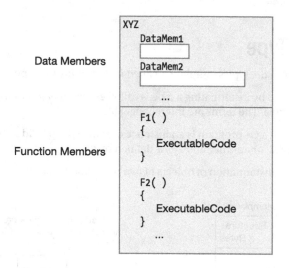

Figure 4-3. *Types specify data members and function members*

Predefined Types

C# provides 16 predefined types, which are shown in Figure 4-4 and listed in Tables 4-1 and 4-2. They include 13 simple types and 3 nonsimple types.

The names of all the predefined types consist of *all lowercase* characters. The predefined simple types include the following:

- Eleven numeric types, including the following:

  - Various lengths of signed and unsigned integer types.

  - Floating-point types—float and double.

  - A high-precision decimal type called decimal. Unlike float and double, type decimal can represent decimal fractional numbers exactly. It's often used for monetary calculations.

- A Unicode character type, called char.

- A Boolean type, called bool. Type bool represents Boolean values and must be one of two values—either true or false.

■ **Note**   Unlike C and C++, in C# numeric values do not have a Boolean interpretation.

The three nonsimple types are the following:

- Type string, which is an array of Unicode characters

- Type object, which is the base type on which all other types are based

- Type dynamic, which is used when using assemblies written in dynamic languages

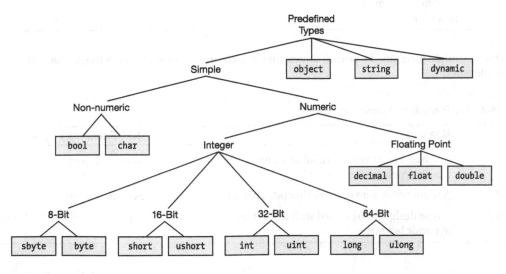

Figure 4-4. *The predefined types*

More About the Predefined Types

All the predefined types are mapped directly to underlying .NET types. The C# type names are simply aliases for the .NET types, so using the .NET names works fine syntactically, although this is discouraged. Within a C# program, you should use the C# names rather than the .NET names.

The predefined simple types represent a single item of data. They're listed in Table 4-1, along with the ranges of values they can represent and the underlying .NET types to which they map.

Table 4-1. *The Predefined Simple Types*

Name	Meaning	Range	.NET Framework Type	Default Value
sbyte	8-bit signed integer	-128 to 127	System.SByte	0
byte	8-bit unsigned integer	0 to 255	System.Byte	0
short	16-bit signed integer	-32,768 to 32,767	System.Int16	0
ushort	16-bit unsigned integer	0 to 65,535	System.UInt16	0
int	32-bit signed integer	-2,147,483,648 to 2,147,483,647	System.Int32	0
uint	32-bit unsigned integer	0 to 4,294,967,295	System.UInt32	0
long	64-bit signed integer	-9,223,372,036,854,775,808 to 9,223,372,036,854,775,807	System.Int64	0
ulong	64-bit unsigned integer	0 to 18,446,744,073,709,551,615	System.UInt64	0
float	Single-precision float	1.5×10^{-45} to 3.4×10^{38}	System.Single	0.0f
double	Double-precision float	5×10^{-324} to 1.7×10^{308}	System.Double	0.0d
bool	Boolean	true, false	System.Boolean	false
char	Unicode character	U+0000 to U+ffff	System.Char	\x0000
decimal	Decimal value with 28-significant-digit precision	$\pm 1.0 \times 10^{28}$ to $\pm 7.9 \times 10^{28}$	System.Decimal	0m

The nonsimple predefined types are somewhat more complex. Table 4-2 shows the predefined nonsimple types.

Table 4-2. *The Predefined Nonsimple Types*

Name	Meaning	.NET Framework Type
object	The base class from which all other types, including the simple types are derived	System.Object
string	A sequence of zero or more Unicode characters	System.String
dynamic	A type designed to be used with assemblies written in dynamic languages	No corresponding .NET type

User-Defined Types

Besides the 16 predefined types provided by C#, you can also create your own user-defined types. There are six kinds of types you can create.

- `class` types

- `struct` types

- `array` types

- `enum` types

- `delegate` types

- `interface` types

You create a type using a *type declaration*, which includes the following information:

- The kind of type you are creating

- The name of the new type

- A declaration (name and specification) of each of the type's members—except for `array` and `delegate` types, which don't have named members

Once you've declared a type, you can create and use objects of the type just as if they were predefined types. Figure 4-5 summarizes the use of predefined and user-defined types. Using predefined types is a one-step process in which you simply instantiate the objects of that type. Using user-defined types is a two-step process. You must first declare the type and then instantiate objects of the type.

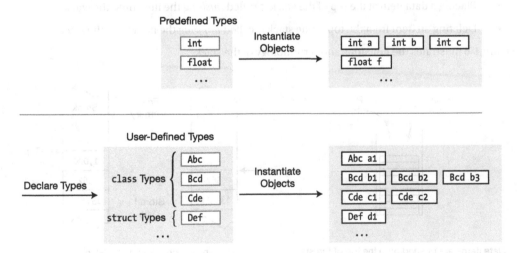

Figure 4-5. *The predefined types require instantiation only. The user-defined types require two steps: declaration and instantiation.*

The Stack and the Heap

While a program is running, its data must be stored in memory. How much memory is required for an item, and where and how it's stored, depends on its type.

A running program uses two regions of memory to store data: the *stack* and the *heap*.

The Stack

The stack is an array of memory that acts as a last-in, first-out (LIFO) data structure. It stores several types of data.

- The values of certain types of variables

- The program's current execution environment

- Parameters passed to methods

The system takes care of all stack manipulation. You, as the programmer, don't need to do anything with it explicitly. But understanding its basic functions will give you a better understanding of what your program is doing when it's running and allow you to better understand the C# documentation and literature.

Facts About Stacks

The general characteristics of stacks are the following:

- Data can be added to and deleted only from the top of the stack.

- Placing a data item at the top of the stack is called *pushing* the item onto the stack.

- Deleting an item from the top of the stack is called *popping* the item from the stack.

Figure 4-6 illustrates the functions and terminology of the stack.

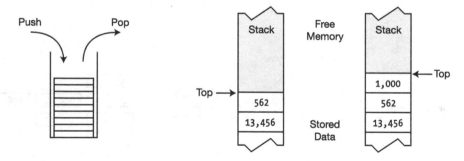

Data items are pushed onto the top of the stack
and popped from the top of the stack.

Pushing an integer (e.g., 1,000) onto
the stack moves the top of the stack up.

Figure 4-6. *Pushing and popping on the stack*

The Heap

The heap is an area of memory where chunks are allocated to store certain kinds of data objects. Unlike the stack, data can be stored and removed from the heap in any order. Figure 4-7 shows a program that has four items stored in the heap.

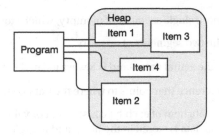

Figure 4-7. *The memory heap*

Although your program can store items in the heap, it cannot explicitly delete them. Instead, the CLR's garbage collector (GC) automatically cleans up orphaned heap objects when it determines that your code can no longer access them. This frees you from what in other programming languages can be an error-prone task. Figure 4-8 illustrates the garbage collection process.

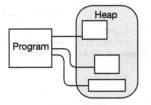

1. The program has stored three objects in the heap.

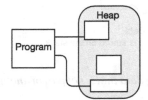

2. Later in the program, one of the objects is no longer used by the program.

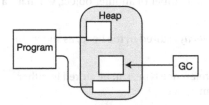

3. The garbage collector finds the orphaned object and releases it.

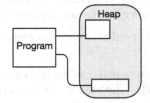

4. After garbage collection, the released object's memory is available for reuse.

Figure 4-8. *Automatic garbage collection in the heap*

Value Types and Reference Types

The *type* of a data item defines how much memory is required to store it and the data members that comprise it. The type also determines where an object is stored in memory—the stack or the heap.

Types are divided into two categories: value types and reference types. Objects of these types are stored differently in memory.

- Value types require only a single segment of memory, which stores the actual data.

- Reference types require two segments of memory.

  - The first contains the actual data—and is always located in the heap.

  - The second is a reference that points to where the data is stored in the heap.

Figure 4-9 shows how a single data item of each type is stored. For value types, data is stored on the stack. For reference types, the actual data is stored in the heap, and the reference is stored on the stack.

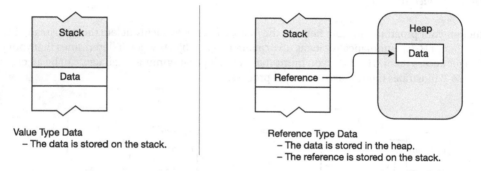

Figure 4-9. *Storing data that is not part of another type*

Storing Members of a Reference Type Object

Although Figure 4-9 shows how data is stored when it isn't a member of another object, when it's a member of another object, data might be stored a little differently.

- The data portion of a reference type object is *always* stored in the heap, as shown in Figure 4-9.

- A value type object, or the reference part of a reference type, can be stored in either the stack or the heap, depending on the circumstances.

Suppose, for example, that you have an instance of a reference type called MyType that has two members—a value type member and a reference type member. How is it stored? Is the value type member stored on the stack and the reference type split between the stack and the heap, as shown in Figure 4-9? The answer is no.

Remember that for a reference type, the data of an instance is *always* stored in the heap. Since both members are part of the object's data, they're both stored in the heap, regardless of whether they are value or reference types. Figure 4-10 illustrates the case of type MyType.

- Even though member A is a value type, it's part of the data of the instance of MyType and is therefore stored with the object's data in the heap.

- Member B is a reference type, and therefore its data portion will always be stored in the heap, as shown by the small box marked "Data." What's different is that its reference is also stored in the heap, inside the data portion of the enclosing MyType object.

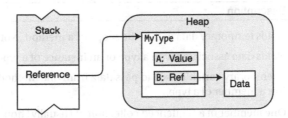

Figure 4-10. *Storage of data as part of a reference type*

■ **Note**   For any object of a reference type, all its data members are stored in the heap, regardless of whether they are of value type or reference type.

Categorizing the C# Types

Table 4-3 shows all the types available in C# and what kinds of types they are—value types or reference types. Each reference type is covered later in the text.

Table 4-3. *Value Types and Reference Types in C#*

	Value Types		Reference Types	
Predefined types	sbyte	byte	float	object
	short	ushort	double	string
	int	uint	char	dynamic
	long	ulong	decimal	
	bool			
User-defined types	struct			class
	enum			interface
				delegate
				array

Variables

A general-purpose programming language must allow a program to store and retrieve data.

- A *variable* is a name that represents data stored in memory during program execution.

- C# provides four kinds of variables, each of which will be discussed in detail. These are listed in Table 4-4.

Table 4-4. *The Four Kinds of Variables*

Name	Description
Local variable	Holds temporary data within the scope of a method. Not a member of a type.
Field	Holds data associated with a type or an instance of a type. Member of a type.
Parameter	A temporary variable used to pass data from one method to another method. Not a member of a type.
Array element	One member of a sequenced collection of (usually) homogeneous data items. Can be either local or a member of a type.

Variable Declarations

A variable must be declared before it can be used. The variable declaration defines the variable and accomplishes two things.

- It gives the variable a name and associates a type with it.

- It allows the compiler to allocate memory for it.

A simple variable declaration requires at least a type and a name. The following declaration defines a variable named var2, of type `int`:

```
Type
 ↓
int var2;
     ↑
    Name
```

For example, Figure 4-11 represents the declaration of four variables and their places on the stack.

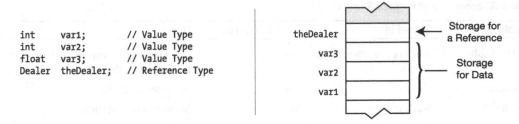

Figure 4-11. *Value type and reference type variable declarations*

Variable Initializers

Besides declaring a variable's name and type, you can optionally use the declaration to initialize its memory to a specific value.

A *variable initializer* consists of an equal sign followed by the initializing value, as shown here:

```
      Initializer
          ↓
int var2 = 17;
```

Local variables without initializers have an undefined value and cannot be used until they have been assigned a value. Attempting to use an undefined local variable causes the compiler to produce an error message.

Figure 4-12 shows a number of local variable declarations on the left and the resulting stack configuration on the right. Some of the variables have initializers, and others do not. Because of automatic initialization, the variable dealer1 in Figure 4-12 will have a value of null, and the variable var1 will have a value of 0, provided that those variables are not declared inside a method.

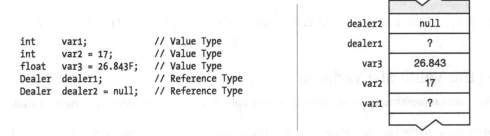

Figure 4-12. *Variable initializers*

Automatic Initialization

Some kinds of variables are automatically set to default values if they are declared without an initializer, and others are not. Variables that are not automatically initialized to default values contain undefined values until the program assigns them a value. Table 4-5 shows which kinds of variables are automatically initialized and which are not. I'll cover each of the five kinds of variables later in the text.

Table 4-5. *Summary of Variable Storage*

Variable	Stored In	Auto-initialized	Use
Local variables	Stack or stack and heap	No	Used for local computation inside a function member
Class fields	Heap	Yes	Members of a class
Struct fields	Stack or heap	Yes	Members of a struct
Parameters	Stack	No	Used for passing values into and out of a method
Array elements	Heap	Yes	Members of an array

Multiple-Variable Declarations

You can declare multiple variables in a single declaration statement.

- The variables in a multiple-variable declaration must all be of the same type.

- The variable names must be separated with commas. Initializers can be included with the variable names.

For example, the following code shows two valid declaration statements with multiple variables. Notice that the initialized variables can be mixed with uninitialized variables as long as they're separated by commas. The last declaration statement shown is invalid because it attempts to declare variables of different types in a single statement.

```
// Variable declarations--some with initializers, some without
int     var3 = 7, var4, var5 = 3;
double var6, var7 = 6.52;
```

```
Type          Different type
  ↓                ↓
int var8,   float var9;        // Error! Can't mix types (int and float)
```

Using the Value of a Variable

A variable name represents the value stored by the variable. You can use the value by using the variable name.

For example, in the following statement, the variable name var2 represents the *value* stored by the variable. That value is retrieved from memory when the statement is executed.

```
Console.WriteLine("{0}", var2);
```

Static Typing and the dynamic Keyword

One thing you'll have noticed is that every variable declaration includes the *type* of the variable. This allows the compiler to determine the amount of memory it will require at run time and which parts should be stored on the stack and which in the heap. The type of the variable is determined at compile time and cannot be changed at run time. This is called *static typing*.

Not all languages, though, are statically typed. Many, including scripting languages such as IronPython and IronRuby, are *dynamically typed*. That is, the type of a variable might not be resolved until run time. Since these are also .NET languages, C# programs need to be able to use assemblies written in these languages. The problem, then, is that C# needs to be able to resolve at compile time a type from an assembly that doesn't resolve its types until run time.

To solve this problem, C# provides the dynamic keyword to represent a specific C# type that knows how to resolve itself at run time.

At compile time, the compiler doesn't do type checking on variables of type dynamic. Instead, it packages up any information about the variable's operations and includes that information with the variable. At run time, that information is checked to make sure it's consistent with the actual type to which the variable was resolved. If it isn't, the run time throws an exception.

Nullable Types

There are situations, particularly when working with databases, where you want to indicate that a variable does not currently hold a valid value. For reference types, you can do this easily, by setting the variable to null. When you define a variable of a value type, however, its memory is allocated whether or not its contents have any valid meaning.

What you would like in this situation is to have a Boolean indicator associated with the variable so that when the value is valid, the indicator is true, and that when the value is not valid, the indicator is false.

Nullable types allow you to create a value type variable that can be marked as valid or invalid so that you can make sure a variable is valid before using it. Regular value types are called *non-nullable types*.. I'll explain the details of nullable types in Chapter 27, when you have a better understanding of C#.

CHAPTER 5

■ ■ ■

Classes: The Basics

© Daniel Solis and Cal Schrotenboer 2018

D. Solis and C. Schrotenboer, *Illustrated C# 7*, https://doi.org/10.1007/978-1-4842-3288-0_5

Overview of Classes

In the previous chapter, you saw that C# provides six user-defined types. The most important of these, and the one we'll cover first, is the *class*. Since the topic of classes in C is a large one, we'll spread its discussion over the next several chapters.

A Class Is an Active Data Structure

Before the days of object-oriented analysis and design, programmers thought of a program as just a sequence of instructions. The focus at that time was on structuring and optimizing those instructions. With the advent of the object-oriented paradigm, the focus changed from optimizing instructions to organizing a program's data and functions into encapsulated sets of logically related data items and functions, called *classes*.

A class is a data structure that can store data and execute code. It contains data members and function members.

- *Data members* store data associated with the class or an instance of the class. Data members generally model the attributes of the real-world object the class represents.

- Function members execute code. These generally model the functions and actions of the real-world object that the class represents.

A C# class can have any number of data and function members. The members can be any combination of nine possible member types. Table 5-1 shows these member types. In this chapter we'll cover fields and methods.

Table 5-1. *Types of Class Members*

Data Members Store Data	Function Members Execute Code	
Fields	Methods	Operators
Constants	Properties	Indexers
	Constructors	Events
	Destructors	

■ **Note** Classes are encapsulated sets of logically related data items and functions that generally represent objects in the real world or a conceptual world.

Programs and Classes: A Quick Example

A running C# program is a group of interacting type objects, most of which are instances of classes. For example, suppose you have a program simulating a poker game. When it's running, it might have an instance of a class called Dealer, whose job is to run the game, and several instances of a class called Player, which represent the players of the game.

The Dealer object stores such information as the current state of the card deck and the number of players. Its actions include shuffling the deck and dealing the cards.

The Player class is very different. It stores such information as the player's name and the amount of money left to bet, and it performs actions such as analyzing the player's current hand and placing bets. Figure 5-1 illustrates the running program. The class names are shown outside the boxes, and the instance names are inside.

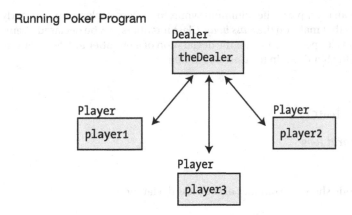

Figure 5-1. *The objects in a running program*

A real program would undoubtedly contain dozens of other classes besides Dealer and Player. These would include classes such as Card and Deck. Each class models some *thing* that is a component of the poker game.

■ **Note**   A running program is a set of objects interacting with each other.

Declaring a Class

Although types int, double, and char are defined in the C# language, classes such as Dealer and Player, as you can probably guess, are not defined by the language. If you want to use them in a program, you'll have to define them yourself. You do this by writing a *class declaration*.

A *class declaration* defines the characteristics and members of a new class. It does not create an instance of the class but creates the template from which class instances will be created. The class declaration provides the following:

- The class name

- The members of the class

- The characteristics of the class

The following is an example of the minimum syntax for a class declaration. The curly braces contain the member declarations that make up the *class body*. Class members can be declared in any order inside the class body. This means it's perfectly fine for the declaration of a member to refer to another member that is not yet defined until further down in the class declaration.

```
Keyword      Class name
   ↓             ↓
class    MyExcellentClass
{
    MemberDeclarations
}
```

The following code shows the outlines of two class declarations:

```
class Dealer           // Class declaration
{
    ...
}


class Player           // Class declaration
{
    ...
}
```

■ **Note**   Since a class declaration "defines" a new class, you will often see a class declaration referred to as a *class definition* both in the literature and in common usage among programmers.

Class Members

Two of the most important class member types are fields and methods. Fields are data members, and methods are function members.

Fields

A *field* is a variable that belongs to a class.

- It can be of any type, either predefined or user-defined.

- Like all variables, fields store data and have the following characteristics:

  - They can be written to.

  - They can be read from.

The minimum syntax for declaring a field is the following:

```
Type
 ↓
Type Identifier;
          ↑
       Field name
```

For example, the following class contains the declaration of field `MyField`, which can store an `int` value:

```
class MyClass
{    Type
       ↓
     int MyField;
            ↑
}        Field name
```

■ **Note**   Unlike C and C++, in C# there are *no global variables* (that is, variables or fields) declared outside of a type. All fields belong to a type and must be declared within their type declaration.

Explicit and Implicit Field Initialization

Since a field is a kind of variable, the syntax for a field initializer is the same as that of the variable initializer shown in the previous chapter.

- A *field initializer* is part of the field declaration and consists of an equal sign followed by an expression that evaluates to a value.

- The initialization value must be determinable at compile time.

```
class MyClass
{
    int F1 = 17;
}
```
               ↑
         Field initializer

- If no initializer is used, the compiler sets the value of a field to a default value, determined by the type of the field. Table 4-1 (in Chapter 4) gives the default values for the simple types. To summarize them, the default value for each type is 0 and is false for bool. The default for reference types is null.

For example, the following code declares four fields. The first two fields are initialized implicitly. The second two fields are initialized explicitly with initializers.

```
class MyClass
{
    int    F1;              // Initialized to 0    - value type
    string F2;              // Initialized to null - reference type

    int    F3 = 25;         // Initialized to 25
    string F4 = "abcd";     // Initialized to "abcd"
}
```

Declarations with Multiple Fields

You can declare multiple fields *of the same type* in the same statement by separating the names with commas. You cannot mix different types in a single declaration. For example, you can combine the four preceding field declarations into two statements, with the exact same semantic result.

```
int    F1, F3 = 25;
string F2, F4 = "abcd";.
```

Methods

A method is a named block of executable code that can be executed from many different parts of the program, and even from other programs. (There are also anonymous methods, which aren't named—but we'll cover those in Chapter 14.)

When a method is *called*, or *invoked*, it executes the method's code and then returns to the code that called it and continues executing the calling code. Some methods return a value to the position from which they were called; others do not. Methods correspond to member functions in C++.

The minimum syntax for declaring a method includes the following components:

- *Return type*: This states the type of value the method returns. If a method doesn't return a value, the return type is specified as void.

- *Name*: This is the name of the method.

- *Parameter list*: This consists of at least an empty set of matching parentheses. If there are parameters (which we'll cover in the next chapter), they're listed between the parentheses.

- *Method body*: This consists of a matching set of curly braces containing the executable code.

For example, the following code declares a class with a simple method called PrintNums. From the declaration, you can tell the following about PrintNums:

- The return type is specified as void; hence, it returns no value.

- It has an empty parameter list.

- It contains two lines of code in its method body. The first prints the number 1, and the second prints 2.

```
class SimpleClass
{
   Return type      Parameter list
       ↓                 ↓
   void PrintNums()
   {
      Console.WriteLine("1");
      Console.WriteLine("2");
   }
}
```

■ **Note**   Unlike C and C++, in C# there are *no global functions* (that is, methods or functions) declared outside of a type declaration. Also unlike C and C++, in C# there is no "default" return type for a method. All methods must include a return type or list it as void.

Creating Variables and Instances of a Class

The class declaration is just the blueprint from which instances of the class are created. Once a class is declared, you can create instances of the class.

- Classes are reference types, which, as you will remember from the previous chapter, means that they require memory both for the reference to the data and for the actual data.

- The reference to the data is stored in a variable of the class type. So, to create an instance of the class, you need to start by declaring a variable of the class type. If the variable isn't initialized, its value is undefined.

Figure 5-2 illustrates how to define the variable to hold the reference. At the top of the code on the left is a declaration for class Dealer. After that is a declaration for class Program, which contains method Main. Main declares variable theDealer of type Dealer. Since the variable is uninitialized, its value is undefined, as shown on the right in the figure.

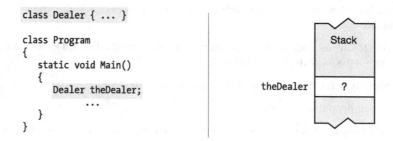

Figure 5-2. *Allocating memory for the reference of a class variable*

Allocating Memory for the Data

Declaring the variable of the class type allocates the memory to hold the reference, but not the memory to hold the actual data of the class object. To allocate memory for the actual data, you use the new operator.

- The new operator allocates and initializes memory for an instance of the specified type. It allocates the memory from either the stack or the heap, depending on the type.

- Use the new operator to form an object-creation expression, which consists of the following:

  - The keyword new.

  - The name of the type of the instance for which memory is to be allocated.

  - Matching parentheses—which may or may not include parameters. We'll discuss more about the possible parameters later.

Keyword   Parentheses are required.
  ↓   ↓
  new *TypeName* ( )
       ↑
     Type

- If the memory allocated is for a reference type, the object-creation expression returns a reference to the allocated and initialized instance of the object in the heap.

This is exactly what you need to allocate and initialize the memory to hold the class instance data. Use the new operator to create an object-creation expression and assign the value returned by it to the class variable. Here's an example:

```
Dealer theDealer;          // Declare variable for the reference
theDealer = new Dealer();  // Allocate memory for the class object and assign
           ↑               // it to the variable
   Object-creation expression
```

The code on the left in Figure 5-3 shows the new operator used to allocate memory and create an instance of class Dealer, which is then assigned to the class variable. The memory structure is illustrated in the figure, to the right of the code.

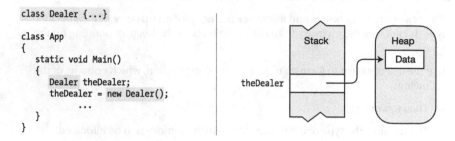

```
class Dealer {...}

class App
{
    static void Main()
    {
        Dealer theDealer;
        theDealer = new Dealer();
            ...
    }
}
```

Figure 5-3. *Allocating memory for the data of a class variable*

Combining the Steps

You can combine the two steps by *initializing* the variable with the object-creation expression.

Declare variable.
↓

Dealer theDealer = new Dealer();   // Declare and initialize
                        ↑
        Initialize with an object-creation expression.

Instance Members

A class declaration acts as a blueprint from which you can create as many instances of the class as you like.

- *Instance members*: Each instance of a class is a separate entity that has its own set of data members, distinct from the other instances of the same class. These are called *instance members* since they are associated with an instance of the class.

- *Static members*: Instance members are the default, but you can also declare members called *static members*, which are associated with the class, not the instance. We'll cover these in Chapter 7.

As an example of instance members, the following code shows the poker program with three instances of class Player. Figure 5-4 shows that each instance has a different value for the Name field.

```
class  Dealer { ... }                    // Declare class
class  Player                            // Declare class
{
   string Name;                          // Field
   ...
}

class Program
{
   static void Main()
   {
      Dealer theDealer = new Dealer();
      Player player1   = new Player();
      Player player2   = new Player();
      Player player3   = new Player();
      ...
   }
}
```

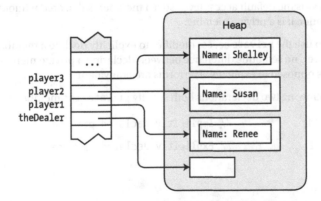

Figure 5-4. *Instance members have distinct values between class objects*

Access Modifiers

From within a class, any function member can access any other member of the class by simply using that member's name.

The *access modifier* is an optional part of a member declaration that specifies what other parts of the program have access to the member. The access modifier is placed before the simple declaration forms. The following is the syntax for fields and methods:

```
Fields
    AccessModifier Type Identifier

Methods
    AccessModifier ReturnType MethodName ()
    {
        ...
    }
```

The five categories of member access are the following. We'll describe the first two in this chapter and the others in Chapter 8.

- Private

- Public

- Protected

- Internal

- Protected internal

Private and Public Access

Private members are accessible only from within the class in which they are declared—other classes cannot see or access them.

- Private access is the default access level, so if a member is declared without an access modifier, it is a private member.

- You can also use the `private` access modifier to explicitly declare a member as private. There's no semantic difference between declaring a private member implicitly as opposed to explicitly. The forms are equivalent.

For example, the following two declarations both specify `private int` members:

```
        int MyInt1;          // Implicitly declared private

  private int MyInt2;        // Explicitly declared private
      ↑
Access modifier
```

Public members of an instance are accessible to other objects in the program. You must use the `public` access modifier to specify public access.

Access modifier
↓
```
public int MyInt;
```

Depicting Public and Private Access

The figures in this text represent classes as labeled boxes, as shown in Figure 5-5.

- The class members are represented as smaller labeled boxes inside the class boxes.

- Private members are represented as enclosed entirely within their class box.

- Public members are represented as sticking partially outside their class box.

```
class Program
{
            int Member1;
    private int Member2;
    public  int Member3;
}
```

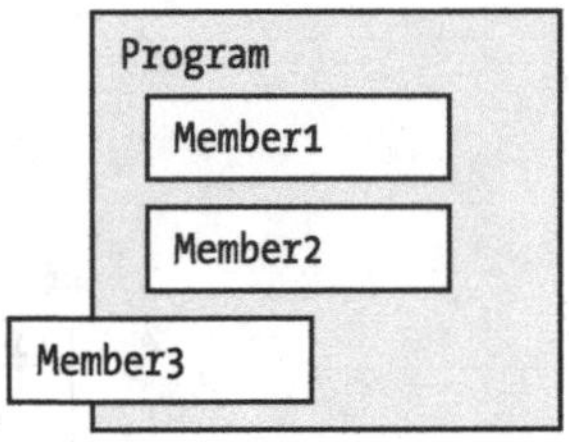

Figure 5-5. *Representing classes and members*

Example of Member Access

Class C1 in the following code declares both public and private fields and methods. Figure 5-6 illustrates the visibility of the members of class C1.

```
class C1
{
    int        F1;              // Implicit private field
    private int F2;             // Explicit private field
    public  int F3;             // Public field

    void DoCalc()               // Implicit private method
    {
        ...
    }

    public int GetVal()         // Public method
    {
        ...
    }
}
```

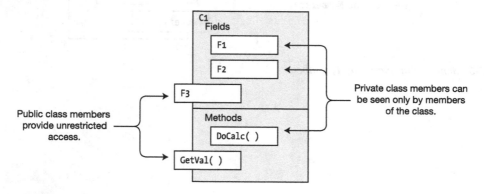

Figure 5-6. *Private and public class members*

Accessing Members from Inside the Class

As mentioned, members of a class can access the other class members by just using their names.

For example, the following class declaration shows the methods of the class accessing the fields and other methods. Even though the fields and two of the methods are declared private, all the members of a class can be accessed by any method (or any function member) of the class. Figure 5-7 illustrates the code.

```
class DaysTemp
{
   // Fields
   private int High = 75;
   private int Low  = 45;

   // Methods
   private int GetHigh()
   {
      return High;                    // Access private field
   }

   private int GetLow()
   {
      return Low;                     // Access private field
   }

   public float Average ()
   {
      return (GetHigh() + GetLow()) / 2;   // Access private methods
   }          ↑        ↑
            Accessing the private methods
}
```

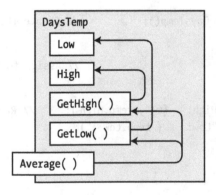

Figure 5-7. *Members within a class can freely access each other*

Accessing Members from Outside the Class

To access a public instance member from outside the class, you must include the variable name and the member name, separated by a period (dot). This is called *dot-syntax notation*; we'll describe it in more detail later.

For example, the second line of the following code shows an example of accessing a method from outside the class:

```
DaysTemp myDt = new DaysTemp();        // Create an object of the class
float fValue  = myDt.Average();        // Access it from outside
                ↑         ↑
        Variable name   Member name
```

As an example, the following code declares two classes: DaysTemp and Program.

- The two fields in DaysTemp are declared public, so they can be accessed from outside the class.

- Method Main is a member of class Program. It creates a variable and object of class DaysTemp, and it assigns values to the fields of the object. It then reads the values of the fields and prints them out.

```
class DaysTemp                                 // Declare class DaysTemp
{
   public int High = 75;
   public int Low  = 45;
}

class Program                                  // Declare class Program
{
   static void Main()
   {           Variable name
                    ↓
      DaysTemp temp = new DaysTemp();           // Create the object
Variable name and field
             ↓
      temp.High = 85;                           // Assign to the fields
      temp.Low  = 60;                  Variable name and field
                                               ↓
      Console.WriteLine("High:    {0}", temp.High );    // Read from fields
      Console.WriteLine($"Low:     { temp.Low }");
   }
}
```

This code produces the following output:

```
High:   85
Low:    60
```

Putting It All Together

The following code creates two instances and stores their references in variables named t1 and t2.
Figure 5-8 illustrates t1 and t2 in memory. The code demonstrates the following three actions discussed so
far in the use of a class:

- Declaring a class

- Creating instances of the class

- Accessing the class members (that is, writing to a field and reading from a field)

```
class DaysTemp                         // Declare the class
{
    public int High, Low;              // Declare the instance fields
    public int Average()               // Declare the instance method
    {
        return (High + Low) / 2;
    }
}

class Program
{
    static void Main()
    {
        // Create two instances of DaysTemp
        DaysTemp t1 = new DaysTemp();
        DaysTemp t2 = new DaysTemp();

        // Write to the fields of each instance
        t1.High = 76;    t1.Low = 57;
        t2.High = 75;    t2.Low = 53;

        // Read from the fields of each instance and call a method of
        // each instance
        Console.WriteLine("t1: {0}, {1}, {2}",
                            t1.High, t1.Low, t1.Average() );
        Console.WriteLine("t2: {0}, {1}, {2}",
                            t2.High, t2.Low, t2.Average() );
                              ↑        ↑         ↑
    }                       Field    Field    Method

}
```

This code produces the following output:

```
t1: 76, 57, 66
t2: 75, 53, 64
```

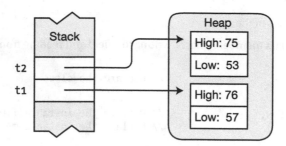

Figure 5-8. *Memory layout of instances t1 and t2*

Throughout this book examples of both the old and new string syntax will be used because it's important to understand and be able to use either one. While the new syntax is generally preferable because it is easier to read, examples using the old syntax are still occasionally used in this book because they likely constitute 95% of all examples in existing code and online sources. Unless all your work will be in new development, you will mostly encounter the pre-C# 6.0 syntax and it is best to be prepared for that.

CHAPTER 6

■ ■ ■

Methods

© Daniel Solis and Cal Schrotenboer 2018

D. Solis and C. Schrotenboer, *Illustrated C# 7*, https://doi.org/10.1007/978-1-4842-3288-0_6

The Structure of a Method

A *method* is a block of code with a name. You can execute the code from somewhere else in the program by using the method's name. You can also pass data into a method and receive data back as output.

As you saw in the previous chapter, a method is a function member of a class. Methods have two major sections, as shown in Figure 6-1—the method header and the method body.

- The *method header* specifies the method's characteristics, including the following:

  - Whether the method returns data and, if so, what type

  - The name of the method

  - What types of data can be passed to and from the method and how that data should be treated

- The *method body* contains the sequence of executable code statements. Execution starts at the first statement in the method body and continues sequentially through the method

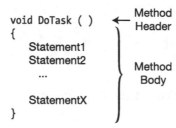

Figure 6-1. *The structure of a method*

The following example shows the the method header. We'll cover each part in the following pages.

```
int MyMethod ( int par1, string par2 )
  ↑       ↑         ↑
Return  Method    Parameter
type    name        list
```

For example, the following code shows a simple method called MyMethod that, in turn, calls the WriteLine method several times:

```
void MyMethod()
{
    Console.WriteLine("First");
    Console.WriteLine("Last");
}
```

Although these first few chapters describe classes, there's another user-defined type called a struct, which we'll cover in Chapter 11. Most of what this chapter covers about class methods is also true for struct methods.

Code Execution in the Method Body

The method body is a *block*, which (as you will recall from Chapter 3) is a sequence of statements between curly braces. A block can contain the following items:

- Local variables
- Flow-of-control constructs
- Method invocations
- Blocks nested within it
- Other methods, known as local functions

Figure 6-2 shows an example of a method body and some of its components.

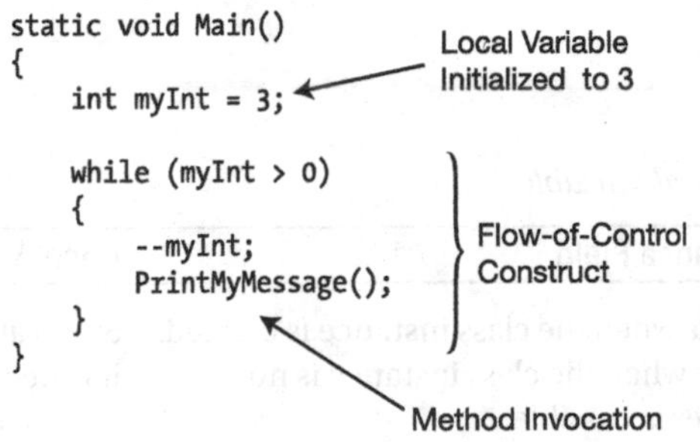

```
static void Main()
{                                    Local Variable
    int myInt = 3;  ◄──────────      Initialized to 3

    while (myInt > 0)
    {                          ⎫
        --myInt;               ⎬     Flow-of-Control
        PrintMyMessage();      ⎭     Construct
    }
}
                                     Method Invocation
```

Figure 6-2. *Method body example*

Local Variables

Like fields, which were covered in Chapter 5, local variables store data. While fields usually store data about the state of the object, local variables are usually created to store data for local, or transitory, computations. Table 6-1 compares and contrasts local variables and instance fields.

The following line of code shows the syntax of local variable declarations. The optional initializer consists of an equal sign followed by a value to be used to initialize the variable

```
          Variable name      Optional initializer
                ↓                    ↓
Type  Identifier = Value;
```

- The existence and lifetime of a local variable is limited to the block in which it is created and the blocks nested within that block.

  - The variable comes into existence at the point at which it is declared.

  - It goes out of existence when the block completes execution.

- You can declare local variables at any position in the method body, but you must declare them before you can use them.

The following example shows the declaration and use of two local variables. The first is of type int, and the second is of type SomeClass.

```
static void Main( )
{
   int myInt    = 15;
   SomeClass sc = new SomeClass();
   ...
}
```

Table 6-1. *Instance Fields vs. Local Variables*

	Instance Field	Local Variable
Lifetime	Starts when the class instance is created. Ends when the class instance is no longer accessible.	Starts at the point in the block where it is declared. Ends when the block completes execution.
Implicit initialization	Initialized to a default value for the type.	No implicit initialization. The compiler produces an error message if nothing is assigned to the variable before it's used.
Storage area	Because instance fields are members of a class, all instance fields are stored in the heap, regardless of whether they're value types or reference types.	Value type: Stored on the stack. Reference type: Reference stored on the stack and data stored in the heap.

Type Inference and the var Keyword

If you look at the following code, you'll see that in supplying the type name at the beginning of the declaration, you are supplying information that the compiler can already infer from the right side of the initialization.

- In the first variable declaration, the compiler can infer that 15 is an int.

- In the second declaration, the object-creation expression on the right side returns an object of type MyExcellentClass.

So, in both cases, including the explicit type name at the beginning of the declaration is redundant.

```
static void Main( )
{
   int total = 15;
   MyExcellentClass mec = new MyExcellentClass();
   ...
}
```

To avoid this redundancy, C# allows you to use the keyword var in place of the explicit type name at the beginning of the variable declaration, as follows:

```
static void Main( )
{ Keyword
     ↓
   var total = 15;
   var mec   = new MyExcellentClass();
   ...

}
```

The var keyword does *not* signal a special kind of variable. It's just syntactic shorthand for whatever type can be inferred from the initialization on the right side of the statement. In the first declaration, it's shorthand for int. In the second, it's shorthand for MyExcellentClass. The preceding code segment with the explicit type names and the code segment with the var keywords are semantically equivalent.

Some important conditions on using the var keyword are the following:

- You can use it only with local variables—not with fields.

- You can use it only when the variable declaration includes an initialization.

- Once the compiler infers the type of a variable, it is fixed and unchangeable.

■ **Note**   The var keyword is *not* like the JavaScript var that can reference different types. It's shorthand for the actual type inferred from the right side of the equal sign. The var keyword *does not change the strongly typed nature of C#*.

Local Variables Inside Nested Blocks

Method bodies can have other blocks nested inside them.

- There can be any number of blocks, and they can be sequential or nested further. Blocks can be nested to any level.

- Local variables can be declared inside nested blocks, and like all local variables, their lifetime and visibility are limited to the block in which they're declared and the blocks nested within it.

Figure 6-3 illustrates the lifetimes of two local variables, showing the code and the state of the stack. The arrows indicate the line that has just been executed.

- Variable var1 is declared in the body of the method, before the nested block.

- Variable var2 is declared inside the nested block. It exists from the time it's declared until the end of the block in which it was declared.

- When control passes out of the nested block, its local variables are popped from the stack.

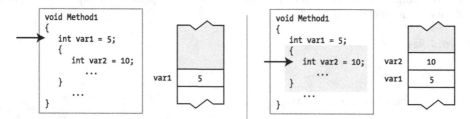

1. Variable var1 is declared before the nested block, and space is allocated for it on the stack.

2. Variable var2 is declared within the nested block, and space is allocated for it on the stack.

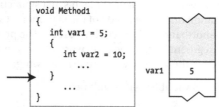

3. When execution passes out of the nested block, var2 is popped from the stack.

Figure 6-3. *The lifetime of a local variable*

■ **Note**   In C and C++ you can declare a local variable, and then within a nested block you can declare another local variable with the same name. The inner name masks the outer name while within the inner scope. In C#, however, you cannot declare another local variable with the same name within the scope of the first name, regardless of the level of nesting.

Local Constants

A local constant is much like a local variable, except that once it is initialized, its value can't be changed. Like a local variable, a local constant must be declared inside a block

The two most important characteristics of a constant are the following:

- A constant *must be initialized* at its declaration.

- A constant *cannot be changed* after its declaration.

The core declaration for a constant is shown here:

Keyword
↓
```
const Type Identifier = Value;
```
↑
Initializer required

The syntax is the same as that of a field or variable declaration, except for the following:

- The addition of the keyword const before the type.

- The mandatory initializer. The initializer value must be determinable at compile time and is usually one of the predefined simple types or an expression made up of them. It can also be the null reference, but it cannot be a reference to an object because references to objects are determined at run time.

■ **Note**   The keyword const is not a modifier but part of the core declaration. It must be placed immediately before the type.

A local constant, like a local variable, is declared in a method body or code block, and it goes out of scope at the end of the block in which it is declared. For example, in the following code, local constant PI, of built-in type double, goes out of scope at the end of method DisplayRadii.

```
void DisplayRadii() {
   const double PI = 3.1416;                  // Declare local constant

   for (int radius = 1; radius <= 5; radius++) {
      double area = radius * radius * PI;      // Read from local constant
      Console.WriteLine
         ($"Radius: { radius }, Area: { area }");
   }
}
```

Flow of Control

Methods contain most of the code for the actions that comprise a program. The remainder is in other function members, such as properties and operators.

The term *flow of control* refers to the flow of execution through a program. By default, program execution moves sequentially from one statement to the next. The flow-of-control statements allow you to modify the order of execution.

In this section, we'll just mention some of the available control statements you can use in your code. Chapter 10 covers them in detail.

- *Selection statements*: These statements allow you to select which statement or block of statements to execute.

    - `if`: Conditional execution of a statement

    - `if...else`: Conditional execution of one statement or another

    - `switch`: Conditional execution of one statement from a set

- *Iteration statements*: These statements allow you to loop, or iterate, on a block of statements.

    - `for`: Loop—testing at the top

    - `while`: Loop—testing at the top

    - `do`: Loop—testing at the bottom

    - `foreach`: Executes once for each member of a set

- *Jump statements*: These statements allow you to jump from one place in the block or method to another.

    - `break`: Exits the current loop

    - `continue`: Goes to the bottom of the current loop

    - `goto`: Goes to a named statement

    - `return`: Returns execution to the calling method

For example, the following method shows two of the flow-of-control statements. Don't worry about the details. (The `==` sign is the equality comparison operator.)

```
void SomeMethod() {
   int intVal = 3;

   if( intVal == 3 )                              // if statement
      Console.WriteLine("Value is 3. ");
   for( int i=0; i<5; i++ )                       // for statement
      Console.WriteLine($"Value of i: { i }");
}
```

Method Invocations

You can call other methods from inside a method body.

- The phrases *call a method* and *invoke a method* are synonymous.

- You call a method by using its name, along with the parameter list, which we'll discuss shortly.

For example, the following class declares a method called PrintDateAndTime, which is called from inside method Main:

```
class MyClass
{
    void PrintDateAndTime()              // Declare the method.
    {
        DateTime dt = DateTime.Now;      // Get the current date and time.
        Console.WriteLine($"{ dt }");    // Write it out.
    }

    static void Main()                   // Declare the method.
    {
        MyClass mc = new MyClass();
        mc.PrintDateAndTime( );          // Invoke the method.
                    ↑          ↑
                  Method     Empty
                   name   parameter list
}
```

Figure 6-4 illustrates the sequence of actions when a method is called.

1. Execution of the current method suspends at that point of the invocation.

2. Control transfers to the beginning of the invoked method.

3. The invoked method executes until it completes.

4. Control returns to the calling method.

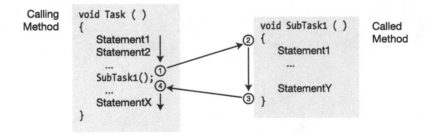

Figure 6-4. *Flow of control when calling a method*

Return Values

A method can return a value to the calling code. The returned value is inserted into the calling code at the position in the expression where the invocation occurred.

To return a value, the method must declare a *return type* before the method name.

- If a method doesn't return a value, it must declare a return type of void.

The following code shows two method declarations. The first returns a value of type int. The second doesn't return a value.

```
Return type
   ↓
 int  GetHour()     { ... }
 void DisplayHour() { ... }
  ↑
No value is returned.
```

A method that declares a return type must return a value from the method by using the following form of the return statement, which includes an expression after the keyword return. Every path through the method must end with a return statement of this form.

```
   return Expression;                    // Return a value.
          ↑
Evaluates to a value of the return type
```

For example, the following code shows a method called GetHour, which returns a value of type int.

```
Return type
   ↓
 int GetHour( )
 {
    DateTime dt = DateTime.Now;      // Get the current date and time.
    int hour    = dt.Hour;          // Get the hour.

    return hour;                     // Return an int.
 }        ↑
    Return statement
```

You can also return objects of user-defined types. For example, the following code returns an object of type MyClass:

Return type — MyClass
     ↓

```
MyClass method3( )
{
   MyClass mc = new MyClass();
   ...
   return mc;                          // Return a MyClass object.

}
```

As another example, in the following code, method GetHour is called in the WriteLine statement in Main and returns an int value to that position in the WriteLine statement.

```
class MyClass
{                   ↓ Return type
   public int GetHour()
   {
      DateTime dt = DateTime.Now;      // Get the current date and time.
      int hour    = dt.Hour;           // Get the hour.

      return hour;                     // Return an int.
   }            ↑
}           Return value


class Program
{
   static void Main()
   {                              Method invocation
      MyClass mc = new MyClass();        ↓
      Console.WriteLine("Hour: {0}", mc.GetHour());
   }                              ↑   ↑
                              Instance Method
}                                name   name
```

The Return Statement and Void Methods

In the previous section, you saw that methods that return a value must contain return statements. Void methods do not require return statements. When the flow of control reaches the closing curly brace of the method body, control returns to the calling code, and no value is inserted back into the calling code.

Often, however, you can simplify your program logic by exiting the method early when certain conditions apply

- You can exit a void method at any time by using the following form of the return statement, with no parameters:

  ```
  return;
  ```

- This form of the return statement can be used only with methods declared void.

For example, the following code shows the declaration of a void method called SomeMethod, which has three possible places it might return to the calling code. The first two places are in branches called if statements, which are covered in Chapter 10. The last place is the end of the method body.

```
Void return type
    ↓
 void SomeMethod()
 {
    ...
    if ( SomeCondition )          // If ...
       return;                    // return to the calling code.
    ...

    if ( OtherCondition )         // If ...
       return;                    // return to the calling code.

    ...

 }                                // Default return to the calling code.
```

The following code shows an example of a void method with a return statement. The method writes out a message only if the time is after noon. The process, which is illustrated in Figure 6-5, is as follows:

- First the method gets the current date and time. (Don't worry about understanding the details of this right now.)

- If the hour is less than 12 (that is, before noon), the return statement is executed, and control immediately returns to the calling method without writing anything to the screen.

- If the hour is 12 or greater, the return statement is skipped, and the code executes the WriteLine statement, which writes an informative message to the screen.

```
class MyClass
{      ↓ Void return type
    void TimeUpdate()
    {
        DateTime dt = DateTime.Now;          // Get the current date and time.
            if (dt.Hour < 12)                // If the hour is less than 12,
                return;                      // then return.
                  ↑
            Return to calling method
        Console.WriteLine("It's afternoon!");   // Otherwise, print message.
    }

    static void Main()
    {
        MyClass mc = new MyClass();          // Create an instance of the class.
        mc.TimeUpdate();                     // Invoke the method.
    }
}
```

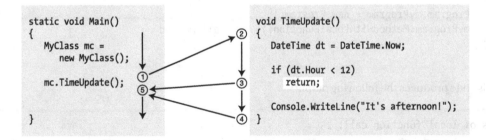

Figure 6-5. *Using a return statement with a void return type*

Local Functions

As just explained, the code inside a method block can call another method. If that other method is in the same class, it can be called simply by using its name and passing any required parameters (described in the next section). If that method is in another class, it must generally be called by using an object instance of the other class. Methods in other classes also must have been declared using the public access modifier.

Beginning with C# 7.0 you can declare a separate method directly inside another method. This isolates the contained method from other code as it can only be called from within the method in which it is contained. When used properly, this can also lead to clearer code and easier maintenance. These contained methods are called *local functions*.

Unlike local variables, which must be declared before they can be used, you can declare a local function at any point within its containing method.

The following code shows an example of a method called MethodWithLocalFunction that contains a local function called MyLocalFunction.

```
class Program
{
    public void MethodWithLocalFunction()
    {
        int MyLocalFunction(int z1)               // Local function declaration
        {
            return z1 * 5;
        }

        int results = MyLocalFunction(5);        // Call local function
        Console.WriteLine($"Results of local function call: {results}");
    }

    static void Main(string[] args)
    {
        Program myProgram = new Program();
        myProgram.MethodWithLocalFunction();   // Call Method
    }
}
```

This code produces the following output:

```
Results of local function call: 25
```

Parameters

So far, you've seen that methods are named units of code that can be called from many places in a program and can return a single value to the calling code. Returning a single value is certainly valuable, but what if you need to return multiple values? Also, it would be useful to be able to pass data into a method when it starts execution. *Parameters* are a special kind of variable that can allow you to do both these things.

Formal Parameters

Formal parameters are local variables that are declared in the method declaration's parameter list, rather than in the body of the method.

The following method header shows the syntax of parameter declarations. It declares two formal parameters—one of type int and the other of type float.

```
public void PrintSum( int x, float y )
{                        ↑
    ...          Formal parameter declarations
}
```

- Because formal parameters are variables, they have a data type and a name, and they can be written to and read from.

- Unlike a method's other local variables, the parameters are defined outside the method body and are initialized before the method starts (except for one type, called *output parameters*, which we'll cover shortly).

- The parameter list can have any number of formal parameter declarations, and the declarations must be separated by commas.

The formal parameters are used throughout the method body, for the most part, just like other local variables. For example, the following declaration of method PrintSum uses two formal parameters, x and y, and a local variable, sum, all of which are of type int.

```
public void PrintSum( int x, int y )
{
    int sum = x + y;
    Console.WriteLine($"Newsflash:  { x } + { y } is { sum  }");
}
```

Actual Parameters

When your code calls a method, the values of the formal parameters must be initialized before the code in the method begins execution. The expressions or variables used to initialize the formal parameters are called the *actual parameters*. They are also sometimes called *arguments*.

- The actual parameters are placed in the parameter list of the method invocation.

- Each actual parameter must match the type of the corresponding formal parameter, or the compiler must be able to implicitly convert the actual parameter to that type. We'll explain the details of conversion from one type to another in Chapter 17.

For example, the following code shows the invocation of method `PrintSum`, which has two actual parameters of data type `int`:

```
PrintSum( 5, someInt );
        ↑    ↑
   Expression  Variable of type int
```

When the method is called, the value of each actual parameter is used to initialize the corresponding formal parameter. The method body is then executed. Figure 6-6 illustrates the relationship between the actual parameters and the formal parameters.

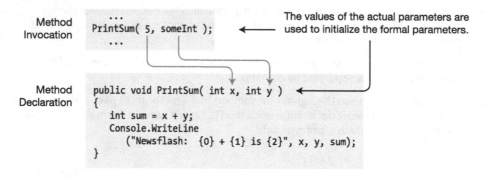

Figure 6-6. *Actual parameters initialize the corresponding formal parameters*

Notice that in the previous example code, and in Figure 6-6, the number of actual parameters matches the number of formal parameters, and each actual parameter matches the type of the corresponding formal parameter. Parameters that follow this pattern are called *positional parameters*. We'll look at some other options shortly. But first we'll look at positional parameters in more detail.

An Example of Methods with Positional Parameters

In the following code, class MyClass declares two methods—one that takes two integers and returns their sum and another that takes two floats and returns their average. In the second invocation, notice that the compiler has implicitly converted the two int values—5 and someInt—to the float type.

```
class MyClass        Formal parameters
{                         ↓
    public int Sum(int x, int y)              // Declare the method.
    {
        return x + y;                         // Return the sum.
    }                      Formal parameters
                              ↓
    public float Avg(float input1, float input2)    // Declare the method.
    {
        return (input1 + input2) / 2.0F;      // Return the average.
    }
}


class Program
{
    static void Main()
    {
        MyClass myT = new MyClass();
        int someInt = 6;

        Console.WriteLine
            ("Newsflash:  Sum: {0} and {1} is {2}",
                5, someInt, myT.Sum( 5, someInt ));      // Invoke the method.
                                      ↑
                              Actual parameters
        Console.WriteLine
            ("Newsflash:  Avg: {0} and {1} is {2}",
                5, someInt, myT.Avg( 5, someInt ));      // Invoke the method.
    }                                 ↑
                              Actual parameters
}
```

This code produces the following output:

```
Newsflash:  Sum: 5 and 6 is 11
Newsflash:  Avg: 5 and 6 is 5.5
```

Value Parameters

There are several kinds of parameters, each of which passes data to and from the method in slightly different ways. The kind we've looked at so far is the default type and is called a *value parameter*.

When you use value parameters, data is passed to the method by copying the value of the actual parameter to the formal parameter. When a method is called, the system does the following:

- It allocates space on the stack for the formal parameters.

- It copies the values of the actual parameters to the formal parameters.

An actual parameter for a value parameter doesn't have to be a variable. It can be any expression evaluating to the matching data type. For example, the following code shows two method calls. In the first, the actual parameter is a variable of type `float`. In the second, it's an expression that evaluates to `float`.

```
float func1( float val )                       // Declare the method.
{                    ↑
               Float data type
   float j = 2.6F;
   float k = 5.1F;
      ...
}

                        Variable of type float
                              ↓
   float fValue1 = func1( k );                  // Method call
   float fValue2 = func1( (k + j) / 3 );        // Method call
   ...
                        Expression that evaluates to a float
```

Before you can use a variable as an actual parameter, that variable must be assigned a value (except in the case of output parameters, which we'll cover shortly). For reference types, the variable can be assigned either an actual reference or `null`.

■ **Note**   Chapter 4 covered *value types*, which, as you will remember, are types that contain their own data. Don't be confused that we're now talking about *value parameters*. They're entirely different. *Value parameters* are parameters where the value of the actual parameter is copied to the formal parameter.

For example, the following code shows a method called MyMethod, which takes two parameters—a variable of type MyClass and an int.

- The method adds 5 both to the int type field belonging to the class and to the int.

- You might also notice that MyMethod uses the modifier static, which we haven't explained yet. You can ignore it for now. We'll explain static methods in Chapter 7.

```
class MyClass
{
   public int Val = 20;                          // Initialize the field to 20.
}

class Program                    Formal parameters
{                                        ↓
   static void MyMethod( MyClass f1, int f2 )
   {
      f1.Val = f1.Val + 5;                        // Add 5 to field of f1 param.
      f2     = f2 + 5;                            // Add 5 to second param.
      Console.WriteLine($"f1.Val: { f1.Val }, f2: { f2 }");
   }

   static void Main()
   {
      MyClass a1 = new MyClass();
      int     a2 = 10;

            Actual parameters
                 ↓
      MyMethod( a1, a2 );                         // Call the method.
      Console.WriteLine($"a1.Val: { a1.Val }, a2: { a2 }");
   }

}
```

This code produces the following output:

```
f1.Val: 25, f2: 15
a1.Val: 25, a2: 10
```

Figure 6-7 illustrates the following about the values of the actual and formal parameters at various stages in the execution of the method:

- Before the method call, variables a1 and a2, which will be used as the actual parameters, are already on the stack.

- By the beginning of the method, the system will have allocated space on the stack for the formal parameters and copied the values from the actual parameters.

  - Since a1 is a reference type, the reference is copied, resulting in both the actual and formal parameters referring to the same object in the heap.

  - Since a2 is a value type, the value is copied, producing an independent data item.

- At the end of the method, both f2 and the field of object f1 have been incremented by 5.

  - After method execution, the formal parameters are popped off the stack.

  - The value of a2, the value type, is unaffected by the activity in the method.

  - The value of a1, the reference type, however, has been changed by the activity in the method.

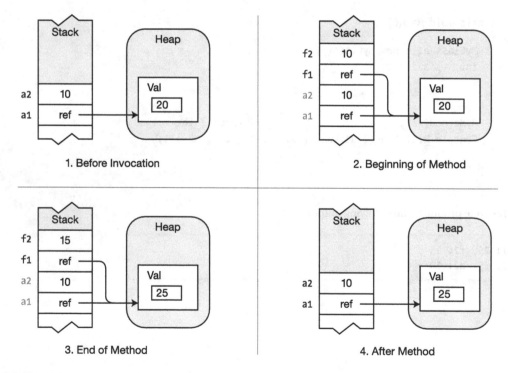

Figure 6-7. Value parameters

Reference Parameters

The second type of parameter is called a *reference parameter*.

- When using a reference parameter, you must use the ref modifier in both the declaration and the invocation of the method.

- The actual parameter *must* be a variable, and it must be assigned to before being used as the actual parameter. If it's a reference type variable, it can be assigned either an actual reference or the value null.

For example, the following code illustrates the syntax of the declaration and invocation:

```
                  Include the ref modifier.
                           ↓
void MyMethod( ref int val )         // Method declaration
{ ... }

int y = 1;                           // Variable for the actual parameter
MyMethod ( ref y );                  // Method call
              ↑
       Include the ref modifier.

MyMethod ( ref 3+5 );                // Error!
              ↑
       Must use a variable
```

In the previous section you saw that for value parameters, the system allocates memory on the stack for the formal parameters. In contrast, reference parameters have the following characteristics:

- They do not allocate memory on the stack for the formal parameters.

- Instead, a formal parameter name acts as an alias for the actual parameter variable, referring to the same memory location.

Since the formal parameter name and the actual parameter name are referencing the same memory location, clearly any changes made to the formal parameter during method execution are visible after the method is completed, through the actual parameter variable.

■ **Note**　Remember to use the ref keyword in both the method declaration *and* the invocation.

For example, the following code shows method MyMethod again, but this time the parameters are reference parameters rather than value parameters:

```
class MyClass
{
   public int Val = 20;                       // Initialize field to 20.
}

class Program          ref modifier        ref modifier
{                          ↓                    ↓
   static void MyMethod(ref MyClass f1, ref int f2)
   {
      f1.Val = f1.Val + 5;                 // Add 5 to field of f1 param.
      f2     = f2 + 5;                     // Add 5 to second param.
      Console.WriteLine($"f1.Val: { f1.Val }, f2: { f2 }");
   }

   static void Main()
   {
      MyClass a1 = new MyClass();
      int a2     = 10;
                 ref modifiers
                  ↓        ↓
      MyMethod(ref a1, ref a2);            // Call the method.
      Console.WriteLine($"a1.Val: { a1.Val }, a2: { a2 }");
   }

}
```

This code produces the following output:

```
f1.Val: 25, f2: 15
a1.Val: 25, a2: 15
```

Notice that the value of f1.Val is the same whether or not the MyClass object f1 is passed to the method by ref or not. This will be discussed in more detail shortly.

Figure 6-8 illustrates the following about the values of the actual and formal parameters at various stages in the execution of the method:

- Before the method call, variables a1 and a2, which will be used as the actual parameters, are already on the stack.

- By the beginning of the method, the names of the formal parameters will have been set as aliases for the actual parameters. Variables a1 and f1 reference the same memory location, and a2 and f2 also reference the same memory location.

- At the end of the method, both f2 and the field of the object of f1 have been incremented by 5.

- After method execution, the names of the formal parameters are gone ("out of scope"), but both the value of a2, which is the value type, and the value of the object pointed at by a1, which is the reference type, have been changed by the activity in the method.

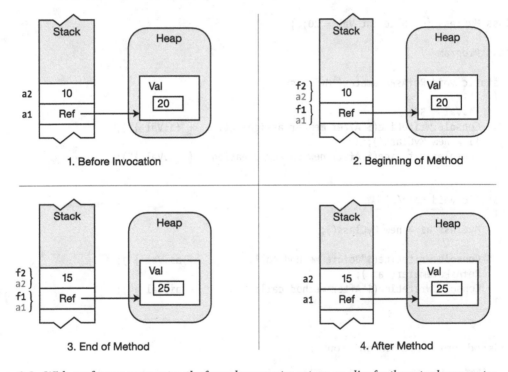

Figure 6-8. With a reference parameter, the formal parameter acts as an alias for the actual parameter

Reference Types As Value and Reference Parameters

In the previous sections you saw that for a reference type object, you can modify its members inside the method call, regardless of whether you send the object in as a value parameter or as a reference parameter. We didn't, however, assign to the formal parameter itself, inside the method. In this section, we'll look at what happens when you assign to the formal parameter of a reference type inside the method. The answer is the following:

- *Passing a reference type object as a value parameter*: If you create a new object inside the method and assign it to the formal parameter, it breaks the connection between the formal parameter and the actual parameter, and the new object does not persist after the method call.

- *Passing a reference type object as a reference parameter*: If you create a new object inside the method and assign it to the formal parameter, that new object persists after the method is ended and is the value referenced by the actual parameter.

The following code shows the first case—using a reference type object as a *value parameter*:

```
class MyClass { public int Val = 20; }

class Program
{
   static void RefAsParameter( MyClass f1 )
   {
      f1.Val = 50;
      Console.WriteLine($"After member assignment:    { f1.Val }");
      f1 = new MyClass();
      Console.WriteLine($"After new object creation:  { f1.Val }");
   }

   static void Main( )
   {
      MyClass a1 = new MyClass();

      Console.WriteLine($"Before method call:         { a1.Val }");
      RefAsParameter( a1 );
      Console.WriteLine($"After method call:          { a1.Val }");
   }
}
```

This code produces the following output:

```
Before method call:        20
After member assignment:   50
After new object creation: 20
After method call:         50
```

Figure 6-9 illustrates the following about the code:

- At the beginning of the method, both the actual parameter and the formal parameter point to the same object in the heap.

- After the assignment to the object's member, they still point at the same object in the heap.

- When the method allocates a new object and assigns it to the formal parameter, the actual parameter (outside the method) still points at the original object, and the formal parameter points at the new object.

- After the method call, the actual parameter points to the original object, and the formal parameter and new object are gone.

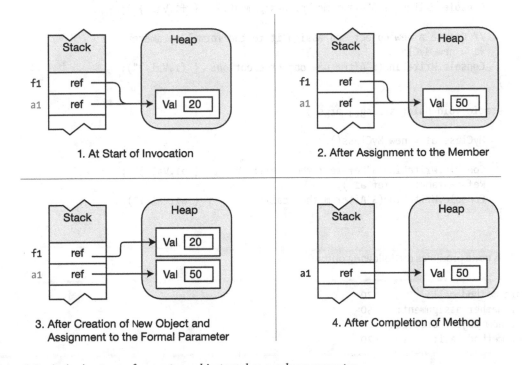

Figure 6-9. *Assigning to a reference type object used as a value parameter*

The following code illustrates the case where a reference type object is used as a reference parameter. The code is the same except for the ref keyword in the method declaration and the method invocation.

```
class MyClass
{
   public int Val = 20;
}

class Program
{
   static void RefAsParameter( ref MyClass f1 )
   {
      // Assign to the object member.
      f1.Val = 50;
      Console.WriteLine($"After member assignment:    { f1.Val }");

      // Create a new object and assign it to the formal parameter.
      f1 = new MyClass();
      Console.WriteLine($"After new object creation: { f1.Val }");
   }

   static void Main( string[] args )
   {
      MyClass a1 = new MyClass();

      Console.WriteLine($"Before method call:        { a1.Val }");
      RefAsParameter( ref a1 );
      Console.WriteLine($"After method call:         { a1.Val }");
   }
}
```

This code produces the following output:

```
Before method call:       20
After member assignment:   50
After new object creation: 20
After method call:         20
```

As you remember, a reference parameter acts as an alias for the formal parameter. This makes the explanation of the previous code easy. Figure 6-10 illustrates the following about the code:

- When the method is invoked, the formal and actual parameters point at the same object in the heap.

- The modification of the member value is seen by both the formal and actual parameters.

- When the method creates a new object and assigns it to the formal parameter, the references of both the formal and actual parameters point to the new object.

- After the method, the actual parameter is left pointing at the object that was created inside the method.

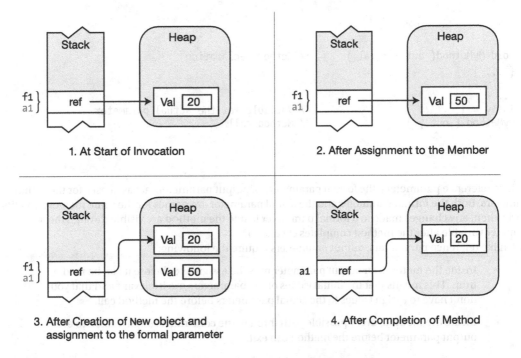

Figure 6-10. *Assigning to a reference type object used as a reference parameter*

Output Parameters

Output parameters are used to pass data from inside the method back out to the calling code. Their behavior is similar to reference parameters. Like reference parameters, output parameters have the following requirements

- You must use a modifier in both the method declaration and the invocation. With output parameters, the modifier is out, rather than ref.

- Like reference parameters, the actual parameter *must* be a variable—it cannot be another type of expression. This makes sense since the method needs a memory location to store the value it's returning.

For example, the following code declares a method called MyMethod, which takes a single output parameter:

```
                   out modifier
                        ↓
void MyMethod( out int val )        // Method declaration
{ ... }

...
int y = 1;                          // Variable for the actual parameter
MyMethod ( out y );                 // Method call
            ↑
       out modifier
```

Like reference parameters, the formal parameters of output parameters act as aliases for the actual parameters. Both the formal parameter and the actual parameter are names for the same memory location. Clearly, then, any changes made to a formal parameter inside the method are visible through the actual parameter variable after the method completes execution.

Unlike reference parameters, output parameters require the following:

- Inside the method, an output parameter must be assigned to before it can be read from. This means that the initial values of the parameters are irrelevant and that you don't have to assign values to the actual parameters before the method call.

- Inside the method, every possible path through the code must assign a value to every output parameter before the method can exit.

Since the code inside the method must write to an output parameter before it can read from it, it is *impossible* to send data *into* a method using output parameters. In fact, if there is any execution path through the method that attempts to read the value of an output parameter before the method assigns it a value, the compiler produces an error message.

```
public void Add2( out int outValue )
{
   int var1 = outValue + 2;   // Error! Can't read from an output parameter
}                             // before it has been assigned to by the method.
```

For example, the following code again shows method MyMethod, but this time using output parameters:

```
class MyClass
{
   public int Val = 20;                    // Initialize field to 20.
}

class Program          out modifier        out modifier
{                           ↓                   ↓
   static void MyMethod(out MyClass f1, out int f2)
   {
      f1 = new MyClass();               // Create an object of the class.
      f1.Val = 25;                      // Assign to   the class field.
      f2      = 15;                      // Assign to the int param.
   }

   static void Main()
   {
      MyClass a1 = null;
      int a2;

      MyMethod(out a1, out a2);          // Call the method.
   }                   ↑        ↑
}                        out modifiers
```

105

Figure 6-11 illustrates the following about the values of the actual and formal parameters at various stages in the execution of the method:

- Before the method call, variables a1 and a2, which will be used as the actual parameters, are already on the stack.

- At the beginning of the method, the names of the formal parameters are set as aliases for the actual parameters. Therefore, variables a1 and f1 reference the same memory location, and a2 and f2 also reference the same memory location. The names a1 and a2 are out of scope and cannot be accessed from inside MyMethod.

- Inside the method, the code creates an object of type MyClass and assigns it to f1. It then assigns a value to f1's field and also assigns a value to f2. The assignments to f1 and f2 are both required since they're output parameters.

- After method execution, the names of the formal parameters are out of scope, but the values of both a1, the reference type, and a2, the value type, have been changed by the activity in the method.

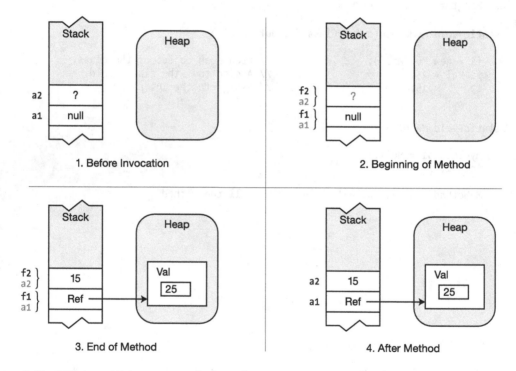

Figure 6-11. *With an output parameter, the formal parameter acts as an alias for the actual parameter but with the additional requirement that it must be assigned to inside the method*

Starting with C# 7.0 you no longer need to predeclare a variable to be used as an out parameter. You can add a variable type to the parameter listing in the method call itself, and it will act as the variable declaration.

For example, in the previous code example, method Main declared variables a1 and a2 and then used them as out parameters in the call to MyMethod, as shown again here:

```
static void Main()
{
    MyClass a1 = null;          // Declare variable to be used as out parameter
    int a2;                     // Declare variable to be used as out parameter

    MyMethod(out a1, out a2);   // Call the method.
}
```

Using the new syntax, however, you can do the following:

- Omit the explicit variable declarations.

- Add the types of the variable directly in the method call.

The following code shows the new form:

```
static void Main()
{
    MyMethod( out MyClass a1, out int a2 );      // Call the method.
}                      ↑                ↑
                  Variable type    Variable type
```

Even though a1 and a2 are declared only in the method call statement itself, they become available to the code in scope after the method call, as shown in the following code:

```
static void Main()
{
    MyMethod(out MyClass a1, out int a2);   // Call the method.
    Console.WriteLine(a2);                  // Use the return value

    a2 += 5;                                // Write to the variable
    Console.WriteLine(a2);
}
```

This code produces the following output:

```
15
20
```

Parameter Arrays

In the parameter types we've covered so far, there must be exactly one actual parameter for each formal parameter. *Parameter arrays* are different in that they allow *zero or more* actual parameters of a particular type for a particular formal parameter. Important points about parameter arrays are the following:

- There can be only one parameter array in a parameter list.

- If there is one, it must be the last parameter in the list.

- All the parameters represented by the parameter array must be of the same type.

To declare a parameter array, you must do the following:

- Use the `params` modifier before the data type.

- Place a set of empty square brackets after the data type.

The following method header shows the syntax for the declaration of a parameter array of type `int`. In this example, formal parameter `inVals` can represent zero or more actual `int` parameters.

```
                    Array of ints
                         ↓
void ListInts( params int[] inVals )
{ ...            ↑          ↑
             Modifier   Parameter name
```

The empty set of square brackets after the type name specifies that the parameter will be an *array* of `ints`. You don't need to worry about the details of arrays here. They're covered in detail in Chapter 13. For our purposes here, though, all you need to know is the following:

- An array is an ordered set of data items of the same type.

- An array is accessed by using a numerical index.

- An array is a reference type and therefore stores all its data items in the heap.

Method Invocation

You can supply the actual parameters for a parameter array in two ways.

- A comma-separated list of elements of the data type. All the elements must be of the type specified in the method declaration.

  ```
  ListInts( 10, 20, 30 );              // Three ints
  ```

- A one-dimensional array of elements of the data type.

  ```
  int[] intArray = {1, 2, 3};
  ListInts( intArray );                // An array variable
  ```

Notice in these examples that you do *not* use the params modifier in the *invocation*. The usage of the modifier in parameter arrays doesn't fit the pattern of the other parameter types.

- The other parameter types are consistent in that they either use a modifier or do not use a modifier.

  - Value parameters take no modifier in either the declaration or the invocation.

  - Reference and output parameters require the modifier in both places.

- The summary for the usage of the params modifier is the following:

  - It is required in the declaration.

  - It is not allowed in the invocation.

Expanded Form

The first form of method invocation, where you use separate actual parameters in the invocation, is sometimes called the *expanded form*.

For example, the declaration of method ListInts in the following code matches all the method invocations after it, even though they have different numbers of actual parameters:

```
void ListInts( params int[] inVals ) { ... }       // Method declaration

...
ListInts( );                        // 0 actual parameters
ListInts( 1, 2, 3 );                // 3 actual parameters
ListInts( 4, 5, 6, 7 );             // 4 actual parameters
ListInts( 8, 9, 10, 11, 12 );       // 5 actual parameters
```

When you use an invocation with separate actual parameters for a parameter array, the compiler does the following:

- It takes the list of actual parameters and uses them to create and initialize an array in the heap.

- It stores the reference to the array in the formal parameter on the stack.

- If there are no actual parameters at the position corresponding to the formal parameter array, the compiler creates an array with zero elements and uses that.

For example, the following code declares a method called ListInts, which takes a parameter array. Main declares three ints and passes them to the array.

```
class MyClass                        Parameter array
{                                         ↓
    public void ListInts( params int[] inVals )
    {
        if ( (inVals != null) && (inVals.Length != 0))
            for (int i = 0; i < inVals.Length; i++)      // Process the array.
            {
                inVals[i] = inVals[i] * 10;
                Console.WriteLine($"{ inVals[i] }");   // Display new value.
            }
    }
}

class Program
{
    static void Main()
    {
        int first = 5, second = 6, third = 7;          // Declare three ints.

        MyClass mc = new MyClass();
        mc.ListInts( first, second, third );           // Call the method.
                          ↑
                    Actual parameters
        Console.WriteLine($"{ first }, { second  }, { third }");
    }

}
```

This code produces the following output:

```
50
60
70
5, 6, 7
```

Figure 6-12 illustrates the following about the values of the actual and formal parameters at various stages in the execution of the method:

- Before the method call, the three actual parameters are already on the stack.

- By the beginning of the method, the three actual parameters will have been used to initialize an array in the heap, and the reference to the array will have been assigned to formal parameter inVals.

- Inside the method, the code first checks to make sure the array reference is not null and then processes the array by multiplying each element in the array by 10 and storing it back.

- After method execution, the formal parameter, inVals, is out of scope.

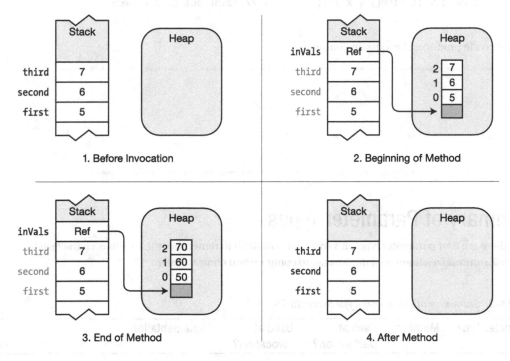

Figure 6-12. Parameter array example

An important thing to remember about parameter arrays is that when an array is created in the heap, the values of the actual parameters are *copied* to the array. In this way, they're like value parameters.

- If the array parameter is a value type, the *values* are copied, and the actual parameters *cannot be affected* inside the method.

- If the array parameter is a reference type, the *references* are copied, and the objects referenced by the actual parameters *can be affected* inside the method.

Arrays As Actual Parameters

You can also create and populate an array before the method call and pass the single array variable as the actual parameter. In this case, the compiler uses *your* array, rather than creating one.

For example, the following code uses method ListInts, declared in the previous example. In this code, Main creates an array and uses the array variable as the actual parameter, rather than using separate integers.

```
static void Main() {
    int[] myArr = new int[] { 5, 6, 7 };      // Create and initialize array.
    MyClass mc = new MyClass();
    mc.ListInts(myArr);                       // Call method to print the values.

    foreach (int x in myArr)
        Console.WriteLine($"{ x }");          // Print out each element.
}
```

This code produces the following output:

```
50
60
70
50
60
70
```

Summary of Parameter Types

Since there are four parameter types, it's sometimes difficult to remember their various characteristics. Table 6-2 summarizes them, making it easier to compare and contrast them.

Table 6-2. *Summary of Parameter Type Syntactic Usage*

Parameter Type	Modifier	Used at Declaration?	Used at Invocation?	Implementation
Value	None			The system copies the value of the actual parameter to the formal parameter.
Reference	ref	Yes	Yes	The formal parameter is an alias for the actual parameter.
Output	out	Yes	Yes	The parameter contains only a returned value. The formal parameter is an alias for the actual parameter.
Array	params	Yes	No	The parameter allows passing a variable number of actual parameters to a method.

Ref Local and Ref Return

Earlier in this chapter you saw that you could pass a reference to an object into a method call using the ref keyword and any changes made to the object would be visible in the calling context when the method returned. The *ref return* feature goes the other direction and lets you send a reference *out of a method* where it can be used in the calling context. A related feature, the *ref local* feature, allows a variable to be an alias for another variable.

We'll start by looking at the ref local feature. The important things to know about the ref local feature are the following:

- Using this feature, you can create an alias of a variable even if the referenced object is a value type!

- Any assignments made to either variable are reflected in the other since they refer to the same object—again, even if it's a value type.

The syntax to create the alias requires two uses of the keyword ref, one in front of the type of the alias declaration and the other on the right side of the assignment operator, in front of the variable being aliased, as shown in the following line:

```
ref int y = ref x;
    ↑           ↑
 Keyword     Keyword
```

The following code shows an example, where the ref local feature is used to create an alias of variable x, called y. When x is changed, so is y and vice versa.

```
class Program {
   static void Main() {
      int x = 2;
      ref int y = ref x;

      Console.WriteLine( $"x = {x},    y = {y}" );
      x = 5;
      Console.WriteLine( $"x = {x},    y = {y}" );
      y = 6;
      Console.WriteLine( $"x = {x},    y = {y}" );
   }
}
```

This code produces the following output:

```
x = 2,    y = 2
x = 5,    y = 5
x = 6,    y = 6
```

But the aliasing feature is not the most common use of the ref local feature. Instead, it's usually used in conjunction with the ref return feature. The *ref return* feature gives you the means to have a method return a reference to a variable, rather than return the variable's value. The additional syntax required here, again, consists of the following two uses of the keyword ref:

- One before the return type declaration of the method

- The other inside the method after the return keyword and before the variable name of the object being returned

The following code shows an example of this. Notice that after the call to the method, when the calling code modifies the ref local variable, the value of the class's field changes.

```csharp
class Simple
{
    private int Score = 5;
            Keyword for ref return method
                    ↓
    public ref int RefToValue()
    {
        return ref Score;
    }         ↑
            Keyword for ref return
    public void Display()
    {
        Console.WriteLine( $"Value inside class object:  {Score}" );
    }
}

class Program
{
    static void Main()
    {
        Simple s = new Simple();
        s.Display();

        ref int v1Outside = ref s.RefToValue();
    }    ↑                      ↑
        Keyword for ref local    Keyword for ref local
        v1Outside = 10;          // Change the value out in the calling scope.
        s.Display();             // Check that the value has changed.
    }

}
```

This code produces the following output:

```
Value inside class object:  5
Value inside class object:  10
```

Another possibly useful example is a twist on the Math library's Max method. With Math.Max you can supply two variables of some numeric type, and the method will return the larger of the two values. Suppose, however, you wanted it to return *a reference to the variable* that contains the higher value—rather than just returning the value. To do this, you could use the ref return feature, as shown in the following code:

```
using static System.Console;

class Program
{
    static ref int Max(ref int p1, ref int p2)
    {
        if ( p1 > p2 )
            return ref p1;    // Return the reference--not the value.
        else
            return ref p2;    // Return the reference--not the value.
    }

    static void Main()
    {
        int v1 = 10;
        int v2 = 20;
        WriteLine("Start");
        WriteLine($"v1: {v1}, v2: {v2}\n");

        ref int max = ref Max(ref v1, ref v2);
        WriteLine("After assignment");
        WriteLine($"max: {max}\n");

        max++;
        WriteLine("After increment");
        WriteLine($"max: {max}, v1: {v1}, v2: {v2}");
    }
}
```

This code produces the following output:

```
Start
v1: 10, v2: 20

After assignment
max: 20

After increment
max: 21, v1: 10, v2: 21
```

Some additional constraints on these features are the following:

- You cannot declare a method with a return type of void as a ref return method.

- A ref return expression cannot return the following:

  - The null value

  - A constant

  - An enumeration member

  - A property of either a class or a struct

  - A pointer to a read-only location

- A ref return expression can only point either to a location that originated in the calling scope or to a field. Hence, it cannot be a variable local to the method.

- A ref local variable can be assigned only one time. That is, it cannot be pointed to a *different* storage location after having once been initialized.

- Even if a method is declared as a ref return method, if a *call* to that method omits the ref keyword, the value returned will be the value, rather than a pointer to the value's memory location.

- If you pass a ref local variable as a regular actual parameter to some other method, that other method gets only a copy of the variable. Even though the ref local variable holds a pointer to a storage location, when it's used in this way, it passes the value rather than the reference.

Method Overloading

A class can have more than one method with the same name. This is called *method overloading*. Each method with the same name must have a different *signature* than the others.

- The signature of a method consists of the following information from the method header of the method declaration:

  - The name of the method

  - The number of parameters

  - The data types and order of the parameters

  - The parameter modifiers

- The return type is not part of the signature—although it's a common mistake to believe that it is.

- Notice that the *names* of the formal parameters are *not* part of the signature.

```
Not part of signature
   ↓
 long AddValues( int a, out int b) { ... }
                        ↑
                    Signature
```

For example, the following four methods are overloads of the method name AddValues:

```
class A
{
    long AddValues( int    a, int    b)          { return a + b;         }
    long AddValues( int    c, int    d, int e)   { return c + d + e;     }
    long AddValues( float f, float g)            { return (long)(f + g); }
    long AddValues( long   h, long   m)          { return h + m;         }
}
```

The following code shows an illegal attempt at overloading the method name AddValues. The two methods differ only in the return types and the names of the formal parameters. But they still have the same signature because they have the same method name; and the number, type, and order of their parameters are the same. The compiler would produce an error message for this code..

```
class B              Signature
{                       ↓
   long AddValues( long   a, long   b) { return a+b; }
   int  AddValues( long   c, long   d) { return c+d; }  // Error, same signature
}                             ↑
                          Signature
```

Named Parameters

So far in our discussion of parameters we've used positional parameters, which, as you'll remember, means that the position of each actual parameter matches the position of the corresponding formal parameter.

Alternatively, C# allows you to use *named parameters*. Named parameters allow you to list the actual parameters in your method invocation in any order, as long as you explicitly specify the names of the parameters. The details are as follows:

- Nothing changes in the declaration of the method. The formal parameters already have names.

- In the method invocation, however, you use the formal parameter name, followed by a colon, in front of the actual parameter value or expression, as shown in the following method invocation. Here a, b, and c are the names of the three formal parameters of method Calc.

```
          Actual parameter values
             ↓      ↓      ↓
c.Calc ( c: 2,  a: 4,  b: 3);
             ↑      ↑      ↑
          Named parameters
```

Figure 6-13 illustrates the structure of using named parameters.

```
class MyClass                          No Change in
{                                      Parameter Declarations
    public int Calc(int a, int b, int c)
    { return (a + b) * c;  }

    static void Main()
    {                                  Parameter Names
        MyClass mc = new MyClass();    Used with Values

        int result = mc.Calc( c: 2, a: 4, b: 3 );

        Console.WriteLine("{0}", result);
    }
}
```

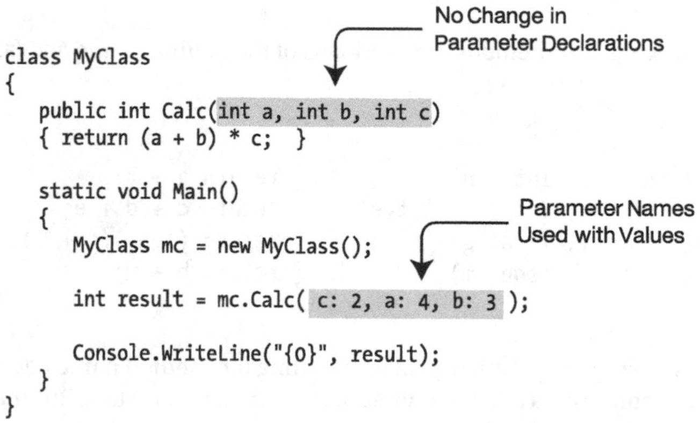

Figure 6-13. *When using named parameters, include the parameter name in the method invocation. No changes are needed in the method declaration.*

You can use both positional and named parameters in an invocation, but if you do, all the *positional parameters must be listed first*. For example, the following code shows the declaration of a method called Calc, along with five different calls to the method using different combinations of positional and named parameters:

```
class MyClass {
    public int Calc( int a, int b, int c )
    { return ( a + b ) * c;  }

    static void Main() {
        MyClass mc = new MyClass( );

        int r0 = mc.Calc( 4, 3, 2 );            // Positional Parameters
        int r1 = mc.Calc( 4, b: 3, c: 2 );      // Positional and Named Parameters
        int r2 = mc.Calc( 4, c: 2, b: 3 );      // Switch order
        int r3 = mc.Calc( c: 2, b: 3, a: 4 );   // All named parameters
        int r4 = mc.Calc( c: 2, b: 1 + 2, a: 3 + 1 ); // Named parameter expressions

        Console.WriteLine($"{ r0 }, { r1 }, { r2 }, { r3 }, { r4 }");
    }
}
```

This code produces the following output:

```
14, 14, 14, 14, 14
```

Named parameters are useful as a means of self-documenting a program in that they can show, at the position of the method call, what values are being assigned to which formal parameters. For example, in the following two calls to method GetCylinderVolume, the second call is a bit more informative and less prone to error:

```
class MyClass {
    double GetCylinderVolume( double radius, double height )
    {
        return 3.1416 * radius * radius * height;
    }

    static void Main( string[] args ) {
        MyClass mc = new MyClass();
        double volume;
                                       ↓    ↓
        volume = mc.GetCylinderVolume( 3.0, 4.0 );
        ...
        volume = mc.GetCylinderVolume( radius: 3.0, height: 4.0 );
    }                                      ↑           ↑
}                                       More informative
```

Optional Parameters

C# also allows *optional parameters*. An optional parameter is a parameter that you can either include or omit when invoking the method.

To specify that a parameter is optional, you need to include a default value for that parameter in the method declaration. The syntax for specifying the default value is the same as that of initializing a local variable, as shown in the method declaration of the following code. In this example,

- Formal parameter b is assigned the default value 3.

- Therefore, if the method is called with only a single parameter, the method will use the value 3 as the initial value of the second parameter.

```
class MyClass                      Optional parameter
{                                        ↓
   public int Calc( int a, int b = 3 )
   {                                      ↑
      return a + b;          Default value assignment
   }

   static void Main()
   {
      MyClass mc = new MyClass();

      int r0 = mc.Calc( 5, 6 );          // Use explicit values.
      int r1 = mc.Calc( 5 );             // Use default for b.

      Console.WriteLine($"{ r0 }, { r1 }");
   }
}
```

This code produces the following output:

11, 8

There are several important things to know about declaring optional parameters.

- Not all types of parameters can be used as optional parameters. Figure 6-14 illustrates when optional parameters can be used.

  - You can use value types as optional parameters as long as the default value is determinable at compile time.

  - You can use a reference type as an optional parameter only if the default value is null.

Parameter Types

Data Types		Value	ref	out	params
	Value Type	Yes	No	No	No
	Reference Type	Only null default	No	No	No

Figure 6-14. *Optional parameters can only be value parameter types*

- All required parameters must be declared before any optional parameters are declared. If there is a params parameter, it must be declared after all the optional parameters. Figure 6-15 illustrates the required syntactic order.

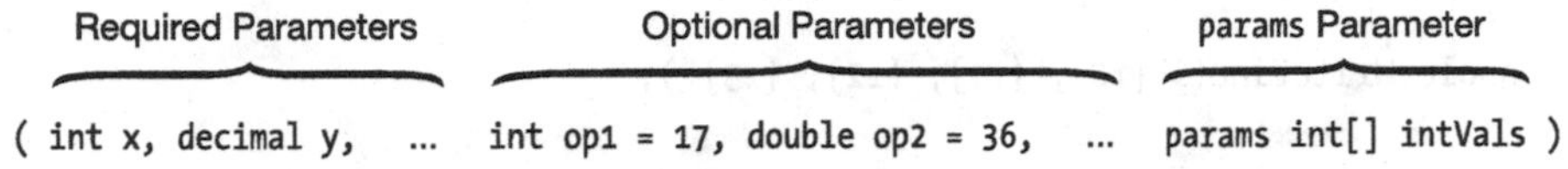

Required Parameters	Optional Parameters	params Parameter

```
( int x, decimal y,   ...   int op1 = 17, double op2 = 36,   ...   params int[] intVals )
```

Figure 6-15. *In the method declaration, optional parameters must be declared after all the required parameters and before the params parameter, if one exists*

As you saw in the previous example, you instruct the program to use the default value of an optional parameter by leaving out the corresponding actual parameter from the method invocation. You can't, however, omit just any combination of optional parameters because in many situations it would be ambiguous as to which optional parameters the method is supposed to use. The rules are as follows:

- You must omit parameters starting from the end of the list of optional parameters and work toward the beginning.

- That is, you can omit the last optional parameter, or the last n optional parameters, but you can't pick and choose to omit any arbitrary optional parameters; they must be taken off the end.

```
class MyClass
{
    public int Calc( int a = 2, int b = 3, int c = 4 )
    {
        return (a + b) * c;
    }

    static void Main( )
    {
        MyClass mc = new MyClass( );
        int r0 = mc.Calc( 5, 6, 7 );    // Use all explicit values.
        int r1 = mc.Calc( 5, 6 );       // Use default for c.
        int r2 = mc.Calc( 5 );          // Use default for b and c.
        int r3 = mc.Calc( );            // Use all defaults.

        Console.WriteLine($"{r0}, {r1}, {r2}, {r3}");
    }
}
```

This code produces the following output:

```
77, 44, 32, 20
```

To omit optional parameters from arbitrary positions within the list of optional parameters, rather than from the end of the list, you must use the names of the optional parameters to disambiguate the assignments. In this case, you're using both the named-parameters and optional-parameters features. The following code illustrates this use of positional, optional, and named parameters:

```
class MyClass
{
   double GetCylinderVolume( double radius = 3.0, double height = 4.0 )
   {
      return 3.1416 * radius * radius * height;
   }

   static void Main( )
   {
      MyClass mc = new MyClass();
      double volume;

      volume = mc.GetCylinderVolume( 3.0, 4.0 );        // Positional
      Console.WriteLine( "Volume = " + volume );

      volume = mc.GetCylinderVolume( radius: 2.0 );     // Use default height
      Console.WriteLine( "Volume = " + volume );

      volume = mc.GetCylinderVolume( height: 2.0 );     // Use default radius
      Console.WriteLine( "Volume = " + volume );

      volume = mc.GetCylinderVolume( );                 // Use both defaults
      Console.WriteLine( "Volume = " + volume );
   }
}
```

This code produces the following output:

```
Volume = 113.0976
Volume = 50.2656
Volume = 56.5488
Volume = 113.0976
```

Stack Frames

So far, you know that local variables and parameters are kept on the stack. In this section, we'll look at that organization a bit further.

When a method is called, memory is allocated at the top of the stack to hold a number of data items associated with the method. This chunk of memory is called the *stack frame* for the method.

- The stack frame contains memory to hold the following:

    - The return address—that is, where to resume execution when the method exits

    - Those parameters that allocate memory—that is, the value parameters of the method, and the parameter array if there is one

    - Various other administrative data items relevant to the method call

- When a method is called, its entire stack frame is pushed onto the stack.

- When the method exits, its entire stack frame is popped from the stack. Popping a stack frame is sometimes called *unwinding* the stack.

For example, the following code declares three methods. Method Main calls MethodA, which calls MethodB, thus creating three stack frames. As the methods exit, the stack unwinds.

```
class Program
{
    static void MethodA( int par1, int par2)
    {
        Console.WriteLine($"Enter MethodA: { par1 }, { par2 }");
        MethodB(11, 18);                      // Call MethodB.
        Console.WriteLine("Exit  MethodA");
    }

    static void MethodB(int par1, int par2)
    {
        Console.WriteLine($"Enter MethodB: { par1 }, { par2 }");
        Console.WriteLine("Exit  MethodB");
    }

    static void Main( )
    {
        Console.WriteLine("Enter Main");
        MethodA( 15, 30);                     // Call MethodA.
        Console.WriteLine("Exit  Main");
    }
}
```

This code produces the following output:

```
Enter Main
Enter MethodA: 15, 30
Enter MethodB: 11, 18
Exit  MethodB
Exit  MethodA
Exit  Main
```

Figure 6-16 shows how the stack frames of each method are placed on the stack when the method is called and how the stack is unwound as the methods complete.

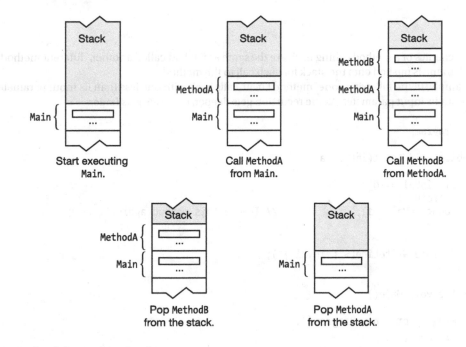

Figure 6-16. *Stack frames in a simple program*

125

Recursion

Besides calling other methods, a method can also call *itself*. This is called *recursion*.

Recursion can produce some very elegant code, such as the following method for computing the factorial of a number. Notice in this example that inside the method, the method calls itself with an actual parameter of one less than its input parameter.

```
int Factorial(int inValue)
{
   if (inValue <= 1)
      return inValue;
   else
      return inValue * Factorial(inValue - 1); // Call Factorial again.
}
                                  ↑
                              Calls itself
```

The mechanics of a method calling itself are the same as if it had called another, different method. A new stack frame is pushed onto the stack for each call to the method.

For example, in the following code, method Count calls itself with one less than its input parameter and then prints out its input parameter. As the recursion gets deeper, the stack gets larger.

```
class Program
{
   public void Count(int inVal)
   {
      if (inVal == 0)
         return;
      Count(inVal - 1);                   // Invoke this method again.
          ↑
      Calls itself
      Console.WriteLine($"{ inVal }");
   }

   static void Main()
   {
      Program pr = new Program();
      pr.Count(3);
   }
}
```

This code produces the following output:

```
1
2
3
```

Figure 6-17 illustrates the code. Notice that with an input value of 3, there are four different, independent stack frames for method Count. Each has its own value for input parameter inVal.

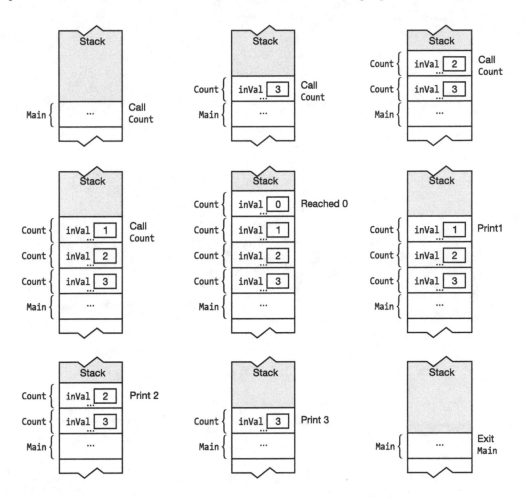

Figure 6-17. *Example of building and unwinding the stack with a recursive method*

CHAPTER 7

■ ■ ■

More About Classes

© Daniel Solis and Cal Schrotenboer 2018   129
D. Solis and C. Schrotenboer, *Illustrated C# 7*, https://doi.org/10.1007/978-1-4842-3288-0_7

Class Members

The previous two chapters covered two of the nine types of class members: fields and methods. In this chapter, we'll introduce all the other class members except events and operators and explain their features. We'll cover events in Chapter 15.

Table 7-1 lists the class member types. Those that have already been introduced are marked with diamonds. Those that are covered in this chapter are marked with a check. Those that will be covered later in the book are marked with empty check boxes.

Table 7-1. *Types of Class Members*

Data Members (Store Data)	Function Members (Execute Code)	
◆ Fields	◆ Methods	❑ Operators
✓ Constants	✓ Properties	✓ Indexers
	✓ Constructors	❑ Events
	✓ Destructors	

Order of Member Modifiers

Previously, you saw that the declarations of fields and methods can include modifiers such as `public` and `private`. In this chapter, we'll discuss a number of additional modifiers. Since many of these modifiers can be used together, the question that arises is, what order do they need to be in?

Class member declaration statements consist of the following: the core declaration, an optional set of *modifiers*, and an optional set of *attributes*. The syntax used to describe this structure is the following. The square brackets indicate that the enclosed set of components is optional.

```
[ attributes ] [ modifiers ]  CoreDeclaration
```

The optional components are the following:

- Modifiers

  - If there are any modifiers, they must be placed before the core declaration.

  - If there are multiple modifiers, they can be in any order.

- Attributes

  - If there are any attributes, they must be placed before the modifiers and core declaration.

  - If there are multiple attributes, they can be in any order.

So far, we've explained only two modifiers: `public` and `private`. We'll cover attributes in Chapter 25. For example, `public` and `static` are both modifiers that can be used together to modify certain declarations. Since they're both modifiers, they can be placed in either order. For example, the following two lines are semantically equivalent:

```
public static int MaxVal;
static public int MaxVal;
```

Figure 7-1 shows the order of the components as applied to the member types shown so far: fields and methods. Notice that the type of the field and the return type of the method are not modifiers—they're part of the core declaration.

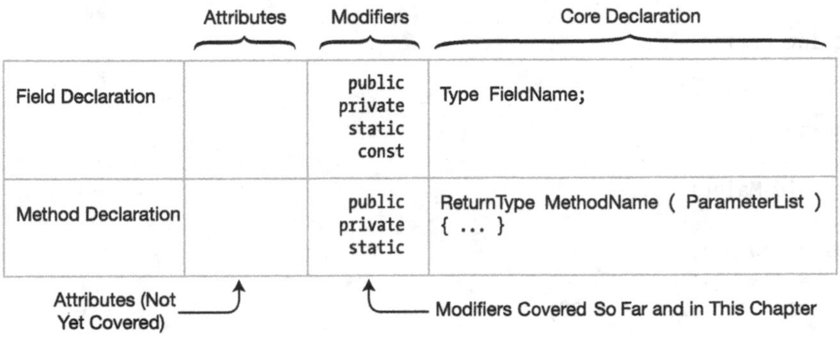

	Attributes	Modifiers	Core Declaration
Field Declaration		public private static const	Type FieldName;
Method Declaration		public private static	ReturnType MethodName (ParameterList) { ... }

Attributes (Not Yet Covered)   Modifiers Covered So Far and in This Chapter

Figure 7-1. *The order of attributes, modifiers, and core declarations*

Instance Class Members

Class members can be associated with an instance of the class or with the class as a whole, that is, to all the instances of the class. By default, members are associated with an instance. You can think of each instance of a class as having its own copy of each class member. These members are called *instance members*.

Changes to the value of one instance field do not affect the values of the members in any other instance. So far, the fields and methods you've seen have all been instance fields and instance methods.

For example, the following code declares a class, D, with a single integer field, Mem1. Main creates two instances of the class. Each instance has its own copy of field Mem1. Changing the value of one instance's copy of the field doesn't affect the value of the other instance's copy. Figure 7-2 shows the two instances of class D.

```
class D
{
    public int Mem1;
}

class Program
{
    static void Main()
    {
        D d1 = new D();
        D d2 = new D();
        d1.Mem1 = 10; d2.Mem1 = 28;

        Console.WriteLine($"d1 = { d1.Mem1 }, d2 = { d2.Mem1 }");
    }
}
```

This code produces the following output:

```
d1 = 10, d2 = 28
```

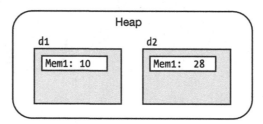

Figure 7-2. *Each instance of class D has its own copy of field Mem1*

Static Fields

Besides instance fields, classes can have what are called *static fields*.

- A static field is *shared* by *all the instances of the class*, and all the instances access the same memory location. Hence, if the value of the memory location is changed by one instance, the change is visible to all the instances.

- Use the `static` modifier to declare a field static, as follows:

```
class D
{
    int Mem1;                   // Instance field
    static int Mem2;            // Static field
        ↑
} Keyword
```

For example, the code on the left in Figure 7-3 declares class D with static field Mem2 and instance field Mem1. Main defines two instances of class D. The figure shows that static field Mem2 is stored separately from the storage of any of the instances. The gray fields inside the instances represent the fact that, from inside an instance method, the syntax to access or update the static field is the same as for any other member field.

- Because Mem2 is static, both instances of class D share a single Mem2 field. If Mem2 is changed, that change is seen from both.

- Member Mem1 is not declared `static`, so each instance has its own distinct copy.

```
class D
{
    int Mem1;
    static int Mem2;
    ...
}

static void Main()
{
    D d1 = new D();
    D d2 = new D();
    ...
}
```

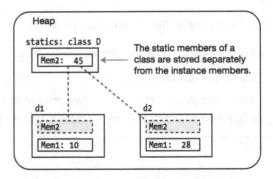

Static field Mem2 is shared by all the instances of class D,
whereas each instance has its own copy of instance field Mem1.

***Figure 7-3.** Static and instance data members*

Accessing Static Members from Outside the Class

In the previous chapter, you saw that dot-syntax notation is used to access public instance members from outside the class. Dot-syntax notation consists of listing the instance name, followed by a dot, followed by the member name.

Static members, like instance members, can also be accessed from outside the class using dot-syntax notation. But since there is no instance, the most common technique for accessing static members uses the *class name*, as shown here:

```
Class name
    ↓
  D.Mem2 = 5;              // Accessing the static class member
    ↑
  Member name
```

Another option to access the member doesn't use any prefix at all, provided that you have included a using static declaration for the specific class to which that member belongs, as shown here:

```
using static System.Console;    // includes, amongst other members, Writeline()
using static System.Math;       // includes, amongst other members, Sqrt()
    ...
WriteLine($"The square root of 16 is { Sqrt(16) }" );
```

This is equivalent to the following:

```
using System;
    ...
Console.WriteLine($"The square root of 16 is { Math.Sqrt(16) }");
```

The using static declaration construct is covered in more detail in Chapter 22.

■ **Note**   You should choose between these two forms of accessing a static member based on which approach makes your code clearer and more understandable to you and to others responsible for maintaining your code.

Example of a Static Field

The following code expands the preceding class D by adding two methods.

- One method sets the values of the two data members.
- The other method displays the values of the two data members.

```
class D
{
    int       Mem1;
    static int Mem2;

    public void SetVars(int v1, int v2) // Set the values
    { Mem1 = v1; Mem2 = v2; }
                  ↑ Access as if it were an instance field

    public void Display( string str )
    { Console.WriteLine("{0}: Mem1= {1}, Mem2= {2}", str, Mem1, Mem2); }
}
                                                              ↑
                                      Access as if it were an instance field
    class Program {
        static void Main()
        {
            D d1 = new D(), d2 = new D();    // Create two instances.

            d1.SetVars(2, 4);               // Set d1's values.
            d1.Display("d1");

            d2.SetVars(15, 17);             // Set d2's values.
            d2.Display("d2");

            d1.Display("d1");               // Display d1 again and notice that the
        }                                   // value of static member Mem2 has changed!
    }
}
```

This code produces the following output:

```
d1: Mem1= 2, Mem2= 4
d2: Mem1= 15, Mem2= 17
d1: Mem1= 2, Mem2= 17
```

Lifetimes of Static Members

The lifetimes for static members are different from those of instance members.

- As you saw previously, instance members come into existence when the instance is created and go out of existence when the instance is destroyed.

- Static members, however, exist and are accessible *even if there are no instances* of the class.

Figure 7-4 illustrates a class, D, with a static field, Mem2. Even though Main doesn't define any instances of the class, it assigns the value 5 to the static field and prints it out with no problem.

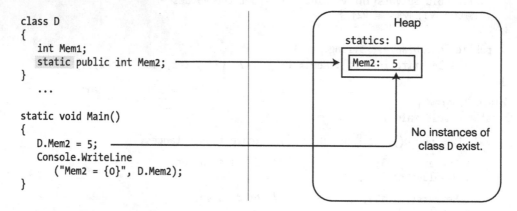

***Figure 7-4.** Static fields with no class instances can still be assigned to and read from because the field is associated with the class, not an instance*

The code in Figure 7-4 produces the following output:

```
Mem2 = 5
```

■ **Note**   Static members exist even if there are no instances of the class. If a static field has an initializer, the field is initialized before the use of any of the class's static fields, but not necessarily at the beginning of program execution.

Static Function Members

Besides static fields, there are also static function members.

- Static function members, like static fields, are independent of any class instance. Even if there are no instances of a class, you can still call a static method.

- Static function members *cannot access instance members*. They can, however, access other static members.

For example, the following class contains a static field and a static method. Notice that the body of the static method accesses the static field.

```
class X
{
   static public int A;                        // Static field
   static public void PrintValA()              // Static method
   {
      Console.WriteLine("Value of A: {0}", A);
   }                                     ↑
}                              Accessing the static field
```

The following code uses class X, defined in the preceding code:

```
class Program
{
   static void Main()
   {
      X.A = 10;              // Use dot-syntax notation
      X.PrintValA();         // Use dot-syntax notation
   } ↑
      Class name
}
```

This code produces the following output:

```
Value of A: 10
```

Figure 7-5 illustrates the preceding code.

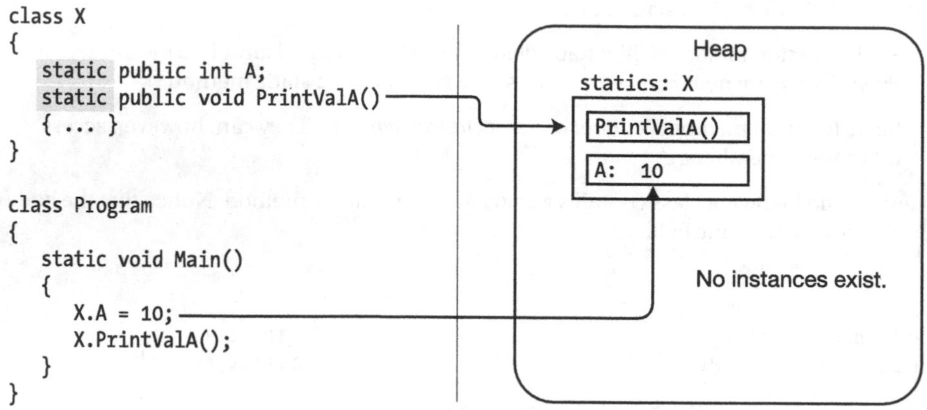
class X
{
static public int A;
static public void PrintValA()
{ ... }
}
class Program
{
static void Main()
{
X.A = 10;
X.PrintValA();
}
}
Heap
statics: X
PrintValA()
A: 10
No instances exist.

Figure 7-5. *Static methods of a class can be called even if there are no instances of the class*

Other Static Class Member Types

The types of class members that can be declared `static` are shown checked in Table 7-2. The other member types cannot be declared `static`.

Table 7-2. *Class Member Types That Can Be Declared Static*

Data Members (Store Data)	Function Members (Execute Code)
✓ Fields	✓ Methods
✓ Types	✓ Properties
Constants	✓ Constructors
	✓ Operators
	Indexers
	✓ Events

Member Constants

Member constants are like the local constants covered in the previous chapter except that they're declared in the class declaration rather than in a method, as shown in the following example:

```
class MyClass
{
    const int IntVal = 100;        // Defines a constant of type int
              ↑           ↑         // with a value of 100.
}          Type       Initializer

const double PI = 3.1416;          // Error: cannot be declared outside a type
                                   // declaration
```

Like local constants, the value used to initialize a member constant must be computable at compile time and is usually one of the predefined simple types or an expression composed of them.

```
class MyClass
{
    const int IntVal1 = 100;
    const int IntVal2 = 2 * IntVal1;  // Fine, since the value of IntVal1
}                                     // was set in the previous line.
```

Like local constants, you cannot assign to a member constant after its declaration.

```
class MyClass
{
    const int IntVal;              // Error: initialization is required.
    IntVal = 100;                  // Error: assignment is not allowed.
}
```

■ **Note**   Unlike C and C++, in C# there are no global constants. Every constant must be declared within a type.

Constants Are Like Statics

Member constants, however, are more interesting than local constants, in that they act like static values. They're "visible" to every instance of the class, and they're available even if there are no instances of the class. Unlike actual statics, constants do not have their own storage locations and are substituted in by the compiler at compile time in a manner similar to #define values in C and C++.

For example, the following code declares class X with constant field PI. Main doesn't create any instances of X, and yet it can use field PI and print its value. Figure 7-6 illustrates the code.

```
class X
{
   public const double PI = 3.1416;
}

class Program
{
   static void Main()
   {
      Console.WriteLine($"pi = { X.PI }");   // Use the const field PI
   }
}
```

This code produces the following output:

```
pi = 3.1416
```

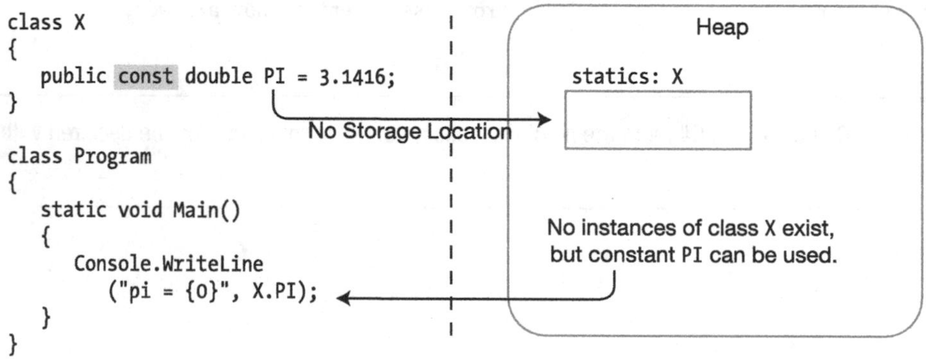

Figure 7-6. *Constant fields act like static fields but do not have a storage location in memory*

Although a constant member acts like a static, you cannot declare a constant as static, as shown in the following line of code:

```
static const double PI = 3.14;      // Error: can't declare a constant as static
```

Properties

A *property* is a member that represents an item of data in a class or class instance. Using a property appears very much like writing to, or reading from, a field. The syntax is the same.

For example, the following code shows the use of a class called MyClass that has both a public field and a public property. From their usage, you cannot tell them apart.

```
MyClass mc = new MyClass();

mc.MyField   = 5;           // Assigning to a field
mc.MyProperty = 10;         // Assigning to a property

Console.WriteLine($"{ mc.MyField } { mc.MyProperty }"); // Read field and property
```

A property, like a field, has the following characteristics:

- It is a named class member.

- It has a type.

- It can be assigned to and read from.

Unlike a field, however, a property is a function member; hence:

- It does not necessarily allocate memory for data storage.

- It executes code.

A property is a named set of two matching methods called *accessors*.

- The set accessor is used for assigning a value to the property.

- The get accessor is used for retrieving a value from the property.

Figure 7-7 shows the representation of a property. The code on the left shows the syntax of declaring a property named MyValue, of type int. The image on the right shows how properties will be represented visually in this text. Notice that the accessors are shown sticking out the back because, as you will soon see, they're not directly callable.

```
int MyValue
{
    set
    {
        SetAccessorCode
    }
    get
    {
        GetAccessorCode
    }
}
```

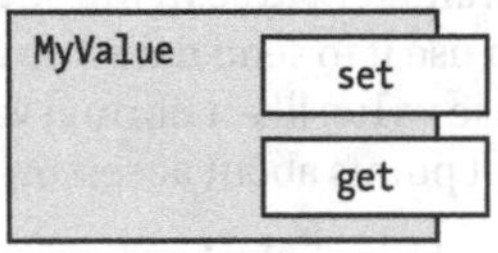

Figure 7-7. An example property named MyValue, of type int

141

Property Declarations and Accessors

The set and get accessors have predefined syntax and semantics. You can think of the set accessor as a method with a single parameter that "sets" the value of the property. The get accessor has no parameters and returns the value of the property.

- The set accessor always has the following:

    - A single, implicit value parameter named value, of the same type as the property

    - A return type of void

- The get accessor always has the following:

    - No parameters

    - A return type of the same type as the property

Figure 7-8 shows the structure of a property declaration. Notice in the figure that neither accessor declaration has *explicit* parameter or return type declarations. They don't need them because they're *implicit* in the type of the property.

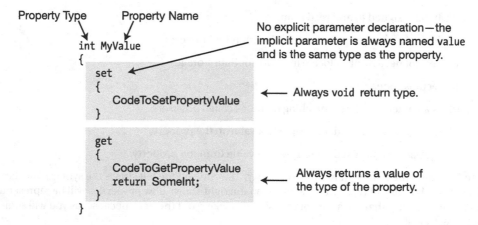

Figure 7-8. *The syntax and structure of a property declaration*

The implicit parameter value in the set accessor is a normal value parameter. Like other value parameters, you can use it to send data into a method body—or in this case, the accessor block. Once inside the block, you can use value like a normal variable, including assigning values to it.

Other important points about accessors are the following:

- All paths through the implementation of a get accessor *must* include a return statement that returns a value of the property type.

- The set and get accessors can be declared in either order, and no methods other than the two accessors are allowed on a property.

A Property Example

The following code shows an example of the declaration of a class called C1, which contains a property named MyValue.

- Notice that the property itself doesn't have any storage. Instead, the accessors determine what should be done with data sent in and what data should be sent out. In this case, the property uses a field called theRealValue for storage.

- The set accessor takes its input parameter, value, and assigns that value to field theRealValue.

- The get accessor just returns the value of field theRealValue.

Figure 7-9 illustrates the code.

```
class C1
{
    private int theRealValue;        // Field: memory allocated

    public int MyValue               // Property: no memory allocated
    {
        set { theRealValue = value; }
        get { return theRealValue;  }
    }
}
```

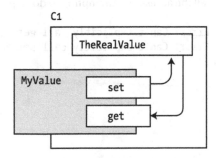

Figure 7-9. *Property accessors often use fields for storage*

Using a Property

As you saw previously, you write to and read from a property in the same way you access a field. The accessors are called implicitly.

- To write to a property, use the property's name on the left side of an assignment statement.

- To read from a property, use the property's name in an expression.

For example, the following code contains an outline of the declaration of a property named MyValue. You write to and read from the property using just the property name, as if it were a field name.

```
int MyValue               // Property declaration
{
    set{ ... }
    get{ ... }
}
...
```
Property name
↓

```
MyValue = 5;              // Assignment: the set method is implicitly called.
z = MyValue;             // Expression: the get method is implicitly called.
```
↑
Property name

The appropriate accessor is called implicitly depending on whether you are writing to or reading from the property. You cannot explicitly call the accessors. Attempting to do so produces a compile error.

```
y = MyValue.get();       // Error! Can't explicitly call get accessor.
MyValue.set(5);          // Error! Can't explicitly call set accessor.
```

Properties and Associated Fields

A property is often associated with a field, as shown in the previous two sections. A common practice is to encapsulate a field in a class by declaring the field private and declaring a public property to give controlled access to the field from outside the class. The field associated with a property is called the *backing field* or *backing store*.

For example, the following code uses the public property MyValue to give controlled access to private field theRealValue:

```
class C1
{
    private int theRealValue = 10;    // Backing Field: memory allocated
    public  int MyValue               // Property: no memory allocated
    {
        set{ theRealValue = value; }  // Sets the value of field theRealValue
        get{ return theRealValue; }   // Gets the value of the field
    }
}

class Program
{
    static void Main()
    {
```
                              Read from the property as if it were a field.
                                        ↓
```
        C1 c = new C1();
        Console.WriteLine("MyValue:  {0}", c.MyValue);

        c.MyValue = 20;          ←  Use assignment to set the value of a property.
        Console.WriteLine("MyValue:  {0}", c.MyValue);
    }
}
```

There are several conventions for naming properties and their backing fields. One convention is to use the same string for both names but use *camel casing* for the field and *Pascal casing* for the property. (Remember that camel casing describes a compound word identifier where the first letter of each word, except the first, is capitalized, and the rest of the letters are lowercase. Pascal casing is where the first letter of each word in the compound is capitalized.) Although this violates the general rule that it's bad practice to have different identifiers that differ only in casing, it has the advantage of tying the two identifiers together in a meaningful way.

Another convention is to use Pascal casing for the property, and then for the field, use the camel case version of the same identifier, with an underscore in front.

The following code shows both conventions:

```
private int firstField;              // Camel casing
public  int FirstField               // Pascal casing
{
   get { return firstField; }
   set { firstField = value; }
}

private int _secondField;            // Underscore and camel casing
public  int SecondField
{
   get { return _secondField; }
   set { _secondField = value; }
}
```

Performing Other Calculations

Property accessors are not limited to just passing values back and forth from an associated backing field; the get and set accessors can perform any, or no, computations. The only action *required* is that the get accessor return a value of the property type.

For instance, the following example shows a valid (but probably useless) property that just returns the value 5 when its get accessor is called. When the set accessor is called, it doesn't do anything. The value of implicit parameter value is ignored.

```
public int Useless
{
   set{ }             // I'm not setting anything.
   get{ return 5; }   // I'm always just returning the value 5.
}
```

The following code shows a more realistic and useful property, where the set accessor performs filtering before setting the associated field. The set accessor sets field theRealValue to the input value—unless the input value is greater than 100. In that case, it sets theRealValue to 100.

```
int theRealValue = 10;                                      // The field
int MyValue                                                 // The property
{
   set { theRealValue = value > 100 ? 100 : value; }        // Conditional operator
   get { return theRealValue; }
}
```

C# 7.0 introduced an alternate syntax for property getters and setters that uses expression bodies. While *expression bodies* (also known as *lambda expressions*) are discussed in more detail in Chapter 14, the new syntax is illustrated here for completeness. This alternate syntax can be used only if the accessor body consists of a single expression.

```
int MyValue
{
   set => value > 100 ? 100 : value;
   get => theRealValue;
}
```

■ **Note**   In the preceding code sample, the syntax between the equal sign and the end of the statement is the *conditional operator*, which we'll cover in greater detail in Chapter 9. The conditional operator is a ternary operator that evaluates the expression in front of the question mark, and if the expression evaluates to true, it returns the expression after the question mark. Otherwise, it returns the expression after the colon. Some people would use and if...then statement here, but the conditional operator is more appropriate, as you'll see when we look at both constructs in Chapter 9.

Read-Only and Write-Only Properties

You can leave one or the other (but not both) of a property's accessors undefined by omitting its declaration.

- A property with only a get accessor is called a *read-only* property. A read-only property is a safe way of passing an item of data out from a class or class instance without allowing the caller to modify the value of the property.

- A property with only a set accessor is called a *write-only* property. Write-only properties are rarely seen because there are very few practical uses for them. If the intention is to trigger a side effect when the value is assigned, you should use a method rather than a property.

- At least one of the two accessors must be defined, or the compiler will produce an error message.

Figure 7-10 illustrates read-only and write-only properties.

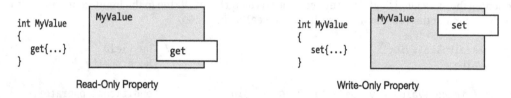

```
int MyValue                MyValue
{                                          
    get{...}                          get
}
```
Read-Only Property

```
int MyValue                MyValue        set
{
    set{...}
}
```
Write-Only Property

***Figure 7-10.** A property can have one or the other of its accessors undefined*

Properties vs. Public Fields

As a matter of preferred coding practice, properties are preferred over public fields for several reasons.

- Since properties are function members, as opposed to data members, they allow you to process the input and output, which you can't do with public fields.

- You can have read-only or write-only properties, but you can't have these characteristics with a field.

- The semantics of a compiled variable and a compiled property are different.

The third point has implications when you release an assembly that is accessed by other code. For example, sometimes you may be tempted to use a public field rather than a property, with the reasoning that if you ever need to add processing to the data held in the field, you can always change the field to a property at a later time. This is true, but if you make that change, you will also have to recompile any other assemblies *accessing* that field because the compiled semantics of fields and properties are different. On the other hand, if you implement it as a property and just change its *implementation*, you won't need to recompile the other assemblies accessing it.

An Example of a Computed, Read-Only Property

In most of the examples so far, the property has been associated with a backing field, and the get and set accessors have referenced that field. However, a property does not have to be associated with a field. In the following example, the get accessor *computes* the return value.

In the code, class RightTriangle represents, not surprisingly, a right triangle. Figure 7-11 illustrates read-only property Hypotenuse.

- It has two public fields that represent the lengths of the two right-angle sides of the triangle. These fields can be written to and read from.

- The third side is represented by property Hypotenuse, which is a read-only property whose return value is based on the lengths of the other two sides. It isn't stored in a field. Instead, it computes the correct value, on demand, for the current values of A and B.

```
class RightTriangle
{
   public double A = 3;
   public double B = 4;
   public double Hypotenuse                 // Read-only property
   {
      get{ return Math.Sqrt((A*A)+(B*B)); }    // Calculate return value
   }
}

class Program
{
   static void Main()
   {
      RightTriangle c = new RightTriangle();
      Console.WriteLine($"Hypotenuse:  { c.Hypotenuse }");
   }
}
```

This code produces the following output:

Hypotenuse: 5

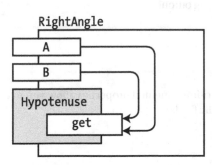

Figure 7-11. *Read-only property Hypotenuse*

Automatically Implemented Properties—Auto-properties

Because properties are so often associated with backing fields, C# provides *automatically implemented properties*, also called *auto-implemented properties* or, more commonly, just *auto-properties*, which allow you to declare the property without declaring a backing field. The compiler creates a hidden backing field for you and automatically hooks up the get and set accessors to it.

The important points about auto-implemented properties are the following:

- You do not declare the backing field—the compiler allocates the storage for you, based on the type of the property.

- You cannot supply the bodies of the accessors—they must be declared simply as semicolons. The get acts as a simple read of the memory, and the set as a simple write. However, because you cannot access the bodies of auto-properties, it is often more difficult to debug your code when using auto-properties.

  Beginning with C# 6.0, you can now use read-only auto-properties. Also, it is now possible to initialize auto-properties as part of their declaration.

The following code shows an example of an automatically implemented property:

```
class C1
{                           ← No declared backing field
    public int MyValue                          // Allocates memory
    {
        set; get;
    }    ↑   ↑
}     The bodies of the accessors are declared as semicolons.

class Program
{
    static void Main()
    {                            Use auto-implemented properties as regular properties.
        C1 c = new C1();                      ↓
        Console.WriteLine("MyValue:  {0}", c.MyValue);

        c.MyValue = 20;
        Console.WriteLine("MyValue:  {0}", c.MyValue);
    }
}
```

This code produces the following output:

```
MyValue:  0
MyValue:  20
```

Besides being convenient, auto-implemented properties allow you to easily insert a property where you might be tempted to declare a public field.

Static Properties

Properties can also be declared `static`. Accessors of static properties, like all static members, have the following characteristics:

- They cannot access instance members of a class—although they can be accessed by them.

- They exist regardless of whether there are instances of the class.

- From inside the class, you reference the static property using just its name.

- From outside the class, you must reference the property either using its class name or using the `using static` construct, as described earlier in this chapter.

The following code shows an example of a class with an auto-implemented static property called `MyValue`. In the first three lines of `Main`, the property is accessed, even though there are no instances of the class. The last line of `Main` calls an instance method that accesses the property from *inside* the class.

```
using System;
using static ConsoleTestApp.Trivial;
namespace ConsoleTestApp
{
    class Trivial {
        public static int MyValue { get; set; }     Accessed from inside the class
        public void PrintValue()                              ↓
        { Console.WriteLine("Value from inside: {0}", MyValue); }
    }

    class Program {                                Accessed from outside the class
        static void Main() {                                 ↓
            Console.WriteLine("Init Value: {0}", Trivial.MyValue);
            Trivial.MyValue = 10;              ← Accessed from outside the class
            Console.WriteLine("New Value : {0}", Trivial.MyValue);

            MyValue = 20;  ← Accessed from outside the class, but no class name because of using static
            Console.WriteLine($"New Value : { MyValue }");

            Trivial tr = new Trivial();
            tr.PrintValue();
        }
    }
}
```

```
Init Value: 0
New Value : 10
New Value : 20
Value from inside: 20
```

Instance Constructors

An *instance constructor* is a special method that is executed whenever a new instance of a class is created.

- A constructor is used to initialize the state of the class instance.
- If you want to be able to create instances of your class from outside the class, you need to declare the constructor public.

Figure 7-12 shows the syntax of a constructor. A constructor looks like the other methods in a class declaration, with the following exceptions:

- The name of the constructor is the same as the name of the class.
- A constructor cannot have a return type.

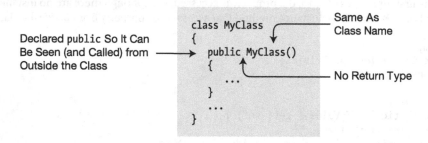

Figure 7-12. *Constructor declaration*

For example, the following class uses its constructor to initialize its fields. In this case, it has a field called TimeOfInstantiation that is initialized with the current date and time.

```
class MyClass
{
   DateTime TimeOfInstantiation;                    // Field
   ...
   public MyClass()                                 // Constructor
   {
      TimeOfInstantiation = DateTime.Now;           // Initialize field
   }
   ...
}
```

■ **Note**   Having just finished the section on static properties, take a closer look at the line that initializes TimeOfInstantiation. The DateTime class (actually it's a struct, but you can think of it as a class since we haven't covered structs yet) is from the BCL, and Now is a *static property* of DateTime. The Now property creates a new instance of the DateTime class, initializes it with the current date and time from the system clock, and returns a reference to the new DateTime instance.

Constructors with Parameters

Constructors are like other methods in the following ways:

- A constructor can have parameters. The syntax for the parameters is exactly the same as for other methods.

- A constructor can be overloaded.

When you use an object-creation expression to create a new instance of a class, you use the new operator followed by one of the class's constructors. The new operator uses that constructor to create the instance of the class.

For example, in the following code, Class1 has three constructors: one that takes no parameters, one that takes an int, and another that takes a string. Main creates an instance using each one.

```
class Class1
{
   int Id;
   string Name;

   public Class1()          { Id=28;    Name="Nemo"; }   // Constructor 0
   public Class1(int val)   { Id=val;   Name="Nemo"; }   // Constructor 1
   public Class1(String name) { Name=name;          }   // Constructor 2

   public void SoundOff()
   { Console.WriteLine($"Name { Name },   Id { Id }"); }
}

class Program
{
   static void Main()
   {
      Class1 a = new Class1(),                    // Call constructor 0.
             b = new Class1(7),                   // Call constructor 1.
             c = new Class1("Bill");              // Call constructor 2.

      a.SoundOff();
      b.SoundOff();
      c.SoundOff();
   }
}
```

This code produces the following output:

```
Name Nemo,    Id 28
Name Nemo,    Id 7
Name Bill,    Id 0
```

153

Default Constructors

If no instance constructor is explicitly supplied in the class declaration, then the compiler supplies an implicit, default constructor, which has the following characteristics:

- It takes no parameters.

- It has an empty body.

If you declare any constructors *at all* for a class, then the compiler does not define the default constructor for the class.

For example, Class2 in the following example declares two constructors:

- Because there is at least one explicitly defined constructor, the compiler does not create any additional constructors.

- In Main, there is an attempt to create a new instance using a constructor with no parameters. Since there *is* no constructor with zero parameters, the compiler produces an error message.

```
class Class2
{
   public Class2(int Value)    { ... }   // Constructor 0
   public Class2(String Value) { ... }   // Constructor 1
}

class Program
{
   static void Main()
   {
      Class2 a = new Class2();   // Error! No constructor with 0 parameters
      ...
   }
}
```

■ **Note**   You can assign access modifiers to instance constructors just as you can to other members. You'll also want to declare the constructors public so that you can create instances from outside the class. You can also create private constructors, which cannot be called from outside the class but can be used from within the class, as you'll see in the next chapter.

Static Constructors

Constructors can also be declared static. While an instance constructor initializes each new instance of a class, a static constructor initializes items at the class level. Generally, static constructors initialize the static fields of the class.

- Class-level items are initialized at the following times:
  - Before any static member is referenced
  - Before any instance of the class is created
- Static constructors are like instance constructors in the following ways:
  - The name of the static constructor must be the same as the name of the class.
  - The constructor cannot return a value.
- Static constructors are unlike instance constructors in the following ways:
  - Static constructors use the static keyword in the declaration.
  - There can be only a single static constructor for a class, and it cannot have parameters.
  - Static constructors cannot have accessibility modifiers.

The following is an example of a static constructor. Notice that its form is the same as that of an instance constructor, but with the addition of the static keyword.

```
class Class1
{
   static Class1 ()
   {
      ...                  // Do all the static initializations.
   }
   ...
```

Other important things you should know about static constructors are the following:

- A class can have both a static constructor and instance constructors.
- Like static methods, a static constructor cannot access instance members of its class and cannot use the this accessor, which we'll cover shortly.
- You cannot explicitly call static constructors from your program. They're called automatically by the system, at some indeterminate time.
  - Before any instance of the class is created
  - Before any static member of the class is referenced

Example of a Static Constructor

The following code uses a static constructor to initialize a private static field named RandomKey, of type Random. Random is a class provided by the BCL to produce random numbers. It's in the System namespace.

```
class RandomNumberClass
{
    private static Random RandomKey;          // Private static field

    static RandomNumberClass()                // Static constructor
    {
        RandomKey = new Random();             // Initialize RandomKey
    }

    public int GetRandomNumber()
    {
        return RandomKey.Next();
    }
}

class Program
{
    static void Main()
    {
        RandomNumberClass a = new RandomNumberClass();
        RandomNumberClass b = new RandomNumberClass();

        Console.WriteLine("Next Random #: {0}", a.GetRandomNumber());
        Console.WriteLine($"Next Random #: { b.GetRandomNumber() }");
    }
}
```

One execution of this code produced the following output:

```
Next Random #: 47857058
Next Random #: 1124842041
```

Object Initializers

So far in the text, you've seen that an object-creation expression consists of the keyword new followed by a class constructor and its parameter list. An *object initializer* extends that syntax by placing a list of member initializations at the end of the expression. An object initializer allows you to set the values of fields and properties when creating a new instance of an object.

The syntax has two forms, as shown here. One form includes the constructor's argument list, and the other doesn't. Notice that the first form doesn't even use the parentheses that would enclose the argument list.

```
                                    Object initializer
                                          ↓
new TypeName          { FieldOrProp = InitExpr, FieldOrProp = InitExpr, ...}
new TypeName(ArgList) { FieldOrProp = InitExpr, FieldOrProp = InitExpr, ...}
                           ↑                        ↑
                      Member initializer       Member initializer
```

For example, for a class named Point with two public integer fields X and Y, you could use the following expression to create a new object:

```
new Point { X = 5, Y = 6 };
              ↑       ↑
           Init X  Init Y
```

Important things to know about object initializers are the following:

- The fields and properties being initialized must be accessible to the code creating the object. For example, in the previous code, X and Y must be public.

- The initialization occurs *after* the constructor has finished execution, so the values might have been set in the constructor and then reset to the same or a different value in the object initializer.

The following code shows an example of using an object initializer. In Main, pt1 calls just the constructor, which sets the values of its two fields. For pt2, however, the constructor sets the fields' values to 1 and 2, and the initializer changes them to 5 and 6.

```
public class Point
{
    public int X = 1;
    public int Y = 2;
}

class Program
{
    static void Main( )
    {                              Object initializer
        Point pt1 = new Point();       ↓
        Point pt2 = new Point   { X = 5, Y = 6 };
        Console.WriteLine("pt1: {0}, {1}", pt1.X, pt1.Y);
        Console.WriteLine($"pt2: { pt2.X }, { pt2.Y }");
    }
}
```

This code produces the following output:

```
pt1: 1, 2
pt2: 5, 6
```

Destructors

Destructors perform actions required to clean up or release unmanaged resources after an instance of a class is no longer referenced. Unmanaged resources are such things as file handles that you've gotten using the Win32 API, or chunks of unmanaged memory. These aren't things you'll get by using .NET resources, so if you stick to the .NET classes, you won't likely have to write destructors for your classes. For this reason, we're going to save the description of destructors until Chapter 27.

The readonly Modifier

A field can be declared with the readonly modifier. The effect is similar to declaring a field as const, in that once the value is set, it cannot be changed.

- While a const field can be initialized only in the field's declaration statement, a readonly field can have its value set in any of the following places:

  - The field declaration statement—like a const.

  - Any of the class constructors. If it's a static field, then it must be done in the static constructor.

- While the value of a const field must be determinable at compile time, the value of a readonly field can be determined at run time. This additional freedom allows you to set different values under different circumstances or in different constructors!

- Unlike a const, which always acts like a static, the following is true of a readonly field:

  - It can be either an instance field or a static field.

  - It has a storage location in memory.

For example, the following code declares a class called Shape, with two readonly fields.

- Field PI is initialized in its declaration.

- Field NumberOfSides is set to either 3 or 4, depending on which constructor is called.

```
class Shape
{   Keyword          Initialized
        ↓                ↓
    readonly double  PI = 3.1416;
    readonly int     NumberOfSides;
       ↑                ↑
    Keyword          Not initialized

    public Shape(double side1, double side2)                    // Constructor
    {
        // Shape is a rectangle
        NumberOfSides = 4;
              ↑
        ... Set in constructor
    }

    public Shape(double side1, double side2, double side3) {  // Constructor
        // Shape is a triangle
        NumberOfSides = 3;
              ↑
        ... Set in constructor
    }
}
```

The this Keyword

The this keyword, used in a class, is a reference to the current instance. It can be used only in the *blocks* of the following class members:

- Instance constructors

- Instance methods

- Instance accessors of properties and indexers (indexers are covered in the next section)

Clearly, since static members are not part of an instance, you cannot use the this keyword inside the code of any static function member. Rather, it is used for the following:

- To distinguish between class members and local variables or parameters

- As an actual parameter when calling a method

For example, the following code declares class MyClass, with an int field and a method that takes a single int parameter. The method compares the values of the parameter and the field and returns the greater value. The only complicating factor is that the names of the field and the formal parameter are the same: Var1. The two names are distinguished inside the method by using the this access keyword to reference the field. (This naming conflict is for example purposes only since you shouldn't use the same name for your member variable and for your parameter name.)

```
class MyClass
{
   int Var1 = 10;
           ↑   Both are called "Var1"     ↓
   public int ReturnMaxSum(int Var1)
   {      Parameter        Field
                  ↓            ↓
      return Var1 > this.Var1
                 ? Var1           // Parameter
                 : this.Var1;     // Field
   }
}
```

```
class Program
{
    static void Main()
    {
        MyClass mc = new MyClass();

        Console.WriteLine($"Max: { mc.ReturnMaxSum(30) }");
        Console.WriteLine($"Max: { mc.ReturnMaxSum(5) }");
    }
}
```

This code produces the following output:

```
Max: 30
Max: 10
```

While it is important to understand the purpose and functionality of the this keyword, its actual usage in your code will likely be relatively rare. See, however, the indexers covered later in this chapter, as well as the extension methods, which are covered in Chapter 18.

Indexers

Suppose you were to define class `Employee`, with three fields of type `string` (as shown in Figure 7-13). You could then access the fields using their names, as shown in the code in `Main`.

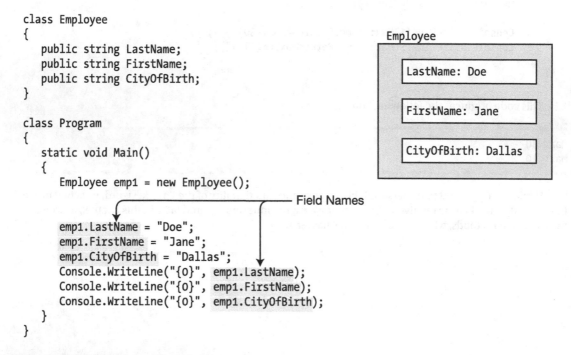

Figure 7-13. *Simple class without indexers*

There are times, however, when it would be convenient to be able to access them with an index, as if the instance were an array of fields. This is exactly what *indexers* allow you to do. If you were to write an indexer for class `Employee`, method `Main` might look like the code in Figure 7-14. Notice that instead of using dot-syntax notation, indexers use *index notation*, which consists of an index between square brackets.

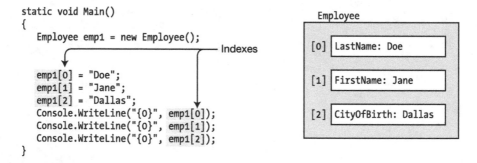

Figure 7-14. *Using indexed fields*

What Is an Indexer?

An indexer is a pair of get and set accessors, similar to those of properties. Figure 7-15 shows the representation of an indexer for a class that can get and set values of type string.

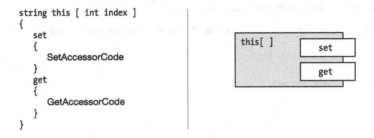

```
string this [ int index ]
{
    set
    {
        SetAccessorCode
    }
    get
    {
        GetAccessorCode
    }
}
```

Figure 7-15. *Representations of an indexer*

Indexers and Properties

Indexers and properties are similar in many ways.

- Like a property, an indexer does not allocate memory for storage.

- Both indexers and properties are used primarily for giving access to *other* data members with which they're associated and for which they provide get and set access.

    - A *property* usually represents a *single* data member.

    - An *indexer* usually represents *multiple* data members.

■ **Note**   You can think of an *indexer* as a *property* that gives get and set access to *multiple data members* of the class. You select which of the many possible data members by supplying an index, which itself can be of any type—not just numeric.

Some additional points you should know about indexers are the following:

- Like a property, an indexer can have either one or both of the accessors.

- Indexers are always instance members; hence, an indexer cannot be declared static.

- Like properties, the code implementing the get and set accessors does not have to be associated with any fields or properties. The code can do anything, or nothing, as long as the get accessor returns some value of the specified type.

Declaring an Indexer

The syntax for declaring an indexer is shown next. Notice the following about indexers:

- An indexer *does not have a name*. In place of the name is the keyword this.

- The parameter list is between *square* brackets.

- There must be at least one parameter declaration in the parameter list.

```
          Keyword      Parameter list
             ↓              ↓
ReturnType this [ Type param1, ... ]
{               ↑               ↑
   get      Square bracket   Square bracket
   {
      ...
   }
   set
   {
      ...
   }
}
```

Declaring an indexer is similar to declaring a property. Figure 7-16 shows the syntactic similarities and differences.

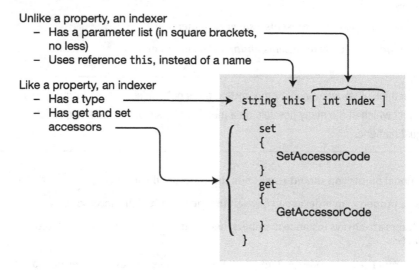

Figure 7-16. *Comparing an indexer declaration to a property declaration*

The Indexer set Accessor

When the indexer is the target of an assignment, the set accessor is called and receives two items of data, as follows:

- An implicit parameter, named value, which holds the data to be stored

- One or more index parameters that represent where it should be stored

```
emp[0] = "Doe";
```
       ↑   ↑
     Index   Value
   parameter

Your code in the set accessor must examine the index parameters, determine where the data should be stored, and then store it.

Figure 7-17 shows the syntax and meaning of the set accessor. The left side of the figure shows the actual syntax of the accessor declaration. The right side shows the semantics of the accessor if it were written using the syntax of a normal method. The figure on the right shows that the set accessor has the following semantics:

- It has a void return type.

- It uses the same parameter list as that in the indexer declaration.

- It has an implicit value parameter named value, of the same type as the indexer.

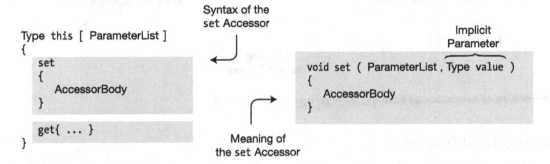

Figure 7-17. *The syntax and meaning of the set accessor declaration*

The Indexer get Accessor

When the indexer is used to retrieve a value, the get accessor is called with one or more index parameters. The index parameters represent which value to retrieve.

```
string s = emp[0];
                ↑
        Index parameter
```

The code in the get accessor body must examine the index parameters, determine which field they represent, and return the value of that field.

Figure 7-18 shows the syntax and meaning of the get accessor. The left side of the figure shows the actual syntax of the accessor declaration. The right side shows the semantics of the accessor if it were written using the syntax of a normal method. The semantics of the get accessor are as follows:

- It has the same parameter list as in the indexer declaration.

- It returns a value of the same type as the indexer.

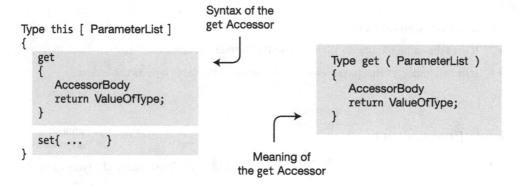

Figure 7-18. *The syntax and meaning of the get accessor declaration*

More About Indexers

As with properties, the get and set accessors cannot be called explicitly. Instead, the get accessor is called automatically when the indexer is used in an expression for a value. The set accessor is called automatically when the indexer is assigned a value with the assignment statement.

When an indexer is "called," the parameters are supplied between the square brackets.

```
Index   Value
  ↓       ↓
emp[0] = "Doe";             // Calls set accessor
string NewName = emp[0];    // Calls get accessor
                    ↑
                  Index
```

Declaring the Indexer for the Employee Example

The following code declares an indexer for the earlier example: class Employee.

- The indexer must read and write values of type string—so string must be declared as the indexer's type. It must be declared public so that it can be accessed from outside the class.

- The three fields in the example have been arbitrarily indexed as integers 0 through 2, so the formal parameter between the square brackets, named index in this case, must be of type int.

- In the body of the set accessor, the code determines which field the index refers to and assigns the value of implicit variable value to it. In the body of the get accessor, the code determines which field the index refers to and returns that field's value.

```
class Employee {
    public string LastName;              // Call this field 0.
    public string FirstName;             // Call this field 1.
    public string CityOfBirth;           // Call this field 2.

    public string this[int index]        // Indexer declaration
    {
        set                              // Set accessor declaration
        {
            switch (index) {
                case 0: LastName = value;
                    break;
                case 1: FirstName = value;
                    break;
                case 2: CityOfBirth = value;
                    break;

                default:                          // (Exceptions in Ch. 23)
                    throw new ArgumentOutOfRangeException("index");
            }
        }

        get                              // Get accessor declaration
        {
            switch (index) {
                case 0: return LastName;
                case 1: return FirstName;
                case 2: return CityOfBirth;

                default:                          // (Exceptions in Ch. 23)
                    throw new ArgumentOutOfRangeException("index");
            }
        }
    }
}
```

167

Another Indexer Example

The following is an additional example that indexes the two int fields of class Class1:

```
class Class1
{
   int Temp0;                         // Private field
   int Temp1;                         // Private field
   public int this [ int index ]      // The indexer
   {
      get
      {
         return ( 0 == index )        // Return value of either Temp0 or Temp1
                    ? Temp0
                    : Temp1;
      }

      set
      {
         if( 0 == index )
            Temp0 = value;            // Note the implicit variable "value".
         else
            Temp1 = value;            // Note the implicit variable "value".
      }
   }
}

class Example
{
   static void Main()
   {
      Class1 a = new Class1();

      Console.WriteLine("Values -- T0: {0},  T1: {1}", a[0], a[1]);
      a[0] = 15;
      a[1] = 20;
      Console.WriteLine($"Values -- T0: { a[0] }, T1: { a[1] }");
   }
}
```

This code produces the following output:

```
Values -- T0: 0,  T1: 0
Values -- T0: 15, T1: 20
```

Indexer Overloading

A class can have any number of indexers, as long as the parameter lists are different; however, it isn't sufficient for the indexer *type* to be different. This is called *indexer overloading* because all the indexers have the same "name"—the this access reference.

For example, the following class has three indexers: two of type string and one of type int. Of the two indexers of type string, one has a single int parameter, and the other has two int parameters.

```
class MyClass
{
    public string this [ int index ]
    {
        get { ... }
        set { ... }
    }

    public string this [ int index1, int index2 ]
    {
        get { ... }
        set { ... }
    }

    public int this [ float index1 ]
    {
        get { ... }
        set { ... }
    }

    ...
}
```

■ **Note**   Remember that the overloaded indexers of a class must have different parameter lists.

Access Modifiers on Accessors

In this chapter, you've seen two types of function members that have get and set accessors: properties and indexers. By default, both a member's accessors have the same access level as the member itself. That is, if a property has an access level of public, then both its accessors have that same access level. The same is true of indexers.

You can, however, assign different access levels to the two accessors. For example, the following code shows a common and important paradigm of declaring a private set accessor and a public get accessor. The get is public because the access level of the property is public.

Notice in this code that although the property can be read from outside the class, it can be set only from inside the class itself, in this case by the constructor. This is an important tool for encapsulation.

```
class Person          Accessors with different access levels
{                          ↓         ↓
    public string Name { get; private set; }
    public Person( string name ) { Name = name; }
}

class Program
{
    static public void Main( )
    {
        Person p = new Person( "Capt. Ernest Evans" );
        Console.WriteLine( $"Person's name is { p.Name }");
    }

}
```

This code produces the following output:

```
Person's name is Capt. Ernest Evans
```

There are several restrictions on the access modifiers of accessors. The most important ones are the following:

- An accessor can have an access modifier only if the member (property or indexer) has both a get accessor and a set accessor.

- Although both accessors must be present, only one of them can have an access modifier.

- The access modifier of the accessor must be *strictly more restrictive* than the access level of the member.

Figure 7-19 shows the hierarchy of access levels. The access level of an accessor must be strictly lower in the chart than the access level of the member.

For example, if a property has an access level of public, you can give any of the four lower access levels on the chart to one of the accessors. But if the property has an access level of protected, the only access modifier you can use on one of the accessors is private.

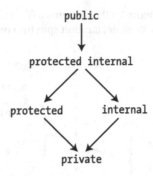

Figure 7-19. *Hierarchy of strictly restrictive accessor levels*

Partial Classes and Partial Types

The declaration of a class can be partitioned among several partial class declarations.

- Each of the partial class declarations contains the declarations of some of the class members.

- The partial class declarations of a class can be in the same file or in different files.

Each partial declaration must be labeled as partial class, in contrast to the single keyword class. The declaration of a partial class looks the same as the declaration of a normal class, other than the addition of the type modifier partial.

```
Type modifier
    ↓
    partial class MyPartClass     // Same class name as following
    {
        member1 declaration
        member2 declaration
            ...
    }
Type modifier
    ↓
    partial class MyPartClass     // Same class name as preceding
    {
        member3 declaration
        member4 declaration
            ...
    }
```

■ **Note**   The type modifier partial is not a keyword, so in other contexts you can use it as an identifier in your program. But when used immediately before the keywords class, struct, or interface, it signals the use of a partial type.

For example, the box on the left of Figure 7-20 represents a file with a class declaration. The boxes on the right of the figure represent that same class declaration split into two files.

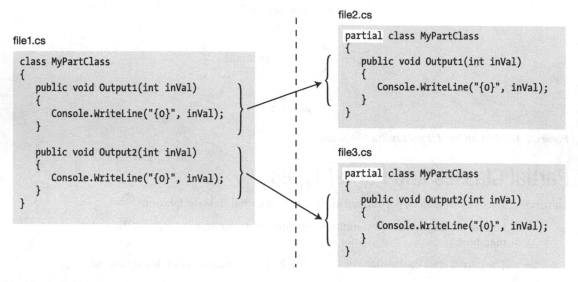

Figure 7-20. *Class split using partial types*

All the partial class declarations comprising a class must be compiled together. A class using partial class declarations has the same meaning as if all the class members were declared within a single class declaration body.

Visual Studio uses this feature in its standard Windows program templates. When you create an ASP. NET project, a Windows Forms project, or a Windows Presentation Foundation (WPF) project from the standard templates, the templates create two class files for each web page, form, or WPF window. In the cases of ASP.NET or Windows Forms, the following is true:

- One file contains the partial class containing the code generated by Visual Studio, declaring the components on the page. You shouldn't modify the partial class in this file since it's regenerated by Visual Studio when you modify the components on the page.

- The other file contains the partial class you use to implement the look and behavior of the components of the page or form.

Besides partial classes, you can create two other partial types, which are the following:

- Partial structs. (Structs are covered in Chapter 11.)

- Partial interfaces. (Interfaces are covered in Chapter 16.)

Partial Methods

Partial methods are methods that are declared in different parts of a partial class. The different parts of the partial method can be declared in different parts of the partial class or in the same part. The two parts of the partial method are the following:

- The defining partial method declaration

  - Lists the signature and return type.

  - The implementation part of the declaration syntax consists of only a semicolon.

- The implementing partial method declaration

  - Lists the signature and return type.

  - The implementation is in the normal format, which, as you know, is a statement block.

The important things to know about partial methods are the following:

- The defining and implementing declarations must match in signature and return type. The signature and return type have the following characteristics:

  - The return type must be void.

  - The signature cannot include access modifiers, *making partial methods implicitly private*.

  - The parameter list cannot contain out parameters.

  - The contextual keyword partial must be included in both the defining and implementing declarations immediately before the keyword void.

- You can have a defining partial method without an implementing partial method. In this case, the compiler removes the declaration and any calls to the method made inside the class. You cannot have an implementing partial method without a defining partial method.

The following code shows an example of a partial method called PrintSum.

- PrintSum is declared in different parts of partial class MyClass: the defining declaration is in the first part, and the implementing declaration is in the second part. The implementation prints out the sum of its two integer parameters.

- Since partial methods are implicitly private, PrintSum cannot be called from outside the class. Method Add is a public method that calls PrintSum.

- Main creates an object of class MyClass and calls public method Add, which calls method PrintSum, which prints out the sum of the input parameters.

```
partial class MyClass
{           Must be void
                ↓
   partial void PrintSum(int x, int y);      // Defining partial method
        ↑                            ↑
   Contextual keyword          No implementation here

   public void Add(int x, int y)
   {
      PrintSum(x, y);
   }
}

partial class MyClass
{
   partial void PrintSum(int x, int y)        // Implementing partial method
   {
      Console.WriteLine("Sum is {0}", x + y);      ← Implementation
   }
}

class Program
{
   static void Main( )
   {
      var mc = new MyClass();
      mc.Add(5, 6);
   }
}
```

This code produces the following output:

```
Sum is 11
```

CHAPTER 8

■ ■ ■

Classes and Inheritance

© Daniel Solis and Cal Schrotenboer 2018
D. Solis and C. Schrotenboer, *Illustrated C# 7*, https://doi.org/10.1007/978-1-4842-3288-0_8

Class Inheritance

Inheritance allows you to define a new class that incorporates and extends an already declared class.

- You can use an existing class, called the *base class*, as the basis for a new class, called the *derived class*. The members of the derived class consist of the following:

  - The members in its own declaration

  - The members of the base class

- To declare a derived class, you add a class-base specification after the class name. The class-base specification consists of a colon, followed by the name of the class to be used as the base class. The derived class is said to directly inherit from the base class listed.

- A derived class is said to extend its base class because it includes the members of the base class plus any additional functionality provided in its own declaration.

- A derived class *cannot delete* any of the members it has inherited.

For example, the following shows the declaration of a class called OtherClass, which is derived from a class called SomeClass:

```
                Class-base specification
                           ↓
class OtherClass : SomeClass
{                        ↑       ↑
    ...                 Colon  Base class

}
```

Figure 8-1 shows an instance of each of the classes. Class SomeClass, on the left, has one field and one method. Class OtherClass, on the right, is derived from SomeClass and contains an additional field and an additional method.

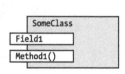

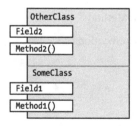

Figure 8-1. *Base class and derived class*

Accessing the Inherited Members

Inherited members are accessed just as if they had been declared in the derived class itself. (Inherited constructors are a bit different—we'll cover them later in the chapter.) For example, the following code declares classes SomeClass and OtherClass, which were shown in Figure 8-1. The code shows that all four members of OtherClass can be seamlessly accessed, regardless of whether they're declared in the base class or the derived class.

- Main creates an object of derived class OtherClass.

- The next two lines in Main call Method1 in the base class, using Field1 from the base class and then Field2 from the derived class.

- The subsequent two lines in Main call Method2 in the *derived class*, again using Field1 from the base class and then Field2 from the derived class.

```
class SomeClass                        // Base class
{
    public string Field1 = "base class field ";
    public void Method1( string value ) {
        Console.WriteLine($"Base class -- Method1:    { value }");
    }
}

class OtherClass: SomeClass {          // Derived class
    public string Field2 = "derived class field";
    public void Method2( string value ) {
        Console.WriteLine($"Derived class -- Method2:  { value }");
    }
}

class Program {
    static void Main() {
        OtherClass oc = new OtherClass();

        oc.Method1( oc.Field1 );       // Base method with base field
        oc.Method1( oc.Field2 );       // Base method with derived field
        oc.Method2( oc.Field1 );       // Derived method with base field
        oc.Method2( oc.Field2 );       // Derived method with derived field
    }
}
```

This code produces the following output:

```
Base class -- Method1:    base class field
Base class -- Method1:    derived class field
Derived class -- Method2: base class field
Derived class -- Method2: derived class field
```

All Classes Are Derived from Class object

All classes, except the special class object, are derived classes, even if they don't have a class-base specification. Class object is the only class that is not derived since it is the base of the inheritance hierarchy.

Classes without a class-base specification are implicitly derived directly from class object. Leaving off the class-base specification is just shorthand for specifying that object is the base class. The two forms are semantically equivalent, as shown in Figure 8-2.

```
class SomeClass                 class SomeClass : object
{                               {
    ...                             ...
}                               }
```

Figure 8-2. *The class declaration on the left implicitly derives from class object, while the one on the right explicitly derives from object. The two forms are semantically equivalent.*

Other important facts about class derivation are the following:

- A class declaration can have only a single class listed in its class-base specification. This is called *single inheritance*.

- Although a class can directly inherit from only a single base class, there is no limit to the *level* of derivation. That is, the class listed as the base class might be derived from another class, which is derived from another class, and so forth, until you eventually reach object.

Base class and *derived class* are relative terms. All classes are derived classes, either from object or from another class—so generally when we call a class a derived class, we mean that it is immediately derived from some class other than object. Figure 8-3 shows a simple class hierarchy. After this, we won't show object in the figures since all classes are ultimately derived from it.

```
class SomeClass
{ ... }

class OtherClass: SomeClass
{ ... }

class MyNewClass: OtherClass
{
    ...
}
```

| MyNewClass |
| OtherClass |
| SomeClass |
| object |

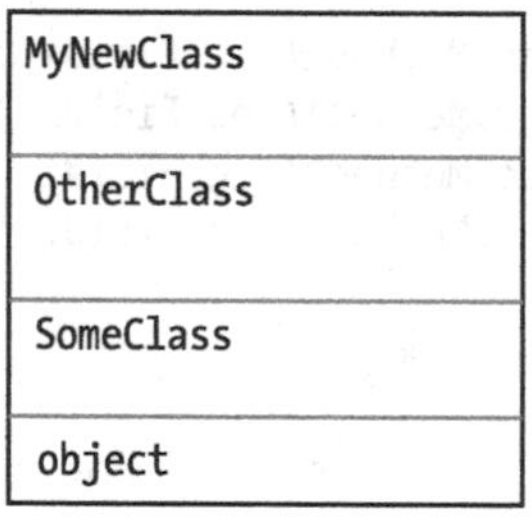

Figure 8-3. *A class hierarchy*

Masking Members of a Base Class

A derived class cannot delete any of the members it has inherited; it can, however, mask a base class member with a member of the same name. This is extremely useful, and one of the major features of inheritance.

For example, you might want to inherit from a base class that has a particular method. That method, although perfect for the class in which it is declared, may not do exactly what you want in the derived class. In such a case, what you want to do is to mask the base class method with a new member declared in the derived class. Some important aspects of masking a base class member in a derived class are the following:

- To mask an inherited *data* member, declare a new member of the same type and with the same *name*.

- To mask an inherited function member, declare a new function member with the same signature. Remember that the signature consists of the name and parameter list but does not include the return type.

- To let the compiler know that you're purposely masking an inherited member, use the new modifier. Without it, the program will compile successfully, but the compiler will warn you that you're hiding an inherited member.

- You can also mask static members.

The following code declares a base class and a derived class, each with a string member called Field1. The keyword new is used to explicitly tell the compiler to mask the base class member. Figure 8-4 illustrates an instance of each class.

```
class SomeClass                          // Base class
{
   public string Field1;
   ...
}

class OtherClass : SomeClass             // Derived class
{
   new public string Field1;             // Mask base member with same name
     ↑
   Keyword
```

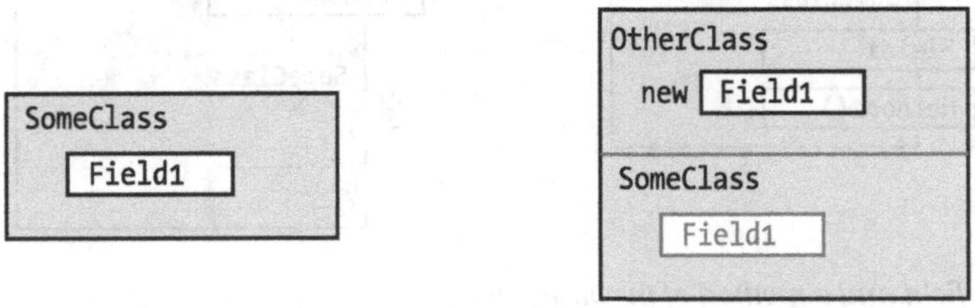

Figure 8-4. *Masking a field of a base class*

In the following code, OtherClass derives from SomeClass but hides both its inherited members. Note the use of the new modifier. Figure 8-5 illustrates the code.

```
class SomeClass                                    // Base class
{
    public string Field1 = "SomeClass Field1";
    public void    Method1(string value)
        { Console.WriteLine($"SomeClass.Method1:  { value }"); }
}


class OtherClass : SomeClass                       // Derived class
{  Keyword
   ↓
    new public string Field1 = "OtherClass Field1"; // Mask the base member.
    new public void    Method1(string value)        // Mask the base member.
      ↑  { Console.WriteLine($"OtherClass.Method1:  { value }"); }
}  Keyword


class Program
{
    static void Main()
    {
        OtherClass oc = new OtherClass();          // Use the masking member.
        oc.Method1(oc.Field1);                     // Use the masking member.
    }
}
```

This code produces the following output:

```
OtherClass.Method1:  OtherClass Field1
```

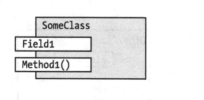
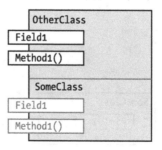

Figure 8-5. *Hiding a field and a method of the base class*

Base Access

If your derived class absolutely must access a hidden inherited member, you can access it by using a *base access* expression. This expression consists of the keyword base, followed immediately by a period and the name of the member, as shown here:

```
Console.WriteLine("{0}", base.Field1);
                          ↑
                    Base access
```

For example, in the following code, derived class OtherClass hides Field1 in its base class but accesses it by using a base access expression.

```
class SomeClass {                                        // Base class
   public string Field1 = "Field1 -- In the base class";
}

class OtherClass : SomeClass {                           // Derived class

   new  public string Field1= "Field1 -- In the derived class";
     ↑                      ↑
   Hides the field in the base class
   public void PrintField1()
   {
      Console.WriteLine(Field1);          // Access the derived class.
      Console.WriteLine(base.Field1);     // Access the base class.
   }                              ↑
}                            Base access

class Program {
   static void Main()
   {
      OtherClass oc = new OtherClass();
      oc.PrintField1();
   }
}
```

This code produces the following output:

```
Field1 -- In the derived class
Field1 -- In the base class
```

If you find that your program's code is frequently using this feature—that is, accessing a hidden inherited member—you might want to reevaluate the design of your classes. Generally there are more elegant designs, but the feature is there if there's a situation where nothing else will do.

Using References to a Base Class

An instance of a derived class consists of an instance of the base class plus the additional members of the derived class. A reference to the derived class points to the whole class object, including the base class part.

If you have a reference to a derived class object, you can get a reference to just the base class part of the object by *casting* the reference to the type of the base class by using the *cast operator*. The cast operator is placed in front of the object reference and consists of a set of parentheses containing the name of the class being cast to. Casting is covered in detail in Chapter 17. The effect of casting a derived class object to the base class object is that the resulting variable has access only to members of the base class (except in the case of an overridden method, discussed in a moment).

The next few sections cover accessing an object by using a reference to the base class part of the object. We'll start by looking at the two lines of code that follow, which declare references to objects. Figure 8-6 illustrates the code and shows the parts of the object seen by the different variables.

- The first line declares and initializes variable derived, which then contains a reference to an object of type MyDerivedClass.

- The second line declares a variable of the base class type, MyBaseClass, and casts the reference in derived to that type, giving a reference to the base class part of the object.

  - The reference to the base class part is stored in variable mybc, on the left side of the assignment operator.

  - The reference to the base class part cannot "see" the rest of the derived class object because it's "looking" at it through a reference to the base type.

```
MyDerivedClass derived = new MyDerivedClass();     // Create an object.
MyBaseClass mybc       = (MyBaseClass) derived;     // Cast the reference.
```

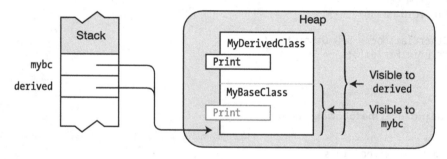

Figure 8-6. *Reference derived can see the entire MyDerivedClass object, while mybc can see only the MyBaseClass part of the object*

The following code shows the declaration and use of these two classes. Figure 8-7 illustrates the object and references in memory.

Main creates an object of type MyDerivedClass and stores its reference in variable derived. Main also creates a variable of type MyBaseClass and uses it to store a reference to the base class portion of the object. When the Print method is called on each reference, the call invokes the implementation of the method that the reference can see, producing different output strings.

```
class MyBaseClass
{
   public void Print()
   {
      Console.WriteLine("This is the base class.");
   }
}
class MyDerivedClass : MyBaseClass
{
   public int var1;

   new public void Print()
   {
      Console.WriteLine("This is the derived class.");
   }
}
class Program
{
   static void Main()
   {
      MyDerivedClass derived = new MyDerivedClass();
      MyBaseClass mybc = (MyBaseClass)derived;
                          ↑
                    Cast to base class
      derived.Print();           // Call Print from derived portion.
      mybc.Print();              // Call Print from base portion.
      // mybc.var1 = 5;          // Error:  base class reference cannot
                                 // access derived class members.
   }
}
```

This code produces the following output:

```
This is the derived class.
This is the base class.
```

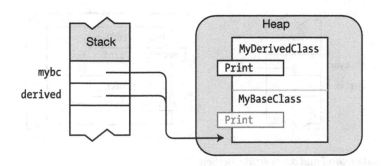

Figure 8-7. *A reference to the derived class and the base class*

Virtual and Override Methods

In the previous section, you saw that when you access an object of a derived class by using a reference to the base class, you get only the members from the base class. *Virtual methods* allow a reference to the base class to access "up into" the derived class.

You can use a reference to a base class to call a method in the *derived class* if the following are true:

- The method in the derived class and the method in the base class each have the same signature and return type.

- The method in the base class is labeled `virtual`.

- The method in the derived class is labeled `override`.

For example, the following code shows the `virtual` and `override` modifiers on the methods in the base class and derived class:

```
class MyBaseClass                          // Base class
{
    virtual public void Print()
         ↑
    ...
class MyDerivedClass : MyBaseClass         // Derived class
{
    override public void Print()
        ↑
```

Figure 8-8 illustrates this set of `virtual` and `override` methods. Notice how the behavior differs from the previous case, where we used `new` to hide the base class members.

- When the `Print` method is called by using the reference to the base class (`mybc`), the method call is passed up to the derived class and executed, because

  - The method in the base class is marked as `virtual`.

  - There is a matching `override` method in the derived class.

- Figure 8-8 illustrates this by showing the arrow coming out the back of the `virtual` `Print` method and pointing at the override `Print` method.

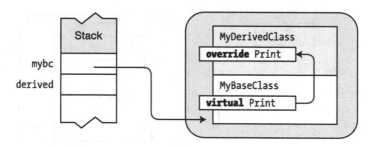

Figure 8-8. *A virtual method and an override method*

The following code is the same as in the previous section, but this time, the methods are labeled virtual and override. This produces a result that is very different from that of the previous example. In this version, calling the method through the base class invokes the method in the derived class.

```
class MyBaseClass
{
    virtual public void Print()
    {
        Console.WriteLine("This is the base class.");
    }
}

class MyDerivedClass : MyBaseClass
{
    override public void Print()
    {
        Console.WriteLine("This is the derived class.");
    }
}

class Program
{
    static void Main()
    {
        MyDerivedClass derived = new MyDerivedClass();
        MyBaseClass mybc        = (MyBaseClass)derived;
                                           ↑
        derived.Print();           Cast to base class
        mybc.Print();
    }
}
```

This code produces the following output:

```
This is the derived class.
This is the derived class.
```

Other important things to know about the virtual and override modifiers are the following:

- The overriding and overridden methods must have the same accessibility. In other words, the overridden method cannot be, for example, private, and the overriding method public.

- You cannot override a method that is static or is not declared as virtual.

- Methods, properties, and indexers (which we covered in the preceding chapter), and another member type, called an *event* (which we'll cover later in the text), can all be declared virtual and override.

185

Overriding a Method Marked override

Overriding methods can occur between any levels of inheritance.

- When you use a reference to the base class part of an object to call an overridden method, the method call is passed up the derivation hierarchy for execution to the *most derived* version of the method marked as override.

- If there are other declarations of the method at higher levels of derivation that are not marked as override, they are not invoked.

For example, the following code shows three classes that form an inheritance hierarchy: MyBaseClass, MyDerivedClass, and SecondDerived. All three classes contain a method named Print, with the same signature. In MyBaseClass, Print is labeled virtual. In MyDerivedClass, it's labeled override. In class SecondDerived, you can declare method Print with either override or new. Let's look at what happens in each case.

```
class MyBaseClass                            // Base class
{
   virtual public void Print()
   { Console.WriteLine("This is the base class."); }
}

class MyDerivedClass : MyBaseClass           // Derived class
{
   override public void Print()
   { Console.WriteLine("This is the derived class."); }
}

class SecondDerived : MyDerivedClass         // Most-derived class
{
   ... // Given in the following pages
}
```

Case 1: Declaring Print with override

If you declare the Print method of SecondDerived as override, then it will override *both the less derived versions* of the method, as shown in Figure 8-9. If a reference to the base class is used to call Print, it gets passed all the way up the chain to the implementation in class SecondDerived.

The following code implements this case. Notice the code in the last two lines of method Main.

- The first of the two statements calls the Print method by using a reference to the most derived class—SecondDerived. This is not calling through a reference to the base class portion, so it will call the method implemented in SecondDerived.

- The second statement, however, calls the Print method by using a reference to the base class—MyBaseClass.

```
class SecondDerived : MyDerivedClass
{
  override public void Print() {
      ↑   Console.WriteLine("This is the second derived class.");
  }
}

class Program
{
    static void Main()
    {
        SecondDerived derived = new SecondDerived(); // Use SecondDerived.
        MyBaseClass mybc = (MyBaseClass)derived;      // Use MyBaseClass.

        derived.Print();
        mybc.Print();
    }

}
```

The result is that regardless of whether Print is called through the derived class or the base class, the method in the most derived class is called. When called through the base class, it's passed up the inheritance hierarchy. This code produces the following output:

```
This is the second derived class.
This is the second derived class.
```

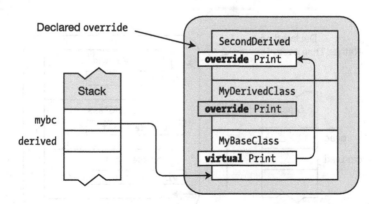

Figure 8-9. *Execution is passed to the top of the chain of multiple levels of override*

Case 2: Declaring Print with new

If instead you declare the Print method of SecondDerived as new, the result is as shown in Figure 8-10. Main is the same as in the previous case.

```
class SecondDerived : MyDerivedClass
{
    new public void Print()
    {
        Console.WriteLine("This is the second derived class.");
    }
}

class Program
{
    static void Main()                                      // Main
    {
        SecondDerived derived = new SecondDerived();        // Use SecondDerived.
        MyBaseClass mybc       = (MyBaseClass)derived;      // Use MyBaseClass.

        derived.Print();
        mybc.Print();
    }
}
```

The result is that when method Print is called through the reference to SecondDerived, the method in SecondDerived is executed, as you would expect. When the method is called through a reference to MyBaseClass, however, the method call is passed up only one level, to class MyDerived, where it is executed. The only difference between the two cases is whether the method in SecondDerived is declared with modifier override or modifier new.

This code produces the following output:

```
This is the second derived class.
This is the derived class.
```

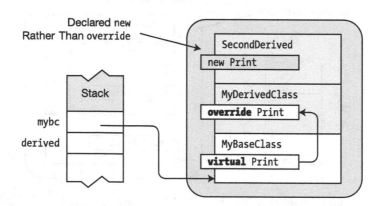

Figure 8-10. *Hiding the overridden methods*

Overriding Other Member Types

In the previous few sections, you've seen how the virtual/override designations work on methods. These work exactly the same way with properties, events, and indexers. For example, the following code shows a read-only property named MyProperty using virtual/override:

```csharp
class MyBaseClass
{
   private int _myInt = 5;
   virtual public int MyProperty
   {
      get { return _myInt; }
   }
}

class MyDerivedClass : MyBaseClass
{
   private int _myInt = 10;
   override public int MyProperty
   {
      get { return _myInt; }
   }
}

class Program
{
   static void Main()
   {
      MyDerivedClass derived = new MyDerivedClass();
      MyBaseClass mybc        = (MyBaseClass)derived;

      Console.WriteLine( derived.MyProperty );
      Console.WriteLine( mybc.MyProperty );
   }
}
```

This code produces the following output:

```
10
10
```

Constructor Execution

In the preceding chapter, you saw that a constructor executes code that prepares a class for use. This includes initializing both the static and instance members of the class. In this chapter, you saw that part of a derived class object is an object of the base class.

- To create the base class part of an object, a constructor for the base class is implicitly called as part of the process of creating the instance.

- Each class in the inheritance hierarchy chain executes its base class constructor before it executes its own constructor body.

For example, the following code shows a declaration of class `MyDerivedClass` and its constructor. When the constructor is called, it calls the parameterless constructor `MyBaseClass()` before executing its own body.

```
class MyDerivedClass : MyBaseClass
{
    MyDerivedClass()           // Constructor uses base constructor MyBaseClass()
    {
        ...
    }
}
```

Figure 8-11 shows the order of construction. When an instance is being created, one of the first things that's done is the initialization of all the instance members of the object. After that, the base class constructor is called. Only then is the body of the constructor of the class itself executed.

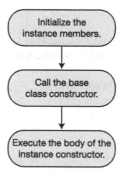

Figure 8-11. *Order of object construction*

For example, in the following code, the values of MyField1 and MyField2 would be set to 5 and 0, respectively, before the base class constructor is called.

```
class MyDerivedClass : MyBaseClass
{
   int MyField1 = 5;                    // 1. Member initialized
   int MyField2;                        //    Member initialized

   public MyDerivedClass()              // 3. Body of constructor executed
   {
      ...
   }
}

class MyBaseClass
{
   public MyBaseClass()                 // 2. Base class constructor called
   {
      ...
   }
}
```

■ **Caution**   Calling a virtual method in a constructor is *strongly discouraged*. The virtual method in the base class would call the override method in the derived class while the base class constructor is being executed. But that would be before the derived constructor's body is executed. It would, therefore, be calling up into the derived class before the class is completely initialized.

Constructor Initializers

By default, the parameterless constructor of the base class is called when an object is being constructed. But constructors can be overloaded, so a base class might have more than one. If you want your derived class to use a specific base class constructor other than the parameterless constructor, you must specify it in a *constructor initializer*.

There are two forms of constructor initializers.

- The first form uses the keyword base and specifies which base class constructor to use.

- The second form uses the keyword this and specifies which other constructor from this class should be used.

A base class constructor initializer is placed after a colon following the parameter list in a class's constructor declaration. The constructor initializer consists of the keyword base and the parameter list of the base constructor to call.

For example, the following code shows a constructor for class MyDerivedClass.

- The constructor initializer specifies that the construction process should call the base class constructor with two parameters, where the first parameter is a string and the second parameter is an int.

- The parameters in the base parameter list must match the *intended base constructor's* parameter list in type and order.

```
                                        Constructor initializer
                                                 ↓
public MyDerivedClass( int x, string s ) : base( s, x )
{                                              ↑
   ...                                       Keyword
```

When you declare a constructor without a constructor initializer, it's a shortcut for the form with a constructor initializer consisting of base(), as illustrated in Figure 8-12. The two forms are semantically equivalent.

```
class MyDerived: MyBase                    class MyDerived: MyBase
{                                          {
   MyDerived()                                MyDerived() : base()
   {                                          {
      ...                                        ...
   }                                          }
   ...                                        ...

Constructor Implicitly Using Base          Constructor Explicitly Using Base
      Constructor MyBase()                       Constructor MyBase()
```

Figure 8-12. *Equivalent forms of a constructor*

The other form of constructor initializer instructs the construction process (actually, the compiler) to use a different constructor from the same class. For example, the following shows a constructor with a single parameter for class MyClass. That single-parameter constructor, however, uses a constructor from the same class, but with two parameters, supplying a default parameter as the second one.

```
                            Constructor initializer
                        _____
                                   ↓
public MyClass(int x):this(x, "Using Default String")
{                       ↑
    ...             Keyword

}
```

Another situation where this comes in particularly handy is where you have several constructors for a class and they have common code that should always be performed at the beginning of the object construction process. In this case, you can factor out that common code and place it in a constructor that is used as a constructor initializer by all the other constructors. In fact, this is a recommended practice since it reduces code duplication.

You might think that you could just declare another method that performs those common initializations and have all the constructors call that method. This isn't as good for several reasons. The first is that the compiler can optimize certain things when it knows a method is a constructor. The second is that there are some things that can be done only in a constructor and not elsewhere. For example, in the previous chapter you learned that readonly fields can be initialized only inside a constructor. You will get a compiler error if you attempt to initialize a readonly field in any other method, even if that method is only called by a constructor. Note, however, that this constraint only applies to readonly fields and not to readonly properties.

Going back to that common constructor, if it can stand on its own as a valid constructor that initializes everything in the class that needs to be initialized, then it's perfectly fine to leave it as a public constructor.

What if, however, it doesn't completely initialize an object? In that case, you mustn't allow that constructor to be callable from outside the class since it would then create incompletely initialized objects. To avoid that problem, you can declare the constructor private instead of public and have it be used only by the other constructors. The following code illustrates this usage:

```
class MyClass
{
    readonly int    firstVar;
    readonly double secondVar;

    public string UserName;
    public int UserIdNumber;

    private MyClass( )              // Private constructor performs initializations
    {                              // common to the other constructors
        firstVar  = 20;
        secondVar = 30.5;
    }

    public MyClass( string firstName ) : this() // Use constructor initializer
    {
        UserName     = firstName;
        UserIdNumber = -1;
    }

    public MyClass( int idNumber ) : this( )    // Use constructor initializer
    {
        UserName     = "Anonymous";
        UserIdNumber = idNumber;
    }
}
```

Class Access Modifiers

A class can be seen and accessed by other classes in the system. This section explains the accessibility of classes. Although we'll use classes in the explanations and examples since that's what we've covered so far in the text, the accessibility rules also apply to the other types we'll cover later.

The term *visible* is sometimes used for the term *accessible*. They can be used interchangeably. There are two levels of class accessibility: public and internal.

- A class marked public can be accessed by code from any assembly in the system. To make a class visible to other assemblies, use the public access modifier, as shown here:

Keyword
↓
```
public class MyBaseClass
{ ...
```

- A class marked internal can be seen only by classes within its own assembly. (Remember from Chapter 1 that an *assembly* is either a program or a DLL. We'll cover assemblies in detail in Chapter 22.)

  - This is the default accessibility level, so unless you explicitly specify the modifier public in the class declaration, code outside the assembly cannot access the class.

  - You can explicitly declare a class as internal by using the internal access modifier.

Keyword
↓
```
internal class MyBaseClass
{ ...
```

Figure 8-13 illustrates the accessibility of internal and public classes from outside the assembly. Class MyClass is not visible to the classes in the assembly on the left because MyClass is marked internal. Class OtherClass, however, is visible to the classes on the left because it's marked public.

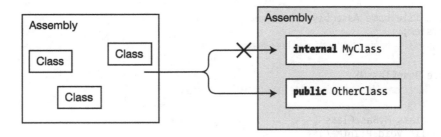

Figure 8-13. *Classes from other assemblies can access public classes but cannot access internal classes*

Inheritance Between Assemblies

So far, we've been declaring derived classes in the same assembly that contains the base class. But C# also allows you to derive a class from a base class defined in a different assembly.

To have your classes derive from a base class in another assembly, the following must be true:

- The base class must be declared public so that it can be accessed from outside its assembly.

- You must include a reference to the assembly containing the base class in the References section of your Visual Studio project. You can find the heading in Solution Explorer.

To make it easier to refer to the classes and types in the other assembly without constantly using their fully qualified names, place a using directive at the top of the source file, with the namespace containing the classes or types you want to access.

■ **Note**   Adding a reference to the other assembly and adding a using directive are two separate things. Adding the reference to the other assembly tells the compiler where the required types are defined. Adding the using directive allows you to reference other classes without having to use their fully qualified names. Chapter 22 covers this in detail.

For example, the following two code segments, from different assemblies, show how easy it is to inherit a class from another assembly. The first code listing creates an assembly that contains the declaration of a class called MyBaseClass, which has the following characteristics:

- It's declared in a source file called Assembly1.cs and inside a namespace declared as BaseClassNS.

- It's declared public so that it can be accessed from other assemblies.

- It contains a single member, a method called PrintMe, which just writes out a simple message identifying the class.

```
// Source file name Assembly1.cs
using System;
          Namespace containing declaration of base class
                      ↓
namespace BaseClassNS
{ Declare the class public so it can be seen outside the assembly.
     ↓
   public class MyBaseClass {
      public void PrintMe() {
         Console.WriteLine("I am MyBaseClass");
      }
   }
}
```

The second assembly contains the declaration of a class called DerivedClass, which inherits from MyBaseClass, declared in the first assembly. The source file is named Assembly2.cs. Figure 8-14 illustrates the two assemblies.

- DerivedClass has an empty body but inherits method PrintMe from MyBaseClass.

- Main creates an object of type DerivedClass and calls its inherited method PrintMe.

```
// Source file name Assembly2.cs
using System;
using BaseClassNS;
        ↑
    Namespace containing declaration of base class
namespace UsesBaseClass
{                     Base class in other assembly
                           ↓
    class DerivedClass: MyBaseClass
    {
        // Empty body
    }

    class Program {
        static void Main( )
        {
            DerivedClass mdc = new DerivedClass();
            mdc.PrintMe();
        }
    }

}
```

This code produces the following output:

```
I am MyBaseClass
```

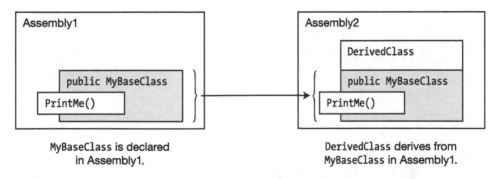

Figure 8-14. *Inheriting across assemblies*

Member Access Modifiers

The previous two sections explained class accessibility. With class accessibility, there are only two modifiers—internal and public. This section covers *member accessibility*. Class accessibility describes the visibility of a class; member accessibility describes the visibility of the members of a class object.

Each member declared in a class is visible to various parts of the system, depending on the access modifier assigned to it in its class declaration. You've seen that private members are visible only to other members of the same class, while public members can be visible to classes outside the assembly as well. In this section, we'll look again at the public and private access levels, as well as the three other levels of accessibility.

Before looking at the specifics of member accessibility, there are some general things we need to mention first.

- All members explicitly declared in a class's declaration are visible to each other, regardless of their accessibility specification.

- Inherited members are not explicitly declared in a class's declaration, so, as you'll see, inherited members might or might not be visible to members of a derived class.

- The following are the names of the five member access levels. So far, we've only introduced public and private.

  - public

  - private

  - protected

  - internal

  - protected internal

- You must specify member access levels on a per-member basis. If you don't specify an access level for a member, its implicit access level is private.

- A member cannot be more accessible than its class. That is, if a class has an accessibility level limiting it to the assembly, individual members of the class cannot be seen outside the assembly, regardless of their access modifiers, even public.

Regions Accessing a Member

A class specifies which of its members can be accessed by other classes by labeling its members with access modifiers. You've already seen the public and private modifiers. The following declaration shows a class that has declared members with each of the five access levels:

```
public class MyClass
{
    public             int Member1;
    private            int Member2;
    protected          int Member3;
    internal           int Member4;
    protected internal int Member5;
    ...
```

Another class—say, class B—can or cannot access these members based on two of its characteristics, which are the following:

- Whether class B is derived from class MyClass
- Whether class B is in the same assembly as class MyClass

These two characteristics yield four groups, as illustrated in Figure 8-15. In relation to class MyClass, another class can be any of the following:

- In the same assembly and derived from MyClass (bottom right)
- In the same assembly but not derived from MyClass (bottom left)
- In a different assembly and derived from MyClass (top right)
- In a different assembly and not derived from MyClass (top left)

These characteristics are used to define the five access levels, which we'll cover in the next section.

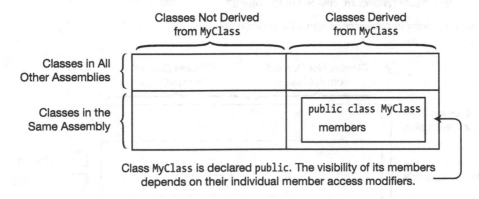

Figure 8-15. *Areas of accessibility*

Public Member Accessibility

The public access level is the least restrictive. All classes both inside and outside the assembly have free access to the member. Figure 8-16 illustrates the accessibility of a public class member of MyClass.

To declare a member public, use the public access modifier, as shown.

Keyword
↓
```
public int Member1;
```

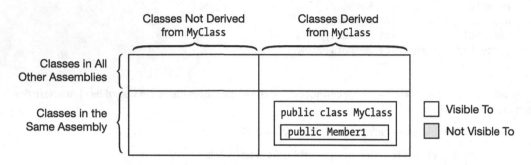

Figure 8-16. *A public member of a public class is visible to all classes in the same assembly and other assemblies*

Private Member Accessibility

The private access level is the most restrictive.

- A private class member can be accessed only by members of its own class. It cannot be accessed by other classes, including classes that are derived from it.

- A private member can, however, be accessed by members of classes nested in its class. *Nested classes* are covered in Chapter 27.

Figure 8-17 illustrates the accessibility of a private member.

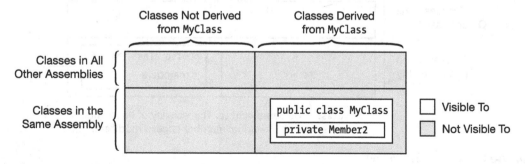

Figure 8-17. *A private member of any class is visible only to members of its own class (or nested classes)*

Protected Member Accessibility

The protected access level is like the private access level except that it also allows classes derived from the class to access the member. Figure 8-18 illustrates protected accessibility. Notice that even classes outside the assembly that are derived from the class have access to the member.

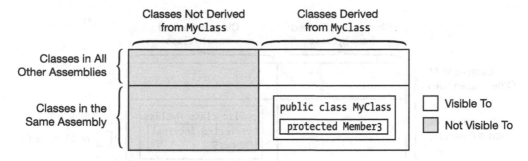

Figure 8-18. *A protected member of a public class is visible to members of its own class and classes derived from it. The derived classes can even be in other assemblies.*

Internal Member Accessibility

Members marked internal are visible to all the classes in the assembly, but not to classes outside the assembly, as illustrated in Figure 8-19.

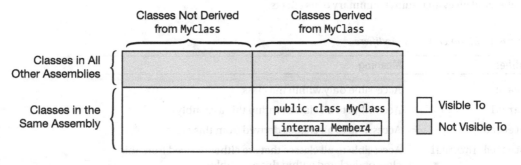

Figure 8-19. *An internal member of a public class is visible to members of any class in the same assembly, but not to classes outside the assembly*

Protected Internal Member Accessibility

Members marked protected internal are visible to all the classes that inherit from the class and also to all classes inside the assembly, as shown in Figure 8-20. Notice that the set of classes allowed access is the combined set of classes allowed by the protected modifier plus the set of classes allowed by the internal modifier. Notice that this is the *union* of protected and internal—not the intersection.

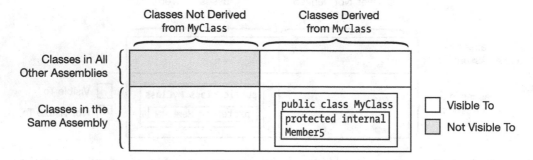

Figure 8-20. *A protected internal member of a public class is visible to members of classes in the same assembly and to members of classes derived from that class. It's not visible to classes in other assemblies that are not derived from the class.*

Summary of Member Access Modifiers

The following two tables summarize the characteristics of the five member access levels. Table 8-1 lists each modifier and gives an intuitive summary of its effects.

Table 8-1. *Member Access Modifiers*

Modifier	Meaning
private	Accessible only within the class
internal	Accessible to all classes within this assembly
protected	Accessible to all classes derived from this class
protected internal	Accessible to all classes that are either derived from this class or declared within this assembly
public	Accessible to any class

Figure 8-21 shows the relative accessibility of the five member access modifiers.

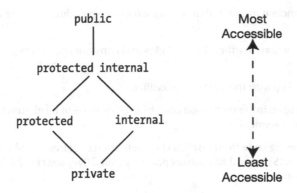

Figure 8-21. *Relative accessibility of the various member access modifiers*

Table 8-2 lists the access modifiers down the left side of the table and the categories of classes across the top. *Derived* refers to classes derived from the class declaring the member. *Nonderived* means classes not derived from the class declaring the member. A check in a cell means that the category of class can access members with the corresponding modifier.

Table 8-2. *Summary of Member Accessibility*

	Classes in Same Assembly		Classes in Different Assembly	
	Nonderived	Derived	Nonderived	Derived
private				
internal	✓	✓		
protected		✓		✓
protected internal	✓	✓		✓
public	✓	✓	✓	✓

Abstract Members

An *abstract member* is a function member that is designed to be overridden. An abstract member has the following characteristics:

- It must be a function member. That is, fields and constants cannot be abstract members.

- It must be marked with the `abstract` modifier.

- It must not have an implementation code block. The code of an abstract member is represented by a semicolon.

For example, the following code from inside a class definition declares two abstract members: an abstract method called `PrintStuff` and an abstract property called `MyProperty`. Notice the semicolons in place of the implementation blocks.

```
Keyword              Semicolon in place of implementation
   ↓                              ↓
abstract public void PrintStuff(string s);

abstract public int MyProperty
{
    get;   ← Semicolon in place of implementation
    set;   ← Semicolon in pla ce of implementation

}
```

Abstract members can be declared only in *abstract classes*, which we'll look at in the next section. Four types of members can be declared as abstract.

- Methods

- Properties

- Events

- Indexers

Other important facts about abstract members are the following:

- Abstract members, although they must be overridden by a corresponding member in a derived class, *cannot* use the `virtual` modifier in addition to the `abstract` modifier.

- As with virtual members, the implementation of an abstract member in a derived class must specify the `override` modifier.

Table 8-3 compares and contrasts virtual members and abstract members.

Table 8-3. *Comparing Virtual and Abstract Members*

	Virtual Member	**Abstract Member**
Keyword	`virtual`	`abstract`
Implementation body	Has an implementation body	No implementation body—semicolon instead
Overridden in a derived class	*Can* be overridden—using `override`	*Must* be overridden—using `override`
Types of members	Methods Properties Events Indexers	Methods Properties Events Indexers

Abstract Classes

Abstract classes are designed to be inherited from. An *abstract class* can be used only as the base class of another class.

- You cannot create instances of an abstract class.

- An abstract class is declared using the `abstract` modifier.

Keyword
↓
```
abstract class MyClass
{
   ...

}
```

- An abstract class can contain abstract members or regular, nonabstract members. The members of an abstract class can be any combination of abstract members and normal members with implementations.

- An abstract class can itself be derived from another abstract class. For example, the following code shows one abstract class derived from another:

```
abstract class AbClass                    // Abstract class
{
   ...
}

abstract class MyAbClass : AbClass        // Abstract class derived from
{                                         // an abstract class
   ...
}
```

- Any class derived from an abstract class must implement all the abstract members of the class by using the `override` keyword, unless the derived class is itself abstract.

Example of an Abstract Class and an Abstract Method

- The following code shows an abstract class called AbClass with two methods.
- The first method is a normal method with an implementation that prints out the name of the class. The second method is an abstract method that must be implemented in a derived class. Class DerivedClass inherits from AbClass and implements and overrides the abstract method. Main creates an object of DerivedClass and calls its two methods.

```
Keyword
   ↓
abstract class AbClass                              // Abstract class
{
    public void IdentifyBase()                      // Normal method
    { Console.WriteLine("I am AbClass"); }
    Keyword
      ↓
  abstract public void IdentifyDerived();           // Abstract method
}

class DerivedClass : AbClass                        // Derived class
{   Keyword
      ↓
  override public void IdentifyDerived()            // Implementation of
    { Console.WriteLine("I am DerivedClass"); }     // abstract method
}

class Program
{
    static void Main()
    {
        // AbClass a = new AbClass();       // Error.  Cannot instantiate
        // a.IdentifyDerived();             // an abstract class.

        DerivedClass b = new DerivedClass(); // Instantiate the derived class.
        b.IdentifyBase();                    // Call the inherited method.
        b.IdentifyDerived();                 // Call the "abstract" method.
    }
}
```

This code produces the following output:

```
I am AbClass
I am DerivedClass
```

Another Example of an Abstract Class

The following code shows the declaration of an abstract class that contains data members as well as function members. Remember that data members—fields and constants—cannot be declared as abstract.

```
abstract class MyBase        // Combination of abstract and nonabstract members
{
   public int SideLength        = 10;          // Data member
   const  int TriangleSideCount = 3;           // Data member

   abstract public void PrintStuff( string s );  // Abstract method
   abstract public int  MyInt { get; set; }      // Abstract property

   public int PerimeterLength( )                  // Regular, nonabstract method
   { return TriangleSideCount * SideLength; }
}

class MyClass : MyBase
{
   public override void PrintStuff( string s )   // Override abstract method
   { Console.WriteLine( s ); }

   private int _myInt;
   public override int MyInt                      // Override abstract property
   {
      get { return _myInt; }
      set { _myInt = value; }
   }
}

class Program
{
   static void Main( string[] args )
   {
      MyClass mc = new MyClass( );
      mc.PrintStuff( "This is a string." );
      mc.MyInt = 28;
      Console.WriteLine( mc.MyInt );
      Console.WriteLine($"Perimeter Length: { mc.PerimeterLength( ) }");
   }
}
```

This code produces the following output:

```
This is a string.
28
Perimeter Length: 30
```

Sealed Classes

In the previous section, you saw that an abstract class must be used as a base class—it cannot be instantiated as a stand-alone class object. The opposite is true of a *sealed class*.

- A sealed class can be instantiated only as a stand-alone class object—it cannot be used as a base class.

- A sealed class is labeled with the `sealed` modifier.

For example, the following class is a sealed class. Any attempt to use it as the base class of another class will produce a compile error.

```
Keyword
   ↓
sealed class MyClass
{
    ...
}
```

Static Classes

A static class is a class where all the members are static. Static classes are used to group data and functions that are not affected by instance data. A common use of a static class might be to create a math library containing sets of mathematical methods and values.

The important things to know about a static class are the following:

- The class itself must be marked static.

- All the members of the class must be static.

- The class can have a static constructor, but it cannot have an instance constructor since you cannot create an instance of the class.

- Static classes are implicitly sealed. That is, you cannot inherit from a static class.

You access the members of a static class just as you would access any static member—by using the class name and the member name. Also, starting with C# 6.0 you can access members of a static class without the class name provided that you have a using static directive. Using directives are discussed in detail in Chapter 22.

The following code shows an example of a static class:

```
Class must be marked static
    ↓
static public class MyMath   {
   public static float PI = 3.14f;
   public static bool IsOdd(int x)
               ↑          { return x % 2 == 1; }
         Members must be static
               ↓
   public static int Times2(int x)
                    { return 2 * x; }
}

class Program    {
   static void Main( )
   {                                    Use class name and member name.
      int val = 3;                                   ↓
      Console.WriteLine("{0} is odd is {1}.", val,  MyMath.IsOdd(val));
      Console.WriteLine($"{ val } * 2 = { MyMath.Times2(val) }.");
   }
}
```

This code produces the following output:

```
3 is odd is True.
3 * 2 = 6.
```

Extension Methods

So far in this text, every method you've seen has been associated with the class in which it is declared. The *extension method* feature extends that boundary, allowing you to write methods associated with classes *other than the class in which they are declared.*

To see how you might use this feature, take a look at the following code. It contains class MyData, which stores three values of type double, and contains a constructor and a method called Sum, which returns the sum of the three stored values.

In real-world development, extension methods are an incredibly useful tool. In fact, almost the entire library of LINQ queries is implemented via extension methods. LINQ is covered in Chapter 20.

```
class MyData
{
   private double D1;                                    // Fields
   private double D2;
   private double D3;

   public MyData(double d1, double d2, double d3)        // Constructor
   {
      D1 = d1; D2 = d2; D3 = d3;
   }

   public double Sum()                                   // Method Sum
   {
      return D1 + D2 + D3;
   }
}
```

This is a pretty limited class, but suppose it would be more useful if it contained another method, which returned the average of the three data points. With what you know so far about classes, there are several ways you might implement the additional functionality:

- If you have the source code and can modify the class, you could, of course, just add the new method to the class.

- If, however, you can't modify the class—for example, if the class is in a third-party class library—then, as long as it isn't sealed, you could use it as a base class and implement the additional method in a class derived from it.

If, however, you don't have access to the code, the class is sealed, or there is some other design reason that prevents either of these solutions from working, then you will have to write a method in another class that uses the publicly available members of the class.

For example, you might write a class like the one in the following code. The code contains a static class called ExtendMyData, which contains a static method called Average, which implements the additional functionality. Notice that the method takes an instance of MyData as a parameter.

```
static class ExtendMyData        Instance of MyData class
{                                          ↓
                                     _____
   public static double Average( MyData md  )
   {
      return md.Sum() / 3;
   }        ↑
}    Use the instance of MyData.


class Program
{
   static void Main()
   {                                          Instance of MyData
                                                      ↓
      MyData md = new MyData(3, 4, 5);
      Console.WriteLine("Average: {0}", ExtendMyData.Average(md));
   }                                                 ↑
                                            Call the static method.
}
```

This code produces the following output:

```
Average: 4
```

Although this is a perfectly fine solution, it would be more elegant if you could call the method on the class instance itself, rather than creating an instance of another class to act on it. The following two lines of code illustrate the difference. The first uses the method just shown—invoking a static method on an instance of another class. The second shows the form we would like to use—invoking an instance method on the object itself.

```
ExtendMyData.Average( md )        // Static invocation form
md.Average();                     // Instance invocation form
```

Extension methods allow you to use the second form, even though the first form would be the normal way of writing the invocation.

By making a small change in the declaration of method Average, you can use the instance invocation form. The change you need to make is to add the keyword this before the type name in the parameter declaration, as shown following. Adding the this keyword to the first parameter of the static method of the static class changes it from a regular method of class ExtendMyData into an *extension method* of class MyData. You can now use both invocation forms.

```
Must be a static class
     ↓
static class ExtendMyData
{   Must be public and static              Keyword and type
            ↓                                    ↓
    public static double Average( this MyData md )
    {
        ...
    }
}
```

The important requirements for an extension method are the following:

- The class in which the extension method is declared must be declared static.

- The extension method itself must be declared static.

- The extension method must contain as its first parameter type the keyword this, followed by the name of the class it is extending.

Figure 8-22 illustrates the structure of an extension method.

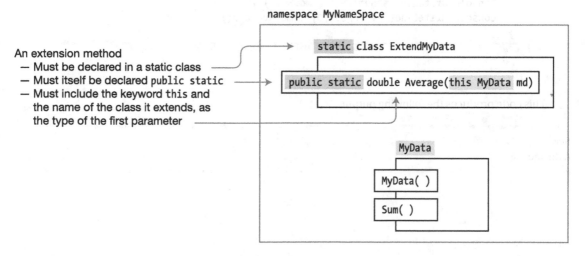

Figure 8-22. *The structure of an extension method*

The following code shows a full program, including class MyData and extension method Average, declared in class ExtendMyData. Notice that method Average is invoked exactly as if it were an *instance member* of MyData! Figure 8-22 illustrates the code. Classes MyData and ExtendMyData together act like the desired class, with three methods.

```
namespace ExtensionMethods
{
    sealed class MyData
    {
        private double D1, D2, D3;
        public MyData(double d1, double d2, double d3)
        { D1 = d1; D2 = d2; D3 = d3; }

        public double Sum() { return D1 + D2 + D3; }
    }

    static class ExtendMyData            Keyword and type
    {                                          ↓
        public static double Average(this MyData md)
        {            ↑
            Declared static
            return md.Sum() / 3;
        }
    }

    class Program
    {
        static void Main()
        {
            MyData md = new MyData(3, 4, 5);
            Console.WriteLine($"Sum:     { md.Sum() }");
            Console.WriteLine("Average: {0}", md.Average());
        }                                       ↑
    }                          Invoke as an instance member of the class
}
```

This code produces the following output:

```
Sum:     12
Average: 4
```

Naming Conventions

Writing programs requires coming up with lots of names—names for classes, variables, methods, properties, and lots of things we haven't covered yet. When you're reading through a program, using naming conventions is an important method of giving you a clue as to the kinds of objects you're dealing with.

We touched a bit on naming in Chapter 7, but now that you know more about classes, we can give you more details. Table 8-4 gives the three main naming styles and how they're commonly used in .NET programs.

Table 8-4. *Commonly Used Identifier Naming Styles*

Style Name	Description	Recommended Use	Examples
Pascal casing	Each word in the identifier is capitalized.	Use for type names and member names visible outside the class. These include the names of the following: classes, methods, namespaces, properties, and public fields.	CardDeck, DealersHand
Camel casing	Each word in the identifier, except the first, is capitalized.	Use for local variable names and the names of formal parameters in method declarations.	totalCycleCount, randomSeedParam
Camel case with leading underscore	This is a camel-cased identifier that starts with an underscore.	Use for the names of private and protected fields.	_cycleCount, _selectedIndex

One major pillar of maintainable code is the use of accurate, self-descriptive variable names (a policy that does not generally apply to books such as this one, articles, and code samples where other considerations apply). When it comes to variable names, brevity needs to bow to the adage that "haste makes waste."

Not everyone agrees with these conventions, especially the leading-underscore part. Some find the leading underscore very useful, while others find it exceedingly ugly. Microsoft itself seems conflicted on the issue as well. In its suggested conventions, Microsoft doesn't include the leading underscore as an option. But in much of its own code, developers use it.

Throughout the rest of this book we'll adhere to Microsoft's officially recommended convention of using camel casing for private and protected fields.

One last word about underscores is that they aren't generally used in the body of an identifier, except in the names of event handlers, which we'll cover in Chapter 15.

CHAPTER 9

■ ■ ■

Expressions and Operators

© Daniel Solis and Cal Schrotenboer 2018

D. Solis and C. Schrotenboer, *Illustrated C# 7*, https://doi.org/10.1007/978-1-4842-3288-0_9

Expressions

This chapter defines expressions and describes the operators provided by C#. It also explains how you can define the C# operators to work with your user-defined classes.

An *operator* is a symbol that represents an operation that returns a single result. An *operand* is a data element used as input by the operator. An operator does the following:

- Takes its operands as input

- Performs an action

- Returns a value, based on the action

An *expression* is a string of operators and operands. The C# operators take one, two, or three operands. The following are some of the constructs that can act as operands:

- Literals

- Constants

- Variables

- Method calls

- Element accessors, such as array accessors and indexers

- Other expressions

Expressions can be combined, using operators, to create more complex expressions, as shown in the following expression with three operators and four operands:

$$\left. \begin{array}{l} \underbrace{a\ +\ b} \\ \underbrace{expr\ +\ c} \\ expr\quad +\ d \end{array} \right\} \quad a\ +\ b\ +\ c\ +\ d$$

Evaluating an expression is the process of applying each operator to its operands, in the proper sequence, to produce a value.

- The value is returned to the position at which the expression was evaluated. There, it might in turn be used as an operand in an enclosing expression.

- Besides the value returned, some expressions also have side effects, such as setting a value in memory.

Literals

Literals are numbers or strings typed into the source code that represent a specific, set value of a specific type.

For example, the following code shows literals of six types. Notice, for example, the difference between the double literal and the float literal.

```
static void Main()           Literals
{                               ↓
    Console.WriteLine("{0}", 1024);          // int literal
    Console.WriteLine("{0}", 3.1416);        // double literal
    Console.WriteLine("{0}", 3.1416F);       // float literal
    Console.WriteLine("{0}", true);          // boolean literal
    Console.WriteLine("{0}", 'x');           // character literal
    Console.WriteLine("{0}", "Hi there");    // string literal

}
```

The output of this code is the following:

```
1024
3.1416
3.1416
True
x
Hi there
```

Because literals are written into the source code, their values must be known at compile time. Several of the predefined types have their own forms of literal.

- Type bool has two literals: true and false. Note that these, like all C# keywords, are lowercase.

- For reference type variables, literal null means that the variable does not point to data in memory.

Integer Literals

Integer literals are the most commonly used literals. They are written as a sequence of decimal digits, with the following characteristics:

- No decimal point

- An optional suffix to specify the type of the integer

For example, the following lines show four literals for the integer 236. Each is interpreted by the compiler as a different type of integer, depending on its suffix.

```
236             // int
236L            // long
236U            // unsigned int
236UL           // unsigned long
```

Integer-type literals can also be written in hexadecimal (hex) form. The digits must be hex digits (0 through *F*), and the string must be prefaced with either 0x or 0X (numeral 0, letter *x*).

A third format for integer-type literals is binary notation. All digits must be either 0 or 1 and must be preceded by either 0b or 0B (numeral 0, letter *b*).

■ **Note**   Only integer-type literals can be expressed in hex or binary form. Hex and binary notation are specified with a prefix, while the actual data type is specified using a suffix.

Figure 9-1 shows the forms of the integer literal formats. Components with names in square brackets are optional.

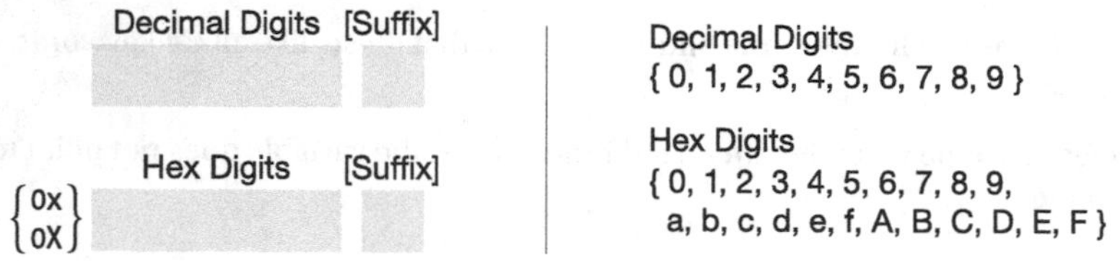

Figure 9-1. *The integer literal formats*

Table 9-1 lists the integer literal suffixes. For a given suffix, the compiler will interpret the string of digits as the smallest of the four listed integer types that can represent the value without losing data.

For example, take the literals 236 and 5000000000, neither of which has a suffix. Since 236 can be represented with 32 bits, it will be interpreted by the compiler as an int. The second number, however, won't fit into 32 bits, so the compiler will represent it as a long.

Table 9-1. *Integer Literal Suffixes*

Suffix	Integer Type	Notes
None	int, uint, long, ulong	
U, u	uint, ulong	
L, l	long, ulong	Using the lowercase letter *l* is not recommended because it is easily mistaken for the digit 1.
ul, uL, Ul, UL lu, Lu, lU, LU	ulong	Using the lowercase letter *l* is not recommended because it is easily mistaken for the digit 1.

In the preceding example, it wasn't very easy to know exactly how big the number 5000000000 was. Fortunately, you can now insert separators in a numeric literal to make it easier to interpret.

```
Console.WriteLine("5_000_000_000 is much easier to read than 5000000000");
```

Real Literals

C# has three real number data types: float, double, and decimal. These correspond to 32 bits, 64 bits, and 128 bits of precision. All three are floating-point data types, meaning that they are represented internally by two components, one representing the digits comprising the actual number and one, an exponent, that specifies the location of the decimal point. In practical usage, by far the most common real number data type is double.

Literals for real numbers consist of the following:

- Decimal digits

- An optional decimal point

- An optional exponent part

- An optional suffix

For example, the following code shows various formats of literals of the real types:

```
float  f1 = 236F;
double d1 = 236.714;
double d2 = .35192;
double d3 = 6.338e-26;
```

Figure 9-2 shows the valid formats for real literals. Components with names in square brackets are optional. Table 9-2 shows the real suffixes and their meanings.

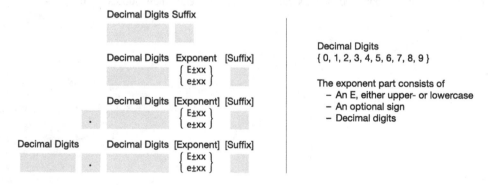

Figure 9-2. *The real literal formats*

Table 9-2. *Suffixes for the Real Literals*

Suffix	Real Type
None	double
F, f	float
D, d	double
M, m	decimal

■ **Note** Real literals without a suffix are of type double, not float!

Character Literals

A character literal consists of a character representation between two single quote marks. Character literals are used to represent single characters (a), nonprinting characters (\n) (newline), or characters that otherwise perform special tasks such as escape (\\). Even though it might require multiple characters to express a character literal, each character literal represents only a single character. To refer to multiple characters, you must use a string literal, as described in the next section.

A character representation can be any of the following: a single character, a simple escape sequence, a hex escape sequence, or a Unicode escape sequence. Important things to know about character literals are the following:

- The type of a character literal is char.

- A *simple escape sequence* is a backslash followed by a single character.

- A hex escape sequence is a backslash, followed by an uppercase or lowercase *x*, followed by up to four hex digits.

- A Unicode escape sequence is a backslash, followed by an uppercase or lowercase *u*, followed by up to four hex digits.

For example, the following code shows various formats of character literals:

```
char c1 = 'd';              // Single character
char c2 = '\n';             // Simple escape sequence
char c3 = '\x0061';         // Hex escape sequence
char c4 = '\u005a';         // Unicode escape sequence
```

Table 9-3 shows some of the important special characters and their encodings.

Table 9-3. *Important Special Characters*

Name	Escape Sequence	Hex Encoding
Null	\0	0x0000
Alert	\a	0x0007
Backspace	\b	0x0008
Horizontal tab	\t	0x0009
New line	\n	0x000A
Vertical tab	\v	0x000B
Form feed	\f	0x000C
Carriage return	\r	0x000D
Double quote	\"	0x0022
Single quote	\'	0x0027
Backslash	\\	0x005C

String Literals

String literals use double quote marks rather than the single quote marks used in character literals. There are two types of string literals.

- Regular string literals

- Verbatim string literals

A regular string literal consists of a sequence of characters between a set of double quotes. A regular string literal can include the following:

- Characters

- Simple escape sequences

- Hex and Unicode escape sequences

Here are some examples:

```
string st1 = "Hi there!";
string st2 = "Val1\t5, Val2\t10";
string st3 = "Add\x000ASome\u0007Interest";
```

A verbatim string literal is written like a regular string literal but is prefaced with an @ character. The important characteristics of verbatim string literals are the following:

- Verbatim literals differ from regular string literals in that escape sequences within the string are not evaluated. Everything between the set of double quotes—including what would normally be considered escape sequences—is printed exactly as it is listed in the string.

- The only exceptions with verbatim literals are sets of contiguous double quotes, which are interpreted as a single double quote character.

For example, the following code compares some regular and verbatim string literals:

```
string rst1 = "Hi there!";
string vst1 = @"Hi there!";

string rst2 = "It started, \"Four score and seven...\"";
string vst2 = @"It started, ""Four score and seven...""";

string rst3 = "Value 1 \t 5, Val2 \t 10";      // Interprets tab esc sequence
string vst3 = @"Value 1 \t 5, Val2 \t 10";     // Does not interpret tab

string rst4 = "C:\\Program Files\\Microsoft\\";
string vst4 = @"C:\Program Files\Microsoft\";

string rst5 = " Print \x000A Multiple \u000A Lines";
string vst5 = @" Print
 Multiple
 Lines";
```

Printing these strings produces the following output:

```
Hi there!
Hi there!

It started, "Four score and seven..."
It started, "Four score and seven..."

Value 1        5, Val2        10
Value 1 \t 5, Val2 \t 10

C:\Program Files\Microsoft\
C:\Program Files\Microsoft\

 Print
 Multiple
 Lines

 Print
 Multiple
 Lines
```

■ **Note** The compiler saves memory by having identical string literals share the same memory location in the heap.

Order of Evaluation

An expression can be made up of many nested subexpressions. The order in which the subexpressions are evaluated can make a difference in the final value of the expression.

For example, given the expression 3 * 5 + 2, there are two possible results depending on the order in which the subexpressions are evaluated, as shown in Figure 9-3.

- If the multiplication is performed first, the result is 17.

- If the 5 and the 2 are added together first, the result is 21.

Figure 9-3. *Simple order of evaluation*

Precedence

You know from your grade-school days that in the preceding example, the multiplication must be performed before the addition because multiplication has a higher precedence than addition. But unlike grade-school days, where you had four operators and two levels of precedence, things are a bit more complex with C#, which has more than 45 operators and 14 levels of precedence.

Table 9-4 shows the complete list of operators and the precedence of each. The table lists the highest precedence operators at the top and continues to the lowest precedence operators at the bottom.

Table 9-4. *Operator Precedence: Highest to Lowest*

Category	Operators
Primary	a.x, f(x), a[x], x++, x--, new, typeof, checked, unchecked
Unary	+, -, !, ~, ++x, --x, (T)x
Multiplicative	*, /, %
Additive	+, -
Shift	<<, >>
Relational and type	<, >, <=, >=, is, as
Equality	==, !=
Logical AND	&
Logical XOR	^
Logical OR	|
Conditional AND	&&
Conditional OR	||
Conditional	?:
Assignment	=, *=, /=, %=, +=, -=, <<=, >>=, &=, ^=, |=

Associativity

When the compiler is evaluating an expression where all the operators have different levels of precedence, then each subexpression is evaluated, starting at the one with the highest level and working down the precedence scale.

But what if two sequential operators have the same level of precedence? For example, given the expression 2 / 6 * 4, there are two possible evaluation sequences.

(2 / 6) * 4 = 4/3

or

2 / (6 * 4) = 1/12

When sequential operators have the same level of precedence, the order of evaluation is determined by *operator associativity*. That is, given two operators of the same level of precedence, one or the other will have precedence, depending on the operators' associativity. Some important characteristics of operator associativity are the following and are summarized in Table 9-5.

- *Left-associative* operators are evaluated from left to right.

- *Right-associative* operators are evaluated from right to left.

- Binary operators, except the assignment operators, are left-associative.

- The assignment operators and the conditional operator are right-associative.

Therefore, given these rules, the preceding example expression should be grouped left to right, giving (2 / 6) * 4, which yields 4/3.

Table 9-5. *Summary of Operator Associativity*

Type of Operator	Associativity
Assignment operators	Right-associative
Other binary operators	Left-associative
Conditional operator	Right-associative

You can explicitly set the order of evaluation of the subexpressions of an expression by using parentheses. Parenthesized subexpressions have the following qualities:

- They override the precedence and associativity rules.

- They are evaluated in order from the innermost nested set to the outermost.

Simple Arithmetic Operators

The simple arithmetic operators perform the four basic arithmetic operations and are listed in Table 9-6. These operators are binary and left-associative.

Table 9-6. *The Simple Arithmetic Operators*

Operator	Name	Description
+	Addition	Adds the two operands.
-	Subtraction	Subtracts the second operand from the first.
*	Multiplication	Multiplies the two operands.
/	Division	Divides the first operand by the second. Integer division rounds the result toward 0 to the nearest integer.

The arithmetic operators perform the standard arithmetic operations on all the predefined simple arithmetic types.

The following are examples of the simple arithmetic operators:

```
int x1 = 5 + 6;          double d1 = 5.0 + 6.0;
int x2 = 12 - 3;         double d2 = 12.0 - 3.0;
int x3 = 3 * 4;          double d3 = 3.0 * 4.0;
int x4 = 10 / 3;         double d4 = 10.0 / 3.0;

byte b1 = 5 + 6;
sbyte sb1 = 6 * 5;
```

The Remainder Operator

The remainder operator (%) divides the first operand by the second operand, ignores the quotient, and returns the remainder. Table 9-7 gives its description.

The remainder operator is binary and left-associative.

Table 9-7. *The Remainder Operator*

Operator	Name	Description
%	Remainder	Divides the first operand by the second operand and returns the remainder

The following lines show examples of the integer remainder operator:

- 0 % 3 = 0, because 0 divided by 3 is 0 with a remainder of 0.

- 1 % 3 = 1, because 1 divided by 3 is 0 with a remainder of 1.

- 2 % 3 = 2, because 2 divided by 3 is 0 with a remainder of 2.

- 3 % 3 = 0, because 3 divided by 3 is 1 with a remainder of 0.

- 4 % 3 = 1, because 4 divided by 3 is 1 with a remainder of 1.

The remainder operator can also be used with real numbers to give *real remainders*.

```
Console.WriteLine("0.0f % 1.5f is {0}" , 0.0f % 1.5f);
Console.WriteLine("0.5f % 1.5f is {0}" , 0.5f % 1.5f);
Console.WriteLine("1.0f % 1.5f is {0}" , 1.0f % 1.5f);
Console.WriteLine("1.5f % 1.5f is {0}" , 1.5f % 1.5f);
Console.WriteLine("2.0f % 1.5f is {0}" , 2.0f % 1.5f);
Console.WriteLine("2.5f % 1.5f is {0}" , 2.5f % 1.5f);
```

This code produces the following output:

```
0.0f % 1.5f is 0           // 0.0 / 1.5 = 0 remainder 0
0.5f % 1.5f is 0.5         // 0.5 / 1.5 = 0 remainder .5
1.0f % 1.5f is 1           // 1.0 / 1.5 = 0 remainder 1
1.5f % 1.5f is 0           // 1.5 / 1.5 = 1 remainder 0
2.0f % 1.5f is 0.5         // 2.0 / 1.5 = 1 remainder .5
2.5f % 1.5f is 1           // 2.5 / 1.5 = 1 remainder 1
```

Relational and Equality Comparison Operators

The relational and equality comparison operators are binary operators that compare their operands and return a value of type bool. Table 9-8 lists these operators.

The relational and equality operators are binary and left-associative.

Table 9-8. *The Relational and Equality Comparison Operators*

Operator	Name	Description
<	Less than	true if the first operand is less than the second operand; false otherwise
>	Greater than	true if the first operand is greater than the second operand; false otherwise
<=	Less than or equal to	true if the first operand is less than or equal to the second operand; false otherwise
>=	Greater than or equal to	true if the first operand is greater than or equal to the second operand; false otherwise
==	Equal to	true if the first operand is equal to the second operand; false otherwise
!=	Not equal to	true if the first operand is not equal to the second operand; false otherwise

A binary expression with a relational or equality operator returns a value of type bool.

■ **Note** Unlike C and C++, numbers in C# do not have a Boolean interpretation.

```
int x = 5;
if( x )          // Wrong.  x is of type int, not type boolean.
   ...
if( x == 5 )     // Fine, since expression returns a value of type boolean
   ...
```

When printed, the Boolean values true and false are represented by the string output values True and False.

```
int x = 5, y = 4;
Console.WriteLine($"x == x is { x == x }");
Console.WriteLine($"x == y is { x == y }" );
```

This code produces the following output:

```
x == x is True
x == y is False
```

Comparison and Equality Operations

When comparing most reference types for equality, only the references are compared.

- If the references are equal—that is, if they point to the same object in memory—the equality comparison is `true`; otherwise, it is `false`, even if *the two separate objects* in memory are *exactly equivalent* in every other respect.

- This is called a *shallow comparison*.

- Figure 9-4 illustrates the comparison of reference types.

- On the left of the figure, the references held by both a and b are the same, so a comparison would return `true`.

- On the right of the figure, the references are not the same, so even if the contents of the two `AClass` objects were exactly the same, the comparison would return `false`.

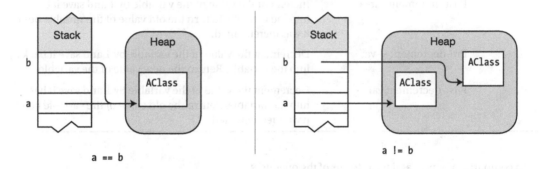

Figure 9-4. *Comparing reference types for equality*

Objects of type `string` are also reference types but are compared differently. When strings are compared for equality, they are compared for length and case-sensitive content.

- If two strings have the same length and the same case-sensitive content, the equality comparison returns `true`, even if they occupy different areas of memory.

- This is called a *deep comparison*.

Delegates, which are covered in Chapter 14, are also reference types and also use deep comparison. When delegates are compared for equality, the comparison returns `true` if both delegates are `null` or if both have the same number of members in their invocation lists and the invocation lists match.

When comparing numeric expressions, the types and values are compared. When comparing enum types, the comparisons are done on the underlying values of the operands. Enums are covered in Chapter 12.

Increment and Decrement Operators

The increment operator adds 1 to the operand. The decrement operator subtracts 1 from the operand. Table 9-9 lists the operators and their descriptions.

These operators are unary and have two forms, the *pre-* form and the *post-* form, which act differently.

- In the pre- form, the operator is placed before the operand; for example, ++x and --y.

- In the post- form, the operator is placed after the operand; for example, x++ and y--.

Table 9-9. *The Increment and Decrement Operators*

Operator	Name	Description
++	Pre-increment ++var	Increment the value of the variable by 1 and save it back into the variable. Return the new value of the variable.
	Post-increment var++	Increment the value of the variable by 1 and save it back into the variable. Return the old value of the variable before it was incremented.
--	Pre-decrement --var	Decrement the value of the variable by 1 and save it back into the variable. Return the new value of the variable.
	Post-decrement var--	Decrement the value of the variable by 1 and save it back into the variable. Return the old value of the variable before it was decremented.

In comparing the pre- and post- forms of the operators,

- The final, stored value of the operand variable after the statement is executed is the same regardless of whether the pre- or post- form of the operator is used.

- The only difference is the value *returned* by the operator to the expression.

Table 9-10 shows an example summarizing this behavior.

Table 9-10. *Behavior of Pre- and Post-Increment and Decrement Operators*

	Starting Expression: x = 10	Value Returned to the Expression	Value of Variable After Evaluation
Pre-increment	++x	11	11
Post-increment	x++	10	11
Pre-decrement	--x	9	9
Post-decrement	x--	10	9

For example, the following is a simple demonstration of the four different versions of the operators. To show the different results on the same input, the value of the operand x is reset to 5 before each assignment statement.

```
int x = 5, y;
y = x++;   // result: y: 5, x: 6
Console.WriteLine($"y: { y }, x: { x }");

x = 5;
y = ++x;   // result: y: 6, x: 6
Console.WriteLine($"y: { y }, x: { x }");

x = 5;
y = x--;   // result: y: 5, x: 4
Console.WriteLine($"y: { y }, x: { x }");

x = 5;
y = --x;   // result: y: 4, x: 4
Console.WriteLine($"y: { y }, x: { x }");
```

This code produces the following output:

```
y: 5, x: 6
y: 6, x: 6
y: 5, x: 4
y: 4, x: 4
```

Conditional Logical Operators

The logical operators are used for comparing or negating the logical values of their operands and returning the resulting logical value. Table 9-11 lists the operators.

The logical AND and logical OR operators are binary and left-associative. The logical NOT is unary.

Table 9-11. *The Conditional Logical Operators*

Operator	Name	Description
&&	Logical AND	true if both operands are true; false otherwise
||	Logical OR	true if at least one operand is true; false otherwise
!	Logical NOT	true if the operand is false; false otherwise

The syntax for these operators is the following, where Expr1 and Expr2 evaluate to Boolean values:

```
Expr1 && Expr2
Expr1 || Expr2
    !    Expr
```

The following are some examples:

```
bool bVal;
bVal = (1 == 1) && (2 == 2);      // True, both operand expressions are true
bVal = (1 == 1) && (1 == 2);      // False, second operand expression is false

bVal = (1 == 1) || (2 == 2);      // True, both operand expressions are true
bVal = (1 == 1) || (1 == 2);      // True, first operand expression is true
bVal = (1 == 2) || (2 == 3);      // False, both operand expressions are false

bVal = true;                      // Set bVal to true.
bVal = !bVal;                     // bVal is now false.
```

The conditional logical operators operate in "short-circuit" mode, meaning that, if after evaluating Expr1 the result can already be determined, then it skips the evaluation of Expr2. The following code shows examples of expressions in which the value can be determined after evaluating the first operand:

```
bool bVal;
bVal = (1 == 2) && (2 == 2);    // False, after evaluating first expression

bVal = (1 == 1) || (1 == 2);    // True, after evaluating first expression
```

Because of the short-circuit behavior, do not place expressions with desired side effects (such as changing a value) in Expr2 since they might not be evaluated. In the following code, the post-increment of variable iVal would not be executed because after the first subexpression is executed, it can be determined that the value of the entire expression is false.

```
bool bVal; int iVal = 10;

    bVal = (1 == 2) && (9 == iVal++);   // result:  bVal = False, iVal = 10
            ↑                ↑
          False        Never evaluated
```

Logical Operators

The bitwise logical operators are often used to set the bit patterns for parameters to methods. Table 9-12 lists the bitwise logical operators.

These operators, except for the bitwise negation operator, are binary and left-associative. The bitwise negation operator is unary.

Table 9-12. *The Logical Operators*

Operator	Name	Description
&	Bitwise AND	Produces the bitwise AND of the two operands. The resulting bit is 1 only if both operand bits are 1.
|	Bitwise OR	Produces the bitwise OR of the two operands. The resulting bit is 1 if either corresponding operand bit is 1.
^	Bitwise XOR	Produces the bitwise XOR of the two operands. The resulting bit is 1 if one, but not both, of the corresponding operand bits is 1.
~	Bitwise negation	Each bit in the operand is switched to its opposite. This produces the one's complement of the operand. (The *one's complement* of a number is the inversion of every bit of its binary representation. That is, every 0 is switched to 1, and every 1 is switched to 0.)

The binary bitwise operators compare the corresponding bits at each position in each of their two operands, and they set the bit in the return value according to the logical operation.

Figure 9-5 shows four examples of the bitwise logical operations.

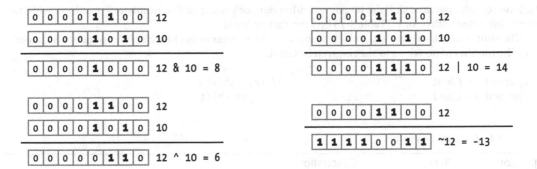

Figure 9-5. *Examples of bitwise logical operators*

The following code implements the preceding examples:

```
const byte x = 12, y = 10;
sbyte a;

a = x & y;        //  a = 8
a = x | y;        //  a = 14
a = x ^ y;        //  a = 6
a = ~x;           //  a = -13
```

Shift Operators

The bitwise shift operators shift the bit pattern either right or left a specified number of positions, with the vacated bits filled with 0s or 1s. Table 9-13 lists the shift operators.

The shift operators are binary and left-associative. The syntax of the bitwise shift operators is shown here. The number of positions to shift is given by Count.

```
Operand << Count                        // Left shift
Operand >> Count                        // Right shift
```

Table 9-13. *The Shift Operators*

Operator	Name	Description
<<	Left shift	Shifts the bit pattern left by the given number of positions. The bits shifted off the left end are lost. Bit positions opening up on the right are filled with 0s.
>>	Right shift	Shifts the bit pattern right by the given number of positions. Bits shifted off the right end are lost.

For the vast majority of programming in C#, you don't need to know anything about the hardware underneath. If you're doing bitwise manipulation of signed numbers, however, it can be helpful to know about the numeric representation. The underlying hardware represents signed binary numbers in a form called *two's complement*. In two's-complement representation, positive numbers have their normal binary form. To negate a number, you take the bitwise negation of the number and add 1 to it. This process turns a positive number into its negative representation, and vice versa. In two's complement, all negative numbers have a 1 in the leftmost bit position. Figure 9-6 shows the negation of the number 12.

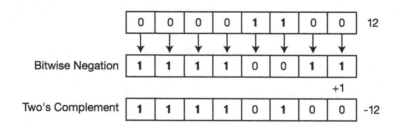

Figure 9-6. *To get the negation of a two's-complement number, take its bitwise negation and add 1*

The underlying representation is important when shifting signed numbers because the result of shifting an integral value one bit to the left is the same as multiplying it by two. Shifting it to the right is the same as dividing it by two.

If, however, you were to shift a negative number to the right and the leftmost bit were to be filled with a 0, it would produce the wrong result. The 0 in the leftmost position would indicate a positive number. But this is incorrect, because dividing a negative number by 2 doesn't produce a positive number.

To address this situation, when the operand is a signed integer, if the leftmost bit of the operand is a 1 (indicating a negative number), bit positions opening up on the left are filled with 1s rather than 0s. This maintains the correct two's-complement representation. For positive or unsigned numbers, bit positions opening up on the left are filled with 0s.

Figure 9-7 shows how the expression 14 << 3 would be evaluated in a byte. This operation causes the following:

- Each of the bits in the operand (14) is shifted three places to the left.

- The three bit positions vacated on the right end are filled with 0s.

- The resulting value is 112.

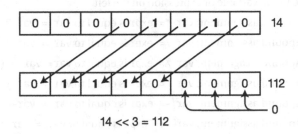

Figure 9-7. *Example of left shift of three bits*

Figure 9-8 illustrates bitwise shift operations.

0	0	0	0	**1**	**1**	**1**	0	14
0	**1**	**1**	**1**	0	0	0	0	14 << 3 = 112

0	0	0	0	**1**	**1**	**1**	0	14
0	0	0	0	0	0	0	**1**	14 >> 3 = 1

Figure 9-8. *Bitwise shifts*

The following code implements the preceding examples:

```
int a, b, x = 14;

a = x << 3;              // Shift left
b = x >> 3;              // Shift right

Console.WriteLine($"{ x } << 3 = { a }");
Console.WriteLine($"{ x } >> 3 = { b }");
```

This code produces the following output:

```
14 << 3 = 112
14 >> 3 = 1
```

Assignment Operators

The assignment operators evaluate the expression on the right side of the operator and use that value to set the value of the variable expression on the left side of the operator. Table 9-14 lists the assignment operators.

The assignment operators are binary and right-associative.

Table 9-14. *The Assignment Operators*

Operator	Description
=	Simple assignment; evaluate the expression on the right, and assign the returned value to the variable or expression on the left.
*=	Compound assignment; var *= expr is equal to var = var * (expr).
/=	Compound assignment; var /= expr is equal to var = var / (expr).
%=	Compound assignment; var %= expr is equal to var= var % (expr).
+=	Compound assignment; var += expr is equal to var = var + (expr).
-=	Compound assignment; var -= expr is equal to var = var- (expr).
<<=	Compound assignment; var <<= expr is equal to var = var << (expr).
>>=	Compound assignment; var >>= expr is equal to var = var >> (expr).
&=	Compound assignment; var &= expr is equal to var = var & (expr).
^4=	Compound assignment; var ^= expr is equal to var = var ^ (expr).
|=	Compound assignment; var |= expr is equal to var = var | (expr).

The syntax is as follows:

```
VariableExpression Operator Expression
```

For simple assignment, the expression to the right of the operator is evaluated, and its value is assigned to the variable on the left.

```
int x;
x = 5;
x = y * z;
```

Remember that an assignment expression is an *expression* and therefore returns a value to its position in the statement. The value of an assignment expression is the value of the left operand, after the assignment is performed. So, in the case of expression x = 10, the value 10 is assigned to variable x. The value of x, which is now 10, becomes the value of the whole expression.

Since an assignment is an expression, it can be part of a larger expression, as shown in Figure 9-9. The evaluation of the expression is as follows:

- Since assignment is right-associative, evaluation starts at the right and assigns 10 to variable x.

- That expression is the right operand of the assignment to variable y, so the value of x, which is now 10, is assigned to y.

- The assignment to y is the right operand for the assignment to z—leaving all three variables with the value 10.

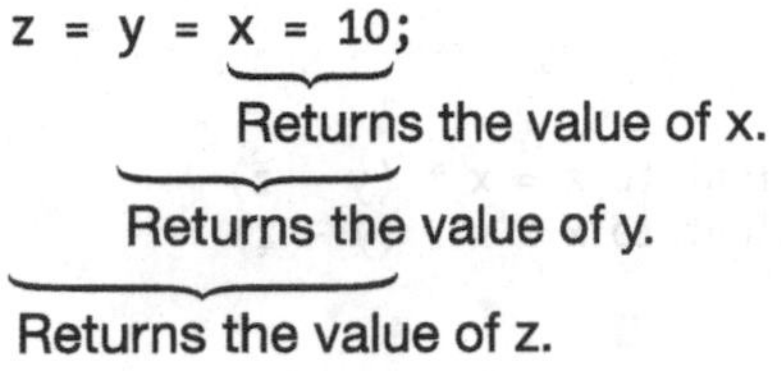

$$z = y = x = 10;$$

Returns the value of x.

Returns the value of y.

Returns the value of z.

Figure 9-9. *An assignment expression returns the value of its left operand after the assignment has been performed*

The types of objects that can be on the left side of an assignment operator are the following. They are discussed later in the text.

- Variables (local variables, fields, parameters)
- Properties
- Indexers
- Events

Compound Assignment

Frequently, you'll want to evaluate an expression and add the results to the current value of a variable, as shown here:

```
x = x + expr;
```

The compound assignment operators allow a shorthand method for avoiding the repetition of the left-side variable on the right side under certain common circumstances. For example, the following two statements are semantically equivalent, but the second is shorter and just as easy to understand.

```
x = x + (y - z);
x += y - z;
```

The other compound assignment statements are analogous.

```
                        Notice the parentheses.
                            ↓         ↓
x *= y - z;      // Equivalent to x = x * (y - z)
x /= y - z;      // Equivalent to x = x / (y - z)

...
```

The Conditional Operator

The conditional operator is a powerful and succinct way of returning one of two values, based on the result of a condition. Table 9-15 shows the operator.

The conditional operator is ternary.

Table 9-15. *The Conditional Operator*

Operator	Name	Description
?:	Conditional operator	Evaluates an expression and returns one of two values, depending on whether the expression returns true or false

The syntax for the conditional operator is shown next. It has a test expression and two result expressions.

- Condition must return a value of type bool.

- If Condition evaluates to true, then Expression1 is evaluated and returned. Otherwise, Expression2 is evaluated and returned.

```
Condition ? Expression1 : Expression2
```

The conditional operator can be compared with the if...else construct. For example, the following if... else construct checks a condition, and if the condition is true, the construct assigns 5 to variable intVar. Otherwise, it assigns it the value 10.

```
if ( x < y )                                    // if...else
   intVar = 5;
else
   intVar = 10;
```

The conditional operator can perform the same operation in a less verbose form, as shown in the following statement:

```
intVar = x < y ? 5 : 10;                        // Conditional operator
```

Placing the condition and each return expression on separate lines, as in the following code, makes the intent very easy to understand.

```
intVar = x < y
       ? 5
       : 10;
```

Figure 9-10 compares the two forms shown in the example.

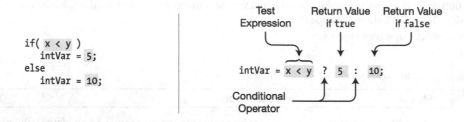

Figure 9-10. *The conditional operator vs. if...else*

For example, the following code uses the conditional operator three times—once in each of the WriteLine statements. In the first instance, it returns either the value of x or the value of y. In the second two instances, it returns either the empty string or the string "not".

```
int x = 10, y = 9;
int highVal = x > y                        // Condition
                ? x                        // Expression 1
                : y;                       // Expression 2
Console.WriteLine($"highVal:  { highVal }\n");

Console.WriteLine("x is{0} greater than y" ,
                  x > y                    // Condition
                  ? ""                     // Expression 1
                  : " not" );              // Expression 2
y = 11;
Console.WriteLine("x is{0} greater than y" ,
                  x > y                    // Condition
                  ? ""                     // Expression 1
                  : " not" );              // Expression 2
```

This code produces the following output:

```
highVal:  10

x is greater than y
x is not greater than y
```

■ **Note** The if...else statement is a flow-of-control *statement*. It should be used for *doing* one or the other of two *actions*. The conditional operator returns an *expression*. It should be used for *returning* one or the other of two *values*.

Unary Arithmetic Operators

The unary operators set the sign of a numeric value. They are listed in Table 9-16.

- The unary positive operator simply returns the value of the operand.
- The unary negative operator returns the value of the operand subtracted from 0.

Table 9-16. *The Unary Operators*

Operator	Name	Description
+	Positive sign	Returns the numeric value of the operand
-	Negative sign	Returns the numeric value of the operand subtracted from 0

For example, the following code shows the use and results of the operators:

```
int x = +10;        // x = 10
int y = -x;         // y = -10
int z = -y;         // z = 10
```

User-Defined Type Conversions

User-defined conversions are discussed in greater detail in Chapter 17, but we'll mention them here as well because they are operators.

- You can define both implicit and explicit conversions for your own classes and structs. This allows you to convert an object of your user-defined type to some other type, and vice versa.

- C# provides implicit and explicit conversions.

  - With an *implicit conversion*, the compiler automatically makes the conversion, if necessary, when it is resolving what types to use in a particular context.

  - With an *explicit conversion*, the compiler will make the conversion only when an explicit cast operator is used.

The syntax for declaring an implicit conversion is the following. The `public` and `static` modifiers are required for all user-defined conversions.

```
             Required                Target                Source
                ↓                      ↓                     ↓
public static implicit operator TargetType ( SourceType Identifier )
{
    ...
    return ObjectOfTargetType;
}
```

The syntax for the explicit conversion is the same, except that `explicit` is substituted for `implicit`.
The following code shows an example of declarations for conversion operators that will convert an object of type `LimitedInt` to type `int`, and vice versa:

```
class LimitedInt                      Target      Source
{                                       ↓           ↓
    public static implicit operator int (LimitedInt li)     // LimitedInt to int
    {
        return li.TheValue;
    }                                          Target      Source
                                                 ↓           ↓
    public static implicit operator LimitedInt (int x)     // int to LimitedInt
    {
        LimitedInt li = new LimitedInt();
        li.TheValue = x;
        return li;
    }

    private int _theValue = 0;
    public int TheValue{ ... }
}
```

For example, the following code reiterates and uses the two type-conversion operators just defined. In Main, an int literal is converted into a LimitedInt object, and in the next line, a LimitedInt object is converted into an int.

```
class LimitedInt
{
    const int MaxValue = 100;
    const int MinValue = 0;

    public static implicit operator int(LimitedInt li)       // Convert type
    {
        return li.TheValue;
    }

    public static implicit operator LimitedInt(int x)        // Convert type
    {
        LimitedInt li = new LimitedInt();
        li.TheValue = x;
        return li;
    }

    private int mTheValue = 0;
    public int TheValue {                                    // Property
        get { return mTheValue; }
        set
        {
            if (value < MinValue)
                mTheValue = 0;
            else
                mTheValue = value > MaxValue
                             ? MaxValue
                             : value;
        }
    }
}

class Program {
    static void Main()                                       // Main
    {
        LimitedInt li = 500;                                 // Convert 500 to LimitedInt
        int value     = li;                                 // Convert LimitedInt to int

        Console.WriteLine($"li: { li.TheValue }, value: { value }");
    }
}
```

This code produces the following output:

```
li: 100, value: 100
```

Explicit Conversion and the Cast Operator

The preceding example code showed the implicit conversion of the int to a LimitedInt type and the implicit conversion of a LimitedInt type to an int. If, however, you had declared the two conversion operators as explicit, you would have had to explicitly use cast operators when making the conversions.

A *cast operator* consists of the name of the type to which you want to convert the expression, inside a set of parentheses. For example, in the following code, method Main casts the value 500 to a LimitedInt object.

```
                       Cast operator
                            ↓
LimitedInt li = (LimitedInt) 500;
```

For example, here is the relevant portion of the code, with the changes marked:

```
                            ↓
public static explicit operator int(LimitedInt li)
{
    return li.TheValue;
}
                     ↓
public static explicit operator LimitedInt(int x)
{
    LimitedInt li = new LimitedInt();
    li.TheValue   = x;
    return li;
}

static void Main()
{
                          ↓
    LimitedInt li = (LimitedInt) 500;
    int value     = (int) li;
                      ↑
    Console.WriteLine($"li: { li.TheValue }, value: { value }");

}
```

In both versions of the code, the output is the following:

```
li: 100, value: 100
```

There are two other operators that take a value of one type and return a value of a different, specified type. These are the is operator and the as operator. These are covered at the end of Chapter 17.

Operator Overloading

The C# operators, as you've seen, are defined to work using the predefined types as operands. If confronted with a user-defined type, an operator simply would not know how to process it. Operator overloading allows you to define how the C# operators should operate on operands of your user-defined types.

- Operator overloading is available only for classes and structs.

- You can overload an operator x for use with your class or struct by declaring a method named operator x that implements the behavior (for example, operator +, operator -, and so on).

  - The overload methods for unary operators take a single parameter of the class or struct type.

  - The overload methods for binary operators take two parameters, at least one of which must be of the class or struct type.

```
public static LimitedInt operator -(LimitedInt x)            // Unary
public static LimitedInt operator +(LimitedInt x, double y)  // Binary
```

The declaration of an operator overload method requires the following:

- The declaration must use both the static and public modifiers.

- The operator must be a member of the class or struct for which it is an operator.

For example, the following code shows two of the overloaded operators of class LimitedInt: the addition operator and the negation operator. You can tell that it is negation, not subtraction, because the operator overload method has only a single parameter and is therefore unary, whereas the subtraction operator is binary.

```
class LimitedInt Return
{      Required          Type       Keyword   Operator     Operand
          ↓               ↓            ↓         ↓            ↓
    public static LimitedInt operator + (LimitedInt x, double y)
    {
        LimitedInt li = new LimitedInt();
        li.TheValue = x.TheValue + (int)y;
        return li;
    }

    public static LimitedInt operator - (LimitedInt x)
    {
        // In this strange class, negating a value just sets it to 0.
        LimitedInt li = new LimitedInt();
        li.TheValue = 0;
        return li;
    }
    ...

}
```

Example of Operator Overloading

The following example shows the overloads of three operators for class LimitedInt: negation, subtraction, and addition:

```
class LimitedInt
{
   const int MaxValue = 100;
   const int MinValue = 0;

   public static LimitedInt operator -(LimitedInt x)
   {
      // In this strange class, negating a value just sets its value to 0.
      LimitedInt li = new LimitedInt();
      li.TheValue = 0;
      return li;
   }

   public static LimitedInt operator -(LimitedInt x, LimitedInt y)
   {
      LimitedInt li = new LimitedInt();
      li.TheValue = x.TheValue - y.TheValue;
      return li;
   }

   public static LimitedInt operator +(LimitedInt x, double y)
   {
      LimitedInt li = new LimitedInt();
      li.TheValue = x.TheValue + (int)y;
      return li;
   }

   private int _theValue = 0;
   public int TheValue
   {
      get { return _theValue; }
      set
      {
         if (value < MinValue)
            _theValue = 0;
         else
            _theValue = value > MaxValue
                              ? MaxValue
                              : value;
      }
   }
}
```

```
class Program
{
    static void Main()
    {
        LimitedInt li1 = new LimitedInt();
        LimitedInt li2 = new LimitedInt();
        LimitedInt li3 = new LimitedInt();
        li1.TheValue = 10; li2.TheValue = 26;
        Console.WriteLine($" li1: { li1.TheValue }, li2: { li2.TheValue }");

        li3 = -li1;
        Console.WriteLine($"-{ li1.TheValue } = { li3.TheValue }");

        li3 = li2 - li1;
        Console.WriteLine($" { li2.TheValue } - { li1.TheValue } = { li3.TheValue }");

        li3 = li1 - li2;
        Console.WriteLine($" { li1.TheValue } - { li2.TheValue } = { li3.TheValue }");
    }
}
```

This code produces the following output:

```
li1: 10, li2: 26
-10 = 0
26 - 10 = 16
10 - 26 = 0
```

■ **Note**   Your overloaded operators should conform to the intuitive meanings of the operators.

Restrictions on Operator Overloading

Not all operators can be overloaded, and there are restrictions on the types of overloading that can be done. The important things you should know about the restrictions on operator overloading are described later in the section. Only the following operators can be overloaded. Prominently missing from the list is the assignment operator.

> *Overloadable unary operators:* +, -, !, ~, ++, --, true, false

> *Overloadable binary operators:* +, -, *, /, %, &, |, ^, <<, >>, ==, !=, >, <, >=, <=

You *cannot* do the following things with operator overloading:

- Create a new operator

- Change the syntax of an operator

- Redefine how an operator works on the predefined types

- Change the precedence or associativity of an operator

The increment and decrement operators are overloadable. For each of these operations, you write a piece of code that either increments or decrements the object: whatever that means for your user-defined type.

- At runtime, when your code performs a *pre-* operation (pre-increment or pre-decrement) on your object, the following happens:

  - Your increment or decrement code is executed on the object.

  - The object is returned.

- At runtime, when your code performs a *post-* operation (post-increment or post-decrement) on your object, the following happens:

  - If it's a value type, the system makes a copy of the object. If it's a reference type, a copy of the *reference* is made.

  - Your increment or decrement code is executed on the object.

  - The saved operand is returned.

If your operand object is a value type object, this should all work fine. But you need to be a bit careful when your user-defined type is a reference type.

For a reference type object, the *pre-* operations should work fine because no copies are made. But for the *post-* operations, since the *copy* that's saved is a *copy of the reference*, this means that both the original reference and the copy are pointing at the same object. Then, when the second step is performed, the increment or decrement code is executed on that object. This means that the saved reference points to an object is no longer in its original state. Returning this reference to the altered object is probably not what was expected.

The following code illustrates the difference between the post-increment when applied to a value type object as opposed to a reference type object. If you run this code twice, where the first time the MyType user-defined type is a struct, you'll get one result. If you run it again but change the type of MyType to a class, you'll get a different answer.

```
using static System.Console;

public struct MyType          // Run twice; once as a struct and again as a class.
{
   public int X;
   public MyType( int x )
   {
      X = x;
   }

   public static MyType operator ++( MyType m )
   {
      m.X++;
      return m;
   }
}

class Test
{
   static void Show( string message, MyType tv )
   {
      WriteLine( $"{message} {tv.X}" );
   }

   static void Main()
   {
      MyType tv = new MyType( 10 );
      WriteLine( "Pre-increment" );
      Show( "Before   ", tv );
      Show( "Returned ", ++tv );
      Show( "After    ", tv );
      WriteLine();

      tv = new MyType( 10 );
      WriteLine( "Post-increment" );
      Show( "Before   ", tv );
      Show( "Returned ", tv++ );
      Show( "After    ", tv );
   }
}
```

When you run the previous code with MyType as a struct, the results are the following, as you would expect (hope).

```
Pre-increment
Before     10
Returned   11
After      11

Post-increment
Before     10
Returned   10
After      11
```

When you run the code with MyType as a class (i.e., a reference type), the post-increment value of the returned object has already been incremented—which might not be what you were hoping for.

```
Pre-increment
Before     10
Returned   11
After      11

Post-increment
Before     10
Returned   11     <-- Not what you would expect.
After      11
```

The typeof Operator

The typeof operator returns the System.Type object of any type given as its parameter. From this object, you can learn the characteristics of the type. (There is only one System.Type object for any given type.) You cannot overload the typeof operator. Table 9-17 lists the operator's characteristics.

The typeof operator is unary.

Table 9-17. *The typeof Operator*

Operator	Description
typeof	Returns the System.Type object of a given type

The following is an example of the syntax of the typeof operator. Type is a class in the System namespace.

```
Type t = typeof ( SomeClass )
```

For example, the following code uses the typeof operator to get information on a class called SomeClass and to print the names of its public fields and methods.

```
using System.Reflection;   // Use the Reflection namespace to take full advantage
                           // of determining information about a type.
class SomeClass
{
   public int   Field1;
   public int   Field2;

   public void Method1() { }
   public int  Method2() { return 1; }
}

class Program
{
   static void Main()
   {
      Type t = typeof(SomeClass);
      FieldInfo[]  fi = t.GetFields();
      MethodInfo[] mi = t.GetMethods();

      foreach (FieldInfo f in fi)
         Console.WriteLine($"Field : { f.Name }");
      foreach (MethodInfo m in mi)
         Console.WriteLine($"Method: { m.Name }");
   }
}
```

This code produces the following output:

```
Field : Field1
Field : Field2
Method: Method1
Method: Method2
Method: ToString
Method: Equals
Method: GetHashCode
Method: GetType
```

The typeof operator is also called by the GetType method, which is available for every object of every type. For example, the following code retrieves the name of the type of the object:

```
class SomeClass
{
}

class Program
{
    static void Main()
    {
        SomeClass s = new SomeClass();

        Console.WriteLine($"Type s: { s.GetType().Name }");
    }
}
```

This code produces the following output:

```
Type s: SomeClass
```

The nameof Operator

The nameof operator returns a string representation of the item given as its parameter, as shown in Table 9-18.

Table 9-18. *The nameof Operator*

Operator	Description
nameof	Returns the string representation of a variable, type, or member

The following examples show different items that can be passed as the parameter to the nameof operator. The output of each statement is contained in parentheses.

```
string var1 = "Local Variable";
Console.WriteLine (nameof (var1));               // Local Variable ("var1")
Console.WriteLine (nameof (MyClass));            // Class ("MyClass")
Console.WriteLine (nameof (MyClass.Method1));    // Public Method ("Method1")
Console.WriteLine (nameof (parameter1));         // Method Parameter ("parameter1")
Console.WriteLine (nameof (MyClass.Property1));  // Public Property ("Property1")
Console.WriteLine (nameof (MyClass.Field1));     // Public Field ("Field1")
Console.WriteLine (nameof (MyStruct));           // Struct ("MyStruct ")
```

The nameof operator returns only the unqualified name of its argument, even if the argument uses a fully qualified name. And as you can see, the nameof operator also works with static classes and static methods.

```
Console.WriteLine (nameof (System.Math);        // Prints "Math"
Console.WriteLine (nameof (Console.WriteLine);  // Prints "WriteLine"
```

Looking at these examples, it might not be clear as to why you would use the nameof operator when the simple string would suffice. The reason, however, relates to changes in your code. If you use a hard-coded string to refer to the name of any element in a statement, as for example a property called MyPropertyName, in the expression OnPropertyChanged("MyPropertyName"), that hard-coded string will not change if you later change the name of your property. The expression would then refer to a nonexistent property. In the case of OnPropertyChanged, notifications will fail if the passed parameter no longer matches the actual property name.

Other Operators

The operators covered in this chapter are the standard operators for the built-in types. There are other special-usage operators that are dealt with later in the book, along with their operand types. For example, the nullable types have special operators called the *null-coalescing operator* and the *null-conditional operator*, which are described in Chapter 27 along with a more in-depth description of nullable types.

CHAPTER 10

■ ■ ■

Statements

© Daniel Solis and Cal Schrotenboer 2018
D. Solis and C. Schrotenboer, *Illustrated C# 7*, https://doi.org/10.1007/978-1-4842-3288-0_10

What Are Statements?

The statements in C# are similar to those of C and C++. This chapter covers the characteristics of the C# statements, as well as the flow-of-control statements provided by the language.

- A *statement* is a source code instruction describing a type or telling the program to perform an action.

- There are three major categories of statements.

  - *Declaration statements*: Statements that declare types or variables

  - *Embedded statements: Statements that perform actions or manage flow of control*

  - *Labeled statements*: Statements to which control can jump

Previous chapters have covered a number of different declaration statements, including declarations of local variables, classes, and class members. This chapter covers the embedded statements, which do not declare types, variables, or instances. Instead, they use expressions and flow-of-control constructs to work with the objects and variables that have been declared by the declaration statements.

- A *simple statement* consists of an expression followed by a semicolon.

- A *block* is a sequence of statements enclosed by matching curly braces. The enclosed statements can include the following:

  - Declaration statements

  - Embedded statements

  - Labeled statements

  - Nested blocks

The following code gives examples of each:

```
int x = 10;          // Simple declaration
int z;               // Simple declaration

{                    // Start of a block
   int y = 20;       // Simple declaration
   z = x + y;        // Embedded statement
top: y = 30;         // Labeled statement
      ...
   {                 // Start of a nested block
      ...
   }                 // End of nested block
}                    // End of outer block
```

▪ **Note**   A block counts syntactically as a single embedded statement. Anywhere that an embedded statement is required syntactically, you can use a block.

An *empty statement* consists of just a semicolon. You can use an empty statement at any position where the syntax of the language requires an embedded statement but your program logic does not require any action.

For example, the following code shows an example of using the empty statement.

- The second line in the code is an empty statement. It's required because there must be an embedded statement between the if part and the else part of the construct.

- The fourth line is a simple statement, as shown by the terminating semicolon.

```
if( x < y )
   ;                    // Empty statement
else
   z = a + b;           // Simple statement
```

Expression Statements

The previous chapter looked at expressions. Expressions return values, but they can also have *side effects*.

- A side effect is an action that affects the state of the program.

- Many expressions are evaluated only for their side effects.

You can create a statement from an expression by placing a statement terminator (a semicolon) after the expression. Any value returned by the expression is discarded. For example, the following code shows an expression statement. It consists of the assignment expression (an assignment operator and two operands) followed by a semicolon. This does the following two things:

- The expression assigns the value on the right of the operator to the memory location referenced by variable x. Although this is probably the main reason for the statement, *this is considered the side effect*.

- After setting the value of x, the expression returns with the new value of x. But there is nothing to receive this return value, so it is ignored.

```
x = 10;
```

The whole reason for evaluating the expression is to achieve the side effect.

Flow-of-Control Statements

C# provides the flow-of-control constructs common to modern programming languages.

- *Conditional execution* executes or skips a section of code depending on a condition. The conditional execution statements are the following:

    - if

    - if...else

    - switch

- *Looping statements* repeatedly execute a section of code. The looping statements are the following:
    - while

    - do

    - for

    - foreach

- *Jump statements* change the flow of control from one section of code to a specific statement in another section of code. The jump statements are the following:

    - break

    - continue

    - return

    - goto

    - throw

Conditional execution and looping constructs (other than foreach) require a test expression, or *condition*, to determine where the program should continue execution.

■ **Note**   Unlike C and C++, in C# test expressions must return a value of type bool. Numbers do not have a Boolean interpretation in C#.

The if Statement

The if statement implements conditional execution. The syntax for the if statement is shown here and is illustrated in Figure 10-1.

- TestExpr must evaluate to a value of type bool.

- If TestExpr evaluates to true, Statement is executed.

- If it evaluates to false, Statement is skipped.

```
if( TestExpr )
    Statement
```

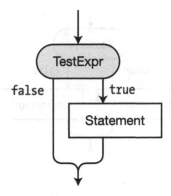

Figure 10-1. *The if statement*

The following code shows examples of if statements:

```
// With a simple statement
if( x <= 10 )
    z = x - 1;          // Single statement--no curly braces needed

// With a block
if( x >= 20 )
{
    x = x - 5;          // Block--curly braces needed
    y = x + z;
}

int x = 5;
if( x )                 // Error: test expression must be a bool, not int
{
    ...
}
```

The if...else Statement

The if...else statement implements a two-way branch. The syntax for the if...else statement is shown here and is illustrated in Figure 10-2.

- If TestExpr evaluates to true, Statement1 is executed.

- Otherwise, Statement2 is executed instead.

```
if( TestExpr )
    Statement1
else
    Statement2
```

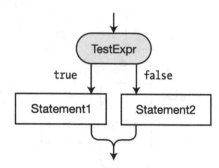

Figure 10-2. *The if...else statement*

The following is an example of the if...else statement:

```
if( x <= 10 )
   z = x - 1;                // Single statement
else
{                           // Multiple statements--block
   x = x - 5;
   y = x + z;
}
```

Of course, Statement1, Statement2, or both could themselves be if or if...else statements, which could be nested further. If you're looking at code containing nested if...else statements and need to determine which else goes with which if, there's a simple rule. Every else belongs to the *closest previous* if that doesn't have an associated else clause.

When Statement2 is an if or if...else statement, it's common to format the construct as in the following code, putting the second if clause on the same line as the else clause. This examples shows two if...else statements, but you can make an arbitrarily long chain.

```
if( TestExpr1 )
    Statement1
else if ( TestExpr2 )
    Statement2
else
    Statement3
```

The while Loop

The while loop is a simple loop construct in which the test expression is performed at the top of the loop. The syntax of the while loop is shown here and is illustrated in Figure 10-3.

- First, TestExpr is evaluated.

- If TestExpr evaluates to false, then execution continues after the end of the while loop.

- Otherwise, when TestExpr evaluates to true, then Statement is executed, and TestExpr is evaluated again. Each time TestExpr evaluates to true, Statement is executed another time. The loop ends when TestExpr evaluates to false.

```
while( TestExpr )
   Statement
```

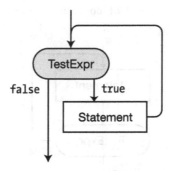

Figure 10-3. *The while loop*

The following code shows an example of the while loop, where the test expression variable starts with a value of 3 and is decremented at each iteration. The loop exits when the value of the variable becomes 0.

```
int x = 3;
while( x > 0 )
{
   Console.WriteLine($"x:  { x }");
   x--;
}
Console.WriteLine("Out of loop");
```

This code produces the following output:

```
x:  3
x:  2
x:  1
Out of loop
```

The do Loop

The do loop is a simple loop construct in which the test expression is performed at the bottom of the loop. The syntax for the do loop is shown here and illustrated in Figure 10-4.

- First, Statement is executed.

- Then, TestExpr is evaluated.

- If TestExpr returns true, then Statement is executed again.

- Each time TestExpr returns true, Statement is executed again.

- When TestExpr returns false, control passes to the statement following the end of the loop construct.

```
do
    Statement
while( TestExpr );          // End of do loop
```

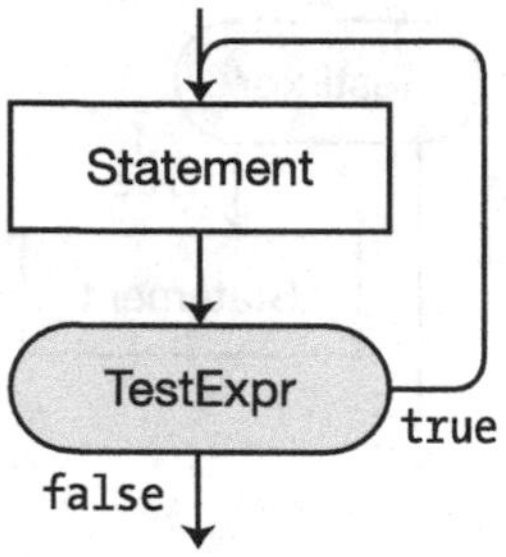

Figure 10-4. *The do loop*

The do loop has several characteristics that set it apart from other flow-of-control constructs. They are the following:

- The body of the loop, Statement, is always executed at least once, even if TestExpr is initially false. The reason for this is that TestExpr isn't evaluated until the bottom of the loop.

- A semicolon is required after the closing parenthesis of the test expression.

The following code shows an example of a do loop:

```
int x = 0;
do
   Console.WriteLine($"x is {x++}");
while (x<3);
        ↑
        Required
```

This code produces the following output:

```
x is 0
x is 1
x is 2
```

The for Loop

The for loop construct executes the body of the loop as long as the test expression returns true when it is evaluated at the top of the loop. The syntax of the for loop is shown here and illustrated in Figure 10-5.

- At the beginning of the for loop, Initializer is executed once.

- TestExpr is then evaluated.

- If TestExpr returns true, Statement is executed, followed by IterationExpr.

- Control then returns to the top of the loop, and TestExpr is evaluated again.

- As long as TestExpr returns true, Statement, followed by IterationExpr, is executed.

As soon as TestExpr returns false, execution continues at the statement following Statement.

```
          Separated by semicolons
              ↓        ↓
for( Initializer ; TestExpr ; IterationExpr )
    Statement
```

Some parts of the statement are optional, and others are required.

- Initializer, TestExpr, and IterationExpr are all optional. Their positions can be left blank. If the TestExpr position is left blank, the test is *assumed to return* true. Therefore, there must be some other means of exiting the statement if the program is to avoid going into an infinite loop.

- The two semicolons are always required as field separators, even if any of the optional items are omitted.

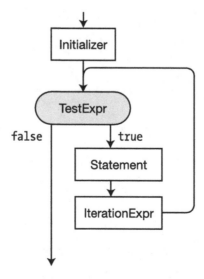

Figure 10-5. *The for loop*

Figure 10-5 illustrates the flow of control through the for statement. You should also know the following about its components:

- Initializer is executed only once, before any other part of the for construct. It is usually used to declare and initialize local values to be used in the loop.

- TestExpr is evaluated to determine whether Statement should be executed or skipped. It must evaluate to a value of type bool. As stated previously, if TestExpr is left blank, it's assumed to always be true.

- IterationExpr is executed immediately after Statement and before returning to the top of the loop to TestExpr.

For example, in the following code,

- Before anything else, the initializer (int i=0) defines a variable called i and initializes its value to 0.

- The condition (i<3) is then evaluated. If it's true, then the body of the loop is executed.

- At the bottom of the loop, after all the loop statements have been executed, the IterationExpr statement is executed—in this case, incrementing the value of i.

```
// The body of this for loop is executed three times.
for( int i=0 ; i<3 ; i++ )
   Console.WriteLine($"Inside loop. i: { i }");

Console.WriteLine("Out of Loop");
```

This code produces the following output:

```
Inside loop.   i:   0
Inside loop.   i:   1
Inside loop.   i:   2
Out of Loop
```

The Scope of Variables in a for Statement

Variables declared in the *initializer,* called *loop variables,* are visible *only within the* for *statement.*

- This is different from C and C++, where the declaration introduces the variable into the enclosing block.

- The following code illustrates this point:

Type is needed here for declaration.
↓
```
for( int i=0; i<10; i++ )   // Variable i is in scope here, and also
   Statement;               // here within the statement.
                            // Here, after the statement, i no longer exists.
```

Type is needed here again because the previous variable i has gone out of existence.
↓
```
for(int i=0; i<10; i++ ) // We need to define a new variable i here,
   Statement;            // the previous one has gone out of existence.
```

The local variables declared within the body of the loop are known only within the loop.

■ **Note**   Loop variables are often given the identifiers i, j, or k. This is a tradition from the old days of FORTRAN programming. In FORTRAN, identifiers that started with the letters *I, J, K, L, M,* and *N* were, by default, of type INTEGER, and you didn't have to declare them. Since loop variables are usually integers, programmers simply used the easy convention of using I as the name of the loop variable. It was short and easy to use, and you didn't have to declare it. If the loop variables had a nested loop, the inner loop variable was usually named J. If there was yet another inner nested loop, that variable was named K.

In general, it's not good to use nondescriptive names as identifiers. But we like the historical connection, and the clarity and brevity, when using these identifiers as loop variables.

Multiple Expressions in the Initializer and Iteration Expression

Both the initializer expression and the iteration expression can contain multiple expressions as long as they are separated by commas.

For example, the following code has two variable declarations in the initializer and two expressions in the iteration expression:

```
static void Main( )
{
    const int MaxI = 5;

              Two declarations        Two expressions
                   ↓                       ↓
    for (int i = 0, j = 10; i < MaxI; i++, j += 10)
    {
        Console.WriteLine($"{ i }, { j }");
    }
}
```

This code produces the following output:

```
0, 10
1, 20
2, 30
3, 40
4, 50
```

The switch Statement

The `switch` statement implements multiway branching. Figure 10-6 shows the syntax and structure of the `switch` statement.

- The `switch` statement has a single parameter generally referred to as the *test* or *matching* expression. Previously, these test expressions had to be one of the following data types: `char`, `string`, `bool`, `integer` (including, for example, `byte`, `int`, or `long`), or enum. C# 7.0 now allows the test expression to be of any type.

- The `switch` statement contains zero or more *switch sections*.

- Each switch section starts with one or more *switch labels*. Each switch label (or the last one if there are multiple switch labels in the same switch section) is followed by a pattern expression that will be compared to the test expression. If both the test and pattern expressions are integral types, the comparison is performed using the C# equality operator (`==`). In all other cases, the comparison is executed using the static method `Object. Equals(test, pattern)`. In other words, for nonintegral types, C# uses a deep comparison.

- Each switch section must adhere to the "no fall through rule." This means that the flow of control of the statement list in the switch section cannot reach the end and meet the next switch section. This rule is usually implemented by ending the statement list with a `break` statement or one of the other four jump statements. Note, however, that the `goto` jump statement cannot be used with nonconstant `switch` expressions.

  - The jump statements are `break`, `return`, `continue`, `goto`, and `throw`. These are described later in this chapter.

  - Of the five jump statements, the `break` statement is the most commonly used for ending a switch section. The `break` statement branches execution to the end of the `switch` statement.

- Switch sections are evaluated in order. If one matches the value of the test expression, its switch section is executed, and then control jumps to the location specified by the jump statement used in that switch section. Since the `break` statement is the most commonly used jump statement, usually control jumps to the first line of executable code following the end of the `switch` statement.

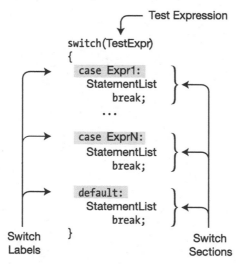

Figure 10-6. Structure of a switch statement

Switch labels have the following form:

```
case PatternExpression:
```
  ↑   ↑
Keyword   Switch label terminator

The flow of control through the structure in Figure 10-6 is the following:

- The test expression (also often referred to as the matching expression), TestExpr, is evaluated at the top of the construct.

- If the value of TestExpr is equal to the value of PatternExpr1, the pattern expression in the first switch label and then the statements in the *statement list* following the switch label are executed, until the one of the jump statements is encountered.

- The default section is optional, but if it is included, it too must end with one of the jump statements.

Figure 10-7 illustrates the general flow of control through a switch statement. You can modify the flow through a switch statement with a goto statement or a return statement.

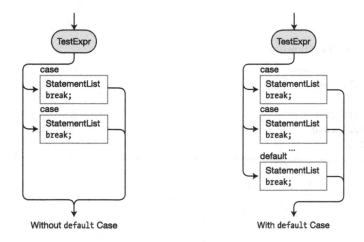

Figure 10-7. The flow of control through a switch statement

A Switch Example Involving Constants

The following code executes the switch statement five times, with the value of x ranging from 1 to 5. From the output, you can tell which case section was executed on each cycle through the loop.

```
for( int x=1; x<6; x++ )
{
   switch( x )                              // Evaluate the value of variable x.
   {
      case 2:                               // If x equals 2
         Console.WriteLine($"x is { x } -- In Case 2");
         break;                             // Go to end of switch.

      case 5:                               // If x equals 5
         Console.WriteLine($"x is { x } -- In Case 5";
         break;                             // Go to end of switch.

      default:                              // If x is neither 2 nor 5
         Console.WriteLine($"x is { x } -- In Default case");
         break;                             // Go to end of switch.
   }
}
```

This code produces the following output:

```
x is 1 -- In Default case
x is 2 -- In Case 2
x is 3 -- In Default case
x is 4 -- In Default case
x is 5 -- In Case 5
```

Other Types of Pattern Expressions

A case label consists of the keyword case followed by a pattern. Patterns can be a simple value such as "Hello" or 55, an expression that evaluates to a simple value, or a type. A pattern can include a filter introduced by the keyword when.

The following code executes a switch statement multiple times by iterating through a collection of objects. From the output, you can tell which case section was executed on each cycle through the loop.

```
public abstract class Shape { }

public class Square : Shape
{
    public double Side {get; set;}
}

public class Circle : Shape
{
    public double Radius {get; set;}
}

public class Triangle : Shape
{
    public double Height {get; set;}
}

class Program
{
    static void Main()
    {
        var shapes = new List<Shape>();
        shapes.Add(new Circle() { Radius = 7 });
        shapes.Add(new Square() { Side = 5 });
        shapes.Add(new Triangle() { Height = 4 });
        var nullSquare = (Square)null;
        shapes.Add(nullSquare);

        foreach (var shape in shapes )
        {
            switch( shape )          //Evaluate the type and/or value of variable shape.
            {
                case Circle circle:                      //Equivalent to if(shape is Circle)
                    Console.WriteLine($"This shape is a circle of radius { circle.Radius }");
                    break;
                case Square square when square.Side > 10:  //Matches only a subset of Squares
                    Console.WriteLine($"This shape is a large square of side { square.Side }");
                    break;
                case Square square:
                    Console.WriteLine($"This shape is a square of side { square.Side }");
                    break;
```

```
            case Triangle triangle:      // Equivalent to if(shape is Triangle)
                Console.WriteLine($"This shape is a triangle of side { triangle.Height }");
                break;
            //case Triangle triangle when triangle.Height < 5:    //Compile error
            //Console.WriteLine($"This shape is a triangle of side { triangle.Height }");
            //break;
            case null:
                Console.WriteLine($"This shape could be a Square, Circle or a Triangle");
                break;
            default:
                throw new ArgumentException(
                message: "shape is not a recognized shape",
                paramName: nameof(shape));
        }
      }
    }
  }
```

This code produces the following output:

```
This shape is a circle of radius 7
This shape is a square of side 5
This shape is a triangle of side 4
This shape could be a Square, Circle or a Triangle
```

In this example, the commented-out code would cause a compile error because this case could never be reached since it is a specific limited case of the immediately preceding general case.

This switch example also illustrates the use of matching variables (circle, square, triangle) to which the test expression (shape) is immediately assigned. Each such variable is in scope until the next jump statement (break, in this case) is reached. It would not be in scope in any other block.

The following code would also cause a compile error. Where there are multiple type patterns in the same switch section, it is not possible to determine at compile time which of these patterns will be matched and, therefore, which variable will be populated. You cannot, therefore, use any of these variables in the statements comprising that section because they might cause a null reference exception.

```
case Square s:
case Circle c:
    Console.WriteLine($"Square has dimensions: { s.Side } x { s.Side }");
    Console.WriteLine($"Found a Circle of radius { c.Radius }");
    break;
```

Note also that there is no requirement that all case expressions must be either constant values or types. These can be intermingled as desired.

More on the switch Statement

A switch statement can have any number of switch sections, including none. The default section is not required, as shown in the following example. It is, however, generally considered good practice to include it, since it can catch potential errors.

For example, the switch statement in the following code has no default section. The switch statement is inside a for loop, which executes the statement five times, with the value of x starting at 1 and ending at 5.

```
for( int x=1; x<6; x++ )
{
    switch( x )
    {
        case 5:
            Console.WriteLine($"x is { x } -- In Case 5");
            break;
    }
}
```

This code produces the following output:

```
x is 5 -- In Case 5
```

The following code has only the default section:

```
for( int x=1; x<4; x++ )
{
    switch( x )
    {
        default:
            Console.WriteLine($"x is { x } -- In Default case");
            break;
    }
}
```

This code produces the following output:

```
x is 1 -- In Default case
x is 2 -- In Default case
x is 3 -- In Default case
```

Switch Labels

The expression following the keyword case in a switch label can be a pattern of any type. Previously (before C# 7.0) it had to be a constant expression and therefore had to be completely evaluable by the compiler at *compile* time. This constraint no longer applies.

For example, Figure 10-8 shows three sample switch statements.

```
const string YES = "yes";        const char LetterB = 'b';      const int Five = 5;

string s = "no";                 char c = 'a';                  int x = 5;
switch (s)                       switch (c)                    switch (x)
{                                {                             {
    case YES:                        case 'a':                     case Five:
        PrintOut("Yes");                 PrintOut("a");                PrintOut("5");
        break;                           break;                        break;

    case "no":                       case LetterB:                 case 10:
        PrintOut("No");                  PrintOut("b");                PrintOut("10");
        break;                           break;                        break;
}                                }                             }
```

Figure 10-8. *Switch statements with different types of switch labels*

■ **Note**   Unlike C and C++, in C# each switch section, including the optional default section, must end with one of the jump statements. In C#, you cannot execute the code in one switch section and then *fall through* to the next.

Although C# does not allow falling through from one switch section to another, you can attach multiple switch labels to any switch section as long as there are *no intervening executable statements* between the switch labels.

For example, in the following code, since there are no executable statements between the first three switch labels, it's fine to have one follow the other. Cases 5 and 6, however, have an executable statement between them, so there must be a jump statement before case 6.

```
switch( x )
{
    case 1:                     // Acceptable
    case 2:
    case 3:
        ...                     // Execute this code if x equals 1, 2, or 3.
        break;
    case 5:
        y = x + 1;
    case 6:                     // Not acceptable because there is no break
                                // or other jump statement

        ...
```

Although the most common way to end a switch section is to use one of the five jump statements, the compiler is smart enough to determine that a particular construct will allow the statement list to meet the "no fall through rule." For example, a while loop where the test condition is the value true will loop forever and will never be able to fall through to the next switch section. The following code shows an example that is perfectly valid:

```
int x = 5;
switch(x)
{
    case 5:
        while (true)    ← This satisfies the "no fall through rule"
            DoStuff();
    default:
        throw new InvalidOperationException();
}
```

Jump Statements

When the flow of control reaches jump statements, program execution is unconditionally transferred to another part of the program. The jump statements are the following:

- `break`
- `continue`
- `return`
- `goto`
- `throw`

This chapter covers the first four of these statements. The `throw` statement is explained in Chapter 23.

The break Statement

Earlier in this chapter you saw the `break` statement used in the `switch` statement. It can also be used in the following statement types:

- `for`
- `foreach`
- `while`
- `do`

In the body of one of these statements, break causes execution to exit the *innermost enclosing loop*.

For example, the following `while` loop would be an infinite loop if it relied only on its test expression, which is always `true`. But instead, after three iterations of the loop, the `break` statement is encountered, and the loop is exited.

```
int x = 0;
while( true )
{
    x++;
    if( x >= 3 )
        break;
}
```

The continue Statement

The continue statement causes program execution to go to the *top* of the *innermost enclosing loop* of the following types:

- while
- do
- for
- foreach

For example, the following for loop is executed five times. In the first three iterations, it encounters the continue statement and goes directly back to the top of the loop, missing the WriteLine statement at the bottom of the loop. Execution only reaches the WriteLine statement during the last two iterations.

```
for( int x=0; x<5; x++ )            // Execute loop five times
{
   if( x < 3 )                      // The first three times
      continue;                     // Go directly back to top of loop

   // This line is only reached when x is 3 or greater.
   Console.WriteLine($"Value of x is { x }");
}
```

This code produces the following output:

```
Value of x is 3
Value of x is 4
```

The following code shows an example of a continue statement in a while loop. This code produces the same output as the preceding for loop example.

```
int x = 0;
while( x < 5 )
{
   if( x < 3 )
   {
      x++;
      continue;                             // Go back to top of loop
   }

   // This line is reached only when x is 3 or greater.
   Console.WriteLine($"Value of x is { x }");
   x++;
}
```

Labeled Statements

A *labeled statement* consists of an identifier, followed by a colon, followed by a statement. It has the following form:

```
Identifier: Statement
```

A labeled statement is executed exactly as if the label were not there and consisted of just the Statement part.

- Adding a label to a statement allows control to be transferred to the statement from another part of the code.

- Labeled statements are allowed only inside blocks.

Labels

Labels have their own declaration space, so the identifier in a labeled statement can be any valid identifier—including those that might be declared in an overlapping scope, such as local variables or parameter names.

For example, the following code shows the valid use of a label with the same identifier as a local variable:

```
{
   int xyz = 0;                           // Variable xyz
      ...
   xyz: Console.WriteLine("No problem.");  // Label xyz
}
```

There are restrictions, however. The identifier cannot be either

- A keyword

- The same as another label identifier with an overlapping scope

The Scope of Labeled Statements

Labeled statements cannot be seen (or accessed) from *outside* the block in which they are declared. The scope of a labeled statement is the following:

- The block in which it is declared

- Any blocks nested inside that block

For example, the code on the left of Figure 10-9 contains several nested blocks, with their scopes marked. There are two labeled statements declared in scope B of the program: increment and end.

- The shaded portions on the right of the figure show the areas of the code in which the labeled statements are in scope.

- Code in scope B, and all the nested blocks, can see and access the labeled statements.

- Code from any of the inner scopes can jump *out* to the labeled statements.

- Code from outside (scope A, in this case) *cannot jump into* a block with a labeled statement.

```
static void Main( )
{ // Scope A

    { // Scope B

    increment: x++;
        { // Scope C

            { // Scope D
            ...
            }
            { // Scope E
            ...
            }
            ...
        }
    end: Console.WriteLine("Exiting");
    }
}
```

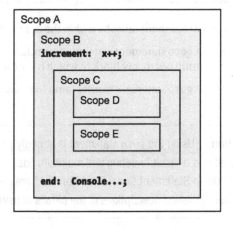

Figure 10-9. *The scope of labels includes nested blocks*

The goto Statement

The goto statement unconditionally transfers control to a *labeled statement*. Its general form is the following, where Identifier is the identifier of a labeled statement:

```
goto Identifier ;
```

For example, the following code shows the simple use of a goto statement:

```
bool thingsAreFine;
while (true)
{
   thingsAreFine = GetNuclearReactorCondition();

   if ( thingsAreFine )
      Console.WriteLine("Things are fine.");
   else
      goto NotSoGood;
}

NotSoGood: Console.WriteLine("We have a problem.");
```

The goto statement must be *within* the scope of the labeled statement.

- A goto statement can jump to any labeled statement within its own block or can jump *out* to any block in which it is nested.

- A goto statement cannot jump *into* any blocks nested within its own block.

■ **Caution**   Using the goto statement is strongly discouraged because it can lead to code that is poorly structured and difficult to debug and maintain. Edsger Dijkstra's 1968 letter to the Communications of the ACM, entitled "Go To Statement Considered Harmful," was an important contribution to computer science; it was one of the first published descriptions of the pitfalls of using the goto statement.

The goto Statement Inside a switch Statement

There are also two other forms of the goto statement, for use inside switch statements. These goto statements transfer control to the correspondingly named switch label in the switch statement. However, it is only possible to use goto labels that reference compile-time constants (as were used in pre-C# 7.0 switch statements).

```
goto case ConstantExpression;
goto default;
goto case PatternExpression;   //Compile error
```

The using Statement

Certain types of unmanaged objects are limited in number or are expensive with system resources. It's important that when your code is done with them, they be released as soon as possible. The using statement helps simplify the process and ensures that these resources are properly disposed of.

A *resource* is a class or struct that implements the System.IDisposable interface. Interfaces are covered in detail in Chapter 16—but in short, an interface is a collection of unimplemented function members that classes and structs can choose to implement. The IDisposable interface contains a single method, named Dispose.

The phases of using a resource are shown in Figure 10-10 and consist of the following:

- Allocating the resource

- Using the resource

- Disposing of the resource

If an unexpected runtime error occurs during the portion of the code using the resource, the code disposing of the resource might not get executed.

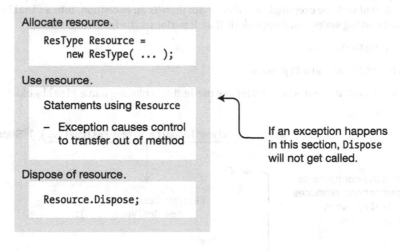

Figure 10-10. *Components of using a resource*

■ **Note**   The using statement is different from using directives (e.g., using System.Math;). The using directives are covered in detail in Chapter 22.

Packaging the Use of a Resource

The using statement helps reduce the potential problem of an unexpected runtime error by neatly packaging the use of a resource.

There are two forms of the using statement. The first form is the following and is illustrated in Figure 10-11.

- The code between the parentheses allocates the resource.

- Statement is the code that uses the resource.

- The using statement *implicitly generates* the code to dispose of the resource.

using (<u>ResourceType Identifier</u> = <u>Expression</u>) <u>Statement</u>
            ↑   ↑

               Allocates resource   Uses resource

Unexpected runtime errors are called *exceptions* and are covered in detail in Chapter 23. The standard way of handling the possibility of exceptions is to place the code that might cause an exception in a try block and place any code that *must* be executed, whether or not there is an exception, into a finally block.

This form of the using statement does exactly that. It performs the following:

- Allocating the resource

- Placing Statement in a try block

- Creating a call to the resource's Dispose method and placing it in a finally block

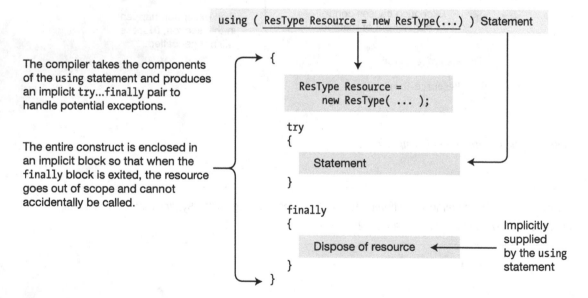

Figure 10-11. *The effect of the using statement*

Example of the using Statement

The following code uses the using statement twice—once with a class called TextWriter and once with a class called TextReader, both from the System.IO namespace. Both classes implement the IDisposable interface, as required by the using statement.

- The TextWriter resource opens a text file for writing and writes a line to the file.

- The TextReader resource then opens the same text file and reads and displays the contents, line by line.

- In both cases, the using statement makes sure that the objects' Dispose methods are called.

- Notice also the difference between the using statements in Main and the using directives on the first two lines.

```
using System;                       // using DIRECTIVE; not using statement
using System.IO;                    // using DIRECTIVE; not using statement

namespace UsingStatement
{
   class Program
   {
      static void Main( )
      {
         // using statement
         using (TextWriter tw = File.CreateText("Lincoln.txt") )
         {
            tw.WriteLine("Four score and seven years ago, ...");
         }

         // using statement
         using (TextReader tr = File.OpenText("Lincoln.txt"))
         {
            string InputString;
            while (null != (InputString = tr.ReadLine()))
               Console.WriteLine(InputString);
         }
      }
   }
}
```

This code produces the following output:

```
Four score and seven years ago, ...
```

Multiple Resources and Nesting

The using statement can also be used with multiple resources of the same type, with the resource declarations separated by commas. The syntax is the following:

```
      Only one type      Resource         Resource
           ↓                 ↓                ↓
using ( ResourceType Id1 = Expr1,   Id2 = Expr2, ... ) EmbeddedStatement
```

For example, in the following code, each using statement allocates and uses two resources:

```
static void Main()
{
   using (TextWriter tw1 = File.CreateText("Lincoln.txt"),
                     tw2 = File.CreateText("Franklin.txt"))
   {
      tw1.WriteLine("Four score and seven years ago, ...");
      tw2.WriteLine("Early to bed; Early to rise ...");
   }

   using (TextReader tr1 = File.OpenText("Lincoln.txt"),
                     tr2 = File.OpenText("Franklin.txt"))
   {
      string InputString;

      while (null != (InputString = tr1.ReadLine()))
         Console.WriteLine(InputString);

      while (null != (InputString = tr2.ReadLine()))
         Console.WriteLine(InputString);
   }
}
```

The using statement can also be nested. In the following code, besides the nesting of the using statements, also note that it is not necessary to use a block with the second using statement because it consists of only a single, simple statement.

```
using ( TextWriter tw1 = File.CreateText("Lincoln.txt") )
{
   tw1.WriteLine("Four score and seven years ago, ...");

   using ( TextWriter tw2 = File.CreateText("Franklin.txt") )   // Nested
      tw2.WriteLine("Early to bed; Early to rise ...");          // Single
}
```

Another Form of the using Statement

Another form of the using statement is the following:

```
 Keyword        Resource      Uses resource
    ↓              ↓               ↓
  using ( Expression ) EmbeddedStatement
```

In this form, the resource is declared before the using statement.

```
TextWriter tw = File.CreateText("Lincoln.txt");              // Resource declared

using ( tw )                                                 // using statement
    tw.WriteLine("Four score and seven years ago, ...");
```

Although this form still ensures that the Dispose method will always be called after you finish using the resource, it does not protect you from attempting to use the resource after the using statement has released its unmanaged resources, leaving it in an inconsistent state. It therefore gives less protection and is discouraged. This form is illustrated in Figure 10-12.

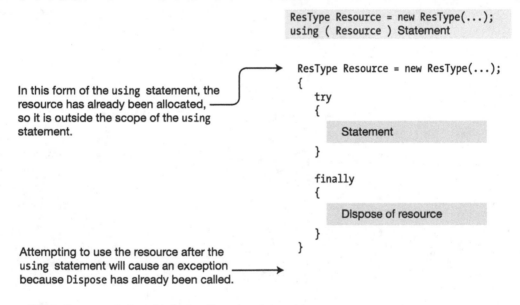

Figure 10-12. *Resource declaration before the using statement*

Other Statements

There are other statements that are associated with particular features of the language. These statements are covered in the sections dealing with those features. The statements covered in other chapters are shown in Table 10-1.

Table 10-1. *Statements Covered in Other Chapters*

Statement	Description	Relevant Chapter
checked, unchecked	These statements control the overflow checking context.	Chapter 17
foreach	This statement iterates through each member of a collection.	Chapters 13 and 19
try, throw, finally	These statements are associated with exceptions.	Chapter 23
return	This statement returns control to the calling function member and can also return a value.	Chapter 6
yield	This statement is used with iterators.	Chapter 19

CHAPTER 11

■ ■ ■

Structs

© Daniel Solis and Cal Schrotenboer 2018

D. Solis and C. Schrotenboer, *Illustrated C# 7*, https://doi.org/10.1007/978-1-4842-3288-0_11

What Are Structs?

Structs are programmer-defined data types, similar to classes. They have data members and function members. Although structs are similar to classes, there are a number of important differences. The most important ones are the following:

- Classes are reference types, and structs are value types.

- Structs are implicitly sealed, which means they cannot be derived from.

The syntax for declaring a struct is similar to that of declaring a class.

```
 Keyword
    ↓
struct StructName
{
   MemberDeclarations
}
```

For example, the following code declares a struct named Point. It has two public fields, named X and Y. In Main, three variables of struct type Point are declared, and their values are assigned and printed out.

```
struct Point
{
   public int X;
   public int Y;
}

class Program
{
   static void Main()
   {
      Point first, second, third;

      first.X  = 10; first.Y = 10;
      second.X = 20; second.Y = 20;
      third.X  = first.X + second.X;
      third.Y  = first.Y + second.Y;

      Console.WriteLine($"first:   { first.X }, { first.Y }");
      Console.WriteLine($"second:  { second.X }, { second.Y }");
      Console.WriteLine($"third:   { third.X }, { third.Y }");
   }
}
```

This code produces the following output:

```
first:    10, 10
second:   20, 20
third:    30, 30
```

Structs Are Value Types

As with all value types, a variable of a struct type contains its own data. Consequently,

- A variable of a struct type cannot be null.

- Two struct variables cannot refer to the same object.

For example, the following code declares a class called CSimple, a struct called Simple, and a variable of each. Figure 11-1 shows how the two would be arranged in memory.

```
class CSimple
{
    public int X;
    public int Y;
}

struct Simple
{
    public int X;
    public int Y;
}

class Program
{
    static void Main()
    {
        CSimple cs = new CSimple();
        Simple  ss = new Simple();
            ...
```

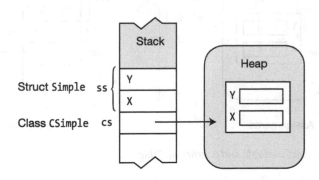

Figure 11-1. *Memory arrangement of a class versus a struct*

Assigning to a Struct

Assigning one struct to another copies the values from one to the other. This is quite different from copying from a class variable, where only the reference is copied.

Figure 11-2 shows the difference between the assignment of a class variable and a struct variable. Notice that after the class assignment, cs2 points at the same object in the heap as cs1. But after the struct assignment, the values of ss2's members are copies of those in ss1.

```
class CSimple
{ public int X; public int Y; }

struct Simple
{ public int X; public int Y; }

class Program
{
   static void Main()
   {
      CSimple cs1 = new CSimple(), cs2 = null;        // Class instances
      Simple  ss1 = new Simple(),  ss2 = new Simple(); // Struct instances

      cs1.X = ss1.X = 5;                   // Assign 5 to ss1.X and cs1.X.
      cs1.Y = ss1.Y = 10;                  // Assign 10 to ss1.Y and cs1.Y.

      cs2 = cs1;                           // Assign class instance.
      ss2 = ss1;                           // Assign struct instance.
   }
}
```

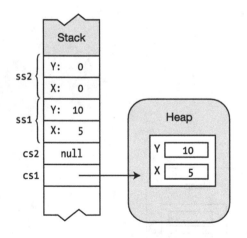
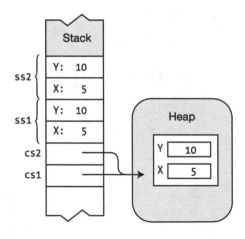

Figure 11-2. *Assigning a class variable and a struct variable*

Constructors and Destructors

Structs can have instance and static constructors, but destructors are not allowed.

Instance Constructors

The language implicitly supplies a parameterless constructor for every struct. This constructor sets each of the struct's members to the default value for that type. Value members are set to their default values. Reference members are set to null.

The predefined parameterless constructor exists for every struct—and you cannot delete or redefine it. You can, however, create additional constructors, as long as they have parameters. Notice that this is different from classes. *For classes*, the compiler supplies an implicit parameterless constructor *only if no other constructors are declared.*

To invoke a constructor, including the implicit parameterless constructor, use the new operator. Notice that the new operator is used even though the memory is not allocated from the heap.

For example, the following code declares a simple struct with a constructor that takes two int parameters. Main creates two instances of the struct—one using the implicit parameterless constructor and the second with the declared two-parameter constructor.

```
struct Simple
{
    public int X;
    public int Y;

    public Simple(int a, int b)                // Constructor with parameters
    {
        X = a;
        Y = b;
    }
}

class Program
{
    static void Main()
    {                    Call implicit constructor
                                  ↓
        Simple s1 = new Simple();
        Simple s2 = new Simple(5, 10);
                              ↑
                        Call constructor
        Console.WriteLine($"{ s1.X },{ s1.Y }");
        Console.WriteLine($"{ s2.X },{ s2.Y }");
    }
}
```

You can also create an instance of a struct without using the new operator. If you do this, however, there are several restrictions, which are the following:

- You cannot use the value of a data member until you have explicitly set it.

- You cannot call *any* function member of the struct until *all* the data members have been assigned.

For example, the following code shows two instances of struct Simple created without using the new operator. When there is an attempt to access s1 without explicitly setting the data member values, the compiler produces an error message. There are no problems reading from s2 after assigning values to its members.

```
struct Simple
{
    public int X;
    public int Y;
}

class Program
{
    static void Main()
    {    No constructor calls
              ↓   ↓
        Simple s1, s2;
        Console.WriteLine("{0},{1}", s1.X, s1.Y);        // Compiler error
                                      ↑      ↑
        s2.X = 5;                    Not yet assigned
        s2.Y = 10;
        Console.WriteLine($"{ s2.X },{ s2.Y }");         // OK
    }
}
```

Static Constructors

As with classes, the static constructors of structs create and initialize the static data members and cannot reference instance members. Static constructors for structs follow the same rules as those for classes, except that parameterless static constructors are permitted.

A static constructor is called before the first of either of the following two actions:

- A call to an explicitly declared constructor

- A reference to a static member of the struct

Summary of Constructors and Destructors

Table 11-1 summarizes the use of constructors and destructors with structs.

Table 11-1. *Summary of Constructors and Destructors*

Type	Description
Instance constructor (parameterless)	Cannot be declared in the program. An implicit constructor is always supplied by the system for all structs. It cannot be deleted or redefined by the program.
Instance constructor (with parameters)	Can be declared in the program.
Static constructor	Can be declared in the program.
Destructor	Cannot be declared in the program. Destructors are not allowed.

Property and Field Initializers

Instance property and field initializers are not allowed in struct declarations, as shown in the following code:

```
struct Simple
{                    Not allowed
                         ↓
    public int x = 0;                 // Compile error
    public int y = 10;                // Compile error
                         ↑
                    Not allowed
    public int prop1 {get; set;} = 5;  //Compile error
}
```

However, both static properties and static fields of a struct can be initialized in their declaration, even though structs themselves cannot be static.

Structs Are Sealed

Structs are always implicitly sealed, and hence you cannot derive other structs from them.

Since structs do not support inheritance, the use of several of the class member modifiers with struct members would not make sense; thus, you cannot use them in their declarations. The modifiers that cannot be used with structs are the following:

- protected

- protected internal

- abstract

- sealed

- virtual

Structs themselves are, under the covers, derived from System.ValueType, which is derived from object.

There are two inheritance-associated keywords that you *can* use with struct members: the new and override modifiers. These keywords are appropriate when creating a member with the same name as a member of the base class System.ValueType, from which all structs are derived.

Boxing and Unboxing

As with other value type data, if you want to use a struct instance as a reference type object, you must make a boxed copy. Boxing is the process of making a reference type copy of a value type variable. Boxing and unboxing are explained in detail in Chapter 17.

Structs As Return Values and Parameters

Structs can be used as return values and parameters.

- *Return value*: When a struct is a return value, a copy is created and returned from the function member.

- *Value parameter*: When a struct is used as a value parameter, a copy of the actual parameter struct is created. The copy is used in the execution of the method.

- *ref and out parameters*: If you use a struct as a ref or out parameter, a reference to the struct is passed into the method so that the data members can be changed.

Additional Information About Structs

Allocating structs requires less overhead than creating instances of a class, so using structs instead of classes can sometimes improve performance—but beware of the high cost of boxing and unboxing.

Finally, some last things you should know about structs are the following:

- The predefined simple types (int, short, long, and so on), although considered primitives in .NET and C#, are all actually implemented under the covers in .NET as structs.

- You can declare partial structs in the same way as partial classes, as described in Chapter 7.

Structs, like classes, can implement interfaces, which will be covered in Chapter 16.

CHAPTER 12

■ ■ ■

Enumerations

■ Enumerations

■ Bit Flags

■ More About Enums

© Daniel Solis and Cal Schrotenboer 2018

D. Solis and C. Schrotenboer, *Illustrated C# 7*, https://doi.org/10.1007/978-1-4842-3288-0_12

Enumerations

An *enumeration*, or enum, is a programmer-defined type, such as a class or a struct.

- Like structs, enums are value types and therefore store their data directly, rather than separately, with a reference and data.

- Enums have only one type of member: named constants with integer values.

The following code shows an example of the declaration of a new enum type called `TrafficLight`, which contains three members. Notice that the list of member declarations is a comma-separated list; there are no semicolons in an enum declaration.

```
Keyword    Enum name
   ↓           ↓
  enum TrafficLight
  {
      Green,    ← Comma separated—no semicolons
      Yellow,   ← Comma separated—no semicolons
      Red
  }
```

Every enum type has an underlying integer type, which by default is `int`.

- Each enum member is assigned a constant value of the underlying type.

- By default, the compiler assigns 0 to the first member and assigns each subsequent member the value one more than the previous member.

For example, in the `TrafficLight` type, the compiler assigns the `int` values 0, 1, and 2 to members `Green`, `Yellow`, and `Red`, respectively. In the output of the following code, you can see the underlying member values by casting them to type `int`. Figure 12-1 illustrates their arrangement on the stack.

```
TrafficLight t1 = TrafficLight.Green;
TrafficLight t2 = TrafficLight.Yellow;
TrafficLight t3 = TrafficLight.Red;

Console.WriteLine($"{ t1 },\t{(int) t1 }");
Console.WriteLine($"{ t2 },\t{(int) t2 }");
Console.WriteLine($"{ t3 },\t{(int) t3 }\n");
                              ↑
                          Cast to int
```

This code produces the following output:

```
Green,   0
Yellow,  1
Red,     2
```

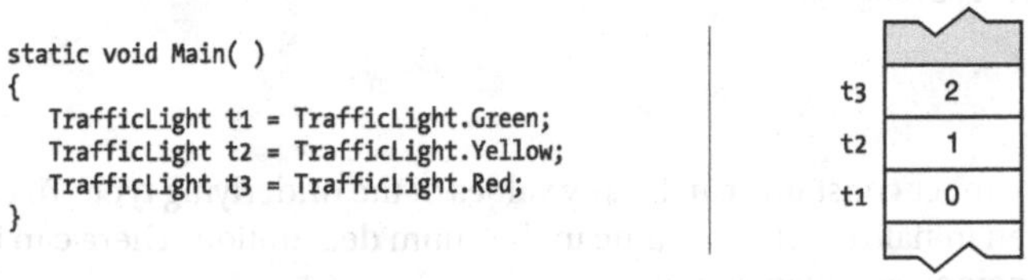

Figure 12-1. *The member constants of an enum are represented by underlying integer values.*

You can assign enum values to variables of the enum type. For example, the following code shows the declaration of three variables of type TrafficLight. Notice that you can assign member literals to variables, or you can copy the value from another variable of same type.

```
class Program
{
   static void Main()
   {     Type    Variable     Member
           ↓        ↓            ↓
       TrafficLight t1 = TrafficLight.Red;      // Assign from member
       TrafficLight t2 = TrafficLight.Green;    // Assign from member
       TrafficLight t3 = t2;                    // Assign from variable

       Console.WriteLine(t1);
       Console.WriteLine(t2);
       Console.WriteLine(t3);
   }
}
```

This code produces the following output. Notice that the member names are printed as strings.

```
Red
Green
Green
```

Setting the Underlying Type and Explicit Values

You can use an integer type other than int by placing a colon and the type name after the enum name. The type can be any integer type. All the member constants are of the enum's underlying type.

```
                Colon
                  ↓
enum TrafficLight : ulong
{                         ↑
    ...         Underlying type
```

The values of the member constants can be any values of the underlying type. To explicitly set the value of a member, use an initializer after its name in the enum declaration. There can be duplicate values, although not duplicate names, as shown here:

```
enum TrafficLight
{
    Green  = 10,
    Yellow = 15,                  // Duplicate values
    Red    = 15                   // Duplicate values
}
```

For example, the code in Figure 12-2 shows two equivalent declarations of enum TrafficLight.

- The code on the left accepts the default type and numbering.

- The code on the right explicitly sets the underlying type to int and sets the members to values corresponding to the default values.

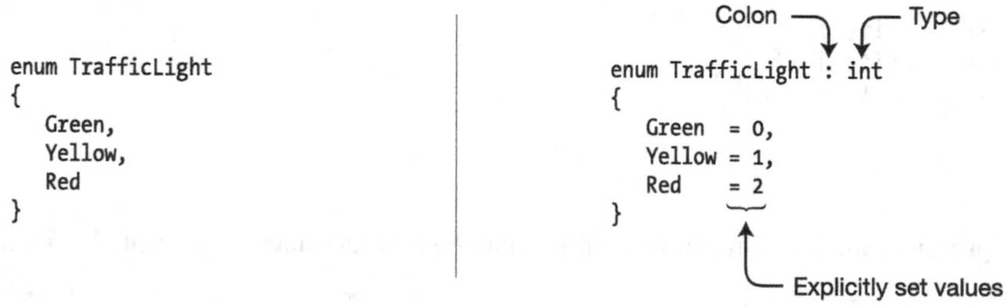

```
enum TrafficLight                      Colon ⌐      ⌐ Type
{                                              ↓    ↓
    Green,                       enum TrafficLight : int
    Yellow,                      {
    Red                              Green  = 0,
}                                    Yellow = 1,
                                     Red    = 2
                                 }
                                          ‿
                                          ↑
                                          └ Explicitly set values
```

Figure 12-2. *Equivalent enum declarations*

Implicit Member Numbering

You can explicitly assign the values for any of the member constants. If you don't initialize a member constant, the compiler implicitly assigns it a value. Figure 12-3 illustrates the rules the compiler uses for assigning those values. The values associated with the member names do not need to be distinct.

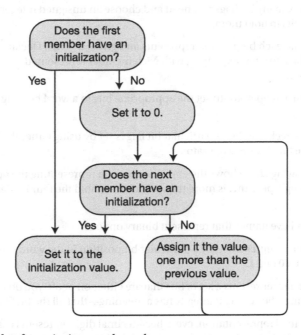

Figure 12-3. *The algorithm for assigning member values*

For example, the following code declares two enumerations. CardSuit accepts the implicit numbering of the members, as shown in the comments. FaceCards sets some members explicitly and accepts implicit numbering of the others.

```
enum CardSuit {
    Hearts,                     // 0  - Since this is first
    Clubs,                      // 1  - One more than the previous one
    Diamonds,                   // 2  - One more than the previous one
    Spades,                     // 3  - One more than the previous one
    MaxSuits                    // 4  - A common way to assign a constant
}                               //        to the number of listed items

enum FaceCards {
    // Member                   // Value assigned
    Jack            = 11,       // 11 - Explicitly set
    Queen,                      // 12 - One more than the previous one
    King,                       // 13 - One more than the previous one
    Ace,                        // 14 - One more than the previous one
    NumberOfFaceCards = 4,      // 4  - Explicitly set
    SomeOtherValue,             // 5  - One more than the previous one
    HighestFaceCard = Ace       // 14 - Ace is defined above
}
```

Bit Flags

Programmers have long used the different bits in a single word as a compact way of representing a set of on/off flags. In this section, we'll call this word the *flag word*. Enums offer a convenient way to implement this.

The general steps are the following:

1. Determine how many bit flags you need and choose an unsigned integer type with enough bits to hold them.

2. Determine what each bit position represents and give it a name. Declare an enum of the chosen integer type, with each member represented by a bit position.

3. Use the bitwise OR operator to set the appropriate bits in a word holding the bit flags.

4. You can then check whether a particular bit flag is set by using either the HasFlag method or the bitwise AND operator.

For example, the following code shows the enum declaration representing the options for a card deck in a card game. The underlying type, uint, is more than sufficient to hold the four bit flags needed. Notice the following about the code:

- The members have names that represent binary options.

  - Each option is represented by a particular bit position in the word. Bit positions hold either a 0 or a 1.

  - Since a bit flag represents a set of bits that are either on or off, you do not want to use 0 as a member value. It already has a meaning—that all the bit flags are off.

- With hexadecimal representation, every hexadecimal digit represents exactly four bits. Because of this direct correlation between the bit patterns and hexadecimal representation, when working with bit patterns, hex is often used rather than decimal representation.

- Starting with C# 7.0, binary representation is also now available.

- Decorating the enum with the Flags attribute is not actually necessary but gives some additional convenience, which we'll discuss shortly. An attribute appears as a string between square brackets, immediately preceding a language construct. In this case, the attribute is immediately before the enum declaration. We'll cover attributes in Chapter 25.

```
[Flags]
enum CardDeckSettings : uint
{
    SingleDeck    = 0x01,        // Bit 0
    LargePictures = 0x02,        // Bit 1
    FancyNumbers  = 0x04,        // Bit 2
    Animation     = 0x08         // Bit 3
}
```

Figure 12-4 illustrates this enumeration.

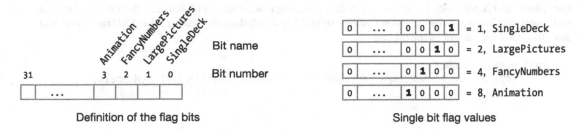

Figure 12-4. *Definition of the flag bits (left), along with their individual representations (right)*

To create a word with the appropriate bit flags, declare a variable of the enum type and use the bitwise OR operator to set the required bits. For example, the following code sets three of the four options in the flag word:

```
     Enum type      Flag word             Bit flags ORed together
         ↓              ↓                         ↓
CardDeckSettings ops =      CardDeckSettings.SingleDeck
                         | CardDeckSettings.FancyNumbers
                         | CardDeckSettings.Animation ;
```

To check whether the flag word has a particular bit flag set, you can use the Boolean HasFlag method of the enum type. You call the HasFlag method on the flag word, passing in the bit flag you're checking for, as shown in the following line of code. If the specified bit flag is set, HasFlag returns true; otherwise, it returns false.

```
bool useFancyNumbers = ops.HasFlag(CardDeckSettings.FancyNumbers);
                           ↑                    ↑
                       Flag word              Bit flag
```

The HasFlag method can also check for multiple bit flags. For example, the following code checks whether the flag word, ops, has both the Animation and FancyNumbers bits set. The code does the following:

- The first statement creates a test word instance, called testFlags, with the Animation and FancyNumbers bits set.

- It then passes testFlags as the parameter to the HasFlag method.

HasFlags checks whether *all* the flags that are set in the test word are also set in the flag word, ops. If they are, then HasFlag returns true. Otherwise, it returns false.

```
CardDeckSettings testFlags =
          CardDeckSettings.Animation | CardDeckSettings.FancyNumbers;

bool useAnimationAndFancyNumbers = ops.HasFlag( testFlags );
                                     ↑              ↑
                                 Flag word      Test word
```

Another method of determining whether one or more particular bits is set is to use the bitwise AND operator. For example, like the previous code, the following code checks a flag word to see whether the FancyNumbers bit flag is set. It does this by ANDing the flag word with the bit flag and then comparing that result with the bit flag. If the bit was set in the original flag word, then the result of the AND operation will have the same bit pattern as the bit flag.

```
bool useFancyNumbers =
    (ops & CardDeckSettings.FancyNumbers) == CardDeckSettings.FancyNumbers;
```

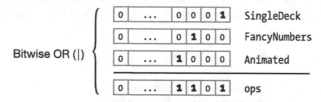

Figure 12-5 illustrates the process of creating the flag word and then using the bitwise AND operation to determine whether a particular bit is set.

Figure 12-5. *Producing a flag word and checking it for a particular bit flag*

The Flags Attribute

The preceding code used the Flags attribute just before declaring the enum, as copied here:

```
[Flags]
enum CardDeckSettings : uint
{
    ...
}
```

The Flags attribute does not change the calculations at all. It does, however, provide several convenient features. First, it informs the compiler, object browsers, and other tools looking at the code that the members of the enum are meant to be combined as bit flags, rather than used only as separate values. This allows the browsers to interpret variables of the enum type more appropriately.

Second, it allows the ToString method of an enum to provide more appropriate formatting for the values of bit flags. The ToString method takes an enum value and compares it to the values of the constant members of the enum. If it matches one of the members, ToString returns the string name of the member.

Examine, for example, the following code, where the enum is not prefaced by the Flags attribute:

```
enum CardDeckSettings : uint
{
    SingleDeck      = 0x01,      // bit 0
    LargePictures   = 0x02,      // bit 1
    FancyNumbers    = 0x04,      // bit 2
    Animation       = 0x08       // bit 3
}

class Program {
    static void Main( ) {
        CardDeckSettings ops;
        ops = CardDeckSettings.FancyNumbers;                        // Set one flag.
        Console.WriteLine( ops.ToString() );

                                                                   // Set two bit flags.
        ops = CardDeckSettings.FancyNumbers | CardDeckSettings.Animation;
        Console.WriteLine( ops.ToString() );                       // Print what?
    }
}
```

This code produces the following output:

```
FancyNumbers
12
```

In this code, method Main does the following:

- Creates a variable of the enum type CardDeckSettings, sets one of its bit flags, and prints out the value of the variable—which is the value FancyNumbers

- Assigns the variable a new value, which consists of two of the bit flags being set, and prints out its value—which is 12

The value 12, displayed as the result of the second assignment, is the value of ops, as an int, since FancyNumbers sets the bit for the value 4, and Animation sets the bit for the value 8—giving an int value of 12. In the WriteLine method following the assignment, when the ToString method tries to look up the name of the enum member with a value of 12, it finds that there is no member with that value—so it just prints out the value.

If, however, we were to add back the Flags attribute before the declaration of the enum, this would tell the ToString method that the bits can be considered separately. In looking up the value, ToString would then find that 12 corresponds to two separate bit flag members—FancyNumbers and Animation—and would return the string containing their names, separated by a comma and a space.

The following shows the result of running the code again, with the `Flags` attribute:

```
FancyNumbers
FancyNumbers, Animation
```

Example Using Bit Flags

The following code puts together all the pieces of using bit flags:

```
[Flags]
enum CardDeckSettings : uint
{
    SingleDeck      = 0x01,      // bit 0
    LargePictures   = 0x02,      // bit 1
    FancyNumbers    = 0x04,      // bit 2
    Animation       = 0x08       // bit 3
}

class MyClass {
    bool UseSingleDeck               = false,
         UseBigPics                  = false,
         UseFancyNumbers             = false,
         UseAnimation                = false,
         UseAnimationAndFancyNumbers = false;

    public void SetOptions( CardDeckSettings ops ) {
        UseSingleDeck   = ops.HasFlag( CardDeckSettings.SingleDeck );
        UseBigPics      = ops.HasFlag( CardDeckSettings.LargePictures );
        UseFancyNumbers = ops.HasFlag( CardDeckSettings.FancyNumbers );
        UseAnimation    = ops.HasFlag( CardDeckSettings.Animation );

        CardDeckSettings testFlags =
                    CardDeckSettings.Animation | CardDeckSettings.FancyNumbers;
        UseAnimationAndFancyNumbers = ops.HasFlag( testFlags );
    }

    public void PrintOptions( )
    {
        Console.WriteLine( "Option settings:" );
        Console.WriteLine($"  Use Single Deck              - { UseSingleDeck }");
        Console.WriteLine($"  Use Large Pictures           - { UseBigPics }");
        Console.WriteLine($"  Use Fancy Numbers            - { UseFancyNumbers }");
        Console.WriteLine($"  Show Animation               - { UseAnimation }");
        Console.WriteLine( "  Show Animation and FancyNumbers - {0}",
                        UseAnimationAndFancyNumbers );
    }
}
```

```
class Program
{
    static void Main( )
    {
        MyClass mc = new MyClass( );
        CardDeckSettings ops = CardDeckSettings.SingleDeck
                             | CardDeckSettings.FancyNumbers
                             | CardDeckSettings.Animation;
        mc.SetOptions( ops );
        mc.PrintOptions( );
    }
}
```

This code produces the following output:

```
Option settings:
   Use Single Deck                    - True
   Use Large Pictures                 - False
   Use Fancy Numbers                  - True
   Show Animation                     - True
   Show Animation and FancyNumbers    - True
```

More About Enums

Enums have only a single member type: the declared member constants.

- You cannot use modifiers with the members. They all implicitly have the same accessibility as the enum.

- The members are static, which, as you'll recall, means that they are accessible even if there are no variables of the enum type.

For example, the following code does not create any variables of the enum TrafficLight type, but because the members are static, they are accessible and can be printed using WriteLine.

```
static void Main()
{
   Console.WriteLine($"{ TrafficLight.Green }");
   Console.WriteLine($"{ TrafficLight.Yellow }");
   Console.WriteLine($"{ TrafficLight.Red }");
}                              ↑         ↑
                         Enum name  Member name
```

- As with all statics, there are two ways of accessing their members.

  - You can use the type name, followed by a dot and the member name, as shown in the previous code and the code samples throughout this chapter.

  - Starting with C# 6.0 you can use the using static directive to avoid the extra work and clutter of having to include the class name with every usage. This can make your code considerably cleaner.

If you use the using static directive for both TrafficLight and the Console class in the previous code, it becomes the following, which is much cleaner and less cluttered:

```
using static TrafficLight;
using static System.Console;
   ...
static void Main()
{
   WriteLine( $"{ Green }" );
   WriteLine( $"{ Yellow }" );
   WriteLine( $"{ Red }" );
}
```

An enum is a distinct type. Comparing enum members of different enum types results in a compile-time error. For example, the following code declares two different enum types with the exact same structure and member names:

- The first if statement is fine because it compares different members from the same enum type.

- The second if statement produces an error because it attempts to compare members from different enum types. This error occurs even though the structures and member names are exactly the same.

```
enum FirstEnum                          // First enum type
{
    Mem1,
    Mem2
}

enum SecondEnum                         // Second enum type
{
    Mem1,
    Mem2
}

class Program
{
    static void Main()
    {
        if (FirstEnum.Mem1 < FirstEnum.Mem2)    // OK--members of same enum type
            Console.WriteLine("True");

        if (FirstEnum.Mem1 < SecondEnum.Mem1)   // Error--different enum types
            Console.WriteLine("True");
    }
}
```

There are also several useful `static` methods of the .NET Enum type, on which enum is based.

- The GetName method takes an enum type object and an integer and returns the name of the corresponding enum member.

- The GetNames method takes an enum type object and returns all the names of all the members in the enum.

The following code shows an example of each of these methods being used. Notice that you have to use the typeof operator to get the enum type object.

```
enum TrafficLight
{
    Green,
    Yellow,
    Red
}

class Program
{
    static void Main()
    {
        Console.WriteLine( "Second member of TrafficLight is {0}\n",
                           Enum.GetName( typeof( TrafficLight ), 1 ) );

        foreach ( var name in Enum.GetNames( typeof( TrafficLight ) ) )
            Console.WriteLine( name );
    }
}
```

This code produces the following output:

```
Second member of TrafficLight is Yellow

Green
Yellow
Red
```

CHAPTER 13

■ ■ ■

Arrays

© Daniel Solis and Cal Schrotenboer 2018

D. Solis and C. Schrotenboer, *Illustrated C# 7*, https://doi.org/10.1007/978-1-4842-3288-0_13

Arrays

An array is a set of uniform data elements represented by a single variable name. The individual elements are accessed using the variable name together with one or more indexes between square brackets, as shown here:

```
Array name  Index
     ↓       ↓
   MyArray[4]
```

Definitions

Let's start with some important definitions having to do with arrays in C#.

- *Elements*: The individual data items of an array are called *elements*. All elements of an array must be of the same type or derived from the same type.

- *Rank/dimensions*: Arrays can have any positive number of dimensions. The number of dimensions an array has is called its *rank*.

- *Dimension length*: Each dimension of an array has a *length*, which is the number of positions in that direction.

- *Array length*: The total number of elements contained in an array, in *all* dimensions, is called the *length* of the array.

Important Details

The following are some important general facts about C# arrays:

- Once an array is created, its size is fixed. C# does not support dynamic arrays.

- Array indexes are *0-based*. That is, if the length of a dimension is n, the index values range from 0 to $n - 1$. For example, Figure 13-1 shows the dimensions and lengths of two example arrays. Notice that for each dimension, the indexes range from 0 to *length* – 1.

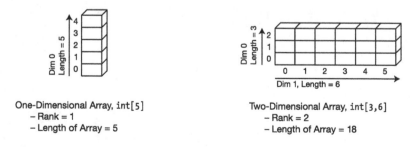

One-Dimensional Array, int[5]
  – Rank = 1
  – Length of Array = 5

Two-Dimensional Array, int[3,6]
  – Rank = 2
  – Length of Array = 18

Figure 13-1. *Dimensions and sizes*

Types of Arrays

C# provides two kinds of arrays.

- One-dimensional arrays can be thought of as a single line, or *vector*, of elements.
- Multidimensional arrays are composed such that each position in the primary vector is itself an array, called a *subarray*. Positions in the subarray vectors can themselves be subarrays.

Additionally, there are two types of multidimensional arrays: *rectangular arrays* and *jagged arrays*; they have the following characteristics:

- Rectangular arrays

    – Are multidimensional arrays where all the subarrays in a particular dimension have the same length

    – Always use a single set of square brackets, regardless of the number of dimensions

    ```
    int x = myArray2[4, 6, 1]     // One set of square brackets
    ```

- Jagged arrays

    – Are multidimensional arrays where each subarray is an independent array

    – Can have subarrays of *different* lengths

    – Use a separate set of square brackets for each dimension of the array

    ```
    jagArray1[2][7][4]            // Three sets of square brackets
    ```

Figure 13-2 shows the kinds of arrays available in C#.

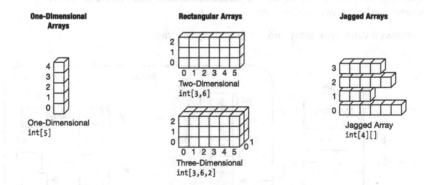

Figure 13-2. One-dimensional, rectangular, and jagged arrays

An Array As an Object

An array instance is an object whose type derives from class System.Array. Since arrays are derived from this BCL base class, they inherit a number of useful members from it, such as the following:

- Rank: A property that returns the number of dimensions of the array

- Length: A property that returns the length (the total number of elements) of the array

Arrays are reference types, and as with all reference types, they have both a reference to the data and the data object itself. The reference is either on the stack or in the heap, and the data object itself is always in the heap. Figure 13-3 shows the memory configuration and components of an array.

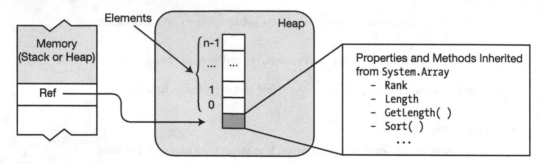

Figure 13-3. *Structure of an array*

Although an array is always a reference type, the elements of the array can be either value types or reference types.

- An array is called a *value type array* if the elements stored are value types.

- An array is called a *reference type array* if the elements stored in the array are references of reference type objects.

Figure 13-4 shows a value type array and a reference type array.

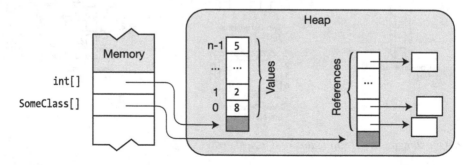

Figure 13-4. *Elements can be values or references.*

One-Dimensional and Rectangular Arrays

Syntactically, one-dimensional arrays and rectangular arrays are similar, so we'll treat them together. We'll then treat jagged arrays separately.

Declaring a One-Dimensional or Rectangular Array

To declare a one-dimensional or rectangular array, use a single set of square brackets between the type and the variable name.

The *rank specifiers* are commas between the brackets. They specify the number of dimensions the array will have. The rank is the number of commas, plus one. For example, having no commas indicates a one-dimensional array, one comma indicates a two-dimensional array, and so forth.

The base type, together with the rank specifiers, is the *type* of the array. For example, the following line of code declares a one-dimensional array of longs. The type of the array is long[ ], which is read as "an array of longs."

```
Rank specifiers = 1
        ↓
long[ ] secondArray;
 ↑
Array type
```

The following code shows examples of declarations of rectangular arrays. Notice the following:

- You can have as many rank specifiers as you need.

- You cannot place array dimension lengths in the array type section. The rank is part of the array's type, but the lengths of the dimensions are *not* part of the type.

- When an array is declared, the *number* of dimensions is fixed. The *length* of the dimensions, however, is not determined until the array is instantiated.

```
Rank specifiers
      ↓
int[,,]   firstArray;              // Array type: 3D array of int
int[,]    arr1;                    // Array type: 2D array of int
long[,,]  arr3;                    // Array type: 3D array of long
 ↑
Array type

long[3,2,6] SecondArray;           // Wrong!  Compile error
     ↑ ↑ ↑
Dimension lengths not allowed!
```

■ **Note**   Unlike in C/C++, in C# the brackets follow the base type, not the variable name.

Instantiating a One-Dimensional or Rectangular Array

To instantiate an array, you use an *array-creation expression*. An array-creation expression consists of the new operator, followed by the base type, followed by a pair of square brackets. The length of each dimension is placed in a comma-separated list between the brackets.

The following are examples of one-dimensional array declarations.

- Array arr2 is a one-dimensional array of four ints.

- Array mcArr is a one-dimensional array of four MyClass references.

Figure 13-5 shows their layouts in memory.

```
                 Four elements
                      ↓
int[]     arr2  = new int[4];
MyClass[] mcArr = new MyClass[4];
                      ↑
           Array-creation expression
```

The following is an example of a rectangular array.

- Array arr3 is a three-dimensional array.

- The length of the array is 3 * 6 * 2 = 36.

Figure 13-5 shows its layout in memory.

```
             Lengths of the dimensions
                      ↓
int[,,] arr3 = new int[3,6,2];
```

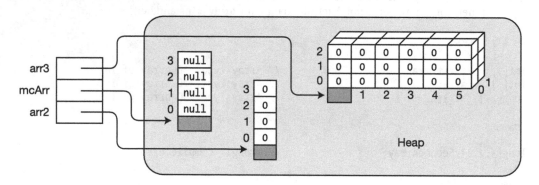

Figure 13-5. *Declaring and instantiating arrays*

■ **Note**   Unlike object-creation expressions, array-creation expressions do not contain parentheses—even for reference type arrays.

Accessing Array Elements

An array element is accessed using an integer value as an index into the array.

- Each dimension uses 0-based indexing.

- The index is placed between square brackets following the array name.

The following code shows examples of declaring, writing to, and reading from a one-dimensional array and a two-dimensional array:

```
int[]  intArr1 = new int[15];       // Declare 1D array of 15 elements.
intArr1[2]     = 10;                // Write to element 2 of the array.
int var1       = intArr1[2];        // Read from element 2 of the array.

int[,] intArr2 = new int[5,10];     // Declare 2D array.
intArr2[2,3]   = 7;                 // Write to the array.
int var2       = intArr2[2,3];      // Read from the array.
```

The following code shows the full process of creating and accessing a one-dimensional array:

```
int[] myIntArray;                           // Declare the array.

myIntArray = new int[4];                    // Instantiate the array.

for( int i=0; i<4; i++ )                    // Set the values.
   myIntArray[i] = i*10;

// Read and display the values of each element.
for( int i=0; i<4; i++ )
   Console.WriteLine($"Value of element { i } = { myIntArray[i] }");
```

This code produces the following output:

```
Value of element 0 is 0
Value of element 1 is 10
Value of element 2 is 20
Value of element 3 is 30
```

Initializing an Array

Whenever an array is created, each of the elements is automatically initialized to the default value for the type. The default values for the predefined types are 0 for integer types, 0.0 for floating-point types, false for Booleans, and null for reference types. For example, the following code creates an array and initializes its four elements to the value 0. Figure 13-6 illustrates the layout in memory.

```
int[] intArr = new int[4];
```

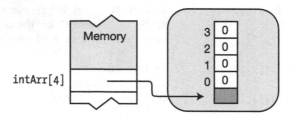

Figure 13-6. *Automatic initialization of a one-dimensional array*

Explicit Initialization of One-Dimensional Arrays

For a one-dimensional array, you can set explicit initial values by including an *initialization list* immediately after the array-creation expression of an array instantiation.

- The initialization values must be separated by commas and enclosed in a set of curly braces.

- The dimension lengths are optional since the compiler can infer the lengths from the number of initializing values.

- Notice that nothing separates the array-creation expression and the initialization list. That is, there is no equal sign or other connecting operator.

For example, the following code creates an array and initializes its four elements to the values between the curly braces. Figure 13-7 illustrates the layout in memory.

```
                               Initialization list
                                      ↓
int[] intArr = new int[] { 10, 20, 30, 40 };
                         ↑
                  No connecting operator
```

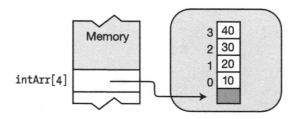

Figure 13-7. *Explicit initialization of a one-dimensional array*

Explicit Initialization of Rectangular Arrays

To explicitly initialize a rectangular array, you need to follow these rules:

- Each *vector of initial values* must be enclosed in curly braces.

- Each *dimension* must also be nested and enclosed in curly braces.

- In addition to the initial values, the initialization lists and components of each dimension must also be separated by commas.

For example, the following code shows the declaration of a two-dimensional array with an initialization list. Figure 13-8 illustrates the layout in memory.

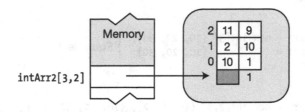

Figure 13-8. *Initializing a rectangular array*

Syntax Points for Initializing Rectangular Arrays

Rectangular arrays are initialized with nested, comma-separated initialization lists. The initialization lists are nested in curly braces. This can sometimes be confusing, so to get the nesting, grouping, and commas right, consider the following tips:

- Commas are used as *separators* between all *elements* and *groups*.

- Commas are *never* placed between left curly braces.

- Commas are *never* placed before a right curly brace.

- If possible, use indentation and carriage returns to arrange the groups so that they're visually distinct.

- Read the rank specifications from left to right, designating the last number as "elements" and all the others as "groups."

For example, read the following declaration as "intArray has four groups of three groups of two elements":

Initialization lists, nested and separated by commas

```
int[,,] intArray = new int[4,3,2] {          ↓          ↓          ↓
                               { {8, 6},   {5,  2}, {12, 9} },
                               { {6, 4},   {13, 9}, {18, 4} },
                               { {7, 2},   {1, 13}, {9,  3} },
                               { {4, 6},   {3,  2}, {23, 8} }
                             };
```

Shortcut Syntax

When combining declaration, array creation, and initialization in a single statement, you can omit the array-creation expression part of the syntax entirely and provide just the initialization portion. Figure 13-9 shows this shortcut syntax.

```
int[] arr1 = new int[3] {10, 20, 30};  }
int[] arr1 =              {10, 20, 30};  } Equivalent


int[,] arr = new int[2,3] {{0, 1, 2}, {10, 11, 12}};  }
int[,] arr =               {{0, 1, 2}, {10, 11, 12}};  } Equivalent
```

Figure 13-9. *Shortcut for array declaration, creation, and initialization*

Implicitly Typed Arrays

So far, we've explicitly specified the array types at the beginnings of all our array declarations. But, like other local variables, your local arrays can also be implicitly typed. This means the following:

- When initializing an array, you can let the compiler infer the array's type from the type of the initializers. This is allowed as long as all the initializers can be implicitly converted to a single type.

- Just as with implicitly typed local variables, use the keyword var instead of the array type.

The following code shows explicit and implicit versions of three array declarations. The first set is a one-dimensional array of ints. The second is a two-dimensional array of ints. The third is an array of strings. Notice that in the declaration of implicitly typed intArr4 you still need to include the rank specifier in the initialization.

```
 Explicit               Explicit
    ↓                       ↓
 int [] intArr1 = new int[] { 10, 20, 30, 40 };
 var    intArr2 = new    [] { 10, 20, 30, 40 };
  ↑                      ↑
 Keyword                Inferred
 int[,] intArr3 = new int[,] { { 10, 1 }, { 2, 10 }, { 11, 9 } };
 var    intArr4 = new    [,] { { 10, 1 }, { 2, 10 }, { 11, 9 } };
                         ↑
                    Rank specifier
 string[] sArr1 = new string[] { "life", "liberty", "pursuit of happiness" };
 var      sArr2 = new       [] { "life", "liberty", "pursuit of happiness" };
```

327

Putting It All Together

The following code puts together all the pieces we've looked at so far. It creates, initializes, and uses a rectangular array.

```
// Declare, create, and initialize an implicitly typed array.
var arr = new int[,] {{0, 1, 2}, {10, 11, 12}};

// Print the values.
for( int i=0; i<2; i++ )
   for( int j=0; j<3; j++ )
      Console.WriteLine($"Element [{ i },{ j }] is { arr[i,j] }");
```

This code produces the following output:

```
Element [0,0] is 0
Element [0,1] is 1
Element [0,2] is 2
Element [1,0] is 10
Element [1,1] is 11
Element [1,2] is 12
```

Jagged Arrays

A jagged array is an array of arrays. Unlike rectangular arrays, the subarrays of a jagged array can have different numbers of elements.

For example, the following code declares a two-dimensional jagged array. Figure 13-10 shows the array's layout in memory.

- The length of the first dimension is 3.

- The declaration can be read as "jagArr is an array of three arrays of ints."

- Notice that the figure shows *four* array objects—one for the top-level array and three for the subarrays.

```
int[][] jagArr = new int[3][];   // Declare and create top-level array.
         ...                     // Declare and create subarrays.
```

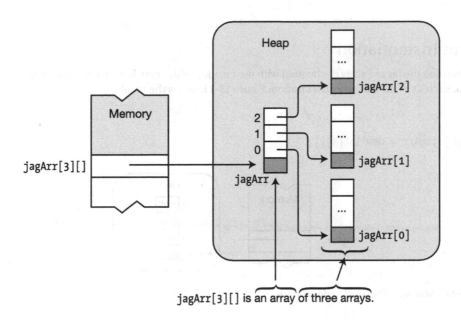

Figure 13-10. A jagged array is an array of arrays

Declaring a Jagged Array

The declaration syntax for jagged arrays requires a separate set of square brackets for each dimension. The number of sets of square brackets in the declaration of the array variable determines the rank of the array.

- A jagged array can be of any number of dimensions greater than one.

- As with rectangular arrays, dimension lengths cannot be included in the array type section of the declaration.

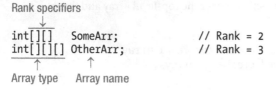

```
Rank specifiers
        ↓
int[][]   SomeArr;          // Rank = 2
int[][][] OtherArr;         // Rank = 3
  ↑         ↑
Array type  Array name
```

Shortcut Instantiation

You can combine the jagged array declaration with the creation of the first-level array using an array-creation expression, such as in the following declaration. Figure 13-11 shows the result.

```
          Three subarrays
               ↓
int[][] jagArr = new int[3][];
```

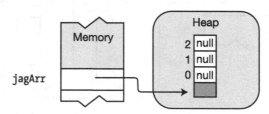

Figure 13-11. *Shortcut first-level instantiation*

You cannot instantiate more than the first-level array in the declaration statement.

```
                 Allowed
                    ↓
int[][] jagArr = new int[3][4];              // Wrong! Compile error
                         ↑
                     Not allowed
```

Instantiating a Jagged Array

Unlike other types of arrays, you cannot fully instantiate a jagged array in a single step. Since a jagged array is an array of independent arrays, each array must be created separately. Instantiating a full jagged array requires the following steps:

1. Instantiate the top-level array.

2. Instantiate each subarray separately, assigning the reference of the newly created array to the appropriate element of its containing array.

For example, the following code shows the declaration, instantiation, and initialization of a two-dimensional jagged array. Notice in the code that the reference to each subarray is assigned to an element in the top-level array. Steps 1 through 4 in the code correspond to the numbered representations in Figure 13-12.

```
int[][] Arr = new int[3][];                  // 1. Instantiate top level.

Arr[0] = new int[] {10, 20, 30};             // 2. Instantiate subarray.
Arr[1] = new int[] {40, 50, 60, 70};         // 3. Instantiate subarray.
Arr[2] = new int[] {80, 90, 100, 110, 120};  // 4. Instantiate subarray.
```

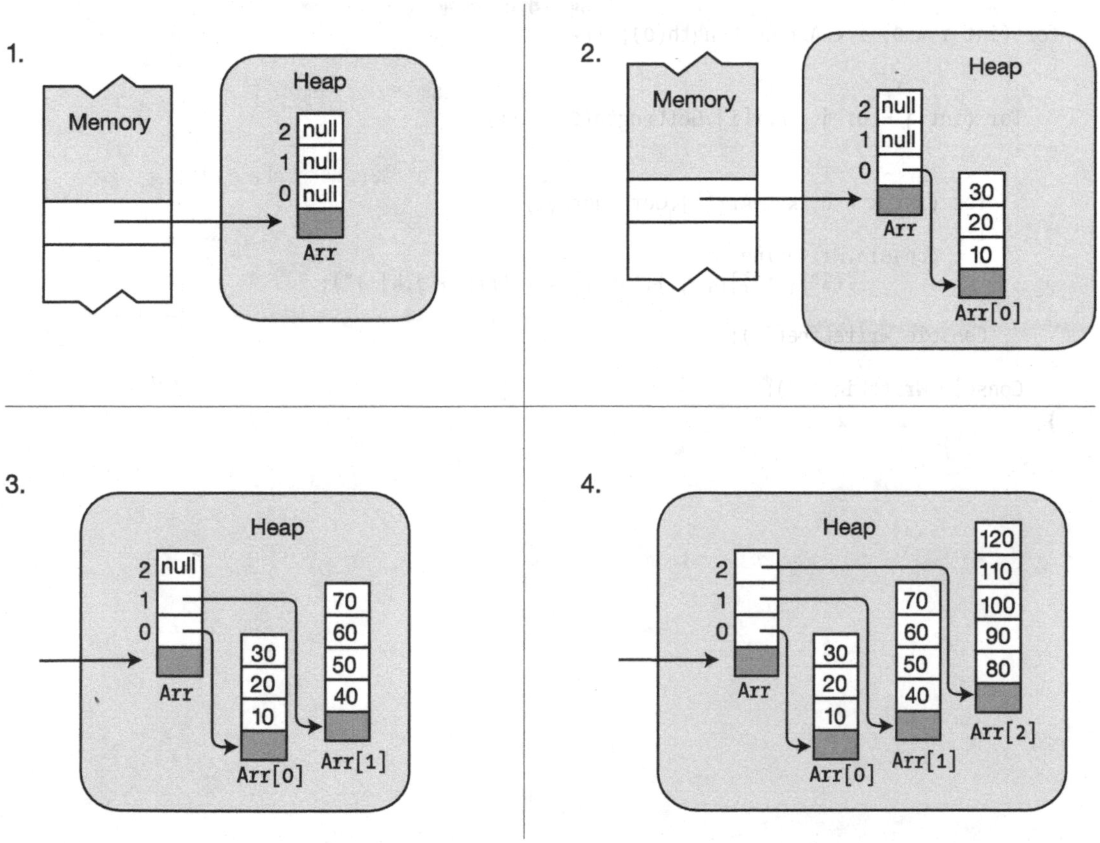

Figure 13-12. *Creating a two-dimensional jagged array*

Subarrays in Jagged Arrays

Since the subarrays in a jagged array are themselves arrays, it's possible to have rectangular arrays inside jagged arrays. For example, the following code creates a jagged array of three two-dimensional rectangular arrays and initializes them with values. It then displays the values. Figure 13-13 illustrates the structure.

The code uses the GetLength(int n) method of arrays, inherited from System.Array, to get the length of the specified dimension of the array.

```
int[][,] Arr;              // An array of 2D arrays
Arr = new int[3][,];       // Instantiate an array of three 2D arrays.

Arr[0] = new int[,] { { 10,  20  },
                      { 100, 200 } };

Arr[1] = new int[,] { { 30,  40,  50  },
                      { 300, 400, 500 } };

Arr[2] = new int[,] { { 60,  70,  80,  90  },
                      { 600, 700, 800, 900 } };
```

```
                              ↓ Get length of dimension 0 of Arr.
for (int i = 0; i < Arr.GetLength(0); i++)
{
                                  ↓ Get length of dimension 0 of Arr[ i ].
   for (int j = 0; j < Arr[i].GetLength(0); j++)
   {
                                      ↓ Get len gth of dimension 1 of Arr[ i ].
      for (int k = 0; k < Arr[i].GetLength(1); k++)
      {
         Console.WriteLine
                 ($"[{ i }][{ j },{ k }] = { Arr[i][j,k] }");
      }
      Console.WriteLine("");
   }
   Console.WriteLine("");
}
```

This code produces the following output:

```
[0][0,0] = 10
[0][0,1] = 20

[0][1,0] = 100
[0][1,1] = 200

[1][0,0] = 30
[1][0,1] = 40
[1][0,2] = 50

[1][1,0] = 300
[1][1,1] = 400
[1][1,2] = 500

[2][0,0] = 60
[2][0,1] = 70
[2][0,2] = 80
[2][0,3] = 90

[2][1,0] = 600
[2][1,1] = 700
[2][1,2] = 800
[2][1,3] = 900
```

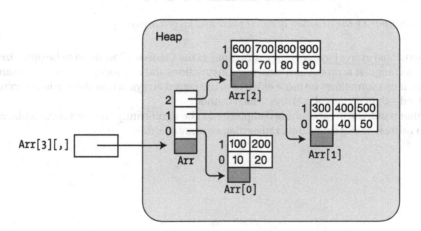

Figure 13-13. *Jagged array of three two-dimensional arrays*

Comparing Rectangular and Jagged Arrays

The structure of rectangular and jagged arrays is significantly different. For example, Figure 13-14 shows the structure of a rectangular three-by-three array, as well as a jagged array of three one-dimensional arrays of length 3.

- Both arrays hold nine integers, but as you can see, their structures are quite different.

- The rectangular array has a single array object, while the jagged array has four array objects.

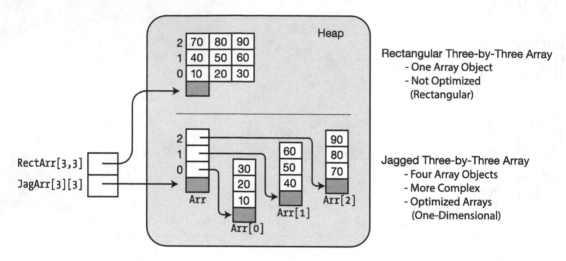

Figure 13-14. *Comparing the structure of rectangular and jagged arrays*

One-dimensional arrays have specific instructions in the CIL that allow them to be optimized for performance. Rectangular arrays do not have these instructions and are not optimized to the same level. Because of this, it can sometimes be more efficient to use jagged arrays of one-dimensional arrays—which can be optimized—than rectangular arrays, which cannot.

On the other hand, the programming complexity can be significantly less for a rectangular array because it can be treated as a single unit, rather than an array of arrays.

The foreach Statement

The foreach statement allows you to sequentially access each element in an array. It's actually a more general construct in that it also works with other collection types—but in this section we'll only discuss its use with arrays. Chapter 19 covers its use with other collection types.

The important points of the foreach statement are the following:

- The *iteration variable* is a temporary variable of the same type as the elements of the array. The foreach statement uses the iteration variable to sequentially represent each element in the array.

- The syntax of the foreach statement is shown next, where

  - Type is the type of the elements of the array. You can explicitly supply its type, or you can use var and let it be implicitly typed and inferred by the compiler since the compiler knows the type of the array.

  - Identifier is the name of the iteration variable.

  - ArrayName is the name of the array to be iterated through.

  - Statement is a simple statement or a block that is executed once for each element in the array.

Explicitly typed iteration variable declaration
         ↓
```
foreach( Type Identifier in ArrayName )
    Statement
```

Implicitly typed iteration variable declaration
         ↓
```
foreach( var Identifier in ArrayName )
    Statement
```

In the following text, we'll sometimes use implicit typing and other times we'll use explicit typing so that you can see the exact type being used. But the forms are semantically equivalent.

The foreach statement works in the following way:

- It starts with the first element of the array and assigns that value to the *iteration variable*.

- It then executes the body of the statement. Inside the body, you can use the iteration variable as a read-only alias for the array element.

- After the body is executed, the foreach statement selects the next element in the array and repeats the process.

In this way, it cycles through the array, allowing you to access each element one by one. For example, the following code shows the use of a foreach statement with a one-dimensional array of four integers:

- The WriteLine statement, which is the body of the foreach statement, is executed once for each of the elements of the array.

- The first time through the loop, iteration variable item has the value of the first element of the array. Each successive time, it has the value of the next element in the array.

```
int[] arr1 = { 10, 11, 12, 13 };
Iteration variable declaration
                    ↓
                 ───────
                                        Iteration variable use
    foreach( int item in arr1 )                ↓
        Console.WriteLine( $"Item Value: { item }");
```

This code produces the following output:

```
Item Value: 10
Item Value: 11
Item Value: 12
Item Value: 13
```

The Iteration Variable Is Read-Only

Since the value of the iteration variable is read-only, clearly it cannot be changed. But this has different effects on value type arrays and reference type arrays.

For value type arrays, this means you cannot change an element of the array when it's being represented by the iteration variable. For example, in the following code, the attempt to change the data in the iteration variable produces a compile-time error message:

```
int[] arr1 = {10, 11, 12, 13};

foreach( int item in arr1 )
    item++;      // Compilation error. Changing variable value is not allowed.
```

For reference type arrays, you still cannot change the iteration variable, but the iteration variable only holds the reference to the data, not the data itself. So although you cannot change the reference, you can change the *data* through the iteration variable.

The following code creates an array of four MyClass objects and initializes them. In the first foreach statement, the data in each of the objects is changed. In the second foreach statement, the changed data is read from the objects.

```
class MyClass {
    public int MyField = 0;
}

class Program {
    static void Main() {
        MyClass[] mcArray = new MyClass[4];                // Create array.
        for (int i = 0; i < 4; i++)
        {
            mcArray[i] = new MyClass();                    // Create class objects.
            mcArray[i].MyField = i;                        // Set field.
        }
        foreach (MyClass item in mcArray)
            item.MyField += 10;                            // Change the data.

        foreach (MyClass item in mcArray)
            Console.WriteLine($"{ item.MyField }");        // Read the changed data.
    }
}
```

This code produces the following output:

```
10
11
12
13
```

The foreach Statement with Multidimensional Arrays

In a multidimensional array, the elements are processed in the order in which the rightmost index is incremented fastest. When the index has gone from 0 to *length* – 1, the next index to the left is incremented, and the indexes to the right are reset to 0.

Example with a Rectangular Array

The following example shows the foreach statement used with a rectangular array:

```
class Program
{
    static void Main()
    {
        int total = 0;
        int[,] arr1 = { {10, 11}, {12, 13} };

        foreach( var element in arr1 )
        {
            total += element;
            Console.WriteLine
                    ($"Element: { element }, Current Total: { total }");
        }
    }
}
```

This code produces the following output:

```
Element: 10, Current Total: 10
Element: 11, Current Total: 21
Element: 12, Current Total: 33
Element: 13, Current Total: 46
```

Example with a Jagged Array

Since jagged arrays are arrays of arrays, you must use separate foreach statements for each dimension in the jagged array. The foreach statements must be nested properly to make sure that each nested array is processed properly.

For example, in the following code, the first foreach statement cycles through the top-level array—arr1—selecting the next subarray to process. The inner foreach statement processes the elements of that subarray.

```
class Program
{
    static void Main( )
    {
        int total       = 0;
        int[][] arr1 = new int[2][];
        arr1[0]        = new int[] { 10, 11 };
        arr1[1]        = new int[] { 12, 13, 14 };

        foreach (int[] array in arr1)        // Process the top level.
        {
            Console.WriteLine("Starting new array");
            foreach (int item in array)      // Process the second level.
            {
                total += item;
                Console.WriteLine
                          ($"  Item: { item }, Current Total: { total }");
            }
        }
    }
}
```

This code produces the following output:

```
Starting new array
  Item: 10, Current Total: 10
  Item: 11, Current Total: 21
Starting new array
  Item: 12, Current Total: 33
  Item: 13, Current Total: 46
  Item: 14, Current Total: 60
```

Array Covariance

Under certain conditions, you can assign an object to an array element even if the object is not of the array's base type. This property of arrays is called *array covariance*. You can use array covariance if the following are true:

- The array is a reference type array.

- There is an implicit or explicit conversion between the type of the object you are assigning and the array's base type.

Since there is always an implicit conversion between a derived class and its base class, you can always assign an object of a derived class to an array declared for the base class.

For example, the following code declares two classes, A and B, where class B derives from class A. The last line shows covariance by assigning objects of type B to array elements of type A. Figure 13-15 shows the memory layout for the code.

```
class A { ... }                              // Base class
class B : A { ... }                          // Derived class

class Program {
   static void Main() {
      A[] AArray1 = new A[3];    // Two arrays of type A[]
      A[] AArray2 = new A[3];    //

      // Normal--assigning objects of type A to an array of type A
      AArray1[0] = new A(); AArray1[1] = new A(); AArray1[2] = new A();

      // Covariant--assigning objects of type B to an array of type A
      AArray2[0] = new B(); AArray2[1] = new B(); AArray2[2] = new B();
   }
}
```

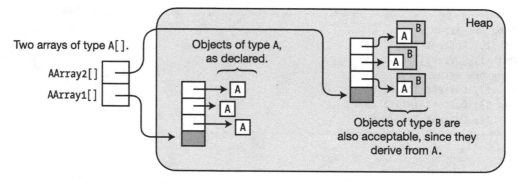

Figure 13-15. *Arrays showing covariance*

■ **Note**   There is no covariance for value type arrays.

Useful Inherited Array Members

We mentioned earlier that C# arrays are derived from class System.Array. From that base class they inherit a number of useful properties and methods. Table 13-1 lists some of the most useful ones.

Table 13-1. *Some Useful Members Inherited by Arrays*

Member	Type	Lifetime	Meaning
Rank	Property	Instance	Gets the number of dimensions of the array
Length	Property	Instance	Gets the total number of elements in all the dimensions of the array
GetLength	Method	Instance	Returns the length of a particular dimension of the array
Clear	Method	Static	Sets a range of elements to 0 or null
Sort	Method	Static	Sorts the elements in a one-dimensional array
BinarySearch	Method	Static	Searches a one-dimensional array for a value, using binary search
Clone	Method	Instance	Performs a shallow copy of the array—copying only the elements, both for arrays of value types and reference types
IndexOf	Method	Static	Returns the index of the first occurrence of a value in a one-dimensional array
Reverse	Method	Static	Reverses the order of the elements of a range of a one-dimensional array
GetUpperBound	Method	Instance	Gets the upper bound at the specified dimension

For example, the following code uses some of these properties and methods:

```
public static void PrintArray(int[] a)
{
    foreach (var x in a)
        Console.Write($"{ x }  ";

    Console.WriteLine("");
}

static void Main()
{
    int[] arr = new int[] { 15, 20, 5, 25, 10 };
    PrintArray(arr);

    Array.Sort(arr);
    PrintArray(arr);

    Array.Reverse(arr);
    PrintArray(arr);

    Console.WriteLine();
    Console.WriteLine($"Rank = { arr.Rank }, Length = { arr.Length }");
    Console.WriteLine($"GetLength(0)     = { arr.GetLength(0) }");
    Console.WriteLine($"GetType()        = { arr.GetType() }");
}
```

This code produces the following output:

```
15   20   5   25   10
5    10   15   20   25
25   20   15   10   5

Rank = 1, Length = 5
GetLength(0)      = 5
GetType()         = System.Int32[]
```

The Clone Method

The Clone method performs a shallow copy of an array. This means that it only creates a clone of the array itself. If it is a reference type array, it does *not* copy the objects referenced by the elements. This has different results for value type arrays and reference type arrays.

- Cloning a value type array results in two independent arrays.

- Cloning a reference type array results in two arrays pointing at the same objects.

The Clone method returns a reference of type object, which must be cast to the array type.

```
int[] intArr1 = { 1, 2, 3 };
                Array type    Returns an object
                   ↓               ↓
int[] intArr2 = (int[]) intArr1.Clone();
```

For example, the following code shows an example of cloning a value type array, producing two independent arrays. Figure 13-17 illustrates the steps shown in the code.

```
static void Main()
{
   int[] intArr1 = { 1, 2, 3 };                            // Step 1
   int[] intArr2 = (int[]) intArr1.Clone();                // Step 2

   intArr2[0] = 100; intArr2[1] = 200; intArr2[2] = 300;   // Step 3
}
```

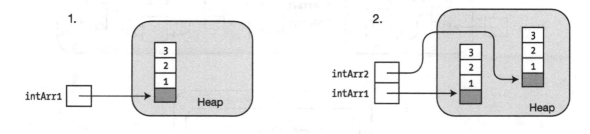

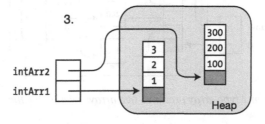

Figure 13-16. *Cloning a value type array produces two independent arrays*

Cloning a reference type array results in two arrays *pointing at the same objects*. The following code shows an example. Figure 13-17 illustrates the steps shown in the code.

```
class A
{
   public int Value = 5;
}

class Program
{
   static void Main()
   {
      A[] AArray1 = new A[3] { new A(), new A(), new A() };    // Step 1
      A[] AArray2 = (A[]) AArray1.Clone();                     // Step 2

      AArray2[0].Value = 100;
      AArray2[1].Value = 200;
      AArray2[2].Value = 300;                                  // Step 3
   }
}
```

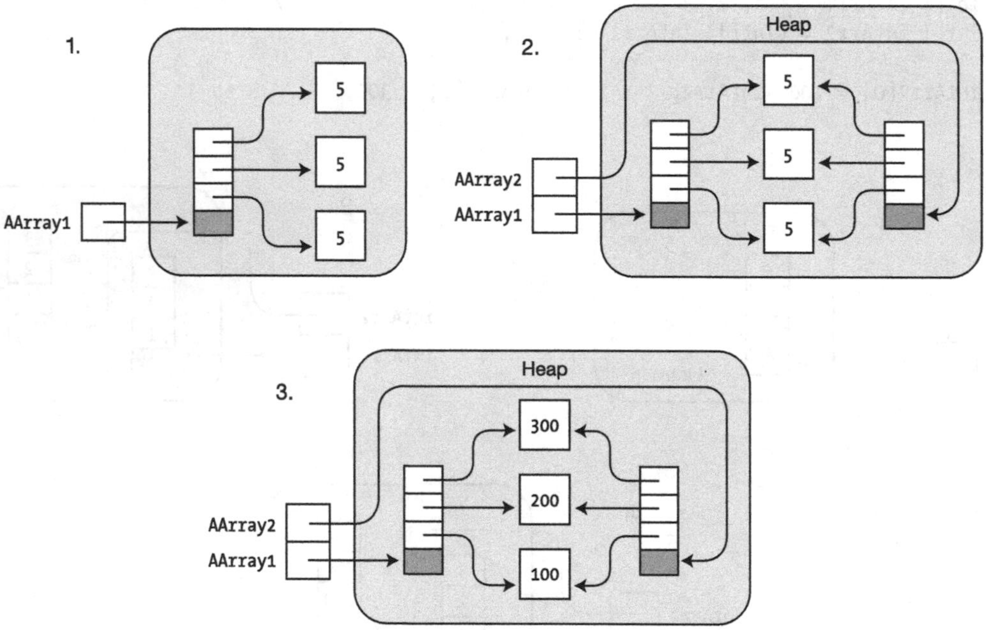

Figure 13-17. Cloning a reference type array produces two arrays referencing the same objects

Comparing Array Types

Table 13-2 summarizes some of the important similarities and differences between the three types of arrays.

Table 13-2. *Summary Comparing Array Types*

Array Type	Array Objects	Syntax		Shape
		Brackets	**Commas**	
One-dimensional • Has optimizing instructions in CIL.	One	Single set	No	One-Dimensional int[3]
Rectangular • Multidimensional. • All subarrays in a multidimensional array must be of the same length.	One	Single set	Yes	Two-Dimensional int[3,6] Three-Dimensional int[3,6,2]
Jagged • Multidimensional. • Subarrays can be of different lengths.	Multiple	Multiple sets	No	Jagged int[4][]

Arrays and Ref Return and Ref Local

We described the ref return and ref local features in detail in Chapter 6. One of their common uses, however, is to pass a reference to an array *element* back to the calling scope, so we'll just give a quick example of that here, now that we've explained arrays.

Remember that using the ref return feature allows you to pass a reference back out of a method as a return value, and a ref local allows you to use that reference in the calling scope. For example, the following code defines a method called PointerToHighestPositive. This method takes an array as its parameter and returns a reference to the element of the array—*not* the int value held in that element. Then, back in the calling scope, you can assign to that element through the ref local.

```
class Program
{               Keyword for ref return method
                        ↓
    public static ref int PointerToHighestPositive(int[] numbers)
    {
        int highest       = 0;
        int indexOfHighest = 0;

        for (int i = 0; i < numbers.Length; i++) {
            if (numbers[i] > highest)
            {
                indexOfHighest = i;
                highest        = numbers[indexOfHighest];
            }
        }

        return ref numbers[indexOfHighest];
    }            ↑
             Keyword for ref return

    static void Main() {
        int[] scores = { 5, 80 };
        Console.WriteLine($"Before: {scores[0]}, {scores[1]}");
        ref int locationOfHigher = ref PointerToHighestPositive(scores);
          ↑                         ↑
      Keyword for ref local     Keyword for ref local
        locationOfHigher = 0;       // Change the value through ref local
        Console.WriteLine($"After : {scores[0]}, {scores[1]}");
    }
}
```

This code produces the following output:

```
Before: 5, 80
After : 5, 0
```

CHAPTER 14

■ ■ ■

Delegates

© Daniel Solis and Cal Schrotenboer 2018
D. Solis and C. Schrotenboer, *Illustrated C# 7*, https://doi.org/10.1007/978-1-4842-3288-0_14

What Is a Delegate?

You can think of a delegate as an object that holds one or more methods. Normally, of course, you wouldn't think of "executing" an *object*, but a delegate is different from a typical object. You can execute a delegate, and when you do so, it executes the method or methods that it "holds."

In this chapter we'll explain the syntax and semantics of creating and using delegates. In later chapters you'll see how you can use delegates to pass executable code from one method to another—and why that's a useful thing.

We'll start with the example code on the next page. Don't worry if everything isn't completely clear at this point, because we'll explain the details of delegates throughout the rest of the chapter.

- The code starts with the declaration of a delegate type called MyDel. (Yes, a delegate *type—not* a delegate *object*. We'll get to this shortly.)

- Class Program declares three methods: PrintLow, PrintHigh, and Main. The delegate object we will create shortly will hold either the PrintLow or PrintHigh method—but which one will be used won't be determined until run time.

- Main declares a local variable called del, which will hold a reference to a delegate object of type MyDel. This doesn't create the object—it just creates the variable that will hold a reference to the delegate object, which will be created and assigned to it several lines below.

- Main creates an object of the .NET class Random, which is a random-number-generator class. The program then calls the object's Next method, with 99 as its input parameter. This returns a random integer between 0 and 99 and stores that value in local variable randomValue;.

- The next line checks whether the random value returned and stored is less than 50. (Notice that we're using the ternary conditional operator here to return one or the other of the delegate objects.)

  - If the value is less than 50, it creates a MyDel delegate object and initializes it to hold a reference to the PrintLow method.

  - Otherwise, it creates a MyDel delegate object that holds a reference to the PrintHigh method.

- Finally, Main *executes* the del delegate object, which executes whichever method (PrintLow or PrintHigh) it's holding.

■ **Note** If you're coming from a C++ background, the fastest way for you to understand delegates is to think of them as type-safe, object-oriented C++ function pointers on steroids.

```
delegate void MyDel(int value);    // Declare delegate TYPE.

class Program
{
   void PrintLow( int value )
   {
      Console.WriteLine($"{ value } - Low Value");
   }

   void PrintHigh( int value )
   {
      Console.WriteLine($"{ value } - High Value");
   }

   static void Main( )
   {
      Program program = new Program();

      MyDel    del;               // Declare delegate variable.

      // Create random-integer-generator object and get a random
      // number between 0 and 99.
      Random   rand     = new Random();
      int randomValue = rand.Next( 99 );

      // Create a delegate object that contains either PrintLow or
      // PrintHigh, and assign the object to the del variable.
      del = randomValue < 50
               ? new MyDel( program.PrintLow  )
               : new MyDel( program.PrintHigh );

      del( randomValue );    // Execute the delegate.
   }
}
```

Because we're using the random-number generator, the program will produce different values on different runs. One run of the program produced the following output:

```
28 - Low Value
```

An Overview of Delegates

Now let's go into the details. A delegate is a user-defined type, just as a class is a user-defined type. But whereas a class represents a collection of data and methods, a delegate holds one or more methods and a set of predefined operations. You use a delegate by performing the following steps. We'll go through each of these steps in detail in the following sections.

1. Declare a delegate type. A delegate declaration looks like a method declaration, except that it doesn't have an implementation block.

2. Declare a delegate variable of the delegate type.

3. Create an object of the delegate type and assign it to the delegate variable. The new delegate object includes a reference to a method that must have the same signature and return type as the delegate type defined in the first step.

4. You can optionally add additional methods into the delegate object. These methods must have the same signature and return type as the delegate type defined in the first step.

5. Throughout your code you can then invoke the delegate, just as it if it were a method. When you invoke the delegate, each of the methods it contains is executed.

In looking at the previous steps, you might have noticed that they're similar to the steps in creating and using a class. Figure 14-1 compares the processes of creating and using classes and delegates.

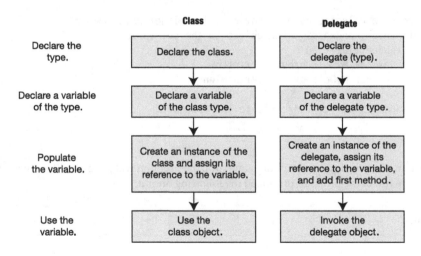

Figure 14-1. *A delegate is a user-defined reference type, like a class*

You can think of a delegate as an object that contains an ordered list of methods with the same signature and return type, as illustrated in Figure 14-2.

- The list of methods is called the *invocation list*.

- Methods held by a delegate *can be from any class or struct,* as long as they match *both* of the following:

  - The delegate's return type

  - The delegate's signature (including `ref` and `out` modifiers)

- Methods in the invocation list can be either instance methods or static methods.

- When a delegate is invoked, each method in its invocation list is executed.

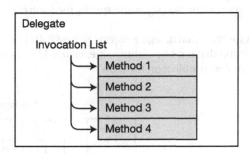

Figure 14-2. *A delegate as a list of methods*

Declaring the Delegate Type

As we stated in the previous section, delegates are types, just as classes are types. And as with classes, a delegate type must be declared before you can use it to create variables and objects of the type. The following example code declares a delegate type:

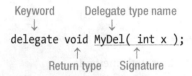

The declaration of a delegate type looks much like the declaration of a method, in that it has both a *return type* and a *signature*. The return type and signature specify the form of the methods that the delegate will accept.

The preceding declaration specifies that delegate objects of type MyDel will only accept methods that have a single int parameter and that have no return value. Figure 14-3 shows a representation of the delegate type on the left and the delegate object on the right.

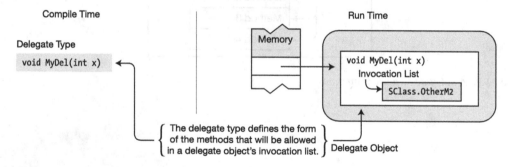

Figure 14-3. *Delegate type and object*

The delegate type declaration differs from a method declaration in two ways. The delegate type declaration

- Is prefaced with the keyword delegate
- Does not have a method body

■ **Note** Even though the delegate type declaration looks like a method declaration, it doesn't need to be declared inside a class because it's a type declaration.

CHAPTER 14 ■ DELEGATES

Creating the Delegate Object

A delegate is a reference type and therefore has both a reference and an object. After a delegate type is declared, you can declare variables and create objects of the type. The following code shows the declaration of a variable of a delegate type:

```
Delegate type    Variable
     ↓              ↓
    MyDel    delVar;
```

There are two ways you can create a delegate object. The first is to use an object-creation expression with the new operator, as shown in the following code. The operand of the new operator consists of the following:

- The delegate type name.

- A set of parentheses containing the name of a method to use as the first member in the invocation list. *The method can be either an instance method or a static method.*

```
                   Instance method
                         ↓
delVar = new MyDel( myInstObj.MyM1 );     // Create delegate and save ref.
dVar   = new MyDel( SClass.OtherM2 );     // Create delegate and save ref.
                         ↑
                   Static method
```

You can also use the shortcut syntax, which consists of just the method specifier, as shown in the following code. This code and the preceding code are semantically equivalent. Using the shortcut syntax works because there is an implicit conversion between a method name and a compatible delegate type.

```
delVar = myInstObj.MyM1;         // Create delegate and save reference.
dVar   = SClass.OtherM2;         // Create delegate and save reference.
```

353

For example, the following code creates two delegate objects: one with an instance method and the other with a static method. Figure 14-4 shows the instantiations of the delegates. This code assumes that there is an object called myInstObj, which is an instance of a class that has defined a method called MyM1, which returns no value and takes an int as a parameter. It also assumes that there is a class called SClass, which has a static method OtherM2 with a return type and signature matching those of delegate MyDel.

```
delegate void MyDel(int x);            // Declare delegate type.
MyDel delVar, dVar;                    // Create two delegate variables.
                    Instance method
                         ↓
delVar = new MyDel( myInstObj.MyM1 );  // Create delegate and save ref.
dVar   = new MyDel( SClass.OtherM2 );  // Create delegate and save ref.
                         ↑
                    Static method
```

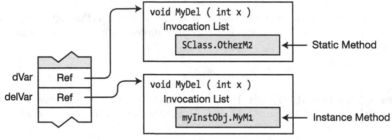

Figure 14-4. *Instantiating the delegates*

Besides allocating the memory for the delegate, creating a delegate object also places the first method in the delegate's invocation list.

You can also create the variable and instantiate the object in the same statement, using the initializer syntax. For example, the following statements also produce the same configuration shown in Figure 14-4:

```
MyDel delVar = new MyDel( myInstObj.MyM1 );
MyDel dVar   = new MyDel( SClass.OtherM2 );
```

The following statements use the shortcut syntax but again produce the results shown in Figure 14-4:

```
MyDel delVar = myInstObj.MyM1;
MyDel dVar   = SClass.OtherM2;
```

Assigning Delegates

Because delegates are reference types, you can change the reference contained in a delegate variable by assigning to it. The old delegate object will be disposed of by the garbage collector (GC) when it gets around to it.

For example, the following code sets and then changes the value of delVar. Figure 14-5 illustrates the code.

```
MyDel delVar;
delVar = myInstObj.MyM1;        // Create and assign the delegate object.

   ...
delVar = SClass.OtherM2;        // Create and assign the new delegate object.
```

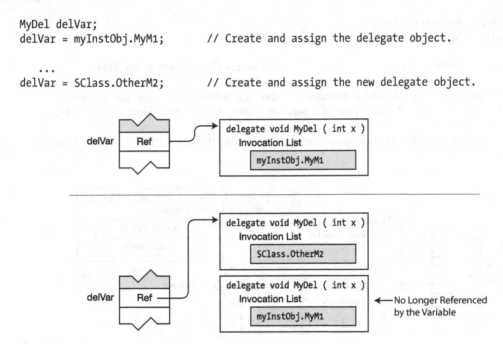

Figure 14-5. *Assigning to a delegate variable*

Combining Delegates

All the delegates you've seen so far have had only a single method in their invocation lists. Delegates can be "combined" by using the addition operator. The result of the operation is the creation of a new delegate, with an invocation list that is the concatenation of copies of the invocation lists of the two operand delegates.

For example, the following code creates three delegates. The third delegate is created from the combination of the first two.

```
MyDel delA = myInstObj.MyM1;
MyDel delB = SClass.OtherM2;

MyDel delC = delA + delB;                    // Has combined invocation list
```

Although the term *combining delegates* might give the impression that the operand delegates are modified, they are not changed at all. In fact, *delegates are immutable*. After a delegate object is created, it cannot be changed.

Figure 14-6 illustrates the results of the preceding code. Notice that the operand delegates remain unchanged.

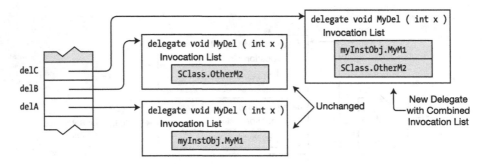

Figure 14-6. *Combining delegates*

Adding Methods to Delegates

Although you saw in the previous section that delegates are, in reality, immutable, C# provides syntax for making it appear that you can add a method to a delegate, using the += operator.

For example, the following code "adds" two methods to the invocation list of the delegate. The methods are added to the bottom of the invocation list. Figure 14-7 shows the result.

```
MyDel delVar  = inst.MyM1;    // Create and initialize.
delVar        += SC1.m3;      // Add a method.
delVar        += X.Act;       // Add a method.
```

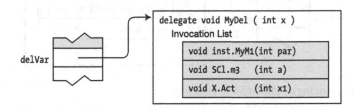

Figure 14-7. *Result of "adding" methods to a delegate. In reality, because delegates are immutable, the resulting delegate with three methods in its invocation list is an entirely new delegate pointed at by the variable.*

What is actually happening, of course, is that when the += operator is used, a new delegate is created, with an invocation list that is the combination of the delegate on the left and the method listed on the right. This new delegate is then assigned to the delVar variable.

You can add a method to a delegate more than once. Each time you add it, it creates a new element in the invocation list.

Removing Methods from a Delegate

You can also remove a method from a delegate, using the -= operator. The following line of code shows the use of the operator. Figure 14-8 shows the result of this code when applied to the delegate illustrated in Figure 14-7.

```
delVar -= SCl.m3;              // Remove the method from the delegate.
```

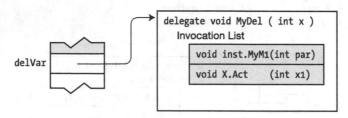

Figure 14-8. *Result of removing a method from a delegate*

As with adding a method to a delegate, the resulting delegate is actually a new delegate. The new delegate is a copy of the old delegate—but its invocation list no longer contains the reference to the method that was removed.

The following are some things to remember when removing methods:

- If there are multiple entries for a method in the invocation list, the -= operator *starts searching at the bottom of the list* and removes the first instance of the matching method it finds.

- Attempting to delete a method that is not in the invocation list has no effect.

- Attempting to invoke an empty delegate throws an exception. You can check whether a delegate's invocation list is empty by comparing the delegate to null. If the invocation list is empty, the delegate is null.

Invoking a Delegate

The important things to know about invoking a delegate are the following:

- You can invoke a delegate in either of two ways. First, you can call the delegate as if it were simply a method. Second, you can use the Invoke method on the delegate.

- Place the parameters within the parentheses of the call, as shown in the next code block. The parameters used to invoke the delegate are used to invoke each of the methods on the invocation list (unless one of the parameters is an output parameter, which we'll cover shortly).

- If a method is in the invocation list more than once, then when the delegate is invoked, the method will be called each time it is encountered in the list.

- The delegate must not be empty (null) when invoked, or it will throw an exception. You can use an if statement to check, or you can use the null conditional operator and the Invoke method.

The following code shows an example of creating and using the delVar delegate, which takes a single integer input value. Invoking the delegate with a parameter causes it to invoke each of the members in its invocation list with the same parameter value. The code shows both ways of invoking the delegate—calling as method and using Invoke. Figure 14-9 illustrates the invocation.

```
MyDel delVar   = inst.MyM1;
delVar        += SC1.m3;
delVar        += X.Act;
    ...
if (delVar != null)
   { delVar(55); }          // Invoke the delegate.
delVar?.Invoke(65);         // Using Invoke with the null conditional operator
    ...
```

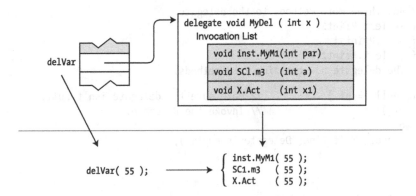

Figure 14-9. *When the delegate is invoked, it executes each of the methods in its invocation list, with the same parameters with which it was called.*

Delegate Example

The following code defines and uses a delegate with no parameters and no return value. Note the following about the code:

- Class Test defines two print functions.

- Method Main creates an instance of the delegate and then adds three more methods.

- The program then invokes the delegate, which calls its methods. Before invoking the delegate, however, it checks to make sure it's not null.

```
// Define a delegate type with no return value and no parameters.
delegate void PrintFunction();

class Test
{
    public void Print1()
    { Console.WriteLine("Print1 -- instance"); }

    public static void Print2()
    { Console.WriteLine("Print2 -- static"); }
}

class Program
{
    static void Main()
    {
        Test t = new Test();      // Create a test class instance.
        PrintFunction pf;         // Create a null delegate.

        pf = t.Print1;            // Instantiate and initialize the delegate.

        // Add three more methods to the delegate.
        pf += Test.Print2;
        pf += t.Print1;
        pf += Test.Print2;
        // The delegate now contains four methods.

        if( null != pf )          // Make sure the delegate isn't null.
            pf();                 // Invoke the delegate.
        else
            Console.WriteLine("Delegate is empty");
    }
}
```

This code produces the following output:

```
Print1 -- instance
Print2 -- static
Print1 -- instance
Print2 -- static
```

Invoking Delegates with Return Values

If a delegate has a return value and more than one method in its invocation list, the following occurs:

- The value returned by the last method in the invocation list is the value returned from the delegate invocation.

- The return values from all the other methods in the invocation list are ignored.

For example, the following code declares a delegate that returns an int value. Main creates an object of the delegate and adds two additional methods. It then calls the delegate in the WriteLine statement and prints its return value. Figure 14-10 shows a graphical representation of the code.

```
delegate int MyDel( );              // Declare delegate with return value.
class MyClass {
   int IntValue = 5;
   public int Add2() { IntValue += 2; return IntValue;}
   public int Add3() { IntValue += 3; return IntValue;}
}

class Program {
   static void Main( ) {
      MyClass mc = new MyClass();
      MyDel mDel = mc.Add2;          // Create and initialize the delegate.
      mDel += mc.Add3;               // Add a method.
      mDel += mc.Add2;               // Add a method.
      Console.WriteLine($"Value: { mDel() }");
   }                                        ↑
}                     Invoke the delegate and use the return value.
```

This code produces the following output:

Value: 12

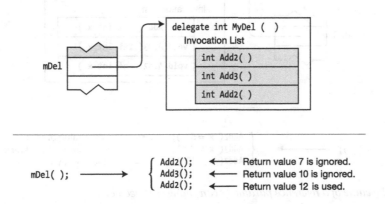

Figure 14-10. *The return value of the last method executed is the value returned by the delegate.*

Invoking Delegates with Reference Parameters

If a delegate has a reference parameter, the value of the parameter can change upon return from one or more of the methods in the invocation list.

When calling the next method in the invocation list, the *new value of the parameter—not the initial value*—is the one passed to the next method. For example, the following code invokes a delegate with a reference parameter. Figure 14-11 illustrates the code.

```
delegate void MyDel( ref int X );

class MyClass {
   public void Add2(ref int x) { x += 2; }
   public void Add3(ref int x) { x += 3; }
   static void Main() {
      MyClass mc = new MyClass();

      MyDel mDel = mc.Add2;
      mDel += mc.Add3;
      mDel += mc.Add2;

      int x = 5;
      mDel(ref x);

      Console.WriteLine($"Value: { x }");
   }
}
```

This code produces the following output:

Value: 12

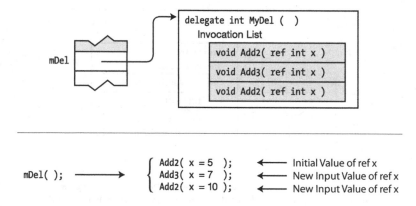

Figure 14-11. *The value of a reference parameter can change between calls*

Anonymous Methods

So far, you've seen that you can use either static methods or instance methods to instantiate a delegate. In either case, the method itself can be called explicitly from other parts of the code and, of course, must be a member of some class or struct.

What if, however, the method is used only one time—to instantiate the delegate? In that case, other than the syntactic requirement for creating the delegate, there is no real need for a separate, named method. Anonymous methods allow you to dispense with the separate, named method.

An *anonymous method* is a method that is declared inline, at the point of instantiating a delegate. For example, Figure 14-12 shows two versions of the same class. The version on the left declares and uses a method named Add20. The version on the right uses an anonymous method instead. The nonshaded code of both versions is identical.

```
class Program                                    class Program
{                                                {
  public static int Add20(int x)
  {
    return x + 20;
  }

  delegate int OtherDel(int InParam);              delegate int OtherDel(int InParam);
  static void Main()                               static void Main()
  {                                                {
    OtherDel del = Add20;                            OtherDel del = delegate(int x)
                                                                   {
                                                                     return x + 20;
                                                                   };
    Console.WriteLine("{0}", del(5));                Console.WriteLine("{0}", del(5));
    Console.WriteLine("{0}", del(6));                Console.WriteLine("{0}", del(6));
  }                                                }
}                                                }
          Named Method                                   Anonymous Method
```

Figure 14-12. Comparing a named method and an anonymous method

Both sets of code in Figure 14-12 produce the following output:

```
25
26
```

Using Anonymous Methods

You can use an anonymous method in the following places:

- As an initializer expression when declaring a delegate variable.

- On the right side of an assignment statement when combining delegates.

- On the right side of an assignment statement adding a delegate to an event. Chapter 15 covers events.

Syntax of Anonymous Methods

The syntax of an anonymous method expression includes the following components:

- The type keyword `delegate`

- The *parameter list*, which can be omitted if the statement block doesn't use any parameters

- The *statement block*, which contains the code of the anonymous method

```
        Parameter
Keyword   list                 Statement block
   ↓       ↓                        ↓
delegate ( Parameters ) { ImplementationCode }
```

Return Type

An anonymous method does not explicitly declare a return type. The behavior of the implementation code itself, however, must match the delegate's return type by returning a value of that type. If the delegate has a return type of void, then the anonymous method code cannot return a value.

For example, in the following code, the delegate's return type is int. The implementation code of the anonymous method must therefore return an int on all pathways through the code.

```
       Return type of delegate type
              ↓
delegate int OtherDel(int InParam);

static void Main()
{
    OtherDel del = delegate(int x)
                {
                      return x + 20 ;                   // Returns an int
                };
        ...
}
```

Parameters

Except in the case of array parameters, the parameter list of an anonymous method must match that of the delegate with respect to the following three characteristics:

- Number of parameters

- Types and positions of the parameters

- Modifiers

You can simplify the parameter list of an anonymous method by leaving the parentheses empty or omitting them altogether, but only if *both* of the following are true:

- The delegate's parameter list does not contain any out parameters.

- The anonymous method does not use *any* parameters.

For example, the following code declares a delegate that does not have any out parameters and an anonymous method that does not use any parameters. Since both conditions are met, you can omit the parameter list from the anonymous method.

```
delegate void SomeDel ( int X );            // Declare the delegate type.
SomeDel SDel = delegate                      // Parameter list omitted
                {
                    PrintMessage();
                    Cleanup();
                };
```

The params Parameters

If the delegate declaration's parameter list contains a params parameter, then the params keyword is omitted from the parameter list of the anonymous method. For example, in the following code,

- The delegate type declaration specifies the last parameter as a params type parameter.

- The anonymous method's parameter list, however, must omit the params keyword.

```
                params keyword used in delegate type declaration
                                    ↓
delegate void SomeDel( int X, params int[] Y);
                    params keyword omitted in matching anonymous method
                                    ↓
SomeDel mDel = delegate (int X, int[] Y)
            {
                ...
            };
```

Scope of Variables and Parameters

The scopes of parameters and local variables declared inside an anonymous method are limited to the body of the implementation code, as illustrated in Figure 14-13.

For example, the following anonymous method defines parameter y and local variable z. After the close of the body of the anonymous method, y and z are no longer in scope. The last line of the code would produce a compile error.

```
delegate void MyDel( int x );
...

MyDel mDel = delegate ( int y )
             {
                 int z = 10;
                 Console.WriteLine("{0}, {1}", y, z);
             };

Console.WriteLine("{0}, {1}", y, z);   // Compile error.
```

Scope of y and z

Out of Scope

Figure 14-13. Scope of variables and parameters

Outer Variables

Unlike the named methods of a delegate, anonymous methods have access to the local variables and environment of the scope surrounding them.

- Variables from the surrounding scope are called *outer variables*.

- An outer variable used in the implementation code of an anonymous method is said to be *captured* by the method.

For example, the code in Figure 14-14 shows variable x defined outside the anonymous method. The code in the method, however, has access to x and can print its value.

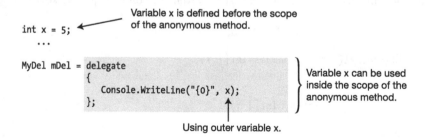

Variable x is defined before the scope of the anonymous method.

```
int x = 5;
...

MyDel mDel = delegate
             {
                 Console.WriteLine("{0}", x);
             };
```

Variable x can be used inside the scope of the anonymous method.

Using outer variable x.

Figure 14-14. Using an outer variable

Extension of a Captured Variable's Lifetime

A captured outer variable remains alive as long as its capturing method is part of the delegate, even if the variable would have normally gone out of scope.

For example, the code in Figure 14-15 illustrates the extension of a captured variable's lifetime.

- Local variable x is declared and initialized inside a block.

- Delegate mDel is then instantiated, using an anonymous method that captures outer variable x.

- When the block is closed, x goes out of scope.

- If the WriteLine statement following the close of the block were to be uncommented, it would cause a compile error because it references x, which is now out of scope.

- The anonymous method inside delegate mDel, however, maintains x in its environment and prints its value when mDel is invoked.

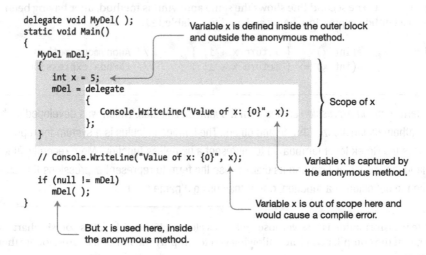

Figure 14-15. *Variable captured in an anonymous method*

The code in the figure produces the following output:

```
Value of x: 5
```

Lambda Expressions

C# 2.0 introduced anonymous methods, which we've just looked at. The syntax for anonymous methods, however, is somewhat verbose and requires information that the compiler itself already knows. Rather than requiring you to include this redundant information, C# 3.0 introduced *lambda expressions*, which pare down the syntax of anonymous methods. You'll probably want to use lambda expressions instead of anonymous methods. In fact, if lambda expressions had been introduced first, there never would have been anonymous methods.

In the anonymous method syntax, the `delegate` keyword is redundant because the compiler can already see that you're assigning the method to a delegate. You can easily transform an anonymous method into a lambda expression by doing the following:

- Delete the `delegate` keyword.

- Place the lambda operator, `=>`, between the parameter list and the body of the anonymous method. The lambda operator is read as "goes to."

The following code shows this transformation. The first line shows an anonymous method being assigned to variable del. The second line shows the same anonymous method, after having been transformed into a lambda expression, being assigned to variable le1.

```
MyDel del = delegate(int x)    { return x + 1; } ;    // Anonymous method
MyDel le1 =           (int x) => { return x + 1; } ;    // Lambda expression
```

■ **Note**   The term *lambda expression* comes from the *lambda calculus*, which was developed in the 1920s and 1930s by mathematician Alonzo Church and others. The lambda calculus is a system for representing functions and uses the Greek letter lambda (λ) to represent a nameless function. More recently, functional programming languages such as Lisp and its dialects use the term to represent expressions that can be used to directly describe the definition of a function, rather than using a name for it.

This simple transformation is less verbose and looks cleaner, but it only saves you six characters. There's more, however, that the compiler can infer, allowing you to simplify the lambda expression further, as shown in the following code.

- From the delegate's declaration, the compiler also knows the types of the delegate's parameters, so the lambda expression allows you to leave out the parameter types, as shown in the assignment to le2.

    - Parameters listed with their types are called *explicitly typed*.

    - Those listed without their types are called *implicitly typed*.

- If there's only a single, implicitly typed parameter, you can leave off the parentheses surrounding it, as shown in the assignment to le3.

- Finally, lambda expressions allow the body of the expression to be either a statement block or an expression. If the statement block contains a single return statement, you can replace the statement block with just the expression that follows the return keyword, as shown in the assignment to le4.

```
MyDel del = delegate(int x)     { return x + 1; } ;     // Anonymous method
MyDel le1 =             (int x) => { return x + 1; } ;    // Lambda expression
MyDel le2 =                 (x) => { return x + 1; } ;    // Lambda expression
MyDel le3 =                  x  => { return x + 1; } ;    // Lambda expression
MyDel le4 =                  x  =>          x + 1    ;    // Lambda expression
```

The final form of the lambda expression has about one-fourth the characters of the original anonymous method and is cleaner and easier to understand.

The following code shows the full transformation. The first line of Main shows an anonymous method being assigned to variable del. The second line shows the same anonymous method, after having been transformed into a lambda expression, being assigned to variable le1.

```
delegate double MyDel(int par);

class Program
{
    static void Main()
    {
        delegate int MyDel(int x);

        MyDel del = delegate(int x) { return x + 1; } ;   // Anonymous method

        MyDel le1 =        (int x) => { return x + 1; } ;  // Lambda expression
        MyDel le2 =            (x) => { return x + 1; } ;
        MyDel le3 =             x  => { return x + 1; } ;
        MyDel le4 =             x  =>          x + 1    ;

        Console.WriteLine($"{ del (12) }");
        Console.WriteLine($"{ le1 (12) }");
        Console.WriteLine($"{ le2 (12) }");
        Console.WriteLine($"{ le3 (12) }");
        Console.WriteLine($"{ le4 (12) }");
    }
}
```

This code produces the following output:

```
13
13
13
13
13
```

Some important points about lambda expression parameter lists are the following:

- The parameters in the parameter list of a lambda expression must match that of the delegate in number, type, and position.

- The parameters in the parameter list of an expression do not have to include the type (i.e., they're *implicitly typed*) unless the delegate has either ref or out parameters—in which case the types are required (i.e., they're *explicitly typed*).

- If there is only a single parameter and it is implicitly typed, the surrounding parentheses can be omitted. Otherwise, they are required.

- If there are no parameters, you must use an empty set of parentheses.

Figure 14-16 shows the syntax for lambda expressions.

```
( Parameter, Parameter, ... )
      ( Parameter )                =>       { Statements }
        Parameter                             Expression
          ( )
```

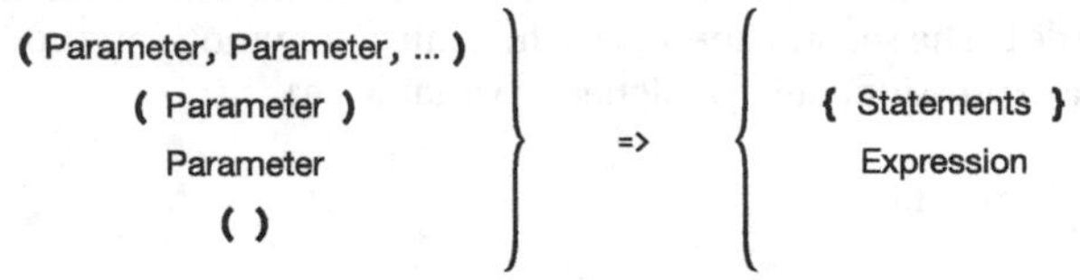

Figure 14-16. *The syntax for lambda expressions consists of the lambda operator, with the parameter section on the left and the lambda body on the right.*

CHAPTER 15

■ ■ ■

Events

© Daniel Solis and Cal Schrotenboer 2018

D. Solis and C. Schrotenboer, *Illustrated C# 7*, https://doi.org/10.1007/978-1-4842-3288-0_15

Publishers and Subscribers

One common requirement in many programs is that when a particular program event occurs, other parts of the program need to be notified that the event has occurred.

One pattern for satisfying this requirement is called the *publisher/subscriber pattern*. In this pattern, a class, called the *publisher*, defines a set of events that other parts of the program might be interested in. Other classes can then "sign up" to be notified by the publisher when these events occur. These *subscriber* classes "sign up" for notification by supplying a method to the publisher. When the event occurs, the publisher "raises the event," and all the methods submitted by the subscribers are executed.

The methods supplied by the subscribers are called *callback methods* because the publisher "calls the subscribers back" by executing their methods. They are also called *event handlers* because they are the code that is called to handle the event. Figure 15-1 illustrates the process, showing the publisher with an event and three subscribers to the event.

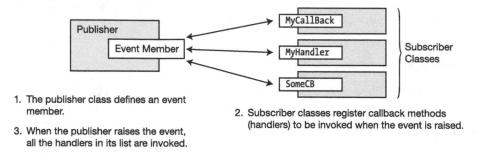

1. The publisher class defines an event member.

2. Subscriber classes register callback methods (handlers) to be invoked when the event is raised.

3. When the publisher raises the event, all the handlers in its list are invoked.

Figure 15-1. *Publishers and subscribers*

The following are some important terms related to events:

- *Publisher*: A class or struct that publishes an event so that other classes can be notified when the event occurs.

- *Subscriber*: A class or struct that registers to be notified when the event occurs.

- *Event handler*: A method that is registered with the publisher, by the subscriber, and is executed when the publisher raises the event. The event handler method can be declared in the same class or struct as the event or in a different class or struct.

- *Raising an event*: The term for *invoking* or *firing* an event. When an event is raised, all the methods registered with that event are invoked.

The preceding chapter covered delegates. Many aspects of events are similar to those of delegates. In fact, an event is like a simpler delegate that is specialized for a particular use. There's good reason for the similarities in the behaviors of delegates and events. An event contains a private delegate, as illustrated in Figure 15-2.

The important things to know about an event's private delegate are the following:

- An *event* gives structured access to its privately controlled delegate. That is, you can't directly access the delegate.

- There are fewer operations available than with a delegate. With an event you can only add and remove event handlers and invoke the event.

- When an event is raised, it invokes the delegate, which sequentially calls the methods in its invocation list.

Notice in Figure 15-2 that only the += and -= operators are sticking out to the left of the event box. This is because they are the only operations (apart from invoking the event itself) allowed on an event.

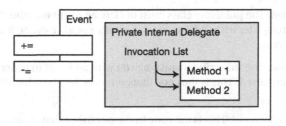

Figure 15-2. *An event has an encapsulated delegate.*

Figure 15-3 illustrates a program with a class called `Incrementer`, which performs a count of some sort.

- `Incrementer` defines an event called `CountedADozen`, which it raises every time it counts another dozen items.

- Subscriber classes `Dozens` and `SomeOtherClass` each have an event handler registered with the `CountedADozen` event.

- Each time the event is raised, the handlers are called.

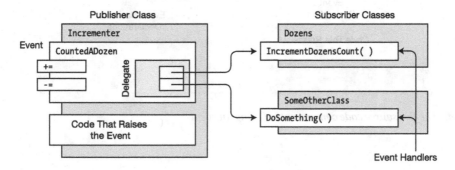

Figure 15-3. *Structure and terminology of a class with an event*

Overview of Source Code Components

There are five pieces of code that need to be in place to use events. These are illustrated in Figure 15-4. We'll cover each of them in the following sections. These pieces of code are the following:

- *Delegate type declaration*: The event and the event handlers must have a common signature and return type, which are specified by the delegate type. described by a delegate type.

- *Event handler declarations*: These are the declarations, in the subscriber classes, of the methods to be executed when the event is raised. These do not have to be explicitly named methods; they can also be anonymous methods or lambda expressions, as described in Chapter 14.

- *Event declaration*: The publisher class must declare an event member that subscribers can register with. When a class declares a `public` event, it is said to have *published the event*.

- *Event registration*: The subscribers must register with an event in order to be notified when it has been raised. This is the code that connects the event handlers to the event.

- *Code that raises the event*: This is the code in the publisher that "fires" the event, causing it to invoke all the event handlers registered with it.

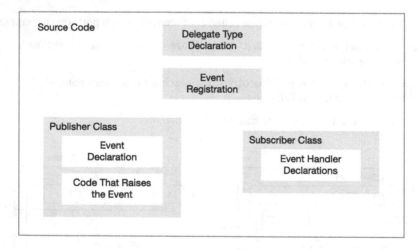

Figure 15-4. *The five source code components of using an event*

Declaring an Event

The publisher must provide the event object. Creating an event is simple—it requires only a delegate type and a name. The syntax for an event declaration is shown in the following code, which declares an event called CountedADozen. Notice the following about event CountedADozen:

- The event is declared inside a class.

- It requires the name of a delegate type. Any event handlers attached to the event (i.e., registered with it) must match the delegate type in signature and return type.

- It is declared public so that other classes and structs can register event handlers with it.

- You do not use an object-creation expression (a new expression) with an event.

```
class Incrementer
{
    public event EventHandler CountedADozen;
}
```

You can declare more than one event in a declaration statement by using a comma-separated list. For example, the following statement declares three events:

```
public event EventHandler MyEvent1, MyEvent2, OtherEvent;
```
                                        ↑
                                   Three events

You can also make events static by including the static keyword, as shown in the following declaration:

```
public static event EventHandler CountedADozen;
```
          ↑
       Keyword

An Event Is a Member

A common error is to think of an event as a type—which it's not. Like a method, or a property, an event is a *member of a class* or a struct, and there are several important ramifications to this.

- Because an event is a member,
  - You cannot declare an event in a block of executable code.
  - It must be declared in a class or struct, with the other members.
- An event member is implicitly and automatically initialized to `null` with the other members.

To declare an event, you must supply the name of a *delegate type*. You can either declare one or use one that already exists. If you declare a delegate type, it must specify the signature and return type of the methods that will be registered by the event.

The BCL declares a delegate called `EventHandler` specifically for use with system events. We'll describe the `EventHandler` delegate later in this chapter.

Subscribing to an Event

Subscribers add event handlers to the event. For an event handler to be added to an event, the handler must have the same return type and signature as the event's delegate.

- Use the += operator to add an event handler to an event, as shown in the following code. The event handler is placed on the right side of the operator.

- The event handler specification can be any of the following:

  - The name of an instance method

  - The name of a static method

  - An anonymous method

  - A lambda expression

For example, the following code adds three methods to event CountedADozen. The first is an instance method. The second is a static method. The third is an instance method, using the delegate form.

```
Class instance                      Instance method
      ↓                                   ↓
incrementer.CountedADozen += IncrementDozensCount;        // Method reference form
incrementer.CountedADozen += ClassB.CounterHandlerB;      // Method reference form
                ↑                        ↑
         Event member              Static method

mc.CountedADozen += new EventHandler(cc.CounterHandlerC); // Delegate form
```

Just as with delegates, you can use anonymous methods and lambda expressions to add event handlers. For example, the following code first uses a lambda expression and then uses an anonymous method:

```
// Lambda expression
incrementer.CountedADozen += () => DozensCount++;

// Anonymous method
incrementer.CountedADozen += delegate { DozensCount++; };
```

Raising an Event

The event member itself just holds the event handlers that need to be invoked. Nothing happens with them unless the event is raised. You need to make sure there is code to do just that, at the appropriate times.

For example, the following code raises event CountedADozen. Notice the following about the code:

- Before raising the event, the code compares it to null to see whether it contains any event handlers. If the event is null, it is empty and cannot be executed.

- The syntax for raising the event is the same as that of invoking a method.

  - Use the name of the event, followed by the parameter list enclosed in parentheses.

  - The parameter list must match the delegate type of the event.

```
if (CountedADozen != null)              // Make sure there are methods to execute.
    CountedADozen (source, args);       // Raise the event.
         ↑                ↑
    Event name       Parameter list
```

Putting together the event declaration and the code to raise the event gives the following class declaration for the publisher. The code contains two members: the event and a method called DoCount, which raises the event when appropriate.

```
class Incrementer
{
    public event EventHandler CountedADozen;   // Declare the event.

    void DoCount(object source, EventArgs args)
    {
        for( int i=1; i < 100; i++ )
            if( i % 12 == 0 )
                if (CountedADozen != null)          // Make sure there are methods to execute.
                    CountedADozen(source, args);
    }                                 ↑
}                              Raise the event.
```

The code in Figure 15-5 shows the whole program, with publisher class Incrementer and subscriber class Dozens. The things to note about the code are the following:

- In its constructor, class Dozens subscribes to the event, supplying method IncrementDozensCount as its event handler.

- In method DoCount in class Incrementer, event CountedADozen is raised each time the method increments another 12 times.

```
delegate void Handler();        Declare the delegate
```

Publisher

```
class Incrementer
{
    public event Handler CountedADozen;        Create and publish an event.

    public void DoCount()
    {
        for ( int i=1; i < 100; i++ )
            if ( i % 12 == 0 && CountedADozen != null )
                CountedADozen();        Raise the event every 12 counts.
    }
}
```

Subscriber

```
class Dozens
{
    public int DozensCount { get; private set; }

    public Dozens( Incrementer incrementer )
    {
        DozensCount = 0;
        incrementer.CountedADozen += IncrementDozensCount;        Subscribe to the event.
    }

    void IncrementDozensCount()
    {                                   Declare the event handler.
        DozensCount++;
    }
}
```

```
class Program
{
    static void Main( )
    {
        Incrementer incrementer = new Incrementer();
        Dozens dozensCounter    = new Dozens( incrementer );

        incrementer.DoCount();
        Console.WriteLine( "Number of dozens = {0}",
                            dozensCounter.DozensCount );
    }
}
```

Figure 15-5. *A complete program with a publisher and a subscriber, showing the five segments of code necessary for using an event*

The code in Figure 15-5 produces the following output:

```
Number of dozens = 8
```

Standard Event Usage

GUI programming is event driven, which means that while the program is running, it can be interrupted at any time by events such as button clicks, key presses, or system timers. When this happens, the program needs to handle the event and then continue on its course.

Clearly, this asynchronous handling of program events is the perfect situation for using C# events. Windows GUI programming uses events so extensively that there is a standard .NET Framework pattern for using them. The foundation of the standard pattern for event usage is the EventHandler delegate type, which is declared in the System namespace. The following line of code shows the declaration of the EventHandler delegate type. The things to notice about the declaration are the following:

- The first parameter is meant to hold a reference to the object that raised the event. It is of type object and can, therefore, match any instance of any type.

- The second parameter is meant to hold state information of whatever type is appropriate for the application.

- The return type is void.

```
public delegate void EventHandler(object sender, EventArgs e);
```

The second parameter in the EventHandler delegate type is an object of class EventArgs, which is declared in the System namespace. You might be tempted to think that since the second parameter is meant for passing data, an EventArgs class object would be able to store data of some sort. You would be wrong.

- The EventArgs class is designed to carry no data. It is used for event handlers that do not need to pass data—and is generally ignored by them.

- If you want to pass data, you must declare a class *derived* from EventArgs, with the appropriate fields to hold the data you want to pass.

Even though the EventArgs class does not actually pass data, it is an important part of the pattern of using the EventHandler delegate. These parameters, of types object and EventArgs, are the base classes for whatever actual types are used as the parameters. This allows the EventHandler delegate to provide a signature that is the lowest common denominator for all events and event handlers, allowing all events to have exactly two parameters, rather than having different signatures for each case.

If we modify the Incrementer program to use the EventHandler delegate, we have the program shown in Figure 15-6. Notice the following about the code:

- The declaration for delegate Handler has been removed since the event uses the system-defined EventHandler delegate.

- The signature of the event handler declaration in the subscriber class must match the signature (and return type) of the event delegate, which now uses parameters of type object and EventArgs. In the case of event handler IncrementDozensCount, the method just ignores the formal parameters.

- The code that raises the event must invoke the event with objects of the appropriate parameter types.

Publisher

```
class Incrementer
{
    public event EventHandler CountedADozen;          Use the system-defined
                                                      EventHandler delegate.
    public void DoCount()
    {
        for ( int i=1; i < 100; i++ )
            if ( i % 12 == 0 && CountedADozen != null )
                CountedADozen(this, null);    Use EventHandler's parameters
    }                                         when raising the event.
}
```

Subscriber

```
class Dozens
{
    public int DozensCount { get; private set; }

    public Dozens( Incrementer incrementer )
    {
        DozensCount = 0;
        incrementer.CountedADozen += IncrementDozensCount;
    }
                                                       The signature of the event
    void IncrementDozensCount(object source, EventArgs e)  handler must match that of
    {                                                      the delegate.
        DozensCount++;
    }
}
```

```
class Program
{
    static void Main( )
    {
        Incrementer incrementer = new Incrementer();
        Dozens dozensCounter    = new Dozens( incrementer );

        incrementer.DoCount();
        Console.WriteLine( "Number of dozens = {0}",
                            dozensCounter.DozensCount );
    }
}
```

Figure 15-6. *The Incrementer program modified to use the system-defined EventHandler delegate*

Passing Data by Extending EventArgs

To pass data in the second parameter of your event handler and adhere to the standard conventions, you need to declare a custom class derived from EventArgs that can store the data you need passed. By convention, the name of the class should end in EventArgs. For example, the following code declares a custom class that can store a string in a field called Message:

```
        Custom class name          Base class
                ↓                      ↓
public class IncrementerEventArgs : EventArgs
{
    public int IterationCount { get; set; }  // Stores an integer
}
```

Now that you have a custom class for passing data in the second parameter of your event handlers, you need a delegate type that uses the new custom class. To obtain this, use the generic version of delegate EventHandler<>. Chapter 18 covers C# generics in detail, so for now you'll just have to watch. To use the generic delegate, do the following, as shown in the subsequent code:

- Place the name of the custom class between the angle brackets.

- Use the entire string wherever you would have used the name of your custom delegate type. For example, this is what the event declaration would look like:

```
            Generic delegate using custom class
                            ↓
public event EventHandler<IncrementerEventArgs> CountedADozen;
                                                       ↑
                                                  Event name
```

Use the custom class and the custom delegate in the other four sections of code dealing with the event. For example, the following code updates the Incrementer code to use the custom EventArgs class called IncrementerEventArgs and the generic EventHandler<IncrementerEventArgs> delegate.

```
public class IncrementerEventArgs : EventArgs    // Custom class derived from EventArgs
{
    public int IterationCount { get; set; }       // Stores an integer
}

class Incrementer           Generic delegate using custom class
{                                         ↓
    public event EventHandler<IncrementerEventArgs> CountedADozen;

    public void DoCount()    Object of custom class
    {                               ↓
        IncrementerEventArgs args = new IncrementerEventArgs();
        for ( int i=1; i < 100; i++ )
            if ( i % 12 == 0 && CountedADozen != null )
            {
                args.IterationCount = i;
```

```
            CountedADozen( this, args );
         }                    ↑
      }                  Pass parameters when raising the event
}

class Dozens
{
   public int DozensCount { get; private set; }

   public Dozens( Incrementer incrementer )
   {
      DozensCount = 0;
      incrementer.CountedADozen += IncrementDozensCount;
   }

   void IncrementDozensCount( object source, IncrementerEventArgs e )
   {
      Console.WriteLine
         ($"Incremented at iteration: { e.IterationCount } in { source.ToString() }" );
      DozensCount++;
   }
}

class Program
{
   static void Main()
   {
      Incrementer incrementer = new Incrementer();
      Dozens dozensCounter    = new Dozens( incrementer );

      incrementer.DoCount();
      Console.WriteLine($"Number of dozens = { dozensCounter.DozensCount }");
   }

}
```

This program produces the following output, which displays the iteration when it was called and the fully qualified class name of the source object. We'll cover fully qualified class names in Chapter 22.

```
Incremented at iteration: 12 in Counter.Incrementer
Incremented at iteration: 24 in Counter.Incrementer
Incremented at iteration: 36 in Counter.Incrementer
Incremented at iteration: 48 in Counter.Incrementer
Incremented at iteration: 60 in Counter.Incrementer
Incremented at iteration: 72 in Counter.Incrementer
Incremented at iteration: 84 in Counter.Incrementer
Incremented at iteration: 96 in Counter.Incrementer
Number of dozens = 8
```

Removing Event Handlers

When you're done with an event handler, you can remove it from the event. You remove an event handler from an event by using the -= operator, as shown in the following line of code:

```
p.SimpleEvent -= s.MethodB;;          // Remove handler MethodB.
```

For example, the following code adds two handlers to event SimpleEvent and then raises the event. Each of the handlers is called and prints out a line of text. The MethodB handler is then removed from the event, and when the event is raised again, only the MethodB handler prints out a line.

```
class Publisher
{
    public event EventHandler SimpleEvent;

    public void RaiseTheEvent() { SimpleEvent( this, null ); }
}

class Subscriber
{
    public void MethodA( object o, EventArgs e ) { Console.WriteLine( "AAA" ); }
    public void MethodB( object o, EventArgs e ) { Console.WriteLine( "BBB" ); }
}

class Program
{
    static void Main( )
    {
        Publisher  p = new Publisher();
        Subscriber s = new Subscriber();

        p.SimpleEvent += s.MethodA;
        p.SimpleEvent += s.MethodB;
        p.RaiseTheEvent();

        Console.WriteLine( "\r\nRemove MethodB" );
        p.SimpleEvent -= s.MethodB;
        p.RaiseTheEvent();
    }
}
```

This code produces the following output:

```
AAA
BBB

Remove MethodB
AAA
```

If a handler is registered more than once with an event, then when you issue the command to remove the handler, only the last instance of that handler is removed from the list.

Event Accessors

The last topic to cover in this chapter is event accessors. We mentioned earlier that the += and -= operators are the only operators allowed for an event. These operators have the well-defined behavior that you've seen so far in this chapter.

It is possible, however, to change these operators' behavior and have the event perform whatever custom code you like when they are used. This is an advanced topic, however, so we'll just mention it here, without going into too much detail.

To change the operation of these operators, you must define event accessors for the event.

- There are two accessors: add and remove.

- The declaration of an event with accessors looks similar to the declaration of a property.

The following example shows the form of an event declaration with accessors. Both accessors have an implicit value parameter called value that takes a reference to either an instance method or a static method.

```
public event EventHandler CountedADozen
{
    add
    {
        ...    // Code to implement the =+ operator
    }

    remove
    {
        ...    // Code to implement the -= operator
    }
}
```

When event accessors are declared, the event does not contain an embedded delegate object. You must implement your own storage mechanism for storing and removing the methods registered with the event.

The event accessors act as *void methods*, meaning that they cannot use return statements that return a value.

CHAPTER 16

Interfaces

© Daniel Solis and Cal Schrotenboer 2018
D. Solis and C. Schrotenboer, *Illustrated C# 7*, https://doi.org/10.1007/978-1-4842-3288-0_16

What Is an Interface?

An *interface* is a reference type that *specifies a set of function members* but does not implement them. That's left to classes and structs that *implement the interface.* This description sounds pretty abstract, so we'll first show you the problem that an interface helps solve, as well as how it solves it.

Take, for example, the following code. If you look at method Main in class Program, you'll see that it creates and initializes an object of class CA and passes the object to method PrintInfo. PrintInfo expects an object of type CA and prints out the information contained in the class object.

```
class CA {
    public string Name;
    public int    Age;
}

class CB {
    public string First;
    public string Last;
    public double PersonsAge;
}

class Program {
    static void PrintInfo( CA item ) {
        Console.WriteLine($"Name: { item.Name }, Age: { item.Age }");
    }

    static void Main() {
        CA a = new CA() { Name = "John Doe", Age = 35 };
        PrintInfo( a );
    }
}
```

Method PrintInfo works great as long as you pass it objects of type CA, but it won't work if you pass it an object of type CB (also shown in the previous code). Suppose, however, that the algorithm in method PrintInfo was so useful that you wanted to be able to apply it to objects of many different classes.

There are several reasons that this won't work with the code as it currently stands. First, PrintInfo's formal parameter specifies that the actual parameter must be an object of type CA, so passing in an object of type CB or any other type would produce a compile error. But even if we could get around that hurdle and somehow pass in an object of type CB, we would still have a problem because CB's structure is different from that of CA. Its fields have different names and types than CA, and PrintInfo doesn't know anything about these fields.

But what if we could create classes in such a way that they could be successfully passed into PrintInfo, and PrintInfo would be able to process them regardless of the structure of the class? Interfaces make this possible.

The code in Figure 16-1 solves the problem by using an interface. You don't need to understand the details yet, but generally, it does the following:

- First, it declares an interface called IInfo that comprises two method declarations— GetName and GetAge—each of which returns a string.

- Classes CA and CB both implement interface IInfo by listing it in their base class lists and then implementing the two methods required by the interface.

- Main then creates instances of CA and CB and passes them to PrintInfo.

- Because the class instances implement the interface, PrintInfo can call the methods, and each class instance executes its method as it was defined in its class declaration.

```
interface IInfo                  ◄──── Declare the interface.
{
    string GetName();
    string GetAge();
}

class CA : IInfo  ◄──── Declare that class CA implements the interface.
{
    public string Name;                    ┌──── Implement the two interface
    public int Age;                        │     methods in class CA.
    public string GetName( ) { return Name; }
    public string GetAge( ) { return Age.ToString( ); }
}

class CB : IInfo  ◄──── Declare that class CB implements the interface.
{
    public string First;
    public string Last;                    ┌──── Implement the two interface
    public double PersonsAge;              │     methods in class CB.
    public string GetName( ) { return First + " " + Last; }
    public string GetAge( )  { return PersonsAge.ToString( ); }
}

class Program
{
    static void PrintInfo( IInfo item )  ◄──── Pass objects as references to the interface.
    {
        Console.WriteLine( "Name: {0}, Age {1}", item.GetName(), item.GetAge() );
    }

    static void Main( )
    {
        CA a = new CA( ) { Name = "John Doe", Age = 35 };
        CB b = new CB( ) { First = "Jane", Last = "Doe", PersonsAge = 33 };

        PrintInfo( a );   ◄──── References to the objects are automatically converted
        PrintInfo( b );         (cast) to references to the interfaces they implement.
    }
}
```

Figure 16-1. *Using an interface to make method PrintInfo usable by any number of classes*

This code produces the following output:

```
Name: John Doe, Age 35
Name: Jane Doe, Age 33
```

Example Using the IComparable Interface

Now that you've seen some of the problems solved by interfaces, we'll show you a second example and go into a bit more detail. Start by taking a look at the following code, which takes an unsorted array of integers and sorts them in ascending order. The code does the following:

- The first line creates an array of five integers that are in no particular order.

- The second line uses the Array class's static Sort method to sort the elements.

- The foreach loop prints them out, showing that the integers are now in ascending order.

```
var myInt = new [] { 20, 4, 16, 9, 2 };      // Create an array of ints.

Array.Sort(myInt);                           // Sort elements by magnitude.

foreach (var i in myInt)                     // Print them out.
   Console.Write($"{ i } ");
```

This code produces the following output:

```
2 4 9 16 20
```

The Array class's Sort method clearly works great on an array of ints, but what would happen if you were to try to use it on an array of one of your own classes, as shown here?

```
class MyClass                         // Declare a simple class.
{
   public int TheValue;
}
   ...
MyClass[] mc = new MyClass[5];        // Create an array of five elements.
   ...                                // Create and initialize the elements.

Array.Sort(mc);                       // Try to use Sort--raises exception.
```

When you try to run this code, it raises an exception instead of sorting the elements. The reason Sort doesn't work with the array of MyClass objects is that it doesn't know how to compare user-defined objects and how to rank their order. The Array class's Sort method depends on an interface called IComparable, which is declared in the BCL. IComparable has a single method named CompareTo.

The following code shows the declaration of the IComparable interface. Notice that the interface body contains the declaration of method CompareTo, specifying that it takes a single parameter of type object. Again, although the method has a name, parameters, and a return type, there is no implementation. Instead, the implementation is represented by a semicolon.

```
        Keyword     Interface name
           ↓            ↓
public interface IComparable
{
    int CompareTo( object obj );
}                              ↑
        Semicolon in place of method implementation
```

Figure 16-2 illustrates interface IComparable. The CompareTo method is shown in gray to illustrate that it doesn't contain an implementation.

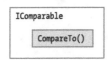

Figure 16-2. *Representation of interface IComparable*

Although the interface declaration doesn't provide an implementation for method CompareTo, the .NET documentation of interface IComparable describes what the method should do, in case you create a class or struct that implements the interface. It says that when method CompareTo is called, it should return one of the following values:

- A negative value, if the current object is less than the parameter object

- A positive value, if the current object is greater than the parameter object

- Zero, if the two objects are considered equal in the comparison

The algorithm used by Sort depends on the fact that it can use the element's CompareTo method to determine the order of two elements. The int type implements IComparable, but MyClass does not, so when Sort tries to call the nonexistent CompareTo method of MyClass, it raises an exception.

You can make the Sort method work with objects of type MyClass by making the class implement IComparable. To implement an interface, a class or struct must do two things.

- It must list the interface name in its base class list.

- It must provide an implementation for each of the interface's members.

For example, the following code updates MyClass to implement interface IComparable. Notice the following about the code:

- The name of the interface is listed in the base class list of the class declaration.

- The class implements a method called CompareTo, whose parameter type and return type match those of the interface member.

- Method CompareTo is implemented to satisfy the definition given in the interface's documentation. That is, it returns a negative 1, positive 1, or 0, depending on its value compared to the object passed into the method.

```
     Interface name in base class list
                    ↓
class MyClass : IComparable
{
    public int TheValue;

    public int CompareTo(object obj)    // Implementation of interface method
    {
        MyClass mc = (MyClass)obj;
        if (this.TheValue < mc.TheValue) return -1;
        if (this.TheValue > mc.TheValue) return  1;
        return 0;
    }
}
```

Figure 16-3 illustrates the updated class. The arrow pointing from the shaded interface method to the class method indicates that the interface method doesn't contain code but is implemented by the class-level method.

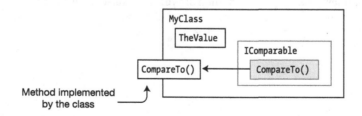

Figure 16-3. *Implementing IComparable in MyClass*

Now that MyClass implements IComparable, Sort will work on it just fine. It would not, by the way, have been sufficient to just declare the CompareTo method—it must be part of implementing the interface, which means placing the interface name in the base class list.

The following shows the complete updated code, which can now use the Sort method to sort an array of MyClass objects. Main creates and initializes an array of MyClass objects and then prints them out. It then calls Sort and prints them out again to show that they've been sorted.

```csharp
class MyClass : IComparable                    // Class implements interface.
{
    public int TheValue;
    public int CompareTo(object obj)           // Implement the method.
    {
        MyClass mc = (MyClass)obj;
        if (this.TheValue < mc.TheValue) return -1;
        if (this.TheValue > mc.TheValue) return 1;
        return 0;
    }
}

class Program {
    static void PrintOut(string s, MyClass[] mc)
    {
        Console.Write(s);
        foreach (var m in mc)
            Console.Write($"{ m.TheValue } ");
        Console.WriteLine("");
    }

    static void Main()
    {
        var myInt = new [] { 20, 4, 16, 9, 2 };

        MyClass[] mcArr = new MyClass[5];      // Create array of MyClass objs.
        for (int i = 0; i < 5; i++)            // Initialize the array.
        {
            mcArr[i] = new MyClass();
            mcArr[i].TheValue = myInt[i];
        }
        PrintOut("Initial Order:  ", mcArr);   // Print the initial array.
        Array.Sort(mcArr);                     // Sort the array.
        PrintOut("Sorted Order:   ", mcArr);   // Print the sorted array.
    }
}
```

This code produces the following output:

```
Initial Order:  20 4 16 9 2
Sorted Order:    2 4 9 16 20
```

Declaring an Interface

The previous section used an interface that was already declared in the BCL. In this section, you'll see how to declare your own interfaces. The important things to know about declaring an interface are the following:

- An interface declaration cannot contain the following:
  - Data members
  - Static members

- An interface declaration can contain only declarations of the following kinds of *nonstatic* function members:
  - Methods
  - Properties
  - Events
  - Indexers

- The declarations of these function members cannot contain any implementation code. Instead, a semicolon must be used in place of the body of each member declaration.

- By convention, interface names begin with an uppercase *I* (e.g., ISaveable).

- Like classes and structs, interface declarations can also be split into partial interface declarations, as described in the "Partial Classes and Partial Types" section of Chapter 7.

The following code shows an example of declaring an interface with two method members:

```
  Keyword     Interface name
     ↓             ↓
interface IMyInterface1                          Semicolon in place of body
{                                                           ↓
    int    DoStuff      ( int nVar1, long lVar2 );
    double DoOtherStuff( string s, long x );
}                                                ↑
                                    Semicolon in place of body
```

There is an important difference between the accessibility of an interface and the accessibility of interface members:

- An interface declaration can have any of the access modifiers public, protected, internal, or private.

- *Members* of an interface, however, are implicitly public, and *no* access modifiers, including public, are allowed.

```
Access modifiers are allowed on interfaces.
      ↓
    public interface IMyInterface2
    {
        private int Method1( int nVar1, long lVar2 );           // Error
    }       ↑
        Access modifiers are NOT allowed on interface members.
```

Implementing an Interface

Only classes or structs can implement an interface. As shown in the Sort example, to implement an interface, a class or struct must

- Include the name of the interface in its base class list

- Supply implementations for each of the interface's members

For example, the following code shows a new declaration for class MyClass, which implements interface IMyInterface1, declared in the previous section. Notice that the interface name is listed in the base class list after the colon and that the class provides the actual implementation code for the interface members.

```
             Colon    Interface name
               ↓          ↓
class MyClass : IMyInterface1
{
   int    DoStuff    ( int nVar1, long lVar2 )
   { ... }                                      // Implementation code

   double DoOtherStuff( string s, long x )
   { ... }                                      // Implementation code

}
```

Some important things to know about implementing interfaces are the following:

- If a class implements an interface, it must implement *all* the members of that interface.

- If a class is derived from a base class and also implements interfaces, the name of the base class must be listed in the base class list *before* any interfaces, as shown following. (Remember that there can only ever be one base class, so any other types listed must be the names of interfaces.)

```
        Base class must be first          Interface names
                   ↓              _____↓_____
class Derived : MyBaseClass, IIfc1, IEnumerable, IComparable
{
   ...
}
```

Example with a Simple Interface

The following code declares an interface named IIfc1, which contains a single method named PrintOut. Class MyClass implements interface IIfc1 by listing it in its base class list and supplying a method named PrintOut that matches the signature and return type of the interface member. Main creates an object of the class and calls the method from the object.

```
interface IIfc1        Semicolon in place of body            // Declare interface.
{                              ↓
    void PrintOut(string s);
}
                    Implement interface
                           ↓
class MyClass : IIfc1                                         // Declare class.
{
    public void PrintOut(string s)                           // Implementation
    {
        Console.WriteLine($"Calling through:  { s }");
    }
}

class Program
{
    static void Main()
    {
        MyClass mc = new MyClass();                          // Create instance.
        mc.PrintOut("object");                              // Call method.
    }

}
```

This code produces the following output:

```
Calling through:  object
```

An Interface Is a Reference Type

An interface is more than just a list of members for a class or struct to implement. It's a reference type.

You cannot access an interface directly through the class object's members. You can, however, get a *reference to the interface* by casting the class object reference to the type of the interface. Once you have a reference to the interface, you can use dot-syntax notation with the reference to call interface members. With this interface, however, you cannot call any members of the class that are not members of that particular interface.

For example, the following code shows an example of getting an interface reference from a class object reference.

- In the first statement, variable mc is a reference to a class object that implements interface IIfc1. The statement explicitly casts that reference to a reference to the interface and assigns it to variable ifc. We could, however, have left out the explicit cast part, and the compiler would implicitly cast it to the right interface, which it can infer from the left side of the assignment.

- The second statement uses the reference to the interface to call the implementation method.

```
   Interface      Cast to interface
      ↓               ↓
IIfc1 ifc = (IIfc1) mc;                 // Get ref to interface.
      ↑               ↑
  Interface ref   Class object ref

ifc.PrintOut ("interface");             // Use ref to interface to call member.
    ↑
Use dot-syntax notation to call through the interface reference.
```

For example, the following code declares an interface and a class that implements it. The code in Main creates an object of the class and calls the implementation method through the class object. It also creates a variable of the interface type, casts the reference of the class object to the interface type, and calls the implementation method through the reference to the interface. Figure 16-4 illustrates the class and the reference to the interface.

```csharp
interface IIfc1
{
   void PrintOut(string s);
}

class MyClass : IIfc1
{
   public void PrintOut(string s)
   {
      Console.WriteLine($"Calling through: { s }");
   }
}

class Program
{
   static void Main()
   {
      MyClass mc = new MyClass();   // Create class object.
      mc.PrintOut("object");        // Call class object implementation method.

      IIfc1 ifc = (IIfc1)mc;        // Cast class object ref to interface ref.
      ifc.PrintOut("interface");    // Call interface method.
   }
}
```

This code produces the following output:

```
Calling through:   object
Calling through:   interface
```

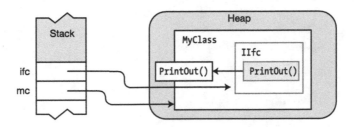

Figure 16-4. *A reference to the class object and a reference to the interface*

Using the as Operator with Interfaces

In the previous section, you saw that you can use the cast operator to get a reference to an object's interface. An even better idea is to use the as operator. The as operator is covered in detail in Chapter 17, but we'll mention it here as well since it's a good choice to use with interfaces.

If you attempt to cast a class object reference to a reference of an interface that the class doesn't implement, the cast operation will raise an exception. You can avoid this problem by using the as operator instead. It works as follows:

- If the class implements the interface, the expression returns a reference to the interface.

- If the class doesn't implement the interface, the expression returns null rather than raising an exception. (*Exceptions* are unexpected errors in the code. We'll cover exceptions in detail in Chapter 23—but you want to avoid exceptions because they significantly slow down the code and can leave the program in an inconsistent state.)

The following code demonstrates the use of the as operator. The first line uses the as operator to obtain an interface reference from a class object. The result of the expression sets the value of b to either null or a reference to an ILiveBirth interface.

The second line checks the value of b and, if it is not null, executes the command that calls the interface member method.

```
         Class object ref     Interface name
                ↓                    ↓
ILiveBirth b = a as ILiveBirth;          // Acts like cast: (ILiveBirth)a
             ↑   ↑
         Interface Operator
            ref
if (b != null)

Console.WriteLine($"Baby is called:{ b.BabyCalled() }");
```

Implementing Multiple Interfaces

In the examples shown so far, the classes have implemented a single interface.

- A class or struct can implement any number of interfaces.

- All the interfaces implemented must be listed in the base class list and separated by commas (following the base class name, if there is one).

For example, the following code shows class MyData, which implements two interfaces: IDataStore and IDataRetrieve. Figure 16-5 illustrates the implementation of the multiple interfaces in class MyData.

```
interface IDataRetrieve { int GetData(); }         // Declare interface.
interface IDataStore    { void SetData( int x ); }  // Declare interface.

            Interface        Interface
                ↓                ↓
class MyData: IDataRetrieve, IDataStore             // Declare class.
{
    int Mem1;                                        // Declare field.
    public int  GetData()          { return Mem1; }
    public void SetData( int x ) { Mem1 = x;     }
}

class Program
{
    static void Main()                               // Main
    {
        MyData data = new MyData();
        data.SetData( 5 );
        Console.WriteLine($"Value = { data.GetData() }");
    }
}
```

This code produces the following output:

```
Value = 5
```

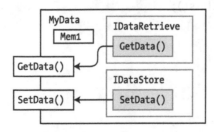

Figure 16-5. *Class implementing multiple interfaces*

Implementing Interfaces with Duplicate Members

Since a class can implement any number of interfaces, it's possible that two or more of the interface members might have the same signature and return type. So, how does the compiler handle that situation?

For example, suppose you had two interfaces—IIfc1 and IIfc2—as shown next. Each interface has a method named PrintOut, with the same signature and return type. If you were to create a class that implemented both interfaces, how should you handle these duplicate interface methods?

```
interface IIfc1
{
    void PrintOut(string s);
}

interface IIfc2
{
    void PrintOut(string t);
}
```

The answer is that if a class implements multiple interfaces, where several of the interfaces have members with the same signature and return type, the class can implement a single member that satisfies all the interfaces containing that duplicated member.

For example, the following code shows the declaration of class MyClass, which implements both IIfc1 and IIfc2. Its implementation of method PrintOut satisfies the requirement for both interfaces.

```
class MyClass : IIfc1, IIfc2             // Implement both interfaces.
{
    public void PrintOut(string s)       // Single implementation for both
    {
        Console.WriteLine($"Calling through: { s }");
    }
}

class Program
{
    static void Main()
    {
        MyClass mc = new MyClass();
        mc.PrintOut("object");
    }
}
```

This code produces the following output:

```
Calling through:  object
```

Figure 16-6 illustrates the duplicate interface methods being implemented by a single class-level method implementation.

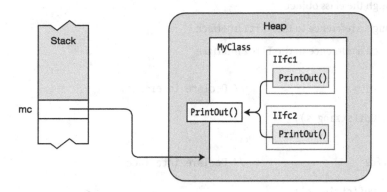

Figure 16-6. *Multiple interfaces implemented by the same class member*

References to Multiple Interfaces

You saw previously that interfaces are reference types and that you can get a reference to an interface by using the as operator or by casting an object reference to the interface type. If a class implements multiple interfaces, you can get separate references for each one.

For example, the following class implements two interfaces with the single method PrintOut. The code in Main calls method PrintOut in three ways.

- Through the class object

- Through a reference to the IIfc1 interface

- Through a reference to the IIfc2 interface

```
interface IIfc1                      // Declare interface.
{
    void PrintOut(string s);
}

interface IIfc2                      // Declare interface
{
    void PrintOut(string s);
}

class MyClass : IIfc1, IIfc2         // Declare class.
{
    public void PrintOut(string s)
    {
        Console.WriteLine($"Calling through: { s }");
    }
}
```

```
class Program
{
   static void Main()
   {
      MyClass mc = new MyClass();

      IIfc1 ifc1 = (IIfc1) mc;               // Get ref to IIfc1.
      IIfc2 ifc2 = (IIfc2) mc;               // Get ref to IIfc2.

      mc.PrintOut("object");                 // Call through class object.

      ifc1.PrintOut("interface 1");          // Call through IIfc1.
      ifc2.PrintOut("interface 2");          // Call through IIfc2.
   }
}
```

This code produces the following output:

```
Calling through:   object
Calling through:   interface 1
Calling through:   interface 2
```

Figure 16-7 illustrates the class object and references to IIfc1 and IIfc2.

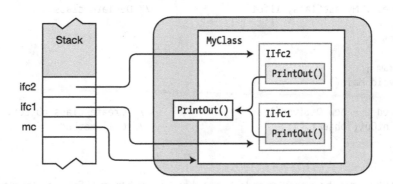

Figure 16-7. *Separate references to different interfaces in the class*

An Inherited Member As an Implementation

A class implementing an interface can inherit the code for an implementation from one of its base classes. For example, the following code illustrates a class inheriting implementation code from a base class.

- IIfc1 is an interface with a method member called PrintOut.

- MyBaseClass contains a method called PrintOut that matches IIfc1's method declaration.

- Class Derived has an empty declaration body but derives from class MyBaseClass and contains IIfc1 in its base class list.

- Even though Derived's declaration body is empty, the code in the base class satisfies the requirement to implement the interface method.

```csharp
interface IIfc1 { void PrintOut(string s); }

class MyBaseClass                               // Declare base class.
{
   public void PrintOut(string s)               // Declare the method.
   {
      Console.WriteLine($"Calling through:  { s }");
   }
}

class Derived : MyBaseClass, IIfc1              // Declare class.
{
}

class Program {
   static void Main()
   {
      Derived d = new Derived();                // Create class object.
      d.PrintOut("object.");                    // Call method.
   }
}
```

Figure 16-8 illustrates the preceding code. Notice that the arrow from IIfc1 goes down to the code in the base class.

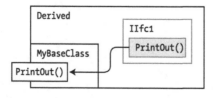

Figure 16-8. *Implementation in the base class*

Explicit Interface Member Implementations

You saw in previous sections that a single class can implement all the members required by multiple interfaces, as illustrated in Figures 17-5 and 17-6.

But what if you want separate implementations for each interface? In this case, you can create what are called *explicit interface member implementations*. An explicit interface member implementation has the following characteristics:

- Like all interface implementations, it is placed in the class or struct implementing the interface.

- It is declared using a *qualified interface name*, which consists of the interface name and member name, separated by a dot.

The following code shows the syntax for declaring explicit interface member implementations. Each of the two interfaces implemented by MyClass implements its own version of method PrintOut.

```
class MyClass : IIfc1, IIfc2
{          Qualified interface name
                    ↓
    void IIfc1.PrintOut (string s)            // Explicit implementation
    { ... }

    void IIfc2.PrintOut (string s)            // Explicit implementation
    { ... }
}
```

Figure 16-9 illustrates the class and interfaces. Notice that the boxes representing the explicit interface member implementations are not shown in gray since they now represent actual code.

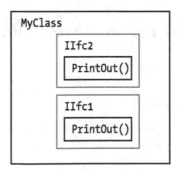

Figure 16-9. *Explicit interface member implementations*

For example, in the following code, class MyClass declares explicit interface member implementations for the members of the two interfaces. Notice that in this example there are only explicit interface member implementations. There is no class-level implementation.

```
interface IIfc1 { void PrintOut(string s); }   // Declare interface.
interface IIfc2 { void PrintOut(string t); }   // Declare interface.

class MyClass : IIfc1, IIfc2
{
       Qualified interface name
               ↓
   void IIfc1.PrintOut(string s)             // Explicit interface member
   {                                         //       implementation
      Console.WriteLine($"IIfc1:  { s }");
   }
           Qualified interface name
                   ↓
   void IIfc2.PrintOut(string s)             // Explicit interface member
   {                                         //       implementation
      Console.WriteLine($"IIfc2:  { s }");
   }
}

class Program
{
   static void Main()
   {
      MyClass mc = new MyClass();            // Create class object.

      IIfc1 ifc1 = (IIfc1) mc;               // Get reference to IIfc1.
      ifc1.PrintOut("interface 1");          // Call explicit implementation.

      IIfc2 ifc2 = (IIfc2) mc;               // Get reference to IIfc2.
      ifc2.PrintOut("interface 2");          // Call explicit implementation.
   }

}
```

This code produces the following output:

```
IIfc1:   interface 1
IIfc2:   interface 2
```

Figure 16-10 illustrates the code. Notice in the figure that the interface methods do not point at class-level implementations but contain their own code. Notice in the figure that we cannot use the mc reference to call the PrintOut methods. There is no class-level PrintOut method.

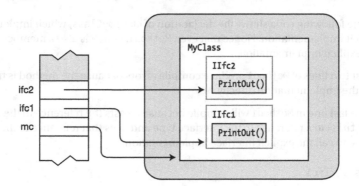

Figure 16-10. *References to interfaces with explicit interface member implementations*

When there is an explicit interface member implementation, a class-level implementation is allowed but not required. The explicit implementation satisfies the requirement that the class or struct must implement the method. You can therefore have any of the following three implementation scenarios:

- A class-level implementation

- An explicit interface member implementation

- Both a class-level and an explicit interface member implementation

Accessing Explicit Interface Member Implementations

An explicit interface member implementation can be accessed *only* through a reference to the interface, as demonstrated in the previous example. This means that even other class members can't directly access them.

For example, the following code shows the declaration of class MyClass, which implements interface IIfc1 with an explicit implementation. Notice that even Method1, which is also a member of MyClass, can't directly access the explicit implementation.

- The first two lines of Method1 produce compile errors because the method is trying to access the implementation directly.

- Only the last line in Method1 will compile because it casts the reference to the current object (this) to a reference to the interface type and uses that reference to the interface to call the explicit interface implementation.

```
class MyClass : IIfc1
{
   void IIfc1.PrintOut(string s)      // Explicit interface implementation
   {
      Console.WriteLine("IIfc1");
   }

   public void Method1()
   {
      PrintOut("...");                // Compile error
      this.PrintOut("...");           // Compile error

      ((IIfc1)this).PrintOut("...");  // OK, call method.
   }
          ↑
   Cast to a reference to the interface
}
```

This restriction has an important ramification for inheritance. Since other fellow class members can't directly access explicit interface member implementations, members of classes derived from the class clearly can't directly access them either. They must always be accessed through a reference to the interface.

Interfaces Can Inherit Interfaces

You saw earlier that interface *implementations* can be inherited from base classes. But an interface itself can inherit from one or more other interfaces.

- To specify that an interface inherits from other interfaces, place the names of the base interfaces in a comma-separated list after a colon following the interface name in the interface declaration, as shown here:

```
        Colon      Base interface list
          ↓              ↓
interface IDataIO : IDataRetrieve, IDataStore
{ ...
```

- Unlike a class, which can have only a single class name in its base class list, an interface can have any number of interfaces in its base interface list.

  - The interfaces in the list can themselves have inherited interfaces.

  - The resulting interface contains all the members it declares, as well as all those of its base interfaces.

The code in Figure 16-11 shows the declaration of three interfaces. Interface IDataIO inherits from the first two. The illustration on the right shows IDataIO encompassing the other two interfaces.

```
interface IDataRetrieve
{ int GetData( ); }

interface IDataStore
{ void SetData( int x ); }

// Derives from the first two interfaces
interface IDataIO: IDataRetrieve, IDataStore
{
}

class MyData: IDataIO {
   int nPrivateData;
   public int GetData( )
        { return nPrivateData; }
   public void SetData( int x )
        { nPrivateData = x; }
}

class Program {
   static void Main( ) {
      MyData data = new MyData ();
      data.SetData( 5 );
      Console.WriteLine("{0}", data.GetData());
   }
}
```

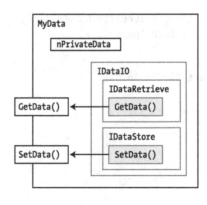

Figure 16-11. *Class implementing interface that inherits from multiple interfaces*

411

Example of Different Classes Implementing an Interface

The following code illustrates several aspects of interfaces that have been covered. The program declares a class called Animal, which is used as a base class for several other classes that represent various types of animals. It also declares an interface named ILiveBirth.

Classes Cat, Dog, and Bird all derive from base class Animal. Cat and Dog both implement the ILiveBirth interface, but class Bird does not.

In Main, the program creates an array of Animal objects and populates it with a class object of each of the three types of animal classes. The program then iterates through the array and, using the as operator, retrieves a reference to the ILiveBirth interface of each object that has one and calls its BabyCalled method.

```
interface ILiveBirth                        // Declare interface.
{
    string BabyCalled();
}

class Animal { }                            // Base class Animal

class Cat : Animal, ILiveBirth              // Declare class Cat.
{
    string ILiveBirth.BabyCalled()
    { return "kitten"; }
}

class Dog : Animal, ILiveBirth              // Declare class Dog.
{
    string ILiveBirth.BabyCalled()
    { return "puppy"; }
}

class Bird : Animal                         // Declare class Bird.
{
}
```

```
class Program
{
   static void Main()
   {
      Animal[] animalArray = new Animal[3];      // Create Animal array.
      animalArray[0] = new Cat();                // Insert Cat class object.
      animalArray[1] = new Bird();               // Insert Bird class object.
      animalArray[2] = new Dog();                // Insert Dog class object.
      foreach( Animal a in animalArray )         // Cycle through array.
      {
         ILiveBirth b = a as ILiveBirth;         // if implements ILiveBirth...
         if (b != null)
            Console.WriteLine($"Baby is called: { b.BabyCalled() }");
      }
   }
}
```

This code produces the following output:

```
Baby is called: kitten
Baby is called: puppy
```

Figure 16-12 illustrates the array and the objects in memory.

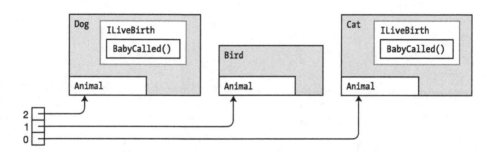

Figure 16-12. *Different object types of base class Animal are interspersed in the array*

413

CHAPTER 17

■ ■ ■

Conversions

What Are Conversions?

To get an understanding of what conversions are, let's start by considering the simple case in which you declare two variables of different types and then assign the value of one (the *source*) to the other (the *target*). Before the assignment can occur, the source value must be converted to a value of the target type. Figure 17-1 illustrates type conversion.

- *Conversion* is the process of taking a value of one type and *using it as* the equivalent value of another type.

- The value resulting from the conversion should be the same as the source value—but in the target type.

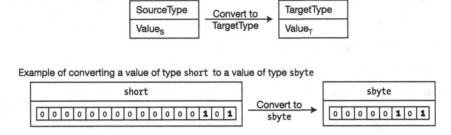

Figure 17-1. *Type conversion*

For example, the code in Figure 17-2 shows the declaration of two variables of different types.

- var1 is of type short, a 16-bit signed integer that is initialized to 5. var2 is of type sbyte, an 8-bit signed integer that is initialized to the value 10.

- The third line of the code assigns the value of var1 to var2. Since these are two different types, the value of var1 must be converted to a value of the same type as var2 before the assignment can be performed. This is performed using the cast expression, which you'll see shortly.

- Notice also that the value and type of var1 are unchanged. Although it is called a conversion, this only means that the source value is used as the value of the target type—not that the source is changed into the target type.

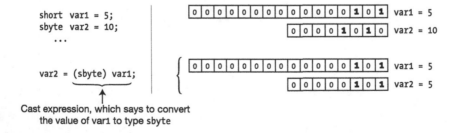

Figure 17-2. *Converting from a short to an sbyte*

Implicit Conversions

For certain types of conversions, there is no possibility of loss of data or precision. For example, it's easy to stuff an 8-bit value into a 16-bit type with no loss of data.

- The language will do these conversions for you automatically. These are called *implicit conversions*.

- When converting from a source type with fewer bits to a target type with more bits, the extra bits in the target need to be filled with either 0s or 1s.

- When converting from a smaller unsigned type to a larger unsigned type, the extra most significant bits of the target are filled with 0s. This is called *zero extension*.

Figure 17-3 shows an example of the zero extension of an 8-bit value of 10 converted to a 16-bit value of 10.

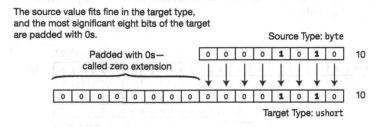

Figure 17-3. *Zero extension in unsigned conversions*

For conversion between signed types, the extra most significant bits are filled with the sign bit of the source expression.

- This maintains the correct sign and magnitude for the converted value.

- This is called *sign extension* and is illustrated in Figure 17-4, first with 10 and then with –10.

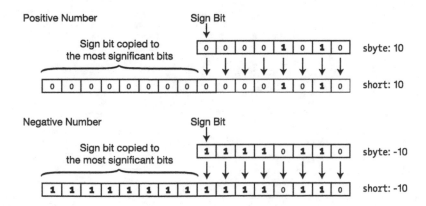

Figure 17-4. *Sign extension in signed conversions*

417

Explicit Conversions and Casting

When you convert from a shorter type to a longer type, it's easy for the longer type to hold all the bits of the shorter type. In other situations, however, the target type might not be able to accommodate the source value without loss of data.

For example, suppose you want to convert a ushort value to a byte.

- A ushort can hold any value between 0 and 65,535.

- A byte can only hold a value between 0 and 255.

- As long as the ushort value you want to convert is less than 256, there won't be any loss of data. If it is greater, however, the most significant bits will be lost.

For example, Figure 17-5 shows an attempt to convert a ushort with a value of 1,365 to a byte, resulting in a loss of data. Not all the significant bits of the source value fit into the target type, resulting in an overflow and loss of data. The source value was 1,365, but the maximum value the target can hold is 255. The resulting value in the byte is 85 instead of 1,365.

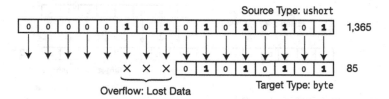

Figure 17-5. *Attempting to convert a ushort to a byte*

Clearly, only a relatively small number (0.4 percent) of the possible unsigned 16-bit ushort values can be safely converted to an unsigned 8-bit byte type without loss of data. The rest result in data *overflow*, yielding different values.

Casting

For the predefined types, C# will automatically convert from one data type to another—but only between those types for which there is no possibility of data loss between the source type and the target type. That is, the language does not provide automatic conversion between two types if there is *any* value of the source type that would lose data if it were converted to the target type. If you want to make a conversion of this type, you must use an *explicit conversion* called a *cast expression*.

The following code shows an example of a cast expression. It converts the value of `var1` to type `sbyte`. A cast expression consists of the following:

- A set of matching parentheses containing the name of the target type
- The source expression, following the parentheses

```
Target type
  ↓
 (sbyte) var1;
           ↑
   Source expression
```

When you use a cast expression, you are explicitly taking responsibility for performing the operation that might lose data. Essentially, you are saying, "In spite of the possibility of data loss, I know what I'm doing, so make this conversion anyway." (Make sure, however, that you *do* know what you're doing.)

For example, Figure 17-6 shows cast expressions converting two values of type `ushort` to type `byte`. In the first case, there is no loss of data. In the second case, the most significant bits are lost, giving a value of 85—which is clearly not equivalent to the source value, 1,365.

```
ushort sh = 10;
byte sb = (byte) sh;
Console.WriteLine
     ("sb:  {0} = 0x{0:X}", sb);

sh = 1365;
sb = (byte) sh;
Console.WriteLine
     ("sb:  {0} = 0x{0:X}", sb);
```

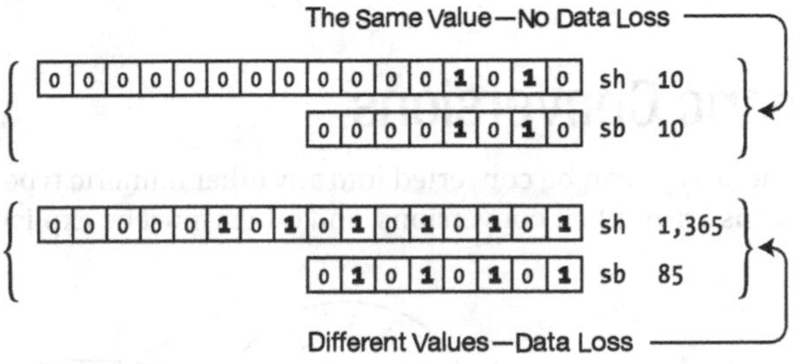

***Figure 17-6.** Casting a ushort to a byte*

The output of the code in the figure shows both the decimal and hexadecimal values of the results and is the following:

```
sb:  10 = 0xA
sb:  85 = 0x55
```

Types of Conversions

There are a number of standard, predefined conversions for the numeric and reference types. The categories are illustrated in Figure 17-7.

- Beyond the standard conversions, you can also define both implicit and explicit conversions for your user-defined types.

- There is also a predefined type of conversion called *boxing*, which converts any value type to either of these:

  - Type object

  - Type System.ValueType

- Unboxing converts a boxed value back to its original type.

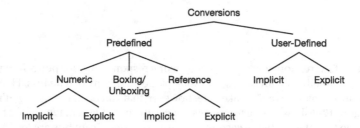

Figure 17-7. *Types of conversions*

Numeric Conversions

Any numeric type can be converted into any other numeric type, as illustrated in Figure 17-8. Some of the conversions are implicit conversions, and others must be explicit.

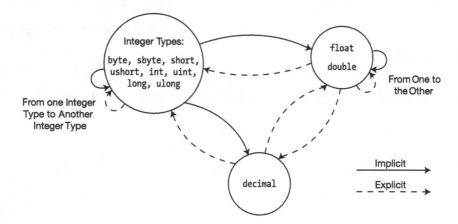

Figure 17-8. *Numeric conversions*

Implicit Numeric Conversions

The implicit numeric conversions are shown in Figure 17-9.

- There is an *implicit conversion* from the source type to the target type if there is a path, following the arrows, from the source type to the target type.

- Any numeric conversion for which there is not a path following the arrows from the source type to the target type must be an *explicit conversion*.

The figure demonstrates that, as you would expect, there is an implicit conversion between numeric types that occupy fewer bits to those that occupy more bits.

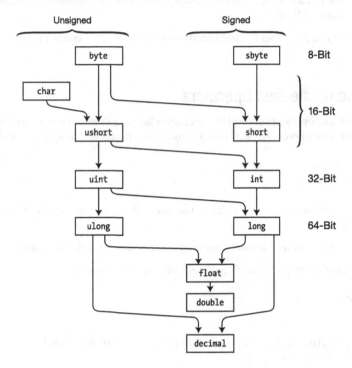

Figure 17-9. *The implicit numeric conversions*

Overflow Checking Context

You've seen that explicit conversions have the possibility of losing data and not being able to represent the source value equivalently in the target type. For integer types, C# provides you with the ability to choose whether the runtime should check the result for overflow when making these types of conversions. It does this through the checked operator and the checked statement.

- Whether a segment of code is checked or not is called its *overflow checking context*.

  - If you designate an expression or segment of code as checked, the CLR will raise an OverflowException exception if the conversion produces an overflow.

  - If the code is not checked, the conversion will proceed regardless of whether there is an overflow.

- By default, if you don't specify checked, the overflow checking context is not checked.

The checked and unchecked Operators

The checked and unchecked operators control the overflow checking context of an expression, which is placed between a set of parentheses. The expression cannot be a method. The syntax is as follows:

```
checked    ( Expression )
unchecked  ( Expression )
```

For example, the following code executes the same conversion—first in a checked operator and then in an unchecked operator.

- In the unchecked context, the overflow is ignored, resulting in the value 208.

- In the checked context, an OverflowException exception is raised.

```
ushort sh = 2000;
byte   sb;

sb = unchecked ( (byte) sh );        // Most significant bits lost
Console.WriteLine($"sb: { sb }");

sb =   checked ( (byte) sh );        // OverflowException raised
Console.WriteLine($"sb: { sb }");
```

This code produces the following output:

```
sb: 208

Unhandled Exception: System.OverflowException: Arithmetic operation resulted in an
overflow. at Test1.Test.Main() in C:\Programs\Test1\Program.cs:line 21
```

The checked and unchecked Statements

The checked and unchecked *operators* that you just saw act on the single expression between the parentheses. The checked and unchecked *statements* perform the same function but control all the conversions in a block of code, rather than in a single expression.

The checked and unchecked statements can be nested to any level. For example, the following code uses checked and unchecked statements and produces the same results as the previous example, which uses checked and unchecked expressions. In this case, however, blocks of code are affected, rather than just expressions.

```
byte sb;
ushort sh = 2000;

checked
{
   unchecked
   {
      sb = (byte) sh;
      Console.WriteLine( $"sb: { sb }" );
   }

   sb = checked((byte) sh);
   Console.WriteLine( $"sb: { sb }" );
}
```

Explicit Numeric Conversions

You've seen that the implicit conversions automatically convert from the source expression to the target type because there is no possible loss of data. With the explicit conversions, however, there is the possibility of losing data—so it's important for you as the programmer to know how a conversion will handle that loss if it occurs.

In this section, we will look at each of the various types of explicit numeric conversions. Figure 17-10 shows the subset of explicit conversions.

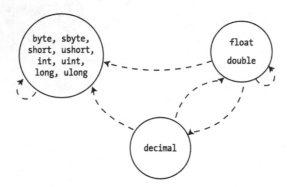

Figure 17-10. *The explicit numeric conversions*

Integer Type to Integer Type

Figure 17-11 shows the behavior of the integer-to-integer explicit conversions. In the checked case, if the conversion loses data, the operation raises an OverflowException exception. In the unchecked case, any lost bits go unreported.

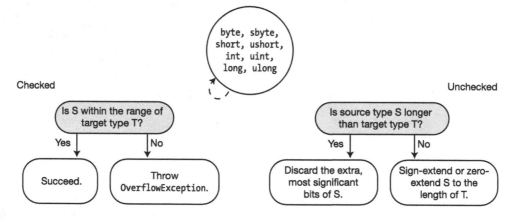

Figure 17-11. *Integer-to-integer explicit conversions*

float or double to Integer Type

When converting a floating-point type to an integer type, the value is rounded toward 0 to the nearest integer. Figure 17-12 illustrates the conversion conditions. If the rounded value is not within the range of the target type, then

- The CLR raises an OverflowException exception if the overflow checking context is checked.

- C# does not define what its value should be if the context is unchecked.

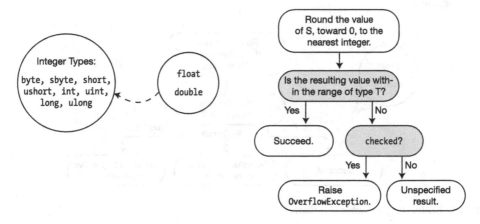

Figure 17-12. *Converting a float or a double to an integer type*

decimal to Integer Type

When converting from decimal to the integer types, the CLR raises an OverflowException exception if the resulting value is not within the target type's range. Figure 17-13 illustrates the conversion conditions.

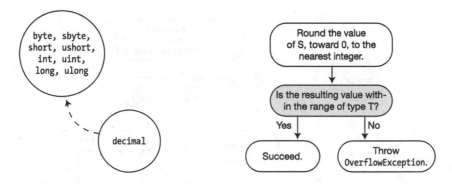

Figure 17-13. *Converting a decimal to an integer type*

double to float

Values of type float occupy 32 bits, and values of type double occupy 64 bits. When a double is rounded to a float, the double type value is rounded to the nearest float type value. Figure 17-14 illustrates the conversion conditions.

- If the value is too small to be represented by a float, the value is set to either positive or negative 0, depending on whether the original value was positive or negative.

- If the value is too large to be represented by a float, the value is set to either positive or negative infinity, depending on whether the original value was positive or negative.

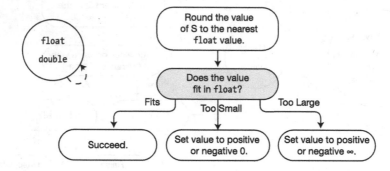

Figure 17-14. *Converting a double to a float*

float or double to decimal

Figure 17-15 shows the conversion conditions for converting from floating-point types to decimal.

- If the value is too small to be represented by the decimal type, the result is set to 0.

- If the value is too large, the CLR raises an OverflowException exception.

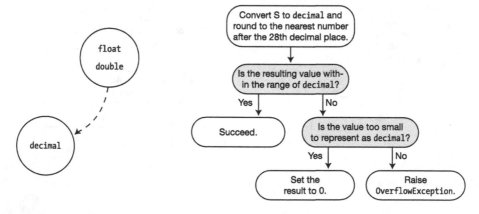

Figure 17-15. *Converting a float or double to a decimal*

decimal to float or double

Conversions from decimal to the floating-point types always succeed. There might, however, be a loss of precision. Figure 17-16 shows the conversion conditions.

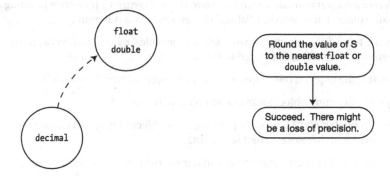

Figure 17-16. *Converting a decimal to a float or double*

Reference Conversions

As you well know by now, reference type objects comprise two parts in memory: the reference and the data.

- Part of the information held by the reference is the *type of the data it is pointing at*.

- A reference conversion takes a source reference and returns a reference pointing at the same place in the heap but "labels" the reference as a different type.

For example, the following code shows two reference variables, myVar1 and myVar2, that point to the same object in memory. The code is illustrated in Figure 17-17.

- To myVar1, the object it references looks like an object of type B—which it is.

- To myVar2, the same object looks like an object of type A.

  - Even though myVar2 is actually pointing at an object of type B, it cannot see the parts of B that extend A and therefore cannot see Field2.

  - The second WriteLine statement would therefore cause a compile error.

Notice that the "conversion" does not change myVar1.

```
class A     { public int Field1; }

class B: A { public int Field2; }

class Program
{
   static void Main( )
   {
      B myVar1 = new B();
```
Return the reference to myVar1 as a reference to a class A.
```
                     ↓
      A myVar2 = (A) myVar1;

      Console.WriteLine($"{ myVar2.Field1 }");        // Fine
      Console.WriteLine($"{ myVar2.Field2 }");        // Compile error!
   }                              ↑
}
                      myVar2 can't see Field2.
```

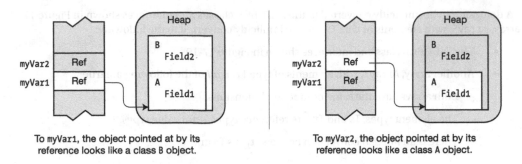

To myVar1, the object pointed at by its
reference looks like a class B object.

To myVar2, the object pointed at by its
reference looks like a class A object.

Figure 17-17. *A reference conversion returns a different type associated with the object*

Implicit Reference Conversions

Just as there are implicit numeric conversions that the language will automatically perform for you, there are also implicit reference conversions. These are illustrated in Figure 17-18.

- All reference types have an implicit conversion to type object.

- Any interface can be implicitly converted to an interface from which it is derived.

- A class can be implicitly converted to

    - Any class in the chain from which it is derived

    - Any interface that it implements

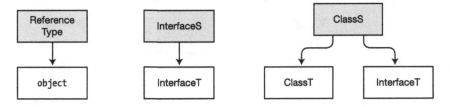

Figure 17-18. *Implicit conversions for classes and interfaces*

A delegate can be implicitly converted to the .NET BCL classes and interfaces shown in Figure 17-19. An array, ArrayS, with elements of type Ts, can be implicitly converted to the following:

- The .NET BCL class and interfaces shown in Figure 17-19

- Another array, ArrayT, with elements of type Tt, if *all* of the following are true:

    - Both arrays have the same number of dimensions.

    - The element types, Ts and Tt, are reference types—not value types.

    - There is an *implicit* conversion between types Ts and Tt.

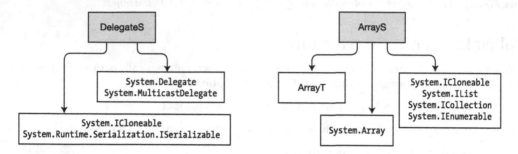

Figure 17-19. *Implicit conversions for delegates and arrays*

Explicit Reference Conversions

Explicit reference conversions are reference conversions from a general type to a more specialized type.

- Explicit conversions include
  - Conversions from an object to any reference type
  - Conversions from a base class to a class derived from it

- The explicit reference conversions are illustrated by reversing each of the arrows in Figures 17-18 and 17-19.

If this type of conversion were allowed without restriction, you could easily attempt to reference members of a class that are not actually in memory. The compiler, however, *does* allow these types of conversions. But when the system encounters them at run time, it raises an exception.

For example, the code in Figure 17-20 converts the reference of base class A to its derived class B and assigns it to variable myVar2.

- If myVar2 were to attempt to access Field2, it would be attempting to access a field in the "B part" of the object, which doesn't exist—causing a memory fault.

- The runtime will catch this inappropriate cast and raise an InvalidCastException exception. Notice, however, that it *does not* cause a compile error.

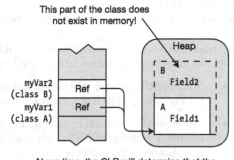

Figure 17-20. *Invalid casts raise runtime exceptions*

Valid Explicit Reference Conversions

There are three situations in which an explicit reference conversion will succeed at run time—that is, not raise an InvalidCastException exception.

The first case is where the explicit conversion is unnecessary—that is, where the language would have performed an implicit conversion for you anyway. For example, in the following code, the explicit conversion is unnecessary because there is always an implicit conversion from a derived class to one of its base classes.

```
class A    { public int Field1; }
class B: A { public int Field2; }
  ...
B myVar1 = new B();
A myVar2 = (A) myVar1;     // Cast is unnecessary; A is the base class of B.
```

The second case is where the source reference is null. For example, in the following code, even though it would normally be unsafe to convert a reference of a base class to that of a derived class, the conversion is allowed because the value of the source reference is null.

```
class A    { public int Field1; }
class B: A { public int Field2; }
  ...
A myVar1 = null;
B myVar2 = (B) myVar1;     // Allowed because myVar1 is null
```

The third case is where the *actual data* pointed to by the source reference could safely be converted implicitly. The following code shows an example, and Figure 17-21 illustrates the code.

- The implicit conversion in the second line makes myVar2 "think" that it is pointing to data of type A, while it is actually pointing to a data object of type B.

- The explicit conversion in the third line is casting a reference of a base class to a reference of one of its derived classes. Normally this would raise an exception. In this case, however, the object being pointed to actually is a data item of type B.

```
class A    { public int Field1; }
class B: A { public int Field2; }
  ...
B myVar1 = new B();
A myVar2 = myVar1;       // Implicitly cast myVar1 to type A.
B myVar3 = (B) myVar2;   // This cast is fine because the data is of type B.
```

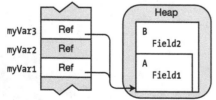 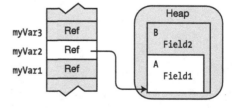

Figure 17-21. *Casting to a safe type*

Boxing Conversions

All C# types, including the value types, are derived from type object. Value types, however, are efficient, lightweight types that do not, by default, include their object component in the heap. When the object component is needed, however, you can use *boxing*, which is an implicit conversion that takes a value type value, creates from it a full reference type object in the heap, and returns a reference to the object.

One of the most common examples of a case where boxing is required is when you pass a value type to a method as a parameter with a data type of object (or some variation thereof). For example, Figure 17-22 shows three lines of code.

- The first two lines of code declare and initialize value type variable i and reference type variable oi.

- In the third line of code, you want to assign the value of variable i to oi. But oi is a reference type variable and must be assigned a reference to an object in the heap. Variable i, however, is a value type and doesn't have a reference to an object in the heap.

- The system therefore boxes the value of i by doing the following:

  - Creating an object of type int in the heap

  - Copying the value of i to the int object

  - Returning the reference of the int object to oi to store as its reference

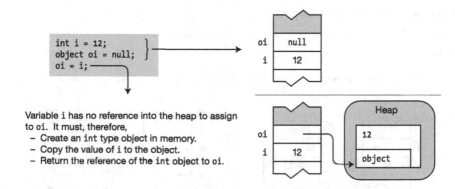

Figure 17-22. *Boxing creates a full reference type object from a value type*

Boxing Creates a Copy

A common misconception about boxing is that it acts upon the item being boxed. It doesn't. It returns a reference type *copy* of the value. After the boxing procedure, there are two copies of the value—the value type original and the reference type copy—each of which can be manipulated separately.

For example, the following code shows the separate manipulation of each copy of the value. Figure 17-23 illustrates the code.

- The first line defines value type variable i and initializes its value to 10.

- The second line creates reference type variable oi and initializes it with the boxed copy of variable i.

- The last three lines of code show i and oi being manipulated separately.

```
int i = 10;                    // Create and initialize value type
    Box i and assign its reference to oi.
            ↓
object oi = i;                 // Create and initialize reference type
Console.WriteLine($"i: { i }, io: { oi }");

i  = 12;
oi = 15;
Console.WriteLine($"i:{i}, io: {oi }");
```

This code produces the following output:

```
i: 10, io: 10
i: 12, io: 15
```

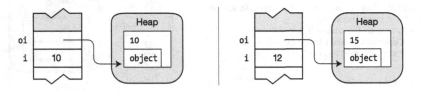

***Figure 17-23.** Boxing creates a copy that can be manipulated separately*

The Boxing Conversions

Figure 17-24 shows the boxing conversions. Any value type ValueTypeS can be implicitly converted to any of types object, System.ValueType, or InterfaceT, if ValueTypeS implements InterfaceT.

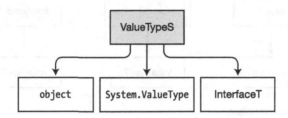

Figure 17-24. *Boxing is the implicit conversion of value types to reference types*

Unboxing Conversions

Unboxing is the process of converting a boxed object back to its value type.

- Unboxing is an explicit conversion.

- The system performs the following steps when unboxing a value to ValueTypeT:

  - It checks that the object being unboxed is actually a boxed value of type ValueTypeT.

  - It copies the value of the object to the variable.

For example, the following code shows an example of unboxing a value.

- Value type variable i is boxed and assigned to reference type variable oi.

- Variable oi is then unboxed, and its value is assigned to value type variable j.

```
static void Main()
{
    int i = 10;
      Box i and assign its reference to oi.
              ↓
    object oi = i;
        Unbox oi and assign its value to j.
               ↓
    int j = (int) oi;
    Console.WriteLine($"i: { i },   oi: { oi },   j: { j }");
}
```

This code produces the following output:

```
i: 10,   oi: 10,   j: 10
```

Attempting to unbox a value to a type other than the original type raises an InvalidCastException exception.

The Unboxing Conversions

Figure 17-25 shows the unboxing conversions.

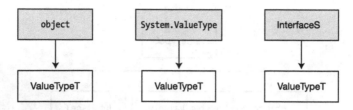

Figure 17-25. *The unboxing conversions*

User-Defined Conversions

Besides the standard conversions, you can also define both implicit and explicit conversions for your own classes and structs.

The syntax for user-defined conversions is shown in the following code.

- The syntax is the same for both implicit and explicit conversion declarations, except for the keywords `implicit` and `explicit`.

- Both the `public` and `static` modifiers are required.

```
      Required                  Operator   Keyword              Source
         ↓                         ↓          ↓                   ↓
public static implicit operator  TargetType ( SourceType  Identifier )
{
              ↑
        Implicit or explicit
    ...
    return ObjectOfTargetType;
}
```

For example, the following shows an example of the syntax of a conversion method that converts an object of type `Person` to an `int`:

```
public static implicit operator int(Person p)
{
    return p.Age;
}
```

Constraints on User-Defined Conversions

There are some important constraints on user-defined conversions. The most important are the following:

- You can only define user-defined conversions for classes and structs.

- You cannot redefine standard implicit or explicit conversions.

- The following are true for source type S and target type T:

  - S and T must be different types.

  - S and T cannot be related by inheritance. That is, S cannot be derived from T, and T cannot be derived from S.

  - Neither S nor T can be an interface type or the type `object`.

  - The conversion operator must be a member of either S or T.

- You cannot declare two conversions, one implicit and the other explicit, with the same source and target types.

Example of a User-Defined Conversion

The following code defines a class called Person that contains a person's name and age. The class also defines two implicit conversions. The first converts a Person object to an int value. The target int value is the age of the person. The second converts an int to a Person object.

```
class Person
{
   public string Name;
   public int    Age;
   public Person(string name, int age)
   {
      Name = name;
      Age = age;
   }

   public static implicit operator int(Person p)   // Convert Person to int.
   {
      return p.Age;
   }

   public static implicit operator Person(int i)   // Convert int to Person.
   {
      return new Person("Nemo", i);      // ("Nemo" is Latin for "No one".)
   }
}
class Program
{
   static void Main( )
   {
      Person bill = new Person( "bill", 25);
```

Convert a Person object to an int.
↓

```
      int age = bill;
      Console.WriteLine($"Person Info: { bill.Name }, { age }");
```

Convert an int to a Person object.
↓

```
      Person anon = 35;
      Console.WriteLine($"Person Info: { anon.Name }, { anon.Age }");
   }
}
```

This code produces the following output:

```
Person Info: bill, 25
Person Info: Nemo, 35
```

If you had defined the same conversion operators as explicit rather than implicit, then you would have needed to use cast expressions to perform the conversions, as shown here:

```
                     Explicit
     ...                ↓
public static explicit operator int( Person p )
{
    return p.Age;
}
...

static void Main( )
{
        ...   Requires cast expression
                ↓
    int age = (int) bill;
  ...
```

Evaluating User-Defined Conversions

The user-defined conversions discussed so far have directly converted the source type to an object of the target type in a single step, as shown in Figure 17-26.

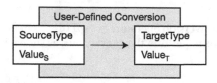

Figure 17-26. *Single-step user-defined conversion*

But user-defined conversions can have up to three steps in the full conversion. Figure 17-27 illustrates these stages, which include the following:

- The preliminary standard conversion

- The user-defined conversion

- The following standard conversion

There is *never* more than a single user-defined conversion in the chain.

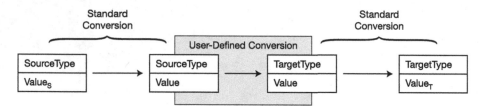

Figure 17-27. *Multistep user-defined conversion*

Example of a Multistep User-Defined Conversion

The following code declares class Employee, which is derived from class Person.

- Several sections ago, the code sample declared a user-defined conversion from class Person to int. So if there is a standard conversion from Employee to Person and one from int to float, you can convert from Employee to float.

  - There is a standard conversion from Employee to Person since Employee is derived from Person.

  - There is a standard conversion from int to float since that is an implicit numeric conversion.

- Since all three parts of the chain exist, you can convert from Employee to float. Figure 17-28 illustrates how the compiler performs the conversion.

```
class Employee : Person { }

class Person
{
    public string Name;
    public int    Age;

    // Convert a Person object to an int.
    public static implicit operator int(Person p)
    {
        return p.Age;
    }
}

class Program
{
    static void Main( )
    {
        Employee bill = new Employee();
        bill.Name = "William";
        bill.Age  = 25;
                     Convert an Employee to a float.
                          ↓
        float fVar = bill;

        Console.WriteLine($"Person Info: { bill.Name }, { fVar }");
    }
}
```

This code produces the following output:

```
Person Info: William, 25
```

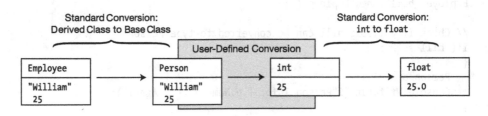

Figure 17-28. *Conversion of Employee to float*

441

The is Operator

As shown previously, some conversion attempts are not successful and raise an InvalidCastException exception at run time. Instead of blindly attempting a conversion, you can use the is operator to check whether a conversion would complete successfully.

The syntax of the is operator is the following, where Expr is the source expression:

```
            Returns a bool
                  ↓
─────────────────────────
Expr is TargetType
```

The operator returns true if Expr can be successfully converted to the target type through any of the following:

- A reference conversion

- A boxing conversion

- An unboxing conversion

For example, the following code uses the is operator to check whether variable bill, of type Employee, can be converted to type Person and then takes the appropriate action.

```csharp
class Employee : Person { }
class Person
{
   public string Name = "Anonymous";
   public int Age    = 25;
}

class Program
{
   static void Main()
   {
      Employee bill = new Employee();

      // Check if variable bill can be converted to type Person
      if( bill is Person )
      {
         Person p = bill;
         Console.WriteLine($"Person Info: { p.Name }, { p.Age }");
      }
   }
}
```

The is operator can be used only for reference conversions and boxing and unboxing conversions. It *cannot* be used for user-defined conversions.

The as Operator

The as operator is like the cast operator, except that it does not raise an exception. If the conversion fails, rather than raising an exception, it returns null.

The syntax of the as operator is the following, where

- Expr is the source expression.

- TargetType is the target type, which must be a reference type.

```
Returns a reference
         ↓
Expr as TargetType
```

Since the as operator returns a reference expression, it can be used as the source for an assignment. For example, variable bill of type Employee is converted to type Person, using the as operator, and is assigned to variable p of type Person. The code then checks to see whether p is null before using it.

```
class Employee : Person { }

class Person
{
   public string Name = "Anonymous";
   public int Age    = 25;
}

class Program
{
   static void Main()
   {
      Employee bill = new Employee();
      Person p;

      p = bill as Person;
      if( p != null )
      {
         Console.WriteLine($"Person Info: { p.Name }, { p.Age }");
      }
   }
}
```

Like the is operator, the as operator can be used only for reference conversions and boxing and unboxing conversions. It *cannot* be used for user-defined conversions or conversions to a value type.

CHAPTER 18

Generics

What Are Generics?

With the language constructs you've learned so far, you can build powerful objects of many different types. You do this mostly by declaring classes that encapsulate the behavior you want and then creating instances of those classes.

All the types used in the class declarations so far have been specific types—either programmer-defined or supplied by the language or the BCL. There are times, however, when a class would be more useful if you could "distill" or "refactor" out its actions and apply them not just to the data types for which they are coded but for other types as well.

Generics allow you to do just that. You can refactor your code and add an additional layer of abstraction so that, for certain kinds of code, the data types are not hard-coded. This is particularly designed for cases in which there are multiple sections of code performing the same instructions but on different data types.

That might sound pretty abstract, so we'll start with an example that should make things clearer.

A Stack Example

Suppose first that you have created the following code, which declares a class called MyIntStack that implements a stack of ints. It allows you to push ints onto the stack and pop them off. This, by the way, isn't the system stack.

```
class MyIntStack                    // Stack for ints
{
   int   StackPointer = 0;
   int[] StackArray;                // Array of int
     ↑                    int
   int                     ↓
   public void Push( int x )        // Input type: int
   {
     ...
   }         int
             ↓
   public int Pop()                 // Return type: int
   {
     ...
   }

     ...
}
```

Suppose now that you would like the same functionality for values of type float. There are several ways you could achieve this. One way is to perform the following steps to produce the subsequent code:

1. Cut and paste the code for class MyIntStack.

2. Change the class name to MyFloatStack.

3. Change the appropriate int declarations to float declarations throughout the class declaration.

```
class MyFloatStack                      // Stack for floats
{
   int    StackPointer = 0;
   float [] StackArray;                 // Array of float
     ↑                    float
   float                    ↓
   public void Push( float x )          // Input type: float
   {
      ...
   }
          float
            ↓
   public float Pop()                   // Return type: float
   {
      ...
   }
   ...
}
```

This method certainly works, but it's error-prone and has the following drawbacks:

*   You need to inspect every part of the class carefully to determine which type declarations need to be changed and which should be left alone.

*   You need to repeat the process for each new type of stack class you need (long, double, string, and so on).

*   After the process, you end up with multiple copies of nearly identical code, taking up additional space.

*   Debugging and maintaining the parallel implementations is inelegant and error-prone.

*   When fixing a bug, you need to fix it in all the parallel implementations—which is annoying and error prone.

Generics in C#

The *generics* feature offers a more elegant way of using a set of code with more than one type. Generics allow you to declare *type-parameterized* code, which you can instantiate with different types. This means you can write the code with "placeholders for types" and then supply the *actual* types when you create an instance of the class.

By this point in the text, you should be familiar with the concept that a type is not an object but a template for an object. In the same way, a generic type is not a type but a template for a type. Figure 18-1 illustrates this point.

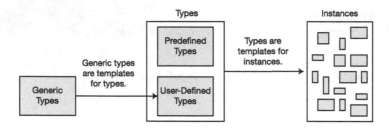

Figure 18-1. *Generic types are templates for types*

C# provides five kinds of generics: classes, structs, interfaces, delegates, and methods. Notice that the first four are types, and methods are members. Figure 18-2 shows how generic types fit in with the other types covered.

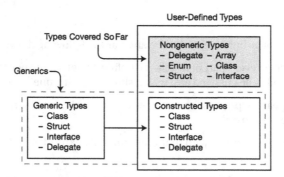

Figure 18-2. *Generics and user-defined types*

Continuing with the Stack Example

In the stack example, with classes MyIntStack and MyFloatStack, the bodies of the declarations of the classes are identical, except at the positions dealing with the type of the value held by the stack.

- In MyIntStack, these positions are occupied by type int.
- In MyFloatStack, they are occupied by float.

You can create a generic class from MyIntStack by doing the following:

1. Take the MyIntStack class declaration, and instead of substituting float for int, substitute the type placeholder T.

2. Change the class name to MyStack.

3. Place the string <T> after the class name.

The result is the following generic class declaration. The string consisting of the angle brackets with the T means that T is a placeholder for a type. (It doesn't have to be the letter T—it can be any identifier.) Everywhere throughout the body of the class declaration where T is located, an actual type will need to be substituted by the compiler.

```
class MyStack<T>
{
    int StackPointer = 0;
    T [] StackArray;

    public void Push(T x ) {...}

    public T Pop() {...}
        ...
}
```

Generic Classes

Now that you've seen a generic class, let's look at generic classes in more detail and see how they're created and used.

As you know, there are two steps for creating and using your own regular, nongeneric classes: declaring the class and creating instances of the class. However, generic classes are not actual classes but templates for classes—so you must first construct actual class types from them. You can then create references and instances from these constructed class types.

Figure 18-3 illustrates the process at a high level. If it's not all completely clear yet, don't worry—we'll cover each part in the following sections.

1. Declare a class, using placeholders for some of the types.

2. Provide *actual* types to substitute in for the placeholders. This gives you an actual class definition, with all the "blanks" filled in. This is called a *constructed type*.

3. Create instances of the constructed type.

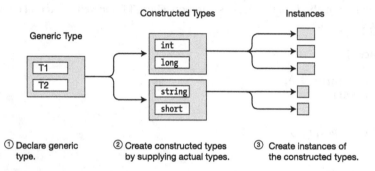

Figure 18-3. Creating instances from a generic type

Declaring a Generic Class

Declaring a simple generic class is much like declaring a regular class, with the following differences:

- You place a matching set of angle brackets after the class name.

- Between the angle brackets, you place a comma-separated list of the placeholder strings that represent the types, to be supplied on demand. These are called *type parameters*.

- You use the type parameters throughout the body of the declaration of the generic class to represent the types that should be substituted in.

For example, the following code declares a generic class called SomeClass. The type parameters are listed between the angle brackets and then used throughout the body of the declaration as if they were real types.

```
            Type parameters
                  ↓
class SomeClass < T1, T2 >
{    Normally, a type would be used in this position.
              ↓
    public T1 SomeVar;
    public T2 OtherVar;
}          ↑

        Normally, a type would be used in this position.
```

There is no special keyword that flags a generic class declaration. Instead, the presence of the type parameter list, demarcated with angle brackets, distinguishes a generic class declaration from a regular class declaration.

Creating a Constructed Type

Once you have declared the generic type, you need to tell the compiler what actual types should be substituted for the placeholders (the type parameters). The compiler takes those actual types and creates a constructed type, which is a template from which it creates actual class objects.

The syntax for creating the constructed type is shown next and consists of listing the class name and supplying real types between the angle brackets, in place of the type parameters. The real types being substituted for the type parameters are called *type arguments*.

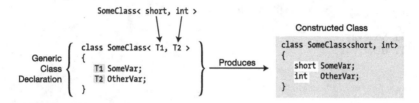

The compiler takes the type arguments and substitutes them for their corresponding type parameters throughout the body of the generic class, producing the constructed type—from which actual class instances are created. Figure 18-4 shows the declaration of generic class SomeClass on the left. On the right, it shows the constructed class created by using the type arguments short and int.

Figure 18-4. *Supplying type arguments for all the type parameters of a generic class allows the compiler to produce a constructed class from which actual class objects can be created.*

Figure 18-5 illustrates the difference between type parameters and type arguments.

- Generic class declarations have *type parameters*, which act as placeholders for types.

- *Type arguments* are the actual types you supply when creating a constructed type.

Type Parameters ⌐

class SomeClass< T1, T2 >
{
    ...
}

Generic Class Declaration

Type Arguments ⌐

SomeClass< short, int >

Constructed Type

Figure 18-5. *Type parameters versus type arguments*

Creating Variables and Instances

A constructed class type is used just like a regular type in creating references and instances. For example, the following code shows the creation of two class objects.

- The first line shows the creation of an object from a regular, nongeneric class. This is a form that you should be completely familiar with by now.

- The second line of code shows the creation of an object from generic class `SomeClass`, instantiated with types `short` and `int`. The form is exactly analogous to the line above it, with the constructed class forms in place of a regular class name.

- The third line is the same semantically as the second line but rather than listing the constructed type on both sides of the equal sign, it uses the `var` keyword to make the compiler use type inference.

```
MyNonGenClass          myNGC = new MyNonGenClass          ();
        Constructed class                    Constructed class
                ↓                                    ↓
SomeClass<short, int>  mySc1 = new SomeClass<short  int>();
var                    mySc2 = new SomeClass<short, int>();
```

As with nongeneric classes, the reference and the instance can be created separately, as shown in Figure 18-6. The figure also shows that what is going on in memory is the same as for a nongeneric class.

- The first line below the generic class declaration allocates a reference in the stack for variable `myInst`. Its value is `null`.

- The second line allocates an instance in the heap and assigns its reference to the variable.

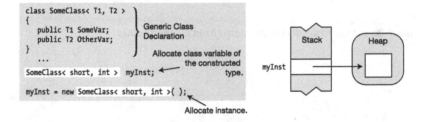

Figure 18-6. *Using a constructed type to create a reference and an instance*

Many different class types can be constructed from the same generic class. Each one is a separate class type, just as if it had its own separate nongeneric class declaration.

For example, the following code shows the creation of two types from generic class SomeClass. The code is illustrated in Figure 18-7.

- One type is constructed with types short and int.

- The other is constructed with types int and long.

```
class SomeClass< T1, T2 >                         // Generic class
{
    public T1 SomeVar;
    public T2 OtherVar;
}

class Program
{
    static void Main()
    {
        var first  =  new SomeClass<short, int >();    // Constructed type
        var second =  new SomeClass<int,   long>();    // Constructed type

        ...
```

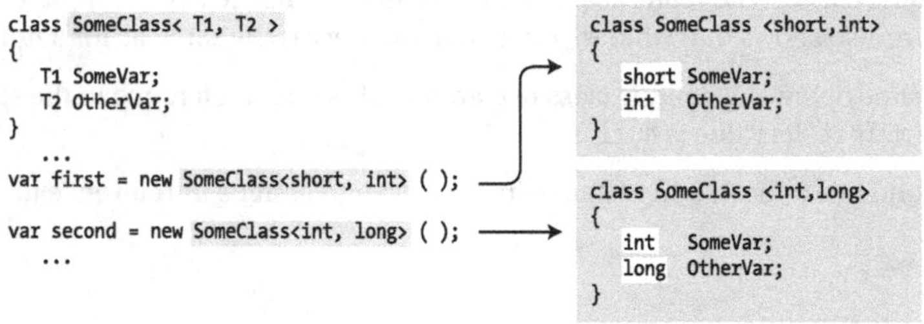

Figure 18-7. *Two different constructed classes created from a generic class*

The Stack Example Using Generics

The following code shows the stack example implemented using generics. Method Main defines two variables: stackInt and stackString. The two constructed types are created using int and string as the type arguments.

```
class MyStack<T>
{
   T[] StackArray;
   int StackPointer = 0;

   public void Push(T x)
   {
      if ( !IsStackFull )
         StackArray[StackPointer++] = x;
   }

   public T Pop()
   {
      return ( !IsStackEmpty )
         ? StackArray[--StackPointer]
         : StackArray[0];
   }

   const int MaxStack = 10;
   bool IsStackFull  { get{ return StackPointer >= MaxStack; } }
   bool IsStackEmpty { get{ return StackPointer <= 0; } }

   public MyStack()
   {
      StackArray = new T[MaxStack];
   }

   public void Print()
   {
      for (int i = StackPointer-1; i >= 0 ; i--)
         Console.WriteLine($"   Value: { StackArray[i] }");
   }

}
```

```
class Program
{
   static void Main( )
   {
      MyStack<int>    StackInt    = new MyStack<int>();
      MyStack<string> StackString = new MyStack<string>();

      StackInt.Push(3);
      StackInt.Push(5);
      StackInt.Push(7);
      StackInt.Push(9);
      StackInt.Print();

      StackString.Push("This is fun");
      StackString.Push("Hi there!   ");
      StackString.Print();
   }
}
```

This code produces the following output:

```
Value: 9
Value: 7
Value: 5
Value: 3

Value: Hi there!
Value: This is fun
```

Comparing the Generic and Nongeneric Stack

Table 18-1 summarizes some of the differences between the initial nongeneric version of the stack and the final generic version of the stack. Figure 18-8 illustrates some of these differences.

Table 18-1. *Differences Between the Nongeneric and Generic Stacks*

	Nongeneric	Generic
Source Code Size	Larger: You need a new implementation for each type.	Smaller: You need only one implementation regardless of the number of constructed types.
Executable Size	The compiled version of each stack is present, regardless of whether it is used.	Only types for which there is a constructed type are present in the executable.
Ease of Writing	Easier to write and read, because it's more concrete.	Harder to write and read, because it's more abstract.
Difficulty to Maintain	More error-prone to maintain, since all changes need to be applied for each applicable type.	Easier to maintain, because modifications are needed in only one place.

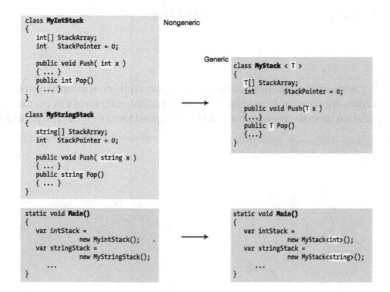

Figure 18-8. *Nongeneric stack versus generic stack*

Constraints on Type Parameters

In the generic stack example, the stack did not do anything with the items it contained other than store them and pop them. It didn't try to add them, compare them, or do anything else that would require using operations of the items themselves. There's good reason for that. Since the generic stack doesn't know the type of the items it will be storing, it can't know what members these types implement.

All C# objects, however, are ultimately derived from class object, so the one thing the stack can be sure of about the items it's storing is that they implement the members of class object. These include methods ToString, Equals, and GetType. Other than that, it can't know what members are available.

As long as your code doesn't access the objects of the types it handles (or as long as it sticks to the members of type object), your generic class can handle any type. Type parameters that meet this constraint are called *unbounded type parameters*. If, however, your code tries to use any other members, the compiler will produce an error message.

For example, the following code declares a class called Simple with a method called LessThan that takes two variables of the same generic type. LessThan attempts to return the result of using the less-than operator. But not all classes implement the less-than operator, so you can't just substitute any class for T. The compiler, therefore, produces an error message.

```
class Simple<T>
{
    static public bool LessThan(T i1, T i2)
    {
        return i1 < i2;                    // Error
    }
    ...
}
```

To make generics more useful, you need to be able to supply additional information to the compiler about what kinds of types are acceptable as arguments. These additional bits of information are called *constraints*. Only types that meet the constraints can be substituted for the given type parameter to produce constructed types.

Where Clauses

Constraints are listed as where clauses.

- Each type parameter that has constraints has its own where clause.

- If a parameter has multiple constraints, they are listed in the where clause, separated by commas.

The syntax of a where clause is the following:

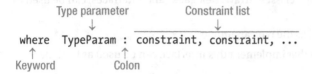

```
             Type parameter          Constraint list
                  ↓          _____↓_____
where  TypeParam : constraint, constraint, ...
  ↑                    ↑
Keyword              Colon
```

The important points about where clauses are the following:

- They're listed after the closing angle bracket of the type parameter list.

- They're not separated by commas or any other token.

- They can be listed in any order.

- The token where is a contextual keyword, so you can use it in other contexts.

For example, the following generic class has three type parameters. T1 is unbounded. For T2, only classes of type Customer or classes *derived from* Customer can be used as type arguments. For T3, only classes that implement interface IComparable can be used as type arguments.

```
           Unbounded   With constraints
               ↓       __↓__     No separators
class MyClass < T1, T2, T3 >        ↓
               where T2: Customer          // Constraint for T2
               where T3: IComparable       // Constraint for T3
{                            ↑
   ...              No separators
}
```

Constraint Types and Order

There are five types of constraints. These are listed in Table 18-2.

Table 18-2. *Types of Constraints*

Constraint Type	Description
ClassName	Only classes of this type or classes derived from it can be used as the type argument.
class	Any reference type, including classes, arrays, delegates, and interfaces, can be used as the type argument.
struct	Any value type can be used as the type argument.
InterfaceName	Only this interface or types that implement this interface can be used as the type argument.
new()	Any type with a parameterless public constructor can be used as the type argument. This is called the *constructor constraint*.

The where clauses can be listed in any order. The constraints in a where clause, however, must be placed in a particular order, as shown in Figure 18-9.

- There can be at most one primary constraint, and if there is one, it must be listed first.

- There can be any number of InterfaceName constraints.

- If the constructor constraint is present, it must be listed last.

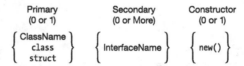

Figure 18-9. *If a type parameter has multiple constraints, they must be in this order*

The following declarations show examples of where clauses:

```
class SortedList<S>
        where S: IComparable<S> { ... }

class LinkedList<M,N>
        where M : IComparable<M>
        where N : ICloneable     { ... }

class MyDictionary<KeyType, ValueType>
        where KeyType : IEnumerable,
        new()                    { ... }
```

Generic Methods

Unlike the other generics, a method is not a type but a member. You can declare generic methods in both generic and nongeneric classes and in structs and interfaces, as shown in Figure 18-10.

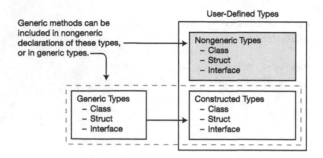

Figure 18-10. *Generic methods can be declared in generic and nongeneric types*

Declaring a Generic Method

Generic methods have a type parameter list and optional constraints.

- Generic methods have two parameter lists.

    - The *type parameter* list, enclosed in angle brackets.

    - The *method parameter* list, enclosed in parentheses.

- To declare a generic method, do the following:

    - Place the type parameter list immediately after the method name and before the method parameter list.

    - Place any constraint clauses after the method parameter list.

```
          Type parameter list          Constraint clauses
                  ↓                            ↓
public void PrintData<S, T> ( S p, T t ) where S: Person
{                              ↑
...                     Method parameter list
}
```

■ **Note**   Remember that the type parameter list goes after the method name and before the method parameter list.

Invoking a Generic Method

To invoke a generic method, supply type arguments with the method invocation, as shown here:

```
        Type arguments
             ↓
    MyMethod<short, int>();
    MyMethod<int, long >();
```

Figure 18-11 shows the declaration of a generic method called DoStuff, which takes two type parameters. Below it are two places where the method is called, each with a different set of type parameters. The compiler uses each of these constructed instances to produce a different version of the method, as shown on the right of the figure.

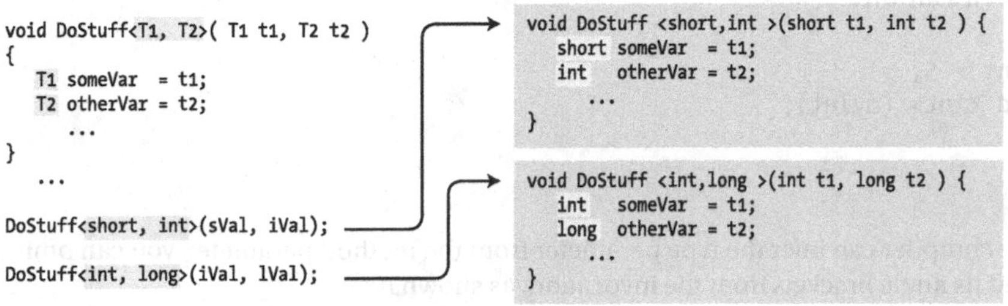

```
void DoStuff<T1, T2>( T1 t1, T2 t2 )              void DoStuff <short,int >(short t1, int t2 ) {
{                                                     short someVar  = t1;
    T1 someVar  = t1;                                 int    otherVar = t2;
    T2 otherVar = t2;                                    ...
      ...                                           }
}
  ...
                                                  void DoStuff <int,long >(int t1, long t2 ) {
DoStuff<short, int>(sVal, iVal);                      int    someVar  = t1;
                                                      long   otherVar = t2;
DoStuff<int, long>(iVal, lVal);                          ...
                                                  }
```

Figure 18-11. *A generic method with two instantiations*

Inferring Types

If you are passing parameters into a method, the compiler can sometimes infer from the types of the *method parameters* the types that should be used as the *type parameters* of the generic method. This can make the method calls simpler and easier to read.

For example, the following code declares MyMethod, which takes a method parameter of the same type as the type parameter.

```
public void MyMethod <T> (T myVal) { ... }
```
                         ↑   ↑
                    Both are of type T

If you invoke MyMethod with a variable of type int, as shown in the following code, the information in the type parameter of the method invocation is redundant, since the compiler can see from the method parameter that it's an int.

```
int myInt = 5;
MyMethod <int> (myInt);
```
          ↑   ↑
        Both are ints

Since the compiler can infer the type parameter from the method parameter, you can omit the type parameter and its angle brackets from the invocation, as shown here:

```
MyMethod(myInt);
```

Example of a Generic Method

The following code declares a generic method called ReverseAndPrint in a nongeneric class called Simple. The method takes as its parameter an array of any type. Main declares three different array types. It then calls the method twice with each array. The first time it calls the method with a particular array, it explicitly uses the type parameter. The second time, the type is inferred.

```
class Simple                                          // Non-generic class
{
   static public void ReverseAndPrint<T>(T[] arr)     // Generic method
   {
      Array.Reverse(arr);
      foreach (T item in arr)                         // Use type argument T.
         Console.Write( $"{ item.ToString() }, ");
      Console.WriteLine("");
   }
}

class Program
{
   static void Main()
   {
      // Create arrays of various types.
      var intArray    = new int[]    { 3, 5, 7, 9, 11 };
      var stringArray = new string[] { "first", "second", "third" };
      var doubleArray = new double[] { 3.567, 7.891, 2.345 };

      Simple.ReverseAndPrint<int>(intArray);          // Invoke method.
      Simple.ReverseAndPrint(intArray);               // Infer type and invoke.

      Simple.ReverseAndPrint<string>(stringArray);    // Invoke method.
      Simple.ReverseAndPrint(stringArray);            // Infer type and invoke.

      Simple.ReverseAndPrint<double>(doubleArray);    // Invoke method.
      Simple.ReverseAndPrint(doubleArray);            // Infer type and invoke.
   }
}
```

This code produces the following output:

```
11, 9, 7, 5, 3,
3, 5, 7, 9, 11,
third, second, first,
first, second, third,
2.345, 7.891, 3.567,
3.567, 7.891, 2.345,
```

Extension Methods with Generic Classes

Extension methods are described in detail in Chapter 8 and work just as well with generic classes. They allow you to associate a static method in one class with a different generic class and to invoke the method as if it were an instance method on a constructed instance of the class.

As with nongeneric classes, an extension method for a generic class must satisfy the following constraints:

- It must be declared static.

- It must be the member of a static class.

- It must contain as its first parameter type the keyword this, followed by the name of the generic class it extends.

The following code shows an example of an extension method called Print on a generic class called Holder<T>:

```
static class ExtendHolder
{
    public static void Print<T>(this Holder<T> h)
    {
        T[] vals = h.GetValues();
        Console.WriteLine($"{ vals[0] },\t{ vals[1] },\t{ vals[2] }");
    }
}

class Holder<T>
{
    T[] Vals = new T[3];

    public Holder(T v0, T v1, T v2)
    { Vals[0] = v0; Vals[1] = v1; Vals[2] = v2; }

    public T[] GetValues() { return Vals; }
}

class Program
{
    static void Main(string[] args) {
        var intHolder    = new Holder<int>(3, 5, 7);
        var stringHolder = new Holder<string>("a1", "b2", "c3");
        intHolder.Print();
        stringHolder.Print();
    }
}
```

This code produces the following output:

```
3,      5,      7
a1,     b2,     c3
```

Generic Structs

Like generic classes, generic structs can have type parameters and constraints. The rules and conditions for generic structs are the same as those for generic classes.

For example, the following code declares a generic struct called `PieceOfData`, which stores and retrieves a piece of data, the type of which is determined when the type is constructed. `Main` creates objects of two constructed types—one using `int` and the other using `string`.

```
struct PieceOfData<T>                          // Generic struct
{
    public PieceOfData(T value) { _data = value; }
    private T _data;
    public  T Data
    {
        get { return _data; }
        set { _data = value; }
    }
}

class Program
{
    static void Main()              Constructed type
    {                                      ↓
        var intData    = new PieceOfData<int>(10);
        var stringData = new PieceOfData<string>("Hi there.");
                                            ↑
                                     Constructed type
        Console.WriteLine($"intData    = { intData.Data }");
        Console.WriteLine($"stringData = { stringData.Data }");
    }
}
```

This code produces the following output:

```
intData    = 10
stringData = Hi there.
```

Generic Delegates

Generic delegates are very much like nongeneric delegates, except that the type parameters determine the characteristics of what methods will be accepted.

- To declare a generic delegate, place the type parameter list in angle brackets after the delegate name and before the delegate parameter list.

Type parameters

```
delegate R MyDelegate<T, R>( T value );
```

Return type   Delegate formal parameter

- Notice that there are two parameter lists: the delegate formal parameter list and the type parameter list.

- The scope of the type parameters includes the following:

  - The return type

  - The formal parameter list

  - The constraint clauses

The following code shows an example of a generic delegate. In Main, generic delegate MyDelegate is instantiated with an argument of type string and initialized with method PrintString.

```
delegate void MyDelegate<T>(T value);              // Generic delegate

class Simple
{
   static public void PrintString(string s)        // Method matches delegate
   {
      Console.WriteLine( s );
   }

   static public void PrintUpperString(string s)   // Method matches delegate
   {
      Console.WriteLine($"{ s.ToUpper() }");
   }
}

class Program
{
   static void Main( )
   {
      var myDel =                                  // Create inst of delegate.
         new MyDelegate<string>(Simple.PrintString);
      myDel += Simple.PrintUpperString;            // Add a second method.

      myDel("Hi There.");                          // Call delegate.
   }
}
```

This code produces the following output:

```
Hi There.
HI THERE.
```

Another Generic Delegate Example

Since C#'s LINQ feature uses generic delegates extensively, it's worth showing another example before we get there. We'll cover LINQ itself, and more about its generic delegates, in Chapter 20.

The following code declares a generic delegate named Func, which takes methods with two parameters and that return a value. The method return type is represented as TR, and the method parameter types are represented as T1 and T2.

```
                            Delegate parameter type
                            ↓    ↓        ↓        ↓
public delegate TR Func<T1, T2, TR>(T1 p1, T2 p2);  // Generic delegate
                    ↑            ↑
class Simple      Delegate return type
{
    static public string PrintString(int p1, int p2) // Method matches delegate
    {
        int total = p1 + p2;
        return total.ToString();
    }
}

class Program
{
    static void Main()
    {
        var myDel =                                  // Create inst of delegate.
            new Func<int, int, string>(Simple.PrintString);

        Console.WriteLine($"Total: { myDel(15, 13) }");  // Call delegate.
    }
}
```

This code produces the following output:

```
Total: 28
```

Generic Interfaces

Generic interfaces allow you to write interfaces where the formal parameters and return types of interface members are generic type parameters. Generic interface declarations are similar to nongeneric interface declarations but have the type parameter list in angle brackets after the interface name.

For example, the following code declares a generic interface called IMyIfc.

- Simple is a generic class that implements generic interface IMyIfc.

- Main instantiates two objects of the generic class: one with type int and the other with type string.

```
              Type parameter
                    ↓
interface IMyIfc<T>                          // Generic interface
{
    T ReturnIt(T inValue);
}
         Type parameter     Generic interface
               ↓                  ↓
class Simple<S> : IMyIfc<S>                   // Generic class
{
    public S ReturnIt(S inValue)             // Implement generic interface.
    { return inValue; }
}

class Program
{
    static void Main()
    {
        var trivInt    = new Simple<int>();
        var trivString = new Simple<string>();

        Console.WriteLine($"{ trivInt.ReturnIt(5) }");
        Console.WriteLine($"{ trivString.ReturnIt("Hi there.") }");
    }
}
```

This code produces the following output:

```
5
Hi there.
```

471

An Example Using Generic Interfaces

The following example illustrates two additional capabilities of generic interfaces:

- Like other generics, instances of a generic interface instantiated with different type parameters are different interfaces.

- You can implement a generic interface in a *nongeneric type*.

For example, the following code is similar to the previous example, but in this case, Simple is a *nongeneric* class that implements a generic interface. In fact, it implements two instances of IMyIfc. One instance is instantiated with type int and the other with type string.

```
interface IMyIfc<T>                        // Generic interface
{
    T ReturnIt(T inValue);
}
              Two different interfaces from the same generic interface
                       ↓              ↓
class Simple : IMyIfc<int>, IMyIfc<string>   // Nongeneric class
{
    public int ReturnIt(int inValue)          // Implement interface using int.
    { return inValue; }

    public string ReturnIt(string inValue)    // Implement interface using string.
    { return inValue; }
}

class Program
{
    static void Main()
    {
        Simple trivial = new Simple();

        Console.WriteLine($"{ trivial.ReturnIt(5) }");
        Console.WriteLine($"{ trivial.ReturnIt("Hi there.") }");
    }
}
```

This code produces the following output:

```
5
Hi there.
```

Generic Interface Implementations Must Be Unique

When implementing an interface in a generic type, there must be no possible combination of type arguments that would create a duplicate interface in the type.

For example, in the following code, class `Simple` uses two instantiations of interface `IMyIfc`.

- The first one is a constructed type, instantiated with type `int`.

- The second one has a type parameter rather than an argument.

There's nothing wrong with the second interface in itself since it's perfectly fine to use a generic interface. The problem here, though, is that it allows a possible conflict because if `int` is used as the type argument to replace `S` in the second interface, then `Simple` would have two interfaces of the same type—which is not allowed.

```
interface IMyIfc<T>
{
    T ReturnIt(T inValue);
}
                    Two interfaces
               _____   _____
                  ↓          ↓
class Simple<S> : IMyIfc<int>, IMyIfc<S>      // Error!
{
    public int ReturnIt(int inValue)   // Implement first interface.
    {
        return inValue;
    }
    public S ReturnIt(S inValue)       // Implement second interface,
    {                                  // but if it's int, it would be
        return inValue;                // the same as the one above.
    }
}
```

■ **Note**   The names of generic interfaces do not clash with nongeneric interfaces. For example, in the preceding code, we could have also declared a nongeneric interface named `IMyIfc`.

Covariance and Contravariance

As you've seen throughout this chapter, when you create an instance of a generic type, the compiler takes the generic type declaration and the type arguments and creates a constructed type. A mistake that people commonly make, however, is to assume that you can assign a delegate of a derived type to a variable of a delegate of a base type. In the following sections, we'll look at this topic, which is called *variance*. There are three types of variance—*covariance*, *contravariance*, and *invariance*.

Covariance

We'll start by reviewing something you've already learned: every variable has a type assigned to it, and you can assign an object of a more derived type to a variable of one of its base types. This is called *assignment compatibility*. The following code demonstrates assignment compatibility with a base class Animal and a class Dog derived from Animal. In Main, you can see that the code creates an object of type Dog and assigns it to variable a2 of type Animal. The output follows the code.

```
class Animal
{  public int NumberOfLegs = 4; }

class Dog : Animal
{ }

class Program
{
   static void Main( )
   {
      Animal a1 = new Animal( );
      Animal a2 = new Dog( );

      Console.WriteLine($"Number of dog legs: { a2.NumberOfLegs }");
   }
}
```

```
Number of dog legs: 4
```

Figure 18-12 illustrates assignment compatibility. In this figure, the boxes showing the Dog and Animal objects also show their base classes.

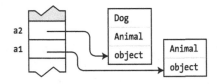

Figure 18-12. *Assignment compatibility means that you can assign a reference of a more derived type to a variable of a less derived type*

Now let's look at a more interesting case by expanding the code in the following ways, as shown in the following code:

- This code adds a generic delegate named Factory, which takes a single type parameter T, takes no method parameters, and returns an object of type T.

- We've added a method named MakeDog that takes no parameters and returns a Dog object. This method, therefore, matches delegate Factory if we use Dog as the type parameter.

- The first line of Main creates a delegate object whose type is delegate Factory<Dog> and assigns its reference to variable dogMaker, of the same type.

- The second line attempts to assign a delegate of type delegate Factory<Dog> to a delegate type variable named animalMaker of type delegate Factory<Animal>.

This second line in Main, however, causes a problem, and the compiler produces an error message saying that it can't implicitly convert the type on the right to the type on the left.

```
class Animal        { public int Legs = 4; }  // Base class
class Dog : Animal { }                        // Derived class

delegate T Factory<T>( );          ← delegate Factory

class Program
{
    static Dog MakeDog( )          ← Method that matches delegate Factory
    {
        return new Dog( );
    }

    static void Main( )
    {
        Factory<Dog>    dogMaker    = MakeDog;   ← Create delegate object.
        Factory<Animal> animalMaker = dogMaker;  ← Attempt to assign delegate object.

        Console.WriteLine( animalMaker( ).Legs.ToString( ) );
    }
}
```

It seems to make sense that a delegate constructed with the base type should be able to hold a delegate constructed with the derived type. So why does the compiler give an error message? Doesn't the principle of assignment compatibility hold?

The principle *does* hold, but it doesn't apply in this situation! The problem is that although Dog derives from Animal, delegate Factory<Dog> does *not* derive from delegate Factory<Animal>. Instead, both delegate objects are peers, deriving from type delegate, which derives from type object, as shown in Figure 18-13. Neither delegate is derived from the other, so assignment compatibility doesn't apply.

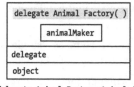

delegate Animal Factory<Animal>()   delegate Dog Factory<Dog>()

Figure 18-13. Assignment compatibility doesn't apply because the two delegates are unrelated by inheritance

Although the mismatch of delegate types doesn't allow assigning one type to the variable of another type, it isn't too bad in this situation, because in the example code, any time we would execute delegate animalMaker, the calling code would expect to have a reference to an Animal object returned. If it returned a reference to a Dog object instead, that would be perfectly fine since a reference to a Dog is a reference to an Animal, by assignment compatibility.

Looking at the situation more carefully, we can see that for any generic delegate, if a type parameter is used *only as an output value*, then the same situation applies. In all such situations, you would be able to use a constructed delegate type created with a derived class, and it would work fine since the invoking code would always be expecting a reference to the base class—which is exactly what it would get.

This constant *relation* between the use of a derived type only as an output value and the validity of the constructed delegate is called *covariance*. To let the compiler know that this is what you intend, you must mark the type parameter in the delegate declaration with the out keyword.

If we change the delegate declaration in the example by adding the out keyword, as shown here, the code compiles and works fine:

```
delegate T Factory<out T>( );
                       ↑
              Keyword specifying covariance
                 of the type parameter
```

Figure 18-14 illustrates the components of covariance in this example.

- The variable on the stack, on the left, is of type delegate T Factory<out T>(), where type variable T is of class Animal.

- The actual constructed delegate in the heap, on the right, was declared with a type variable of class Dog, which is derived from class Animal.

- This is acceptable because when the delegate is called, the calling code receives an object of type Dog, instead of the expected object of type Animal. The calling code can freely operate on the Animal part of the object, as it expects to do.

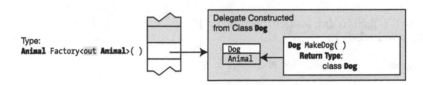

Figure 18-14. *The covariant relationship allows a more derived type to be in return and out positions*

Contravariance

Now that you understand covariance, let's take a look at a related situation. The following code declares a delegate named Action1 that takes a single type parameter and a single method parameter whose type is that of the type parameter, and it returns no value.

The code also contains a method called ActOnAnimal, whose signature and void return type match the delegate declaration.

The first line in Main creates a constructed delegate using type Animal and method ActOnAnimal, whose signature and void return type match the delegate declaration. In the second line, however, the code attempts to assign the reference to this delegate to a stack variable named dog1, of type delegate Action1<Dog>.

```
class Animal { public int NumberOfLegs = 4; }
class Dog : Animal { }

class Program              Keyword for contravariance
{                                 ↓
    delegate void Action1<in T>( T a );

    static void ActOnAnimal( Animal a ) { Console.WriteLine( a.NumberOfLegs ); }

    static void Main( )
    {
        Action1<Animal> act1 = ActOnAnimal;
        Action1<Dog>    dog1 = act1;
        dog1( new Dog() );
    }
}
```

This code produces the following output:

4

Like the previous situation, by default, you can't assign the two incompatible types. But also like the previous situation, there are scenarios where the assignment would work perfectly fine.

In fact, this is true whenever the type parameter is used *only as an input parameter* to the method in the delegate. The reason for this is that even though the invoking code passes in a reference to a more derived class, the method in the delegate is only expecting a reference to a less derived class—which of course it receives and knows how to manipulate.

This relation, allowing a more derived object where a less derived object is expected, is called *contravariance*. To use it, you must use the in keyword with the type parameter, as shown in the code.

Figure 18-15 illustrates the components of contravariance in line 2 of Main.

- The variable on the stack, on the left, is of type delegate void Action1<in T>(T a), where the type variable is of class Dog.

- The actual constructed delegate, on the right, is declared with a type variable of class Animal, which is a base class of class Dog.

- This works fine because when the delegate is called, the calling code passes in an object of type Dog to method ActOnAnimal, which is expecting an object of type Animal. The method can freely operate on the Animal part of the object, as it expects to do.

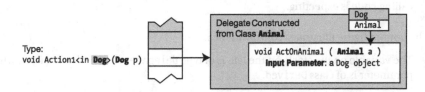

Figure 18-15. *The contravariant relationship allows more derived types to be allowed as input parameters*

Summarizing the Differences Between Covariance and Contravariance

Figure 18-16 summarizes the differences between covariance and contravariance in a generic delegate.

- The top figure illustrates covariance.

  - The variable on the stack, on the left, is of type delegate F<out T>( ), where the type parameter is of a class named Base.

  - The actual constructed delegate, on the right, was declared with a type parameter of class Derived, which is derived from class Base.

  - This works fine because when the delegate is called, the method returns a reference to an object of the derived type, which is also a reference to the base class, which is exactly what the calling code is expecting.

- The bottom figure illustrates contravariance.

  - The variable on the stack, on the left, is of type delegate void F<in T>(T a), where the type parameter is of class Derived.

  - The actual constructed delegate, on the right, was declared with a type parameter of class Base, which is a base class of class Derived.

  - This works fine because when the delegate is called, the calling code passes in an object of the derived type to the method, which is expecting an object of the base type. The method can operate freely on the base part of the object, as it expects to do.

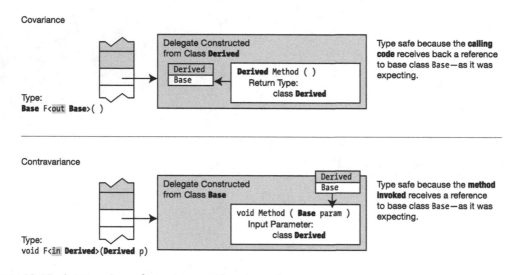

Figure 18-16. *A comparison of covariance and contravariance*

Covariance and Contravariance in Interfaces

You should now have an understanding of covariance and contravariance as it applies to delegates. The same principles apply to interfaces, including the syntax using the out and in keywords in the interface declaration.

The following code shows an example of using covariance with an interface. The things to note about the code are the following:

- The code declares a generic interface with type parameter T. The out keyword specifies that the type parameter is covariant.

- Generic class SimpleReturn implements the generic interface.

- Method DoSomething shows how a method can take an *interface* as a parameter. This method takes as its parameter a generic IMyIfc interface constructed with type Animal.

The code works in the following way:

- The first two lines of Main create and initialize a constructed instance of generic class SimpleReturn, using class Dog.

- The next line assigns that object to a variable on the stack that is declared of constructed interface type IMyIfc<Animal>. Notice several things about this declaration:

    - The type on the left of the assignment is an interface type—not a class.

    - Even though the interface types don't exactly match, the compiler allows them because of the covariant out specifier in the interface declaration.

- Finally, the code calls method DoSomething with the constructed covariant class that implements the interface.

```
class Animal { public string Name; }
class Dog: Animal{ };
                Keyword for covariance
                      ↓
interface IMyIfc<out T>
{
    T GetFirst();
}

class SimpleReturn<T>: IMyIfc<T>
{
    public T[] items = new T[2];
    public T GetFirst() { return items[0]; }
}

class Program
{
    static void DoSomething(IMyIfc<Animal> returner)
    {
        Console.WriteLine( returner.GetFirst().Name );
    }

    static void Main( )
    {
        SimpleReturn<Dog> dogReturner = new SimpleReturn<Dog>();
        dogReturner.items[0] = new Dog() { Name = "Avonlea" };

        IMyIfc<Animal> animalReturner = dogReturner;

        DoSomething(dogReturner);
    }

}
```

This code produces the following output:

Avonlea

More About Variance

The previous two sections explained explicit covariance and contravariance. There is also a situation where the compiler automatically recognizes that a certain constructed delegate is covariant or contravariant and makes the type coercion automatically. This happens when the object hasn't yet had a type assigned to it. The following code shows an example.

The first line of Main creates a constructed delegate of type Factory<Animal> from a method where the return type is a Dog object, not an Animal object. When Main creates this delegate, the method name on the right side of the assignment operator isn't yet a delegate object and hence doesn't have a delegate type. At this point the compiler can determine that the method matches the type of the delegate, with the exception that its return type is of type Dog rather than type Animal. The compiler is smart enough to realize that this is a covariant relation and creates the constructed type and assigns it to the variable.

Compare that with the assignments in the third and fourth lines of Main. In these cases, the expressions on the right side of the equal sign are already delegates and hence have a delegate type. These, therefore, need the out specifier in the delegate declaration to signal the compiler to allow them to be covariant.

```
class Animal { public int Legs = 4; }          // Base class
class Dog : Animal { }                          // Derived class

class Program
{
   delegate T Factory<out T>();

   static Dog MakeDog() { return new Dog(); }

   static void Main()
   {
      Factory<Animal> animalMaker1 = MakeDog;       // Coerced implicitly

      Factory<Dog>    dogMaker     = MakeDog;
      Factory<Animal> animalMaker2 = dogMaker;       // Requires the out specifier

      Factory<Animal> animalMaker3
               = new Factory<Dog>(MakeDog);          // Requires the out specifier
   }
}
```

Here are some other important things you should know about variance:

- As you've seen, variance deals with the issue of where it's safe to substitute a base type for a derived type, and vice versa. Variance, therefore, applies only to reference types—since you can't derive other types from value types.

- Explicit variance, using the in and out keywords, applies only to delegates and interfaces—not classes, structs, or methods.

- Delegate and interface type parameters that don't include either the in or out keyword are called *invariant*. These types cannot be used covariantly or contravariantly.

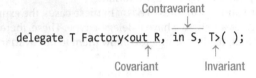

CHAPTER 19

■ ■ ■

Enumerators and Iterators

- Enumerators and Enumerable Types
- The IEnumerator Interface
- The IEnumerable Interface
- The Generic Enumeration Interfaces
- Iterators
- Common Iterator Patterns
- Producing Multiple Enumerables
- Iterators As Properties
- Behind the Scenes with Iterators

© Daniel Solis and Cal Schrotenboer 2018
D. Solis and C. Schrotenboer, *Illustrated C# 7*, https://doi.org/10.1007/978-1-4842-3288-0_19

Enumerators and Enumerable Types

In Chapter 13, you saw that you can use a foreach statement to cycle through the elements of an array. In this chapter, you'll take a closer look at arrays and see why they can be processed by foreach statements. You'll also look at how you can add this capability to your own user-defined classes, using iterators.

Using the foreach Statement

When you use a foreach statement with an array, the statement presents you with each element in the array, one by one, allowing you to read its value. For example, the following code declares an array with four elements and then uses a foreach loop to print out the values of the items:

```
int[] arr1 = { 10, 11, 12, 13 };              // Define the array.

foreach (int item in arr1)                     // Enumerate the elements.
   Console.WriteLine($"Item value:  { item }");
```

This code produces the following output:

```
Item value:  10
Item value:  11
Item value:  12
Item value:  13
```

Why does this work with arrays? The reason is that an array can produce, upon request, an object called an *enumerator*. The enumerator is an object that can return the elements of the array, one by one, in order, as they're requested. The enumerator "knows" the order of the items and keeps track of where it is in the sequence. It then returns the current item when it is requested.

For a type that has an enumerator, there must be a way of retrieving it. The way to retrieve an object's enumerator is to call the object's GetEnumerator method. Types that implement a GetEnumerator method are called *enumerable types*, or just *enumerables*. Arrays are enumerables.

Figure 19-1 illustrates the relationship between enumerables and enumerators.

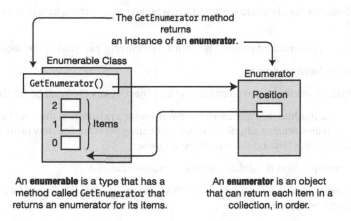

Figure 19-1. *Overview of enumerators and enumerables*

The foreach construct is designed to work with enumerables. As long as the object it's given to iterate over is an enumerable type, such as an array, it performs the following actions:

- It gets the object's enumerator by calling its GetEnumerator method.

- It requests each item from the enumerator and makes it available to your code as the *iteration variable*, which your code can read (but not change).

```
                          Must be enumerable
                                  ↓
foreach( Type VarName in EnumerableObject )
{
    ...
}
```

The IEnumerator Interface

An enumerator implements the IEnumerator interface, which contains three function members: Current, MoveNext, and Reset.

- Current is a property that returns the item at the current position in the sequence.

    - It is a read-only property.

    - It returns a reference of type object, so an object of any type can be returned.

- MoveNext is a method that advances the enumerator's position to the next item in the collection. It also returns a Boolean value, indicating whether the new position is a valid position or is beyond the end of the sequence.

    - If the new position is valid, the method returns true.

    - If the new position isn't valid (that is, the current position is beyond the end), the method returns false.

    - The initial position of the enumerator is *before* the first item in the sequence, so MoveNext must be called *before* the first access of Current.

- Reset is a method that resets the position to the initial state.

Figure 19-2 illustrates a collection of three items, which is shown on the left of the figure, and its enumerator, which is shown on the right. In the figure, the enumerator is an instance of a class called ArrEnumerator.

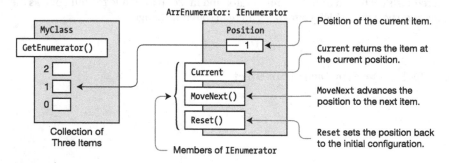

Figure 19-2. *The enumerator for a small collection*

The way the enumerator keeps track of the current item in the sequence is entirely implementation-dependent. It might be implemented as a reference to an object, an index value, or something else entirely. In the case of the built-in single-dimensional array type, it's simply the index of the item.

Figure 19-3 illustrates the states of an enumerator for a collection of three items. The states are labeled 1 through 5.

- Notice that in state 1, the initial position of the enumerator is –1 (that is, before the first element of the collection).

- Each transition between states is caused by a call to MoveNext, which advances the position in the sequence. Each call to MoveNext between states 1 and 4 returns true. In the transition between states 4 and 5, however, the position ends up beyond the last item in the collection, so the method returns false.

- In the final state, any further calls to MoveNext return false. If Current is called, it throws an exception.

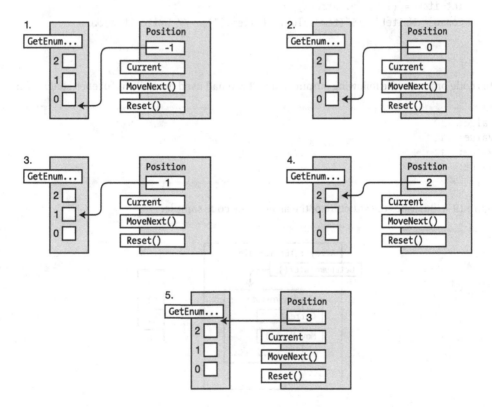

Figure 19-3. *The states of an enumerator*

Given a collection's enumerator, you should be able to simulate a foreach loop by cycling through the items in the collection using the MoveNext and Current members. For example, you know that arrays are enumerable, so the following code does *manually* what the foreach statement does *automatically*. In fact, the C# compiler generates code similar to this (in CIL, of course) when you write a foreach loop.

```
static void Main()
{
    int[] arr1 = { 10, 11, 12, 13 };                  // Create an array.
                       Get and store the enumerator.
                                ↓
    IEnumerator ie = arr1.GetEnumerator();
           Move to the next position.
                    ↓
    while ( ie.MoveNext() )
    {                       Get the current item.
                                ↓
        int item = (int) ie.Current;
        Console.WriteLine($"Item value:  { item }");  // Write it out.
    }
}
```

This code produces the following output, just as if you had used the built-in foreach statement:

```
Item value:   10
Item value:   11
Item value:   12
Item value:   13
```

Figure 19-4 illustrates the structure of the array in the code sample.

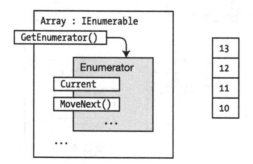

Figure 19-4. *The components of the array in the code sample*

The IEnumerable Interface

An enumerable class is one that implements the IEnumerable interface. The IEnumerable interface has only a single member, method GetEnumerator, which returns an enumerator for the object.

Figure 19-5 shows class MyClass, which has three items to enumerate, and implements the IEnumerable interface by implementing the GetEnumerator method.

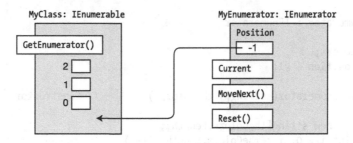

Figure 19-5. *The GetEnumerator method returns an enumerator object for the class*

The following code shows the form for the declaration of an enumerable class:

```
using System.Collections;
                    Implements the IEnumerable interface
                            ↓
class MyClass : IEnumerable
{
    public IEnumerator GetEnumerator { ... }
    ...        ↑
}       Returns an object of type IEnumerator
```

The following code gives an example of an enumerable class that uses an enumerator class called ColorEnumerator, which implements IEnumerator. We'll show the implementation of ColorEnumerator in the next section.

```
using System.Collections;

class MyColors: IEnumerable
{
    string[] Colors = { "Red", "Yellow", "Blue" };

    public IEnumerator GetEnumerator()
    {
        return new ColorEnumerator(Colors);
    }                      ↑
}              An instance of the enumerator class
```

491

Example Using IEnumerable and IEnumerator

The following code shows a full example of an enumerable class called Spectrum and its enumerator class ColorEnumerator. Class Program creates an instance of MyColors in method Main and uses it in a foreach loop.

```
using System;
using System.Collections;

class ColorEnumerator : IEnumerator
{
    string[] Colors;
    int      Position = -1;

    public ColorEnumerator( string[] theColors )        // Constructor
    {
        Colors = new string[theColors.Length];
        for ( int i = 0; i < theColors.Length; i++ )
            Colors[i] = theColors[i];
    }

    public object Current                                // Implement Current.
    {
        get
        {
            if ( Position == -1 )
                throw new InvalidOperationException();
            if ( Position >= Colors.Length )
                throw new InvalidOperationException();

            return Colors[Position];
        }
    }

    public bool MoveNext()                               // Implement MoveNext.
    {
        if ( Position < Colors.Length - 1 )
        {
            Position++;
            return true;
        }
        else
            return false;
    }

    public void Reset()                                  // Implement Reset.
    {
        Position = -1;
    }
}
```

```
class Spectrum : IEnumerable
{
    string[] Colors = { "violet", "blue", "cyan", "green", "yellow", "orange", "red" };

    public IEnumerator GetEnumerator()
    {
        return new ColorEnumerator( Colors );
    }
}

class Program
{
    static void Main()
    {
        Spectrum spectrum = new Spectrum();
        foreach ( string color in spectrum )
            Console.WriteLine( color );
    }
}
```

This code produces the following output:

```
violet
blue
cyan
green
yellow
orange
red
```

The Generic Enumeration Interfaces

The enumeration interfaces we've described so far are nongeneric versions. In reality, you should mostly be using the generic versions of the interfaces, which are IEnumerable<T> and IEnumerator<T>. They're called generic because they use C# generics, which are covered in Chapter 18. Using them is mostly the same as using the nongeneric forms.

The essential differences between the two are the following:

- With the nongeneric interface form

    - The GetEnumerator method of interface IEnumerable returns an enumerator class instance that implements IEnumerator.

    - The class implementing IEnumerator implements property Current, which returns a reference of type object, which you must then cast to the actual type of the object.

- The generic interface inherits from the nongeneric interface. With the generic interface form,

    - The GetEnumerator method of interface IEnumerable<T> returns an instance of a class that implements IEnumerator<T>.

    - The class implementing IEnumerator<T> implements property Current, which returns an instance of the actual type, rather than a reference to the base class object.

    - These are covariant interfaces, so their actual declarations are IEnumerable<out T> and IEnumerator<out T>. As you'll recall from Chapter 18, this means that the objects implementing these interfaces can be of a more derived type.

The most important point to notice, though, is that the nongeneric interface implementations we've been looking at so far are not type safe. They return a reference to type object, which must then be cast to the actual type.

With the *generic interfaces*, however, the enumerator is type safe, returning a reference to the actual type. If you're creating your own enumerables by implementing the interfaces, this is the approach you should take. The nongeneric interface forms are for legacy code developed before C# 2.0 when generics were introduced.

Although the generic versions are the same or easier to use than the nongeneric versions, their structures are a bit more complex. Figures 19-6 and 19-7 illustrate their structures.

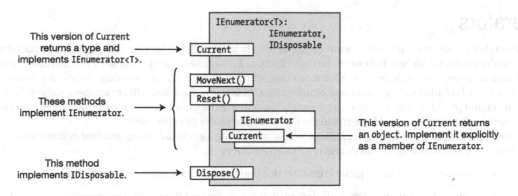

Figure 19-6. *The structure of a class implementing the IEnumerator<T> interface*

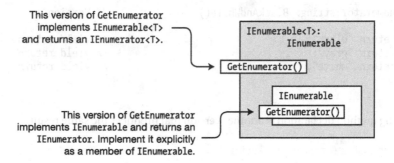

Figure 19-7. *The structure of a class implementing the IEnumerable<T> interface*

Iterators

Enumerable classes and enumerators are used extensively in the .NET collection classes, so it's important that you're familiar with how they work. But now that you know how to create your own enumerable classes and enumerators, you might be pleased to learn that, starting with C# 2.0, the language provides a much simpler way of creating enumerators and enumerables. In fact, the compiler will create them for you. The construct that produces them is called an *iterator*. You can use the enumerators and enumerables generated by iterators wherever you would use manually coded enumerators or enumerables.

Before we explain the details, let's take a look at two examples. The following method declaration implements an iterator that produces and returns an enumerator.

- The iterator returns a generic enumerator that returns three items of type string.

- The yield return statements declare that *this is the next item in the enumeration*.

Return an enumerator that returns strings.
↓

```
public IEnumerator<string> BlackAndWhite()              // Version 1
{
    yield return "black";                              // yield return
    yield return "gray";                               // yield return
    yield return "white";                              // yield return
}
```

The following method declaration is another version that produces the same result:

Return an enumerator that returns strings.
↓

```
public IEnumerator<string> BlackAndWhite()              // Version 2
{
    string[] theColors = { "black", "gray", "white" };

    for (int i = 0; i < theColors.Length; i++)
        yield return theColors[i];                     // yield return
}
```

We haven't explained the yield return statement yet, but on inspecting these code segments, you might have the feeling that something is different about this code. It doesn't seem quite right. What exactly does the yield return statement do?

For example, in the first version, if the method returns on the first yield return statement, then the last two statements can never be reached. If it doesn't return on the first statement but continues through to the end of the method, then what happens to the values? And in the second version, if the yield return statement in the body of the loop returns on the first iteration, then the loop will *never* get to any subsequent iterations.

And besides all that, an enumerator doesn't just return all the elements in one shot—it returns a new value with each access of the Current property. So, how does this give you an enumerator? Clearly this code is different from anything shown before.

Iterator Blocks

An *iterator block* is a code block with one or more yield statements. Any of the following three types of code blocks can be iterator blocks:

- A method body

- An accessor body

- An operator body

Iterator blocks are treated differently than other blocks. Other blocks contain sequences of statements that are treated *imperatively*. That is, the first statement in the block is executed, followed by the subsequent statements, and eventually control leaves the block.

An iterator block, on the other hand, is not a sequence of imperative commands to be executed at one time. Instead, it's declarative; it describes the behavior of the enumerator class you want the compiler to build for you. The code in the iterator block describes how to enumerate the elements.

Iterator blocks have two special statements.

- The yield return statement specifies the next item in the sequence to return.

- The yield break statement specifies that there are no more items in the sequence.

The compiler takes this description of how to enumerate the items and uses it to build an enumerator class, including all the required method and property implementations. The resulting class is nested inside the class where the iterator is declared.

You can have the iterator produce either an enumerator or an enumerable depending on the return type you use for the iterator block, as shown in Figure 19-8.

```
public IEnumerator<string> IteratorMethod()
{
    ...
    yield return ...;
}
```

An iterator that produces an enumerator

```
public IEnumerable<string> IteratorMethod()
{
    ...
    yield return ...;
}
```

An iterator that produces an enumerable

Figure 19-8. *You can have an iterator block produce either an enumerator or an enumerable depending on the return type you specify*

Using an Iterator to Create an Enumerator

The following code illustrates how to use an iterator to create an enumerable class.

- Method BlackAndWhite is an iterator block that produces a method that returns an enumerator for class MyClass.

- MyClass also implements method GetEnumerator, which just calls BlackAndWhite, and returns the enumerator that BlackAndWhite returns to it.

- Notice that in Main, you can use an instance of the class directly in the foreach statement since the class implements GetEnumerator and is therefore enumerable. It doesn't check for the interface—only the implementation of the interface.

```
class MyClass
{
    public IEnumerator<string> GetEnumerator()
    { return BlackAndWhite(); }                 // Returns the enumerator
            Returns an enumerator
                    ↓
    public IEnumerator<string> BlackAndWhite()  // Iterator
    {
        yield return "black";
        yield return "gray";
        yield return "white";
    }
}
class Program
{
    static void Main()
    {
        MyClass mc = new MyClass();
                Use the instance of MyClass.
                        ↓
        foreach (string shade in mc)
            Console.WriteLine(shade);
    }
}
```

This code produces the following output:

```
black
gray
white
```

Figure 19-9 shows the code for MyClass on the left and the resulting objects on the right. Notice how much is built for you automatically by the compiler.

- The iterator's code is shown on the left side of the figure and shows that its return type is IEnumerator<string>.

- On the right side of the figure, the diagram shows that the nested class implements IEnumerator<string>.

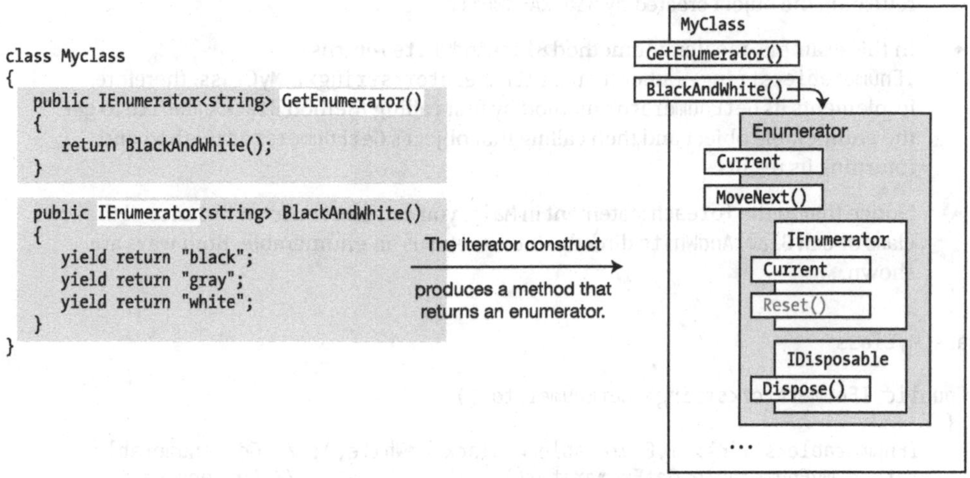

Figure 19-9. *An iterator block that produces an enumerator*

499

Using an Iterator to Create an Enumerable

The previous example created a class comprising two parts: the iterator that produced the method that returned an enumerator and the GetEnumerator method that returned that enumerator. In this example, the iterator produces an *enumerable* rather than an *enumerator*. There are some important differences between this example and the last:

- In the previous example, iterator method BlackAndWhite returned an IEnumerator<string>, and MyClass implemented method GetEnumerator by returning the object created by BlackAndWhite.

- In this example, the iterator method BlackAndWhite returns an IEnumerable<string> rather than an IEnumerator<string>. MyClass, therefore, implements its GetEnumerator method by first calling method BlackAndWhite to get the enumerable object and then calling that object's GetEnumerator method and returning its results.

- Notice that in the foreach statement in Main, you can either use an instance of the class or call BlackAndWhite directly since it returns an enumerable. Both ways are shown.

```
class MyClass
{
   public IEnumerator<string> GetEnumerator()
   {
      IEnumerable<string> myEnumerable = BlackAndWhite(); // Get enumerable.
      return myEnumerable.GetEnumerator();                // Get enumerator.
   }          Returns an enumerable
                          ↓
   public IEnumerable<string> BlackAndWhite()
   {
      yield return "black";
      yield return "gray";
      yield return "white";
   }
}

class Program
{
   static void Main()
   {
      MyClass mc = new MyClass();
                        Use the class object.
                              ↓
      foreach (string shade in mc)
         Console.Write($"{ shade }  ");
                              Use the class iterator  method.
                                   ↓
      foreach (string shade in mc.BlackAndWhite())
         Console.Write($"{ shade }  ");
   }
}
```

This code produces the following output:

```
black   gray   white   black   gray   white
```

Figure 19-10 illustrates the generic enumerable produced by the enumerable iterator in the code.

- The iterator's code is shown on the left side of the figure and shows that its return type is IEnumerable<string>.

- On the right side of the figure, the diagram shows that the nested class implements both IEnumerator<string> and IEnumerable<string>.

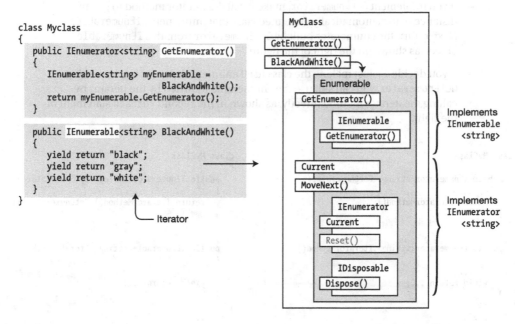

Figure 19-10. *The compiler produces a class that is enumerable and returns an enumerator. It also produces the method, BlackAndWhite, that returns the Enumerable object.*

Common Iterator Patterns

The previous two sections showed that you can create an iterator to return either an *enumerable* or an *enumerator*. Figure 19-11 summarizes how to use the common iterator patterns.

- When you implement an iterator that returns an enumerator, you must make the *class* enumerable by implementing GetEnumerator so that it returns the enumerator returned by the iterator. This is shown on the left of the figure.

- In a class, when you implement an iterator that returns an enumerable, you can make this class itself enumerable or not by either making it implement GetEnumerator or not.

  - If you implement GetEnumerator, make it call the iterator method to get an instance of the automatically generated class that implements IEnumerable. Next, return the enumerator built by GetEnumerator from this IEnumerable object, as shown on the right of the figure.

  - If you decide against making the class itself enumerable by not implementing GetEnumerator, you can still use the enumerable returned by the iterator by calling the iterator method directly, as shown in the second foreach statement on the right.

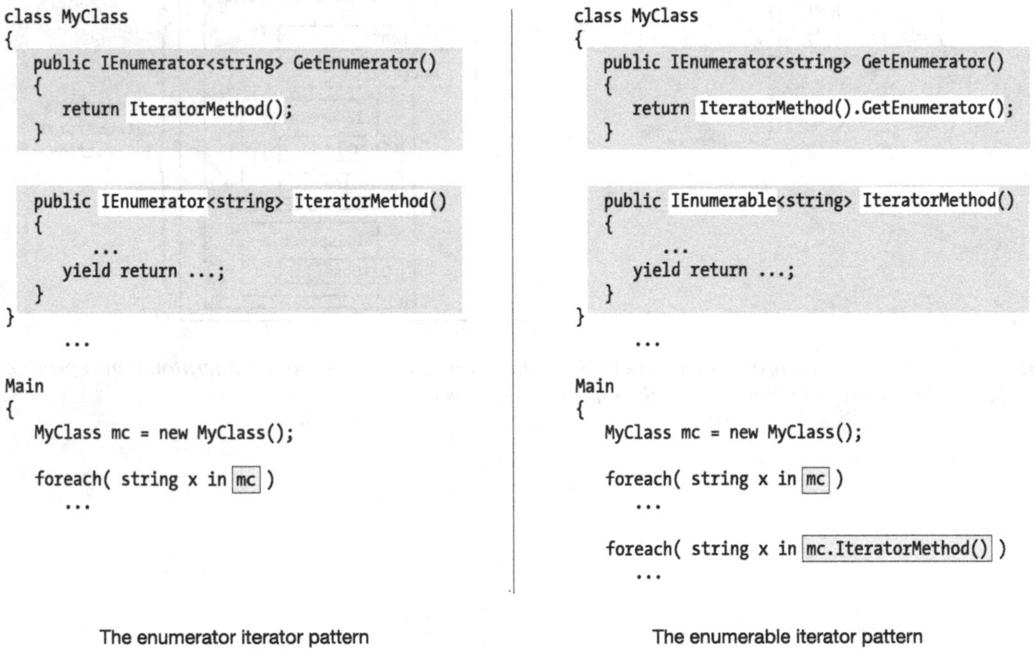

```
class MyClass
{
    public IEnumerator<string> GetEnumerator()
    {
        return IteratorMethod();
    }


    public IEnumerator<string> IteratorMethod()
    {
        ...
        yield return ...;
    }
}
    ...

Main
{
    MyClass mc = new MyClass();

    foreach( string x in mc )
        ...
```

```
class MyClass
{
    public IEnumerator<string> GetEnumerator()
    {
        return IteratorMethod().GetEnumerator();
    }


    public IEnumerable<string> IteratorMethod()
    {
        ...
        yield return ...;
    }
}
    ...

Main
{
    MyClass mc = new MyClass();

    foreach( string x in mc )
        ...

    foreach( string x in mc.IteratorMethod() )
        ...
```

The enumerator iterator pattern   The enumerable iterator pattern

Figure 19-11. *The common iterator patterns*

Producing Multiple Enumerables

In the following example, class Spectrum has two enumerable iterators—one enumerating the colors of the spectrum from the ultraviolet end to the infrared end, and the other in the opposite direction. Notice that although it has two methods that return enumerables, the class itself is not enumerable since it doesn't implement GetEnumerator.

```
using System;
using System.Collections.Generic;

class Spectrum
{
    string[] colors = { "violet", "blue", "cyan", "green", "yellow", "orange", "red" };
                    Returns an enumerable
                    ↓
    public IEnumerable<string> UVtoIR()
    {
        for ( int i=0; i < colors.Length; i++ )
            yield return colors[i];
    }
                    Returns an enumerable
                    ↓
    public IEnumerable<string> IRtoUV()
    {
        for ( int i=colors.Length - 1; i >= 0; i-- )
            yield return colors[i];
    }
}
class Program
{
    static void Main()
    {
        Spectrum spectrum = new Spectrum();

        foreach ( string color in spectrum.UVtoIR() )
            Console.Write($"{ color }  " );
        Console.WriteLine();

        foreach ( string color in spectrum.IRtoUV() )
            Console.Write($"{ color }  " );
        Console.WriteLine();
    }
}
```

This code produces the following output:

```
violet  blue  cyan  green  yellow  orange  red
red  orange  yellow  green  cyan  blue  violet
```

Iterators As Properties

The previous example used iterators to produce a class with two enumerables. This example shows two things. First, it uses iterators to produce a class with two enumerators. Second, it shows how iterators can be implemented as *properties* rather than methods.

The code declares two properties that define two different enumerators. The GetEnumerator method returns one or the other of the two enumerators, depending on the value of the Boolean variable _listFromUVtoIR. If _listFromUVtoIR is true, then the UVtoIR enumerator is returned. Otherwise, the IRtoUV enumerator is returned.

```
using System;
using System.Collections.Generic;

class Spectrum {
   bool _listFromUVtoIR;

   string[] colors = { "violet", "blue", "cyan", "green", "yellow", "orange", "red" };

   public Spectrum( bool listFromUVtoIR )
   {
      _listFromUVtoIR = listFromUVtoIR;
   }

   public IEnumerator<string> GetEnumerator()
   {
      return _listFromUVtoIR
                  ? UVtoIR
                  : IRtoUV;
   }

   public IEnumerator<string> UVtoIR
   {
      get
      {
         for ( int i=0; i < colors.Length; i++ )
            yield return colors[i];
      }
   }

   public IEnumerator<string> IRtoUV
   {
      get
      {
         for ( int i=colors.Length - 1; i >= 0; i-- )
            yield return colors[i];
      }
   }
}
```

```
class Program
{
   static void Main()
   {
      Spectrum startUV = new Spectrum( true );
      Spectrum startIR = new Spectrum( false );

      foreach ( string color in startUV )
         Console.Write($"{ color } " );
      Console.WriteLine();

      foreach ( string color in startIR )
         Console.Write($"{ color } " );
      Console.WriteLine();
   }
}
```

This code produces the following output:

```
violet  blue  cyan  green  yellow  orange  red
red  orange  yellow  green  cyan  blue  violet
```

Behind the Scenes with Iterators

The following are some other important things to know about iterators:

- Generic iterators require the System.Collections.Generic namespace, so you should include it with a using directive.

- In the compiler-generated enumerators, the Reset method is not supported. It is implemented since it is required by the interface, but the implementation throws a System.NotSupportedException exception if it is called. Notice that the Reset method is shown grayed out in Figure 19-9.

Behind the scenes, the enumerator class generated by the compiler is a state machine with four states.

- *Before*: The initial state before the first call to MoveNext.

- *Running*: The state entered when MoveNext is called. While in this state, the enumerator determines and sets the position for the next item. It exits the state when it encounters a yield return, a yield break, or the end of the iterator body.

- *Suspended*: The state where the state machine is waiting for the next call to MoveNext.

- *After*: The state where there are no more items to enumerate.

If the state machine is in either the *before or suspended state* and there is a call to the MoveNext method, it goes into the running state. In the *running* state, it determines the next item in the collection and sets the position.

If there are more items, the state machine goes into the *suspended* state. If there are no more items, it goes into the *after* state, where it remains. Figure 19-12 shows the state machine.

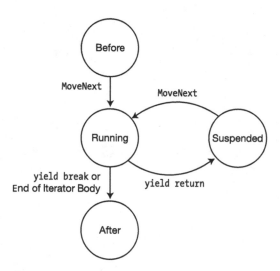

Figure 19-12. *An iterator state machine*

CHAPTER 20

■ ■ ■

Introduction to LINQ

© Daniel Solis and Cal Schrotenboer 2018

D. Solis and C. Schrotenboer, *Illustrated C# 7*, https://doi.org/10.1007/978-1-4842-3288-0_20

What Is LINQ?

In a relational database system, data is organized into nicely normalized tables and accessed with a simple but powerful query language—SQL. SQL can work with any set of data in a database because the data is organized into tables, following strict rules.

In a program, as opposed to a database, however, data is stored in class objects or structs that are all vastly different. As a result, there's been no general query language for retrieving data from data structures. The method of retrieving data from objects has always been custom-designed as part of the program. LINQ, however, makes it easy to query collections of objects.

The following are the important high-level characteristics of LINQ:

- LINQ stands for *Language Integrated Query* and is pronounced "link."

- LINQ is an extension of the .NET Framework and allows you to query collections of data in a manner similar to using SQL to query databases.

- With LINQ you can query data from databases, collections of objects, XML documents, and more.

The following code shows a simple example of using LINQ. In this code, the data source being queried is simply an array of ints. The definition of the query is the statement with the from and select keywords. Although the query is *defined* in this statement, it's not actually performed until the result is required in the foreach statement at the bottom.

```
static void Main()
{
    int[] numbers = { 2, 12, 5, 15 };          // Data source

    IEnumerable<int> lowNums =                 // Define and store the query.
                    from n in numbers
                    where n < 10
                    select n;

    foreach (var x in lowNums)                 // Execute the query.
        Console. Write($"{ x }, ");
}
```

This code produces the following output:

```
2, 5,
```

LINQ Providers

In the previous example, the data source was simply an array of ints, which is an in-memory object of the program. LINQ, however, can work with many different types of data sources, such as SQL databases, XML documents, and a host of others. For every data source type, however, under the covers there must be a module of code that implements the LINQ queries in terms of that data source type. These code modules are called *LINQ providers*. The important points about LINQ providers are the following:

- Microsoft provides LINQ providers for a number of common data source types, as shown in Figure 20-1.

- You can use any LINQ-enabled language (C# in this case) to query any data source type for which there is a LINQ provider.

- New LINQ providers are constantly being produced by third parties for all sorts of data source types.

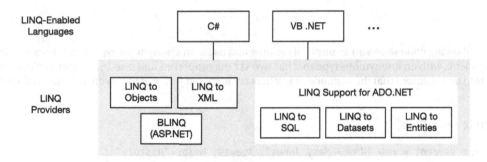

Figure 20-1. *The architecture of LINQ, the LINQ-enabled languages, and LINQ providers*

There are entire books dedicated to LINQ in all its forms and subtleties, but that's clearly beyond the scope of this chapter. Instead, this chapter will introduce you to LINQ and explain how to use it with program objects (LINQ to Objects) and XML (LINQ to XML).

Anonymous Types

Before getting into the details of LINQ's querying features, we'll start by covering a language feature that allows you to create unnamed class types. These are called, not surprisingly, *anonymous types*. Anonymous types are often used for the results of LINQ queries.

Chapter 7 covered *object initializers*, which allow you to initialize the fields and properties of a new class instance when using an object-creation expression. Just to remind you, this kind of object-creation expression consists of three components: the keyword new, the class name or constructor, and the object initializer. The object initializer consists of a comma-separated list of member initializers between a set of curly braces.

Creating a variable of an anonymous type uses the same form—but without the class name or constructor. The following line of code shows the object-creation expression form of an anonymous type:

```
No class name        Anonymous object initializer
   ↓                        ↓
new  { FieldProp = InitExpr, FieldProp = InitExpr, ...}
          ↑                      ↑
      Member initializer     Member initializer
```

The following code shows an example of creating and using an anonymous type. It creates a variable called student, with an anonymous type that has two string properties and one int property. Notice in the WriteLine statement that the instance's members are accessed just as if they were members of a named type.

```
static void Main( )
{
    var student = new {Name="Mary Jones", Age=19, Major="History"};
      ↑                 ↑
Must use var           Anonymous object initializer
    Console.WriteLine($"{ student.Name }, Age { student.Age }, Major: { student.Major }");
}
```

This code produces the following output:

```
Mary Jones, Age 19, Major: History
```

Important things to know about anonymous types are the following:

- Anonymous types can be used only with local variables, not with class members.

- Since an anonymous type doesn't have a name, you must use the var keyword as the variable type.

- You cannot assign to the properties of an object of an anonymous type. The properties created by the compiler for an anonymous type are read-only properties.

When the compiler encounters the object initializer of an anonymous type, it creates a new class type with a private name that it constructs. For each member initializer, it infers its type and creates a read-only property to access its value. The property has the same name as the member initializer. Once the anonymous type is constructed, the compiler creates an object of that type.

Besides the assignment form of member initializers, anonymous type object initializers also allow two other forms: simple identifiers and member access expressions. These forms, called *projection initializers*, don't use assignment expressions. Instead, they use either an identifier or the name of a member of an object being accessed as the name for the anonymous type member. The following variable declaration shows all three forms. The first member initializer is in the assignment form. The second is a member access expression, and the third is an identifier.

```
var student = new { Age = 19, Other.Name, Major };
```

For example, the following code shows how this is used. Notice that the projection initializers must be defined before the declaration of the anonymous type. Major is a local variable, and Name is a static field of class Other.

```
class Other
{
    static public string Name = "Mary Jones";
}

class Program
{
    static void Main()
    {
        string Major = "History";
                          Assignment form          Identifier
                               ↓                        ↓
        var student = new { Age = 19, Other.Name, Major};
                                          ↑
                                    Member access
        Console.WriteLine($"{student.Name }, Age {student.Age }, Major: {student.Major}");
    }
}
```

This code produces the following output:

```
Mary Jones, Age 19, Major: History
```

The projection initializer form of the object initializer just shown has exactly the same result as the assignment form shown here:

```
var student = new { Age = Age, Name = Other.Name, Major = Major};
```

If the compiler encounters another anonymous object initializer with the same parameter names, with the same inferred types, and in the same order, it reuses the anonymous type already created and just creates a new instance—not a new anonymous type.

Method Syntax and Query Syntax

LINQ provides two syntactic forms for specifying queries: query syntax and method syntax.

- Method syntax uses standard method invocations. The methods are from a set called the standard query operators, which we'll describe later in the chapter.

- Query syntax looks very much like an SQL statement. Query syntax is written in the form of query expressions.

- You can combine both forms in a single query.

Query syntax is a *declarative* form, which means that your query describes what you want returned but doesn't specify how to perform the query. Method syntax is an *imperative* form, which specifies an exact order in which query methods are to be called. Queries expressed using query syntax are translated by the C# compiler into method invocation form. There is no difference in runtime performance between the two forms.

Microsoft recommends using query syntax because it's more readable and more clearly states your query intentions and is therefore less error-prone. There are some operators, however, that can only be written using method syntax.

The following code shows the two forms and an example of the combined form. In the method syntax part, notice that the parameter of the Where method uses a lambda expression, as was described in Chapter 14. We'll cover its use in LINQ a bit later in the chapter.

```
static void Main( )
   {
      int[] numbers = { 2, 5, 28, 31, 17, 16, 42 };

      var numsQuery = from n in numbers                    // Query syntax
                      where n < 20
                      select n;

      var numsMethod = numbers.Where(N => N < 20);         // Method syntax

      int numsCount = (from n in numbers                   // Combined
                       where n < 20
                       select n).Count();

      foreach (var x in numsQuery)
         Console.Write($"{ x }, ");
      Console.WriteLine();

      foreach (var x in numsMethod)
         Console.Write($"{ x }, ");
      Console.WriteLine();

      Console.WriteLine(numsCount);
   }
```

This code produces the following output:

```
2, 5, 17, 16,
2, 5, 17, 16,
4
```

Query Variables

A LINQ query can return one of two types of results: an *enumeration*, which lists the items that satisfy the query parameters; or a single value, called a *scalar*, which is some form of summary of the results that satisfied the query.

In the following example code, the following happens:

- The first statement creates an array of ints and initializes it with three values.

- The second statement specifies a LINQ query that enumerates the results of the query.

- The third statement executes the query and then calls a LINQ method (Count) that returns the count of the items returned from the query. We'll cover operators that return scalars, such as Count, later in this chapter.

```
int[] numbers = { 2, 5, 28 };

IEnumerable<int> lowNums = from n in numbers          // Returns an enumerator
                           where n < 20
                           select n;

int numsCount = (from n in numbers                    // Returns an int
                 where n < 20
                 select n).Count();
```

The variable on the left of the equal sign of the second and third statements is called the *query variable*. Although the types of the query variables (IEnumerable<T> and int) are given explicitly in the example statements, you could also have used the var keyword in place of the type names and had the compiler infer the types of the query variables.

It's important to understand how query variables are used. After executing the preceding code, query variable lowNums does *not* contain the results of the query. Instead, the compiler has created code that will be run to execute the query if it's called upon to do so later in the code.

Query variable numsCount, however, contains an actual integer value, which can be obtained only by actually running the query.

The differences in the timing of the execution of the queries can be summarized as follows:

- If a query expression returns an enumeration, the query is not executed until the enumeration is processed.

- If the enumeration is processed multiple times, the query is executed multiple times.

- If the data changes between the time the enumeration is produced and the time the query is executed, the query is run on the new data.

- If the query expression returns a scalar, the query is executed immediately, and the result is stored in the query variable.

The Structure of Query Expressions

A query expression consists of a `from` clause followed by a query body, as illustrated in Figure 20-2. Some of the important things to know about query expressions are the following:

- The clauses must appear in the order shown.

- The two parts that are required are the `from` clause and the `select...group` clause.

- The other clauses are optional.

- In a LINQ query expression, the `select` clause is at the end of the expression. This is different from SQL, where the `SELECT` statement is at the beginning of a query. One of the reasons for using this position in C# is that it allows Visual Studio's IntelliSense to give you more options while you're entering code.

- There can be any number of `from...let...where` clauses, as illustrated in the figure.

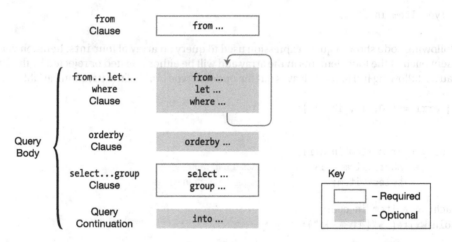

Figure 20-2. *The structure of a query statement consists of a from clause followed by a query body*

The from Clause

The from clause specifies the data collection that is to be used as the data source. It also introduces the iteration variable. The important points about the from clause are the following:

- The *iteration variable* sequentially represents each element in the data source.

- The syntax of the from clause is shown next, where

  - Type is the type of the elements in the collection. This is optional because the compiler can infer the type from the collection.

  - Item is the name of the iteration variable.

  - Items is the name of the collection to be queried. The collection must be enumerable, as described in Chapter 19.

```
         Iteration variable declaration
                    ↓
from Type Item in Items
```

The following code shows a query expression used to query an array of four ints. Iteration variable item will represent each of the four elements in the array and will be either selected or rejected by the where and select clauses following it. This code leaves out the optional type (int) of the iteration variable.

```
int[] arr1 = {10, 11, 12, 13};
                  Iteration variable
                        ↓
var query = from item in arr1
            where item < 13        ← Uses the iteration variable
            select item;           ← Uses the iteration variable

foreach( var item in query )
Console.Write( $"{item }," );
```

This code produces the following output:

```
10, 11, 12,
```

Figure 20-3 shows the syntax of the from clause. Again, the type specifier can be replaced by the keyword var since it can be inferred by the compiler. There can be any number of optional join clauses.

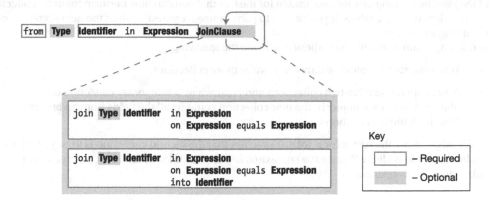

Figure 20-3. *The syntax of the from clause*

Although there is a strong similarity between the LINQ from clause and the foreach statement, there are several major differences.

- The foreach statement imperatively specifies that the items in the collection are to be considered in order, from the first to the last. The from clause declaratively states that each item in the collection must be considered but does not assume an order.

- The foreach statement executes its body at the point in the code where it is encountered. The from clause, on the other hand, does not execute anything. It creates a behind-the-scenes code object that can execute the query later. The query is executed only if the program's flow of control encounters a statement that accesses the query variable.

The join Clause

The join clause in LINQ is much like the JOIN clause in SQL. If you're familiar with joins from SQL, then joins in LINQ will be nothing new for you, except for the fact that you can now perform them on collections of objects as well as database tables. If you're new to joins or need a refresher, then the next section should help clear things up for you.

The first important things to know about a join are the following:

- You use a join to combine data from two or more collections.

- A join operation takes two collections and creates a new temporary collection of objects, where each object in the new collection contains all the fields from an object from both initial collections.

The following shows the syntax for a join. It specifies that the second collection is to be joined with the collection in the previous clause. Notice the contextual keyword equals, which must be used to compare the fields, rather than the == operator.

```
  Keyword            Keyword              Keyword          Keyword
    ↓                  ↓                    ↓                ↓
  join  Identifier in Collection2  on  Field1 equals Field2
              ↑                             ↑
        Specify additional collection    The fields to compare
          and ID to reference it.            for equality
```

Figure 20-4 illustrates the syntax for the join clause.

```
        join  Type  Identifier   in  Expression
                                 on  Expression equals Expression


        join  Type  Identifier   in  Expression
                                 on  Expression equals Expression
                                 into  Identifier
```

Figure 20-4. *Syntax for the join clause*

The following annotated statement shows an example of the join clause:

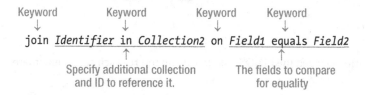

```
                   First collection and ID
                   _____
                           ↓              Item from first collection   Item from second
  var query = from s in students                    ↓                       ↓
              join c in studentsInCourses on  s.StID equals c.StID
                           ↑                          ↑
                   Second collection and ID       Fields to compare
```

What Is a Join?

A join in LINQ takes two collections and creates a new collection where each element has members from the elements of the two original collections.

For example, the following code declares two classes: Student and CourseStudent.

- Objects of type Student contain a student's last name and student ID number.

- Objects of type CourseStudent represent a student that is enrolled in a course and contain the course name and a student ID number.

```
public class Student
{
    public int    StID;
    public string LastName;
}

public class CourseStudent
{
    public string CourseName;
    public int    StID;
}
```

Figure 20-5 shows the situation in a program where there are three students and three courses, and the students are enrolled in various courses. The program has an array called students, of Student objects, and an array called studentsInCourses, of CourseStudent objects, which contains one object for every student enrolled in each course.

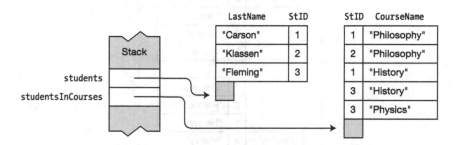

Figure 20-5. Students enrolled in various courses

Suppose now that you want to get the last name of every student in a particular course. The students array has the last names but not the class enrollment information. The studentsInCourses array has the course enrollment information but not the student names. But we can tie this information together using the student ID number (StID), which is common to the objects of both arrays. You can do this with a join on the StID field.

Figure 20-6 shows how the join works. The left column shows the students array, and the right column shows the studentsInCourses array. If we take the first student record and compare its ID with the student ID in each studentsInCourses object, we find that two of them match, as shown at the top of the center column. If we then do the same with the other two students, we find that the second student is taking one course, and the third student is taking two courses.

The five grayed objects in the middle column represent the join of the two arrays on field StID. Each object contains three fields: the LastName field from the Students class, the CourseName field from the CourseStudent class, and the StID field common to both classes.

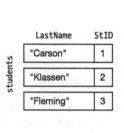
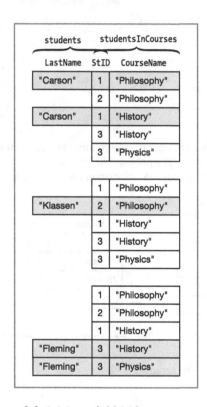
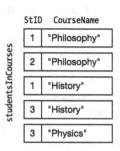

Figure 20-6. *Two arrays of objects and their join on field StId*

The following code puts the whole example together. The query finds the last names of all the students taking the history course.

```csharp
class Program
{
    public class Student {                              // Declare classes.
        public int     StID;
        public string LastName;
    }

    public class CourseStudent {
        public string CourseName;
        public int     StID;
    }

    static Student[] students = new Student[] {
        new Student { StID = 1, LastName = "Carson"  },
        new Student { StID = 2, LastName = "Klassen" },
        new Student { StID = 3, LastName = "Fleming" },
    };
                                                        // Initialize arrays.
    static CourseStudent[] studentsInCourses = new CourseStudent[] {
        new CourseStudent { CourseName = "Art",      StID = 1 },
        new CourseStudent { CourseName = "Art",      StID = 2 },
        new CourseStudent { CourseName = "History",  StID = 1 },
        new CourseStudent { CourseName = "History",  StID = 3 },
        new CourseStudent { CourseName = "Physics",  StID = 3 },
    };

    static void Main( )
    {
        // Find the last names of the students taking history.
        var query = from s in students
                    join c in studentsInCourses on s.StID equals c.StID
                    where c.CourseName == "History"
                    select s.LastName;

        // Display the names of the students taking history.
        foreach (var q in query)
            Console.WriteLine($"Student taking History:  { q }");
    }
}
```

This code produces the following output:

```
Student taking History:   Carson
Student taking History:   Fleming
```

The from ... let ... where Section in the Query Body

The optional from...let...where section is the first section of the query body. It can have any number of any of the three clauses that comprise it—the from clause, the let clause, and the where clause. Figure 20-7 summarizes the syntax of the three clauses.

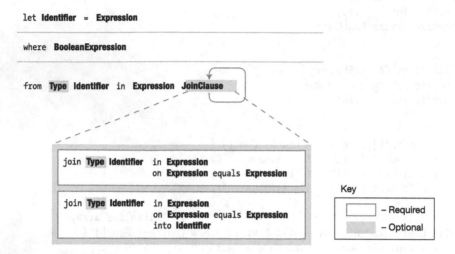

Figure 20-7. *The syntax of the from . . . let . . . where clause*

The from Clause

You saw that a query expression starts with a required from clause, which is followed by the query body. The body itself can start with any number of additional from clauses, where each subsequent from clause specifies an additional source data collection and introduces a new iteration variable for use in further evaluations. The syntax and meanings of all the from clauses are the same.

The following code shows an example of this use.

- The first from clause is the required clause of the query expression.

- The second from clause is the first clause of the query body.

- The select clause creates objects of an anonymous type.

```
static void Main()
{
   var groupA = new[] { 3, 4, 5, 6 };
   var groupB = new[] { 6, 7, 8, 9 };

   var someInts = from a in groupA             ← Required first from clause
                  from b in groupB             ← First clause of query body
                  where a > 4 && b <= 8
                  select new {a, b, sum = a + b}; ← Object of anonymous type

   foreach (var x in someInts)
      Console.WriteLine(x);
}
```

This code produces the following output:

```
{ a = 5, b = 6, sum = 11 }
{ a = 5, b = 7, sum = 12 }
{ a = 5, b = 8, sum = 13 }
{ a = 6, b = 6, sum = 12 }
{ a = 6, b = 7, sum = 13 }
{ a = 6, b = 8, sum = 14 }
```

The let Clause

The let clause takes the evaluation of an expression and assigns it to an identifier to be used in other evaluations. The syntax of the let clause is the following:

```
let Identifier = Expression
```

For example, the query expression in the following code pairs each member of array groupA with each element of array groupB. The where clause eliminates each set of integers from the two arrays where the sum of the two is not equal to 12.

```
static void Main()
{
    var groupA = new[] { 3, 4, 5, 6 };
    var groupB = new[] { 6, 7, 8, 9 };

    var someInts = from a in groupA
                   from b in groupB
                   let sum = a + b          ← Store result in new variable.
                   where sum == 12
                   select new {a, b, sum};

    foreach (var a in someInts)
        Console.WriteLine(a);
}
```

This code produces the following output:

```
{ a = 3, b = 9, sum = 12 }
{ a = 4, b = 8, sum = 12 }
{ a = 5, b = 7, sum = 12 }
{ a = 6, b = 6, sum = 12 }
```

The where Clause

The where clause eliminates items from further consideration if they don't meet the specified condition. The syntax of the where clause is the following:

```
where BooleanExpression
```

Important things to know about the where clause are the following:

- A query expression can have any number of where clauses, as long as they are in the from...let...where section.

- An item must satisfy all the where clauses to avoid elimination from further consideration.

The following code shows an example of a query expression that contains two where clauses. The where clauses eliminate each set of integers from the two arrays where the sum of the two is not greater than or equal to 11 and the element from groupA is not the value 4. Each set of elements selected must satisfy the conditions of *both* where clauses.

```
static void Main()
{
    var groupA = new[] { 3, 4, 5, 6 };
    var groupB = new[] { 6, 7, 8, 9 };

    var someInts = from int a in groupA
                   from int b in groupB
                   let sum = a + b
                   where sum >= 11        ← Condition 1
                   where a == 4           ← Condition 2
                   select new {a, b, sum};

    foreach (var a in someInts)
        Console.WriteLine(a);
}
```

This code produces the following output:

```
{ a = 4, b = 7, sum = 11 }
{ a = 4, b = 8, sum = 12 }
{ a = 4, b = 9, sum = 13 }
```

The orderby Clause

The orderby clause takes an expression and returns the result items in order according to the expression.

Figure 20-8 shows the syntax of the orderby clause. The optional keywords ascending and descending set the direction of the order. *Expression* is usually a field of the items. The field doesn't have to be a numeric field. It can be another orderable type such as a string, as well.

- The default ordering of an orderby clause is ascending. You can, however, explicitly set the ordering of the elements to either ascending or descending using the ascending and descending keywords.

- There can be any number of orderby clauses, and they must be separated by commas.

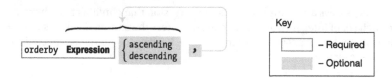

Figure 20-8. *The syntax of the orderby clause*

The following code shows an example of student records ordered by the ages of the students. Notice that the array of student information is stored in an array of anonymous types.

```
static void Main( ) {
   var students = new []        // Array of objects of an anonymous type
   {
      new { LName="Jones",   FName="Mary",   Age=19, Major="History" },
      new { LName="Smith",   FName="Bob",    Age=20, Major="CompSci" },
      new { LName="Fleming", FName="Carol",  Age=21, Major="History" }
   };

   var query = from student in students
               orderby student.Age        ← Order by Age.
               select student;

   foreach (var s in query) {
      Console.WriteLine($"{ s.LName }, { s.FName }:  { s.Age }, { s.Major }");
   }
}
```

This code produces the following output:

```
Jones, Mary:  19, History
Smith, Bob:  20, CompSci
Fleming, Carol:  21, History
```

The select . . . group Clause

There are two types of clauses that make up the select...group section: the select clause and the group...by clause. While the clauses that precede the select...group section specify the data sources and which objects to choose, the select...group section does the following:

- The select clause specifies which parts of the chosen objects should be selected. It can specify any of the following:

  - The entire data item

  - A field from the data item

  - A new object comprising several fields from the data item (or any other value, for that matter)

- The group...by clause is optional and specifies how the chosen items should be grouped. We'll cover the group...by clause later in this chapter.

Figure 20-9 shows the syntax for the select...group clause.

```
select  Expression
_____

group  Expression1  by  Expression2
```

Figure 20-9. *The syntax of the select . . . group clause*

The following code shows an example of using the select clause to select the entire data item. First, the program creates an array of objects of an anonymous type. The query expression then uses the select statement to select each item in the array.

```
using System;
using System.Linq;
class Program {
    static void Main() {
        var students = new[]         // Array of objects of an anonymous type
        {
            new { LName="Jones",   FName="Mary",  Age=19, Major="History" },
            new { LName="Smith",   FName="Bob",   Age=20, Major="CompSci" },
            new { LName="Fleming", FName="Carol", Age=21, Major="History" }
        };

        var query = from s in students
                      select s;

        foreach (var q in query)
            Console.WriteLine($"{ q.LName }, { q.FName }:  { q.Age }, { q.Major }");
    }
}
```

This code produces the following output:

```
Jones, Mary:  19, History
Smith, Bob:  20, CompSci
Fleming, Carol:  21, History
```

You can also use the select clause to choose particular fields of the object. For example, if you substitute the following two statements for the corresponding two statements in the previous example, the code selects only the last name of the student.

```
var query = from s in students
              select s.LName;

foreach (var q in query)
    Console.WriteLine(q);
```

With this substitution, the program produces the following output, printing only the last names:

```
Jones
Smith
Fleming
```

Anonymous Types in Queries

The result of a query can consist of items from the source collections, fields from the items in the source collections, or anonymous types.

You can create an anonymous type in a select clause by placing curly braces around a comma-separated list of fields you want to include in the type. For example, to make the code in the previous section select just the names and majors of the students, you could use the following syntax:

```
select new { s.LastName, s.FirstName, s.Major };
                  ↑
            Anonymous type
```

The following code creates an anonymous type in the select clause and uses it later in the WriteLine statement:

```
using System;
using System.Linq;

class Program
{
    static void Main()
    {
        var students = new[]        // Array of objects of an anonymous type
        {
            new { LName="Jones",   FName="Mary",  Age=19, Major="History" },
            new { LName="Smith",   FName="Bob",   Age=20, Major="CompSci" },
            new { LName="Fleming", FName="Carol", Age=21, Major="History" }
        };

        var query = from s in students
                    select new { s.LName, s.FName, s.Major };
                                 ↑
                        Create anonymous type.
        foreach (var q in query)
            Console.WriteLine($"{ q.FName } { q.LName } -- { q.Major}");
    }                             ↑            ↑             ↑
}                          Access fields of anonymous type
```

This code produces the following output:

```
Mary Jones -- History
Bob Smith -- CompSci
Carol Fleming -- History
```

The group Clause

The group clause groups the selected objects according to a specified criterion. For example, with the array of students in the previous examples, the program could group the students according to their majors.

The important things to know about the group clause are the following:

- When items are included in the result of the query, they're placed in groups according to the value of a particular field. The property on which items are grouped is called the *key*.

- A query with the group clause does not return an enumeration of the items from the original source. Instead, it returns an enumerable that enumerates the groups of items that have been formed.

- The groups themselves are enumerable and can enumerate the actual items.

An example of the syntax of the group clause is the following:

```
group student by student.Major;
      ↑                ↑
   Keyword          Keyword
```

For example, the following code groups the students according to their majors:

```
static void Main( )
{
    var students = new[]          // Array of objects of an anonymous type
    {
        new { LName="Jones",   FName="Mary",  Age=19, Major="History" },
        new { LName="Smith",   FName="Bob",   Age=20, Major="CompSci" },
        new { LName="Fleming", FName="Carol", Age=21, Major="History" }
    };

    var query = from student in students
                group student by student.Major;

    foreach (var g in query)              // Enumerate the groups.
    {
        Console.WriteLine("{0}", g.Key);
                                  ↑
                            Grouping key
        foreach (var s in g)              // Enumerate the items in the group.
            Console.WriteLine($"    { s.LName }, { s.FName }");
    }
}
```

This code produces the following output:

```
History
      Jones, Mary
      Fleming, Carol
CompSci
      Smith, Bob
```

Figure 20-10 illustrates the object that is returned from the query expression and stored in the query variable.

- The object returned from the query is an `IEnumerable<IGrouping>` that enumerates the groups resulting from the query.

- Each group is distinguished by a field called Key.

- Each group is itself enumerable and can enumerate its items.

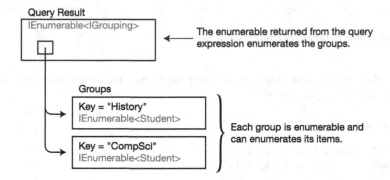

Figure 20-10. *The group clause returns a collection of collections of objects rather than a collection of objects.*

Query Continuation: The into Clause

A query continuation clause takes the result of one part of a query and assigns it a name so that it can be used in another part of the query. Figure 20-11 shows the syntax for query continuation.

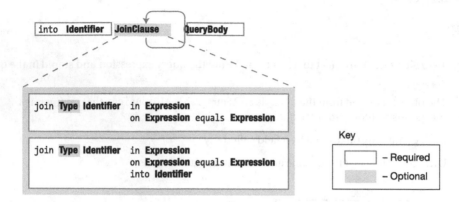

Figure 20-11. *The syntax of the query continuation clause*

For example, the following query joins groupA and groupB and names the result groupAandB. It then performs a simple select from groupAandB.

```
static void Main()
{
    var groupA = new[] { 3, 4, 5, 6 };
    var groupB = new[] { 4, 5, 6, 7 };

    var someInts = from a in groupA
                   join b in groupB on a equals b
                   into groupAandB                    ← Query continuation
                   from c in groupAandB
                   select c;
    foreach (var v in someInts)
        Console.Write($"{ v } ");
}
```

This code produces the following output:

```
4   5   6
```

The Standard Query Operators

The standard query operators comprise a set of methods called an *application programming interface* (API) that lets you query any .NET array or collection. Important characteristics of the standard query operators are the following:

- The standard query operators use method syntax.

- Some operators return IEnumerable objects (or other sequences), while others return scalars. Operators that return scalars execute their queries immediately and return a value instead of an enumerable object. The "ToCollection" operators such as ToArray() and ToList() also execute immediately.

- Many of these operators take a predicate as a parameter. A predicate is a method that takes an object as a parameter and returns true or false depending on whether the object meets some criterion.

The collection objects queried are called *sequences* and must implement the IEnumerable<T> interface, where T is a type.

The following code shows an example of the use of operators Sum and Count, which return ints. Notice the following about the code:

- The operators are used as methods *directly on the sequence of objects*, which in this case is the array numbers.

- The return type is not an IEnumerable object but an int.

```
class Program
{
    static int[] numbers = new int[] {2, 4, 6};

    static void Main( )
    {
        int total    = numbers.Sum();
        int howMany = numbers.Count();
            ↑              ↑        ↑
        Scalar        Sequence  Operator
        object
        Console.WriteLine($"Total: { total }, Count: { howMany }");
    }
}
```

This code produces the following output:

```
Total: 12, Count: 3
```

There are a number of standard query operators. They operate on one or more sequences. A *sequence* is any class that implements the IEnumerable<> interface. This includes such classes as List<>, Dictionary<>, Stack<>, and Array. The standard query operators can help you query and manipulate objects of these types in powerful ways.

Table 20-1 lists these operators and gives just enough information to let you know the purpose and general idea of each one. Most of them, however, have several overloads, allowing different options and behaviors. You should peruse the list and become familiar with these powerful tools that can save you lots of time and effort. Then when you need to use them, you can look up the full documentation online.

Table 20-1. *The Standard Query Operators*

Operator Name	Description
Where	Filters the sequence, given a selection predicate.
Select	Specifies an object or part of an object for inclusion.
SelectMany	Certain types of queries return collections of collections. This method flattens these results into a single collection.
Take	Takes an input parameter count and returns the first count objects from the sequence.
Skip	Takes an input parameter count and skips the first count objects of the sequence and returns the remaining objects.
TakeWhile	Takes a predicate and starts iterating through the sequence, selecting each item, as long as the predicate evaluates to true for that item. As soon as the predicate returns its first false, that item and the rest of the items are rejected.
SkipWhile	Takes a predicate and starts iterating through the sequence, skipping each item as long as the predicate evaluates to true for that item. As soon as the predicate returns its first false, that item and the rest of the items are returned.
Join	Performs an inner join on two sequences. Joins are described earlier in this chapter.
GroupJoin	A join that produces a hierarchical result, where each element in the first sequence is associated with a collection of elements from the second sequence.
Concat	Concatenates two sequences.
OrderBy/ThenBy	Orders the elements of the sequence in ascending order on one or more keys.
Reverse	Reverses the elements of the sequence.
GroupBy	Groups the elements of the sequence.
Distinct	Eliminates duplicates from the sequence.
Union	Returns the set union of two sequences.
Intersect	Returns the set intersection of two sequences.
Except	Works on two sequences. It returns the set of distinct elements in the first sequence, minus any elements that are also in the second sequence.
AsEnumerable	Returns the sequence as an IEnumerable<T>.
AsQueryable	Converts an IEnumerable to an IQueryable

(continued)

Table 20-1. (*continued*)

Operator Name	Description
ToArray	Returns the sequence as an array.
ToList	Returns the sequence as a List<T>.
ToDictionary	Returns the sequence as a Dictionary<TKey, TElement>.
ToLookup	Returns the sequence as a LookUp<TKey, TElement>.
OfType	Returns the elements of the sequence that are of a particular type.
Cast	Casts all the elements of the sequence to a given type.
SequenceEqual	Returns a Boolean value specifying whether two sequences are equal.
First	Returns the first element of the sequence that matches the predicate. If no element matches the predicate, it throws an InvalidOperationException.
FirstOrDefault	Returns the first element of the sequence that matches the predicate. If no predicate is given, the method returns the first element of the sequence. If no element matches the predicate, it uses the default value for that type.
Last	Returns the last element of the sequence that matches the predicate. If no element matches the predicate, it throws an InvalidOperationException.
LastOrDefault	Returns the last element of the sequence that matches the predicate. If no element matches the predicate, it returns a default value.
Single	Returns the single element from the sequence that matches the predicate. If no elements match or if more than one matches, it throws an exception.
SingleOrDefault	Returns the single element from the sequence that matches the predicate. If no elements match or if more than one matches, it returns a default value.
ElementAt	Given a parameter of n, it returns the n+1th element of the sequence.
ElementAtOrDefault	Given a parameter of n, it returns the n+1th element of the sequence. If the index is out of range, it returns a default value.
DefaultIfEmpty	Supplies a default value if the sequence is empty.
Range	Given a start integer and a count integer, this method returns a sequence of count integers where the first integer has the value start, and each successive element is one more than the previous one.
Repeat	Given an element of type T and a count integer, this method returns a sequence of count copies of element.
Empty	Returns an empty sequence of given type T.
Any	Returns a Boolean value specifying whether any elements in the sequence return true for the predicate.
All	Returns a Boolean value specifying whether all the elements in the sequence return true for the predicate.
Contains	Returns a Boolean value specifying whether the sequence contains the given element.

(*continued*)

Table 20-1. (*continued*)

Operator Name	Description
Count	Returns the number of elements in the sequence as an int. One overload can take a predicate and return the number of elements in the sequence for which the predicate is true.
Sum	Returns the sum of the values in the sequence.
Min	Returns the minimum of the values in the sequence.
Max	Returns the maximum of the values in the sequence.
Average	Returns the average of the values in the sequence.
Aggregate	Successively applies a given function on each element of the sequence.

Signatures of the Standard Query Operators

The standard query operators are methods declared in class System.Linq.Enumerable. These methods, however, aren't just any methods—they're extension methods that extend the generic class IEnumerable<T>.

We covered extension methods in Chapters 8 and 18, but this is a good opportunity for you to see how .NET uses them. This will give you a good model for your own code and also give you a better understanding of the standard query operators.

As a review, recall that extension methods are public, static methods that, although defined in one class, are designed to add functionality to a *different* class—the one listed as the first formal parameter. This formal parameter must be preceded by the keyword this.

For example, the following are the signatures of three of the standard query operators: Count, First, and Where. At first glance, these can be somewhat intimidating. Notice the following about the signatures:

- Since the operators are generic methods, they have a generic parameter (T) associated with their names.

- Since the operators are extension methods that extend class IEnumerable<T>, they satisfy the following syntactic requirements:

  - They're declared public and static.

  - They have the this extension indicator before the first parameter.

  - They have IEnumerable<T> as the first parameter type

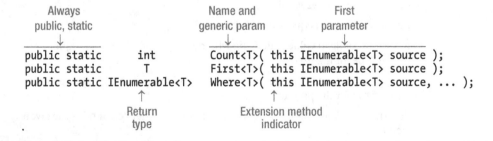

To show the syntactic difference between calling an extension method directly and calling it as an extension, the following code calls the standard query operators `Count` and `First` using both forms. Both operators take only a single parameter—the reference to the `IEnumerable<T>` object.

- The `Count` operator returns a single value, which is the count of all the elements in the sequence.

- The `First` operator returns the first element of the sequence.

The first two times the operators are used in this code, they're called directly, just like normal methods, passing the name of the array as the first parameter. In the following two lines, however, they are called using the extension syntax, as if they were method members of the array. This is valid because .NET class `Array` implements the `IEnumerable` interface.

Notice that in this case no parameter is supplied. Instead, the array name has been moved from the parameter list to before the method name. There it is used as if it contained a declaration of the method.

The method syntax calls and the extension syntax calls are semantically equivalent—only their syntax is different.

```
using System.Linq;
   ...
static void Main( )
{
    int[] intArray = new int[] { 3, 4, 5, 6, 7, 9 };
                                 Array as parameter
                                        ↓
    var count1      = Enumerable.Count(intArray);      // Method syntax
    var firstNum1   = Enumerable.First(intArray);      // Method syntax

    var count2      = intArray.Count();                // Extension syntax
    var firstNum2   = intArray.First();                // Extension syntax
                            ↑
              Array as extended object

    Console.WriteLine($"Count: { count1 }, FirstNumber: { firstNum1 }");
    Console.WriteLine($"Count: { count2 }, FirstNumber: { firstNum2 }");

}
```

This code produces the following output:

```
Count: 6, FirstNumber: 3
Count: 6, FirstNumber: 3
```

Query Expressions and the Standard Query Operators

The set of standard query operators is a set of methods for performing queries. As mentioned at the beginning of the chapter, every query expression can also be written using method syntax with the standard query operators. The compiler translates every query expression into standard query operator form.

Clearly, since all query expressions are translated into the standard query operators, the operators can perform everything done by query expressions. But the operators also give additional capabilities that aren't available in query expression form. For example, operators Sum and Count, which were used in the previous example, can be expressed only using the method syntax.

The two forms, query expressions and method syntax, can, however, be combined. For example, the following code shows a query expression that also uses operator Count. Notice that the query expression part of the statement is inside parentheses, which is followed by a dot and the name of the method.

```
static void Main()
{
    var numbers = new int[] { 2, 6, 4, 8, 10 };

    int howMany = (from n in numbers
                   where n < 7
                   select n).Count();
                        ↑          ↑
                 Query expression     Operator

    Console.WriteLine($"Count: { howMany }");

}
```

This code produces the following output:

```
Count: 3
```

Delegates As Parameters

As you just saw in the previous section, the first parameter of every operator is a reference to an IEnumerable<T> object. The parameters following it can be of any type. Many operators take *generic delegates* as parameters. (Generic delegates were explained in Chapter 18.) The most important thing to recall about generic delegates as parameters is the following:

- Generic delegates are used to supply user-defined code to the operator.

To explain this, we'll start with an example showing several ways you might use the Count operator. The Count operator is overloaded and has two forms. The first form, as you saw in the previous example, has a single parameter that returns the number of elements in the collection. Its signature is repeated here:

```
public static int Count<T>(this IEnumerable<T> source);
```

Suppose, however, that you only want to count the odd elements of the array. To do that, you must supply the Count method with code that determines whether an integer is odd.

To do this, you need to use the second form of the Count method, which is shown next. As its second parameter, it takes a generic delegate. At the point it is invoked, you must supply a delegate object that takes a single input parameter of type T and returns a Boolean value. The return value of the delegate code must specify whether the element should be included in the count.

```
public static int Count<T>(this IEnumerable<T> source,
                                    Func<T, bool> predicate );
                                         ↑
                                  Generic delegate
```

For example, the following code uses this second form of the Count operator to instruct it to include only those values that are odd. It does this by supplying a lambda expression that returns true if the input value is odd and returns false otherwise. (Again, lambda expressions were covered in Chapter 14.) At each iteration through the collection, Count calls this method (represented by the lambda expression) with the current value as input. If the input is odd, the method returns true, and Count includes the element in the total.

```
static void Main()
{
    int[] intArray = new int[] { 3, 4, 5, 6, 7, 9 };

    var countOdd = intArray.Count(n => n % 2 == 1);
                                       ↑
                Lambda expression identifying the odd values
    Console.WriteLine($"Count of odd numbers: { countOdd }");
}
```

This code produces the following output:

```
Count of odd numbers: 4
```

The LINQ Predefined Delegate Types

Like the Count operator from the previous example, many of the LINQ operators require you to supply code that directs how the operator performs its operation. You can do this by using delegate objects as parameters.

Remember from Chapter 14 that you can think of a delegate object as an object that contains a method or list of methods with a particular signature and return type. When the delegate is invoked, the methods it contains are invoked in sequence.

The .NET Framework defines two families of generic delegate types that are used with the standard query operators. (They can also be used anywhere else you might find them useful—not just with the query operators.) These are the Func delegates and the Action delegates. Each set has 19 members.

- The delegate objects you create for use as actual parameters must be of these delegate types or of these forms.

- TR represents the return type and is always *last* in the list of type parameters.

The first four generic Func delegates are listed here. The first form takes no method parameters and returns an object of the return type. The second takes a single method parameter and returns a value, and so forth.

```
public delegate TR Func<out TR>                    ( );
public delegate TR Func<in T1, out TR >            ( T1 a1 );
public delegate TR Func<in T1, in T2, out TR >     ( T1 a1, T2 a2 );
public delegate TR Func<in T1, in T2, in T3, out TR>( T1 a1, T2 a2, T3 a3 );
```
    ↑   ↑   ↑

  Return type   Type parameters   Method parameters

Notice that the return type parameter has the out keyword, making it covariant. It can therefore accept the type declared or any type derived from that type. The input parameters have the in keyword, making them contravariant. They, therefore, can accept the declared type, or any type derived from that type.

With this in mind, if you look again at the declaration of Count, shown next, you see that the second parameter must be a delegate object that takes a single value of some type T as the method parameter and returns a value of type bool. As mentioned earlier in the chapter, a delegate of this form is called a *predicate*

```
public static int Count<T>(this IEnumerable<T> source,
                           Func<T, bool> predicate );
```
                          ↑ ↑

             Parameter type Return type

The first four Action delegates are the following. They're the same as the Func delegates except that they have no return value and hence no return value type parameter. All their type parameters are contravariant.

```
public delegate void Action                        ( );
public delegate void Action<in T1>                 ( T1 a1 );
public delegate void Action<in T1, in T2>          ( T1 a1, T2 a2 );
public delegate void Action<in T1, in T2, in T3>( T1 a1, T2 a2, T3 a3 );
```

Example Using a Delegate Parameter

Now that you better understand Count's signature and LINQ's use of generic delegate parameters, you'll be better able to understand a full example.

The following code declares method IsOdd, which takes a single parameter of type int and returns a bool value specifying whether the input parameter was odd. Method Main does the following:

- Declares an array of ints as the data source.

- Creates a delegate object called MyDel, of type Func<int, bool>, and it uses method IsOdd to initialize the delegate object. Notice that you don't need to declare the Func delegate type because, as you saw, it's already predefined in the .NET Framework.

- Calls Count using the delegate object.

```
class Program
{
    static bool IsOdd(int x)      // Method to be used by the delegate object
    {
        return x % 2 == 1;        // Return true if x is odd.
    }

    static void Main()
    {
        int[] intArray = new int[] { 3, 4, 5, 6, 7, 9 };

        Func<int, bool> myDel = new Func<int, bool>(IsOdd); // Delegate object
        var countOdd = intArray.Count(myDel);               // Use delegate.

        Console.WriteLine($"Count of odd numbers: { countOdd }");
    }
}
```

This code produces the following output:

```
Count of odd numbers: 4
```

Example Using a Lambda Expression Parameter

The previous example used a separate method and a delegate to attach the code to the operator. This required declaring the method, declaring the delegate object, and then passing the delegate object to the operator. This works fine and is exactly the right approach to take if either of the following conditions is true:

- If the method must be called from somewhere in the program other than the place it's used to initialize the delegate object

- If the code in the method body is more than just a statement or two long

If neither of these conditions is true, however, you probably want to use a more compact and localized method of supplying the code to the operator, using a lambda expression.

You can modify the previous example to use a lambda expression by first deleting the IsOdd method entirely and placing the equivalent lambda expression directly at the declaration of the delegate object. The new code is shorter and cleaner and looks like this:

```
class Program
{
    static void Main()
    {
        int[] intArray = new int[] { 3, 4, 5, 6, 7, 9 };
                                    Lambda expression
                                          ↓
        var countOdd = intArray.Count( x => x % 2 == 1 );

        Console.WriteLine($"Count of odd numbers: { countOdd }");
    }
}
```

Like the previous example, this code produces the following output:

```
Count of odd numbers: 4
```

You could also have used an anonymous method in place of the lambda expression, as shown next. This is more verbose, though, and since lambda expressions are equivalent semantically and are less verbose, there's little reason to use anonymous methods anymore.

```
class Program
{
    static void Main( )
    {
        int[] intArray = new int[] { 3, 4, 5, 6, 7, 9 };
                              Anonymous method
                                     ↓
        Func<int, bool> myDel = delegate(int x)
                                {
                                    return x % 2 == 1;
                                };
        var countOdd = intArray.Count(myDel);

        Console.WriteLine($"Count of odd numbers: { countOdd }");
    }
}
```

LINQ to XML

Extensible Markup Language (XML) is an important means of storing and exchanging data. LINQ adds features to the language that make working with XML much easier than previous methods, such as XPath and XSLT. If you're familiar with these methods, you might be pleased to hear that LINQ to XML simplifies the creation, querying, and manipulation of XML in a number of ways, including the following:

- You can create an XML tree in a top-down fashion, with a single statement.

- You can create and manipulate XML in-memory without having an XML document to contain the tree.

- You can create and manipulate string nodes without having a Text subnode.

- One of the huge differences (improvements!) is that you no longer have to traverse an XML tree to search it. Instead, you just query the tree and have it return your result.

Although we won't give a complete treatment of XML, we will start by giving a very brief introduction to it before describing some of the XML manipulation features supplied by LINQ.

Markup Languages

A *markup language* is a set of tags placed in a document to give information *about the information* in the document and to organize its content. That is, the markup tags are not the data of the document—they contain data *about* the data. Data about data is called *metadata*.

A markup language is a defined set of tags designed to convey particular types of metadata about the contents of a document. HTML, for example, is the most widely known markup language. The metadata in its tags contains information about how a web page should be rendered in a browser and how to navigate among the pages using the hypertext links.

While most markup languages contain a predefined set of tags, XML contains only a few defined tags, and the rest are defined by the programmer to represent whatever kinds of metadata are required by a particular document type. As long as the writer and reader of the data agree on what the tags mean, the tags can contain whatever useful information the designers want.

XML Basics

Data in an XML document is contained in an XML tree, which consists mainly of a set of nested elements.

The *element* is the fundamental constituent of an XML tree. Every element has a name and can contain data. Some can also contain other nested elements. Elements are demarcated by opening and closing tags. Any data contained by an element must be between its opening and closing tags.

- An opening tag starts with an open angle bracket, followed by the element name, followed optionally by any attributes, followed by a closing angle bracket.

  `<PhoneNumber>`

- A closing tag starts with an open angle bracket, followed by a slash character, followed by the element name, followed by a closing angle bracket.

  `</PhoneNumber>`

- An element with no content can be represented by a single tag that starts with an open angle bracket, followed by the name of the element, followed by a slash, and is terminated with a closing angle bracket.

  `<PhoneNumber />`

The following XML fragment shows an element named EmployeeName followed by an empty element named PhoneNumber:

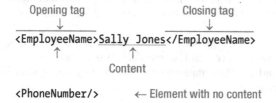

Other important things to know about XML are the following:

- XML documents must have a single root element that contains all the other elements.

- XML tags must be properly nested.

- Unlike HTML tags, XML tags are case-sensitive.

- XML attributes are name-value pairs that contain additional metadata about an element. The value part of an attribute must always be enclosed in quotation marks, which can be either double quotation marks or single quotation marks.

- Whitespace within an XML document is maintained. This is unlike HTML, where whitespace is consolidated to a single space in the output.

The following XML document is an example of XML that contains information about two employees. This XML tree is extremely simple in order to show the elements clearly. The important things to notice about the XML tree are the following:

- The tree contains a root node of type `Employees` that contains two child nodes of type `Employee`.

- Each `Employee` node contains nodes containing the name and phone numbers of an employee.

```
<Employees>
    <Employee>
        <Name>Bob Smith</Name>
        <PhoneNumber>408-555-1000</PhoneNumber>
        <CellPhone />
    </Employee>
    <Employee>
        <Name>Sally Jones</Name>
        <PhoneNumber>415-555-2000</PhoneNumber>
        <PhoneNumber>415-555-2001</PhoneNumber>
    </Employee>
</Employees>
```

Figure 20-12 illustrates the hierarchical structure of the sample XML tree.

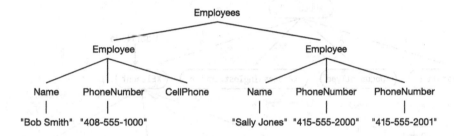

Figure 20-12. *Hierarchical structure of the sample XML tree*

The XML Classes

LINQ to XML can be used to work with XML in two ways. The first way is as a simplified XML manipulation API. The second way is to use the LINQ query facilities you've seen throughout the earlier part of this chapter. We'll start by introducing the LINQ to XML API.

The LINQ to XML API consists of a number of classes that represent the components of an XML tree. The three most important classes you'll use are XElement, XAttribute, and XDocument. There are other classes as well, but these are the main ones.

In Figure 20-12, you saw that an XML tree is a set of nested elements. Figure 20-13 shows the classes used to build an XML tree and how they can be nested.

For example, the figure shows the following:

- An XDocument node can have the following as its direct child nodes:

  - At most, one of each of the following node types: an XDeclaration node, an XDocumentType node, and an XElement node

  - Any number of XProcessingInstruction nodes

- If there is a top-level XElement node under the XDocument, it is the root of the rest of the elements in the XML tree.

- The root element can in turn contain any number of nested XElement, XComment, or XProcessingInstruction nodes, nested to any level.

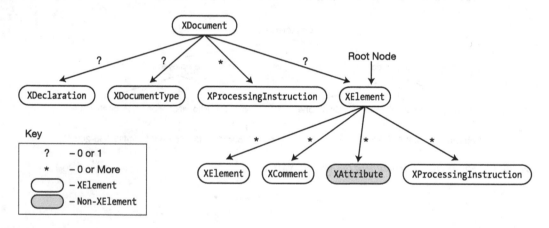

Figure 20-13. *The containment structure of XML nodes*

Except for the XAttribute class, most of the classes used to create an XML tree are derived from a class called XNode and are referred to generically in the literature as *XNodes*. Figure 20-13 shows the XNode classes in white clouds, while the XAttribute class is shown in a gray cloud.

Creating, Saving, Loading, and Displaying an XML Document

The best way to demonstrate the simplicity and usage of the XML API is to show simple code samples. For example, the following code shows how simple it is to perform several of the important tasks required when working with XML.

It starts by creating a simple XML tree consisting of a node called Employees, with two subnodes containing the names of two employees. Notice the following about the code:

- The tree is created with a single statement that creates all the nested elements in place in the tree. This is called *functional construction*.

- Each element is created in place using an object-creation expression, using the constructor of the type of the node.

After creating the tree, the code saves it to a file called EmployeesFile.xml, using XDocument's Save method. It then reads the XML tree back from the file using XDocument's static Load method and assigns the tree to a new XDocument object. Finally, it uses WriteLine to display the structure of the tree held by the new XDocument object.

```
using System;
using System.Xml.Linq;                              // Required namespace

class Program {
    static void Main( ) {
        XDocument employees1 =
            new XDocument(                           // Create the XML document.
                new XElement("Employees",           // Create the root element.
                    new XElement("Name", "Bob Smith"),      // Create element.
                    new XElement("Name", "Sally Jones")     // Create element.
                )
            );

        employees1.Save("EmployeesFile.xml");               // Save to a file.

        // Load the saved document into a new variable.
        XDocument employees2 = XDocument.Load("EmployeesFile.xml");
                              ↑
                         Static method
        Console.WriteLine(employees2);                      // Display document.
    }

}
```

This code produces the following output:

```
<Employees>
  <Name>Bob Smith</Name>
  <Name>Sally Jones</Name>
</Employees>
```

Creating an XML Tree

In the previous example, you saw that you can create an XML document in-memory by using constructors for XDocument and XElement. In the case of both constructors,

- The first parameter is the name of the object.

- The second and following parameters contain the nodes of the XML tree. The second parameter of the constructor is a params parameter and so can have any number of parameters.

For example, the following code produces an XML tree and displays it using the Console.WriteLine method:

```
using System;
using System.Xml.Linq;                      // This namespace is required.

class Program {
   static void Main( ) {
      XDocument employeeDoc =
         new XDocument(                      // Create the document.
            new XElement("Employees",        // Create the root element.
               new XElement("Employee",      // First employee element
                  new XElement("Name", "Bob Smith"),
                  new XElement("PhoneNumber", "408-555-1000") ),

               new XElement("Employee",      // Second employee element
                  new XElement("Name", "Sally Jones"),
                  new XElement("PhoneNumber", "415-555-2000"),
                  new XElement("PhoneNumber", "415-555-2001") )
            )
         );
      Console.WriteLine(employeeDoc);        // Displays the document
   }
}
```

```
<Employees>
  <Employee>
    <Name>Bob Smith</Name>
    <PhoneNumber>408-555-1000</PhoneNumber>
  </Employee>

  <Employee>
    <Name>Sally Jones</Name>
    <PhoneNumber>415-555-2000</PhoneNumber>
    <PhoneNumber>415-555-2001</PhoneNumber>
  </Employee>
</Employees>
```

Using Values from the XML Tree

The power of XML becomes evident when you traverse an XML tree and retrieve or modify values. Table 20-2 shows the main methods used for retrieving data.

Table 20-2. *Methods for Querying XML*

Method Name	Class	Return Type	Description
Nodes	XDocument XElement	IEnumerable<object>	Returns all the children of the current node, regardless of their type
Elements	XDocument XElement	IEnumerable<XElement>	Returns all the current node's XElement child nodes or all the child nodes with a specific name
Element	XDocument XElement	XElement	Returns the current node's first XElement child node or the first child node with a specific name
Descendants	XElement	IEnumerable<XElement>	Returns all the descendant XElement nodes or all the descendant XElement nodes with a specific name, regardless of their level of nesting below the current node
DescendantsAndSelf	XElement	IEnumerable<XElement>	Same as Descendants, but also includes the current node
Ancestors	XElement	IEnumerable<XElement>	Returns all the ancestor XElement nodes or all the ancestor XElement nodes above the current node that have a specific name
AncestorsAndSelf	XElement	IEnumerable<XElement>	Same as Ancestors, but also includes the current node
Parent	XElement	XElement	Returns the parent node of the current node

Some of the important things to know about the methods in Table 20-2 are the following:

- **Nodes**: The Nodes method returns an object of type IEnumerable<object> because the nodes returned might be of different types, such as XElement, XComment, and so on. You can use the type parameterized method OfType<type> to specify what type of nodes to return. For example, the following line of code retrieves only the XComment nodes:

  ```
  IEnumerable<XComment> comments = xd.Nodes().OfType<XComment>();
  ```

- **Elements**: Since retrieving XElements is such a common requirement, there is a shortcut for expression Nodes().OfType<XElement>()—the Elements method.

  - Using the Elements method with no parameters returns all the child XElements.

  - Using the Elements method with a single name parameter returns only the child XElements with that name. For example, the following line of code returns all the child XElement nodes with the name *PhoneNumber*.

  ```
  IEnumerable<XElement> empPhones = emp.Elements("PhoneNumber");
  ```

- **Element**: This method retrieves just the first child XElement of the current node. Like the Elements method, it can be called with either one or no parameters. With no parameters, it gets the first child XElement node. With a single name parameter, it gets the first child XElement node of that name.

- **Descendants** *and* Ancestors: These methods work like the Elements and Parent methods, but instead of returning the immediate child elements or parent element, they include the elements below or above the current node, regardless of the difference in nesting level.

The following code illustrates the `Element` and `Elements` methods:

```csharp
using System;
using System.Collections.Generic;
using System.Xml.Linq;

class Program {
   static void Main( ) {
      XDocument employeeDoc =
         new XDocument(
            new XElement("Employees",
               new XElement("Employee",
                  new XElement("Name", "Bob Smith"),
                  new XElement("PhoneNumber", "408-555-1000")),
               new XElement("Employee",
                  new XElement("Name", "Sally Jones"),
                  new XElement("PhoneNumber", "415-555-2000"),
                  new XElement("PhoneNumber", "415-555-2001"))
            )
         );                      Get first child XElement named "Employees"
                                              ↓
      XElement root = employeeDoc.Element("Employees");
      IEnumerable<XElement> employees = root.Elements();

      foreach (XElement emp in employees)
      {                               Get first child XElement named "Name"
                                                ↓
         XElement empNameNode = emp.Element("Name");
         Console.WriteLine(empNameNode.Value);
                                          Get all child elements named "PhoneNumber"
                                                      ↓
         IEnumerable<XElement> empPhones = emp.Elements("PhoneNumber");
         foreach (XElement phone in empPhones)
            Console.WriteLine($"   { phone.Value }");
      }
   }
}
```

This code produces the following output:

```
Bob Smith
   408-555-1000
Sally Jones
   415-555-2000
   415-555-2001
```

Adding Nodes and Manipulating XML

You can add a child element to an existing element using the Add method. The Add method allows you to add as many elements as you like in a single method call, regardless of the node types you're adding.

For example, the following code creates a simple XML tree and displays it. It then uses the Add method to add a single node to the root element. Following that, it uses the Add method a second time to add three elements—two XElements and an XComment. Notice the results in the output:

```
using System;
using System.Xml.Linq;

class Program
{
    static void Main()
    {
        XDocument xd = new XDocument(              // Create XML tree.
            new XElement("root",
                new XElement("first")
            )
        );

        Console.WriteLine("Original tree");
        Console.WriteLine(xd); Console.WriteLine(); // Display the tree.

        XElement rt = xd.Element("root");          // Get the first element.

        rt.Add( new XElement("second"));           // Add a child element.

        rt.Add( new XElement("third"),             // Add three more children.
                new XComment("Important Comment"),
                new XElement("fourth"));

        Console.WriteLine("Modified tree");
        Console.WriteLine(xd);                      // Display modified tree.
    }
}
```

This code produces the following output:

```
<root>
  <first />
</root>
<root>
  <first />
  <second />
  <third />
  <!--Important Comment-->
  <fourth />
</root>
```

The Add method places the new child nodes after the existing child nodes, but you can place the nodes before and between the child nodes as well, using the AddFirst, AddBeforeSelf, and AddAfterSelf methods.

Table 20-3 lists some of the most important methods for manipulating XML. Notice that some of the methods are applied to the parent node and others to the node itself.

Table 20-3. *Methods for Manipulating XML*

Method Name	Call From	Description
Add	Parent	Adds new child nodes after the existing child nodes of the current node
AddFirst	Parent	Adds new child nodes before the existing child nodes of the current node
AddBeforeSelf	Node	Adds new nodes before the current node at the same level
AddAfterSelf	Node	Adds new nodes after the current node at the same level
Remove	Node	Deletes the currently selected node and its contents
RemoveNodes	Node	Removes the child nodes from an XContainer
SetElement	Parent	Sets the contents of a node

Working with XML Attributes

Attributes give additional information about an XElement node. They're placed in the opening tag of the XML element.

When you functionally construct an XML tree, you can add attributes by just including XAttribute constructors within the scope of the XElement constructor. There are two forms of the XAttribute constructor; one takes a name and a value, and the other takes a reference to an already existing XAttribute.

The following code adds two attributes to root. Notice that both parameters to the XAttribute constructor are strings; the first specifies the name of the attribute, and the second gives the value.

```
XDocument xd = new XDocument(
                          Name     Value
                           ↓        ↓
    new XElement("root",
        new XAttribute("color", "red"),        // Attribute constructor
        new XAttribute("size", "large"),       // Attribute constructor
      new XElement("first"),
      new XElement("second")
    )
);

Console.WriteLine(xd);
```

This code produces the following output. Notice that the attributes are placed inside the opening tag of the element.

```
<root color="red" size="large">
  <first />
  <second />
</root>
```

To retrieve an attribute from an XElement node, use the Attribute method, supplying the name of the attribute as the parameter. The following code creates an XML tree with a node with two attributes—color and size. It then retrieves the values of the attributes and displays them.

```
static void Main( )
{
    XDocument xd = new XDocument(                       // Create XML tree.
        new XElement("root",
            new XAttribute("color", "red"),
            new XAttribute("size", "large"),
            new XElement("first")
        )
    );

    Console.WriteLine(xd); Console.WriteLine();         // Display XML tree.

    XElement rt = xd.Element("root");                   // Get the element.

    XAttribute color = rt.Attribute("color");           // Get the attribute.
    XAttribute size =  rt.Attribute("size");            // Get the attribute.

    Console.WriteLine($"color is { color.Value }");     // Display attr. value.
    Console.WriteLine($"size  is { size.Value }");      // Display attr. value.
}
```

This code produces the following output:

```
<root color="red" size="large">
  <first />
</root>

color is red
size is large
```

To remove an attribute, you can select the attribute and use the Remove method, or you can use the SetAttributeValue method on its parent and set the attribute value to null. The following code demonstrates both methods:

```
static void Main( ) {
   XDocument xd = new XDocument(
      new XElement("root",
         new XAttribute("color", "red"),
         new XAttribute("size", "large"),
         new XElement("first")
      )
   );

   XElement rt = xd.Element("root");            // Get the element.

   rt.Attribute("color").Remove();              // Remove the color attribute.
   rt.SetAttributeValue("size", null);          // Remove the size attribute.

   Console.WriteLine(xd);
}
```

This code produces the following output:

```
<root>
  <first />
</root>
```

To add an attribute to an XML tree or change the value of an attribute, you can use the SetAttributeValue method, as shown in the following code:

```
static void Main( ) {
    XDocument xd = new XDocument(
        new XElement("root",
            new XAttribute("color", "red"),
            new XAttribute("size", "large"),
            new XElement("first")));

    XElement rt = xd.Element("root");            // Get the element.

    rt.SetAttributeValue("size",  "medium");     // Change attribute value.
    rt.SetAttributeValue("width", "narrow");     // Add an attribute.

    Console.WriteLine(xd); Console.WriteLine();
}
```

This code produces the following output:

```
<root color="red" size="medium" width="narrow">
  <first />
</root>
```

Other Types of Nodes

Three other types of nodes used in the previous examples are XComment, XDeclaration, and XProcessingInstruction. They're described in the following sections.

XComment

Comments in XML consist of text between the `<!--` and `-->` tokens. The text between the tokens is ignored by XML parsers. You can insert text in an XML document using the XComment class, as shown in the following line of code:

```
new XComment("This is a comment")
```

This code produces the following line in the XML document:

```
<!--This is a comment-->
```

XDeclaration

XML documents start with a line that includes the version of XML used, the type of character encoding used, and whether the document depends on external references. This is information about the XML, so it's actually metadata about the metadata! This is called the *XML declaration* and is inserted using the XDeclaration class. The following shows an example of an XDeclaration statement:

```
new XDeclaration("1.0", "utf-8", "yes")
```

This code produces the following line in the XML document:

```
<?xml version="1.0" encoding="utf-8" standalone="yes"?>
```

XProcessingInstruction

An XML processing instruction is used to supply additional data about how an XML document should be used or interpreted. Most commonly, processing instructions are used to associate a style sheet with the XML document.

You can include a processing instruction using the XProcessingInstruction constructor, which takes two string parameters—a target and a data string. If the processing instruction takes multiple data parameters, those parameters must be included in the second parameter string of the XProcessingInstruction constructor, as shown in the following constructor code. Notice that in this example, the second parameter is a verbatim string, and literal double quotes inside the string are represented by sets of two contiguous double quote marks.

```
new XProcessingInstruction( "xml-stylesheet",
                            @"href=""stories"", type=""text/css""")
```

This code produces the following line in the XML document:

```
<?xml-stylesheet href="stories.css" type="text/css"?>
```

The following code uses all three constructs:

```
static void Main( )
{
    XDocument xd = new XDocument(
        new XDeclaration("1.0", "utf-8", "yes"),
        new XComment("This is a comment"),
        new XProcessingInstruction("xml-stylesheet",
                              @"href=""stories.css"" type=""text/css"""),
        new XElement("root",
            new XElement("first"),
            new XElement("second")
        )
    );
}
```

This code produces the following output in the output file. Using a WriteLine of xd, however, would not show the declaration statement, even though it's included in the document file.

```
<?xml version="1.0" encoding="utf-8" standalone="yes"?>
<!--This is a comment-->
<?xml-stylesheet href="stories.css" type="text/css"?>
<root>
  <first />
  <second />
</root>
```

Using LINQ Queries with LINQ to XML

You can combine the LINQ to XML API with LINQ query expressions to produce simple yet powerful XML tree searches.

The following code creates a simple XML tree, displays it to the screen, and then saves it to a file called SimpleSample.xml. Although there's nothing new in this code, we'll use this XML tree in the following examples.

```
static void Main( )
{
    XDocument xd = new XDocument(
        new XElement("MyElements",
            new XElement("first",
                new XAttribute("color", "red"),
                new XAttribute("size",  "small")),
            new XElement("second",
                new XAttribute("color", "red"),
                new XAttribute("size",  "medium")),
            new XElement("third",
                new XAttribute("color", "blue"),
                new XAttribute("size",  "large"))));

    Console.WriteLine(xd);                  // Display XML tree.
    xd.Save("SimpleSample.xml");            // Save XML tree.
}
```

This code produces the following output:

```
<MyElements>
  <first color="red" size="small" />
  <second color="red" size="medium" />
  <third color="blue" size="large" />
</MyElements>
```

The following example code uses a simple LINQ query to select a subset of the nodes from the XML tree and then display them in several ways. This code does the following:

- It selects from the XML tree only those elements whose names have five characters. Since the names of the elements are *first, second,* and *third,* only node names *first* and *third* match the search criterion, and therefore those nodes are selected.

- It displays the names of the selected elements.

- It formats and displays the selected nodes, including the node name and the values of the attributes. Notice that the attributes are retrieved using the Attribute method, and the values of the attributes are retrieved with the Value property.

```
static void Main( )
{
    XDocument xd = XDocument.Load("SimpleSample.xml");  // Load the document.
    XElement rt = xd.Element("MyElements");             // Get the root element.

    var xyz = from e in rt.Elements()                  // Select elements whose
              where e.Name.ToString().Length == 5      // names have 5 chars.
              select e;

    foreach (XElement x in xyz)                         // Display the
        Console.WriteLine(x.Name.ToString());          // selected elements.

    Console.WriteLine();
    foreach (XElement x in xyz)
        Console.WriteLine("Name: {0}, color: {1}, size: {2}",
                          x.Name,
                          x.Attribute("color").Value,
                          x.Attribute("size") .Value);
                                  ↑               ↑
                          Get the attribute.    Get the attribute's value.
}
```

This code produces the following output:

```
first
third

Name: first, color: red, size: small
Name: third, color: blue, size: large
```

The following code uses a simple query to retrieve all the top-level elements of the XML tree and creates an object of an anonymous type for each one. The first use of the WriteLine method shows the default formatting of the anonymous type. The second WriteLine statement explicitly formats the members of the anonymous type objects.

```
using System;
using System.Linq;
using System.Xml.Linq;

static void Main( )
{
   XDocument xd = XDocument.Load("SimpleSample.xml"); // Load the document.
   XElement rt = xd.Element("MyElements");            // Get the root element.

   var xyz = from e in rt.Elements()
             select new { e.Name, color = e.Attribute("color") };
                         ↑
   foreach (var x in xyz)      Create an anonymous type.
      Console.WriteLine(x);                           // Default formatting

   Console.WriteLine();
   foreach (var x in xyz)
      Console.WriteLine("{0,-6},   color: {1, -7}", x.Name, x.color.Value);
}
```

This code produces the following output. The first three lines show the default formatting of the anonymous type. The last three lines show the explicit formatting specified in the format string of the second WriteLine method.

```
{ Name = first, color = color="red" }
{ Name = second, color = color="red" }
{ Name = third, color = color="blue" }

first,    color: red
second,   color: red
third,    color: blue
```

From these examples, you can see that you can easily combine the XML API with the LINQ query facilities to produce powerful XML querying capabilities.

■■■

CHAPTER 21

Introduction to Asynchronous Programming

What Is Asynchrony?

When you start a program, the system creates a new *process* in memory. A process is the set of resources that comprise a running program. These include the virtual address space, file handles, and a host of other things required for the program to run.

Inside the process, the system creates a kernel object, called a *thread*, which represents the actual executing program. (*Thread* is short for "thread of execution.") Once the process is set up, the system starts the thread executing at the first statement in method Main.

Some important things to know about threads are the following:

- By default, a process contains only a single thread, which executes from the beginning of the program to the end.

- A thread can spawn other threads so that at any time a process might have multiple threads in various states, executing different parts of the program.

- If there are multiple threads in a process, they all share the process's resources.

- It is threads, not processes, that are the units scheduled by the system for execution on the processor.

All the sample programs shown so far in this book have used only a single thread and have executed sequentially from the first statement in the program to the last. There are many situations, however, where this simple model produces unacceptable behavior, in either performance or end-user experience.

For example, a server program might be constantly initiating connections with other servers and requesting data from them, while at the same time processing the requests from many client programs. These communications tasks usually require a fair amount of time where the program is just waiting for a response from another computer on the network or on the Internet. This significantly decreases performance. Instead of just wasting this time waiting for a response, it would be more efficient to work on other tasks in the meantime and then resume working on the first task when the reply arrives.

Another example would be an interactive GUI program. If the user initiates an operation that takes a significant amount of time, it's unacceptable for the program to freeze on the screen until the action completes. The user should still be able to move the window around on the screen and maybe even cancel the operation.

In this chapter we're going to look at *asynchronous programming*, which is a type of programming where portions of a program's code aren't necessarily executed in the strict order in which the code is written. Sometimes this involves running a section of code on another thread. Other times, however, no new thread is created, but instead, the execution of the code is reordered to make better use of the single thread's capacity.

We'll start by looking at a new feature introduced in C# 5.0 that allows you to build asynchronous methods. It's called the async/await feature. After that we'll look at several features that are part of the .NET Framework, but not built into the C# language, that allow additional forms of asynchrony. These topics include the BackgroundWorker class and an introduction to the .NET Task Parallel Library. Both these topics implement asynchrony by creating new threads. We'll finish the chapter by looking at other ways of producing asynchrony.

A Starting Example

For illustration and comparison, we'll start by looking at an example that does *not* use asynchrony and then compare it to a similar program that uses asynchrony.

In the code sample shown next, method DoRun is a method of class MyDownloadString that does the following:

- It creates and starts an object of class Stopwatch, which is in the System. Diagnostics namespace. It uses this Stopwatch timer to time the various tasks performed in the code.

- It then makes two calls to method CountCharacters, which downloads the content of the web site and returns the number of characters the web site contains. The web site is specified as a URL string given as the second parameter.

- It then makes four calls to method CountToALargeNumber. This method is just make-work that represents a task that takes a certain amount of time. It just loops the given number of times.

- Finally, it prints out the number of characters that were found for the two web sites.

```csharp
using System;
using System.Net;
using System.Diagnostics;

class MyDownloadString {
   Stopwatch sw = new Stopwatch();

   public void DoRun() {
      const int LargeNumber = 6_000_000;
      sw.Start();
      int t1 = CountCharacters( 1, "http://www.microsoft.com" );
      int t2 = CountCharacters( 2, "http://www.illustratedcsharp.com" );
      CountToALargeNumber( 1, LargeNumber );
      CountToALargeNumber( 2, LargeNumber );
      CountToALargeNumber( 3, LargeNumber );
      CountToALargeNumber( 4, LargeNumber );

      Console.WriteLine($"Chars in http://www.microsoft.com      : { t1 }");
      Console.WriteLine($"Chars in http://www.illustratedcsharp.com: { t2 }");
   }

   private int CountCharacters(int id, string uriString ) {
      WebClient wc1 = new WebClient();
      Console.WriteLine( "Starting call {0}    :     {1, 4:N0} ms",
                         id, sw.Elapsed.TotalMilliseconds );
      string result = wc1.DownloadString( new Uri( uriString ) );
      Console.WriteLine( "  Call {0} completed:     {1, 4:N0} ms",
                         id, sw.Elapsed.TotalMilliseconds );
      return result.Length;
   }
```

```
      private void CountToALargeNumber( int id, int value ) {
         for ( long i=0; i < value; i++ )
            ;
         Console.WriteLine( "   End counting {0}  :     {1, 4:N0} ms",
                              id, sw.Elapsed.TotalMilliseconds );
      }
   }

   class Program
   {
      static void Main() {
         MyDownloadString ds = new MyDownloadString();
         ds.DoRun();
      }
   }
```

This code produced the following output on one of its runs. The timing numbers, listed in milliseconds (ms), will be different when you run it.

```
Starting call 1     :          1 ms
   Call 1 completed:        178 ms
Starting call 2     :        178 ms
   Call 2 completed:        504 ms
   End counting 1  :        523 ms
   End counting 2  :        542 ms
   End counting 3  :        561 ms
   End counting 4  :        579 ms
Chars in http://www.microsoft.com          : 1020
Chars in http://www.illustratedcsharp.com: 4699
```

Figure 21-1 summarizes the output, showing a timeline of when the various tasks start and end. Looking at the figure, you'll notice that calls 1 and 2 took the bulk of the time of the method call. But for each of these calls, the vast majority of the time required was just wasted waiting for the responses from the web sites.

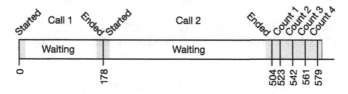

Figure 21-1. *Timeline of the time required for the various tasks in the program*

We could significantly improve the performance of the program if we could initiate both of the CountCharacter calls, and not wait for the results, but go ahead and perform the four calls to CountToALargeNumber and then pick up the results of the two CountCharacter method calls when they're done.

C#'s async/await feature allows you to do exactly that. The code, rewritten to use this feature, is shown next. We'll go into the details of the new feature shortly, but the things to notice in this example are the following:

- When method DoRun calls CountCharactersAsync, CountCharactersAsync returns almost immediately and before it actually does the work of downloading the characters. It returns to the calling method a placeholder object of type Task<int> that represents the work it plans to do, which will eventually "return" an int.

- This allows method DoRun to continue on its way without having to wait for the actual work to be done. Its next statement is another call to CountCharactersAsync, which does the same thing, returning another Task<int> object.

- DoRun can then continue and make the four calls to CountToALargeNumber, while the two calls to CountCharactersAsync continue to do their work—which consists mostly of waiting.

- The last two lines of method DoRun retrieve the results from the Tasks returned by the CountCharactersAsync calls. If a result isn't ready yet, execution blocks and waits until it is.

```
...
using System.Threading.Tasks;

class MyDownloadString
{
    Stopwatch sw = new Stopwatch();

    public void DoRun()  {
        const int LargeNumber = 6_000_000;
        sw.Start();
```
                    Objects that will hold the results
                        ↓
```
        Task<int> t1 = CountCharactersAsync( 1, "http://www.microsoft.com" );
        Task<int> t2 = CountCharactersAsync( 2, "http://www.illustratedcsharp.com" );
        CountToALargeNumber( 1, LargeNumber );
        CountToALargeNumber( 2, LargeNumber );
        CountToALargeNumber( 3, LargeNumber );
        CountToALargeNumber( 4, LargeNumber );
```
                                                                          Get results
                                                                              ↓
```
        Console.WriteLine( "Chars in http://www.microsoft.com        : {0}", t1.Result );
        Console.WriteLine( "Chars in http://www.illustratedcsharp.com: {0}", t2.Result );
    }
```
     Contextual   Type that represents work being done,
       keyword   which will eventually return an int
         ↓   ↓
```
    private async Task<int> CountCharactersAsync( int id, string site ) {
        WebClient wc = new WebClient();
        Console.WriteLine( "Starting call {0}    :      {1, 4:N0} ms",
                           id, sw.Elapsed.TotalMilliseconds );
```
                        Contextual keyword
                             ↓
```
        string result = await wc.DownloadStringTaskAsync( new Uri( site ) );
        Console.WriteLine( "   Call {0} completed:      {1, 4:N0} ms",
                           id, sw.Elapsed.TotalMilliseconds );
        return result.Length;
    }

    private void CountToALargeNumber( int id, int value ) {
        for ( long i=0; i < value; i++ ) ;
        Console.WriteLine( "   End counting {0}   :      {1, 4:N0} ms",
                           id, sw.Elapsed.TotalMilliseconds );
    }
}
class Program {
    static void Main() {
        MyDownloadString ds = new MyDownloadString();
        ds.DoRun();
    }
}
```

One run of this code on our machine produced the following results. Again, your timing results, and possibly the ordering of the lines, will most likely be different than ours.

```
Starting call 1    :        12 ms
Starting call 2    :        60 ms
   End counting 1  :        80 ms
   End counting 2  :        99 ms
   End counting 3  :       118 ms
   Call 1 completed:       124 ms
   End counting 4  :       138 ms
Chars in http://www.microsoft.com        : 1020
   Call 2 completed:       387 ms
Chars in http://www.illustratedcsharp.com: 4699
```

Figure 21-2 summarizes the output, showing a timeline of the modified program. The new version is 32 percent faster than the previous version. It gains this time by performing the four calls to CountToALargeNumber during the time it's waiting for the responses from the web sites in the two CountCharactersAsync method calls. All this was done on the main thread; we did not create any additional threads!

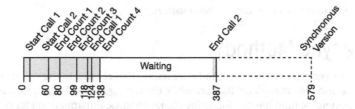

Figure 21-2. *Timeline of the async/await version of the program*

The Structure of the async/await Feature

Now that you've seen an example of an asynchronous method, let's go into the definitions and details.

When a program makes a method call and waits for the method to perform all its processing before continuing, we say that the method call is *synchronous*. This is the default form and is what you've seen in all the chapters previous to this one.

In contrast to that, an *asynchronous* method returns to the calling method before it finishes all its work. C#'s async/await feature allows you to create and use asynchronous methods. The feature comprises three components, as illustrated in Figure 21-3.

- The *calling* method is the method that calls an async method and then continues on its way while the async method performs its tasks, either on the same thread or on a different thread.

- The async method is the method that sets up its work to be done asynchronously and then returns early to the calling method.

- The await expression is used inside the async method and specifies the task that needs to be performed asynchronously. An async method can contain any number of await expressions, although the compiler produces a warning message if there isn't at least one.

We'll cover each of these three components in detail in the coming sections, starting with the syntax and semantics of the async method.

```
class Program
{
    static void Main()
    {
        ...
        Task<int> value = DoAsyncStuff.CalculateSumAsync(5, 6);    Calling Method
        ...
    }
}

static class DoAsyncStuff
{
    public static async Task<int> CalculateSumAsync(int i1, int i2)
    {
        int sum = await TaskEx.Run( () => GetSum( i1, i2 ) );      Async Method
        return sum;
    }
    ...
}
                              Await Expression
```

Figure 21-3. *The overall structure of the async/await feature*

What Is an async Method?

As stated in the previous section, an async method is a method that returns to the calling method before completing all its work and then completes its work while the calling method continues its execution.

Syntactically, an async method has the following characteristics, illustrated in Figure 21-4:

- It has the async method modifier in the method header.

- It contains one or more await expressions. These expressions represent tasks that can be done asynchronously.

- It must have one of the following return types. In the second and third cases—that is, Task and Task<T>—the returned object represents a chunk of work that will be completed in the future, while both the calling method and the async method can continue processing.

    −void
    −Task
    −Task<T>
    −ValueTask<T>

- Any type that has a publicly accessible GetAwaiter method. We'll talk more about GetAwaiter shortly.

- An async method can have any number of formal parameters of any types. None of the parameters, however, can be out or ref parameters.

- By convention, the name of an async method should end with the suffix Async.

- Besides methods, lambda expressions and anonymous methods can also act as async objects.

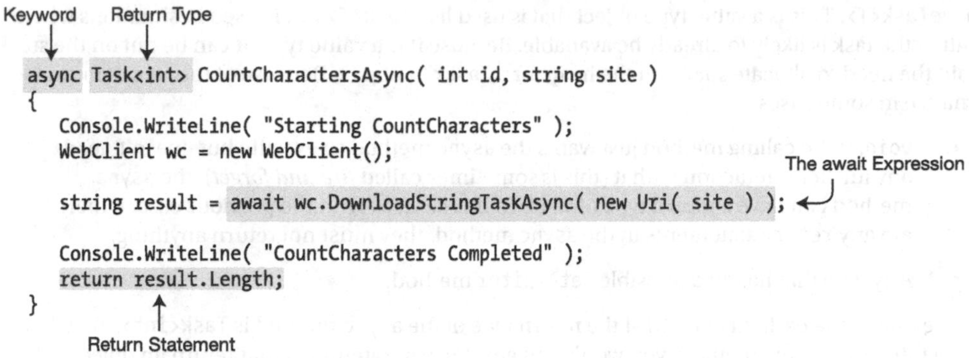

Keyword   Return Type

```
async Task<int> CountCharactersAsync( int id, string site )
{
    Console.WriteLine( "Starting CountCharacters" );
    WebClient wc = new WebClient();

    string result = await wc.DownloadStringTaskAsync( new Uri( site ) );

    Console.WriteLine( "CountCharacters Completed" );
    return result.Length;
}
```

The await Expression

Return Statement

Figure 21-4. The structure of an async method

Figure 21-4 highlights the components of an async method, which we can now look at in more detail. The first item is the async keyword.

- An async method must have the async keyword in its method header, and it must be before the return type.

- This async keyword doesn't do anything more than signal that the method contains one or more await expressions. That is, it doesn't, in itself, create any asynchrony.

- The async keyword is a *contextual keyword*, meaning that in positions other than as a method modifier (or lambda or anonymous method modifier), async can be used as an identifier.

The return type must be one of the following types. Notice that three of the return types include the Task class. When referring to the class we'll use the capitalized form (since that's the name of the class) and the syntax typeface. We'll use the lowercase form in the general sense to indicate a set of work that needs to be done.

- Task: If the calling method doesn't need a return value from the async method but needs to be able to check on the async method's state, then the async method can return an object of type Task. In this case, if there are any return statements in the async method, they must not return anything. The following code sample is from a calling method:

```
Task someTask = DoStuff.CalculateSumAsync(5, 6);
    ...
someTask.Wait();
```

- Task<T>: If the calling method is to receive a value of type T back from the call, the return type of the async method must be Task<T>. The calling method will then get the value of type T by reading the Task's Result property, as shown in the following code:

```
Task<int> value    = DoStuff.CalculateSumAsync( 5, 6 );
    ...
Console.WriteLine($"Value: { value.Result }");
```

ValueTask<T>: This is a value type object that is used like Task<T> but is used in situations where the result of the task is likely to already be available. Because it is a value type, it can be put on the stack and avoid the need to allocate space on the heap for a Task<T> object. Because of this, it can improve performance in some cases.

- void: If the calling method just wants the async method to execute but doesn't need any further interaction with it (this is sometimes called *fire and forget*), the async method can have a return type of void. In this case, as with the previous case, if there are any return statements in the async method, they must not return anything.

- Any type that has an accessible GetAwaiter method.

Notice that in the earlier Figure 21-4 the return type of the async method is Task<int>. Yet when you inspect the body of the method, you won't find any return statements that return an object of type Task<int>. There is, however, a single return statement at the end of the method that returns a value of type int. We can generalize this observation to the following, which we'll look at in more detail shortly:

- Any async method with a return type of Task<T> must return a value of type T or a type implicitly convertible to T.

Figures 21-5, 21-6, 21-7 and 21-8 show the architectures required for the interactions between the calling method and the async method for different kinds of return types.

```csharp
using System;
using System.Threading.Tasks;

class Program
{
    static void Main() {
        Task<int> value = DoAsyncStuff.CalculateSumAsync( 5, 6 );
        // Do other processing ...
        Console.WriteLine( "Value: {0}", value.Result );
    }
}

static class DoAsyncStuff
{
    public static async Task<int> CalculateSumAsync(int i1, int i2)   {
        int sum = await Task.Run( () => GetSum( i1, i2 ) );
        return sum;
    }

    private static int GetSum( int i1, int i2 ) { return i1 + i2; }
}
```

Figure 21-5. *Using an async method that returns a Task<int> object*

```
using System;
using System.Threading.Tasks;

class Program
{
   static void Main() {
      Task someTask = DoAsyncStuff.CalculateSumAsync(5, 6);
      // Do other processing
      someTask.Wait();
      Console.WriteLine( "Async stuff is done" );
   }
}

static class DoAsyncStuff
{
   public static async Task CalculateSumAsync( int i1, int i2 ) {
      int value = await Task.Run( () => GetSum( i1, i2 ) );
      Console.WriteLine("Value: {0}", value );
   }

   private static int GetSum( int i1, int i2 ) { return i1 + i2; }
}
```

Figure 21-6. Using an async method that returns a Task object

The code in Figure 21-7 uses the Thread.Sleep method to pause the main thread so that it doesn't exit before the async method has finished.

```
using System;
using System.Threading;
using System.Threading.Tasks;

class Program
{
    static void Main() {
        DoAsyncStuff.CalculateSumAsync(5, 6);
        // Do other processing
        Thread.Sleep( 200 );
        Console.WriteLine( "Program Exiting" );
    }
}

static class DoAsyncStuff
{
    public static async void CalculateSumAsync(int i1, int i2) {
        int value = await Task.Run( () => GetSum( i1, i2 ) );
        Console.WriteLine( "Value: {0}", value );
    }

    private static int GetSum(int i1, int i2) { return i1 + i2; }
}
```

Figure 21-7. *Using a fire-and-forget async method*

The code in Figure 21-8 shows the use of a ValueTask return type.

```
using System;
using System.Threading.Tasks;

class Program
{
    static void Main()
    {
        ValueTask<int> value = value = DoAsyncStuff.CalculateSumAsync( 0, 6 );
        // Do other processing.
        Console.WriteLine( $"Value: { value.Result }" );
        value = DoAsyncStuff.CalculateSumAsync( 5, 6 );
        // Do other processing.
        Console.WriteLine( $"Value: { value.Result }" );
    }

    static class DoAsyncStuff
    {
        public static async ValueTask<int> CalculateSumAsync(int i1, int i2)
        {
            if(i1 == 0)  // if i1 == 0, then the long running task can be avoided
            {
                return i2;
            }
            int sum = await Task<int>.Run( () => GetSum( i1, i2 ) );
            return sum;
        }

        private static int GetSum(int i1, int i2) { return i1 + i2; }
    }
}
```

Figure 21-8. *Using an async method that returns a ValueTask<int> object*

The Flow of Control in an Async Method

The structure of the body of an `async` method has three distinct regions, which are illustrated in Figure 21-9. We'll cover the `await` expression in detail in the next section, but in this section you can get an overview of its position and role. The three regions are the following:

- *Before the first* `await` *expression*: This includes all the code at the beginning of the method up until the first `await` expression. This region should contain only a small amount of code that doesn't require too much processing.

- *The* `await` *expression*: This expression represents the task to be performed asynchronously.

- *The continuation*: This is the rest of the code in the method, following the `await` expression. This is packaged up along with its execution environment, which includes the information about which thread it's on, the values of the variables currently in scope, and other things it'll need in order to resume execution later, after the `await` expression completes.

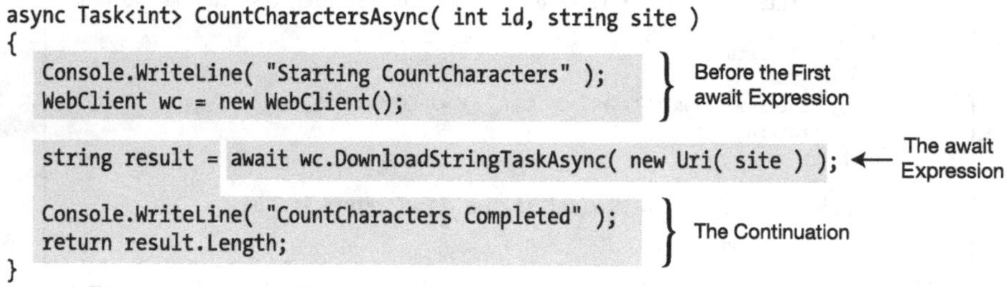

```
async Task<int> CountCharactersAsync( int id, string site )
{
    Console.WriteLine( "Starting CountCharacters" );        } Before the First
    WebClient wc = new WebClient();                           await Expression

    string result = await wc.DownloadStringTaskAsync( new Uri( site ) );  ←  The await
                                                                              Expression

    Console.WriteLine( "CountCharacters Completed" );       } The Continuation
    return result.Length;
}
```

Figure 21-9. *The code regions of an async method*

Figure 21-10 summarizes the flow of control through an async method. It starts with the code before the first await expression and executes normally (synchronously) until it encounters the first await. This region actually ends at the first await expression, where the await's task has not already completed (which should be the vast majority of the time). If the await's task has already completed, the method continues executing synchronously. The process is repeated if another await is encountered.

When the await expression is reached, the async method returns control to the calling method. If the method's return type is of type Task, Task<T>, or ValueTask<T>, the method creates a Task or ValueTask object that represents both the task to be done asynchronously and the continuation and returns that Task or ValueTask to the calling method.

There are now two flows of control: the one in the async method and the one in the calling method. The code in the async method does the following:

- It executes, asynchronously, its await expression's awaitable task.

- When the await expression is done, it executes the continuation. The continuation itself might have other await expressions, which are handled the same way. That is, each await expression is executed asynchronously, followed by the execution of its continuation.

- When the continuation encounters a return statement or the end of the method, the following happens:

  - If the method's return type is void, the flow of control exits.

  - If the method's return type is Task, the continuation sets the status properties on the Task and exits. If the return type is a Task<T> or ValueTask<T>, the continuation additionally sets the Result property of the object.

In the meantime, the code in the calling method continues on its course, having received the Task<T> object or ValueTask<T> object back from the async method. When it needs the actual result value, it references the Result property of the Task or ValueTask object. If, by that point, the async method has set that property, the calling method retrieves the value and continues. Otherwise, it halts and waits for the property to be set before continuing.

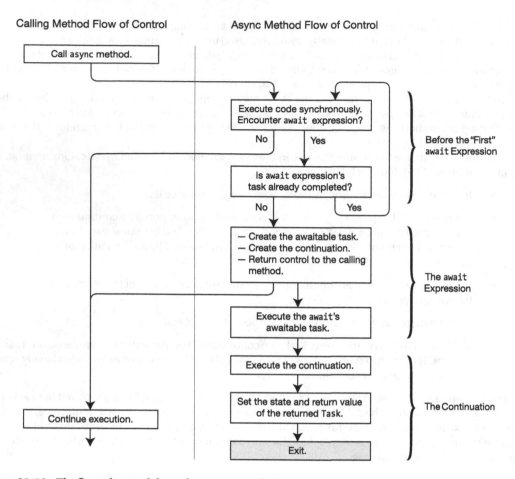

Figure 21-10. The flow of control through an async method

One thing that people are sometimes confused about is the type of the object returned when the first await in the async method is encountered. The type returned is *the type listed as the return type in the header of the async method*, which might have nothing to do with the type of the value returned by the await expression.

In the following code, for example, the await expression returns a string. But during execution of the method, when that await expression is reached, the async method returns to the calling method an object of Task<int> because that's the return type of the method.

```
private async Task<int> CountCharactersAsync( string site )
{
   WebClient wc = new WebClient();

   string result = await wc.DownloadStringTaskAsync( new Uri( site ) );

   return result.Length;
}
```

Another potentially confusing thing is that when the async method "returns" as the result of a return statement in the method or by reaching the end of the method, it doesn't actually return *to* anything—it just exits.

The await Expression

The await expression specifies a task to be done asynchronously. The syntax of the await expression is shown next and consists of the await keyword followed by an awaitable object, which is called the *task*. The task might or might not be an object of type Task. By default, this task is run asynchronously on the current thread.

```
await task
```

An awaitable object is an instance of an *awaitable type*. An awaitable type is one that has a method named GetAwaiter, which takes no parameters and returns an object of a type called an *awaiter*, which has the following members:

```
bool IsCompleted { get; }
void OnCompleted(Action);
```

It also has one of the following:

```
void GetResult();
T GetResult(); (where T is any type)
```

In reality, however, you rarely need to build your own awaitable. Instead, you should use the Task or ValueTask classes, which are awaitable and are probably all that most programmers will ever need with regard to awaitables.

With .NET 4.5, Microsoft released a large number of new and reworked asynchronous methods, throughout the BCL, that return objects of type Task<T>. You can plug these right into your await expressions, and they'll work asynchronously on your current thread.

In many of our previous examples, we've been using the WebClient.DownloadStringTaskAsync method. This is one of these asynchronous methods. The following code is an example of its usage:

```
Uri site       = new Uri("http://www.illustratedcsharp.com" );
WebClient wc   = new WebClient();
string result = await wc.DownloadStringTaskAsync( site );
                            ↑
                Returns a Task<string>
```

Although there are now a number of BCL methods that return objects of type Task<T>, you'll most likely have your own methods that you will want to use as the task for an await expression. The easiest way to do that is to create a Task from your method using the Task.Run method. One important fact about the Task.Run method is that it runs your method on a different thread.

One signature of the Task.Run method is the following, which takes a Func<TReturn> delegate as a parameter. You'll remember from Chapter 20 that Func<TReturn> is a predefined delegate that takes no parameters and returns a value of type TReturn.

```
Task Run( Func<TReturn> func )
```

So, to pass your method to the Task.Run method, you need to create a delegate from it. The following code shows three ways to do this. In the code, method Get10 has a form compatible with a Func<int> delegate since it takes no parameters and returns an int.

- In the first instance, which is in the first two lines of method DoWorkAsync, a Func<int> delegate named ten is created using Get10. That delegate is then used in the Task.Run method in the next line.

- In the second instance, a Func<int> delegate is created right in the Task.Run method's parameter list.

- The last instance doesn't use the Get10 method at all. It uses the return statement that comprises the body of the Get10 method and uses it as the body of a lambda expression compatible with a Func<int> delegate. The lambda expression is implicitly converted to the delegate.

```csharp
class MyClass
{
    public int Get10()                          // Func<int> compatible
    {
        return 10;
    }

    public async Task DoWorkAsync()
    {
        Func<int> ten = new Func<int>(Get10);
        int a = await Task.Run(ten);

        int b = await Task.Run(new Func<int>(Get10));

        int c = await Task.Run(() => { return 10; });

        Console.WriteLine($"{ a } { b } { c }");
    }

class Program
{
    static void Main()
    {
        Task t = (new MyClass()).DoWorkAsync();
        t.Wait();
    }
}
```

This code produces the following output:

```
10   10   10
```

In the previous example code, we used the signature for Task.Run that takes a Func<TResult> as the parameter. There are a total of eight overloads for the method, which are shown in Table 21-1. Table 21-2 shows the signatures of the four delegate types that can be used.

Table 21-1. *The Return Types and Signatures of the Task.Run Overloads*

Return Type	Signature
Task	Run(Action action)
Task	Run(Action action, CancellationToken token)
Task\<TResult\>	Run(Func\<TResult\> function)
Task\<TResult\>	Run(Func\<TResult\> function, CancellationToken token)
Task	Run(Func\<Task\> function)
Task	Run(Func\<Task\> function, CancellationToken token)
Task\<TResult\>	Run(Func\<Task\<TResult\>\> function)
Task\<TResult\>	Run(Func\<Task\<TResult\>\> function, CancellationToken token)

Table 21-2. *The Types of Delegates That Can Be Sent to a Task.Run Method As the First Parameter*

Delegate Type	Delegate Signature	Meaning
Action	void Action()	A method that takes no parameters and returns no value
Func\<TResult\>	TResult Func()	A method that takes no parameters and returns an object of type T
Func\<Task\>	Task Func()	A method that takes no parameters and returns a simple Task object
Func\<Task\<TResult\>\>	Task\<TResult\> Func()	A method that takes no parameters and returns an object of type Task\<T\>

The following code shows four await statements that use the Task.Run method to run methods with the four different delegate types:

```
static class MyClass
{
    public static async Task DoWorkAsync()
    {                                    Action
                                          ↓
        await Task.Run(() => Console.WriteLine(5.ToString()));
                                        TResult Func()
                                          ↓
        Console.WriteLine((await Task.Run(() => 6)).ToString());
                                     Task Func()
                                          ↓
        await Task.Run(() => Task.Run(() => Console.WriteLine(7.ToString())));
                            Task<TResult> Func()
                                          ↓
        int value = await Task.Run(() => Task.Run(() => 8));
        Console.WriteLine(value.ToString());
    }
}

class Program
{
    static void Main()
    {
        Task t = MyClass.DoWorkAsync();
        t.Wait();
        Console.WriteLine("Press Enter key to exit");
        Console.Read();
    }
}
```

This code produces the following output:

```
5
6
7
8
```

The await expression can be used anywhere any other expression can be used (as long as it's inside an async method). In the previous code, the four await expressions are used in three different positions.

- The first and third instances use the await expression as a statement.

- In the second instance, the await expression is used as the parameter to the WriteLine method call.

- The fourth instance uses the await expression as the right-hand side of an assignment statement.

Suppose, however, that you have a method that doesn't match any of the four delegate forms. For example, suppose you have a method named GetSum that takes two int values as input and returns the sum of the two values. This isn't compatible with any of the four acceptable delegates. To get around this, you can create a lambda function in the form of an acceptable Func delegate, whose sole action is to run the GetSum method, as shown in the following line of code:

```
int value = await Task.Run(() => GetSum(5, 6));
```

The lambda function () => GetSum(5, 6) satisfies the Func<TResult> delegate because it is a method that takes no parameters but returns a single value. The following code shows a full example:

```
static class MyClass
{
    private static int GetSum(int i1, int i2)
    {
        return i1 + i2;
    }

    public static async Task DoWorkAsync()
    {                                    TResult Func()
                                              ↓
        int value = await Task.Run( () => GetSum(5, 6) );
        Console.WriteLine(value.ToString());
    }
}

class Program
{
    static void Main()
    {
        Task t = MyClass.DoWorkAsync();
        t.Wait();
        Console.WriteLine("Press Enter key to exit");
        Console.Read();
    }
}
```

This code produces the following output:

```
11
Press Enter key to exit
```

Cancelling an async Operation

Some of the .NET asynchronous methods allow you to request that they abort their execution. You can also build this feature into your own async methods. There are two classes in the System.Threading.Tasks namespace that are designed for this purpose: CancellationToken and CancellationTokenSource.

- A CancellationToken object contains the information about whether a task should be cancelled.

- A task that has a CancellationToken object needs to periodically inspect it to see what the token's state is. If the CancellationToken object's IsCancellationRequested property is set to true, the task should halt its operations and return.

- A CancellationToken is nonreversible and can be used only once. That is, once its IsCancellationRequested property is set to true, it can't be changed.

- A CancellationTokenSource object creates a CancellationToken object, which can then be given to various tasks. Any objects holding a CancellationTokenSource can call its Cancel method, which sets the CancellationToken's IsCancellationRequested property to true.

The following code shows how the CancellationTokenSource and CancellationToken classes are used to implement cancellation. Notice that the process is *cooperative*. That is, the fact that you call Cancel on the CancellationTokenSource doesn't, in itself, cancel the operation. Instead, all it does is set the state of the CancellationToken's IsCancellationRequested property to true. It's up to the code containing the CancellationToken to inspect it and see whether it should stop its execution and return.

The following code shows the use of the cancellation classes. The code as it's written does not cancel the async method but contains two commented lines in the middle of method Main that invoke the cancellation action.

```
class Program
{
    static void Main()
    {
        CancellationTokenSource cts    = new CancellationTokenSource();
        CancellationToken          token = cts.Token;

        MyClass mc   = new MyClass();
        Task t       = mc.RunAsync( token );

        //Thread.Sleep( 3000 );     // Wait 3 seconds.
        //cts.Cancel();             //cancel the operation.

        t.Wait();
        Console.WriteLine($"Was Cancelled: { token.IsCancellationRequested }");
    }
}
```

```
class MyClass
{
   public async Task RunAsync( CancellationToken ct )
   {
      if ( ct.IsCancellationRequested )
         return;
      await Task.Run( () => CycleMethod( ct ), ct );
   }

   void CycleMethod( CancellationToken ct )
   {
      Console.WriteLine( "Starting CycleMethod" );
      const int max = 5;
      for ( int i=0; i < max; i++ )
      {
         if ( ct.IsCancellationRequested )      // Monitor the CancellationToken.
            return;
         Thread.Sleep( 1000 );
         Console.WriteLine($"   { i+1 } of { max } iterations completed");
      }
   }
}
```

The first run, leaving the lines commented, does not cancel the task and produces the following output:

```
Starting CycleMethod
   1 of 5 iterations completed
   2 of 5 iterations completed
   3 of 5 iterations completed
   4 of 5 iterations completed
   5 of 5 iterations completed
Was Cancelled: False
```

If you uncomment the Thread.Sleep and Cancel statements in method Main, the task is cancelled after three seconds, and the execution produces the following output:

```
Starting CycleMethod
   1 of 5 iterations completed
   2 of 5 iterations completed
   3 of 5 iterations completed
Was Cancelled: True
```

Exception Handling and the await Expression

You can use await expressions inside a try statement just as you would with any other expression, and the try...catch...finally constructs work as you would hope.

The following code shows an example of an await expression with a task that throws an exception. The await expression is inside a try block, which handles the exception in the normal way.

```
class Program
{
    static void Main(string[] args)
    {
        Task t = BadAsync();
        t.Wait();
        Console.WriteLine($"Task Status   : { t.Status }");
        Console.WriteLine($"Task IsFaulted: { t.IsFaulted }");
    }

    static async Task BadAsync()
    {
        try
        {
            await Task.Run(() => { throw new Exception(); });
        }
        catch
        {
            Console.WriteLine("Exception in BadAsync");
        }
    }
}
```

This code produces the following output:

```
Exception in BadAsync
Task Status   : RanToCompletion
Task IsFaulted: False
```

Notice in the output that even though the Task threw an Exception, at the end of Main, the Task's status is RanToCompletion. This might be a bit surprising since the async method threw an exception. The reason for this, though, is that the following two conditions are true: (1) the Task wasn't cancelled, and (2) there were no *unhandled* exceptions. Similarly, the IsFaulted property is set to False because there were no unhandled exceptions.

Beginning with C# 6.0, you can also use await expressions in catch and finally blocks. You might use this to perform logging or some other long-running task where the initial exception would not require the termination of your application. If the error is serious enough to prevent your application from continuing, there's little benefit to be gained from performing the catch or finally task in an asynchronous manner.

If, however, this new asynchronous task also generates an exception, any existing exception information would be lost, making debugging the original error more difficult.

Waiting Synchronously for Tasks in the Calling Method

The calling method can make any number of calls to various async methods and receive Task objects from them. Your code might then continue, doing various tasks, but then get to a point where it wants to wait for a particular Task object to complete before continuing further. To do this, the Task class provides instance method Wait, which you call on a Task object.

The following code shows an example of its use. In the code, the calling method DoRun calls async method CountCharactersAsync and receives a Task<int>. It then calls the Wait method on the Task instance to wait until the Task finishes. When it finishes, it displays the result message.

```
static class MyDownloadString
{
    public static void DoRun()
    {
        Task<int> t = CountCharactersAsync( "http://www.illustratedcsharp.com" );
        Wait until the Task t completes.
              ↓
        t.Wait();
        Console.WriteLine($"The task has finished, returning value { t.Result }.");
    }

    private static async Task<int> CountCharactersAsync( string site )
    {
        string result = await new WebClient().DownloadStringTaskAsync( new Uri( site ) );
        return result.Length;
    }
}

class Program
{
    static void Main()
    {
        MyDownloadString.DoRun();
    }
}
```

This code produces the following output:

```
The task has finished, returning value 4699.
```

The Wait method is for use with a single Task object. But you can also wait on a set of Task objects. Given a set of Tasks, you can wait until all of them are completed, or you can wait until one of them completes. The methods you use to do this are the following two static methods on the Task class:

- WaitAll

- WaitAny

These are synchronous methods that return no value. That is, they stop and wait until their constraint is satisfied, before continuing.

We'll start by looking at a simple program that has a method called DoRun, which calls an async method twice, getting back two Task<int> objects in return. The method then continues on its way, checking and printing out whether the tasks are completed. It then goes to the end of the method and waits on the Console.Read call before completing. The Console.Read method waits for a character received from the keyboard. We put this here because otherwise the main method would exit before the asynchronous task was finished.

The program, as written, doesn't use the wait methods, but it contains a commented section in the middle of DoRun that contains the wait code, which we'll use shortly, to compare against the results of this version.

```
class MyDownloadString
{
    Stopwatch sw = new Stopwatch();

    public void DoRun()
    {
        sw.Start();

        Task<int> t1 = CountCharactersAsync( 1, "http://www.microsoft.com" );
        Task<int> t2 = CountCharactersAsync( 2, "http://www.illustratedcsharp.com" );

        //Task.WaitAll( t1, t2 );
        //Task.WaitAny( t1, t2 );

        Console.WriteLine( "Task 1:  {0}Finished", t1.IsCompleted ? "" : "Not " );
        Console.WriteLine( "Task 2:  {0}Finished", t2.IsCompleted ? "" : "Not " );
        Console.Read();
    }

    private async Task<int> CountCharactersAsync( int id, string site )
    {
        WebClient wc = new WebClient();
        string result = await wc.DownloadStringTaskAsync( new Uri( site ) );
        Console.WriteLine( "   Call {0} completed:   {1, 4:N0} ms",
                                        id, sw.Elapsed.TotalMilliseconds );
        return result.Length;
    }
}
```

```
class Program
{
   static void Main()
   {
      MyDownloadString ds = new MyDownloadString();
      ds.DoRun();
   }
}
```

This code produces the following output. Notice that neither Task had completed when they were checked with the IsCompleted method.

```
Task 1:  Not Finished
Task 2:  Not Finished
   Call 1 completed:      166 ms
   Call 2 completed:      425 ms
```

If we uncomment the first line of commented code in the middle of DoRun, as shown in the following two lines of code, the method passes the two tasks that we list as parameters to the WaitAll method. The code will then stop and wait until both tasks have completed before continuing execution.

```
Task.WaitAll( t1, t2 );
//Task.WaitAny( t1, t2 );
```

When we run the code with this configuration, the result is the following:

```
   Call 1 completed:      137 ms
   Call 2 completed:      601 ms
Task 1:  Finished
Task 2:  Finished
```

If we modify the section again to comment out the WaitAll method call and uncomment the WaitAny method call, the code looks like the following:

```
//Task.WaitAll( t1, t2 );
Task.WaitAny( t1, t2 );
```

In this case, the WaitAny call halts until at least one of the Tasks completes. When we run the code again, the results are the following:

```
   Call 1 completed:      137 ms
Task 1:  Finished
Task 2:  Not Finished
   Call 2 completed:      413 ms
```

There are four overloads each for the WaitAll and WaitAny methods, allowing different ways of continuing execution other than completion of the tasks. The different overloads allow you to set a timeout or to use a CancellationToken to force continuation of the process. Table 21-3 shows the overloads for the methods.

Table 21-3. *The Task.WaitAll and WaitAny Overloaded Methods*

Signature	Description
void WaitAll(params Task[] tasks)	Wait for all the Tasks in a set to complete.
bool WaitAll(Task[] tasks, int millisecondsTimeout)	Wait for every Task in a set to complete. If it doesn't happen within the timeout period, return false and continue execution.
void WaitAll(Task[] tasks, CancellationToken token)	Wait for all the Tasks in a set to complete or for a signal from a CancellationToken to cancel.
bool WaitAll(Task[] tasks, TimeSpan span)	Wait for every Task in a set to complete. If it doesn't happen within the timeout period, return false and continue execution.
bool WaitAll(Task[] tasks, int millisecondsTimeout, CancellationToken token)	Wait for all the Tasks in a set to complete or for a signal from a CancellationToken to cancel. If it doesn't happen within the timeout period, return false and continue execution.
void WaitAny(params Task[] tasks)	Wait for any one of a set of tasks to complete.
bool WaitAny (Task[] tasks, int millisecondsTimeout)	Wait for any one of a set of tasks to complete. If it doesn't happen within the timeout period, return false and continue execution.
void WaitAny (Task[] tasks, CancellationToken token)	Wait for any one of a set of tasks to complete or for a signal from a CancellationToken to cancel.
bool WaitAny (Task[] tasks, TimeSpan span)	Wait for any one of a set of tasks to complete. If it doesn't happen within the timeout period, return false and continue execution.
bool WaitAny (Task[] tasks, int millisecondsTimeout, CancellationToken token)	Wait for any one of a set of tasks to complete or for a signal from a CancellationToken to cancel. If it doesn't happen within the timeout period, return false and continue execution.

Waiting Asynchronously for Tasks in the async Method

In the previous section, you learned how to wait synchronously for Task completion. Sometimes, however, in your async method, you will want to wait on Tasks as your await expression. This allows your async method to return to the calling method but allows the async method to wait for completion of one or all of a set of tasks. The calls that allow this are the Task.WhenAll and Task.WhenAny methods. These methods are called *combinators*.

The following code shows an example of using the Task.WhenAll method. This method waits asynchronously, without requiring time on the main thread, until all the Tasks associated with it are completed. Notice that the await expression's task is the Task.WhenAll call.

```csharp
using System;
using System.Collections.Generic;
using System.Net;
using System.Threading.Tasks;

class MyDownloadString
{
    public void DoRun()
    {
        Task<int> t = CountCharactersAsync( "http://www.microsoft.com",
                                    "http://www.illustratedcsharp.com");

        Console.WriteLine( "DoRun:  Task {0}Finished", t.IsCompleted ? "" : "Not " );
        Console.WriteLine( "DoRun:  Result = {0}", t.Result );
    }

    private async Task<int> CountCharactersAsync(string site1, string site2 )
    {
        WebClient wc1 = new WebClient();
        WebClient wc2 = new WebClient();
        Task<string> t1 = wc1.DownloadStringTaskAsync( new Uri( site1 ) );
        Task<string> t2 = wc2.DownloadStringTaskAsync( new Uri( site2 ) );

        List<Task<string>> tasks = new List<Task<string>>();
        tasks.Add( t1 );
        tasks.Add( t2 );

        await Task.WhenAll( tasks );

        Console.WriteLine( "    CCA:  T1 {0}Finished", t1.IsCompleted ? "" : "Not " );
        Console.WriteLine( "    CCA:  T2 {0}Finished", t2.IsCompleted ? "" : "Not " );

        return t1.IsCompleted ? t1.Result.Length : t2.Result.Length;
    }
}
```

```
class Program
{
    static void Main()
    {
        MyDownloadString ds = new MyDownloadString();
        ds.DoRun();
    }
}
```

This code produces the following output:

```
DoRun:  Task Not Finished
   CCA:  T1 Finished
   CCA:  T2 Finished
DoRun:  Result = 1020
```

The Task.WhenAny combinator waits asynchronously until one of the Tasks associated with it completes. If you change the await expression to use the Task.WhenAny method instead of the Task.WhenAll method and rerun the program, it produces the following output:

```
DoRun:  Task Not Finished
   CCA:  T1 Finished
   CCA:  T2 Not Finished
DoRun:  Result = 1020
```

The Task.Delay Method

The Task.Delay method creates a Task object that stops its own processing on the thread and completes after a set amount of time passes. Unlike Thread.Sleep, however, which blocks work on the thread, Task.Delay does not block the thread, so it can continue processing other work.

The following code shows an example of using the Task.Delay method:

```
class Simple
{
    Stopwatch sw = new Stopwatch();

    public void DoRun()
    {
        Console.WriteLine( "Caller: Before call" );
        ShowDelayAsync();
        Console.WriteLine( "Caller: After call" );
    }

    private async void ShowDelayAsync ( )
    {
        sw.Start();
        Console.WriteLine($"   Before Delay: { sw.ElapsedMilliseconds }");
        await Task.Delay( 1000 );
        Console.WriteLine($"   After Delay : { sw.ElapsedMilliseconds }");
    }
}

class Program
{
    static void Main()
    {
        Simple ds = new Simple ();
        ds.DoRun();
        Console.Read();
    }
}
```

This code produces the following output:

```
Caller: Before call
   Before Delay: 0
Caller: After call
   After Delay : 1007
```

There are four overloads for the Delay method, allowing for different ways of specifying the time period and also allowing for a CancellationToken object. Table 21-4 shows the four overloads for the method.

Table 21-4. *The Overloads of the Task.Delay Method*

Signature	Description
Task Delay(int millisecondsDelay)	Returns a Task object that completes after the delay period, which is given in milliseconds.
Task Delay(TimeSpan delay)	Returns a Task object that completes after the delay period, which is given as a .NET TimeSpan object.
Task Delay(int millisecondsDelay, CancellationToken token)	Returns a Task object that completes after the delay period, given in milliseconds, but can be cancelled using the cancellation token.
Task Delay(TimeSpan delay, CancellationToken token)	Returns a Task object that completes after the delay period, given as a .NET TimeSpan object, but can be cancelled using the cancellation token.

Async Operations in GUI Programs

Although all the code in this chapter so far has been for console applications, asynchronous methods are particularly useful for GUI programs.

The reason for this is that GUI programs are designed such that almost every change in the display, including servicing button clicks, displaying labels, and moving the window itself, must be done on the main GUI thread. The way this is implemented in Windows programs is through the use of messages, which are placed into a *message queue*, which is managed by the *message pump*.

The message pump takes a message out of the queue and calls that message's handler code. When the handler code finishes, the message pump gets the next message and repeats the cycle.

Because of this architecture, it's important that handler code be short so that it doesn't hold up the process and block other GUI actions from being processed. If the handler code for a particular message takes a long time, a message backlog builds up in the message queue, and the program becomes unresponsive because none of those messages can be handled until the long-running handler is finished.

Figure 21-11 shows two versions of a window from a WPF program. The window consists of a status label and a button underneath it. The intention of the programmer was that the program user would click the button and the button's handler code would do the following:

- Disable the button so that the user can't click it again while the handler is working

- Change the message to "Doing Stuff" so that the user knows the program is working

- Have the program sleep for four seconds—simulating some work

- Change the message back to the original message and reenable the button

The screenshot on the right of the figure illustrates what the programmer expected the window to look like for the four seconds after the button is pressed. It turns out, however, that that wasn't the result. When the programmer clicked the button, nothing appeared to happen at all, and when he tried to move the window around on the screen several seconds after clicking the button, the window was frozen on the screen and wouldn't move—until after the four seconds were done, when the window all of a sudden lurched to the new position.

Before the Button is Pressed

After the Button is Pressed

Figure 21-11. *A simple WPF program with a button and a status string*

■ **Note**   WPF is Microsoft's replacement for the Windows Forms GUI programming framework. For further information about WPF programming, please see Apress book *Illustrated WPF* (Apress, 2009), by Daniel Solis.

To re-create this WPF program, called MessagePump, in Visual Studio, do the following:

1. Select the File ➤ New ➤ Project menu item, which pops up the New Project window.

2. On the pane on the left of the window, open the Installed Templates section, if it's not already open.

3. Under the C# category, click the Windows entry. This populates the center pane with the installed Windows Classic Desktop program templates.

4. Click WPF App (.NET Framework), and then at the bottom of the window, enter MessagePump in the Name text box. Below that, select a location and click the OK button.

5. Modify the XAML markup in file MainWindow.xaml to be the same as the following markup. This creates the window with the status label and the button.

```
<Window x:Class="MessagePump.MainWindow"
        xmlns="http://schemas.microsoft.com/winfx/2006/xaml/presentation"
        xmlns:x="http://schemas.microsoft.com/winfx/2006/xaml"
        Title="Pump" Height="120" Width="200  ">
    <StackPanel>
        <Label Name="lblStatus" Margin="10,5,10,0" >Not Doing Anything</Label>
        <Button Name="btnDoStuff" Content="Do Stuff" HorizontalAlignment="Left"
                Margin="10,5" Padding="5,2" Click="btnDoStuff_Click"/>
    </StackPanel>
</Window>
```

6. Modify the code-behind file, MainWindow.xaml.cs, so that it matches the following C# code:

```
using System.Threading;
using System.Threading.Tasks;
using System.Windows;
namespace MessagePump
{
    public partial class MainWindow : Window
    {
        public MainWindow()
        {
            InitializeComponent();
        }
        private void btnDoStuff_Click( object sender, RoutedEventArgs e )
        {
            btnDoStuff.IsEnabled = false;
            lblStatus.Content    = "Doing Stuff";
            Thread.Sleep( 4000 );
            lblStatus.Content    = "Not Doing Anything";
            btnDoStuff.IsEnabled = true;
        }
    }
}
```

When you run the program, you'll find that its behavior matches the preceding description, which is that the button isn't disabled and the status label doesn't change, and if you try to move the window, it won't move until the four seconds have passed.

The reason for this possibly surprising behavior is simple. Figure 21-12 illustrates the situation. When the button is clicked, a button Click message is placed on the message queue. The message pump removes the message from the queue and starts the button click's handler code—which is method btnDoStuff_Click. The btnDoStuff_Click handler places on the queue the messages that will trigger the behaviors we want, as shown on the right side of the figure. But none of those messages can be executed until the handler itself exits, which isn't until after it sleeps for four seconds and exits. Then all those things happen, but they're too quick to see.

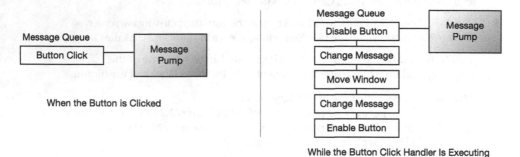

Figure 21-12. *The message pump dispatches messages from the front of the message queue. While the button message handler is executing, messages for the other actions build up on the queue and can't be executed until it's done.*

If, however, we could have the handler put the first two messages onto the queue and then take itself off the processor and only have itself put back into the queue when the four seconds are finished, then those and any other messages could be processed during the waiting time, and the process would perform as we wanted and would remain responsive.

We can accomplish this easily using the async/await feature, as shown next in the modified version of the handler code. When the await statement is reached, the handler returns to the calling method and is taken off the processor, allowing other messages to be processed—including the two it just put on. After the awaitable task finishes (the Task.Delay, in this case), the continuation (the rest of the method) is scheduled back onto the thread.

```
private async void btnDoStuff_Click( object sender, RoutedEventArgs e )
{
    btnDoStuff.IsEnabled = false;
    lblStatus.Content    = "Doing Stuff";

    await Task.Delay( 4000 );

    lblStatus.Content    = "Not Doing Anything";
    btnDoStuff.IsEnabled = true;
}
```

Task.Yield

The Task.Yield method creates an awaitable that immediately returns. Awaiting a Yield allows the async method to return to the calling method while continuing on in the async method's code. You can think of this as leaving the front of the message queue and going to the back of the line in order to allow other tasks to get time on the processor.

The following sample code shows an async method that yields control every 1,000 times through a loop it executes. Each time it executes the Yield method it allows other tasks in the thread to execute.

```
static class DoStuff
{
   public static async Task<int> FindSeriesSum( int i1 )
   {
      int sum = 0;
      for ( int i=0; i < i1; i++ )
      {
         sum += i;
         if ( i % 1000 == 0 )
            await Task.Yield();
      }
      return sum;
   }
}

class Program
{
   static void Main()
   {
      Task<int> value = DoStuff.FindSeriesSum( 1_000_000 );
      CountBig( 100_000 );  CountBig( 100_000 );
      CountBig( 100_000 );  CountBig( 100_000 );
      Console.WriteLine( $"Sum: { value.Result }");
   }

   private static void CountBig( int p )
   {
      for ( int i=0; i < p; i++ )
         ;
   }
}
```

This code produces the following output:

```
Sum: 1783293664
```

The Yield method can be extremely useful in GUI programs to break up large chunks of work and let other tasks use the processor.

Using an async Lambda Expression

So far in this chapter you've seen only async *methods*. But if you recall, we stated that you can also use async anonymous methods and async lambda expressions. These constructs are particularly useful for event handlers with only a small amount of work. The following code snippet shows a lambda expression being registered as the event handler for a button click event:

```
startWorkButton.Click += async ( sender, e ) =>
   {
      // Do the Click handler work.
   };
```

The following is a short WPF program showing its use. The following is the code-behind:

```
using System.Threading.Tasks;
using System.Windows;

namespace AsyncLambda
{
   public partial class MainWindow : Window
   {
      public MainWindow()
      {
         InitializeComponent();
                           Async lambda expression
                                    ↓
         startWorkButton.Click += async ( sender, e ) =>
            {
               SetGuiValues( false, "Work Started" );
               await DoSomeWork();
               SetGuiValues( true, "Work Finished" );
            };
      }

      private void SetGuiValues(bool buttonEnabled, string status)
      {
         startWorkButton.IsEnabled = buttonEnabled;
         workStartedTextBlock.Text = status;
      }

      private Task DoSomeWork()
      {
         return Task.Delay( 2500 );
      }
   }
}
```

The following markup is the XAML file for the program:

```
<Window x:Class="AsyncLambda.MainWindow"
        xmlns="http://schemas.microsoft.com/winfx/2006/xaml/presentation"
        xmlns:x="http://schemas.microsoft.com/winfx/2006/xaml"
        Title="Async Lambda" Height="115" Width="150">
    <StackPanel>
        <TextBlock Name="workStartedTextBlock" Margin="10,10"/>
        <Button Name="startWorkButton" Width="100" Margin="4" Content="Start Work" />
    </StackPanel>
</Window>
```

This program produces a window with the three states shown in Figure 21-13.

Before Button Press   While Work in Progress   After Work Finished

Figure 21-13. *The output of the example program AsyncLambda*

A Full GUI Example

We've covered the `async`/`await` components one piece at a time. In this section we want you to see a complete WPF GUI program that includes a status bar and cancellation.

The sample program presents the screenshot shown on the left in Figure 21-14. When you click the button, the program begins to process and updates the progress bar. If you let the processing go to completion, it displays the message box shown at the top on the right of the figure. If you click the Cancel button before processing is complete, the program displays the message box shown at the bottom on the right of the figure.

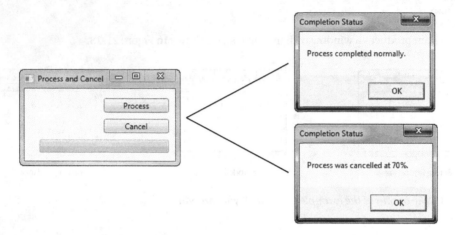

Figure 21-14. *Screenshots from a simple WPF program that implements a status bar and cancellation*

To re-create the program, create a new WPF application called `WpfAwait`. Modify the XAML markup in file `MainWindow.xaml` so that it matches the following:

```xml
<Window x:Class="WpfAwait.MainWindow"
        xmlns="http://schemas.microsoft.com/winfx/2006/xaml/presentation"
        xmlns:x="http://schemas.microsoft.com/winfx/2006/xaml"
        Title="Process and Cancel" Height="150  " Width="250">
    <StackPanel>
        <Button Name="btnProcess" Width="100" Click="btnProcess_Click"
                HorizontalAlignment="Right" Margin="10,15,10,10">Process</Button>
        <Button Name="btnCancel" Width="100" Click="btnCancel_Click"
                HorizontalAlignment="Right" Margin="10,0">Cancel</Button>
        <ProgressBar Name="progressBar" Height="20" Width="200" Margin="10"
                     HorizontalAlignment="Right"/>
    </StackPanel>
</Window>
```

Modify the code-behind file, MainWindow.xaml.cs, so that it matches the following:

```
using System.Threading;
using System.Threading.Tasks;
using System.Windows;
namespace WpfAwait
{
    public partial class MainWindow : Window
    {
        CancellationTokenSource cancellationTokenSource;
        CancellationToken       cancellationToken;

        public MainWindow()
        { InitializeComponent(); }

        private async void btnProcess_Click( object sender, RoutedEventArgs e )
        {
            btnProcess.IsEnabled = false;

            cancellationTokenSource = new CancellationTokenSource();
            cancellationToken       = cancellationTokenSource.Token;

            int completedPercent = 0;
            for ( int i = 0; i < 10; i++ )
            {
                if ( cancellationToken.IsCancellationRequested )
                    break;
                try   We'll cover try/catch statements in the Exceptions chapter
                {
                    await Task.Delay( 500, cancellationToken );
                    completedPercent = ( i + 1 ) * 10;
                }
                catch ( TaskCanceledException ex )
                { completedPercent = i * 10; }
                progressBar.Value = completedPercent;
            }

            string message = cancellationToken.IsCancellationRequested
                    ? string.Format( $"Process was cancelled at { completedPercent }%." )
                    : "Process completed normally.";
            MessageBox.Show( message, "Completion Status" );

            progressBar.Value    = 0;
            btnProcess.IsEnabled = true;
            btnCancel.IsEnabled  = true;
        }

        private void btnCancel_Click( object sender, RoutedEventArgs e )
        {
            if ( !btnProcess.IsEnabled )
            {
                btnCancel.IsEnabled = false;
                cancellationTokenSource.Cancel();
            }
        }
    }
}
```

The BackgroundWorker Class

In the previous sections you learned how to use the async/await feature to process tasks asynchronously. In this section, you'll learn another means of doing asynchronous work—in this case, on a background thread. The async/await feature works best for a small, discrete task that needs to be done in the background.

Sometimes, however, you might want to set up another thread that is continuously running in the background performing work and occasionally communicating with the main thread. The BackgroundWorker class is perfect for this. Figure 21-15 shows the key members of the class.

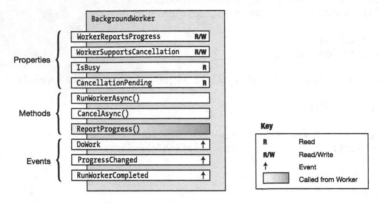

Figure 21-15. *The key members of the BackgroundWorker class*

- The first two properties shown in the figure are used to set whether the background task can report its progress to the main thread and whether it supports cancellation from the main thread. You use the third property to find out whether the background task is running.

- The class has three events, which are used to signal different program events and states. You need to write event handlers for these events to take whatever actions are appropriate for your program.

    - The DoWork event is raised when the background thread starts.

    - The ProgressChanged event is raised when the background task reports progress.

    - The RunWorkerCompleted event is raised when the background worker exits.

- The three methods are used to initiate actions or change state.

    - Calling the RunWorkerAsync method retrieves a background thread that executes the DoWork event handler.

    - Calling the CancelAsync method sets the CancellationPending property to true. It is the responsibility of the DoWork event handler to inspect this property to determine whether it should stop its processing.

    - The ReportProgress method can be called by the DoWork event handler (from the *background thread*) when it wants to report its progress to the main thread.

To use a BackgroundWorker class object, you need to write the following event handlers. The first is required since it contains the code you want to be executed in the background thread. The other two are optional, and you can include them or not, depending on what your program needs.

606

- The handler attached to the DoWork event contains the code you want executed in the background on a separate thread.

  – In Figure 21-16, this handler is named DoTheWork and is in a gradient-shaded box to illustrate that it's executed in the background thread.

  – The DoWork event is raised when the main thread calls the BackgroundWorker object's RunWorkerAsync method.

- The background thread communicates with the main thread by calling the ReportProgress method. When this happens, the ProgressChanged event is raised, and the main thread can handle the event with the handler attached to the ProgressChanged event.

- The handler attached to the RunWorkerCompleted event contains the code to be executed on the main thread after the background thread completes the execution of the DoWork event handler.

Figure 21-16 shows the structure of a program, with the event handlers attached to the events of the BackgroundWorker object.

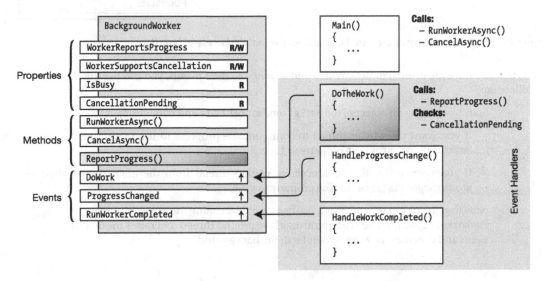

Figure 21-16. *Your code must supply event handlers for the events that control the flow through execution of the tasks*

The delegates for these event handlers are the following. Each takes an object reference as the first parameter and a specialized subclass of the EventArgs class as the second parameter.

```
void DoWorkEventHandler               ( object sender, DoWorkEventArgs e )

void ProgressChangedEventHandler      ( object sender, ProgressChangedEventArgs e )

void RunWorkerCompletedEventHandler ( object sender, RunWorkerCompletedEventArgs e)
```

Figure 21-17 illustrates the structure of the EventArg classes used by these event handlers.

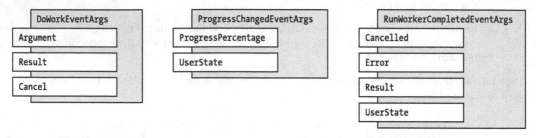

Figure 21-17. *The EventArg classes used by the BackgroundWorker event handlers*

When you have the event handlers written and attached to their events, you can use the class by doing the following:

- Start by creating an object of the BackgroundWorker class and configuring it.

  - If you want the worker thread to communicate progress to the main thread, then set the WorkerReportsProgress property to true.

  - If you want to be able to cancel the worker thread from the main thread, then set the WorkerSupportsCancellation property to true.

- Now that the object is configured, you can start it by calling the object's RunWorkerAsync method. This retrieves a background thread that raises the DoWork event and executes the event's handler in the background.

Now you have both the main thread and the background thread running. While the background thread is running, you can continue processing on the main thread.

In the main thread, if you've enabled the WorkerSupportsCancellation property, then you can call the object's CancelAsync method. As with the CancellationToken that you saw at the beginning of the chapter, this does not cancel the background thread. Instead, it sets the object's CancellationPending property to true. The DoWork event handler code running on the background thread needs to periodically check the CancellationPending property to see whether it should exit.

The background thread, in the meantime, continues to perform its computational tasks, as well as doing the following:

- If the WorkerReportsProgress property is true and the background thread has progress to report to the main thread, then it must call the BackgroundWorker object's ReportProgress method. This raises the ProgressChanged event in the main thread, which runs the corresponding event handler.

- If the WorkerSupportsCancellation property is enabled, then the DoWork event handler code should regularly check the CancellationPending property to determine whether it has been cancelled. If so, it should exit.

- If the background thread finishes its processing without being cancelled, it can return a result to the main thread by setting the Result field in the DoWorkEventArgs parameter shown previously in Figure 21-17.

When the background thread exits, the RunWorkerCompleted event is raised, and its handler is executed on the main thread. The RunWorkerCompletedEventArgs parameter can contain information from the now completed background thread, such as the return value and whether the thread was cancelled.

Example of the BackgroundWorker Class in a WPF Program

Since the BackgroundWorker class is primarily used with GUI programming, the following program shows its use in a simple WPF program.

This program produces the window shown on the left in Figure 21-18. When you click the Process button, it starts the background thread, which reports to the main thread every half-second and increments the progress bar at the top by 10 percent. At completion, it shows the dialog box on the right of the figure.

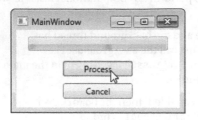

Figure 21-18. *The example WPF program using the BackgroundWorker class*

To re-create this WPF program, use Visual Studio to create a new WPF application named SimpleWorker. Modify your MainWindow.xaml file to match the following listing:

```
<Window x:Class="SimpleWorker.MainWindow"
        xmlns="http://schemas.microsoft.com/winfx/2006/xaml/presentation"
        xmlns:x="http://schemas.microsoft.com/winfx/2006/xaml"
        Title="MainWindow" Height="150  " Width="250">
   <StackPanel>
      <ProgressBar Name="progressBar" Height="20" Width="200" Margin="10"/>
      <Button Name="btnProcess" Width="100" Click="btnProcess_Click"
             Margin="5">Process</Button>
      <Button Name="btnCancel" Width="100" Click="btnCancel_Click"
             Margin="5">Cancel</Button>
   </StackPanel>
</Window>
```

Modify the MainWindow.xaml.cs file to match the following listing:

```
using System.Windows;
using System.ComponentModel;
using System.Threading;

namespace SimpleWorker {
   public partial class MainWindow : Window {
      BackgroundWorker bgWorker = new BackgroundWorker();

      public MainWindow() {
         InitializeComponent();

         // Set BackgroundWorker properties
         bgWorker.WorkerReportsProgress     = true;
         bgWorker.WorkerSupportsCancellation = true;
```

```csharp
      // Connect handlers to BackgroundWorker object.
      bgWorker.DoWork                += DoWork_Handler;
      bgWorker.ProgressChanged       += ProgressChanged_Handler;
      bgWorker.RunWorkerCompleted    += RunWorkerCompleted_Handler;
   }

   private void btnProcess_Click( object sender, RoutedEventArgs e ) {
      if ( !bgWorker.IsBusy )
         bgWorker.RunWorkerAsync();
   }

   private void ProgressChanged_Handler( object sender,
                                    ProgressChangedEventArgs args ) {
      progressBar.Value = args.ProgressPercentage;
   }

   private void DoWork_Handler( object sender, DoWorkEventArgs args ) {
      BackgroundWorker worker = sender as BackgroundWorker;

      for ( int i = 1; i <= 10; i++ )
      {
         if ( worker.CancellationPending )
         {
            args.Cancel = true;
            break;
         }
         else
         {
            worker.ReportProgress( i * 10 );
            Thread.Sleep( 500 );
         }
      }
   }

   private void RunWorkerCompleted_Handler( object sender,
                                    RunWorkerCompletedEventArgs args ) {
      progressBar.Value = 0;

      if ( args.Cancelled )
         MessageBox.Show( "Process was cancelled.", "Process Cancelled" );
      else
         MessageBox.Show( "Process completed normally.", "Process Completed" );
   }

   private void btnCancel_Click( object sender, RoutedEventArgs e )
   {
      bgWorker.CancelAsync();
   }
   }
}
```

Parallel Loops

In this section we'll take an abbreviated look at the Task Parallel Library. The Task Parallel Library is a library of classes in the BCL that greatly simplifies parallel programming. Covering the library in detail is far more than we can do in this chapter. So, unfortunately, we've had to settle for whetting your appetite by introducing just two of its simple constructs that you can learn and use quickly and easily. These are the `Parallel.For` loop and the `Parallel.ForEach` loop. These constructs are in the `System.Threading.Tasks` namespace.

By this point in the book we're sure you're quite familiar with C#'s standard `for` and `foreach` loops. These are common and tremendously powerful constructs. Many times when using these constructs, each iteration depends on a calculation or action in the previous iteration. But this isn't always the case. If the iterations are independent of each other and you're running on a multiprocessor machine, it might be a huge advantage if you could put different iterations on different processors and process them in parallel. This is exactly what the `Parallel.For` and `Parallel.ForEach` constructs do.

These constructs are in the form of methods with input parameters. There are 12 overloads of the `Parallel.For` method, but the simplest has the signature shown in the following line of code:

```
void Parallel.For( int fromInclusive, int toExclusive, Action<int> body );
```

The parameters are the following:

- The `fromInclusive` parameter is the first integer in the iteration series.

- The `toExclusive` parameter is an integer that is *one greater than the last index* in the iteration series. That is, it's the same as comparing using the expression index < ToExclusive.

- The body is a delegate that takes a single input parameter. The code of body is executed once per iteration.

The following code is an example using the `Parallel.For` construct. It iterates from 0 to 14 (remember that the 15 listed as the actual parameter is one more than the top iteration index) and prints out the iteration index and the square of the index. This application fits the requirement that each iteration is independent of any other iteration. Notice also that you must use the `System.Threading.Tasks` namespace.

```
using System;
using System.Threading.Tasks;          // Must use this namespace

namespace ExampleParallelFor
{
   class Program
   {
      static void Main( )
      {
         Parallel.For( 0, 15, i =>
            Console.WriteLine($"The square of { i } is { i * i }"));
      }
   }
}
```

One run of this code on my PC with a two-core processor produced the following output. Notice that you're not guaranteed any particular order of the iterations.

```
The square of 0 is 0
The square of 7 is 49
The square of 8 is 64
The square of 9 is 81
The square of 10 is 100
The square of 11 is 121
The square of 12 is 144
The square of 13 is 169
The square of 3 is 9
The square of 4 is 16
The square of 5 is 25
The square of 6 is 36
The square of 14 is 196
The square of 1 is 1
The square of 2 is 4
```

Another example is the following code. This program fills an integer array, in parallel, with the square of the iteration index.

```csharp
class Program
{
    static void Main()
    {
        const int maxValues = 50;
        int[] squares = new int[maxValues];

        Parallel.For( 0, maxValues, i => squares[i] = i * i );
    }
}
```

In this example, even though the iterations might be executed in parallel and in any order, the end result is an array containing the first 50 squares—in order!

The other parallel loop construct is the Parallel.ForEach method. There are more than a dozen overloads for this method, but the simplest is the following:

- The TSource is the type of object in the collection.
- The source is the collection of TSource objects.
- The body is the lambda expression to be applied to each element of the collection.

```
static ParallelLoopResult ForEach<TSource>( IEnumerable<TSource> source,
                                            Action<TSource> body)
```

An example of using the Parallel.ForEach method is the following code. In this case, TSource is string, and the source is a string[].

```
using System;
using System.Threading.Tasks;

namespace ParallelForeach1 {
    class Program {
        static void Main()
        {
            string[] squares = new string[]
                    { "We", "hold", "these", "truths", "to", "be", "self-evident",
                      "that", "all", "men", "are", "created", "equal"};

            Parallel.ForEach( squares,
                s => Console.WriteLine
                        ( string.Format($"\"{ s }\" has { s.Length } letters") ));
        }
    }
}
```

One run of this code on our PC with a two-core processor produced the following output, but the order might change each time:

```
"We" has 2 letters
"equal" has 5 letters
"truths" has 6 letters
"to" has 2 letters
"be" has 2 letters
"that" has 4 letters
"hold" has 4 letters
"these" has 5 letters
"all" has 3 letters
"men" has 3 letters
"are" has 3 letters
"created" has 7 letters
"self-evident" has 12 letters
```

Other Asynchronous Programming Patterns

For most of the asynchronous code you'll be producing, you'll probably be using the `async`/`await` feature, the `BackgroundWorker` class covered in the first part of this chapter, or the Task Parallel Library. There might still be occasions, however, where you'll need to use the older patterns for producing asynchronous code. For completeness, we'll cover these patterns, starting with this section to the end of the chapter. After learning these older patterns, you'll have a greater appreciation for how much simpler life is with the `async`/`await` feature.

Chapter 14 covered the topic of delegates, and you saw that when a delegate object is invoked, it invokes the methods contained in its invocation list. This is done synchronously, just as if the methods had been called by the program.

If a delegate object has only a single method (which we'll call the *referenced method*) in its invocation list, it can execute that method asynchronously. The delegate class has two methods, called `BeginInvoke` and `EndInvoke`, that are used to do this. You use these methods in the following way:

- When you call the delegate's `BeginInvoke` method, it starts its referenced method executing on a separate thread and then returns immediately to the initial thread. The initial thread then continues on while the referenced method executes in parallel.

- When your program wants to retrieve the results of the completed asynchronous method, it either checks the `IsCompleted` property of the `IAsyncResult` returned by `BeginInvoke` or calls the delegate's `EndInvoke` method to wait for the delegate to finish.

Figure 21-19 shows the three standard patterns for using this process. In all three patterns, the initial thread initiates an asynchronous method call and then does some additional processing. The patterns differ, however, in the ways in which the initial thread receives the information that the spawned thread has completed.

- In the *wait-until-done* pattern, after spawning the asynchronous method and doing some additional processing, the initial thread halts and waits for the spawned thread to finish before continuing.

- In the *polling* pattern, the initial thread checks periodically whether the spawned thread has completed, and if not, it continues additional processing.

- In the *callback* pattern, the initial thread continues execution without waiting or checking whether the spawned thread has completed. Instead, when the referenced method in the spawned thread finishes, it calls a callback method, which handles the results of the asynchronous method before calling EndInvoke.

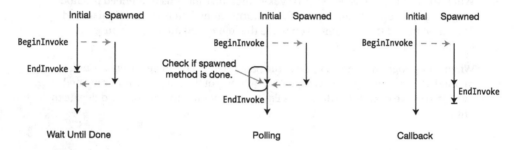

Figure 21-19. *The standard patterns for asynchronous method calls*

BeginInvoke and EndInvoke

Before we look at examples of these asynchronous programming patterns, let's take a closer look at the BeginInvoke and EndInvoke methods. Some of the important things to know about BeginInvoke are the following:

- When calling BeginInvoke, the actual parameters in the parameter list consist of the following:

  - The parameters required by the referenced method

  - Two additional parameters, called the callback parameter and the state parameter

- BeginInvoke retrieves a thread from the thread pool and starts the referenced method running on the new thread.

- BeginInvoke returns to the calling thread a reference to an object implementing the IAsyncResult interface. This interface reference contains information about the current state of the asynchronous method on the thread pool thread. The initial thread then continues execution.

The following code shows an example of calling a delegate's BeginInvoke method. The first line declares a delegate type called MyDel. The next line declares a method called Sum, which matches the delegate.

- The following line declares a delegate object called del, of the delegate type MyDel, and initializes its invocation list with the Sum method.

- Finally, the last line of code calls the BeginInvoke method of the delegate object and supplies it with the two delegate parameters 3 and 5 and the two BeginInvoke parameters callback and state, which are set to null in this example. When executed, the BeginInvoke method performs two actions.

  - It gets a thread from the thread pool and starts method Sum running on the new thread, supplying it with 3 and 5 as its actual parameters.

- It collects information about the state of the new thread and makes it available through a reference to an interface of type IAsyncResult, which it returns to the calling thread. The calling thread, in this example, stores it in a variable called iar.

```
delegate long MyDel( int first, int second );        // Delegate declaration
    ...
static long Sum(int x, int y){ return x + y; }        // Method matching delegate
    ...
MyDel del        = new MyDel(Sum);                     // Create delegate object
IAsyncResult iar = del.BeginInvoke( 3, 5, null, null );
     ↑                  ↑               ↑      ↑
Information about   Invoke delegate   Delegate  Extra
   new thread       asynchronously     params   params
```

You use the EndInvoke method to retrieve the values returned by the asynchronous method call and to release resources used by the thread. EndInvoke has the following characteristics:

- It takes as a parameter the reference to the IAsyncResult returned by the BeginInvoke method and finds the thread it refers to.

- If the thread pool thread has exited, EndInvoke does the following:

  - It cleans up the exited thread's loose ends and disposes of its resources.

  - It finds the value returned by the referenced method and returns that value as its return value.

- If the thread pool thread is still running when EndInvoke is called, the calling thread stops and waits for it to finish before cleaning up and returning the value. Because EndInvoke cleans up after the spawned thread, you must make sure that an EndInvoke is called for each BeginInvoke.

- If the asynchronous method triggers an exception, the exception is raised when EndInvoke is called.

The following line of code shows an example of calling EndInvoke to retrieve the value from an asynchronous method. You must always include the reference to the IAsyncResult object as a parameter.

```
              Delegate object
                    ↓
long result = del.EndInvoke( iar );
     ↑                          ↑
Return value  from          IAsyncResult
asynchronous method           object
```

EndInvoke supplies all the output from the asynchronous method call, including ref and out parameters. If a delegate's referenced method has ref or out parameters, they must be included in EndInvoke's parameter list before the reference to the IAsyncResult object, as shown here:

```
long result = del.EndInvoke(out someInt, iar);
     ↑                          ↑        ↑
Return value from              Out    IAsyncResult
asynchronous method         parameter   object
```

The Wait-Until-Done Pattern

Now that you understand the BeginInvoke and EndInvoke delegate methods, we can look at the asynchronous programming patterns. The first one we'll look at is the wait-until-done pattern. In this pattern, the initial thread initiates an asynchronous method call, does some additional processing, and then stops and waits until the spawned thread finishes. It's summarized as follows:

```
IAsyncResult iar = del.BeginInvoke( 3, 5, null, null );
    // Do additional work in the calling thread, while the method
    // is being executed asynchronously in the spawned thread.
    ...
long result = del.EndInvoke( iar );
```

The following code shows a full example of this pattern. This code uses the Sleep method of the Thread class to suspend itself for 100 milliseconds (1/10 of a second). 100 ms isn't very long to wait. But if we change it to 10 seconds, it's insufferable. The Thread class is in the System.Threading namespace.

```
using System;
using System.Threading;                          // For Thread.Sleep()

delegate long MyDel( int first, int second );    // Declare delegate type.

class Program {
    static long Sum(int x, int y)                // Declare method for async.
    {
        Console.WriteLine("                       Inside Sum");
        Thread.Sleep(100);

        return x + y;
    }
    static void Main( ) {
        MyDel del = new MyDel(Sum);

        Console.WriteLine( "Before BeginInvoke" );
        IAsyncResult iar = del.BeginInvoke(3, 5, null, null); // Start async
        Console.WriteLine( "After  BeginInvoke" );

        Console.WriteLine( "Doing stuff" );

        long result = del.EndInvoke( iar );    // Wait for end and get result
        Console.WriteLine($"After  EndInvoke: { result }");
    }
}
```

This code produces the following output:

```
Before BeginInvoke
After  BeginInvoke
Doing stuff
                    Inside Sum
After  EndInvoke: 8
```

The AsyncResult Class

Now that you've seen BeginInvoke and EndInvoke in action in their simplest forms, it's time to take a closer look at IAsyncResult, which is an integral part of using these methods.

BeginInvoke returns a reference to an IAsyncResult interface that is implemented by a class of type AsyncResult. The AsyncResult class represents the state of the asynchronous method. Figure 21-20 shows a representation of some of the important parts of the class. The important things to know about the class are the following:

- When you call a delegate object's BeginInvoke method, the system creates an object of the class AsyncResult. It doesn't, however, return a reference to the class object. Instead, it returns a reference to the *interface* contained in the object—IAsyncResult.

- An AsyncResult object contains a property called AsyncDelegate, which returns a reference to the delegate that was invoked to start the asynchronous method. This property, however, is part of the class object but not part of the interface.

- The IsCompleted property returns a Boolean value indicating whether the asynchronous method has completed.

- The AsyncState property returns a reference to the object that was listed as the state parameter in the BeginInvoke method invocation. It returns a reference of type object. We'll explain this in the section on the callback pattern.

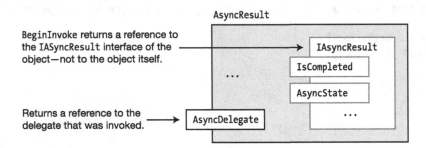

Figure 21-20. An AsyncResult class object

The Polling Pattern

In the polling pattern, the initial thread initiates an asynchronous method call, does some additional processing, and then uses the IsCompleted method of the IAsyncResult object to check periodically whether the spawned thread has completed. If the asynchronous method has completed, the initial thread calls EndInvoke and continues. Otherwise, it does some additional processing and checks again later. The "processing" in this example just consists of counting from 0 to 10,000,000.

```
delegate long MyDel(int first, int second);
class Program
{
    static long Sum(int x, int y)
    {
        Console.WriteLine("                    Inside Sum");
        Thread.Sleep(100);

        return x + y;
    }

    static void Main()
    {
        MyDel del = new MyDel(Sum);    Spawn asynchronous method.
                                    ↓
        IAsyncResult iar = del.BeginInvoke(3, 5, null, null); // Start async.
        Console.WriteLine("After BeginInvoke");
      Check whether the asynchronous method is done.
                            ↓
        while ( !iar.IsCompleted )
        {
            Console.WriteLine("Not Done");

            // Continue processing, even though in this case it's just busywork.
            for (long i = 0; i < 10_000_000; i++)
                ;                                   // Empty statement
        }
        Console.WriteLine("Done");
                    Call EndInvoke to get result and clean up.
                            ↓
        long result = del.EndInvoke(iar);
        Console.WriteLine($"Result: { result }");
    }

}
```

This code produces the following output:

```
After BeginInvoke
Not Done
                Inside Sum
Not Done
Not Done
Done
Result: 8
```

The Callback Pattern

In the previous two patterns, wait-until-done and polling, the initial thread continues with its flow of control only after it knows that the spawned thread has completed. It then retrieves the results and continues.

The callback pattern is different in that once the initial thread spawns the asynchronous method, it goes on its way without synchronizing with it again. When the asynchronous method call completes, the system invokes a user-supplied method to handle its results and to call the delegate's EndInvoke method. This user-defined method is called a *callback method,* or just a *callback.*

The two extra parameters at the end of the BeginInvoke parameter list are used with the callback method as follows:

- The first of the two parameters, the callback parameter, is the name of the callback method.

- The second parameter, the state parameter, can be either null or a reference to an object you want passed into the callback method. You'll be able to access this object through the method's IAsyncResult parameter using its AsyncState property. The type of this parameter is object.

The Callback Method

The signature and return type of the callback method must be of the form described by the AsyncCallback delegate type. This form requires that the method take a single parameter of type IAsyncResult and have a void return type, as shown here:

```
void AsyncCallback( IAsyncResult iar )
```

There are several ways you can supply the callback method to the BeginInvoke method. Since the callback parameter in BeginInvoke is a delegate of type AsyncCallback, you can supply it as a delegate, as shown in the first code statement that follows. Or you can just supply the name of the callback method and let the compiler create the delegate for you. Both forms are semantically equivalent.

```
                          Create a delegate with the callback method.
IAsyncResult iar1 =                        ↓
    del.BeginInvoke(3, 5, new AsyncCallback(CallWhenDone), null);

                             Just use the callback method's name.
                                          ↓
IAsyncResult iar2 = del.BeginInvoke(3, 5,CallWhenDone, null);
```

The second additional BeginInvoke parameter (which is the last one in the parameter list) is used to send an object to the callback method. It can be an object of any type since the parameter is of type object. Inside the callback method you'll have to cast it to the correct type.

Calling EndInvoke Inside the Callback Method

Inside the callback method, your code should call the delegate's EndInvoke method and take care of handling the output results of the asynchronous method execution. To call the delegate's EndInvoke method, though, you need a reference to the delegate object, which is in the initial thread—not here in the spawned thread.

If you're not using BeginInvoke's state parameter for anything else, you can use it to send the delegate reference to the callback method, as shown here:

```
        Delegate object                    Send delegate object as state param.
              ↓                                            ↓
IAsyncResult iar =del.BeginInvoke(3, 5, CallWhenDone, del);
```

Otherwise, you can extract the delegate's reference from the IAsyncResult object sent into the method as the parameter. This is shown in the following code and illustrated in Figure 21-21.

- The single parameter to the callback method is a reference to the IAsyncResult interface of the asynchronous method that has just completed. Remember that the IAsyncResult interface object is inside the AsyncResult class object.

- Although the IAsyncResult interface doesn't have a reference to the delegate object, the AsyncResult class object enclosing it *does* have a reference to the delegate object. So, the first line inside the example method body gets a reference to the class object by casting the interface reference to the class type. Variable ar now has a reference to the class object.

- With the reference to the class object, you can now use the AsyncDelegate property of the class object and cast it to the appropriate delegate type. This gives you the delegate reference, which you can then use to call EndInvoke.

```
using System.Runtime.Remoting.Messaging;        // Contains AsyncResult class

void CallWhenDone( IAsyncResult iar )
{
   AsyncResult ar = (AsyncResult) iar;          // Get class object reference.
   MyDel del = (MyDel) ar.AsyncDelegate;        // Get reference to delegate.

   long Sum = del.EndInvoke( iar );             // Call EndInvoke.
      ...
}
```

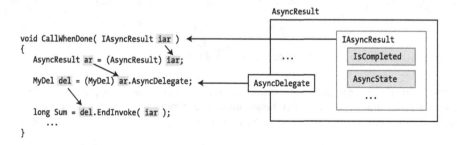

Figure 21-21. *Extracting the delegate's reference inside the callback method*

The following code puts it all together and is an example of using the callback pattern:

```csharp
using System;
using System.Runtime.Remoting.Messaging;        // To access the AsyncResult type
using System.Threading;

delegate long MyDel(int first, int second);

class Program
{
    static long Sum(int x, int y)
    {
        Console.WriteLine("                        Inside Sum");
        Thread.Sleep(100);
        return x + y;
    }
    static void CallWhenDone(IAsyncResult iar)
    {
        Console.WriteLine("                        Inside CallWhenDone.");
        AsyncResult ar = (AsyncResult) iar;
        MyDel del = (MyDel)ar.AsyncDelegate;

        long result = del.EndInvoke(iar);
        Console.WriteLine
            ("                        The result is: {0}.", result);
    }
    static void Main()
    {
        MyDel del = new MyDel(Sum);

        Console.WriteLine("Before BeginInvoke");
        IAsyncResult iar =
            del.BeginInvoke(3, 5, new AsyncCallback(CallWhenDone), null);

        Console.WriteLine("Doing more work in Main.");
        Thread.Sleep(500);
        Console.WriteLine("Done with Main. Exiting.");
    }
}
```

This code produces the following output:

```
Before BeginInvoke
Doing more work in Main.
                    Inside Sum
                    Inside CallWhenDone.
                    The result is: 8.
Done with Main. Exiting.
```

Timers

Timers provide another way to run an asynchronous method on a regular, recurring basis. Although there are several Timer classes available in the .NET BCL, we'll describe the one in the System.Threading namespace.

The important things to know about this timer class are the following:

- The timer uses a callback method that is called each time the timer expires. The callback method must be in the form of the TimerCallback delegate, which has the following form. It takes a single parameter of type object and has a void return type.

```
void TimerCallback( object state )
```

- When the timer expires, the system sets up the callback method on a thread from the thread pool, supplies the state object as its parameter, and starts it running.

- You can set a number of the timer's characteristics, including the following:

  - The dueTime is the amount of time before the first call of the callback method. If dueTime is set to the special value Timeout.Infinite, the timer will not start. If it's set to 0, the callback is called immediately.

  - The period is the amount of time between each successive call of the callback method. If its value is set to Timeout.Infinite, the callback won't be called after the first time.

  - The state is either null or a reference to an object to be passed to the callback method each time it's executed.

The constructor for the Timer class takes as parameters the name of the callback method, the dueTime, the period, and the state. There are several constructors for Timer; the one that's probably the most commonly used has the following form:

```
Timer( TimerCallback callback, object state, uint dueTime, uint period )
```

The following code statement shows an example of the creation of a Timer object:

```
                      Name of            Call first time after
                   the callback.         2000 milliseconds.
                         ↓                       ↓
Timer myTimer = new Timer ( MyCallback, someObject, 2000, 1000 );
                                 ↑                       ↑
                            Object to pass          Call every
                            to the callback.    1000 milliseconds.
```

Once a Timer object is created, you can change its dueTime or period using the Change method.

The following code shows an example of using a timer. The Main method creates the timer so that it will call the callback for the first time after two seconds and once every second after that. The callback method simply prints out a message, including the number of times it's been called.

```
using System;
using System.Threading;

namespace Timers
{
    class Program
    {
        int TimesCalled = 0;

        void Display (object state)
        {
            Console.WriteLine($"{ (string)state } { ++TimesCalled }");
        }

        static void Main( )
        {
            Program p = new Program();

            Timer myTimer = new Timer
                (p.Display, "Processing timer event", 2000, 1000);
            Console.WriteLine("Timer started.");

            Console.ReadLine();
        }
    }

}
```

First callback at 2 seconds
↓
↑
Repeat every second.

This code produces the following output before being terminated after about five seconds:

```
Timer started.
Processing timer event 1
Processing timer event 2
Processing timer event 3
Processing timer event 4
```

There are several other timer classes supplied by the .NET BCL, each having its own uses. The other timer classes are the following:

- `System.Windows.Forms.Timer`: This class is used in Windows Forms applications to periodically place `WM_TIMER` messages into the program's message queue. When the program gets the message from the queue, it processes the handler *synchronously* on the main user interface thread. This is extremely important in Windows Forms applications.

- `System.Timers.Timer`: This class is more extensive and contains a number of members for manipulating the timer through properties and methods. It also has a member event called `Elapsed`, which is raised when each period expires. This timer can run on either a user interface thread or a worker thread.

Namespaces and Assemblies

© Daniel Solis and Cal Schrotenboer 2018

D. Solis and C. Schrotenboer, *Illustrated C# 7*, https://doi.org/10.1007/978-1-4842-3288-0_22

Referencing Other Assemblies

In Chapter 1, you took a high-level look at the compilation process. You saw that the compiler takes the source code file and produces an output file called an *assembly*. This chapter takes a closer look at assemblies and how they are produced and deployed. It also covers how namespaces help organize types.

All the programs you've seen so far have, for the most part, declared and used their own classes. In many projects, however, you will want to use classes or types from other assemblies. These other assemblies might come from the BCL or a third-party vendor, or they might have been created by you. These are called *class libraries*, and the names of their assembly files generally end with the .dll extension rather than the .exe extension.

Suppose, for example, that you want to create a class library that contains classes and types that can be used by other assemblies. The source code for a simple library is shown in the following example and is contained in a file called SuperLib.cs. The library contains a single public class called SquareWidget. Figure 22-1 illustrates the production of the DLL.

```
public class SquareWidget
{
   public double SideLength = 0;
   public double Area
   {
      get { return SideLength * SideLength; }
   }
}
```

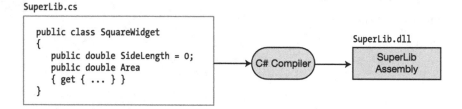

Figure 22-1. *The SuperLib source code and the resulting assembly*

To create a class library using Visual Studio, select the Class Library template from the installed Windows templates. Specifically, when in Visual Studio, do the following:

1. Select File ➤ New ➤ Project, and the New Project window will open.

2. In the left pane, on the Installed ➤ Templates panel, find the Visual C# node and select it.

3. In the middle pane, select the class library template for the platform you're targeting. There are now at least five platforms or types of class libraries. For our example, we'll select Class Library (.NET Framework).

Suppose also that you are writing a program called `MyWidgets` and you want to use the `SquareWidget` class. The code for the program is in a file called `MyWidgets.cs` and is shown next. The code simply creates an object of type `SquareWidget` and uses the object's members.

```
using System;

class WidgetsProgram
{
   static void Main( )
   {
      SquareWidget sq = new SquareWidget();   // From class library
           ↑
         Not declared in this assembly
      sq.SideLength = 5.0;                     // Set the side length.
      Console.WriteLine(sq.Area);             // Print out the area.
   }      ↑
}   Not declared in this assembly
```

Notice that the code doesn't declare class `SquareWidget`. Instead, you use the class defined in `SuperLib`. When you compile the `MyWidgets` program, however, the compiler must be aware that your code uses assembly `SuperLib` so it can get the information about class `SquareWidget`. To do this, you need to give the compiler a *reference* to the assembly by giving its name and location.

In Visual Studio, you can add references to a project in the following way:

- Select Solution Explorer and find the References folder underneath the project name. The References folder contains a list of the assemblies used by the project.

- Right-click the References folder and select Add Reference. There are five tabs from which to choose, allowing you to find the class library in different ways.

- For our program, select the Browse tab, browse to the DLL file containing the SquareWidget class definition, and select it.

- Click the OK button, and the reference will be added to the project.

After you've added the reference, you can compile MyWidgets. Figure 22-2 illustrates the full compilation process.

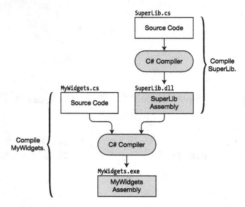

Figure 22-2. *Referencing another assembly*

The mscorlib Library

There's a class library that we've been using in almost every example in the book so far. It is the one that contains the Console class. The Console class is defined in an assembly called mscorlib in a file called mscorlib.dll. You won't find this assembly listed in the References folder, however. Assembly mscorlib contains the definitions of the C# types and the basic types for most .NET languages. It must always be referenced when compiling a C# program, so Visual Studio doesn't bother showing it in the References folder.

When you take into account mscorlib, the compilation process for MyWidgets looks more like the representation shown in Figure 22-3. After this, we'll assume the use of the mscorlib assembly without representing it again.

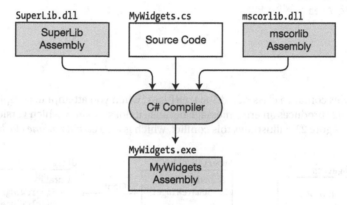

Figure 22-3. *Referencing class libraries*

Now suppose that your program has been working fine with the SquareWidget class, but you want to expand its capabilities to use a class called CircleWidget, which is defined in a different assembly, called UltraLib. The MyWidgets source code now looks like the following. It creates a SquareWidget object as defined in SuperLib and a CircleWidget object as defined in UltraLib.

```
class WidgetsProgram
{
    static void Main( )
    {
        SquareWidget sq = new SquareWidget();        // From SuperLib
        ...

        CircleWidget circle = new CircleWidget();    // From UltraLib
        ...
    }
}
```

The source code for class library UltraLib is shown in the following example. Notice that besides class CircleWidget, like library SuperLib, it also declares a class called SquareWidget. You can compile UltraLib to a DLL and add it to the list of references in project MyWidgets.

```
public class SquareWidget
{
   ...
}

public class CircleWidget
{
   public double Radius = 0;
   public double Area
   {
      get { ... }
   }
}
```

Since both libraries contain a class called SquareWidget, when you attempt to compile program MyWidgets, the compiler produces an error message because it doesn't know which version of class SquareWidget to use. Figure 22-4 illustrates this conflict, which is also called a *name clash*.

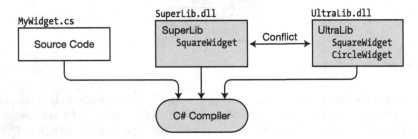

Figure 22-4. *Since assemblies SuperLib and UltraLib both contain declarations for a class called SquareWidget, the compiler doesn't know which one to instantiate*

Namespaces

In the MyWidgets example, since you have the source code, you can solve the name clash by just changing the name of the SquareWidget class in either the SuperLib source code or the UltraLib source code. But what if these libraries had been developed by separate companies, and you didn't have the source code? Suppose that SuperLib was produced by a company called MyCorp and UltraLib was produced by the ABCCorp company. In that case, you wouldn't be able to use them together if you used any classes or types where there was a clash.

As you can imagine, with your development machine containing assemblies produced by dozens, if not hundreds, of different companies, there is likely to be a certain amount of duplication in the names of classes. It would be a shame if you couldn't use two assemblies in the same program just because they happened to have type names in common.

Suppose, however, that MyCorp had a policy of prefacing all its classes with a string that consisted of the company name followed by the product name followed by the descriptive class name. Suppose further that ABCCorp had the same policy. In that case, the three class names in our example would be named MyCorpSuperLibSquareWidget, ABCCorpUltraLibSquareWidget, and ABCCorpUltraLibCircleWidget, as shown in Figure 22-5. These are perfectly valid class names, and there's little chance of the classes in one company's library conflicting with those of another company.

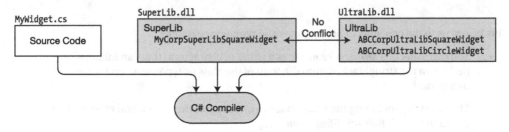

Figure 22-5. *With disambiguating strings prefaced to the class names, there is no conflict between the libraries*

Our example program, however, would need to use these long names and would look like the following:

```
class WidgetsProgram
{
    static void Main( )
    {
        MyCorpSuperLibSquareWidget sq
                = new MyCorpSuperLibSquareWidget();        // From SuperLib
        ...

        ABCCorpUltraLibCircleWidget circle
                = new ABCCorpUltraLibCircleWidget();       // From UltraLib
        ...
    }
}
```

Although this solves the conflict problem, these new, disambiguated names are harder to read and clumsy to work with, even with IntelliSense.

Suppose, however, that in addition to the characters normally allowed in an identifier, you could also use the period character within the string—although still not at the beginning or end of the class name. In this case, we could make the names more understandable, such as MyCorp.SuperLib.SquareWidget, ABCCorp.UltraLib.SquareWidget, and ABCCorp.UltraLib.CircleWidget. Now the code would look like the following:

```
class WidgetsProgram
{
    static void Main( )
    {
        MyCorp.SuperLib.SquareWidget sq
                = new MyCorp.SuperLib.SquareWidget();      // From SuperLib
        ...

        ABCCorp.UltraLib.CircleWidget circle
                = new ABCCorp.UltraLib.CircleWidget();     // From UltraLib
        ...
    }
}
```

This brings us to the concepts of namespaces and namespace names.

- You can think of a *namespace name* as a string of characters (that can include periods in the string) tacked onto the front of the class or type name and separated by a period.

- The full string including the namespace name, separating period, and class name is called the class's *fully qualified name*.

- A *namespace* is the *set of classes and types* that share that namespace name.

Figure 22-6 illustrates these definitions.

Figure 22-6. *A namespace is the set of type definitions that share the same namespace name*

You can use namespaces to group a set of types together and give them a name. Generally, you want namespace names to be descriptive of the types contained by the namespace and to be distinct from other namespace names.

You create a namespace by declaring the namespace in the source file that contains your type declarations. The following shows the syntax for declaring a namespace. You then declare all your classes and other types between the curly braces of the namespace declaration. These are then the *members* of the namespace.

```
  Keyword      Namespace name
    ↓              ↓
namespace NamespaceName
{
    TypeDeclarations
}
```

The following code shows how the programmers at MyCorp could create the `MyCorp.SuperLib` namespace and declare the `SquareWidget` class inside it:

```
  Company name   Period
          ↓  ↓
namespace MyCorp.SuperLib
{
    public class SquareWidget
    {
        public double SideLength = 0;
        public double Area
        {
            get { return SideLength * SideLength; }
        }
    }
}
```

Now, when the MyCorp company ships you the updated assembly, you can use it by modifying your MyWidgets program, as shown here:

```
class WidgetsProgram
{
    static void Main( )
    {
        MyCorp.SuperLib.SquareWidget sq = new MyCorp.SuperLib.SquareWidget();

        CircleWidget circle = new CircleWidget();
        ...
```

Now that you have explicitly specified the SuperLib version of SquareWidget in your code, the compiler will no longer have a problem distinguishing the classes. The fully qualified name is a bit long to type, but at least you can now use both libraries. A little later in the chapter, we'll cover the using alias directive for solving the inconvenience of having to repeatedly type in the fully qualified name.

If the UltraLib assembly were also updated with a namespace by the company that produced it (ABCCorp), then the compile process would be as shown in Figure 22-7.

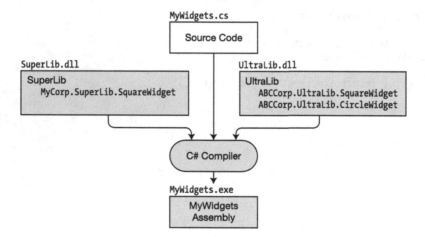

Figure 22-7. *Class libraries with namespaces*

Namespace Names

As you saw, the name of a namespace can contain the name of the company that created the assembly. Besides identifying the company, the name is also used to help programmers get a quick idea of the kinds of types defined in the namespace.

Some important points about the names of namespaces are the following:

- A namespace name can be any valid identifier, as described in Chapter 3. As with any identifier, the string is case-sensitive.

- Additionally, a namespace name can include any number of period characters. You can use this to organize types into hierarchies.

For example, Table 22-1 gives the names of some of the namespaces in the .NET BCL.

Table 22-1. *Sample Namespaces from the BCL*

System	System.IO
System.Data	Microsoft.CSharp
System.Drawing	Microsoft.VisualBasic

Namespace naming guidelines suggest the following:

- Start namespace names with the company name.

- Follow the company name with the technology name.

- Do not name a namespace with the same name as a class or type.

For example, the software development department of the Acme Widget Company develops software in the following three namespaces, one of which shown in the following code:

- AcmeWidgets.SuperWidget

- AcmeWidgets.Media

- AcmeWidgets.Games

```
namespace AcmeWidgets.SuperWidget
{
   class SPDBase ...
   ...
}
```

More About Namespaces

There are several other important things you should know about namespaces.

- Every type name in a namespace must be different from all the others.

- The types in a namespace are called *members* of the namespace.

- A source file can contain any number of namespace declarations, either sequentially or nested.

Figure 22-8 shows a source file on the left that declares two namespaces sequentially, with several types in each one. Notice that even though the namespaces contain several class names in common, they are differentiated by their namespace names, as shown in the assembly at the right of the figure.

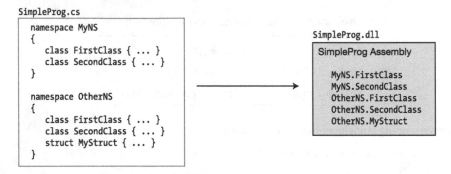

Figure 22-8. *Multiple namespaces in a source file*

The .NET Framework BCL offers thousands of defined classes and types to choose from in building your programs. To help organize this vast array of available functionality, types with related functionality are declared in the same namespace. The BCL uses more than 100 namespaces to organize its types.

Namespaces Spread Across Files

A namespace is not closed. This means you can add more type declarations to it by declaring it again, either later in the source file or in another source file.

For example, Figure 22-9 shows the declaration of three classes, all in the same namespace but declared in separate source files. The source files can be compiled into a single assembly, as shown in Figure 22-9, or into separate assemblies, as shown in Figure 22-10.

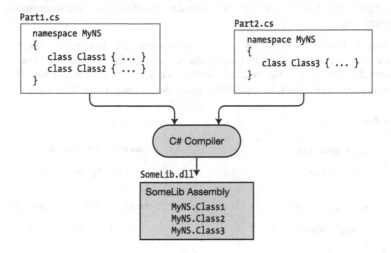

Figure 22-9. *A namespace can be spread across source files and compiled to a single assembly*

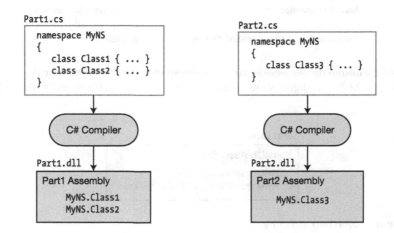

Figure 22-10. *A namespace can be spread across source files and compiled to separate assemblies*

Nesting Namespaces

Namespaces can be nested, producing a *nested namespace*. Nesting namespaces allows you to create a conceptual hierarchy of types.

There are two ways you can declare a nested namespace.

- *Textual nesting*: You can create a nested namespace by placing its declaration inside the declaration body of the enclosing namespace. This is illustrated on the left in Figure 22-11. In this example, namespace OtherNs is nested in namespace MyNamespace.

- *Separate declaration*: You can also create a separate declaration for the nested namespace, but you must use its fully qualified name in the declaration. This is illustrated on the right in Figure 22-11. Notice that in the declaration of nested namespace OtherNs, the fully qualified name MyNamespace.OtherNS is used.

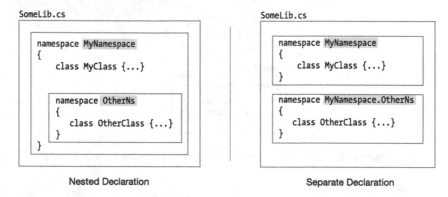

Nested Declaration   Separate Declaration

Figure 22-11. *The two forms of declaring a nested namespace are equivalent*

Both forms of the nested namespace declarations shown in Figure 22-11 produce the same assembly, as illustrated in Figure 22-12. The figure shows the two classes declared in file SomeLib.cs, with their fully qualified names.

```
SomeLib.dll
┌──────────────────────────────────────────┐
│ SomeLib Assembly                          │
│                                           │
│   MyNamespace.MyClass                     │
│   MyNamespace.OtherNS.OtherClass          │
└──────────────────────────────────────────┘
```

Figure 22-12. *Nested namespace structure*

Although the nested namespace is inside the enclosing namespace, its members are *not* members of the enclosing namespace. A common misconception is that since the nested namespace is inside the enclosing namespace, the members of the nested namespace must be a subset of the enclosing namespace. This is not true; the namespaces are separate.

The using Directives

Fully qualified names can be quite long, and using them throughout your code can become quite cumbersome. There are three compiler directives, however, that allow you to avoid having to use fully qualified names—the using *namespace directive* and the using *alias directive*.

Two important points about the using directives are the following:

- They must be placed at the top of the source file, *before any type declarations*.
- They apply for all the namespaces in the current source file.

The using Namespace Directive

You saw in the MyWidgets example several sections back that you can specify a class by using the fully qualified name. You can avoid having to use the long name by placing using namespace directives at the top of the source file.

The using namespace directive instructs the compiler that you will be using types from certain specific namespaces. You can then go ahead and use the simple class names without having to fully qualify them.

When the compiler encounters a name that is not in the current namespace, it checks the list of namespaces given in the using namespace directives and appends the unknown name to the first namespace in the list. If the resulting fully qualified name matches a class in this assembly or a referenced assembly, the compiler uses that class. If it does not match, it tries the next namespace in the list.

The using namespace directive consists of the keyword using, followed by a namespace identifier.

```
Keyword
   ↓
using System;
         ↑
     Name of namespace
```

One method we have been using throughout the text is the WriteLine method, which is a member of class Console, in the System namespace. Rather than use its fully qualified name throughout the code, we simplified our work just a bit, by the use of the using namespace directive at the top of the code.

For example, the following code uses the using namespace directive in the first line to state that the code uses classes or other types from the System namespace.

```
using System;                               // using namespace directive
    ...
System.Console.WriteLine("This is text 1"); // Use fully qualified name.
Console.WriteLine("This is text 2");        // Use directive.
```

The using Alias Directive

The using alias directive allows you to assign an alias for either of the following:

- A namespace

- A type in a namespace

For example, the following code shows the use of two using alias directives. The first directive instructs the compiler that identifier Syst is an alias for namespace System. The second directive says that identifier SC is an alias for class System.Console.

```
 Keyword Alias   Namespace
    ↓      ↓         ↓
  using Syst = System;
  using SC   = System.Console;
    ↑    ↑           ↑
 Keyword Alias      Class
```

The following code uses these aliases. All three lines of code in Main call the System.Console. WriteLine method.

- The first statement in Main uses the alias for a *namespace*—System.

- The second statement uses the fully qualified name of the method.

- The third statement uses the alias for a *class*—Console.

```
using Syst = System;                  // using alias directive
using SC   = System.Console;          // using alias directive

namespace MyNamespace
{
   class SomeClass
   {
      static void Main()
      { Alias for namespace
           ↓
         Syst.Console.WriteLine  ("Using the namespace alias.");
         System.Console.WriteLine("Using fully qualified name.");
         SC.WriteLine            ("Using the type alias");
          ↑
      } Alias for class
   }
}
```

The using static Directive

As previously described in Chapters 6 and 7, you can use the `using static` directive to reference specific classes, structs, or enums within a given namespace. This permits the static members of that class, struct, or enum to be accessed without any prefix.

A `using static` directive begins with a standard `using` namespace directive such as `using System`, inserts the keyword static after the keyword `using`, and appends the name of the applicable class, struct, or enum. The result would be something like this:

```
Keyword   Keyword
   ↓         ↓
using static System.Math;        //System.Math is a fully qualified type name
                ↑      ↑
           Namespace  Class
```

With this `using static` directive in place, all static members of the `System.Math` class can be referenced in code without any prefix, as for example the following:

```
var squareRoot = Sqrt(16);
```

With only a standard `using` namespace directive, this would read instead as follows:

```
using System;
var squareRoot = Math.Sqrt(16);
```

It is not required that the class specified in a `using static` directive be itself static. Any of such types may contain instance members, although such instance members are not imported by a `using static` directive. Inherited members are also not imported, although nested types declared within the specified type are included.

The principal advantage of the `using static` directive, in addition to shorter code, is that it excludes members of other classes, structs, or enums belonging to the same namespace. This reduces the possibility of name collisions.

■ **Note** The `using static` directive only includes static members of the specified class, struct, or enum. Just because a given type is static does not mean that all of its members will also be static.

The Structure of an Assembly

As you saw in Chapter 1, an assembly does not contain native machine code, but Common Intermediate Language (CIL) code. It also contains everything needed by the just-in-time (JIT) compiler to convert the CIL into native code at run time, including references to other assemblies it references. The file extension for an assembly is generally .exe or .dll.

Most assemblies are composed of a single file. Figure 22-13 illustrates the four main sections of an assembly.

- The assembly *manifest* contains the following:

  - The identity of the assembly

  - A list of the files that make up the assembly

  - A map of where things are in the assembly

  - Information about other assemblies that are referenced

- The type metadata section contains the information about all the types defined in the assembly. This information contains everything there is to know about each type.

- The CIL section contains all the intermediate code for the assembly.

- The *resources* section is optional but can contain graphics or language resources.

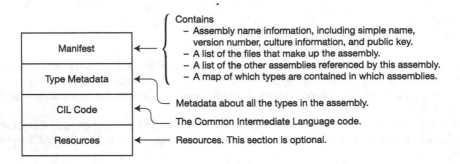

Figure 22-13. *The structure of a single-file assembly*

Assembly code files are called *modules*. Although most assemblies comprise a single module, some have more. For an assembly with multiple modules, one file is the *primary module*, and the others are *secondary modules*.

- The primary module contains the manifest of the assembly and references to the secondary modules.

- The file names of secondary modules end with the extension .netmodule.

- Multiple-file assemblies are considered a single unit. They are deployed together and versioned together.

Figure 22-14 illustrates a multifile assembly with secondary modules.

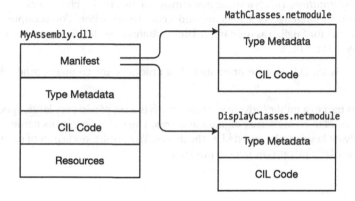

Figure 22-14. *A multifile assembly*

The Identity of an Assembly

In the .NET Framework, the file names of assemblies are not as important as in other operating systems and environments. What is much more important is the *identity* of an assembly.

The identity of an assembly has four components that together should uniquely identify it. These four components are the following:

- *Simple name*: This is just the file name without the file extension. Every assembly has a simple name. It is also called the *assembly name* or the *friendly name*.

- *Version number*: This consists of a string of four period-separated integers, in the form `MajorVersion.MinorVersion.Build.Revision`—for example, `2.0.35.9`.

- *Culture information*: This is a string that consists of two to five characters representing a language, or a language and a country or region. For example, the culture name for English as used in the United States is `en-US`. For German as used in Germany, it is `de-DE`.

- *Public key hash*: This 16-byte string should be unique to the company producing the assembly.

The public key is part of a public/private key pair, which is a set of two very large, specially chosen numbers that can be used to create secure digital signatures. The public key, as its name implies, can be made public. The private key must be guarded by the owner. The public key is part of the assembly's identity. We will look at the use of the private key later in this chapter.

The components of an assembly's name are embedded in the assembly's manifest. Figure 22-15 illustrates this section of the manifest.

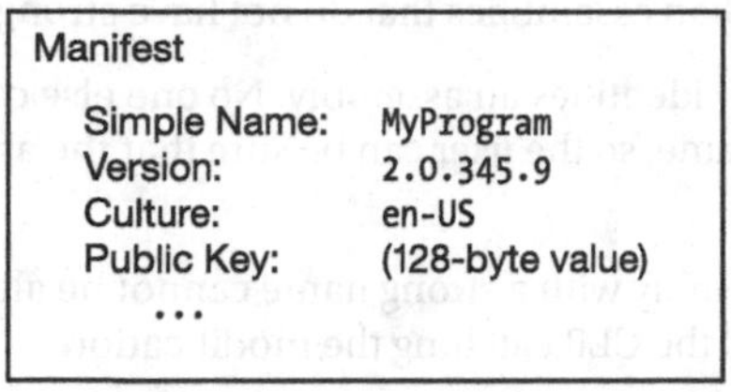

Manifest
Simple Name: MyProgram
Version: 2.0.345.9
Culture: en-US
Public Key: (128-byte value)
...

Figure 22-15. *The components of an assembly identity in the manifest*

Figure 22-16 shows some of the terms used in the .NET documentation and literature regarding the identity of an assembly.

Identity: All four of the components listed at the right together constitute the identity of an assembly.
Fully qualified name: A textual listing of the simple name, version, culture, and the public key, represented by a 16-byte public key token.
Display name: Same as fully qualified name.
Simple Name
Version
Culture
Public Key

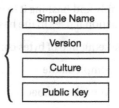

Figure 22-16. *Terms for an assembly's identity*

Strongly Named Assemblies

A *strongly named* assembly is one that has a unique digital signature attached to it. Strongly named assemblies are much more secure than assemblies that do not have strong names, for the following reasons:

- A strong name uniquely identifies an assembly. No one else can create an assembly with the same strong name, so the user can be sure that the assembly came from the claimed source.

- The contents of an assembly with a strong name cannot be altered without the security components of the CLR catching the modification.

A *weakly named* assembly is one that is not strongly named. Since a weakly named assembly does not have a digital signature, it is inherently insecure. Because a chain is only as strong as its weakest link, by default, strongly named assemblies can only access other strongly named assemblies. You will only see the mismatch at run time. (There's also a way to allow "partially trusted callers," but we won't be covering that topic.)

The programmer does not produce the strong name. The compiler produces it by taking information about the assembly and hashing it to create a unique digital signature that it attaches to the assembly. The pieces of information it uses in the hash process are the following:

- The sequence of bytes composing the assembly

- The simple name

- The version number

- The culture information

- The public/private key pair

■ **Note**　There is some diversity in the nomenclature surrounding strong names. What we're calling *strongly named* is often referred to as "strong-named." What we're calling *weakly named* is sometimes referred to as "not strong-named" or "assembly with a simple name."

Creating a Strongly Named Assembly

To strongly name an assembly using Visual Studio, you must have a copy of the public/private key pair file. If you don't have a key file, you can have Visual Studio generate one for you. You can then do the following:

1. Open the properties of the project.

2. Select the Signing tab.

3. Select the Sign the Assembly check box, and enter the location of the key file or create a new one.

When you compile the code, the compiler produces a strongly named assembly. Figure 22-17 illustrates the inputs and output of the compiler.

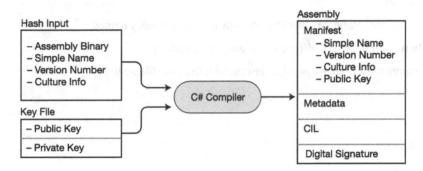

Figure 22-17. *Creating a strongly named assembly*

It is extremely important that you guard your private key. If someone has your public/private key pair, they can create and distribute software masquerading as you.

■ **Note**   To create a strongly named assembly, you can also use a tool called the Strong Name tool (sn.exe), which is installed automatically when you install Visual Studio. This is a command-line tool that allows you to sign assemblies and also provides a number of other options for managing your keys and signatures. This is useful if you need more options than are available with the Visual Studio IDE. You can find the details for using the Strong Name tool online.

Private Deployment of an Assembly

Deploying a program on a target machine can be as simple as creating a directory on the machine and copying the application to it. If the application doesn't need other assemblies (such as DLLs) or if the required DLLs are in the same directory, the program should work just fine where it is. Programs deployed this way are called *private assemblies*, and this method of deployment is called *xcopy* deployment.

Private assemblies can be placed in almost any directory and are self-sufficient as long as all the files on which they depend are in the same directory. In fact, you could have several directories in various parts of the file system, each with the identical set of assemblies, and they would all work fine in their various locations.

Some important things to know about private assembly deployment are the following:

- The directory in which the private assemblies are placed is called the *application directory*.

- A private assembly can be either strongly named or weakly named.

- There is no need to register components in the registry.

- To uninstall a private assembly, just delete it from the file system.

Shared Assemblies and the GAC

Private assemblies are very useful, but sometimes you'll want to put a DLL in a central place so that a single copy can be shared by other assemblies on the system. .NET has such a repository, called the *global assembly cache* (GAC). An assembly placed into the GAC is called a *shared assembly*.

Some important facts about the GAC are the following:

- Only strongly named assemblies can be added to the GAC.

- Although earlier versions of the GAC accepted only files with the .dll extension, you can now add assemblies with the .exe extension as well.

- The GAC is located in a subdirectory of the Windows system directory. Before .NET 4.0 it was located in \Windows\Assembly. Starting with .NET 4.0 it is located in \Windows\Microsoft.NET\assembly.

Installing Assemblies into the GAC

When you attempt to install an assembly into the GAC, the security components of the CLR must first verify that the digital signature on the assembly is valid. If there is no digital signature or if it is invalid, the system will not install it into the GAC.

This is a one-time check, however. After an assembly is in the GAC, no further checks are required when it is referenced by a running program.

The gacutil.exe command-line utility allows you to add and delete assemblies from the GAC and list the assemblies it contains. The three most useful flags are the following:

- /i: Inserts an assembly into the GAC

- /u: Uninstalls an assembly from the GAC

- /l: Lists the assemblies in the GAC

Side-by-Side Execution in the GAC

After an assembly is deployed to the GAC, it can be used by other assemblies in the system. Remember, however, that an assembly's identity consists of all four parts of the fully qualified name. So, if the version number of a library changes or if it has a different public key, these differences specify different assemblies.

The result is that there can be many different assemblies in the GAC that have the same file name. Although they have the same file name, *they are different assemblies* and coexist perfectly fine together in the GAC. This makes it easy for different applications to use different versions of the same DLL at the same time since they are different assemblies with different identities. This is called *side-by-side execution.*

Figure 22-18 illustrates four different DLLs in the GAC that all have the same file name—MyLibrary. dll. Looking at the figure, you can see that the first three come from the same company, because they have the same public key, and the fourth comes from a different source, since it has a different public key. These versions differ as follows:

- An English version 1.0.0.0, from company A

- An English version 2.0.0.0, from company A

- A German version 1.0.0.0, from company A

- An English version 1.0.0.0, from company B

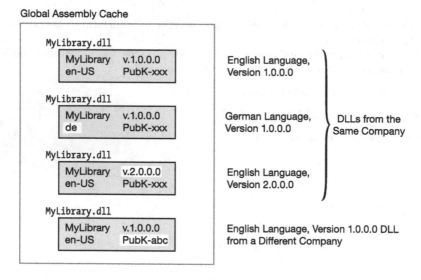

Figure 22-18. *Four different side-by-side DLLs in the GAC*

Configuration Files

Configuration files contain information about the application, for use by the CLR at run time. They can instruct the CLR to do such things as use a different version of a DLL or look in additional directories when searching for a DLL referenced by the program.

Configuration files consist of XML code and don't contain C# code. The details of writing the XML code are beyond the scope of this text, but you should understand the purpose of configuration files and how they are used. One way they are used is to update an application assembly to use the new version of a DLL.

Suppose, for example, that you have an application that references a DLL in the GAC. The identity of the reference in the application's manifest must exactly match the identity of the assembly in the GAC. If a new version of the DLL is released, it can be added to the GAC, where it can happily coexist with the old version.

The application, however, still has embedded in its manifest the identity of the old version of the DLL. Unless you recompile the application and make it reference the new version of the DLL, it will continue to use the old version. That's fine, if that's what you want.

If, however, you do not want to recompile the application but want it to use the new DLL, then you can update the information in the configuration file telling the CLR to use the new version rather than the old version. The configuration file is in the application directory.

Figure 22-19 illustrates objects in the runtime process. The `MyProgram.exe` application on the left calls for version 1.0.0.0 of `MyLibrary.dll`, as indicated by the dashed arrow. But the application has a configuration file, which instructs the CLR to load version 2.0.0.0 instead. Notice that the name of the configuration file consists of the full name of the executable file including the extension, plus the additional extension `.config`.

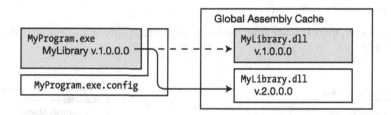

Figure 22-19. *Using a configuration file to bind to a new version*

An example of a simple config file is the following:

```xml
<?xml version="1.0" encoding="utf-8" ?>
<configuration>
    <startup>
        <supportedRuntime version="v4.0" sku=".NETFramework,Version=v4.5.2" />
    </startup>
</configuration>
```

Delayed Signing

It is important that companies carefully guard the private key of their official public/private key pair. Otherwise, if untrustworthy people were to obtain it, they could publish code masquerading as the company's code. To avoid this, companies clearly cannot allow free access to the file containing their public/ private key pair. In large companies, the final strong naming of an assembly is often performed at the very end of the development process, by a special group with access to the key pair.

This can cause problems, though, in the development and testing processes for several reasons. First, since the public key is one of the four components of an assembly's identity, the identity can't be set until the public key is supplied. Also, a weakly named assembly cannot be deployed to the GAC. Both the developers and testers need to be able to compile and test the code in the way it will be deployed on release, including its identity and location in the GAC.

To allow for this, there is a modified form of assigning a strong name, called *delayed signing*, or *partial signing*, that overcomes these problems but does not release access to the private key.

In delayed signing, the compiler uses only the public key of the public/private key pair. The public key can then be placed in the manifest to complete the assembly's identity. Delayed signing also uses a block of 0s to reserve space for the digital signature.

To create a delay-signed assembly consists of two major steps. You must create a copy of the key file that has only the public key, rather than the public/private key pair. And you must add an additional attribute called DelaySignAttribute to the assembly scope of the source code and set its value to true.

Figure 22-20 shows the input and output for producing a delay-signed assembly. Notice the following in the figure:

- In the input, the DelaySignAttribute is located in the source files, and the key file contains only the public key.

- In the output, there is space reserved for the digital signature at the bottom of the assembly.

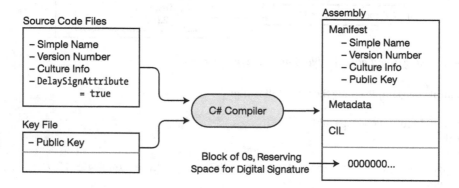

Figure 22-20. *Creating a delay-signed assembly*

If you try to deploy the delay-signed assembly to the GAC, the CLR will not allow it because it's not strongly named. To deploy it on a particular machine, you must first issue a command-line command that disables the GAC's signature verification on that machine, for this assembly only, and allows it to be installed in the GAC. To do this, issue the following command from the Visual Studio command prompt:

```
sn -vr MyAssembly.dll
```

You've now looked at weakly named assemblies, delay-signed assemblies, and strongly named assemblies. Figure 22-21 summarizes the differences in their structures.

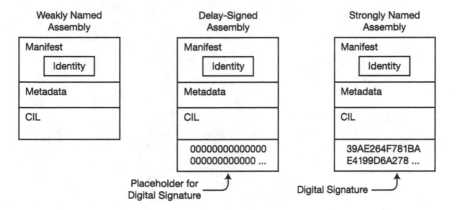

Figure 22-21. *The structures of different assembly signing stages*

CHAPTER 23

■ ■ ■

Exceptions

© Daniel Solis and Cal Schrotenboer 2018

D. Solis and C. Schrotenboer, *Illustrated C# 7*, https://doi.org/10.1007/978-1-4842-3288-0_23

What Are Exceptions?

An *exception* is a runtime error in a program that violates a system or application constraint, or a condition that is not expected to occur during normal operation. Examples are when a program tries to divide a number by zero or tries to write to a read-only file. When these occur, the system catches the error and *raises* an exception.

If the program has not provided code to handle the exception, the system will halt the program. For example, the following code raises an exception when it attempts to divide by zero:

```
static void Main()
{
   int x = 10, y = 0;
   x /= y;                 // Attempt to divide by zero--raises an exception
}
```

When this code is run, the system displays the following error message:

```
Unhandled Exception: System.DivideByZeroException: Attempted to divide by zero.
      at Exceptions_1.Program.Main() in C:\Progs\Exceptions\Program.cs:line 12
```

In the absence of an exception handler, your application will stop (crash) and present your user with a very unfriendly error message. The goal of exception handling is to respond to exceptions with one or more of the following actions:

- Take corrective actions in the limited number of cases where that is possible in order to permit your application to continue running

- Log information about the exception so that it can be addressed by your development team

- Clean up any external resources such as database connections that might otherwise remain open

- Display a user-friendly message to your users

Since continuing to run your application in an unstable or unknown condition is generally a bad idea, once these actions have been performed and no corrective action is possible, your application should terminate.

The try Statement

The try statement allows you to designate blocks of code to be guarded for exceptions and to supply code to handle them if they occur. The try statement consists of three sections, as shown in Figure 23-1.

- The try *block* contains the code that is being guarded for exceptions.

- The catch clauses section contains one or more catch clauses. These are blocks of code to handle the exceptions. They are also known as *exception handlers*.

- The finally *block* contains code to be executed under all circumstances, whether or not an exception is raised.

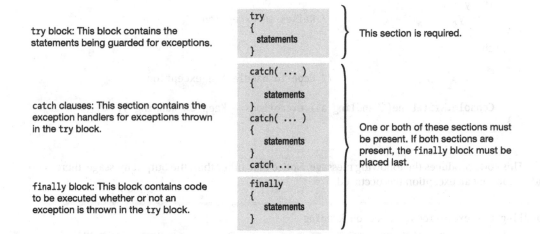

try block: This block contains the statements being guarded for exceptions.

catch clauses: This section contains the exception handlers for exceptions thrown in the try block.

finally block: This block contains code to be executed whether or not an exception is thrown in the try block.

```
try
{
    statements
}
```
This section is required.

```
catch( ... )
{
    statements
}
catch( ... )
{
    statements
}
catch ...
```
One or both of these sections must be present. If both sections are present, the finally block must be placed last.

```
finally
{
    statements
}
```

Figure 23-1. *Structure of the try statement*

Handling the Exception

The previous example showed that attempting to divide by zero causes an exception. You can modify the program to handle that exception by placing the code inside a try block and supplying a simple catch clause. When the exception is raised, it is caught and handled in the catch block.

```
static void Main()
{
   int x = 10;

   try
   {
      int y = 0;
      x /= y;                    // Raises an exception
   }
   catch
   {
      ...                        // Code to handle the exception

      Console.WriteLine("Handling all exceptions - Keep on Running");
   }
}
```

This code produces the following message. Notice that, other than the output message, there is no indication that an exception has occurred.

```
Handling all exceptions - Keep on Running
```

The Exception Classes

There are many different types of exceptions that can occur in a program. The BCL defines a number of exception classes, each representing a specific type. When one occurs, the CLR creates an exception object for the type and looks for an appropriate catch clause to handle it.

All exception classes are ultimately derived from the System.Exception class, which in turn is derived from System.Object. Figure 23-2 shows a portion of the exception inheritance hierarchy.

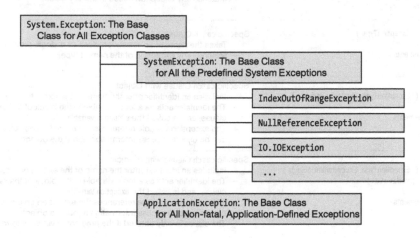

Figure 23-2. *Structure of the exception hierarchy*

An exception object contains read-only properties with information about the exception that caused it. This information can be helpful to you for debugging your application to prevent similar exceptions from occurring in the future. Table 23-1 shows some of these properties.

Table 23-1. *Selected Properties of an Exception Object*

Property	Type	Description
Message	string	This property contains an error message explaining the cause of the exception.
StackTrace	string	This property contains information describing where the exception occurred.
InnerException	Exception	If the current exception was raised by another exception, this property contains a reference to the previous exception.
Source	string	If not set by an application-defined exception, this property contains the name of the assembly where the exception originated.

The catch Clause

The catch clause handles exceptions. There are four forms, allowing different levels of processing. Figure 23-3 shows the forms.

```
catch                                  General catch Clause
{                                        – Does not have a parameter list after the catch keyword.
   Statements                            – Matches any exception raised in the try block.
}
```

```
catch( ExceptionType )                 Specific catch Clause
{                                        – Takes the name of an exception class as a single parameter.
   Statements                            – Matches any exception of the named type.
}
```

```
catch( ExceptionType ExceptionVariable )  Specific catch Clause with Object
{                                          – Includes an identifier after the name of the exception class.
   Statements                              – The identifier acts as a local variable in the block of the catch
}                                            clause, and is called the exception variable.
                                           – The exception variable references the exception object, and
                                             can be used to access information about the object.
```

```
catch( ExceptionType ExceptionVariable )  Specific catch Clause with Predicate
when( predicate )                          – Includes an identifier after the name of the exception class.
{                                          – The identifier acts as a local variable in the block of the catch
   Statements                                clause, and is called the exception variable.
}                                          – The exception variable references the exception object, and
                                             can be used to access information about the object.
                                           – The clause is only entered if the predicate evaluates to true.
```

Figure 23-3. *The four forms of the catch clause*

We'll start by looking at the first three forms and give examples of the second and third forms. With that as background, we'll then look at the fourth form.

The *general* catch clause can accept any exception but can't determine the type of exception that caused it. This allows only general processing and cleanup for whatever exception might occur.

The *specific* catch clause form takes the name of an exception class as a parameter. It matches exceptions of the specified class or exception classes derived from it.

The *specific* catch *clause with object* form gives you the most information about the exception. It matches exceptions of the specified class, or exception classes derived from it. It gives you a reference to the exception object created by the CLR by assigning it to the *exception variable*. You can access the exception variable's properties within the block of the catch clause to get specific information about the exception raised.

For example, the following code handles exceptions of type IndexOutOfRangeException. When an exception of this type occurs, a reference to the actual exception object is passed into the code with parameter name e. The three WriteLine statements each read a string field from the exception object.

```
         Exception type    Exception variable
              ↓                  ↓
catch ( DivideByZeroException e )
{                                   Accessing the exception variables
                                              ↓
    Console.WriteLine( "Message: {0}", e.Message );
    Console.WriteLine( "Source:  {0}", e.Source );
    Console.WriteLine( "Stack:   {0}", e.StackTrace );
```

Examples Using Specific catch Clauses

Going back to our divide-by-zero example, the following code modifies the previous catch clause to specifically handle exceptions of the DivideByZeroException class. While in the previous example the catch clause would handle any exception raised in the try block, by contrast the current example will handle only those of the DivideByZeroException class.

```
int x = 10;
try
{
   int y = 0;
   x /= y;                        // Raises an exception
}                  Exception type
                         ↓
catch ( DivideByZeroException )
{
   ...
   Console.WriteLine("Handling an exception.");
}
```

You could further modify the catch clause to use an exception variable. This allows you to access the exception object inside the catch block.

```
int x = 10;
try
{
   int y = 0;
   x /= y;                        // Raises an exception
}            Exception type      Exception variable
                    ↓                   ↓
catch ( DivideByZeroException  e )
{                                Accessing the exception variables
                                         ↓
   Console.WriteLine("Message: {0}", e.Message );
   Console.WriteLine("Source:  {0}", e.Source );
   Console.WriteLine("Stack:   {0}", e.StackTrace );
}
```

On our computer, this code produces the following output. On your machine, the file path in the third and fourth lines will be different and will match the location of your project and solution directories.

```
Message: Attempted to divide by zero.
Source:  Exceptions 1
Stack:      at Exceptions_1.Program.Main() in C:\Progs\Exceptions 1\
Exceptions 1\Program.cs:line 14
```

Exception Filters

The fourth form of catch clause was added in C# 6.0 and is like the third form in that an exception object is passed into the handler, but in this case only if the object matches a specific condition, called a *filter*. So instead of a single handler that addresses all possible exceptions of a particular exception type, there can be more than one handler for an exception type. This allows you to write smaller, more focused exception handlers, without having numerous if statements inside a single handler.

In the following example, notice that both catch clauses handle the HttpRequestException. The first one is called if the Message field of the exception contains the string "307". The second one is called if the Message field contains the string "301". If the Message field contains both strings, only the first catch clause is called since regardless of how many clauses might match, *only the first matching clause is ever executed*.

```
try
{
    ... Execute some web request
}
catch ( HttpRequestException e ) when ( e.Message.Contains("307") )
{
    ... Take some action
}
catch ( HttpRequestException e ) when ( e.Message.Contains("301") )
{
    ... Take some other action
}
```

Important characteristics of the when clause of a filter are the following:

- It must contain a predicate expression, which is an expression that returns a value of either true or false.

- It cannot be asynchronous.

- It shouldn't use any long-running operations.

- Any exception that occurs within the predicate expression is ignored. This makes it more difficult to debug your predicate expression, but it preserves the information needed to debug your original application error.

The catch Clauses Section

The purpose of a catch clause is to allow you to handle an exception in an elegant way. If your catch clause is of the form that takes a parameter, then the system has set the exception variable to a reference to the exception object, which you can inspect to determine the cause of the exception. If the exception was the result of a previous exception, you can get a reference to that previous exception's object from the variable's InnerException property.

The catch clauses section can contain multiple catch clauses. Figure 23-4 shows a summary of the catch clauses section.

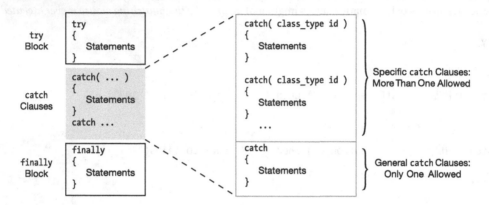

Figure 23-4. *Structure of the catch clauses section of a try statement*

When an exception is raised, the system searches the list of catch clauses in order, and the first catch clause that matches the type of the exception object is executed. Because of this, there are two important rules in ordering the catch clauses. They are the following:

- The specific catch clauses must be ordered with the most specific exception types first, progressing to the most general. For example, if you declare an exception class *derived from* NullReferenceException, the catch clause for your derived exception type should be listed before the catch clause for NullReferenceException.

- If there is a general catch clause, it must be last, after all specific catch clauses. Using the general catch clause is discouraged because it can hide bugs by allowing the program to continue execution when your code *should* be handling the error in a specific way. It can also leave the program in an unknown state. Therefore, you should use one of the specific catch clauses if at all possible.

The finally Block

If a program's flow of control enters a try statement that has a finally block, the finally block is *always* executed. Figure 23-5 shows the flow of control.

- If no exception occurs inside the try block, then at the end of the try block, control skips over any catch clauses and goes to the finally block.

- If an exception occurs inside the try block, then the appropriate catch clause in the catch clauses section is executed, followed by execution of the finally block.

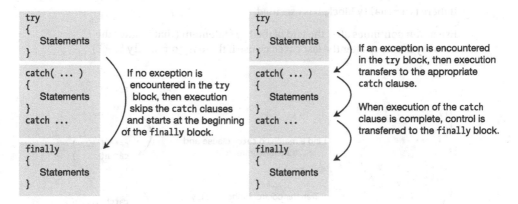

Figure 23-5. Execution of the finally block

The finally block will always be executed before returning to the calling code, even if a try block has a return statement or an exception is thrown in the catch block. For example, in the following code, there is a return statement in the middle of the try block that is executed under certain conditions. This does not allow it to bypass the finally statement.

```
try
{
   if (inVal < 10) {
      Console.Write("First Branch  - ");
      return;
   }
   else
      Console.Write("Second Branch - ");
}
finally
{
   Console.WriteLine("In finally statement");
}
```

This code produces the following output when variable inVal has the value 5:

```
First Branch  - In finally statement
```

Finding a Handler for an Exception

When a program raises an exception, the system checks to see whether the program has provided a handler for it. Figure 23-6 shows the flow of control.

- If the exception occurred inside a try block, the system will check to see whether any of the catch clauses can handle the exception.

- If an appropriate catch clause is found, then the following happens:

  - The catch clause is executed.

  - If there is a finally block, it is executed.

  - Execution continues after the end of the try statement (that is, after the finally block, or after the last catch clause if there is no finally block).

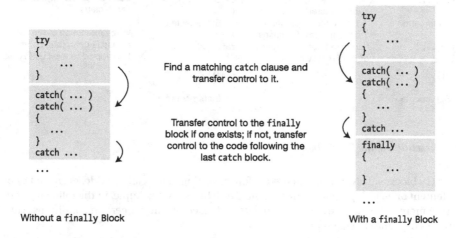

Figure 23-6. *Exception with handler in current try statement*

Searching Further

If the exception was raised in a section of code that was not guarded by a try statement or if the try statement does not have a matching exception handler, the system will have to look further for a matching handler. It will do this by searching down the call stack, in sequence, to see whether there is an enclosing try block with a matching handler.

Figure 23-7 illustrates the search process. On the left of the figure is the calling structure of the code, and on the right is the call stack. The figure shows that Method2 is called from inside the try block of Method1. If an exception occurs inside the try block in Method2, the system does the following:

- First, it checks to see whether Method2 has exception handlers that can handle the exception.

  - If so, Method2 handles it, and program execution continues.

  - If not, the system continues down the call stack to Method1, searching for an appropriate handler.

- If Method1 has an appropriate catch clause, the system does the following:

  - It goes back to the top of the call stack—which is Method2.

  - It executes Method2's finally block and pops Method2 off the stack.

  - It executes Method1's catch clause and its finally block.

- If Method1 doesn't have an appropriate catch clause, the system continues searching down the call stack.

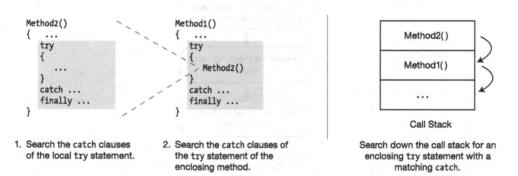

Figure 23-7. Searching down the call stack

General Algorithm

Figure 23-8 shows the general algorithm for handling an exception.

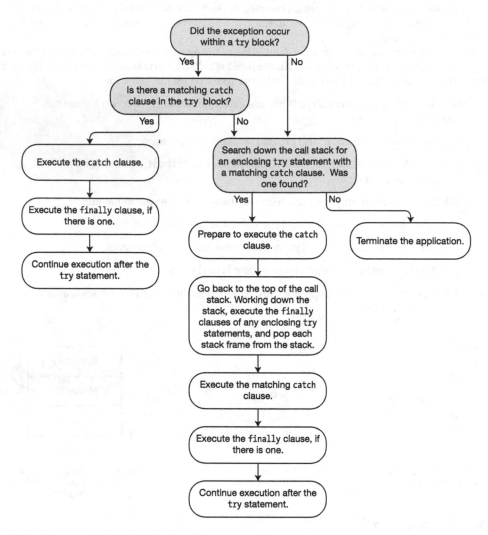

Figure 23-8. *The general algorithm for handling an exception*

Example of Searching Down the Call Stack

In the following code, Main starts execution and calls method A, which calls method B. A description and diagram of the process are given after the code and in Figure 23-9.

```
class Program
{
   static void Main()
   {
      MyClass MCls = new MyClass();
      try
         { MCls.A(); }
      catch ( DivideByZeroException )
         { Console.WriteLine("catch clause in Main()"); }
      finally
         { Console.WriteLine("finally clause in Main()"); }
      Console.WriteLine("After try statement in Main.");
      Console.WriteLine("              -- Keep running.");
   }
}

class MyClass
{
   public void A()
   {
      try
         { B(); }
      catch ( NullReferenceException )
         { Console.WriteLine("catch clause in A()"); }
      finally
         { Console.WriteLine("finally clause in A()"); }
   }

   void B()
   {
      int x = 10, y = 0;
      try
         { x /= y; }
      catch ( IndexOutOfRangeException )
         { Console.WriteLine("catch clause in B()"); }
      finally
         { Console.WriteLine("finally clause in B()"); }
   }
}
```

This code produces the following output:

```
finally clause in B()
finally clause in A()
catch clause in Main()
finally clause in Main()
After try statement in Main.
            -- Keep running.
```

1. Main calls A, which calls B, which encounters a DivideByZeroException exception.

2. The system checks B's catch section for a matching catch clause. Although it has one for IndexOutOfRangeException, it doesn't have one for DivideByZeroException.

3. The system then moves down the call stack and checks A's catch section, where it finds that A also doesn't have a matching catch clause.

4. The system continues down the call stack and checks Main's catch clause section, where it finds that Main does have a DivideByZeroException catch clause.

5. Although the matching catch clause has now been located, it is not executed yet. Instead, the system goes back to the top of the stack, executes B's finally clause, and pops B from the call stack.

6. The system then moves to A, executes its finally clause, and pops A from the call stack.

7. Finally, Main's matching catch clause is executed, followed by its finally clause. Execution then continues after the end of Main's try statement.

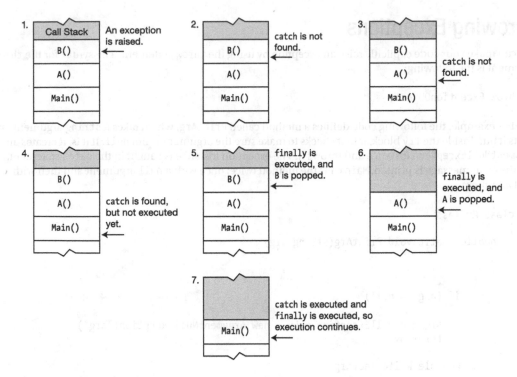

Figure 23-9. *Searching the stack for an exception handler*

Throwing Exceptions

You can make your code explicitly raise an exception by using the throw statement. The syntax for the throw statement is the following:

```
throw ExceptionObject;
```

For example, the following code defines a method called PrintArg, which takes a string argument and prints it out. Inside the try block, it first checks to make sure the argument is not null. If it is, it creates an ArgumentNullException instance and throws it. The exception instance is caught in the catch statement, and the error message is printed. Main calls the method twice: once with a null argument and then with a valid argument.

```
class MyClass
{
   public static void PrintArg(string arg)
   {
      try
      {
         if (arg == null)                            Supply name of null argument.
         {                                                      ↓
            ArgumentNullException myEx = new ArgumentNullException("arg");
            throw myEx;
         }
         Console.WriteLine(arg);
      }
      catch (ArgumentNullException e)
      {
         Console.WriteLine($"Message:  { e.Message }");
      }
   }
}
class Program
{
   static void Main()
   {
      string s = null;
      MyClass.PrintArg(s);
      MyClass.PrintArg("Hi there!");
   }
}
```

This code produces the following output:

```
Message:  Value cannot be null.
Parameter name: arg
Hi there!
```

Throwing Without an Exception Object

The throw statement can also be used without an exception object, inside a catch block.

- This form rethrows the current exception, and the system continues its search for additional handlers for it.

- This form can be used only inside a catch statement.

For example, the following code rethrows the exception from inside the first catch clause:

```
class MyClass
{
    public static void PrintArg(string arg)
    {
        try
        {
            try
            {
                if (arg == null)                              Supply name of null argument.
                {                                                          ↓
                    ArgumentNullException myEx = new ArgumentNullException("arg");
                    throw myEx;
                }
                Console.WriteLine(arg);
            }
            catch (ArgumentNullException e)
            {
                Console.WriteLine($"Inner Catch:  { e.Message }");
                throw;
            }      ↑
        }  Rethrow the exception, with no additional parameters.
        catch
        {
            Console.WriteLine("Outer Catch:  Handling an Exception.");
        }
    }
}

class Program {
    static void Main() {
        string s = null;
        MyClass.PrintArg(s);
        MyClass.PrintArg("Hi there!");
    }
}
```

This code produces the following output:

```
Inner Catch:  Value cannot be null.
Parameter name: arg
Outer Catch:  Handling an Exception.
Hi there!
```

Throw Expressions

As you saw in previous chapters, C# has both statements and expressions. There are locations in the code where statements are not permitted and expressions are required, as well as vice versa. In the previous sections of this chapter, all of the uses of throw have been statements. Starting with C# 7.0, you can now use throw expressions in places that require expressions.

Throw statements and throw expressions are syntactically identical. You do not need to actually specify one or the other. Rather, when the compiler sees that it needs a throw expression, it will use one for you; the same happens for a throw statement.

For example, you can now use a throw statement as the second operand of a null coalescing operator. Remember that the null coalescing operator consists of two operands separated by ??. The first operand must be nullable and is tested to determine whether it is null. If not, its value is used. But if the first operand is null, the second operand is used instead. The following code shows an example that is now valid:

```
private int mSecurityCode;
public int SecurityCode
{
    get => mSecurityCode;
    set => mSecurityCode = value ??
                throw new ArgumentNullException("Security Code may not be null");
}
```

Before C# 7.0, this code would have generated a compile-time error because only an expression was permitted as the second operand of the null coalescing operator.

Another C# construct that requires expressions is the conditional operator. A throw expression can now be used as either the second or third operand in this operator. The following code shows an example:

```
class Program
{
    static string SecretCode { get { return "Roses are red"; } }
    static void Main()
    {
        bool safe = false;
        try
        {
            string secretCode = safe
                ? SecretCode
                : throw new Exception("Not safe to get code.");
            Console.WriteLine($"Code is: {secretCode}.");
        }
        catch (Exception e)
        {
            Console.WriteLine($"{ e.Message }");
        }
    }
}
```

This code produces the following output:

```
Not safe to get code.
```

CHAPTER 24

■ ■ ■

Preprocessor Directives

What Are Preprocessor Directives?

The source code specifies the definition of a program. The *preprocessor directives* instruct the compiler how to treat the source code. For example, under certain conditions, you might want the compiler to ignore portions of the code, and under other conditions, you might want that code compiled. The preprocessor directives give you those options and several others.

In C and C++ there is an actual preprocessor phase, in which the preprocessor goes through the source code and prepares an output stream of text to be processed by the subsequent compilation phase. In C# there is no actual preprocessor. The "preprocessor" directives are handled by the compiler. The term, however, remains.

General Rules

Some of the most important syntactic rules for preprocessor directives are the following:

- Preprocessor directives must be on lines separate from C# code.

- Unlike C# statements, preprocessor directives are not terminated with a semicolon.

- Every line containing a preprocessor directive must start with the # character.

  - There can be space before the # character.

  - There can be space between the # character and the directive.

- End-of-line comments are allowed.

- Delimited comments are *not* allowed in a preprocessor directive line.

The following code illustrates these rules:

```
                         No semicolon
                             ↓
    #define PremiumVersion              // OK

Space before
  ↓
      #define BudgetVersion             // OK
  #    define MediumVersion             // OK
  ↑
Space between                          Delimited comments are not allowed.
                                                   ↓
    #define SuperVersion                /* all bells & whistles */
                                        End-of-line comments are fine.
                                                   ↓
    #define LowCostVersion              // Stripped-down version
```

Table 24-1 lists the preprocessor directives.

Table 24-1. *Preprocessor Directives*

Directive	Summary of Meaning
#define identifier	Defines a compilation symbol.
#undef identifier	Undefines a compilation symbol.
#if expression	If the expression is true, the compiler compiles the following section.
#elif expression	If the expression is true, the compiler compiles the following section.
#else	If the previous #if or #elif expression is false, the compiler compiles the following section.
#endif	Marks the end of an #if construct.
#region name	Marks the beginning of a region of code; has no compilation effect.
#endregion name	Marks the end of a region of code; has no compilation effect.
#warning message	Displays a compile-time warning message.
#error message	Displays a compile-time error message.
#line indicator	Changes the line numbers displayed in compiler messages.
#pragma warning	Gives you options for modifying the behavior of compiler warning messages.

The #define and #undef Directives

A *compilation symbol* is an identifier that has only two possible states. It is either *defined* or *undefined*. A compilation symbol has the following characteristics:

- It can be any identifier except true or false. This includes C# keywords and identifiers declared in your C# code—both of which are fine.

- It has no value. Unlike in C and C++, it does not represent a string.

As shown in Table 24-1,

- The #define directive declares a compilation symbol.

- The #undef directive undefines a compilation symbol.

```
#define PremiumVersion
#define EconomyVersion
   ...
#undef PremiumVersion
```

The #define and #undef directives can be used only at the top of a source file, before any C# code is listed. After the C# code has started, the #define and #undef directives can no longer be used.

```
using System;                        // First line of C# code
#define PremiumVersion               // Error

namespace Eagle
{
   #define PremiumVersion            // Error
   ...
```

The scope of a compilation symbol is limited to a single source file. Redefining a symbol that is already defined is perfectly fine—as long as it's before any C# code, of course.

```
#define AValue
#define BValue
#define AValue                       // Redefinition is fine.
```

Defining an identifier is the equivalent of setting its value to true. Undefining an identifier is the equivalent of setting its value to false. Even though that identifier must be defined outside any C# code, it can be used within the C# code, typically in an #if #else construct.

```
#define debug
static void Main()
{
   #if debug
      // Enable verbose logging
   #else
      // Optimize for performance
   #endif

      ...
}
```

Conditional Compilation

Conditional compilation allows you to mark a section of source code to be either compiled or skipped, depending on whether a particular compilation symbol is defined.

There are four directives for specifying conditional compilation.

- `#if`
- `#else`
- `#elif`
- `#endif`

A *condition* is a simple expression that returns either `true` or `false`.

- A condition can consist of a single compilation symbol or an expression of symbols and operators, as summarized in Table 24-2. Subexpressions can be grouped with parentheses.
- The literals `true` and `false` can also be used in conditional expressions.

Table 24-2. *Conditions Used in the #if and #elif Directives*

Parameter Type	Meaning	Evaluation
Compilation symbol	Identifier, defined (or not) using the `#define` directive	True: If the symbol has been defined using a `#define` directive False: Otherwise
Expression	Constructed using symbols and the operators !, ==, !=, &&, and ||	True: If the expression evaluates to `true` False: Otherwise

The following are examples of conditional compilation conditions:

```
              Expression
                  ↓
#if !DemoVersion
   ...
#endif            Expression
                      ↓
#if (LeftHanded && OemVersion) || FullVersion
   ...
#endif

#if true    // The following code segment will always be compiled.
   ...
#endif
```

The Conditional Compilation Constructs

The #if and #endif directives are the matching demarcations of a conditional compilation construct. Whenever there is an #if directive, there must also be a matching #endif.

Figure 24-1 illustrates the #if and #if...#else constructs.

- If the condition in the #if construct evaluates to true, the code section following it is compiled. Otherwise, it is skipped.

- In the #if...#else construct, if the condition evaluates to true, *CodeSection1* is compiled. Otherwise, *CodeSection2* is compiled.

Figure 24-1. *The #if and #else constructs*

For example, the following code illustrates a simple #if...#else construct. If the symbol RightHanded is defined, the code between the #if and the #else is compiled. Otherwise, the code between the #else and the #endif is compiled.

```
...
#if RightHanded
    // Code implementing right-handed functionality
    ...
#else
    // Code implementing left-handed functionality
    ...
#endif
```

Figure 24-2 illustrates the #if...#elif and #if...#elif...#else constructs.

- In the #if...#elif construct,

    – If *Cond1* evaluates to true, *CodeSection1* is compiled, and compilation continues after the #endif.

    – Otherwise, if *Cond2* evaluates to true, *CodeSection2* is compiled, and compilation continues after the #endif.

    – This continues until either a condition evaluates to true or all the conditions have returned false. If that's the case, none of the code sections in the construct are compiled, and compilation continues after the #endif.

- The #if...#elif...#else construct works the same way, except that if no condition is true, then the code section after the #else is then compiled, and compilation continues after the #endif.

Figure 24-2. *The #if...#elif construct (left) and the #if...#elif...#else construct (right)*

The following code demonstrates the #if...#elif...#else construct. The string containing the description of the version of the program is set to various values, depending on which compilation symbol is defined.

```
#define DemoVersionWithoutTimeLimit

using System;

class demo
{
    static void Main()
    {
        const int intExpireLength = 30;
        string strVersionDesc = null;
        int intExpireCount = 0;

#if DemoVersionWithTimeLimit
        intExpireCount = intExpireLength;
        strVersionDesc = "This version of Supergame Plus will expire in 30 days";

#elif DemoVersionWithoutTimeLimit
        strVersionDesc = "Demo Version of Supergame Plus";

#elif OEMVersion
        strVersionDesc = "Supergame Plus, distributed under license";

#else
        strVersionDesc = "The original Supergame Plus!!";

#endif

        Console.WriteLine(strVersionDesc);
    }
}
```

This code produces the following output:

```
Demo Version of Supergame Plus
```

Diagnostic Directives

Diagnostic directives produce user-defined compile-time warning and error messages.

The following is the syntax of the diagnostic directives. The messages are strings, but notice that unlike normal C# strings, they do not have to be enclosed in quotation marks.

```
#warning Message
```

```
#error Message
```

When the compiler reaches a diagnostic directive, it writes out the associated message. The diagnostic directive messages are listed by the compiler along with any compiler-generated warning and error messages.

For example, the following code shows an #error directive and a #warning directive.

- The #error directive is inside an #if construct so that it will be generated only if the conditions on the #if directive are met. When the condition evaluates to true, the build fails.

- The #warning directive is a reminder to the programmer to come back and clean up a section of code.

```
#define RightHanded
#define LeftHanded

#if RightHanded && LeftHanded
#error Can't build for both RightHanded and LeftHanded
#endif

#warning Remember to come back and clean up this code!
```

Line Number Directives

Line number directives can do several things, including the following:

- Change the apparent line numbers reported by the compiler's warning and error messages

- Change the apparent file name of the source file being compiled

- Hide a sequence of lines from the interactive debugger

The syntax for the #line directives is the following:

```
#line integer        // Sets line number of next line to value of integer
#line "filename"      // Sets the apparent file name
#line default         // Restores real line number and file name

#line hidden          // Hides the following code from stepping debugger
#line                 // Stops hiding from debugger
```

The #line directive with an integer parameter causes the compiler to consider that value to be the line number of the following line of code. Numbering of the subsequent lines continues, based on that line number.

- To change the apparent file name, use the file name, inside double quotes, as the parameter. The double quotes are required.

- To return to true line numbering and the true file name, use default as the parameter.

- To hide a segment of code from the step-through-code feature of the interactive debugger, use hidden as the parameter. To stop hiding, use the directive with no parameter. This feature has so far mostly been used in ASP.NET and WPF for hiding compiler-generated code.

The following code shows examples of the line number directives:

```
#line 226
    x = y + z;               // Now considered by the compiler to be line 226
    ...

#line 330 "SourceFile.cs"   // Changes the reported line number and file name
    var1 = var2 + var3;
    ...

#line default               // Restores true line numbers and file name
```

Region Directives

The region directive allows you to mark, and optionally name, a section of code. A region consists of a #region directive and an #endregion directive somewhere below it. Regions can make navigating through your code easier by exposing only the area of your code that you currently want to work on. They also allow you to organize your code by placing, for example, all properties in the same location and all methods in another specified location. The characteristics of a region are the following:

- A #region directive is placed on the line above the section of code you want to mark, and an #endregion directive is placed after the last line of code in the region.

- A #region directive can take an optional string of text following it on the line. The string serves as the name of the region.

- Regions can have other regions nested inside them.

  - Regions can be nested to any level.

  - An #endregion directive always matches the first *unmatched* #region directive above it.

Although region directives are ignored by the compiler, they can be used by source code tools. Visual Studio, for example, allows you to easily hide or display regions.

As an example, the following code has a region called Constructors, which encloses the two constructors of class MyClass. In Visual Studio, you can collapse this region to a single line when you don't want to see it in the code and then expand it again when you need to work on it or add another constructor.

```
#region Constructors
   MyClass()
   { ... }

   MyClass(string s)
   { ... }
#endregion
```

Regions can be nested, as shown in Figure 24-3.

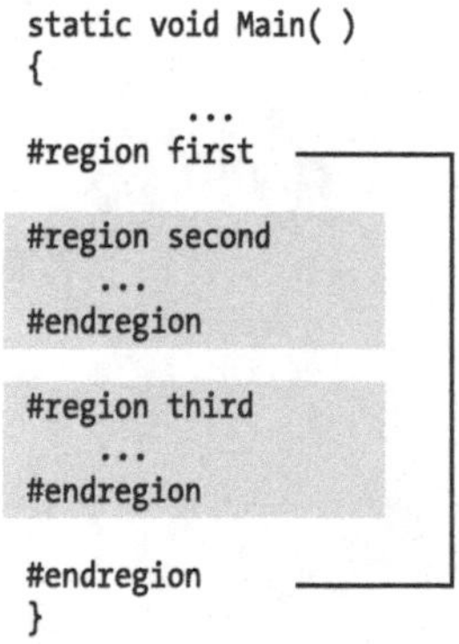

Figure 24-3. *Nested regions*

691

The #pragma warning Directive

The #pragma warning directive allows you to turn off warning messages and to turn them back on.

- To turn off warning messages, use the disable form with a comma-separated list of warning numbers you want to turn off.

- To turn warning messages back on, use the restore form with a list of the warning numbers you want to turn back on.

For example, the following code turns off two warning messages: 618 and 414. Further down in the code, it turns on messages for 618 but leaves the messages for 414 turned off.

```
                         Warning messages to turn off
                              ↓
#pragma warning disable 618, 414

    ...        Messages for the listed warnings are off in this section of code.

#pragma warning restore 618
```

If you use either form without a warning number list, the command then applies to all warnings. For example, the following code turns off, and then restores, all warning messages.

```
#pragma warning disable

    ...        All warning messages are turned off in this section of code.

#pragma warning restore

    ...        All warning messages are turned back on in this section of code.
```

CHAPTER 25

■ ■ ■

Reflection and Attributes

© Daniel Solis and Cal Schrotenboer 2018
D. Solis and C. Schrotenboer, *Illustrated C# 7*, https://doi.org/10.1007/978-1-4842-3288-0_25

Metadata and Reflection

Most programs are written to work on data. They read, write, manipulate, and display data. (Graphics are a form of data.) For some types of programs, however, the data they manipulate is not numbers, text, or graphics, but information about programs and program types.

- Data about programs and their classes is called *metadata* and is stored in the programs' assemblies.

- A program can look at the metadata of other assemblies or of itself, while it's running. When a running program looks at its own metadata, or that of other programs, it's called *reflection*.

An object browser is an example of a program that displays metadata. It can read assemblies and display the types they contain, along with all the characteristics and members.

This chapter will look at how your programs can reflect on data using the Type class and how you can add metadata to your types using *attributes*.

■ **Note**   To use reflection, you must use the System.Reflection namespace.

The Type Class

Throughout this text we've described how to declare and use the types available in C#. These include the predefined types (int, long, string, and so on), types from the BCL (Console, IEnumerable, and so on), and user-defined types (MyClass, MyDel, and so on). Every type has its own members and characteristics.

The BCL declares an abstract class called Type, which is designed to contain the characteristics of a type. Using objects of this class allows you to get information about the types your program is using.

Since Type is an abstract class, it cannot have actual instances. Instead, at run time, the CLR creates instances of a class *derived* from Type (RuntimeType) that contains the type information. When you access one of these instances, the CLR returns a reference, not of the derived type but of the base class Type. For simplicity's sake, though, throughout the rest of the chapter, we'll call the object pointed at by the reference an object of type Type, although technically it's an object of a derived type that is internal to the BCL.

The following are important things to know about Type:

- For every type used in a program, the CLR creates a Type object that contains the information about the type.

- Regardless of the number of instances of a type that are created, there is only a single Type object associated with all the instances.

Figure 25-1 shows a running program with two MyClass objects and an OtherClass object. Notice that although there are two instances of MyClass, there is only a single Type object representing it.

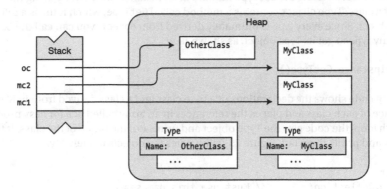

Figure 25-1. *The CLR instantiates objects of type Type for every type used in a program*

You can get almost anything you need to know about a type from its Type object. Table 25-1 lists some of the more useful members of the class.

Table 25-1. *Selected Members of Class System.Type*

Member	Member Type	Description
Name	Property	Returns the name of the type.
Namespace	Property	Returns the namespace containing the type declaration.
Assembly	Property	Returns the assembly in which the type is declared. If the type is generic, it returns the assembly in which the type is defined.
GetFields	Method	Returns a list of the type's fields.
GetProperties	Method	Returns a list of the type's properties.
GetMethods	Method	Returns a list of the type's methods.

Getting a Type Object

You can get a Type object by using the GetType method of an instance object or by using the typeof operator with the name of a class. Type object contains a method called GetType, which returns a reference to an instance's Type object. Since every type is ultimately derived from object, you can call the GetType method on an object of any type to get its Type object, as shown here:

```
Type t = myInstance.GetType();
```

The following code shows the declarations of a base class and a class derived from it. Method Main creates an instance of each class and places the references in an array called bca for easy processing. Inside the outer foreach loop, the code gets the Type object and prints out the name of the class. It then gets the fields of the class and prints them out. Figure 25-2 illustrates the objects in memory.

```
using System;
using System.Reflection;        // Must use this namespace

class BaseClass
{
   public int BaseField = 0;
}

class DerivedClass : BaseClass
{
   public int DerivedField = 0;
}

class Program
{
   static void Main( )
   {
      var bc = new BaseClass();
      var dc = new DerivedClass();

      BaseClass[] bca = new BaseClass[] { bc, dc };

      foreach (var v in bca)
      {
         Type t = v.GetType();                      // Get the type.

         Console.WriteLine($"Object type : { t.Name }");

         FieldInfo[] fi = t.GetFields();            // Get the field information.
         foreach (var f in fi)
            Console.WriteLine($"      Field : { f.Name }");
         Console.WriteLine();
      }
   }
}
```

This code produces the following output:

```
Object type : BaseClass
       Field : BaseField

Object type : DerivedClass
       Field : DerivedField
       Field : BaseField
```

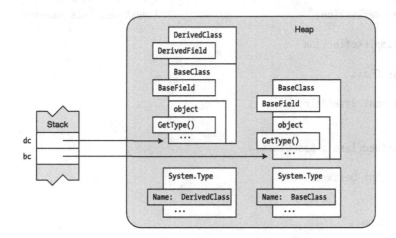

Figure 25-2. *The base class and derived class objects along with their Type objects*

You can also use the typeof operator to get a Type object. Just supply the name of the type as the operand, and it returns a reference to the Type object, as shown here:

```
Type t = typeof( DerivedClass );
         ↑              ↑
      Operator    Type you want the Type object for
```

The following code shows a simple example of using the typeof operator:

```
using System;
using System.Reflection;                        // Must use this namespace

namespace SimpleReflection
{
   class BaseClass
   {
      public int BaseField;
   }

   class DerivedClass : BaseClass
   {
      public int DerivedField;
   }

   class Program
   {
      static void Main()
      {
         Type tbc = typeof(DerivedClass);        // Get the type.
         Console.WriteLine($"Object type : { tbc.Name }");
         FieldInfo[] fi = tbc.GetFields();
         foreach (var f in fi)
             Console.WriteLine($"      Field : { f.Name }");
      }
   }
}
```

This code produces the following output:

```
Object type : DerivedClass
      Field : DerivedField
      Field : BaseField
```

What Is an Attribute?

An *attribute* is a language construct that allows you to add metadata to a program's assembly. It's a special type of class for storing information about program constructs.

- The program construct to which you apply an attribute is called its *target*.

- Programs designed to retrieve and use metadata, such as object browsers, are said to be *consumers* of the attributes.

- There are attributes that are predefined in .NET, and you can also declare custom attributes.

Figure 25-3 gives an overview of the components involved in using attributes and illustrates the following points about them:

- You *apply* attributes to program constructs in the source code.

- The compiler takes the source code and produces metadata from the attributes and then places that metadata in the assembly.

- Consumer programs can access the metadata of the attributes along with the metadata for the rest of the components of the program. Notice that the compiler both produces and consumes attributes.

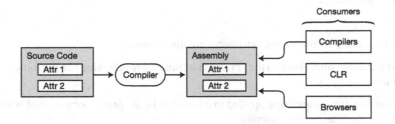

Figure 25-3. *The components involved with creating and using attributes*

By convention, attribute names use Pascal casing and end with the suffix `Attribute`. When applying an attribute to a target, however, you can leave off the suffix. For example, for attributes `SerializableAttribute` and `MyAttributeAttribute`, you can use the short names `Serializable` and `MyAttribute` when applying them to a construct.

Applying an Attribute

Rather than starting with a description of how to create attributes, we're going to start by showing how to use attributes that are already defined. That way, you can get an idea of how they might be useful.

The purpose of an attribute is to tell the compiler to emit a certain set of metadata about a program construct and place it in the assembly. You do this by *applying* the attribute to the construct.

- You apply an attribute by placing an *attribute section* immediately before the construct.

- An *attribute section* consists of square brackets enclosing an attribute name and sometimes a parameter list.

For example, the following code shows the headings of two classes. The first few lines of code show an attribute named Serializable applied to class MyClass. Notice that Serializable has no parameter list. The second class declaration has an attribute called MyAttribute, which has a parameter list with two string parameters.

```
[ Serializable ]                              // Attribute
public class MyClass
{ ...

[ MyAttribute("Simple class", "Version 3.57") ]   // Attribute with parameters
public class MyOtherClass
{ ...
```

Some important things to know about attributes are the following:

- Most attributes apply only to the construct immediately following the attribute section or sections.

- A construct with an attribute applied to it is said to be *decorated*, or *adorned*, with the attribute. Both terms are common.

Predefined, Reserved Attributes

In this section we'll look at several attributes predefined and reserved by .NET.

The Obsolete Attribute

Over a program's lifetime, it may go through many different releases, possibly over a period of years. Later in its life cycle you will often write a new method that supersedes an older method that performed a similar function. For many reasons, you might want to leave alone all the old code that calls the older, now obsolete method, but have the newer code call the new method.

When this happens, you will want your team members, or programmers who work on the code at a later time, to use the new method rather than the old method. To help warn them against using the old method, you can use the `Obsolete` attribute to mark the old method as obsolete and to display a helpful warning message when the code is compiled. The following code shows an example of its use:

```
class Program          Apply attribute.
{                           ↓
    [Obsolete("Use method SuperPrintOut")]    // Apply attribute to method.
    static void PrintOut(string str) {
        Console.WriteLine(str);
    }
    static void Main(string[] args) {
        PrintOut("Start of Main");              // Invoke obsolete method.
    }
}
```

Notice that method `Main` calls `PrintOut` even though it's marked as obsolete. In spite of this, the code compiles and runs fine and produces the following output:

```
Start of Main
```

During compilation, though, the compiler produces the following CS0618 warning message in the Visual Studio output window to inform you that you're using an obsolete construct:

```
'AttrObs.Program.PrintOut(string)' is obsolete: 'Use method SuperPrintOut'
```

Another overload of the `Obsolete` attribute takes a second parameter, of type `bool`. This parameter specifies whether to flag the usage as an error instead of just a warning. The following code specifies that it should be flagged as an error:

```
                          Flag as an error.
                                ↓
[ Obsolete("Use method SuperPrintOut", true) ]   // Apply attribute to method.
static void PrintOut(string str)
{ ...
```

The Conditional Attribute

The Conditional attribute allows you to instruct the compiler to either include or exclude all the *invocations* of a particular method. To use the Conditional attribute, apply it to the method declaration, along with a compilation symbol as a parameter. Important characteristics of the conditional attribute are the following:

- If the compilation symbol is defined, the compiler includes the code for all the invocations of the method, the way it would for any normal method.

- If the compilation symbol is *not* defined, the compiler *omits* all the method invocations throughout the code.

- The CIL code defining the method itself is always included in the assembly. It's just the invocations that are either inserted or omitted.

- Besides using the Conditional attribute on a method, you can also use it on a class, as long as the class is derived from the Attribute class. We won't be covering using Conditional for this case.

The rules for using the Conditional attribute on a method are the following:

- The method must be a method of a class or struct.

- The method must be of type void.

- The method cannot be declared as an override, but it can be marked as virtual.

- The method cannot be the implementation of an interface method.

For example, in the following code, the Conditional attribute is applied to the declaration of a method called TraceMessage. The attribute has a single parameter, which in this case is the string DoTrace.

- When the compiler is compiling the code, it checks whether there is a compilation symbol named DoTrace defined.

- If DoTrace is defined, the compiler places in the code all the calls to method TraceMessage, as usual.

- If there is no DoTrace compilation symbol defined, it doesn't output code for any of the calls to TraceMessage.

```
                    Compilation symbol
                          ↓
[Conditional( "DoTrace" )]
static void TraceMessage(string str)
{
    Console.WriteLine(str);
}
```

Example of the Conditional Attribute

The following code shows a full example of using the Conditional attribute.

- Method Main contains two calls to method TraceMessage.

- The declaration for method TraceMessage is decorated with the Conditional attribute, which has the compilation symbol DoTrace as its parameter. So if DoTrace is defined, the compiler will include the code for all the calls to TraceMessage.

- Since the first line of code defines a compilation symbol named DoTrace, the compiler will include the code for both calls to TraceMessage.

```
#define DoTrace
using System;
using System.Diagnostics;

namespace AttributesConditional
{
    class Program
    {
        [Conditional( "DoTrace" )]
        static void TraceMessage(string str)
        { Console.WriteLine(str); }

        static void Main( )
        {
            TraceMessage("Start of Main");
            Console.WriteLine("Doing work in Main.");
            TraceMessage("End of Main");
        }
    }
}
```

This code produces the following output:

```
Start of Main
Doing work in Main.
End of Main
```

If you comment out the first line so that DoTrace is not defined, the compiler will not insert the code for the two calls to TraceMessage. This time, when you run the program, it produces the following output:

```
Doing work in Main.
```

The Caller Information Attributes

The caller information attributes allow you to access source code information about the file path, the line number, and the name of the calling member.

- The three attribute names are CallerFilePath, CallerLineNumber, and CallerMemberName.

- These attributes can only be used with optional parameters on methods.

The following code declares a method named MyTrace, which uses the three caller information attributes on its three optional parameters. If the method is called with explicit values for those parameters, the values of the actual parameters will be used. In the call from Main, shown next, however, no explicit values are supplied, so the system supplies the source code's file path, the line number of the line where the method was called, and the name of the member calling the method.

```
using System;
using System.Runtime.CompilerServices;

public static class Program
{
    public static void MyTrace( string message,
                                [CallerFilePath]   string fileName = "",
                                [CallerLineNumber] int lineNumber = 0,
                                [CallerMemberName] string callingMember = "" )
    {
        Console.WriteLine($"File:        { fileName }");
        Console.WriteLine($"Line:        { lineNumber }");
        Console.WriteLine($"Called From: { callingMember }");
        Console.WriteLine($"Message:     { message }");
    }

    public static void Main()
    {
        MyTrace( "Simple message" );
    }
}
```

This code produces the following output:

```
File:        c:\TestCallerInfo\TestCallerInfo\Program.cs
Line:        19
Called From: Main
Message:     Simple message
```

The DebuggerStepThrough Attribute

Many times when you're debugging code and stepping through it line by line, there are certain methods that you don't want the debugger to step into; you just want it to execute the method and step to the line following the method call. The DebuggerStepThrough attribute instructs the debugger to execute the target code without stepping into it.

In my own code, this is the attribute we find most useful on a regular basis. Some methods are so small and obviously correct that it's just annoying to have to step through them repeatedly when debugging. Use this attribute with care, though, because you don't want to exclude code that might contain a bug.

Important things to know about DebuggerStepThrough are the following:

- This attribute is in the System.Diagnostics namespace.

- You can use this attribute on classes, structs, constructors, methods, or accessors.

The following extremely contrived code shows the attribute used on an accessor and a method. If you step through this code in your debugger, you'll find that the debugger doesn't enter the IncrementFields method or the set accessor of the X property.

```
using System;
using System.Diagnostics;         // Required for this DebuggerStepThrough
class Program
{
   int x = 1;
   int X
   {
      get { return x; }
      [DebuggerStepThrough]       // Don't step through the set accessor.
      set
      {
         x = x * 2;
         x += value;
      }
   }

   public int Y { get; set; }

   public static void Main()
   {
      Program p = new Program();
      p.IncrementFields();
      p.X = 5;
      Console.WriteLine( $"X = { p.X }, Y = { p.Y }" );
   }

   [DebuggerStepThrough]          // Don't step through this method.
   void IncrementFields()
   {
      X++; Y++;
   }
}
```

Other Predefined Attributes

The .NET Framework predefines a number of attributes that are understood and interpreted by the compiler and the CLR. Table 25-2 lists some of these. The table uses the short names, without the "Attribute" suffix. For example, the full name of CLSCompliant is CLSCompliantAttribute.

Table 25-2. *Important Attributes Defined in .NET*

Attribute	Meaning
CLSCompliant	Declares that the publicly exposed members should be checked by the compiler for compliance with the CLS. Compliant assemblies can be used by any .NET-compliant language.
Serializable	Declares that the construct can be serialized.
NonSerialized	Declares that the construct cannot be serialized.
DLLImport	Declares that the implementation is unmanaged code.
WebMethod	Declares that the method should be exposed as part of an XML web service.
AttributeUsage	Declares what types of program constructs the attribute can be applied to. This attribute is applied to attribute declarations.

More About Applying Attributes

The simple attributes shown so far have used a single attribute applied to a method. This section describes other types of attribute usage.

Multiple Attributes

You can apply multiple attributes to a single construct.

- Multiple attributes can be listed in either of the following formats:
  - Separate attribute sections, one after another. Usually these are stacked on top of each other, on separate lines.
  - A single attribute section, with the attributes separated by commas.
- You can list the attributes in any order.

For example, the following code shows the two ways of applying multiple attributes. The sections of code are equivalent.

```
[ Serializable ]                                                      // Stacked
[ MyAttribute("Simple class", "Version 3.57") ]

[ MyAttribute("Simple class", "Version 3.57"), Serializable ]        // Comma separated
              ↑                    ↑
           Attribute           Attribute
```

Other Types of Targets

Besides classes, you can also apply attributes to other program constructs, such as fields and properties. The following declaration shows an attribute on a field and multiple attributes on a method:

```
[MyAttribute("Holds a value", "Version 3.2")]          // On a field
public int MyField;

[Obsolete]                                             // On a method
[MyAttribute("Prints out a message.", "Version 3.6")]
public void PrintOut()
{
   ...
```

You can also explicitly label attributes to apply to a particular target construct. To use an explicit target specifier, place the target type, followed by a colon, at the beginning of the attribute section. For example, the following code decorates the *method* with an attribute and also applies an attribute to the *return value*.

Explicit target specifier
↓
```
[method: MyAttribute("Prints out a message.", "Version 3.6")]
[return: MyAttribute("This value represents ...", "Version 2.3")]
public long ReturnSetting()
{
   ...
```

The C# language defines ten standard attribute targets, which are listed in Table 25-3. Most of the target names are self-explanatory, but type covers classes, structs, delegates, enums, and interfaces. The typevar target name specifies type parameters to constructs that use generics.

Table 25-3. *Attribute Targets*

event	field
method	param
property	return
type	typevar
assembly	module

Global Attributes

You can also use an explicit target specifier to set attributes at the assembly and module level by using the assembly and module target names. (Assemblies and modules were explained in Chapter 22.) Some important points about assembly-level attributes are the following:

- Assembly-level attributes must be placed *outside any namespace scope* and are usually placed in the AssemblyInfo.cs file.

- The AssembyInfo.cs file usually contains metadata about the company, product, and copyright information.

The following are lines from an AssemblyInfo.cs file:

```
[assembly: AssemblyTitle("SuperWidget")]
[assembly: AssemblyDescription("Implements the SuperWidget product.")]
[assembly: AssemblyConfiguration("")]
[assembly: AssemblyCompany("McArthur Widgets, Inc.")]
[assembly: AssemblyProduct("Super Widget Deluxe")]
[assembly: AssemblyCopyright("Copyright © McArthur Widgets 2012")]
[assembly: AssemblyTrademark("")]
[assembly: AssemblyCulture("")]
```

Custom Attributes

You've probably noticed that the syntax for applying an attribute is very different from anything you've seen so far. From that, you might get the impression that attributes are an entirely different type of construct. They're not—they're just a special kind of class.

Some important points about attribute classes are the following:

- User-defined attribute classes are called *custom attributes*.

- All attribute classes are derived from class System.Attribute.

Declaring a Custom Attribute

Declaring an attribute class is, for the most part, the same as declaring any other class. There are, however, several things to be aware of.

- To declare a custom attribute, do the following:

  - Declare a class derived from System.Attribute.

  - Give it a name ending with the suffix Attribute.

- For security, it's generally suggested that you declare your attribute classes as sealed.

For example, the following code shows the beginning of the declaration of attribute MyAttributeAttribute:

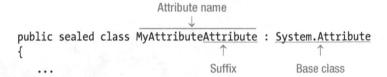

```
                              Attribute name
                      _____
                              ↓
public sealed class MyAttributeAttribute : System.Attribute
{                                    ↑                ↑
    ...                            Suffix         Base class
```

Since an attribute holds information about the target, the public members of an attribute class generally consist only of the following:

- Fields

- Properties

- Constructors

Using Attribute Constructors

Attributes, like other classes, have constructors. Every attribute must have at least one public constructor.

- As with other classes, if you don't declare a constructor, the compiler will produce an implicit, public, parameterless constructor for you.

- Attribute constructors, like other constructors, can be overloaded.

- When declaring the constructor, you must use the full class name, including the suffix. You can only use the shortened name when *applying* an attribute.

For example, with the following constructor, if the method name did not include the suffix, the compiler would produce an error message:

```
                            Suffix
                              ↓
                          _____
public MyAttributeAttribute(string desc, string ver)
{
   Description  = desc;
   VersionNumber = ver;
}
```

Specifying the Constructor

When you apply an attribute to a target, you are specifying which constructor should be used to create the instance of the attribute. The parameters listed in the attribute application are the actual parameters for the constructor.

For example, in the following code, MyAttribute is applied to a field and to a method. For the field, the declaration specifies a constructor with a single string parameter. For the method, it specifies a constructor with two string parameters.

```
[MyAttribute("Holds a value")]                // Constructor with one string
public int MyField;

[MyAttribute("Version 1.3", "Galen Daniel")]   // Constructor with two strings
public void MyMethod()
{ ...
```

Other important points about attribute constructors are the following:

- When applying an attribute, the actual parameters for the constructor must be constant expressions whose values can be determined at compile time.

- If you apply an attribute constructor with no parameters, you can leave off the parentheses. For example, both classes in the following code use the parameterless constructor for the attribute MyAttr. The meanings of the two forms are the same.

```
[MyAttr]
class SomeClass ...

[MyAttr()]
class OtherClass ...
```

Using the Constructor

Notice that you never explicitly call the constructor. Instead, an instance of an attribute is created, and its constructor called *only when an attribute consumer accesses the attribute*. This is very different from other class instances, which are created at the position where you use an object-creation expression. Applying an attribute is a declarative statement that does not determine when an object of the attribute class should be constructed.

Figure 25-4 compares the use of a constructor for a regular class and the use of a constructor with attributes.

- The imperative statement says, in effect, "Create a new class object here."

- The declarative statement says "This attribute is associated with this target, and in case the attribute needs to be constructed, use this constructor."

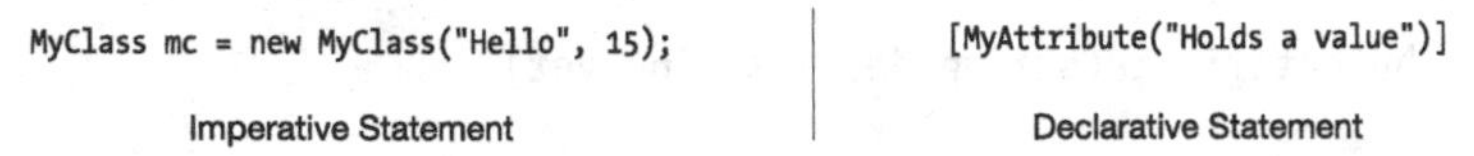

```
MyClass mc = new MyClass("Hello", 15);        [MyAttribute("Holds a value")]

          Imperative Statement                     Declarative Statement
```

Figure 25-4. *Comparing the use of constructors*

Positional and Named Parameters in Constructors

Like the methods and constructors of regular classes, the attribute constructors can also use positional and named parameters.

The following code shows the application of an attribute using a positional parameter and two named parameters:

```
       Positional parameter          Named parameter           Named parameter
              ↓                            ↓                         ↓
[MyAttribute("An excellent class", Reviewer="Amy McArthur", Ver="0.7.15.33")]
                                        ↑                        ↑
                                    Equal sign               Equal sign
```

The following code shows the declaration of the attribute class, as well as its application on class MyClass. Notice that the constructor *declaration* lists only a single formal parameter. And yet, by using named parameters, you can give the constructor three actual parameters. The two named parameters set the values of fields Ver and Reviewer.

```
public sealed class MyAttributeAttribute : System.Attribute
{
    public string Description;
    public string Ver;
    public string Reviewer;

    public MyAttributeAttribute(string desc)  // Single formal parameter
    {
        Description = desc;
    }
}
                                Three actual parameters
                                        ↓
[MyAttribute("An excellent class", Reviewer="Amy McArthur", Ver="7.15.33")]
class MyClass
{
    ...
}
```

■ **Note**   As with methods, if the constructor requires any positional parameters, they must be placed before any named parameters.

Restricting the Usage of an Attribute

You've seen that you can apply attributes to classes. But attributes *themselves* are classes, and there is one important predefined attribute that you can apply to your custom attributes: the AttributeUsage attribute. You can use it to restrict the usage of an attribute to a specific set of target types.

For example, if you want your custom attribute MyAttribute to be applied only to methods, you could use the following form of AttributeUsage:

```
                         Only to methods
                               ↓
[ AttributeUsage( AttributeTargets.Method ) ]
public sealed class MyAttributeAttribute : System.Attribute
{ ...
```

AttributeUsage has three important public properties, which are listed in Table 25-4. The table shows the names of the properties and their meanings. For the second two properties, it also shows their default values.

Table 25-4. *Public Properties of AttributeUsage*

Name	Meaning	Default
ValidOn	Stores a list of the types of targets to which the attribute can be applied. The first parameter of the constructor must be an enum value of type AttributeTargets.	
Inherited	A Boolean value that specifies whether the attribute can be inherited by derived classes of the decorated type.	true
AllowMultiple	A Boolean value that specifies whether the target can have multiple instances of the attribute applied to it.	false

The Constructor for AttributeUsage

The constructor for AttributeUsage takes a single, positional parameter that specifies which target types are allowed for the attribute. It uses this parameter to set its ValidOn property. The acceptable target types are members of the AttributeTargets enumeration. Table 25-5 shows the complete set of the members of the AttributeTargets enumeration.

You can combine the usage types by using the bitwise OR operator. For example, the attribute declared in the following code can be applied only to methods and constructors:

```
                                        Targets
                                          ↓
[ AttributeUsage( AttributeTargets.Method | AttributeTargets.Constructor ) ]
public sealed class MyAttributeAttribute  : System.Attribute
{ ...
```

Table 25-5. *Members of Enum AttributeTargets*

All	Assembly	Class	Constructor
Delegate	Enum	Event	Field
GenericParameter	Interface	Method	Module
Parameter	Property	ReturnValue	Struct

When you apply AttributeUsage to an attribute declaration, the constructor will have at least the one required parameter, which contains the target types to be stored in ValidOn. You can also optionally set the Inherited and AllowMultiple properties by using named parameters. If you don't set them, they'll have their default values, as shown in Table 25-4.

As an example, the next code block specifies the following about MyAttribute:

- MyAttribute must be applied only to classes.

- MyAttribute is not inherited by classes derived from classes to which it is applied.

- There cannot be multiple instances of MyAttribute applied to the same target.

```
[ AttributeUsage( AttributeTargets.Class,      // Required, positional
                  Inherited = false,           // Optional, named
                  AllowMultiple = false ) ]    // Optional, named
public sealed class MyAttributeAttribute : System.Attribute
{ ...
```

Suggested Practices for Custom Attributes

The following practices are strongly suggested when writing custom attributes:

- The attribute class should represent some state of the target construct.

- If the attribute requires certain fields, include a constructor with positional parameters to collect that data, and let optional fields be initialized with named parameters, as needed.

- Don't implement public methods or other function members other than properties.

- For additional security, declare the attribute class as sealed.

- Use the AttributeUsage attribute on your attribute declaration to explicitly specify the set of attribute targets.

The following code illustrates these guidelines:

```
[AttributeUsage( AttributeTargets.Class )]
public sealed class ReviewCommentAttribute : System.Attribute
{
   public string Description   { get; set; }
   public string VersionNumber { get; set; }
   public string ReviewerID    { get; set; }

   public ReviewCommentAttribute(string desc, string ver)
   {
      Description   = desc;
      VersionNumber = ver;
   }
}
```

Accessing an Attribute

At the beginning of the chapter, you saw that you can access information about a type using its Type object. You can access custom attributes in the same way. There are two methods of Type that are particularly useful in this: IsDefined and GetCustomAttributes.

Using the IsDefined Method

You can use the IsDefined method of the Type object to determine whether a particular attribute is applied to a particular class.

For example, the following code declares an attributed class called MyClass and also acts as its own attribute consumer by accessing an attribute declared and applied in the program itself. At the top of the code are declarations of the attribute ReviewComment and the class MyClass, to which it is applied. The code does the following:

- First, Main creates an object of the class. It then retrieves a reference to the Type object by using the GetType method, which it inherited from its base class, object.

- With the reference to the Type object, it can call the IsDefined method to find out whether attribute ReviewComment is applied to this class.

    - The first parameter takes a Type object of the *attribute* you are checking for.

    - The second parameter is of type bool and specifies whether to search the inheritance tree of MyClass to find the attribute.

```
[AttributeUsage(AttributeTargets.Class)]
public sealed class ReviewCommentAttribute : System.Attribute
{... }

[ReviewComment("Check it out", "2.4")]
class MyClass {  }

class Program
{
    static void Main()
    {
        MyClass mc = new MyClass(); // Create an instance of the class.
        Type t = mc.GetType();      // Get the Type object from the instance.
        bool isDefined =            // Check the Type for the attribute.
            t.IsDefined(typeof(ReviewCommentAttribute), false);

        if( isDefined )
            Console.WriteLine($"ReviewComment is applied to type { t.Name }");
    }
}
```

```
ReviewComment is applied to type MyClass
```

Using the GetCustomAttributes Method

The GetCustomAttributes method of the Type class returns an array of the attributes applied to a construct.

- The actual object returned is an array of objects, which you must then cast to the correct attribute type.

- The Boolean parameter specifies whether to search the inheritance tree to find the attributes.

  ```
  object[] AttArr = t.GetCustomAttributes(false);
  ```

- When the GetCustomAttributes method is called, an instance of each attribute associated with the target is created.

The following code uses the same attribute and class declarations as the previous example. But in this case, it doesn't just determine whether an attribute is applied to the class. Instead, it retrieves an array of the attributes applied to the class and cycles through them, printing out their member values.

```
using System;

[AttributeUsage( AttributeTargets.Class )]
public sealed class MyAttributeAttribute : System.Attribute
{
   public string Description    { get; set; }
   public string VersionNumber { get; set; }
   public string ReviewerID     { get; set; }

   public MyAttributeAttribute( string desc, string ver )
   {
      Description   = desc;
      VersionNumber = ver;
   }
}

[MyAttribute( "Check it out", "2.4" )]
class MyClass
{
}
```

```
class Program
   {
      static void Main()
      {
         Type t = typeof( MyClass );
         object[] AttArr = t.GetCustomAttributes( false );

         foreach ( Attribute a in AttArr )
         {
            MyAttributeAttribute attr = a as MyAttributeAttribute;
            if ( null != attr )
            {
               Console.WriteLine($"Description    : { attr.Description }");
               Console.WriteLine($"Version Number : { attr.VersionNumber }");
               Console.WriteLine($"Reviewer ID    : { attr.ReviewerID }");
            }
         }
      }
   }
```

This code produces the following output:

```
Description    : Check it out
Version Number : 2.4
Reviewer ID    :
```

CHAPTER 26

■ ■ ■

What's New in C# 6 and 7

© Daniel Solis and Cal Schrotenboer 2018

D. Solis and C. Schrotenboer, *Illustrated C# 7*, https://doi.org/10.1007/978-1-4842-3288-0_26

What's New

This chapter summarizes the changes made to the C# language since the previous revision of this book, which covered C# up through version 5.0. Most of these changes, however, are enhancements to existing functionality or alternate syntax for expressing a given construct in a slightly different manner. Therefore, understanding these changes requires an understanding of the existing functionality of the current syntax.

The main body of this book has been updated to include the impact of all the changes enumerated in this chapter. In some cases, such as for the nameof operator, the discussion in the main body is more extensive than given here, and in other cases the reverse is true. That is because of the nature of the coverage in the main body and the fact that certain concepts apply at more than one location. For example, where the new item actually represents a new feature in the C# language and thus a new section in the main body of the book, this chapter will include only a brief summary. For each feature, the section in this chapter states whether the primary discussion of the feature is in this chapter or can be found elsewhere in the text.

String Interpolation (C# 6.0)

The primary discussion of string interpolation is in Chapter 3. In addition, string interpolation has been used throughout the text, although not in all cases. Currently, the vast bulk of the C# code base uses the old-style string formatting. For this reason, we've used both forms throughout this text.

Chapter 3 described how to incorporate the value of variables into a format string using substitution markers, which consist of a set of curly braces containing a number. The number corresponds to a position in a comma-separated list of values at the end of the statement. The Console.WriteLine statement in the following code shows an example:

```
string myPet = "Spot";
int age     = 4;
string color = "black and white";
Console.WriteLine("My dog's name is {0}. He is {1} years old. His color is {2}.",
        myPet, age, color);
```

Not only is this syntax verbose but can be confusing when the numbers are out of sequence or are used multiple times. Moreover, as you can see, reading the WriteLine statement forces your eyes to move back and forth between the string and the list of replacement variables.

C# 6.0 simplified this construct with what is called *string interpolation*. This allows each set of curly braces to directly contain the replacement variable, as shown in the following statement:

```
Console.WriteLine(
    $"My dog's name is {myPet}. He is {age} years old. His color is {color}.");
```

To tell the compiler that the string must be interpreted using string interpolation, you must put the $ character in front of the first quotation mark. String interpolation retains the ability to use special formatting for numbers and dates using the same syntax as in `String.Format`.

```
double swanLakePrice = 100.0;
Console.WriteLine($"The cost of a ticket to the ballet is {swanLakePrice :C}");
```

This code produces the following output:

```
The cost of a ticket to the ballet is $100.00.
```

String interpolation doesn't just work with `Console.WriteLine`. It can be used in `String.Format`, as shown in the following code:

```
string name      = "Aiden";
string technology = "Cold Fusion";
string s;

s = String.Format("{0} is working on {1}.", name, technology);
Console.WriteLine(s);

s = String.Format($"{ name } is working on { technology }.");
Console.WriteLine(s);
```

This code produces the following output:

```
Aiden is working on Cold Fusion.
Aiden is working on Cold Fusion.
```

Auto-Property Initializers

This is the only discussion of auto-property initializers. As described in Chapter 6, auto-properties are a short form of property declaration where the compiler produces code for creating and managing an invisible backing field associated with the property. Previously, auto-properties could be initialized only in a constructor or in a method. Now they can also be initialized as part of the property declaration itself, as has always been the case for regular (nonauto) properties. Some developers prefer to perform all initializations in the constructor, and others prefer to perform the initializations in the property declaration. Now you have both these options for auto-properties as well.

```
public double Length { get; set; } = 42.5;
```

You can use this technique even with setters that are internal, protected, internal protected, or private.

```
private double Length { get; private set; } = 42.5;
```

This option is even available for read-only auto-properties, as described in the next section.

```
public double Length { get; } = 42.5;
```

Any expression can be used for an initializer provided that it can be resolved to a literal.

```
const  double myConstant         = 42;
public double Length { get; set; } = myConstant + .5;
```

On the other hand, initializers cannot refer to nonstatic properties, fields, or methods.

```
private double myField            = 42.5;
public double Length { get; set; } = myField;              // Compile error
    ...
private double myProperty { get; set; } = 42.5;
public  double Length     { get; set; } = myProperty;     // Compile error
    ...
```

An example of a good place to always initialize a new object is the case of collections. If you don't initialize a collection before attempting to add items to it, you'll get a null reference exception. For example, initializing the list in the following line of code sets it ready for use:

```
public List<double> Areas { get; set; } = new List<double>();  //ready for use
```

Auto-property initializers also apply to structs as long as the properties are static.

```
struct MyStruct
{
    static double Length  { get; set; } = 42.5;
    double        Length2 { get; set; } = 42.5;    // Compile error - not static
}
```

Read-Only Auto-Properties (C# 6.0)

Read-only auto properties are primarily discussed in Chapter 7.

Previously if you wanted to declare a read-only property, the closest you could come would have been to use a private setter. Although this prevents users of your class from changing the property's value, it could still be changed from other locations within your class.

```
public string CompanyName { get; private set; }
```

Now it is possible to simply omit the setter entirely. In this case, the property must be initialized either in the declaration (discussed in the next section) or in the constructor.

```
public string CompanyName { get; }
```

Getter-only auto-properties are available in both classes and structs. This is a welcome addition in the case of structs given the best-practice recommendation that structs be immutable.

Expression-Bodied Members (C# 6.0 and 7.0)

This is the primary discussion of expression-bodied members. This feature was introduced in C# 6.0 and extended to additional member types in C# 7.0.

Previously, the body of all methods and get properties consisted of the code, enclosed within a set of curly braces, and the curly braces were required. Now, however, we have another option in certain cases. If the body of the function consists of a single expression, we can use a short-form syntax called an *expression body*. Important characteristics of expression-bodied members are the following:

- The code must consist of a single expression, followed by a semicolon.

  - For member types that return a value, the evaluated value of the expression is used as the return value. For members that do not have return types, nothing is returned.

- There must be no beginning or ending curly braces.

- The lambda operator (=>) is used between the parameter list and the expression comprising the body of the function.

- In C# 6, the feature became available for methods and property get accessors. With C# 7, the availability of the feature was expanded to constructors, finalizers, property set accessors, and indexers.

For example, the following method declaration uses the original method body syntax that does not use expression body syntax. It consists of a statement between the curly braces.

```
public string GetWineGrowingRegion(string countryName, string regionName)
{
    return countryName + ":" + regionName;
}
```

Using the expression-bodied form, this code can be rewritten more succinctly as the following, with the lambda operator and no curly braces. Notice that the statement has been replaced by an expression.

```
public string GetWineGrowingRegion(string countryName, string regionName)
                                   => countryName + ":" + regionName;
```

The following shows an example of a read-only property:

```
public string MyFavoriteWineGrowingRegion => "Sonoma County";
```

You cannot use expression-bodied members with automatically implemented read/write properties. Nor is it permissible, in this context, to use accessor lists with an expression body.

```
public int AreaCode          { get; set; } = 408;
public int CentralOfficeCode { get; set; } = 428;
public int LineNumber        { get; set; } = 4208;
```
                         Accessor list.
                             ↓
```
public string PhoneNumber { get; }
              => $"({AreaCode}) {CentralOfficeCode}-{LineNumber}";  // Compile error
```
      No accessor list.
                             ↓
```
public string PhoneNumber
              => $"({AreaCode}) {CentralOfficeCode}-{LineNumber}";  // OK
```

using static (C# 6.0)

The primary discussion of the using static feature is in Chapter 7. It's also discussed in Chapter 22.

Before C# 6, if you wanted to use the static member of a class or struct, you had to include the class or struct name. For example, throughout this text we have been using the WriteLine method, which is a static member of the Console class. We've used this as shown in the following code:

```
using System;                    // System is the namespace
    ...
Console.WriteLine("Hello");      // Console is the class
Console.WriteLine("Goodbye");
```

It can get quite tedious, however, to qualify each of the method calls if it's used many times in a source file. C# 6 has reduced this inconvenience by introducing the using static feature. To use this feature, you include a using static statement at the top of the source file, where the using static keywords are followed by the fully qualified name of the class or struct that contains the static member. Now you can freely use any static members in that type, without having to preface them with the type name, as shown in the following code:

```
Using static System.Console;    // System is the namespace, Console is the class
    ...
WriteLine("Hello");             // Class name not needed
WriteLine("Goodbye");           // Class name not needed
```

You can use the using static feature with classes, structs, and enums.

The using static feature is particularly convenient with enums since enums have always required the type name prefaced to any of their members, and code typically tests agains many of the enum members, as shown in the following code where both the Saturday and Sunday members of enum DayOfWeek must be qualified with the enum name:

```
DateTime day = new DateTime(2020, 1, 25);
if (day.DayOfWeek == DayOfWeek.Monday    ||
    day.DayOfWeek == DayOfWeek.Tuesday   ||
    day.DayOfWeek == DayOfWeek.Wednesday ||
    day.DayOfWeek == DayOfWeek.Thursday  ||
    day.DayOfWeek == DayOfWeek.Friday)
```

You can make the code of the if statement significantly less verbose by using the using static statement, as shown in the following code:

```
using static System.DayOfWeek;
    ...
DateTime day = new DateTime(2020, 1, 25);
if (day.DayOfWeek == Monday    ||
    day.DayOfWeek == Tuesday   ||
    day.DayOfWeek == Wednesday ||
    day.DayOfWeek == Thursday  ||
    day.DayOfWeek == Friday)
```

Null Conditional Operator (C# 6.0)

The primary discussion of the null conditional operator is in Chapter 27.

The null conditional operator is designed to help prevent null reference exceptions that would arise when an attempt is made to access a member of a null object. For example, the following lines of code would both generate runtime exceptions if the Students array is null:

```
Student[] students     = null;
int studentCount       = students.Length;    // Produces an exception.
Student firstStudent = students[0];          // Produces an exception
```

You can use the null conditional operator to avoid the null reference exception, as shown in the following example:

```
int? studentCount      = students?.Length;
Student firstStudent = students?[0];
```

Using await in catch and finally (C# 6.0)

Using await in catch and finally blocks is also discussed in Chapter 21.

When the async/await construct was introduced in C# 5.0, you could not place await clauses in catch or finally blocks. This restriction has been removed.

As described in Chapter 23, you implement a catch block to respond to an exception arising in your code. One of the common tasks inside a catch block is to log information to a file for future reference by a developer assigned to investigate the exception. But writing to disk is a time-consuming process, and it might not be optimal to wait synchronously for the write operation to complete before continuing processing. With await operations now allowed, you can perform the logging asynchronously while continuing with processing.

A finally block contains code that you want executed regardless of whether an exception has occurred. Again, for performance reasons, you might want to execute some or all of these statements asynchronously.

In either case (a catch or finally block), if the asynchronous task generates an exception, it will be passed to the first applicable upstream block. In that case, the exception that originally triggered statement execution in the catch or finally block would be lost.

The nameof Operator (C# 6.0)

The primary description of the nameof operator is in Chapter 9, which deals with expressions and operators.

The nameof operator is a new operator that takes as its single parameter a variable name, a type name, or a member name. The operator returns the string representation of the name of its parameter. For example, when writing and debugging code, you might use the WriteLines in the following code to output to the console when execution enters and exits the method. This will allow you to follow the sequence of execution. This code will let you know whether execution entered the method and whether it exited the method.

```
static void SomeMethod()
{
    WriteLine($"SomeMethod: Entering");
        ...
    WriteLine($"SomeMethod: Exiting");
}
```

This is fine unless you use Visual Studio's Rename feature to change the name of the method. In this case, the method name strings in the WriteLine statements will no longer match the new method name. If, however, you use the nameof operator, as shown in the following code, the Rename operation will also automatically change the strings in the nameof parameter, and everything will remain in sync.

```
static void SomeMethod()
{
    WriteLine($"{nameof(SomeMethod)}: Entering");
        ...
    WriteLine($"{nameof(SomeMethod)}: Exiting");
}
```

Exception Filters (C# 6.0)

The primary discussion of exception filters is in Chapter 23.

Exception filters allow you to apply conditions to catch clauses in a manner similar to WHERE clauses in SQL or LINQ. The condition consists of any expression that can be resolved to a Boolean value, surrounded by parentheses. If the condition is satisfied, the code in the catch clause is executed; if the condition is not satisfied, the catch block is skipped. Be careful, however, because exception filters use the keyword when instead of the more common where. (As described in Chapter 18, the keyword where is used to provide constraints for generic classes.)

Common usages of exception filters would include testing the exception Message property to search for a particular case. It was already possible to specify the Type property of an exception for the catch block as its parameter. The following code shows an example of an exception filter for the catch clause. In this case, the catch body would be entered only if the string returned by the exception Message property contained the string "404".

```
try
{
    ...
}
catch (Exception ex) when (ex.Message.Contains("404"))
{
    ...
}
```

Previously, you would have had to use an if clause inside the catch block to check for the condition. Unfortunately, however, if the condition of the if clause is not met and you rethrow the exception, you lose the information about the original exception, namely, any information about variables in the call stack between the original throw point and the new throw point. If, however, you use an exception filter and the if condition is not satisfied, the original exception object remains unchanged.

```
try
{
    ...
}
catch (Exception ex) when
{
    if (ex.Message.Contains("404"))
    { ... }
    else
    {
        throw              // Lose original exception information
    }
}
```

Index Initializers (C# 6.0)

This is the only discussion of index initializers.

C# 6.0 introduced an additional syntax for initializing data structures with indexers, such as `Dictionary` objects. Previously to initiate such an object, you would supply the values as a list of ordered pairs at the end of the variable definition, as shown in the following code:

```
var favoriteCities = new Dictionary<int, string>
{
    {0, "Oxford"},
    {1, "Paris"},
    {2, "Barcelona"}
};
```

This code is equivalent to the following code, which calls the `Dictionary` constructor, followed by three calls to the Add method:

```
var favoriteCities = new Dictionary<int, string>();
favoriteCities.Add(0, "Oxford");
favoriteCities.Add(1, "Paris");
favoriteCities.Add(2, "Barcelona");
```

Since dictionaries have indexers, you can use the new index initialization syntax as follows:

```
var favoriteCities = new Dictionary<int, string>
{
    [0] = "Oxford",
    [1] = "Paris",
    [2] = "Barcelona"
};
```

This form is equivalent to the following code:

```
var favoriteCities = new Dictionary<int, string>();
favoriteCities[0]  = "Oxford";
favoriteCities[1]  = "Paris";
favoriteCities[2]  = "Barcelona";
```

These forms of initialization appear similar, but there are subtle differences. Collection initialization implicitly calls the collection's Add method, while index initialization does not call an Add method but instead assigns a value to the element specified by the index. While there is probably no practical impact of this difference in the case of a `Dictionary`, there are differences in other circumstances.

In the first place, collection initialization requires a collection that implements the IEnumerable interface and a public Add method. Index initialization requires neither of these. It only requires that the class (or struct) contain an indexer. This is obviously an advantage because classes don't implement the IEnumerable interface or lack an Add method.

An even more significant difference involves collections that do not automatically expand when using index initialization syntax. Consider the case of using index initialization with a `List` instead of a `Dictionary`, as in the following code:

```
var lstFavoriteCities = new List<string>();

lstFavoriteCities[0] = "Oxford";
lstFavoriteCities[1] = "Paris";
lstFavoriteCities[2] = "Barcelona";

Console.WriteLine(lstFavoriteCities[2]);
```

While this code will compile fine, at run time it will throw an `ArgumentOutOfRange` exception because the `List` object has no elements, and therefore you can't assign values to those nonexistent elements.

For collection types that would allow you to use either collection initialization or index initialization, such as `Dictionary`, you cannot combine the syntaxes in the same statement. For example, the following code will produce a compile error:

```
var favoriteCities = new Dictionary<int, string>
{
    {0, "Oxford"},
    [1] = "Paris",
    {2, "Barcelona"}
};
```

Finally, if your initializer contains duplicate indexes, later ones will overwrite earlier ones. For example, in the case of the following code, the resulting `Dictionary` will have only two elements, `Oxford` and `Barcelona`:

```
var favoriteCities = new Dictionary<int, string>
{
    [0] = "Oxford",
    [1] = "Paris",
    [1] = "Barcelona"
};
```

Extension Methods for Collection Initializers (C# 6.0)

This is the only discussion of using extension methods for collection initialization. Extension methods are discussed in Chapter 8.

When you create a collection in C#, you generally do it by using the new keyword, as in the following example:

```
var customers = new List<Customer>();
```

After this statement has executed, your list contains exactly zero customers. To actually put customers into your list, you can either use collection initialization or explicitly call the List's Add method, as shown in the following code:

```
var customer1 = new Customer(Name = "Willem", Age = 35);
var customer2 = new Customer(Name = "Sandra", Age = 32);

// Collection initialization
var customers = new List<Customer>() { customer1, customer2 };
```

Collection initialization works because after the compiler adds the code to call the constructor, it adds calls to the object's Add method for you. Other .NET collections such as Arrays and ObservableCollections also have an Add method and can therefore also use collection initialization.

Suppose, however, that you define your own custom collection that is a wrapper around a .NET collection. Your custom collection might not have an Add method. It might instead have a method with a different name that funnels objects to the internal collection's Add method.

Consider, for example, the case of a magazine publisher that has the following class representing the collection of its subscribers. As you can see, the actual collection is an internal object of type List. The Subscriptions class has a method called Subscribe but does not expose a public Add method.

```
public class Subscriptions : IEnumerable<Customer>
{
    private List<Customer> _subscribers = new List<Customer>();

    public void Subscribe(Customer c)
    {
        _subscribers.Add(c);
    }

    ... // Other members
}
```

Because the Subscriptions class doesn't have an Add method, the following line of code will fail:

```
var customers = new Subscription() { customer1, customer2 };
```

Starting with C# 6.0, however, you can make it work by implementing an extension method named Add to call the Subscribe method in the Subscriptions class. The following code shows the extension method:

```
public static class SubscriptionExtensions
{
    public static void Add( this Subscriptions s, Customer c ) // Extension method
    {
        s.Subscribe( c );
    }
}

public class Customer
{   public string Name{ get; set; } public Customer( string name ) { Name = name; }}

public class Subscriptions : IEnumerable<Customer>
{
    private List<Customer> mSubscribers = new List<Customer>();

    public IEnumerator<Customer> GetEnumerator()
    { return mSubscribers.GetEnumerator(); }

    IEnumerator IEnumerable.GetEnumerator()
    { throw new System.NotImplementedException(); }

    public void Subscribe( Customer c )
    {
        mSubscribers.Add( c );
    }
}

class Program
{
    public static void Main()
    {
        var customer1 = new Customer( "Willem" );
        var customer2 = new Customer( "Sandra" );

        // Collection initialization
        var customers = new Subscriptions() { customer1, customer2 };

        foreach ( Customer c in customers )
            WriteLine( $"Name: {c.Name}" );
    }
}
```

So although C# still requires a public Add method, this requirement can now be satisfied by an extension method. Note, however, that the requirement that the collection must support the IEnumerable interface has not been relaxed.

Improved Overload Resolution (C# 6.0)

This is the only discussion of improved overload resolution; for context, see Tables 21-1 and 21-2.

Finally, C# 6.0 added a feature that instructs the compiler to prefer Task.Run(Func<Task>()) over Task.Run(Action). Previously, this situation would have generated a compile error. The example given in the Microsoft documentation uses the following code:

```
static Task DoThings()
{
    return Task.FromResult(0);
}
Task.Run(DoThings);      //Previously Error due to ambiguity, now works fine
```

ValueTuples (C# 7.0)

The primary explanation of ValueTuples is contained in Chapter 27.

Although C# methods can return only a single return object, there are a number of techniques for returning multiple values to a calling scope. These include out and ref variables, class-level variables, custom classes or structs, anonymous classes, or tuples. Each of these techniques has its own set of advantages and disadvantages.

Essentially, a tuple is an ordered collection of elements that might or might not have the same data type. A tuple is just a convenient way to refer to and manipulate this collection of elements by using a comma-separated list surrounded by parentheses.

```
(string, int) CreateSampleTuple()
{
    return ("Paul", 39);
}

var myTuple = CreateSampleTuple();
Console.WriteLine($"Name:  { myTuple.Item1 }  Age: {myTuple.Item2}");
```

In general, tuples were easy to create but relatively inconvenient to use in the calling scope because the tuple's elements could be referred to only by the nondescriptive names Item1, Item2, and so on. Additionally, since tuples were classes, a reference type, they required processing cycles to be created on the heap and then later needed to be garbage collected when no longer referenced.

C# 7.0 introduced a new type called the ValueTuple, which is a struct, thereby enabling a performance gain over the Tuple. Moreover, elements belonging to a ValueTuple can be named, thereby making the code significantly clearer.

Pattern Matching with is (C# 7.0)

This is the primary discussion of pattern matching with the is operator. We'll start with a quick review of the function of the is operator.

The is operator is used to determine whether a particular object is of a specified type. Recall that C# supports both inheritance and interface implementation. Moreover, while any given class can directly inherit only from a single class, its parent class might in turn have inherited from another base class, and so on. And although C# does not permit multiple inheritance, any given class can implement any number of interfaces.

Given this complexity, the is operator is capable of testing not only for the current class type but also for any level of base class, as well as whether any specified interface is supported. The following sample program illustrates these points:

```
public interface IOne
{
    int SampleIntProperty { get; set; }
}
public interface ITwo
{
    int SampleIntProperty2 { get; set; }
}
public class BaseClass
{
    public string SampleStringProperty { get; set; }
}
public class DerivedClass : BaseClass, IOne, ITwo
{
    public int SampleIntProperty  { get; set; }
    public int SampleIntProperty2 { get; set; }
}

class Program
{
    static void Main(string[] args)
    {
        var dc = new DerivedClass();
        if (dc is DerivedClass)
        { Console.WriteLine("Derived Class found"); }

        if (dc is BaseClass)
        { Console.WriteLine("Base Class found"); }

        if (dc is IOne)
        { Console.WriteLine("Interface One found"); }

        if (dc is ITwo)
        { Console.WriteLine("Interface Two found"); }
    }
}
```

This code produces the following output:

```
Derived Class found
Base Class found
Interface One found
Interface Two found
```

After testing whether a given object is of a particular type, it has previously been necessary to then cast that object to the specified type if you wanted a reference to that type.

```
if(myEmployee is Supervisor)
{
    var mySupervisor = (Supervisor)myEmployee;
    // Proceed to access Supervisor class members
}
```

It was also possible to implement casting of this sort using the as operator.

```
var mySupervisor = myEmployee as Supervisor;
if (mySupervisor != null)
{
    // Proceed to access Supervisor class members
}
```

With C# 7, the is operator type syntax has been simplified, and the assignment can automatically take place in a variable placed immediately after the test class (or other type). The enhanced is operator not only tests the type of a variable but, if the variable passes that test, simultaneously assigns it to a new variable of the specified type. This new variable is called the *match variable*.

```
if (myEmployee is Supervisor mySupervisor)
{
    // The mySupervisor variable is immediately available for use, provided
    // that the is test is satisfied.
    Console.WriteLine($"My supervisor's name is { mySupervisor.Name }");
}
```

In fact, this newly assigned match variable is even available *in the expression* containing the is test.

```
If (myEmployee is Supervisor mySupervisor && mySupervisor.Name == "Fred") ...
```

The match variable is only in scope in the test block.

```
If (myEmployee is Supervisor mySupervisor)
{
    // mySupervisor variable is in scope here
}
Console.WriteLine($"My supervisor's name is { mySupervisor.Name }"); //Error
                                                // mySupervisor is out of scope
                                                here
```

The is operator now also works with value types as well as reference types. This means that you can now test for structs as well as classes.

Pattern Matching with switch (C# 7.0)

The primary discussion of pattern matching with switch is in Chapter 10. The following is a summary.

In general, a switch statement is preferable to a long sequence of if else statements. C# 7.0 has made a number of significant improvements to the switch statement. The new features of the switch statement expand its previous capabilities.

Previously, switch statements were restricted to compile-time constants. These consisted of the following: char, string, bool, integer (including byte, int, or long), or enum. Now the switch statement is no longer limited to only these constants. Instead, you can now test using types of any sort, including user-defined types: class, struct, array, enum, delegate, and interface. Any of these types can now be used in a switch statement, as shown in the following example:

```csharp
using static System.Console;

public abstract class Investment
{
    public string Name          { get; set; }
    public double MinPurchaseAmt { get; set; }
}

public class Stock       : Investment { }
public class Bond        : Investment { }
public class BankAccount : Investment { }
public class RealEstate  : Investment { }

class Program
{
    static void Main()
    {
        var myStock = new Stock() { Name = "Tesla", MinPurchaseAmt = 1000 };
        var myBond  = new Bond()  { Name = "California Municipal", MinPurchaseAmt = 500 };
        var myBankAccount  = new BankAccount() { Name = "ABC Bank", MinPurchaseAmt = 10 };
        var myBankAccount2 = new BankAccount() { Name = "XYZ Bank", MinPurchaseAmt = 20 };
        var myRealEstate   =
                new RealEstate() { Name = "My Vacation Home", MinPurchaseAmt = 100_000 };

        CheckInvestmentType(myStock);
        CheckInvestmentType(myBond);
        CheckInvestmentType(myBankAccount);
        CheckInvestmentType(myBankAccount2);
        myBankAccount2 = null;
        CheckInvestmentType(myBankAccount2);
        CheckInvestmentType(myRealEstate);
    }
```

```
public static void CheckInvestmentType (Investment investment)
{
    switch (investment)
    {
        case Stock stock:
            WriteLine($"This investment is a stock named {stock.Name}");
            break;
        case Bond bond:
            WriteLine($"This investment is a bond named {bond.Name}");
            break;
        case BankAccount bankAccount when bankAccount.Name.Contains("ABC") :
            WriteLine($"This investment is my ABC Bank account");
            break;
        case BankAccount bankAccount:
            WriteLine($"This investment is any bank account other than ABC Bank");
            break;
        case null:
            WriteLine("For whatever reason, this investment is null. ");
            break;
        default:
            WriteLine("The default case will always be evaluated last. ");
            WriteLine("Even if its position is not last.");
            break;
    }
}
```

This code produces the following output:

```
Notice the numeric separator in the previous line
Notice the using static declaration, above.
This investment is a stock named Tesla
This investment is a bond named California Municipal
This investment is my ABC Bank account
This investment is any bank account other than ABC Bank
For whatever reason, this investment is null.
The default case will always be evaluated last.
Even if its position is not last.
```

All type patterns have an implicit when clause with the condition when [type] is not null. This prevents the first type in the switch statement from matching any null value, thereby triggering the statements in its switch block, most likely with undesirable results. You can either add a special case statement to handle null cases or allow null cases to be handled in the default block. Notice that in the preceding example when myBankAccount2 was null, it did not match on case BankAccount bankAccount.

Unlike previously, the order of case statements now matters. Before C# 7.0, all cases had to contain constant values. Since these values were always mutually exclusive, their sequence was unimportant. Now that switch statement cases can often overlap with other cases, order becomes important. It is now necessary to put all specific cases earlier in the list than more general cases. In the previous example, it was imperative that the case BankAccount bankAccount when bankAccount.Name.Contains("ABC") preceded the generic case for BankAccount. If the order had been reversed, the compiler would have generated a compile error.

Notice also the use of the when keyword as a filter on the case statement to limit its applicability to a subset of the general condition. This is essentially taking on the "pattern matching with is" semantics. Moreover, you can use a match variable in the accompanying when clause because the when clause will be evaluated only if the variable has been populated.

There is, however, one exception to the new rule that case order matters: the default case. The default case will always be evaluated last regardless of where it appears in the list. Accordingly, you should put the default case last, so as not to give the mistaken impression that it might be evaluated at a different point.

Custom Deconstruct (C# 7.0)

This is the primary discussion of custom deconstruction.

When ValueTuples were added to C#, one of the features for this new data structure was the ability to deconstruct the ValueTuple into its component elements in a calling scope. The following example illustrates how this works:

```
public static (string name, string course) GetStudentEnrollmentInfo(int id)
{
    // Retrieve values from database
    return ("Connor", "Computer Science");
}

// In the calling scope
var student = GetStudentEnrollmentInfo(49);
Console.WriteLine($"Student name:  { student.name } Course: { student.course }");
```

Without the deconstruct feature, it would have been necessary to refer to the ValueTuple's elements by the nondescriptive names Item1, Item2, and so on.

```
Console.WriteLine($"Student name:  { student.Item1 } Course: { student.Item2 }");
```

This deconstruction applies when the ValueTuple has been returned from a method. It's not necessary if it has been constructed in the current scope.

```
(string name, string course) myValueTuple = ("Daniel", "Particle Physics");
Console.WriteLine
    ($"Student name:  { myValueTuple.name }   Course: { myValueTuple.course }");
```

This deconstruction feature is not limited to ValueTuples. Any type can be deconstructed provided that it implements a Deconstruct method that uses the appropriate out parameters.

```
public class GeoLocation
{
    public double Latitude   { get; set; }
    public double Longitude  { get; set; }
    public string NorthSouth { get; set; }
    public string EastWest   { get; set; }

    public GeoLocation(double latitude, string northSouth,
                       double longitude, string eastWest)
    {
        Latitude   = latitude;
        NorthSouth = northSouth;
        Longitude  = longitude;
        EastWest   = eastWest;
    }
}
```

```
public void Deconstruct(out double latitude, out string northSouth,
                        out double longitude, out string eastWest)
   {
      latitude   = Latitude;
      northSouth = NorthSouth;
      longitude  = Longitude;
      eastWest   = EastWest;
   }
}
   ...
(double latitude, string northSouth, double longitude, string eastWest) =
                           new GeoLocation(51.4769, "N", 0.0, "W");
Console.WriteLine("The Greenwich Observatory is located at {0}{1}, {2}{3}.",
      latitude, northSouth, longitude, eastWest);
```

It even works if the deconstruct method is an extension method. (Extension methods are discussed in detail in Chapter 8.) This can be useful if the class is a sealed class to which you have no access. Imagine that the GeoLocation class in the previous example did not have a Deconstruct method and you were unable to add one to that class. In that case, you could define the following extension method to provide the necessary support for deconstruction:

```
public static class Extensions
{
   public static void Deconstruct(this GeoLocation geoLocation,
               out double latitude,  out string northSouth,
               out double longitude, out string eastWest)
   {
      latitude   = geoLocation.Latitude;
      northSouth = geoLocation.NorthSouth;
      longitude  = geoLocation.Longitude;
      eastWest   = geoLocation.EastWest;
   }
}
   ...

(double latitude, string northSouth, double longitude, string eastWest) =
                           new GeoLocation(40.6892, "N", 74.0445, "W");
Console.WriteLine("The Statue of Liberty in New York is located at {0}{1}, {2}{3}.",
         latitude, northSouth, longitude, eastWest);
```

Binary Literals and Numeric Separators (C# 7.0)

The primary discussion of binary literals and numeric separators is in Chapter 9.

C# previously already had hex notation for expressing integer type values. A hex representation of an integer begins with the two-character string 0x or 0X. Hex numbers are commonly used to represent colors or memory locations. The following is an example of a color specification:

```
const int fillColor = 0xff0517AF;        //Equivalent to 4278523823 (base 10)
```

C# 7.0 added binary literal notation so that you can now represent an integer as a series of 0s and 1s. A binary representation of an integer begins with the two-character string 0b or 0B. Colors represented in hex typically contain two-character blocks, where each block represents one of the color components: transparency (optional), red, green, and blue. The fill color value specified previously would have the following components expressed in binary:

```
int transparency = 0b11111111;
int red          = 0b00000101;
int green        = 0b00010111;
int blue         = 0b10101111;
```

Because binary notation is quite verbose, it can often be difficult to read. To make things easier, you can now insert any number of underscores as visual numeric separators.

The following shows the same values using numeric separators:

```
int transparency2 = 0b11_11_11_11;
int red2          = 0b0000_0101;
int green2        = 0b0001_0111;
int blue2         = 0b1010_1111;
```

You cannot, however, use a numeric separator next to the binary prefix character as in 0b_1111_1111. The following is a color specification in component form, expressed in hex:

```
int transparency3 = 0xff;
int red3          = 0x05;
int green3        = 0x17;
int blue3         = 0xAF;
```

Notice that the data type in all of these examples is int. Binary and hex notation are simply ways of expressing these integer values. You can confirm this by printing out each value, as shown here:

```
Console.WriteLine("Binary:  " + transparency);
Console.WriteLine("Binary with separators:  " + transparency2);
Console.WriteLine("Hex:  " + transparency3);
```

This produces the following output:

```
Binary: 255
Binary with separators: 255
Hex: 255
```

Binary notation also works with other members of the integer (nonfloating type) family of data types such as byte, sbyte, short, ushort, uint, long, and ulong.

Numeric separators can also be used with *any* type of number, not just hex or binary and not just integers.

```
long currentEstimatedNoOfGalaxiesInUniverse = 1_800_000_000_000;  //1.8 trillion
decimal myDesiredBankAccount = 9_999_999.99M;
```

Numeric separators are significant only for viewing a number in code. They do not affect the value of the number or how it is displayed when printed out.

```
Console.WriteLine(currentEstimatedNoOfGalaxiesInUniverse);
Console.WriteLine($"My desired bank account: ${myDesiredBankAccount}");
```

Printing these values produces the following output:

```
1800000000000
My desired bank account: $9999999.99
```

There are, however, a number of constraints in the use of numeric separators. You cannot use a binary separator in the following situations:

- As either the first or last character in any number. Prohibited: _0001_0110 or 0001_0110_ OK: 0001_0110

- Either before or after a decimal point. Prohibited: 11_.11 or 11._11 OK: 1_1.11 or 11.1_1

- Either before or after an exponential character. Prohibited: 22.2_e2 or 22.2e_2 OK: 2_2.2e2 or 2.2e2_2

- Either before or after a type specifier Prohibited: float x = 10.7_f; or decimal y = 33.33m_;

- Either before or after a hexadecimal or binary prefix character Prohibited: 0_x10AD or 0x_10AD or 0_b1011 or 0b_1011 OK: 0x10_AD or 0b10_11)

Out Variables (C# 7.0)

The principal discussion of output parameters is in Chapter 6.

C# 7.0 made a small syntactic change to the treatment of out variables. As you know, out variables are one way of returning more than one value from a method. (Other options are ref variables, tuples, and class data members such as fields or properties.)

Previously, the out variable had to be declared before the call to the method in which it is used. Now you can skip the separate declaration and instead declare the out variable in the method argument list. Even though this out variable is declared within the scope of the method, it is nevertheless available throughout the containing block.

Since the out parameter is not declared on a separate line, it is not possible to inadvertently assign it a value, which would, in any event, be ignored within the method. Nor is it possible to accidentally try to use the variable before the method is called.

A common usage for out parameters is the TryParse family of methods, which return a bool value indicating success or failure, along with an out parameter that is populated with a value only if the parse was successful. The following code shows an example of the new syntax and semantics:

```
public int? OutParameterSampleMethod()
{
    if (!int.TryParse(input, out int result))
    {
        return null;
    }
    return result;
}
```

While syntactically you can use var notation instead of specifying the actual datatype of the out variable, you should use this with caution (or not at all) and only when the data type will be evident to any developer with responsibility to maintain your code. For example, the following code illustrates the ambiguity. The out parameters are declared as var types. But even in this simple case the types of both age and supervisorId are ambiguous. Both might be integers, but they might also be strings. Specifying the actual data type would eliminate any possibility for confusion.

```
public void GetEmployeeDetails
                  (int employeeId, out var name, out var age, out var supervisorId)
{
    // Logic assigning values to name, age and employeeId
}
```

All out variables that are declared inline must be assigned a value inside the method. However, if a method has any variables about which you don't care, you can use the discard character (_) to signal that intention. The following code calls the GetEmployeeDetails method but asks for only name and supervisorId values.

```
GetEmployeeDetails(employeeId, out string name, out _, out int supervisorId);
```

Local Functions (C# 7.0)

The primary discussion of local functions is in Chapter 6.

Assume that you have a small method that you only need to call from one specific other method. The normal place for method declarations is directly within the class. To restrict access to that method, you would normally make it private, which would prevent it from being called from any class other than the one in which it is declared. In that case, even classes derived from your class could not call your private function, but it could still be called from anywhere within the class itself. Moreover, since your method would be in scope from anywhere within your class, it would automatically be included in IntelliSense, thereby adding unnecessary noise to the list of members.

To guarantee that your method cannot be called from any other location—as well as making access to it convenient for review or maintenance—you can now place the method directly in the body of the method from which it is called. These are called *local functions* and can even be placed in a constructor or in either the getter or setter of a property.

```
static void Main()
{
    List<string> data = GetDataFromDb();
    foreach(var item in data)
    {
Console.WriteLine(ReplaceEmptyStringWithElipsis(item));
    }
    string ReplaceEmptyStringWithElipsis(string input)
    {
        if(string.IsNullOrEmpty(input)) return "...";
        return input;
    }
}
```

Inside the code, the ReplaceEmptyStringWithElipsis method can be useful if you are exporting a report to Excel and would like empty cells to contain ".." instead of just being blank. Since most, if not all, reports have more than one column, you would likely want to call this method multiple times from within the method that inserts your data into Excel. Making this method a local function is convenient because it places the method immediately adjacent to the place where it is used.

Local functions have all the capabilities of regular methods, including the ability to be asynchronous, generic, or dynamic. In addition, local functions can access any variables that are available in their containing scope. Since these variables are passed to the local function by reference, if they are modified within the local function, the new value will persist in the calling scope.

```
class Program
{
    static void Main()
    {
        var corvette = GetRemainingRange(.25, 24, "British");
        Console.WriteLine($"Remaining range is {corvette.distance} {corvette.units}");

        var prius = GetRemainingRange(.04, 12, "Metric");
        Console.WriteLine($"Remaining range is {prius.distance} {prius.units}");
    }

    // This method returns a ValueTuple.
    public static (double distance, string units) GetRemainingRange
            (double fuelConsumptionRate, double remainingFuel, string systemOfUnits)
    {
        string units = string.Empty;

        switch (systemOfUnits)
        {
            case "Metric":
                units = "Kilometers";
                break;
```

```
        case "British":
            units = "Miles";
            break;
    }
    //Notice that this local function has no parameters
    double CalculateRemainingRange()
    {
        return remainingFuel / fuelConsumptionRate;
    }
    return (CalculateRemainingRange(), units);
    }
}
```

This code produces the following output:

```
Remaining range is 96 Miles
Remaining range is 300 Kilometers
```

You cannot use an access specifier with a local function since access is implicitly confined to the calling scope. Also, while a local function can be declared within a static method, you cannot use the static keyword with the local function.

You can position a local function at any place within the body of its calling method. You do not have to define it before it can be used. At run time, the compiler converts your local function into a private method, thereby making the location irrelevant.

While there is no specific limit regarding the length of a local function, it's really just intended for simple methods. Since local functions don't allow you to do anything you couldn't already do using other constructs, the key determinants of whether to use a local functions is whether it adds clarity or convenience.

Ref Locals (Ref Variables) and Ref Returns (C# 7.0)

Since both ref locals and ref returns are new features of C# and not a refinement of an existing feature, they are discussed in detail in a new section at the end of Chapter 13.

C# has long permitted a variable to be passed to a method by reference instead of by value. In such a case, any changes to that variable within the method are reflected in the calling scope. C# 7.0 has extended this treatment to allow a method to pass a reference to some storage location as the return value of that method. This returned reference can be stored in a variable, which is then referred to as a *ref local* or *ref variable*. A ref variable holds a pointer to a storage location instead of the actual value residing at that location. As such, any subsequent changes made to that ref variable in the calling scope will change the value at the referenced storage location.

The main purpose of introducing ref returns and ref variables is to enhance performance by allowing direct changes to a value in a given storage location instead of requiring that value to first be copied one or more times.

More Expression-Bodied Members (C# 7.0)

This is the primary discussion of the C# 7.0 expression body extensions.

As previously mentioned in the discussion of new C# 6.0 features, the term *expression-bodied member* refers to a short-form syntax where a single-line statement is introduced with the lambda symbol (=>) instead of being placed in a set of curly braces. C# 6.0 allowed expression-bodied members only with respect to methods and read-only properties. C# 7.0 extends this and now permits expression-bodied members in constructors, in destructors, and in the get and set accessors of properties and indexers, as shown in the following code:

```
//Constructor
public MyClass (string var1) => this.Var1 = var1;

//Destructor
~MyClass() => Console.WriteLine( "Unmanaged resources have been released ");

public string Area
{
  get => mArea;
  set => mArea = value;
}
```

If either the set or get accessor requires multiple statements, the conventional syntax is required for both of them.

Throw Expressions (C# 7.0)

The primary discussion of throw expressions is in Chapter 23.

The throw keyword is used to trigger an exception to indicate an error state. For example, when Visual Studio autocreates a new method for you, it always includes the following one line of code inside that new method:

```
throw new NotImplementedException();
```

This line of code is a statement, not an expression. Recall that a statement is a source code instruction that tells a program to perform an action. An expression is a sequence of operators and operands that returns a value.

Since the pre-C# 7.0 throw keyword was permitted only in statements, it could not be used in certain situations where an expression was required. Examples of these situations include conditional expressions, null coalescing expressions, and some lambda expressions. Even though throw expressions have the identical syntax to throw statements, they can now be used in any of these formerly unavailable situations.

One of the most common examples where throw expressions will be useful involves the null coalescing operator. This operator, which is covered in Chapter 27, has two operands, both of which must be expressions. The first operand is nullable, and when it resolves to null, the second, non-nullable expression, is used instead. Previously, since throw only took the form of a statement, it could not be used as the second operand.

```
bool? success = LoadResource();
var resourceLoadResult =
        success ?? throw new InvalidOperationException("Resource load failed");
```

Expanded Async Return Types (C# 7.0)

Although this is the primary discussion of expanded async return types, they are mentioned throughout the discussion of async/await in Chapter 21.

Prior to C# 7.0 async methods were limited to only three return types: Task (where the async operation does not return a value), void (for use in void asynchronous event handlers), and Task<TResult>. Now async methods can also return any type that has an accessible GetAwaiter method.

As a practical matter, since creating a satisfactory "task-like" type satisfies the new requirements is a complex task, in most cases the newly permissible return type will be a ValueTask<TResult>. To use that type, you must add the System.Threading.Tasks.Extensions NuGet package to your project.

Unlike Task and Task<TResult>, which are both reference types, ValueTask<TResult> is a value type and therefore resides on the stack instead of on the heap. The purpose of ValueTasks is to improve performance in certain cases where the return value is known without needing to perform the asynchronous operation, which otherwise would be awaited. This can happen, for example, if the return value is retrieved from the cached store of a previous invocation.

CHAPTER 27

■ ■ ■

Other Topics

© Daniel Solis and Cal Schrotenboer 2018

D. Solis and C. Schrotenboer, *Illustrated C# 7*, https://doi.org/10.1007/978-1-4842-3288-0_27

Overview

In this chapter, we'll cover a number of other topics that are important in using C# but that don't fit neatly into one of the other chapters. These include string handling, nullable types, the Main method, documentation comments, and nested types.

Strings

The BCL provides a number of classes that make string handling easy. The C# predefined type string represents the .NET class System.String. The most important things to know about strings are the following:

- Strings are arrays of Unicode characters.

- Strings are immutable—they cannot be changed.

The string type has many useful string-manipulation members. Table 27-1 shows some of the most useful members.

Table 27-1. *Useful Members of the string Type*

Member	Type	Meaning
Length	Property	Returns the length of the string.
Concat	Static method	Returns a string that is the concatenation of its argument strings.
Contains	Method	Returns a bool value indicating whether the argument is a substring of the object string.
Format	Static method	Returns a formatted string.
Insert	Method	Takes as parameters a string and a position and creates and returns a new copy of the object string, with the parameter string inserted at the given position.
Remove	Method	Returns a copy of the string in which a substring has been removed.
Replace	Method	Returns a copy of the string in which a substring has been replaced.
Split	Method	Returns an array of strings that contains substrings from the original string. For an input parameter, you supply the method with a set of delimiters that separate the desired substrings.
Substring	Method	Retrieves a substring from the string.
ToLower	Method	Returns a copy of the string in which the alphabetic characters are all lowercase.
ToUpper	Method	Returns a copy of the string in which the alphabetic characters are all uppercase.

The names of many of the methods in Table 27-1 sound as if they're changing the string object. Actually, they're not changing the strings but returning new copies. For a string, any "change" allocates a new immutable string.

For example, the following code declares and initializes a string called s. The first WriteLine statement calls the ToUpper method on s, which returns a copy of the string in all uppercase. The last line prints out the value of s, showing that it's unchanged.

```
string s = "Hi there.";

Console.WriteLine($"{ s.ToUpper() }");        // Print uppercase copy
Console.WriteLine($"{ s }");                  // String is unchanged
```

This code produces the following output:

```
HI THERE.
Hi there.
```

In our own coding, one of the methods listed in the table that we find very useful is the Split method. It splits a string into a set of substrings and returns them in an array. You pass the method an array of delimiters that are used to determine where to split the string, and you can specify what it should do with empty elements in the output array. The original string, of course, remains unchanged.

The following code shows an example of using the Split method. In this example, the set of delimiters consists of the space character and four punctuation marks.

```
class Program {
   static void Main() {
      string s1 = "hi there! this, is: a string.";
      char[] delimiters = { ' ', '!', ',', ':', '.' };
      string[] words = s1.Split( delimiters, StringSplitOptions.RemoveEmptyEntries );
      Console.WriteLine($"Word Count: { words.Length }\n\rThe Words...");
      foreach ( string s in words )
         Console.WriteLine($"   { s }");
   }
}
```

This code produces the following output:

```
Word Count: 6
The Words...
   hi
   there
   this
   is
   a
   string
```

The StringBuilder Class

The StringBuilder class helps you dynamically and efficiently produce strings while reducing the number of copies being made.

- The StringBuilder class is a member of the BCL, in namespace System.Text.

- A StringBuilder object is a *mutable* array of Unicode characters.

For example, the following code declares and initializes a StringBuilder object and prints its resulting string value. The fourth line changes the actual object by replacing part of the internal array of characters. Now when you print its string value by implicitly calling ToString, you can see that, unlike an object of type string, the StringBuilder object actually changes.

```
using System;
using System.Text;

class Program
{
    static void Main()
    {
        StringBuilder sb = new StringBuilder( "Hi there." );
        Console.WriteLine($"{ sb.ToString() }");              // Print string.

        sb.Replace( "Hi", "Hello" );                          // Replace a substring.
        Console.WriteLine($"{ sb.ToString() }");              // Print changed string.
    }
}
```

This code produces the following output:

```
Hi there.
Hello there.
```

When a StringBuilder object is created based on a given string, the class allocates a buffer longer than the actual current string length. As long as the changes made to the string can fit in the buffer, no new memory is allocated. If changes to the string require more space than is available in the buffer, a new, larger buffer is allocated, and the characters are copied to it. Like the original buffer, this new buffer also has extra space.

To get the string corresponding to the StringBuilder content, you simply call its ToString method.

Parsing Strings to Data Values

Strings are arrays of Unicode characters. For example, string "25.873" is six characters long and is *not* a number. Although it looks like a number, you cannot perform arithmetic functions on it. "Adding" two strings produces their concatenation.

- *Parsing* allows you to take a string that *represents* a value and convert it into an actual, typed value.

- All the predefined, simple types have a static method called Parse, which takes a string representing a value and converts it into an actual value of the type.

- If the string cannot be parsed, the system raises an exception.

The following statement shows an example of the syntax of using a Parse method. Notice that Parse is static, so you need to invoke it by using the name of the target type.

```
double d1 = double.Parse("25.873");
             ↑              ↑
        Target type    String to be converted
```

The following code shows an example of parsing two strings to values of type double and then adding them:

```
static void Main()
{
   string s1 = "25.873";
   string s2 = "36.240";

   double d1 = double.Parse(s1);
   double d2 = double.Parse(s2);

   double total = d1 + d2;
   Console.WriteLine($"Total:  { total }");
}
```

This code produces the following output:

Total: 62.113

■ **Note**   A common misconception about Parse is that since it operates on a string, it is thought of as a member of the string class. It is not. Parse is not a single method at all, but a number of methods implemented by the *target* types.

The disadvantage of the Parse methods is that they throw an exception if they can't successfully parse the string to the target type. Exceptions are expensive operations, and you should try to programmatically avoid them if you can. The TryParse method allows you to do that. The important things to know about TryParse are the following:

- Every built-in type that has a Parse method also has a TryParse method.

- The TryParse method takes two parameters and returns a bool.

  - The first parameter is the string you're trying to parse.

  - The second is an out parameter of a reference to a variable of the target type.

  - If TryParse succeeds, the parsed value is assigned to the out parameter, and it returns true. Otherwise, it returns false.

In general, you should use TryParse rather than Parse to avoid possibly throwing an exception. The following code shows two examples of using the int.TryParse method:

```
class Program
{
    static void Main( )
    {
        string parseResultSummary;
        string stringFirst = "28";
        int intFirst;                    Input string      Output variable
                                              ↓                 ↓
        bool success = int.TryParse( stringFirst, out intFirst );

        parseResultSummary = success
                           ? "was successfully parsed"
                           : "was not successfully parsed";
        Console.WriteLine($"String { stringFirst } { parseResultSummary }");

        string stringSecond = "vt750";
        int intSecond;           Input string      Output variable
                                     ↓                 ↓
        success = int.TryParse( stringSecond, out intSecond );

        parseResultSummary = success
                           ? "was successfully parsed"
                           : "was not successfully parsed";
        Console.WriteLine($"String { stringSecond } { parseResultSummary }" );
    }
}
```

This code produces the following output:

```
String 28 was successfully parsed
String vt750 was not successfully parsed
```

More About the Nullable Types

In Chapter 4 you got a quick description of nullable types. As you'll remember, nullable types allow you to create a value type variable that can be marked as valid or invalid, effectively letting you set a value type variable to null. We wanted to introduce nullable types in Chapter 4 with the other built-in types, but now that you know more about C#, it's a good time to cover their more intricate aspects.

Just to review, a nullable type is always based on another type, called the *underlying type*, that has already been declared.

- You can create a nullable type from any value type, including the predefined, simple types.

- You cannot create a nullable type from a reference type or another nullable type.

- You do not explicitly declare a nullable type in your code. Instead, you declare a *variable of a nullable type*. The compiler implicitly creates the nullable type for you.

To create a variable of a nullable type, simply add a question mark to the end of the name of the underlying type, in the variable declaration. Unfortunately, this syntax makes it appear that you have a lot of questions about your code. (Just kidding—but it is kind of ugly.)

For example, the following code declares a variable of the nullable int type. Notice that the suffix is attached to the *type* name—not the variable name.

```
Suffix
  ↓
int? myNInt = 28;
  ↑
The name of the nullable type includes the suffix.
```

With this declaration statement, the compiler takes care of producing both the nullable type and the variable of that type. Figure 27-1 shows the structure of this nullable type. It contains the following:

- An instance of the underlying type

- Several important read-only properties

  - Property HasValue is of type bool and indicates whether the value is valid.

  - Property Value is the same type as the underlying type and returns the value of the variable—if the variable is valid.

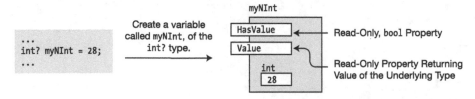

Figure 27-1. *A nullable type contains an object of the underlying type in a struct, with two read-only properties*

Using a nullable type is almost the same as using a variable of any other type. Reading a variable of a nullable type returns its value. You must, however, make sure that the variable is not null. Attempting to read the value of a null variable produces an exception.

- As with any variable, to retrieve its value, you just use its name.

- To check whether a nullable type has a value, you can compare it to null or check its HasValue property.

```
int? myInt1 = 15;
        Compare to null.
            ↓
if ( myInt1 != null )
    Console.WriteLine("{0}", myInt1);
                      ↑
                Use variable name.
```

15

You can easily convert between a nullable type and its corresponding non-nullable type. The important things you need to know about nullable type conversions are the following:

- There is an *implicit* conversion between a non-nullable type and its nullable version. That is, no cast is needed.

- There is an *explicit* conversion between a nullable type and its non-nullable version.

For example, the following lines show conversion in both directions. In the first line, a literal of type int is implicitly converted to a value of type int? and is used to initialize the variable of the nullable type. In the second line, the variable is explicitly converted to its non-nullable version.

```
int? myInt1 = 15;            // Implicitly convert int (15) to int?
int  regInt = (int) myInt1;  // Explicitly convert int? to int
```

Assigning to a Nullable Type

You can assign three kinds of values to a variable of a nullable type:

- A value of the underlying type
- A value of the same nullable type
- The value null

The following code shows an example of each of the three types of assignment:

```
int? myI1, myI2, myI3;

myI1 = 28;                              // Value of underlying type
myI2 = myI1;                            // Value of nullable type
myI3 = null;                            // null

Console.WriteLine( $"myI1: { myI1 }, myI2: { myI2 }, myI3: { myI3 }" );
```

This code produces the following output:

```
myI1: 28, myI2: 28, myI3:
```

The Null Coalescing Operator

The standard arithmetic and comparison operators also handle nullable types. There is also a special operator called the *null coalescing operator*, which returns a non-null value to an expression, in case a nullable type variable is null.

The null coalescing operator consists of two contiguous question marks and has two operands.

- The first operand is a variable of a nullable type.

- The second is a non-nullable value of the underlying type.

- If, at run time, the first operand (the nullable operand) evaluates to null, the non-nullable operand is returned as the result of the expression.

```
                            Null coalescing operator
                                       ↓
int? myI4 = null;
Console.WriteLine("myI4: {0}", myI4 ?? -1);

myI4 = 10;
Console.WriteLine("myI4: {0}", myI4 ?? -1);
```

This code produces the following output:

```
myI4: -1
myI4: 10
```

When comparing two values of the same nullable type and both are null, the equality comparison operators (== and !=) consider them equal. For example, in the following code, the two nullable ints are set to null. The equality comparison operator declares them equal.

```
int? i1 = null, i2 = null;               // Both are null.

if (i1 == i2)                            // Operator returns true.
    Console.WriteLine("Equal");
```

This code produces the following output:

```
Equal
```

The Null Conditional Operator

If you have a reference variable that is null and you attempt to access a member through that null reference, the program will throw a NullReferenceException. One way to avoid this is to use the two-step process of first checking whether the reference is null and then using it only if it is not null. The null conditional operator, which consists of the two-character string ?., allows you to perform the operation in a single step. It checks whether the reference variable is null or contains an object reference. If it's null, the operator returns null. If it's not null, it accesses the member.

The following code shows the two methods:

```
Student[] students = null;
int? studentCount = 5;

if ( students != null )                 // Checking for null before accessing
    studentCount = students.Length;     // Accessing non-null reference
Console.WriteLine( $"studentCount: { studentCount }" );

studentCount = students?.Length;        // Using the null conditional operator
Console.WriteLine( $"studentCount: { studentCount }" );
```

The results are the following:

```
studentCount: 5
studentCount:
```

In looking at the code, we notice that the forms are not completely equivalent.

- If students is non-null, then the two-step process and the null conditional operator both execute the Length property of array students and assign the value to studentCount.

- If students is null, then the following is true:

    - The two-step process makes no assignment to studentCount.

    - The null conditional operator assigns null to studentCount.

There is a second form of the operator that is used with arrays or indexes. When using it in this case, you omit the period character and follow the question mark immediately with the left bracket of the index indicator. The following line of code shows this form:

```
Student student = students?[7];
```

In this code, if the array students is not null, then the eighth element of the array is returned. If the students array is not null but has no members, you will get an ArgumentOutOfRangeException.

Since the purpose of this operator is to test for null, it can be applied only to objects that can have a null reference. The following code will not compile. Instead, you will receive this warning message: "Operator '?' cannot be applied to operand of type 'int.'"

```
int length = 7;
int strLength = length?.ToString()
```

The null conditional operator can be chained. This means that as soon as any of the null conditional operations detects a null, the process is short-circuited and downstream invocations are not evaluated, and the expression returns null. For example, if any of the collections in the following example are null, supervisorPhoneNumber will be assigned null. Assuming that none of the collections is empty, no exceptions will be thrown.

```
var supervisorPhoneNumber = Employees?[0].Supervisors?[0].PhoneNumbers?[0].ToString();
```

When the null conditional operator is used with a member that returns a value type, it always returns a nullable version of that type.

```
var studentCount = students?.Count;
```

In this example, studentCount will be an int?, not simply an int. The following example won't compile because there is no implicit conversion between int? and int.

```
int studentCount = students?.Count;
```

When the null conditional operator is used with a member that is a reference type, the return value will match the member type.

```
var studentCounsellor = students?[0].Counsellor;
```

Just because students is not null will not guarantee that studentCounsellor is also not null. In this example, studentCounsellor might be null if either the students reference or the studentCounsellor member is null.

As described in Chapter 14, one of the most common usages of the null conditional operator is expected to be for delegate invocation. So instead of the following three lines of code,

```
if(handler != null)
{
    handler(this, args)
}
```

we can use the following line of code:

```
handler?.Invoke(this, args);
```

It can also be useful to combine the usage of the null conditional operator with the null coalescing operator, as shown in the following example, which provides a default value instead of a null:

```
int studentCount = Students?.Count ?? 0;
```

Notice that in this case, by comparison to one of the previous examples, studentCount can be typed as an int because regardless of whether students is null, this expression returns an integer value and never a null.

Using Nullable User-Defined Types

So far, you've seen nullable forms of the predefined, simple types. You can also create nullable forms of user-defined value types. These bring up additional issues that don't arise when using the simple types.

The main issue is access to the members of the encapsulated underlying type. A nullable type doesn't directly expose any of the members of the underlying type. For example, take a look at the following code and its representation in Figure 27-2. The code declares a struct (which is a value type) called MyStruct, with two public fields.

- Since the fields of the struct are public, they can easily be accessed in any instance of the struct, as shown on the left of the figure.

- The nullable version of the struct, however, exposes the underlying type only through the Value property and doesn't *directly* expose any of its members. Although the members are public to the struct, they are not public to the nullable type, as shown on the right of the figure.

```
struct MyStruct                                     // Declare a struct.
{
   public int X;                                    // Field
   public int Y;                                    // Field
   public MyStruct(int xVal, int yVal)              // Constructor
   { X = xVal;   Y = yVal; }
}

class Program {
   static void Main()
   {
      MyStruct? mSNull = new MyStruct(5, 10);
      ...
```

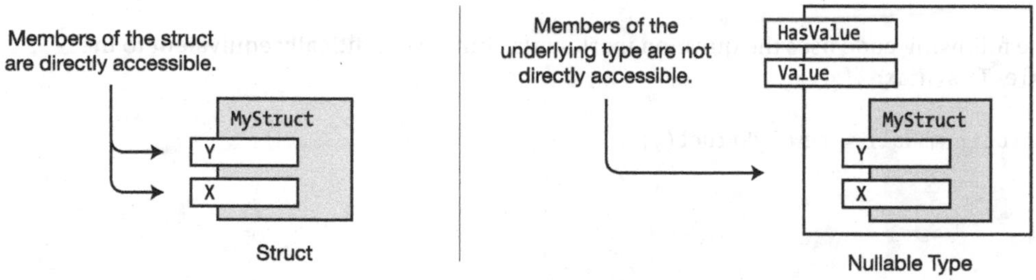

Figure 27-2. The accessibility of the members of a struct is different from that of the nullable type

For example, the following code uses this struct and creates variables of both the struct and the corresponding nullable type. In the third and fourth lines of code, the values of the struct's variables are read directly. In the fifth and sixth lines, they must be read from the value returned by the nullable's Value property.

```
MyStruct  mSStruct = new MyStruct(6, 11);      // Variable of struct
MyStruct? mSNull   = new MyStruct(5, 10);      // Variable of nullable type
                                   Struct access
                                         ↓

Console.WriteLine("mSStruct.X: {0}", mSStruct.X);
Console.WriteLine("mSStruct.Y: {0}", mSStruct.Y);

Console.WriteLine("mSNull.X: {0}",   mSNull.Value.X);
Console.WriteLine("mSNull.Y: {0}",   mSNull.Value.Y);
                                         ↑
                                   Nullable type access
```

Nullable<T>

Nullable types are implemented by using a .NET type called System.Nullable<T>, which uses the C# generics feature. The question mark syntax of C# nullable types is just shortcut syntax for creating a variable of type Nullable<T>, where T is the underlying type. Nullable<T> takes the underlying type, embeds it in a structure, and provides the structure with the properties, methods, and constructors of the nullable type (but not the underlying type).

You can use either the generics syntax of Nullable<T> or the C# shortcut syntax. The shortcut syntax is easier to write and to understand and is less prone to errors. The following code uses the Nullable<T> syntax with struct MyStruct, declared in the preceding example, to create a variable called mSNull of type Nullable<MyStruct>:

```
Nullable<MyStruct> mSNull = new Nullable<MyStruct>();
```

The following code uses the question mark syntax but is semantically equivalent to the Nullable<T> syntax:

```
MyStruct? mSNull = new MyStruct();
```

Method Main

Every C# program must have one entry point—a method that must be called Main.

In the sample code throughout this text, we've used a version of Main that takes no parameters and returns no value. There are, however, four forms of Main that are acceptable as the entry point to a program. These forms are the following:

- static void Main()   {...}
- static void Main(string[] args) {...}
- static int Main()   {...}
- static int Main(string[] args) {...}

The first two forms don't return a value to the execution environment when the program terminates. The second two forms return an int value. A return value, if one is used, is generally used to report success or failure of the program, where 0 is generally used to indicate success.

The second and fourth forms allow you to pass actual parameters, also called *arguments*, from the command line into the program, when it starts. Some important characteristics of command-line arguments are the following:

- There can be zero or more command-line arguments. Even if there are no arguments, the args parameter is not null. Instead, it is an array with no elements.

- The arguments are separated by spaces or tabs.

- Each argument is interpreted by the program as a string, but you don't need to enclose it in quotation marks on the command line.

For example, the following program, called CommandLineArgs, accepts command-line arguments and prints out each argument supplied:

```
class Program
{
    static void Main(string[] args)
    {
        foreach (string s in args)
            Console.WriteLine(s);
    }
}
```

You can execute this program from the Windows Command Prompt program. The following command line executes program CommandLineArgs with five arguments:

CommandLineArgs Jon Peter Beth Julia Tammi
      ↑   ↑
   Executable   Arguments
    Name

This produces the following output:

```
Jon
Peter
Beth
Julia
Tammi
```

Other important things to know about Main are the following:

- Main must always be declared static.
- Main can be declared in either a class or a struct.

A program can contain only one declaration of the four acceptable entry point forms of Main. You can, however, legally declare other methods named Main, as long as they don't have any of the four entry point forms—but doing this is inviting confusion.

Accessibility of Main

Main can be declared public or private.

- If Main is declared private, other assemblies cannot access it, and only the operating system can start the program.
- If Main is declared public, other assemblies can execute it.

The operating system, however, *always* has access to Main, regardless of its declared access level or the declared access level of the class or struct in which it is declared.

By default, when Visual Studio creates a project, it creates a program outline where Main is implicitly private. You can always add the public modifier if you need to do so.

Documentation Comments

The documentation comments feature allows you to include documentation of your program in the form of XML elements. We covered XML in Chapter 20. Visual Studio even assists you in inserting the elements and will read them from your source file and copy them to a separate XML file for you.

Figure 27-3 gives an overview of using XML comments. This includes the following steps:

- You can use Visual Studio to produce the source file with the embedded XML. Visual Studio can automatically insert most of the important XML elements.

- Visual Studio reads the XML from the source code file and copies the XML code to a new file.

- Another program, called a *documentation compiler*, can take the XML file and produce various types of documentation files from it.

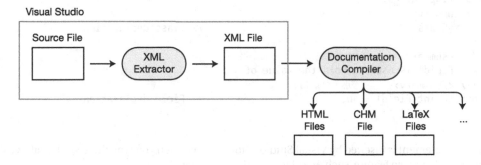

Figure 27-3. *The XML comments process*

Earlier versions of Visual Studio contained an elementary documentation compiler, but it was removed before the release of Visual Studio 2005. Microsoft has developed a new documentation compiler called Sandcastle, which it used to generate the .NET Framework documentation. You can learn more about it and download it for free from `http://sandcastle.codeplex.com`.

Inserting Documentation Comments

Documentation comments start with three consecutive forward slashes.

- The first two slashes indicate to the compiler that this is an end-of-line comment and should be ignored in the parsing of the program.

- The third slash indicates that it's a documentation comment.

For example, in the following code, the first four lines show documentation comments about the class declaration. They use the <summary> XML tag. Above the declaration of the field are three lines documenting the field—again using the <summary> tag.

```
/// <summary>          ← Open XML tag for the class.
/// This is class MyClass, which does the following wonderful things, using
/// the following algorithm. ... Besides those, it does these additional
/// amazing things.
/// </summary>         ← Close XML tag.
class MyClass                                    // Class declaration
{
    /// <summary>      ← Open XML tag for the field.
    /// Field1 is used to hold the value of ...
    /// </summary>     ← Close XML tag.
    public int Field1 = 10;                      // Field declaration
    ...
```

Each XML element is inserted by Visual Studio automatically when you type three slashes above the declaration of a language feature, such as a class or a class member.

For example, the following code shows two slashes above the declaration of class MyClass:

```
//
class MyClass
{ ...
```

As soon as you add the third slash, Visual Studio immediately expands the comment to the following code, without your having to do anything. You can then type anything you want on the documentation comment lines between the tags.

```
/// <summary>          Automatically inserted
///                    Automatically inserted
/// </summary>         Automatically inserted
class MyClass
{ ...
```

Using Other XML Tags

In the preceding examples, you saw the use of the summary XML tag. There are also a number of other tags that C# recognizes. Table 27-2 lists some of the most important.

Table 27-2. *Documentation Code XML Tags*

Tag	Meaning
<code>	Formats the enclosing lines in a font that looks like code
<example>	Marks the enclosing lines as an example
<param>	Marks a parameter for a method or constructor and allows a description
<remarks>	Describes a type declaration
<returns>	Describes a return value
<seealso>	Creates a *See Also* entry in the output document
<summary>	Describes a type or a type member
<value>	Describes a property

Nested Types

Types are usually declared directly inside a namespace. You can, however, also declare types inside a class or struct declaration.

- Types declared inside another type declaration are called *nested types*. Like all type declarations, nested types are templates for an instance of the type.

- A nested type is declared like a member of the *enclosing type*.

    - A nested type can be any type.

    - An enclosing type can be either a class or a struct.

For example, the following code shows class MyClass, with a nested class called MyCounter:

```
class MyClass                    // Enclosing class
{
    class MyCounter              // Nested class
    {
        ...
    }
    ...
}
```

Declaring a type as a nested type often makes sense if it's only meant to be used as a helper for the enclosing type.

Don't be confused by the term *nested*. Nested refers to the location of the *declaration*—not the location in memory of any *instances*. Although a nested type's declaration is inside the enclosing type's declaration, objects of the nested type are not necessarily enclosed in objects of the enclosing type. Objects of the nested type—if any are created at all—are located in memory wherever they would have been located had they not been declared inside another type.

For example, Figure 27-4 shows objects of types MyClass and MyCounter, as outlined in the preceding code. The figure additionally shows a field called Counter, in class MyClass, that is a reference to an object of the nested class, which is located elsewhere in the heap.

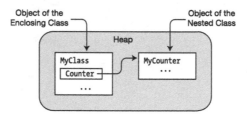

Figure 27-4. *Nesting refers to the location of the declaration, not the location of objects in memory*

Example of a Nested Class

The following code fleshes out classes MyClass and MyCounter into a full program. MyCounter implements an integer counter that starts at 0 and can be incremented using the ++ operator. When the constructor for MyClass is called, it creates an instance of the nested class and assigns the reference to the field. Figure 27-5 illustrates the structure of the objects in the code.

```
class MyClass {
    class MyCounter                                        // Nested class
    {
        public int Count { get; private set; }

        public static MyCounter operator ++( MyCounter current )
        {
            current.Count++;
            return current;
        }
    }

    private MyCounter counter;                             // Field of nested class type

    public MyClass() { counter = new MyCounter(); }        // Constructor

    public int Incr() { return ( counter++ ).Count; }      // Increment method.
    public int GetValue() { return counter.Count; }        // Get counter value.
}

class Program    {
    static void Main() {
        MyClass mc = new MyClass();                        // Create object.

        mc.Incr(); mc.Incr();  mc.Incr();                  // Increment it.
        mc.Incr(); mc.Incr();  mc.Incr();                  // Increment it.

        Console.WriteLine($"Total:  { mc.GetValue() }");   // Print its value.
    }
}
```

This code produces the following output:

```
Total:   6
```

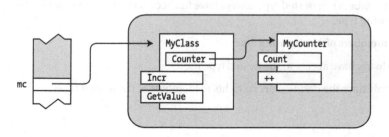

Figure 27-5. *Objects of a nested class and its enclosing class*

Visibility and Nested Types

In Chapter 9, you learned that classes, and types in general, can have an access level of either `public` or `internal`. Nested types, however, are different in that they have *member accessibility* rather than *type accessibility*. Therefore, the following hold for nested types:

- A nested type declared inside a class can have any one of the five class member accessibility levels of `public`, `protected`, `private`, `internal`, or `protected internal`.

- A nested type declared inside a struct can have any one of the three struct member accessibility levels of `public`, `internal`, or `private`.

In both cases, the default access level of a nested type is `private`, which means it cannot be seen outside the enclosing type.

The relationship between the members of the enclosing class and the nested class is a little less straightforward and is illustrated in Figure 27-6. The nested type has complete access to the members of the enclosing type, regardless of their declared accessibility, including members that are `private` and `protected`.

The relationship, however, is not symmetrical. Although the members of the enclosing type can always see the nested type declaration and create variables and instances of it, they do not have complete access to the nested type's members. Instead, their access is limited to the declared access of the nested class members—just as if the nested type were a separate type. That is, they can access the `public` and `internal` members but cannot access the `private` or `protected` members of the nested type.

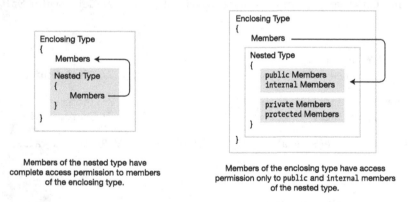

Members of the nested type have complete access permission to members of the enclosing type.

Members of the enclosing type have access permission only to public and internal members of the nested type.

Figure 27-6. *Accessibility between nested type members and enclosing type members*

You can summarize this relationship as follows:

- The members of a nested type always have full access rights to members of the enclosing type.

- The members of an enclosing type

  - Always have access to the nested type itself

  - Only have the *declared access* rights to members of the nested type

The visibility of nested types can also affect the inheritance of base members. If the enclosing class is a derived class, a nested type can hide a base class member with the same name. As always, use the new modifier with the declaration of the nested class to make the hiding explicit.

A this reference within a nested type refers to the *object of the nested type*—not the object of the enclosing type. If an object of the nested type needs access to the enclosing type, it must have a reference to it. You can give it this access by having the enclosing object supply its this reference as a parameter to the nested type's constructor, as shown in the following code:

```
class SomeClass {                             // Enclosing class
    int Field1 = 15, Field2 = 20;             // Fields of enclosing class
    MyNested mn = null;                       // Reference to nested class

    public void PrintMyMembers() {
        mn.PrintOuterMembers();               // Call method in nested class.
    }

    public SomeClass() {                      // Constructor
        mn = new MyNested(this);              // Create instance of nested class.
    }                    ↑
                    Pass in the reference to the enclosing class.
    class MyNested                            // Nested class declaration
    {
        SomeClass sc = null;                  // Reference to enclosing class

        public MyNested(SomeClass SC)         // Constructor of the nested class
        {
            sc = SC;                          // Store reference to enclosing class.
        }

        public void PrintOuterMembers()
        {
            Console.WriteLine($"Field1: { sc.Field1 }");   // Enclosing field
            Console.WriteLine($"Field2: { sc.Field2 }");   // Enclosing field
        }
    }                                         // End of nested class
}

class Program {
    static void Main( ) {
        SomeClass MySC = new SomeClass();
        MySC.PrintMyMembers();
    }
}
```

This code produces the following output:

```
Field1: 15
Field2: 20
```

Destructors and the Dispose Pattern

In Chapter 7 we looked at constructors, which create and set up a class object for use. A class can also have a *destructor*, which can perform actions required to clean up or release unmanaged resources after an instance of a class is no longer referenced. Unmanaged resources are things such as file handles you've gotten using the Win32 API or chunks of unmanaged memory. These aren't things you'll get by using .NET resources, so if you stick to the .NET classes, you won't likely have to write many destructors.

The important things to know about destructors are the following:

- There can be only a single destructor per class.

- A destructor cannot have parameters.

- A destructor cannot have accessibility modifiers.

- A destructor has the same name as the class but is preceded by a tilde character (pronounced "TIL-duh").

- A destructor only acts on instances of classes; hence, there are no static destructors.

- *You cannot call a destructor explicitly in your code.* Instead, the system calls it during the garbage collection process, when the garbage collector analyzes your code and determines that there are no longer any possible paths through your code that reference the object.

For example, the following code illustrates the syntax for a destructor of a class called `Class1`:

```
Class1
{
   ~Class1()                    // The destructor
   {
      CleanupCode
   }
   ...
}
```

Some important guidelines for using destructors are the following:

- Don't implement a destructor if you don't need one. They can be expensive in terms of performance.

- A destructor should only release external resources that the object owns.

- A destructor shouldn't access other objects because you can't assume that those objects haven't already been destroyed.

■ **Note**   Before the release of version 3.0 of C#, destructors were sometimes called *finalizers*. You might sometimes still run across this term in the literature and in the .NET API method names.

The Standard Dispose Pattern

Unlike a C++ destructor, a C# destructor is not called immediately when an instance goes out of scope. In fact, there's no way of knowing when the destructor will be called. Furthermore, as previously mentioned, you cannot explicitly call a destructor. All you know is that the system will call it at some point before the object is removed from the managed heap.

If your code contains unmanaged resources that need to be released as soon as possible, you shouldn't leave that task for the destructor, since there's no guarantee that the destructor will run any time soon. Instead, you should adopt what's called the *standard dispose pattern*.

The standard dispose pattern comprises the following characteristics:

- Your class with the unmanaged resources should implement the IDisposable interface, which consists of a single method named Dispose. Dispose contains the cleanup code that releases the resources.

- When your code is finished with the resources and you want them released, your program code should call the Dispose method. Notice that it is *your code*, not the system, that calls Dispose.

- Your class should also implement a destructor, which calls the Dispose method, in case the Dispose doesn't get called previously.

This can be a bit confusing, so let me summarize the pattern. You want to put all the cleanup code in a method called Dispose, which your code calls when it's done with the resources. As a backup, in case Dispose isn't called, your class destructor should call Dispose. If, on the other hand, Dispose *is* called, then you want to tell the garbage collector not to call the destructor since the cleanup has already been handled by Dispose.

Your destructor and Dispose code should follow the following guidelines:

- Write the logic of your destructor and Dispose methods such that, if for some reason your code doesn't get to call Dispose, your destructor will call it and thus release the resources.

- At the end of the Dispose method should be a call to the GC.SuppressFinalize method, which tells the CLR not to call this object's destructor since the cleanup has already been done.

- Implement the code in Dispose so that it's safe for the method to be called more than once. That is, write it in such a way that if it has already been called, then any subsequent invocations will not do any additional work and will not raise an exception.

The following code shows the standard dispose pattern, which is illustrated in Figure 27-7. The important things about the code are the following:

- There are two overloads of the Dispose method: the public one and the protected one. The protected overload is the one that contains the code for the actual cleanup.

- The public version is the one you'll call explicitly from your code to execute the cleanup. It, in turn, calls the protected version.

- The destructor calls the protected version.

- The bool parameter to the protected version allows the method to know where it's being called from—the destructor or somewhere else in the code. This is important for it to know because it does slightly different things depending on which it is. You can find the details in the following code:

```
class MyClass : IDisposable
{
    bool disposed = false;                          // Disposal status

    public void Dispose()
    {                                                             ⌉
        Dispose( true );                                         │  Public Dispose
        GC.SuppressFinalize(this);                              │
    }                                                            ⌋

    ~MyClass()                                                   ⌉
    {                                                             │  Destructor
        Dispose(false);                                          │
    }                                                            ⌋

    protected virtual void Dispose(bool disposing)               ⌉
    {                                                             │
        if (disposed == false)                                   │
        {                                                         │
            if (disposing == true)                               │
            {                                                     │
                // Dispose the managed resources.                │
                ...                                               │  Factored Dispose
            }                                                     │
                                                                  │
            // Dispose the unmanaged resources.                  │
            ...                                                   │
        }                                                         │
        disposed = true;                                         │
    }                                                            ⌋
}
```

public void Dispose( )

protected virtual
void Dispose(bool disposing)

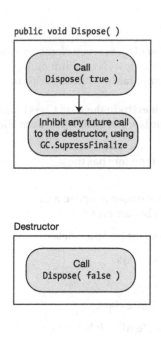

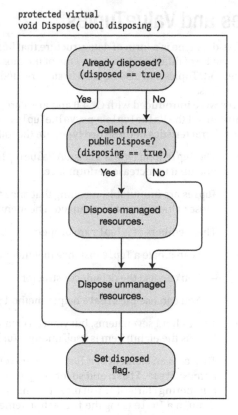

Figure 27-7. *The standard dispose pattern*

Comparing Constructors and Destructors

Table 27-3 provides a summary and comparison of when constructors and destructors are called.

Table 27-3. *Constructors and Destructors*

		When and How Often Called
Instance	Constructor	Called once on the creation of each new instance of the class.
	Destructor	Called for each instance of the class, at some point after the program flow can no longer access the instance.
Static	Constructor	Called only once—either before the first access of any static member of the class or before any instances of the class are created—whichever is first.
	Destructor	Does not exist. Destructors work only on instances.

Tuples and ValueTuples

The Tuples data type is a form of data structure that holds an ordered list of up to seven elements, where the elements can be of different data types. One of the most common uses for tuples is to return multiple values from a method. Tuples can also be used to store related data, usually temporarily, without having to create a full-blown class.

Tuples were introduced with C# 4.0 and are a predefined class that exists in the Base Class Library. C# 7.0 introduced the ValueTuple type. ValueTuples do not replace Tuples, and both types are available. Important characteristics of these two types are the following:

- The Tuple data type is a class. A ValueTuple is a struct and therefore has the potential to increase performance.

- Tuples are immutable, meaning that once their elements have been assigned a value, those values cannot be changed. The members of ValueTuples are mutable.

- The members of a Tuple are properties. The members of a ValueTuple are fields.

- You can create a Tuple instance in either of the following two ways:

  - You can use the default constructor.

  - You can use the Create helper method provided by the Tuple class.

- Tuples hold seven items, but you can create and access a tuple with eight items, as long as the eighth item is itself another Tuple.

- To access an element of a Tuple, you use one of the eight (nondescriptive) property names: Item1, Item2, and so forth, up to Item8. Notice that *there is no* Item0; numbering starts at 1. You must use this accessing method. You cannot cycle through a Tuple using the foreach statement, and you cannot index into it using square braces.

The following code shows both methods of creating a Tuple and how to access the Tuple objects. These Tuples represent the difference in average global temperature from a baseline temperature.[1]

---

[1]NASA has determined a baseline temperature by taking the average of the yearly temperatures between 1951 and 1980, throwing away the outliers, and averaging the results. The values in the tuples are the differences between the average temperature of a particular year and the baseline value. The figures and methodology are from https://climate.nasa.gov/vital-signs/global-temperature.

```
public Tuple<double, double, double, double, double, double>
{
   public Tuple<double, double, double, double, double, double>
   TempDifferenceConst()
   {
      // Using the constructor
      return new Tuple<double, double, double, double, double, double>
                     ( 0.03, 0.00, 0.20, 0.34, 0.52, 0.63 );
   }

   public Tuple<double, double, double, double, double, double>
   TempDifferenceCreate()
   {
      // Using the Create method is more compact
      return Tuple.Create( 0.03, 0.00, 0.20, 0.34, 0.52, 0.63 );
   }
}

class Program
{
   static void Main()
   {
      GlobalTemp gt = new GlobalTemp();

      var tdTuple = gt.TempDifferenceCreate();
      WriteLine( "Temp increase 1950's to 2000: {0}C.", tdTuple.Item5);

      tdTuple = gt.TempDifferenceConst();
      WriteLine( "Temp increase 1950's to 2010: {0}C.", tdTuple.Item6 );
   }
}
```

While the syntax using the Create method for creating a Tuple is more compact, you still have to use the property names Item1, etc., to access the elements. As you can see, in the absence of descriptive element names, it is easy to become confused, resulting in possible runtime errors or, even worse, in logic errors.

C# has solved the element naming problem with a new ValueTuple class. This class is available starting with C# 7.0 and .NET Framework 4.7.

The following code restates the previous examples using a ValueTuple in place of a Tuple. Notice the following about the code:

- The creation of the ValueTuple is implicit, performed simply by passing the correct number of elements of the correct data types.

- The ValueTuple return data type can be recognized by the comma-separated list of elements surrounded by parentheses.

- The methods' return types include names for the ValueTuples' elements. *These names become available in the calling scope to reference individual elements.* If you don't specify names for the elements in the return type list, the old default names of Item1, Item2, etc., still apply.

The following code shows the same example as the previous code but uses ValueTuples rather than Tuples:

```
class GlobalTemp
{
    public (double d1960, double d1970, double d1980,
            double d1990, double d2000, double d2010)
    TempDifferenceUsingValueTupleCtor()
    {
        // Using the constructor
        return new ValueTuple<double, double, double,
                double, double, double>(0.03, 0.00, 0.20, 0.34, 0.52, 0.63);
    }

    public (double d1960, double d1970, double d1980,
            double d1990, double d2000, double d2010)
    TempDifferenceUsingValueTuple()
    {
        // Implicit creation
        return (0.03, 0.00, 0.20, 0.34, 0.52, 0.63);
    }
}

class Program
{
    static void Main()
    {
        GlobalTemp gt = new GlobalTemp();

        var tdVTuple = gt.TempDifferenceUsingValueTupleCtor();
        WriteLine( "Temp increase 1950's to 2000: {0}C.", tdVTuple.d2000 );
                                                                    ↑
                                The parameter name is visible!
        tdVTuple = gt.TempDifferenceUsingValueTuple();
        WriteLine( "Temp increase 1950's to 2010: {0}C.", tdVTuple.d2010);
    }                                                              ↑
}                                       The parameter name is visible!
```

This code produces the following output:

```
Temp increase 1950's to 2000: 0.52C.
Temp increase 1950's to 2010: 0.63C.
```

Interoperating with COM

Although this text doesn't cover COM programming, C# 4.0 has several language features specifically to make COM programming easier. One of these is the *omit ref* feature, which allows you to call a COM method without using the ref keyword when you don't need to use the value passed back by the method.

For example, if Microsoft Word is installed on the machine your program is running on, you can use Word's spell-checker functionality in your own program. The method you would use to do this is the CheckSpelling method on the Document class, which is in the Microsoft.Office.Tools.Word namespace. This method has 12 parameters, and all of them are ref parameters. Without this feature you would have to supply reference variables for each of the parameters, even if you didn't need to use them to pass data to the method or to receive data from the method. Omitting the ref keyword *works only with COM methods*—with anything else, you'll still get a compile error.

This code might look something like the following code. Notice the following about this code:

- The call in the fourth line uses only the second and third parameters, which are Booleans. But since the method requires ref parameters, you have to create two object type variables, ignoreCase and alwaysSuggest, to hold the values.

- The third line creates a variable called optional, of type object, for the other ten parameters.

```
object ignoreCase    = true;
object alwaysSuggest = false;              Objects to hold Boolean variables
object optional      = Missing.Value; _____↓_____ _____↓_____
tempDoc.CheckSpelling( ref optional,  ref ignoreCase, ref alwaysSuggest,
    ref optional, ref optional, ref optional, ref optional, ref optional,
    ref optional, ref optional, ref optional, ref optional );
```

With the omit ref feature, we can clean this up considerably since we don't have to use the ref keyword on those parameters from which we don't need the output, and we can use inline bools for the two parameters we care about. The simplified code looks like the following:

```
                                 bool   bool
object optional = Missing.Value;  ↓      ↓
tempDoc.CheckSpelling( optional, true, false,
    optional, optional, optional, optional,
    optional, optional, optional, optional, optional );
```

We can also use the optional parameters feature. Using both features—omit ref and optional parameters—together makes the final form much less cumbersome than the original.

```
tempDoc.CheckSpelling( Missing.Value, true, false );
```

The following code includes this method in a complete program. To compile this code, you need to have Visual Studio Tools for Office (VSTO) installed on your machine, and you must add a reference in your project to the `Microsoft.Office.Interop.Word` assembly. For the compiled code to run, you must also have Microsoft Word installed on your machine.

```
using System;
using System.Reflection;

class Program
{
    static void Main()
    {
        Console.WriteLine( "Enter a string to spell-check:" );
        string stringToSpellCheck = Console.ReadLine();

        string spellingResults;
        int errors = 0;
        if ( stringToSpellCheck.Length == 0 )
            spellingResults = "No string to check";
        else
        {
            Microsoft.Office.Interop.Word.Application app =
                        new Microsoft.Office.Interop.Word.Application();

            Console.WriteLine( "\nChecking the string for misspellings ..." );
            app.Visible = false;

            Microsoft.Office.Interop.Word._Document tempDoc = app.Documents.Add( );

            tempDoc.Words.First.InsertBefore( stringToSpellCheck );
            Microsoft.Office.Interop.Word.ProofreadingErrors
                                spellErrorsColl = tempDoc.SpellingErrors;
            errors = spellErrorsColl.Count;

            //1.  Without using optional parameters
            //object ignoreCase    = true;
            //object alwaysSuggest = false;
            //object optional      = Missing.Value;
            //tempDoc.CheckSpelling( ref optional, ref ignoreCase, ref alwaysSuggest,
            //    ref optional, ref optional, ref optional, ref optional, ref optional,
            //    ref optional, ref optional, ref optional, ref optional );

            //2. Using the "omit ref" feature
            object optional = Missing.Value;
            tempDoc.CheckSpelling( optional, true, false, optional, optional, optional,
                        optional, optional, optional, optional, optional, optional );

            //3. Using "omit ref" and optional parameters
            //tempDoc.CheckSpelling( Missing.Value, true, false );
```

```
        app.Quit(false);
        spellingResults = errors + " errors found";
    }

    Console.WriteLine( spellingResults );
    Console.WriteLine( "\nPress <Enter> to exit program." );
    Console.ReadLine();
  }
}
```

When you run this code, it produces the console window shown in Figure 27-8, which asks you to enter a string that you want to run through the spell-checker. When it receives the string, it opens Word and runs the spell-checker on it. When that happens, you'll see Word's spell-checker window appear, as shown in Figure 27-9.

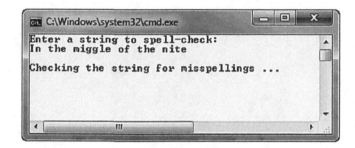

Figure 27-8. *The console window that asks for the string to send to Word's spell-checker*

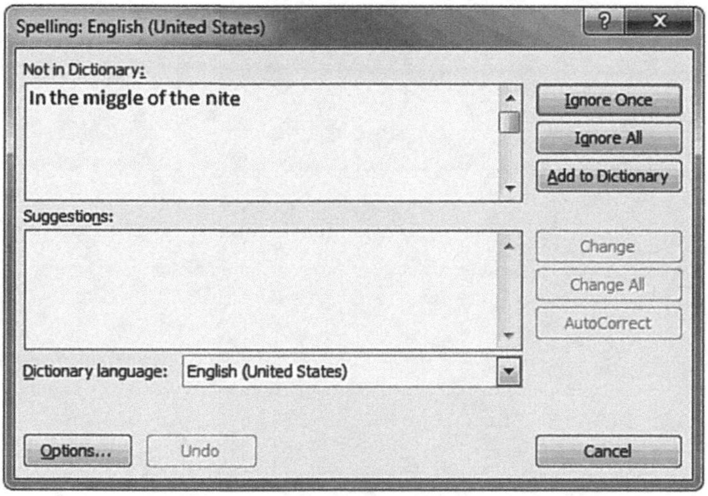

Figure 27-9. *Word's spell-checker created using COM calls from the console program*

Index

© Daniel Solis and Cal Schrotenboer 2018
D. Solis and C. Schrotenboer, *Illustrated C# 7*, https://doi.org/10.1007/978-1-4842-3288-0

■ H

■ I

Get the eBook for only $5!

Why limit yourself?

With most of our titles available in both PDF and ePUB format, you can access your content wherever and however you wish—on your PC, phone, tablet, or reader.

Since you've purchased this print book, we are happy to offer you the eBook for just $5.

To learn more, go to http://www.apress.com/companion or contact support@apress.com.

Apress®

Printed in the United States
By Bookmasters